AF251259

OBJECTS OF VIRTUE

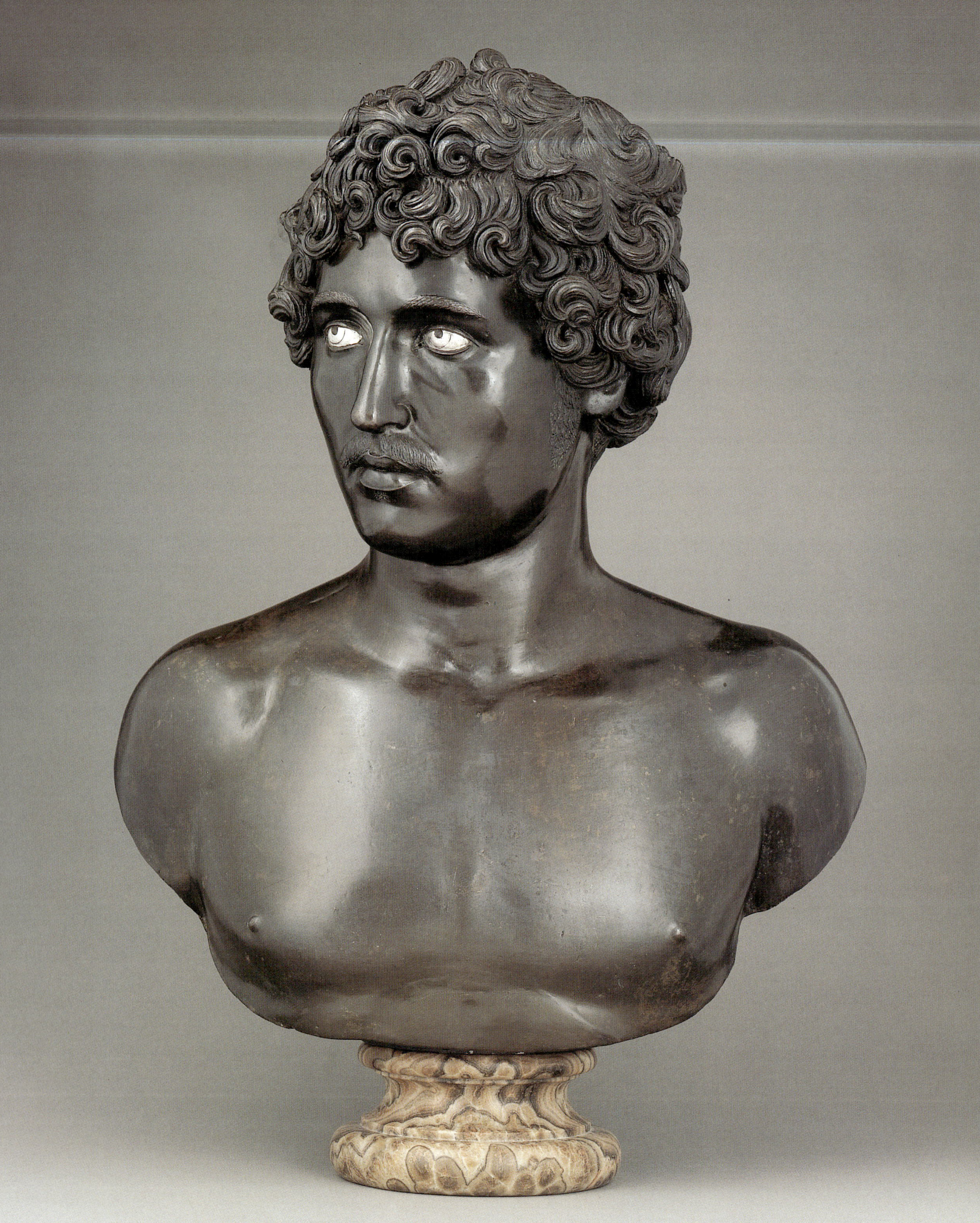

OBJECTS OF VIRTUE

Art in Renaissance Italy

Luke Syson and Dora Thornton

The J. Paul Getty Museum

Los Angeles

Acknowledgements

This book could not have been written without the help of Andrew Burnett and John Cherry, who continued to support the project even when it took much longer than was originally planned, and who shared their expertise with us so generously. Within the unique scholarly community of The British Museum, we should like to single out Philip Attwood, Hugo Chapman, Antony Griffiths, Paul Roberts, Judy Rudoe and Jonathan Williams for their invaluable help and encouragement. Special thanks go to our two departmental photographers, Stephen Dodd and Saul Peckham, and to Tom Cochrane and Lisa Baylis in Prints and Drawings, for their contribution to the book. We are also grateful to Emma Way and Teresa Francis of The British Museum Press; to our editor, Laura Brockbank; to her assistant, Natasha Coates; the copy editor, Barbara Horn; the proofreader, Penny Housden; the indexer, Suzanne Atkin; and the designer, James Shurmer, for their work and for their patience in putting the book together. We were fortunate to have the help of Xavier Salomon as a voluntary assistant during the writing of the book. Beyond The British Museum, we owe particular thanks to Timothy Wilson, who has read and commented on parts of the text in detail and who has generously allowed us to draw upon arguments that first appeared in an unpublished lecture delivered in 1999 to the Society of Antiquaries: 'Dusty artists: the status and aspirations of Renaissance pottery painters'. We are also grateful to Denise Allen, Caroline Elam, Reino Liefkes, Nicholas Penny, Patricia Rubin, Jeffrey Spier, Evelyn Welch and Alison Wright for their comments on drafts of the text or particular chapters. Jeremy Warren also gave us invaluable information and encouragement.

We would also like to thank the following for their assistance of various kinds: Giovanni Agosti, Marta Ajmar, Andrea Bayer, Diane Bilbey, Alison Brown, Duncan Bull, Lorne Campbell, Stephen Campbell, Tom Campbell, Dawson Carr, Keith Christiansen, Georgia Clarke, James Draper, David Ekserdjian, Laurie and Peter Fusco, Charlotte Gere, Dillian Gordon, Philippa Jackson, Lauren Jacobi, Karen Lamberti, David Landau, Isabella Lodi-Fè, Kent Lydecker, John Mallet, Patrick McCray, Peta Motture, Jacqueline Musacchio, Carol Plazzotta, Julia Poole, Anthony Ray, Marie-Laure de Rochebrune, Ruth Rubinstein, Marco Spallanzani, Bette Talvacchia, Peter Thornton, Thomas Tuohy, Paola Venturelli, Clare Vincent, Susan Walker, Ute Wartenberg, Giles Waterfield, Ernst Wegelin and Antoine Wilmering. Errors of fact or interpretation are, of course, our own.

Finally, we would like to dedicate this book to our families and 'families'.

© 2001 The Trustees of the British Museum
Published in the United States of America in 2001 by the J. Paul Getty Museum
Getty Publications
1200 Getty Center Drive, Suite 500
Los Angeles, California 90049-1682
www.getty.edu

LIBRARY OF CONGRESS CONTROL NUMBER: 2001094212
ISBN: 0-89236-657-5

AT THE J. PAUL GETTY MUSEUM
Christopher Hudson, *Publisher*
Mark Greenberg, *Editor in Chief*

Jacket design by Agnes Anderson

AT THE BRITISH MUSEUM
Barbara Horn, *Copy Editor*
Suzanne Atkin, *Indexer*

Designed and typeset in Monotype Garamond by James Shurmer

Printed in Slovenia by Korotan

FRONTISPIECE Pier Jacopo Alari-Bonacolsi, *called* Antico. Italian (Mantua), ca. 1460–1528. *Bust of a Young Man*, ca. 1520. Bronze with silver eyes, 54.6 cm (21½ in.). Los Angeles, J. Paul Getty Museum 86.SB.688

Contents

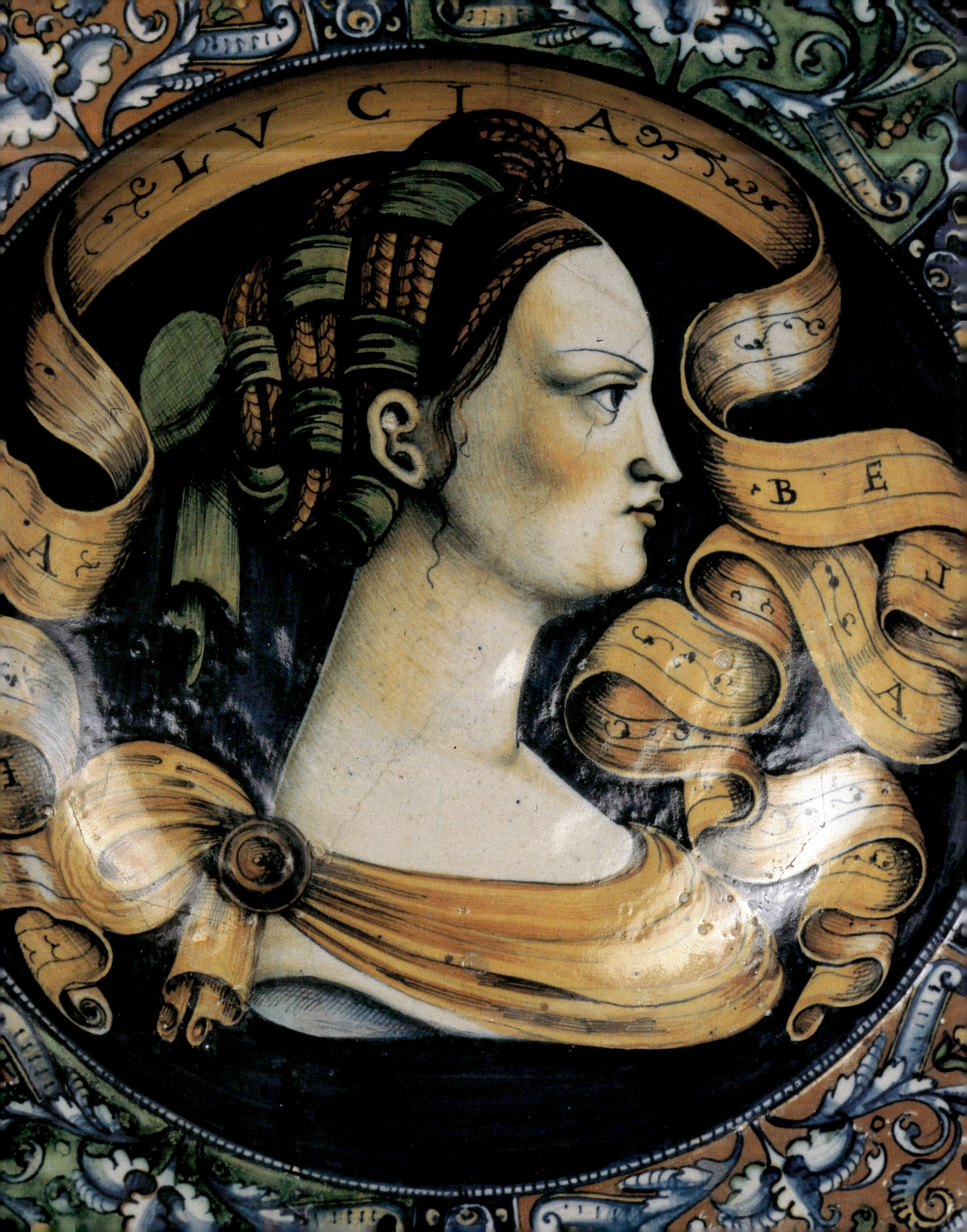
LVCIA
BE
A

Introduction

The illustration opposite shows the profile of a young and (as we are told in the accompanying legend) 'beautiful' woman. Her hair, some of it probably false, is elaborately plaited and wound with a cloth around her head; around her shoulders she wears a classically inspired swathe of drapery – something between a scarf and a toga – fastened with a large shoulder brooch. The image is dated 1524 and, according to the scrolling inscription, the woman is called Lucia, described in Italian as beautiful – *bella* – and as divine, a goddess – *diva* – a word, both Latin and vernacular, whose presence can be explained by reference to the legends of ancient coins that marked the posthumous deification of ancient Roman empresses. The subject is therefore presented as both modern and ancient, and the roundel containing the head is framed by elegant acanthus ornament copied from surviving fragments of Roman sculptural relief. This may be a tribute to a particular woman, perhaps a local beauty, a wife or a wife-to-be. It is certainly an idealized portrait, but perhaps no more so than the various celebrated portraits of unidentified *belle* painted in Italy in the early sixteenth century by artists like Raphael and Titian. Here, the artist and place of production is unknown, though it was probably made at a pottery centre in the Marches or Umbria. Despite its anonymity, this image was evidently made, like the portraits from which it derives, to be enjoyed for its loveliness – for its accomplished artistry – and appreciated for its classical allusions. At the same time, however, there is a significant difference between this work and a canvas or panel executed by Raphael or Titian. Although it is painted, this is not just a painting; it is also a dish (fig. 1).

Its form and medium – tin-glazed ceramic – therefore suggest another function beyond straightforward aesthetic response. Even though it may have decorated a wall or stood on a *credenza* for part or all of its contemporary life, this is an object that is ostensibly utilitarian, something on which to present food and from which to eat. As such, in terms of much traditional art history, it becomes immediately problematic. It is true that it cannot be treated as art for art's sake. Rather it belongs to that nebulous category, the applied arts. That is not to imply that its artistry is necessarily an extra or secondary ingredient. Instead, it should be recognized that specific utility could be inseparably combined with 'artistic' appearance to transmit a single message. The first owner of this plate signalled by its possession and, probably, display that he or she not only needed to eat but had the money and discrimination to dine off the most technologically advanced and aesthetically ambitious tableware of the day.

This is a book about the contemporary meanings and interpretation of many such art objects: furniture, jewellery or vessels made of gold, silver and bronze, precious and semi-precious stones, glass and ceramic. The function of other Renaissance objects was rather less practical – bronze statuettes or medals, or engraved gems, for example – but their purchase, possession and display in the domestic interior was understood to convey

Detail of fig. 1,
see page 9

something of the individual histories, status and 'character' of their owners. These classes of object have traditionally been neglected by many mainstream art historians as the 'minor arts'. Like the kinds of domestic canvas and panel painting (especially those made for the ornamentation of furniture) that assuredly come into this category, however, artistry was a key ingredient, and none of these art objects can be considered independently of one another. As such this is unashamedly a book about art and its contemporary understanding. More than that, it concerns art objects of high quality purchased and commissioned by the most educated and wealthy men and women of Italy, those who could afford to discriminate and to parade their discrimination. We are, therefore, dealing with the material culture of the elite. Moreover, we look at the production of objects as it affected their status and significance and we mention their cost only when this was a relevant factor in contemporary interpretation. The book does not deal with economic history or attempt an analysis of Renaissance consumerism. And, in contrast with many who have looked at the minor and applied arts, we are not concerned to attribute objects to people or places except insomuch as, once again, authorship and origin might have significantly affected the reception of particular pieces.

The fact that we chose to open the book by discussing a single object is significant. If this is cultural history, it is one that is largely determined by the close study of surviving art objects and by the way in which they were made, documented, classified and discussed by contemporaries. It might be argued that the principal task of museum curators is to explain why certain objects in their care came to be made; why they look the way they do; and (perhaps to a lesser extent) how it is that these, rather than other kinds of objects recorded in contemporary sources, have come to survive. Thus 'things' are inevitably the starting point for anything we do, and to that extent, at least, this is conventional museum scholarship. That said, the book is not intended as a guide to the Italian Renaissance collections that can be seen and studied at The British Museum (and we are conscious, for example, that nowhere in the book can be found any reference to the Museum's important collections of coins, scientific instruments or seal-dies). Nevertheless, in writing a book of this kind we have inevitably been faced with an almost infinite number of choices as to what material and, indeed, which individual objects to discuss: why deal with ceramics or glass rather than with printing; with fifteenth-century goldsmiths' work and sixteenth-century ceramic painting, as opposed to tapestry, textiles or wood-carving? We hope that the answers to these questions have not been entirely arbitrary. In the first place, we considered it sensible to shape the contents of this book to no small extent by the types of object that The British Museum has collected over nearly two hundred and fifty years – those, in many instances, with which we are most familiar. Gaps in our discussion therefore sometimes mirror gaps in the British Museum's pattern of collecting. However, at the same time, we wished to present particular groups of contextualized objects in a series of case studies which illuminate particular issues. We have therefore chosen to frame our treatment of glass and ceramics as an examination of the value (in its broadest sense) of technological innovation, and the way in which this was perceived and appraised by contemporaries. In some instances objects in the Museum's collection provided a springboard rather than a complete picture; we considered, for example, that our discussion of

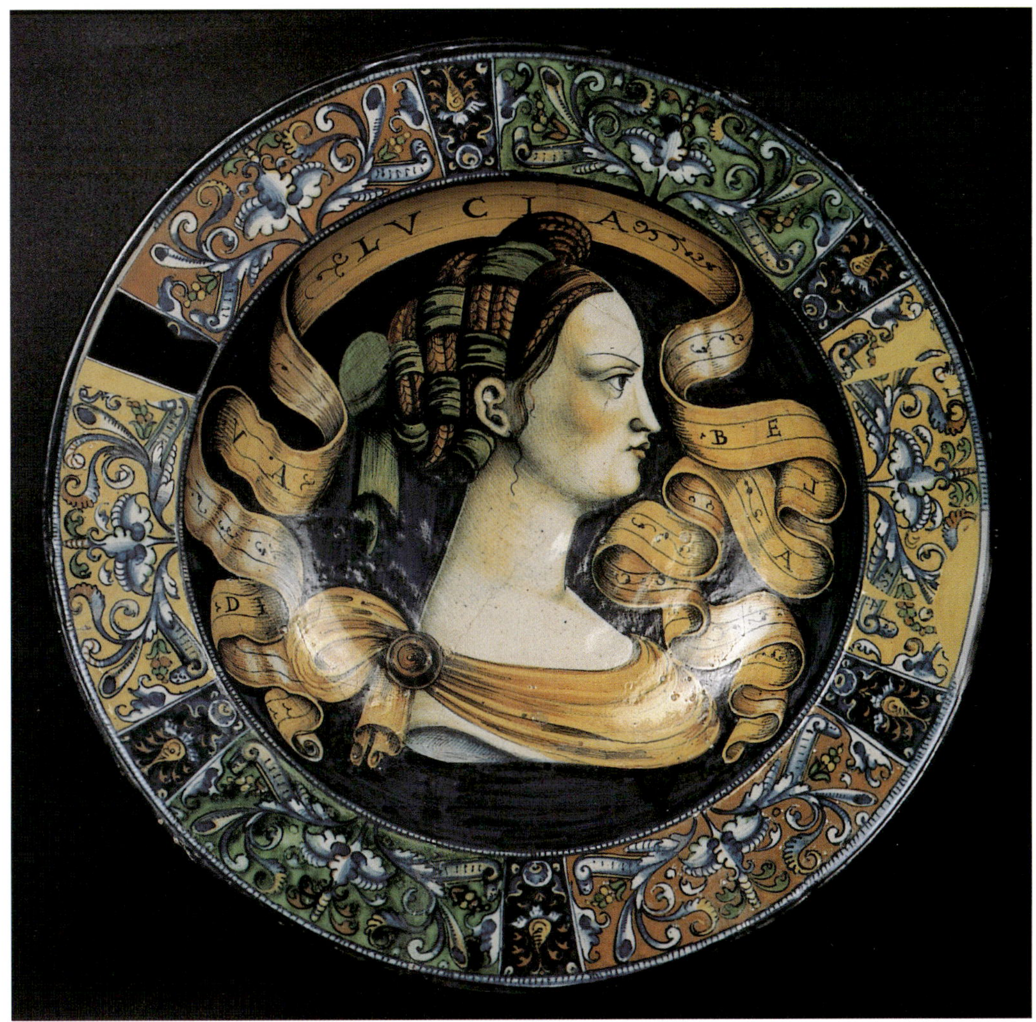

the impact of the study and growing appreciation of Greek and Roman artefacts on the language of Renaissance art should not be confined just to the medals collected by The British Museum but should include Renaissance bronze and marble sculpture, which is not to be found there. In general, however, throughout the book the reader should be aware that the objects for discussion have been selected as paradigmatic, that what can be said, for example, of painting from one city (Milan or, most often, Florence in this book) might often be said of painting from another (Ferrara, Perugia or Venice), or that the design process for goldsmiths' work, and what it implied about the appreciation of the finished objects, might equally apply to tapestries or wooden inlay. We have tried to make it clear when and why we regard particular objects as being somehow unique or exceptional.

Other similar choices have had to be made about the chronological span of this book and its regional biases. We start at the beginning of the fifteenth century. Once again this choice is dictated, in part, by the very limited survival rate of domestic art objects from Italy before *c.*1400. However, just as important is the fact that this period marks the beginning of widespread humanist educational practices, leading to the establishment among the ruling elite of a more or less common frame of intellectual and aesthetic reference. It has been less easy to settle upon a cut-off point. We finish, effectively, with the end of the period known as the High Renaissance, the time that is most marked by its adherence to classically inspired rule-making. When we spill into the 1530s or 1540s, we consider, in the main, artists and patrons in places where the mainstreams of Italian culture were not affected by the invasion of foreign powers; it will be noticed, for example, that mention of Milanese art dries up after the fall of the Sforza regime and the takeover of the duchy by the French. After the mid-sixteenth century we consider that almost everywhere there existed a greater trans-European mentality, one that has been discussed in detail elsewhere.

We have attempted, as far as possible, to look at art made and owned throughout the Italian peninsula. In doing so, we have also tried to preserve a sense of geographical and regional difference. Nevertheless, partly in the interests of preventing the book expanding to unmanageable proportions, we have often chosen to focus attention on specific cities in the pursuit of particular enquiries. We do not pretend to be comprehensive. Rome, for example, has its moment of glory in our chapter on the impact of the antique; Venice appears chiefly as a centre of glass production; Florence is central to our discussion of the objects associated with marriage rituals; while Naples, and the dynastic regimes of the Marches and the North (Urbino, Ferrara, Mantua and Milan) might emerge as places where aesthetic issues were discussed especially ardently by humanists, as places where individual artists were highly prized, or as specialist centres of production for different kinds of goods. We are, once again, aware that, in making decisions of this kind, certain places have received pretty short shrift.

This book seeks to show how art objects of all sorts tell stories, and how they transmit different messages, depending not just on their perceived functions or the artistic languages they employ but also on the interpretive glosses that owners chose to place on them. In many cases, common meanings were determined by an alliance of interests: the attempts of members of an elite to distinguish themselves from more ordinary mortals through their buying, and the scholarly commentators (often themselves financially dependent on the same elite patrons who were purchasing and commissioning art) who both shaped and recorded their choices. It was not enough that Renaissance art objects were – or could be – expensive; they had also to convey other, more abstract qualities, which were presented as those of their owners. Thus the book begins with a selective examination of the critical language applied to art and the social expectations that terms, particularly Renaissance terms, like magnificent, noble or splendid imply. The word 'Renaissance' itself, applied here as much, or more, to a way of thinking as to a period, is justified by the fact that many of the ways in which art objects were viewed was dictated by a self-conscious return to the values of antiquity as they could be divined through the study of ancient texts and, perhaps to a lesser extent, artefacts. This is the intellectual background against which much of the contemporary interpretation – and indeed production – should be seen. The aim was often to produce objects of virtue, by which we mean not just pieces that contained virtuoso craftsmanship or artistry (the usual sense of the word) but also objects that showed off the defined virtues of their owners. These virtues were communicated by objects in isolation and by their association with particular events and rituals. Thus our second chapter looks at specific moments in the public and private lives of men and women when objects might come most into play: birth, death and, above all, betrothal and marriage.

In the third chapter we go on to show how the derivation of a critical terminology had an impact on the appearance of objects themselves. If definitions of appropriate virtues depended on readings of Aristotle or Cicero, then the objects used to encapsulate or represent them might also be expected to look antique. An element of their 'ancient' appearance depended on their makers' ability accurately to imitate the material remains of these inspirational cultures. This desire for authenticity is exemplified in a 'philological' approach to making, adopted by those sculptors and goldsmiths who not only executed medals and statuary but also dealt in antiquities or authenticated them for potential buyers. A key aspect of the ancient discussion of art was the emphasis on the individual talents of artists. Chapter Four therefore looks at the ingredients of artistry and reputation, and how these considerations affected the meanings of Renaissance art objects. Goldsmiths and goldsmiths' work once again come to the fore; it turns out that it was in part through the design of objects in gold and silver that artists with different primary specialities could exhibit the special talents that might establish their claims to be artists. And the involvement of figures as famous as Mantegna or Michelangelo could, in turn, add to the already considerable intrinsic value of such objects.

The perceived worth of an object did not, however, necessarily depend on the use of expensive raw materials or on the direct participation of famous artists. In Chapter Five we show that the value conferred by the art of design could be allied with new technologies to make objects that were acclaimed as 'valuable', and seen as proving not just the parity but the superiority of the modern to the ancient. We have chosen to contrast glass, an ancient medium that was revived and increasingly refined, with tin-glazed maiolica, on which the brilliant and varied pigments were regarded approvingly as improvements on any known models from classical antiquity. The last chapter asks different but related questions: what effect did the fact that a range of art objects were reckoned to be conveyers of particular meanings have on the perceived status of their makers? And what impact did the reputation of a maker – one who would now be defined as an artisan or craftsman – have on the kinds of objects made? Many of the objects in this book have since suffered from a lack of scholarly or aesthetic esteem. This was particularly marked in the late sixteenth century as the result of a division – promoted by many theorists and some interested painters and sculptors – between artists and (lumped together) artisans. The latter were perceived as being reliant on greater creative spirits for the non-technical aspects of their works. It would not be right to say that such distinctions were not made during the period under discussion, but they were made differently. By setting the life and work of the ceramics painter Xanto Avelli into a broader context, and in particular the use he made of prints after drawings by Raphael and other renowned painters, we show that definitions of individual creativity did not depend, as they often do today, on notions of inspired genius but might be defined through what an artist – even a ceramic painter – might have learned and selected from his forebears and his peers. This concluding discussion of Xanto's work illustrates just that concept of *arte* as it was defined by the ancients, and taken up by the humanist readers, with whom we begin.

Chapter One

Defining Social Virtues

Arguments about the consistency of human behaviour over time are essentially inconclusive. There is no sensible way of judging if the men and women of Renaissance Italy were better, or kinder, or nicer than those who came before or after. But it is possible to detect differences in the ways in which they defined and assessed good behaviour. Many fifteenth-century men and women – above all those who were keenly aware of their ancient history – believed they were living in the dawn of a new age; one which was to see the renewal and reappraisal of the values of Greece and Rome and the rivalling of classical achievement. While the teachings of the Church remained dominant, writers (and their readers) added extra imperatives to the ingredients of admirable conduct, codifying a new set of social virtues as distinguishing features of the ruling elite. Dynastic regimes in Naples and the city states of northern Italy might suddenly change or falter due to internecine squabbling, war or the dubious legitimacy of claimants; such shifts might alter the political emphasis from rule by hereditary right to rule chiefly by virtue of personal acclaim. The emergence of a mercantile economy in many cities from the thirteenth century, growing wealth, and an expanding world of material goods made it all the more necessary for the ruling families of the cities of Renaissance Italy to develop legitimating guidelines for political and social behaviour, individual conduct and personal or familial status.[1] Traditional models of behaviour were therefore reassessed and reworked, and certain kinds of social rituals and exchanges, many of which incorporated art objects, were ever more self-consciously envisaged as performances of ancient Greek and Roman notions of friendship, justice, liberality, grace, modesty or learning (depending on the socio-political context, and on the protagonist's gender).[2] The investigation of the nature of social virtues and how they were to be expressed in public were thus accompanied by a reappraisal of the status and significance of art objects.

Models and definitions

Awareness of these concepts of virtue was not new; nor were the rites of passage associated with birth, marriage and death that were employed to show them off. The difference lay in the fact that, from the end of the Trecento, many forms of ritualized behaviour and social interaction were newly and explicitly defined through the reading and analysis of ancient texts – historical, philosophical and poetic. In 1422 Guarino da Verona (fig. 2), soon to become the humanist teacher of Leonello d'Este, the future marquis of Ferrara, wrote 'What better goal can there be for our thoughts and efforts than the arts, precepts and studies by which we may come to guide, order and govern ourselves, our households and our political offices?'[3] His funeral oration written by his pupil, the poet Lodovico Carbone, reiterated the notion that the study of ancient literature bred virtue:

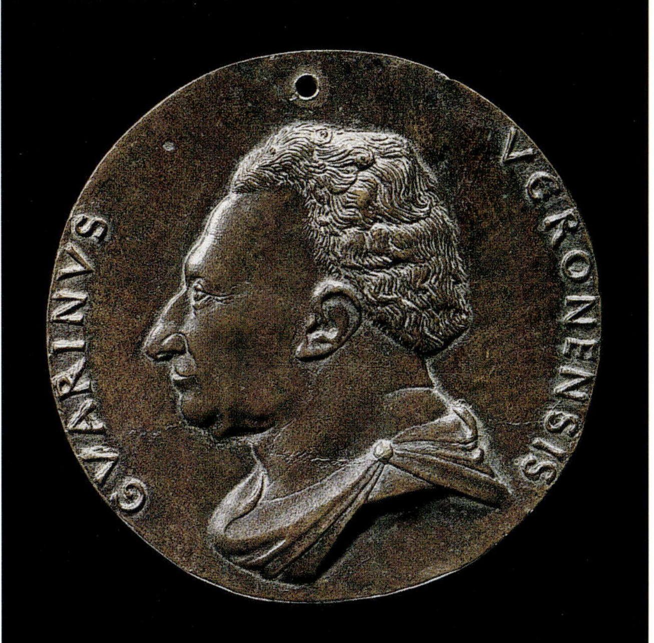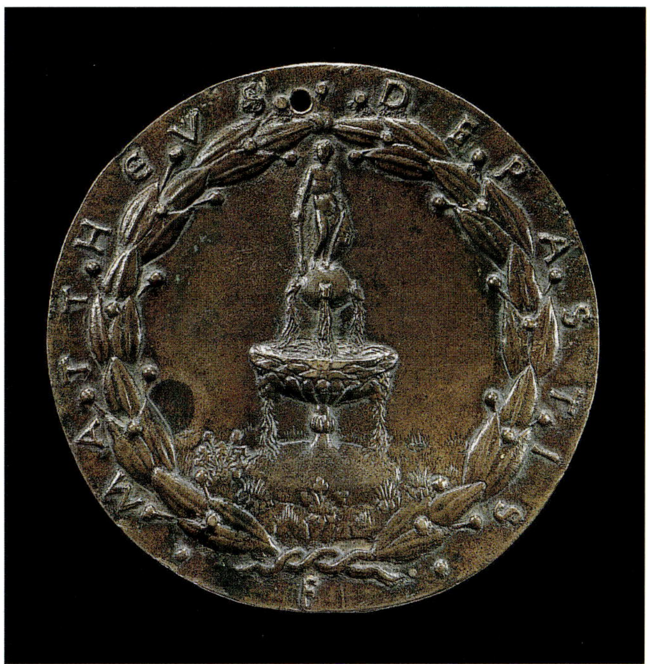

2 Matteo de' Pasti, portrait medal of Guarino da Verona; cast bronze; Rimini, *c*.1450–5. The British Museum, London

It was shameful how little the men of Ferrara knew of letters before the arrival of Guarino … Priscian was lost in oblivion, Servius was unheard of, the works of Cicero were unknown and it was considered miraculous if someone mentioned Salust, or Caesar, or Livy, or if anyone aspired to understand the ancient authors … But after a propitious star had brought this divine individual to Ferrara, there followed an extraordinary transformation in competence … from all quarters they came to listen to that most felicitous voice … No-one was considered noble, no-one as leading a blameless life, unless he had followed Guarino's courses. So that in a short space of time our citizens were led out of the deepest shadows into a true and brilliant light, and all suddenly became eloquent, learned, elegant and felicitous of speech.[4]

However rarified abstract concepts of ancient virtue may have been (and however little they may actually have affected the daily, pragmatic decision-making processes of men and women), the humanist educations of the most powerful men, and to a lesser extent of women from the same ruling families, ensured that knowledge of a codified set of ancient virtues formed a conceptual framework against which current actions could be publicly measured and judged. Professional and semi-professional humanist scholars were employed by rich and powerful patrons to forge links between models from the past and prescribed moral conduct in the present. They wrote a whole series of treatises and guidebooks to modern life, full of advice on everything from magnanimity to matrimony; from deportment and dress to household management.[5] In these books humanist authors were doing more than merely applying fashionable glosses to traditional and current behaviour: they were trying to improve civic societies along classical lines. During this period, for example, medieval codes of chivalry were reappraised and were advertised as being classical, as well as Christian, in origin.[6] Reference to chivalric ideals and imagery was therefore seen as one way of translating the perceived glory of ancient Rome into contemporary life.[7] Such treatises were frequently dedicated by humanists to a patron.

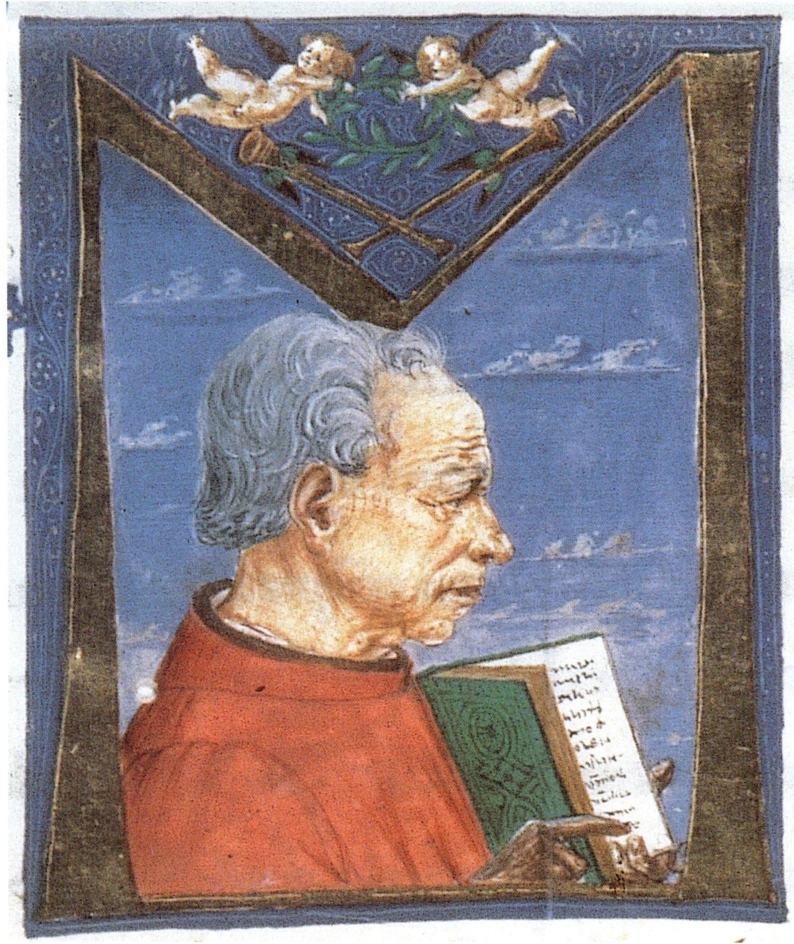

3 Francesco d'Antonio del Chierico (attributed), illuminated portrait initial of Poggio Bracciolini; tempera and gilding on parchment, from Poggio Bracciolini, *Collected Works*; Florence, *c*.1455–60, Urb. lat. 224, fol. 2r. Biblioteca Apostolica Vaticana, Vatican

This was a way of ensuring properly 'liberal' reward, but it also tied the recipient into the value system propounded in the text. In 1416 Francesco Barbaro, for example, wrote his treatise *On Wifely Duties*, one of a number of such texts, as a guidebook for Ginevra Cavalcanti, the new wife of Lorenzo de' Medici, younger brother of the more famous Cosimo.[8] Poggio Bracciolini (fig. 3) dedicated his book *On Nobility* to Gherardo da Como, whom Poggio considered to be an equal to the ancients in virtue and learning.[9] In April 1474 Lorenzo de' Medici – the Magnificent – thanked Bartolomeo Platina for a copy of his treatise on good citizenship, *De optimo cive*, and paid him 100 ducats. Here Platina had acted cannily. The work paid for by Lorenzo was very nearly identical to Platina's book *On the Prince,* which he had earlier dedicated to Federico Gonzaga, Marquis of Mantua.[10]

The form and language of certain much-read modern texts, even if their content was sometimes necessarily new, had to follow ancient precedent, albeit by inventively combining sources rather than by literal emulation. Even Bartolomeo Platina's *On Honourable Pleasure and Good Health*, published in Venice in 1475, a treatise on food and drink in which he collected a mixture of Arabic sources and the recipes of the celebrated cook Martino da Como, follows the structure of the Roman cookery book written in the first century by Apicius.[11] These delicate allusions may have been recognized by their more erudite readers. However, the primary teaching method of the humanist was less dependent on detailed knowledge of Latin (still less Greek). An education in virtue usually centred around the exemplar: an ancient figure whose described actions might make him or her the model of a particular virtue. Such a course was advocated by Leon Battista Alberti (fig. 4), who believed that fathers could mould their sons through praising the virtues of good men and condemning the vices of the wicked.[12]

And the Florentine Matteo Palmieri proposed that only by constantly drumming the actions of these ancient heroes into the heads of unruly adolescents would one arrive at adult men who possessed proper *virtù civile*: a potent combination of prudence, justice, strength and modesty.[13] Thus the histories and biographies of the emperors by, for example, Livy and Suetonius were much read, documented frequently in the fast-growing libraries of the ruling elite, and were among the earliest printed books to appear in Venice and Rome in the early 1470s. Just as influential was Plutarch's *Parallel Lives*, which, even before it was published in Venice by Nicolaus Jensen in 1478,[14] had been translated from Greek by, among many other professional humanists, Francesco Barbaro and Guarino, whom we have already met, and Leonardo Bruni and Francesco Filelfo, who will reappear. Plutarch's book on the virtues of women fulfilled much the same function by providing *exempla* of female virtue. The genre was revived in the Trecento and, by the fifteenth century, collections began to include biographies of contemporaries and the recently dead, though men and women were normally separated. The groups of pagan, Jewish and Christian women promoted as exemplary by, for example, Vespasiano da Bisticci or Sabadino degli Arienti, were augmented by the biographies of famous contemporaries, women like Bianca Maria Visconti, Duchess of Milan.[15] Female virtue came now to be

4 Matteo de' Pasti, portrait medal of Leon Battista Alberti; cast bronze; Rimini, *c.*1450–5. The British Museum, London

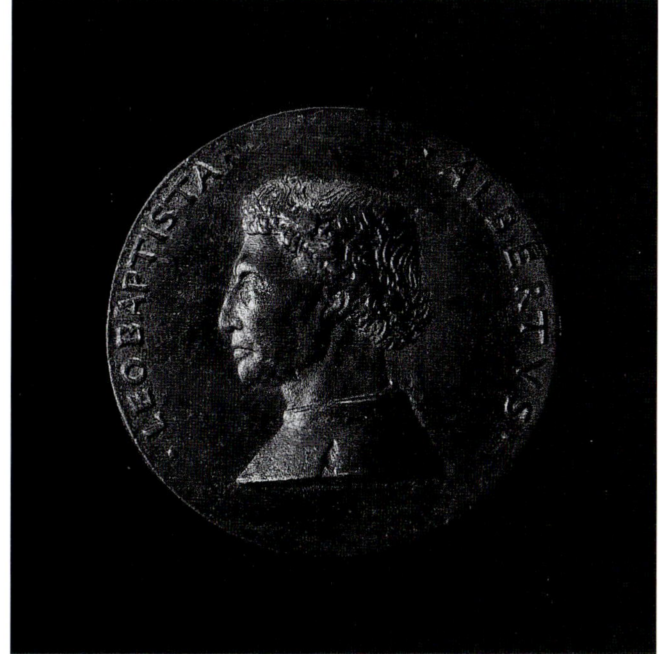
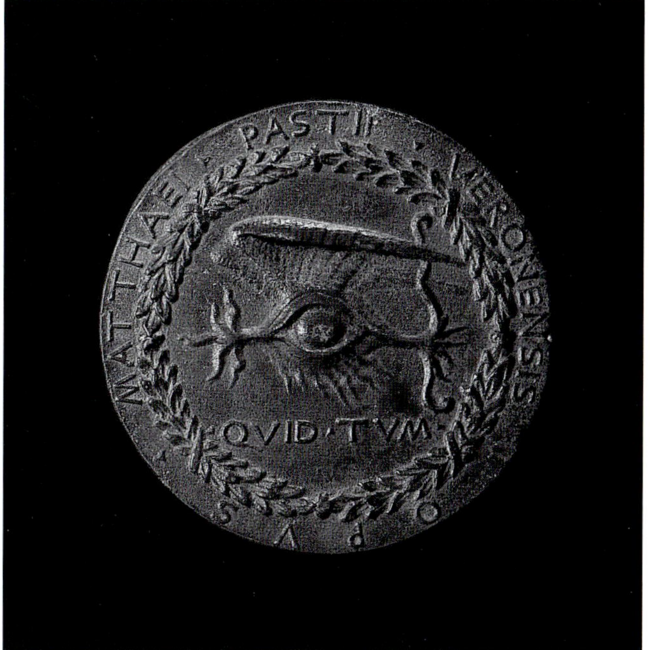

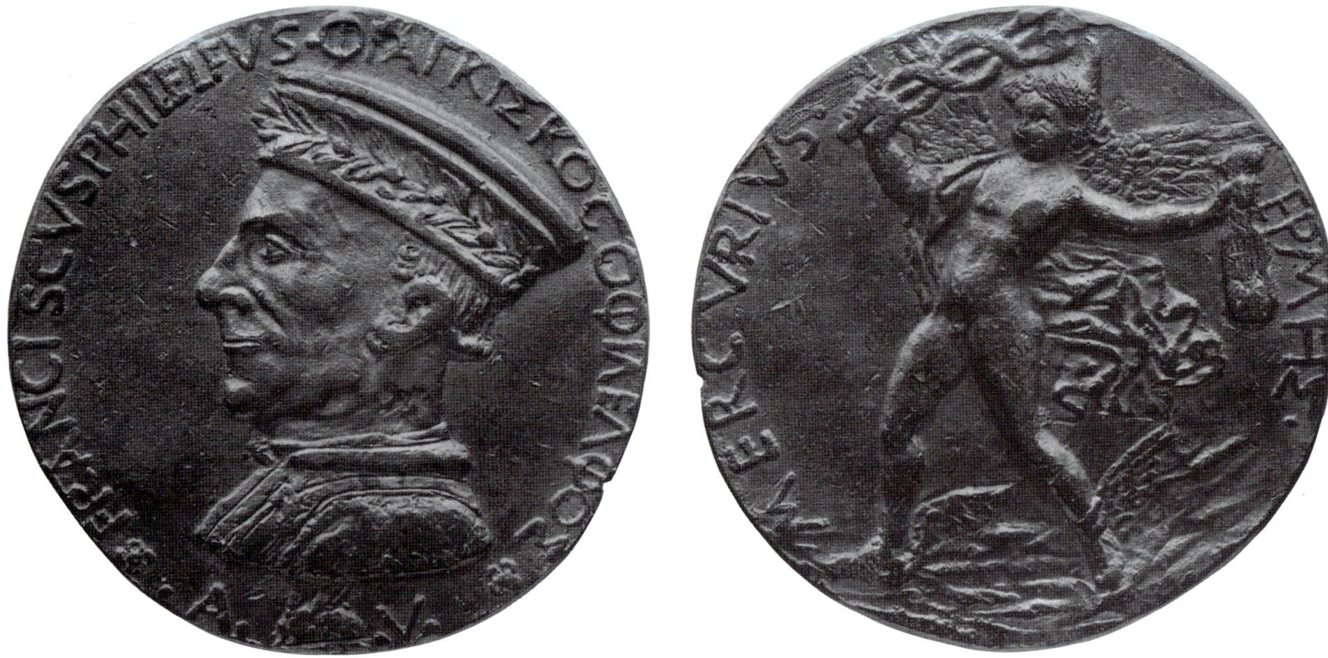

argued as much through the virtuous behaviour of contemporary women as by reference to the deeds of ancient heroines, with a corresponding emphasis on conjugal virtues, especially chastity in marriage.[16]

The scholars who wrote the biographies of famous men of antiquity and translated many of the ancient texts also wrote propagandist biographies of their peers and rulers, poetical panegyrics, and funeral orations that made explicit comparisons between, for example, Alfonso of Aragon (the Magnanimous), King of Naples; the Visconti and Sforza dukes of Milan; the Este and Gonzaga rulers of Ferrara and Mantua; the great Medici banking family of Florence; and their ancient Greek and Roman forebears.[17] This fact could not help but shape their accounts of the lives of their patrons, even if their patrons had not already been keen to establish just such connections.

What effect, then, did this thinking have on patterns of consumption in fifteenth-century Italy? It is evident that the buying and commissioning of art objects of different kinds was advocated and justified as a means of building an individual's honour and public reputation. Libraries, the repositories of virtue, were much valued. Books themselves, containing ancient texts, and the modern writings emulating them, became precious in their own right as art objects that could be sumptuously decorated and illustrated, and elaborately bound.[18] It was not unusual for a patron such as Domenico Malatesta Novello, the educated lord of Cesena, to petition a humanist like Francesco Filelfo (fig. 5) for Latin translations of famous Greek texts (and other patrons were reliant on Italian translations of Latin prose). In 1453 Domenico asked Filelfo for a translation of part of Plutarch's *Lives*, to which the humanist responded the next year by dedicating his translated biographies of Galba and Otho to his patron. The result was three manuscripts of great beauty (fig. 6), containing illuminated portraits of Plutarch's subjects by a group

5 Antonio Averlino, called Filarete, portrait medal of Francesco Filelfo; cast bronze; Milan, *c*.1447. Kunsthistorisches Museum, Vienna

of leading manuscript illuminators, thought by some to have included the most famous artist of his day, Pisanello.[19] Other manuscripts emphasize the concept of exemplarity in their illuminations. Valerius Maximus's *Memorable Acts and Sayings of the Ancient Romans* was a particularly well-read text in the fifteenth century, useful for teaching because the author had arranged the virtuous narratives of famous men according to the virtue they embodied. A manuscript illuminated before 1485 by Gaspare da Padova for Cardinal Giovanni of Aragon, son of the king of Naples, and now in the New York Public Library, shows how particular protagonists were selected to stand for a specific virtue (fig. 7). The frontispiece has profile 'portraits' of four ancient figures (one mythological) embodying the four virtues of Prudence, Temperance, Fortitude and Justice. The female personifications of these virtues are set above them; Hercules is paired with Fortitude, the emperor Augustus with Prudence.[20]

The focus on antiquity introduced new subjects for art objects. Just as books containing ancient texts and humanist treatises found their place in libraries alongside religious and chivalric writings, so a plethora of images derived from ancient texts – narrative *istorie*, moralized mythologies and single exemplary figures – jostled for space with more traditional subjects inside Renaissance palaces. From the Trecento, when Giotto painted a series of frescoes of famous men in the Neapolitan palace of King Robert of Anjou, the

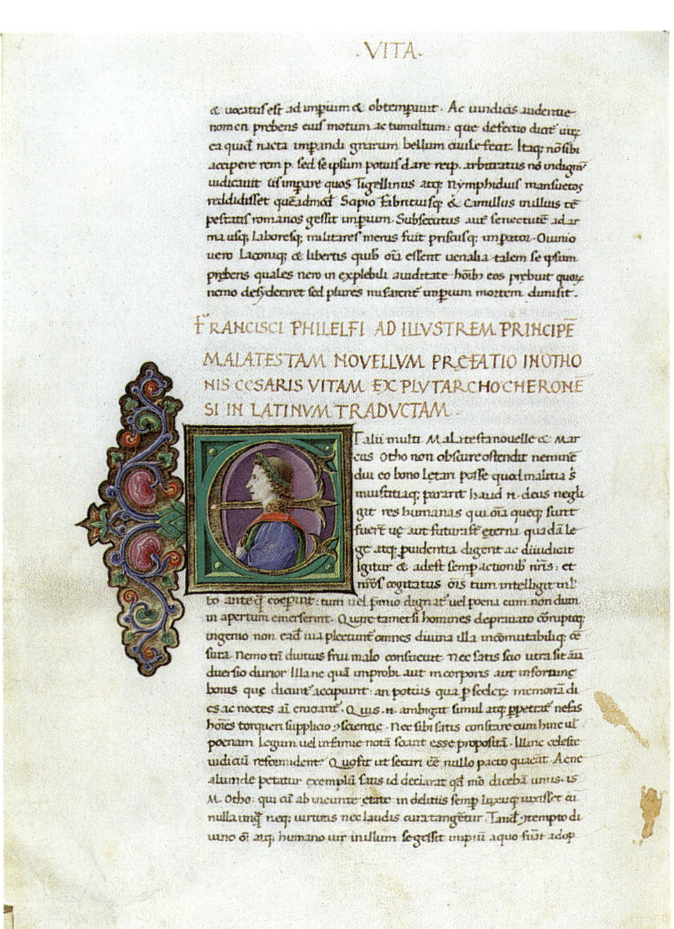

6 Illuminated portrait initial of Emperor Otho; tempera on parchment, from Plutarch, *Parallel Lives*; Cesena, *c.*1453. MS S.XV.2, fol. 233v. Biblioteca Malatestiana, Cesena

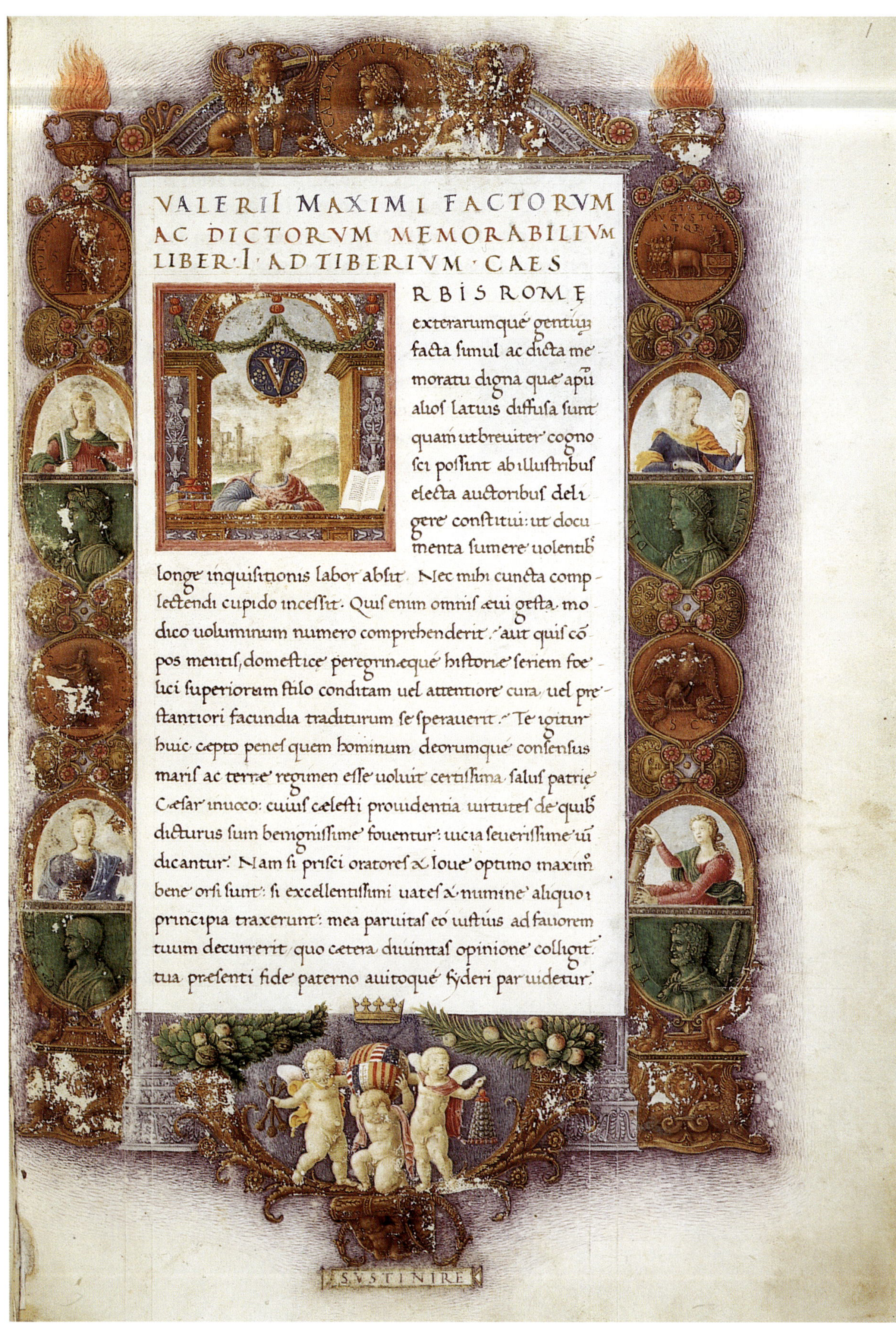

VALERII MAXIMI FACTORVM
AC DICTORVM MEMORABILIVM
LIBER I AD TIBERIVM CAES

RBIS ROMÆ
exterarumque gentiuṃ
facta simul ac dicta me
moratu digna quæ apũ
alios latius diffusa sunt
quam ut breuiter cogno
sci possint ab illustribus
electa auctoribus deli
gere constitui: ut docu
menta sumere uolentib

longe inquisitionis labor absit. Nec mihi cuncta comp
lectendi cupido incessit. Quis enim omnis æui gesta mo
dico uoluminum numero comprehenderit: aut quis có
pos mentis, domestice peregrinæque historiæ seriem foe
lici superioram stilo conditam uel attentiore cura, uel præ
stantiori facundia traditurum se sperauerit. Te igitur
huic cæpto penes quem hominum deorumque consensus
maris ac terræ regimen esse uoluit certissima salus patriæ
Cæsar inuoco: cuius cælesti prouidentia uirtutes de quib
dicturus sum benigniscime fouentur: uicia seuerissime ú
dicantur. Nam si prisci oratores a Ioue optimo maximú
bene orsi sunt: si excellentiscimi uates a numine aliquoi
principia traxerunt: mea paruitas eo iustius ad fauorem
tuum decurrerit, quo cetera diuinitas opinione colligit
tua presenti fide paterno auitoque syderi par uidetur.

depiction of historic (or pseudo-historic) *exempla* became a feature of the ornamentation of public spaces.[21] In the second half of the fifteenth century such series became more intimate, becoming standard features in the decoration of the domestic interior. Paolo Cortesi, writing at the beginning of the sixteenth century, was not the first to discuss such images as suitable decoration for a palace:

It seems to us, however, that painting would be a more frugal and advantageous manner of decoration than [terracotta, statuary or stucco], since men are fascinated by the type of painting by which they may benefit from the lessons of history brought to life. For, by the striking, life-like imitation of the thing represented in the paintings, either the appetite of the soul is aroused or virtue is spurred....[22]

Some cycles seem deliberately to have eliminated biblical and chivalric figures to give them a more undiluted classical emphasis. In the mid-1480s, for example, Eleonora of Aragon, daughter of the Neapolitan king and duchess of Ferrara, had the court artist Ercole de' Roberti paint a series of suicidal ancient heroines – Lucretia, Portia (fig. 8)

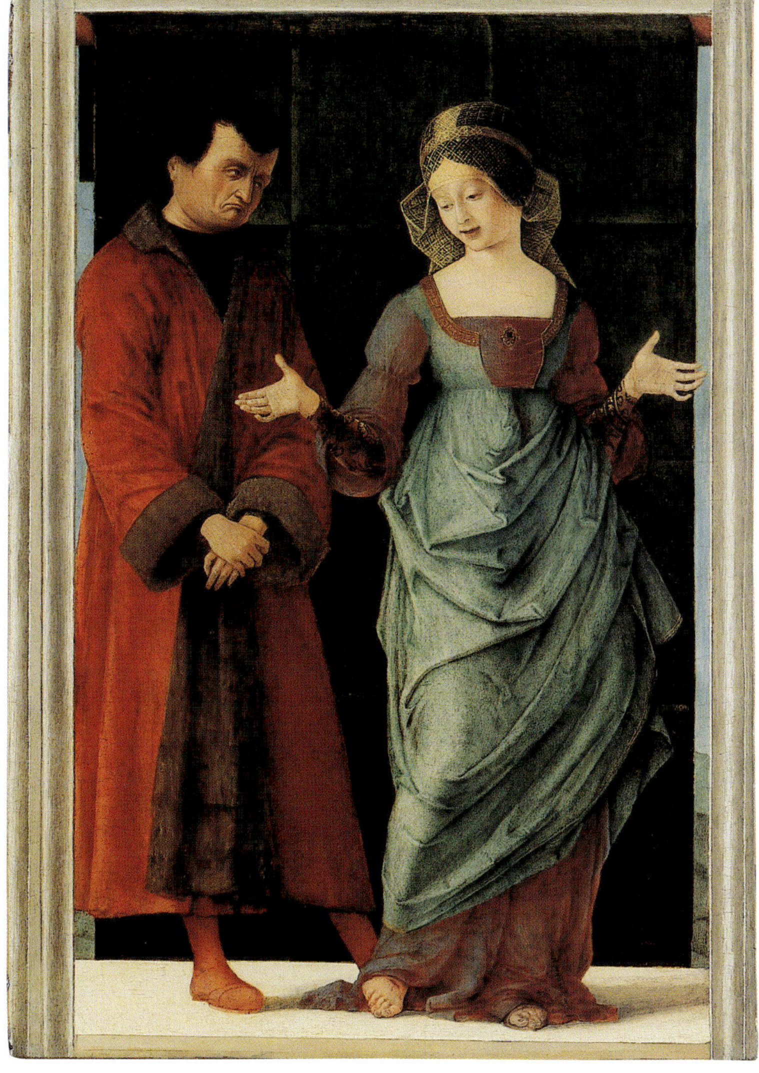

8 Ercole de' Roberti, *Portia and Brutus*; tempera and oil on panel; Ferrara, *c.*1486. Kimbell Art Museum, Fort Worth, Texas

(*Opposite page*)
7 Gaspare da Padova (attributed), illuminated frontispiece with border including figures of cardinal virtues and ancient exemplars, Roman coins, sphinxes (with script attributed to Antonio Sinibaldi); tempera and gilding on parchment, from Valerius Maximus, *Facta et dicta memorabilia*; Rome, *c.*1480–5. Spencer MS 20, fol. 1r. New York Public Library, New York

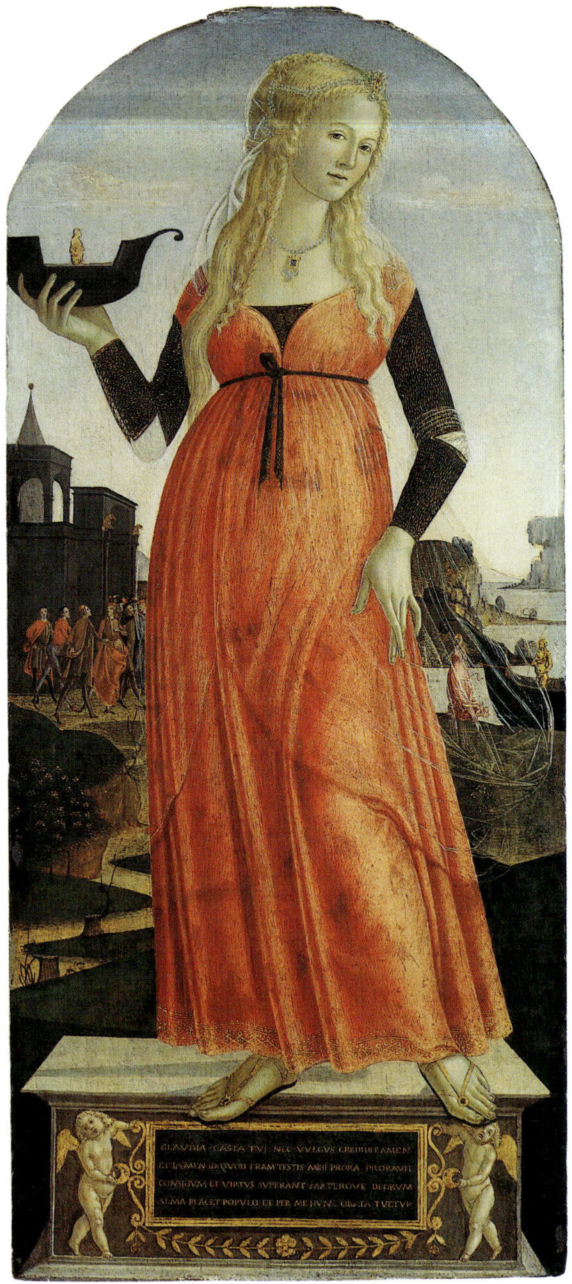

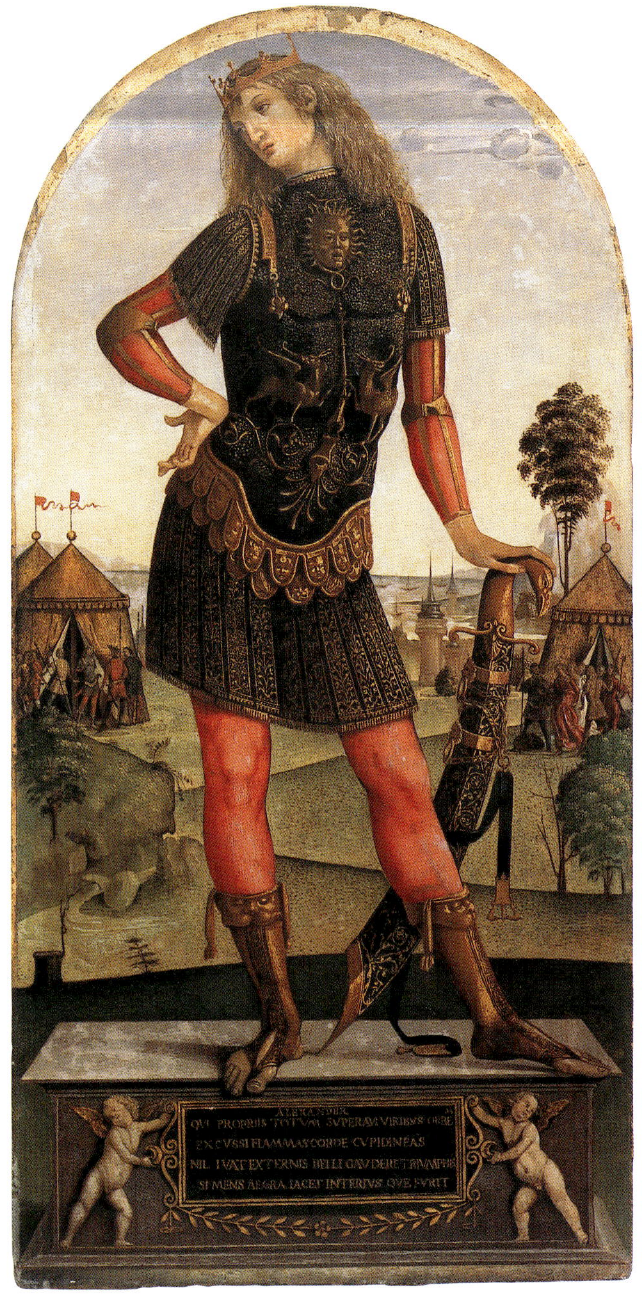

and the unnamed wife of Hasdrubal – to illustrate the motto of her royal father, King Ferrante of Naples, *Malo mori, quam foedari* (I prefer Death to Dishonour).[23] All of the iconographies find their sources in Valerius Maximus. The citizens of Siena seem to have made a speciality of such cycles. One for a member of the Piccolomini family was executed by a group of painters in the early 1490s, perhaps to mark a marriage with the powerful Placidi family, embodying the virtues of continence, chastity and conjugal love. In this instance Valerius Maximus was amplified by reference to accounts by Ovid and Plutarch (figs 9, 10).[24] The heroes and heroines are posed like statues on plinths, on which are placed explanatory Latin inscriptions provided by an anonymous humanist. Didactic narratives and the 'portrait' heads of exemplary men and women were also affixed to smaller art objects. Writing instruments and utensils and *pastiglia* boxes (boxes

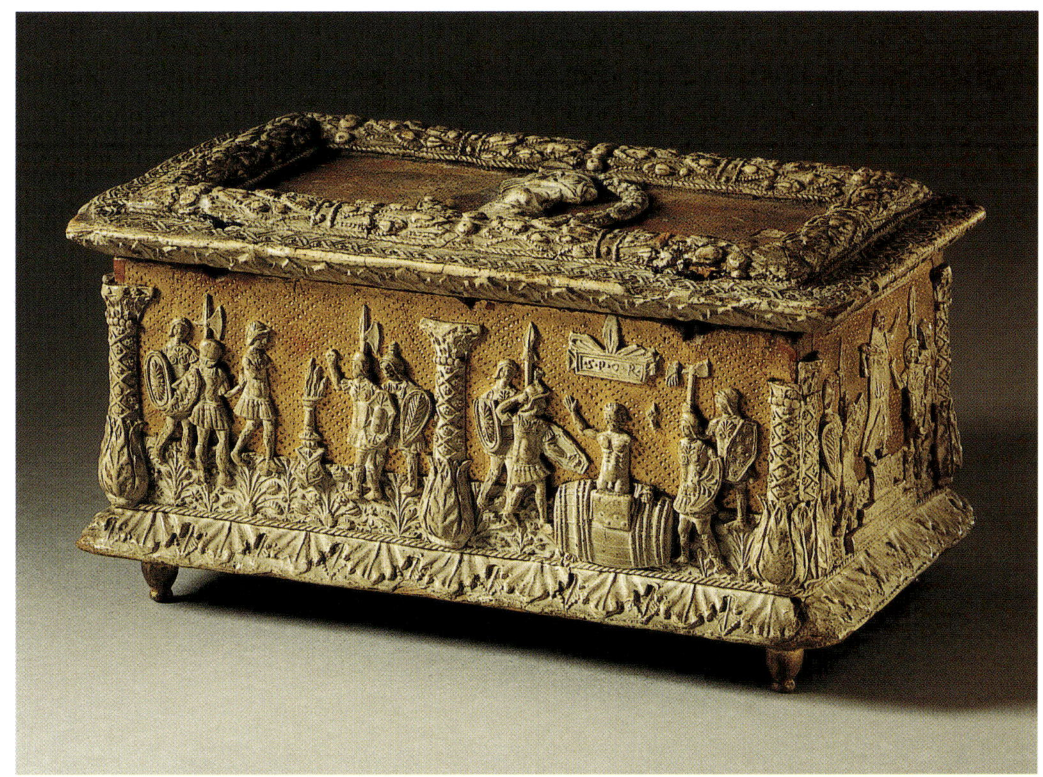

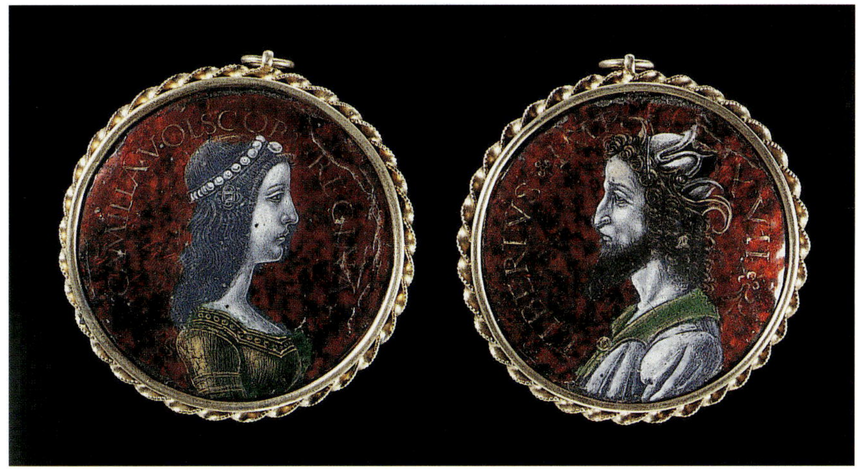

decorated with stamped reliefs), for example, used in both the study and the bedchamber, commonly featured well-known narratives – of Mucius Scaevola, Coriolanus and other heroes – taken from ancient writers (fig. 11). A rare group of enamelled roundels in The British Museum, depicting four figures from ancient history (and mythology), including Camilla and Tiberius, were executed, probably in Milan, to be attached to a valuable piece of furniture or perhaps a book binding (fig. 12).

The concept of exemplarity was extended to contemporaries. Paolo Cortesi again on the pictures to be seen every morning in bedchambers:

… pictures should be symbols of virtue so that … the soul will be excited to similar virtuous acts [throughout the day]. Thus Francesco Sforza [Duke of Milan] should be represented practising, as he did daily, his aim with a javelin, which is a symbol of prudent judgement in foretelling the

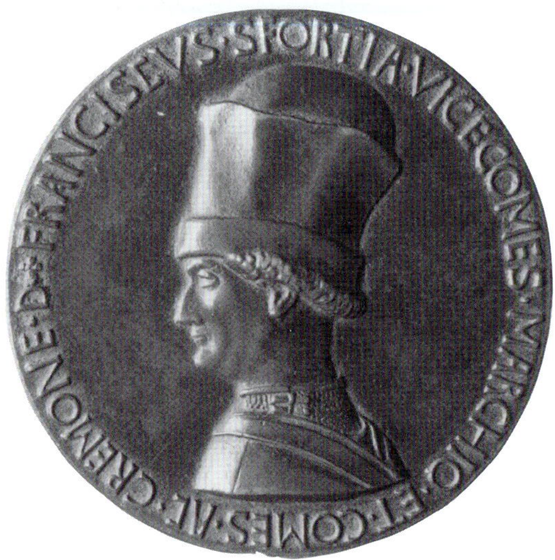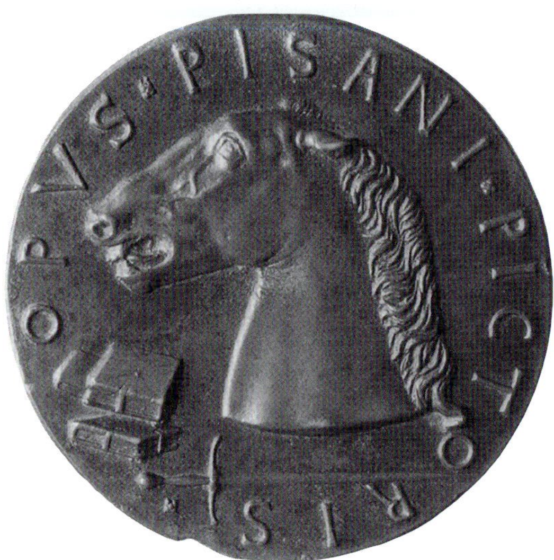

13 Pisanello, portrait medal of Francesco Sforza; cast bronze; Milan (?), *c.*1441. Münzkabinett, Staatliche Museen zu Berlin

outcome of wars. His life certainly offers examples of domestic virtues [*exempla … domestica*] which a cardinal can imitate at home.[25]

By identifying the duke of Milan as the paradigm of military prudence, Cortesi seems to accept the messages of virtue carried on the reverses of so many of the commemorative portrait medals of the period. Pisanello's medal of Francesco, executed in *c.*1441 before he wrested power in Milan, celebrates his virtues as one of Italy's leading *condottieri* (fig. 13).[26] This man might make his living by the sale of his military prowess, the medal informs us, but in doing so he takes full account of the *humanae litterae;*[27] the image of a sword and a horse's head is combined with a pile of three books. He becomes the exemplary learned soldier. Other Quattrocento medals of princely subjects amplify the portraits on their obverses with reverse emblems and allegories – even little narratives – of wisdom, faith, fortitude and so on, which magnified the professed individual virtues of these dynastic rulers, reinforcing the political claims. The virtue of liberality was much stressed, a concept that incorporated a prince's rewarding of virtue in his subjects. In 1449 Pisanello conveyed the 'Augustan' *liberalitas* of Alfonso V of Aragon, King of Naples, by showing the eagle, sitting back to allow the lesser birds of prey to feast on a dead hind (fig. 14).[28] The reverse image, illustrating the same theme, of a medal struck in about 1497 by Gian Marco Cavalli is more straightforward (fig. 15).[29] Cavalli seems likely, from the style of the piece, to have been working from designs provided by Andrea Mantegna, with whom he was to collaborate on other projects. Francesco Gonzaga, Marquis of Mantua, is depicted as an armoured figure rewarding two of his subjects. The Latin inscription LIBERALITAS is accompanied by another that translates as 'To give is divine, to accept is human', a nice distinction between noble giver and humble receiver.

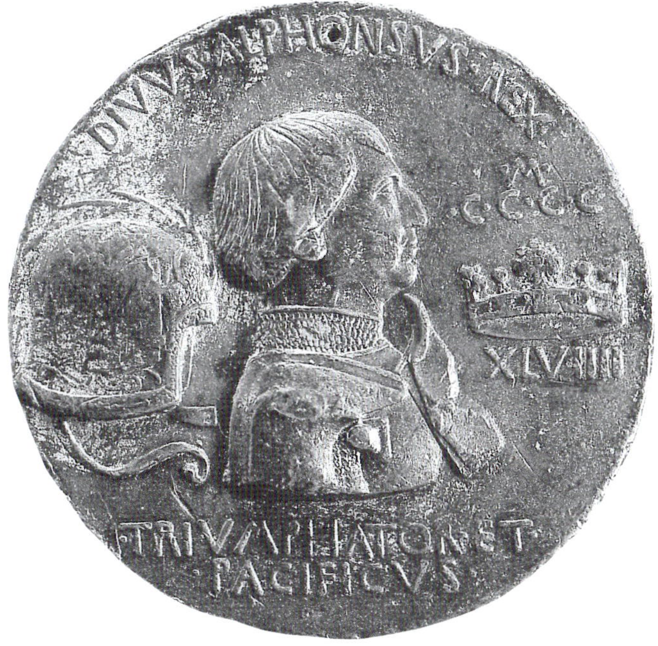
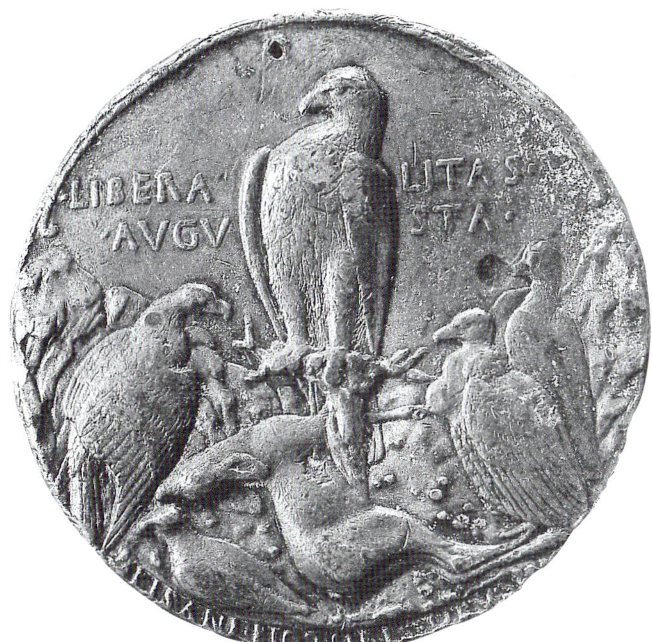

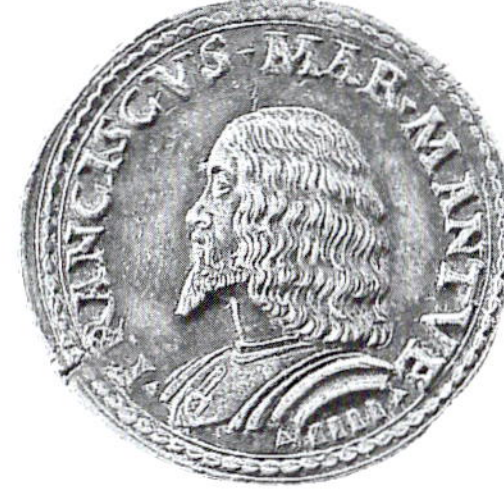
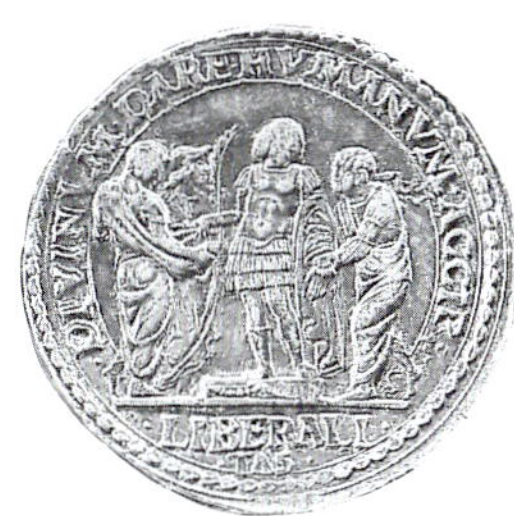

14 Pisanello (and workshop), portrait medal of Alfonso of Aragon; cast lead; Naples, 1449. The British Museum, London

15 Gian Marco Cavalli after Andrea Mantegna (?), portrait medal of Francesco Gonzaga; struck bronze; Mantua, *c*.1497. The British Museum, London

Magnificence and money

Spending money on art became in itself an outward sign of particular virtues. Central to this way of thinking were the concepts of nobility, magnificence, splendour and *gentilezza*. While wealth was a necessary precondition to the pursuit of these virtues, it was now regarded as an instrument whereby an individual could self-consciously construct a sense of his own dignity and self-esteem. Renaissance writers analysed the way in which personal honour and reputation could derive from public display, as long as the expenditure involved on such things as buildings and ceremonial was appropriate to one's status, and that the results exhibited taste and good judgement.[30] Discussion of the concept of nobility, for instance, placed a renewed emphasis on certain forms of behaviour, rather than on noble birth, in a society in which, with new money flowing, traditional feudal models were becoming eroded. It was viewed as an exclusively urban phenomenon. Poggio Bracciolini in his treatise *On Nobility* put these words into the mouth of Niccolò Niccoli: 'Nobility is gained and exercised best in cities, among people, and less easily among wild beasts in solitude or in dealings with farmers.'[31] How then was nobility to manifest itself in the objects patrons had around them? In the large part dedicated to ancient *exempla* in Platina's book *On the Prince*, the author cites Valerius Maximus's narratives of nobility. Many of the series of ancient rulers and statesmen whose actions are described befriended other men, less well-born perhaps, but who were nevertheless called 'noble' on account of their accomplishments: nobility expressed by its mutual recognition.[32] If a patron was to be able to express, visually (and therefore publicly), his own nobility by the acknowledgement of the artistic nobility of painters, sculptors and goldsmiths, new definitions of their crafts were required.

Such definitions were not slow in coming. We will see that certain materials were sometimes described as 'noble'. More importantly, in the climax to his treatise *On Painting* of 1435–6 (the Latin version of which was dedicated to Gian Francesco Gonzaga, Marquis of Mantua), Alberti called painting 'this most noble art' (*hanc nobilissimam artem*).[33] The term is echoed by the Florentine Lorenzo Ghiberti in his *Commentaries*, when he praised the Trecento Sienese painter Ambrogio Lorenzetti as, among other things, a 'most noble draughtsman'.[34] Indeed, in the first half of the Quattrocento, at just the time Bracciolini was developing his theories of what was noble, the use of the word to describe works of art seems to have spread beyond the narrow confines of humanist Florence. In a little-known chronicle by the painter Giovanni di Mastro Pedrino of Forlì, he recorded events of 1432, when Pope Eugenius IV furnished a 'most beautiful palace' to lodge the visiting Holy Roman Emperor, Sigismund IV. The Pope prepared 'several noble jewels to give him, among which he had painted a most noble little panel [*nobilissima toaletta*] by the hand of [Pisanello]'.[35] The central place given to Pisanello's picture in this account may reflect the biases of the painter-narrator. However, even allowing for status-enhancing exaggeration, his story shows that painting had become an art form that could comprise a central element in noble gift-giving between the two most powerful men of Western Europe.

Even more than nobility, the concept of magnificence was central to the commissioning and ownership of art objects. This was a quality expressed through 'spending in order to achieve sumptuousness, greatness and sublimity', in the words of one Quattrocento humanist, Sabadino degli Arienti.[36] It was a quick route to social and political acceptance, according to the opinion expressed in Alberti's dialogue *On the Family*: 'One can gain fame and authority by adopting riches in ample and noble things with much largesse and magnificence.'[37] All commentators agreed that magnificence was characterized by luxurious display, ceremonial, gift-giving, and expenditure on large public projects such as buildings.[38] Derived from Aristotle's *Nicomachean Ethics* and developed by medieval Christian writers such as Thomas Aquinas, magnificence was traditionally regarded as a princely virtue, expressed through magnanimity and largesse.[39] Magnificence in behaviour, appearance and possessions was therefore expected of rulers and princes, and especially of cardinals as princes of the Church, as a public assertion of power.[40] It signalled civility and a certain level of cultural attainment. Yet all humanists agreed that a magnificent appearance was essential in a ruler, even if it were not the outward expression of other intellectual and moral qualities.[41]

For princes and cardinals to spend money was nothing new. Ground-breaking, however, was the link between conspicuous expenditure and classical virtue and, in particular, the extension and adaptation of the concept of magnificence to a new ruling elite.[42] A lavish manuscript with illuminations attributed to Francesco Rosselli (fig. 16), containing translations from Greek into Latin of Aristotle's philosophical works, including the *Ethics,* was made for Lorenzo de' Medici, a demonstration in itself of the

(Opposite page)
16 Francesco Rosselli (attributed), illuminated frontispiece with portrait initial of Aristotle; portrait roundel of Cosimo de' Medici, and medal of his son Piero de' Medici; cameos of Roman emperors (script by Gonsalvo Fernandez de Heredia); tempera and gilding on parchment from Aristotle, *Physics, Metaphysics, On the Soul, On the Heavens, Nicomachean Ethics,* fol. 2r; Florence, *c.*1473–8. Biblioteca Medicea Laurenziana, 84, 1, Florence

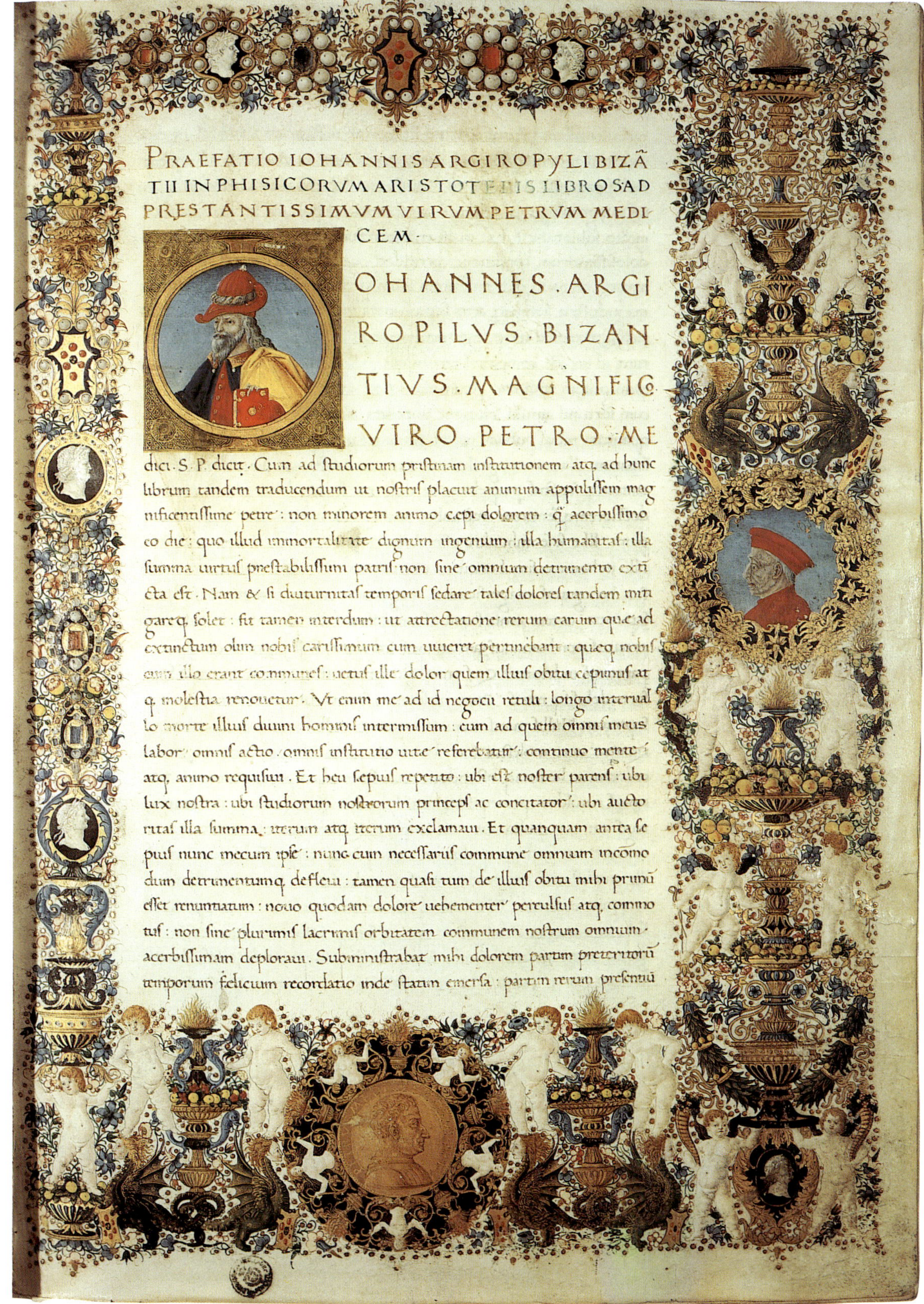

PRAEFATIO IOHANNIS ARGIROPYLI BIZÃ
TII IN PHISICORVM ARISTOTELIS LIBROS AD
PRESTANTISSIMVM VIRVM PETRVM MEDI
CEM
OHANNES . ARGI
ROPILVS . BIZAN
TIVS . MAGNIFIC
VIRO . PETRO . ME
dici . S. P. dicit . Cum ad studiorum pristinam institutionem . atq̃, ad hunc
librum tandem traducendum ut nostris placuit animum appulissem mag
nificentissime petre : non minorem animo cepi dolorem : q̃ acerbissimo
eo die : quo illud immortalitate dignum ingenium : illa humanitas : illa
summa uirtus prestabilissum patris non sine omnium detrimento exti
cta est . Nam & si diuturnitas temporis sedare tales dolores tandem miti
gareq̃ solet : fit tamen interdum : ut attrectatione rerum carum que ad
extinctum olim nobis carissimum cum uiueret pertinebant : queq̃ nobis
cum illo erant communes : uetus ille dolor quem illius obitu cepimus at
q̃ molestia renouetur . Vt enim me ad id negocii retuli : longo interual
lo morte illius diuini hominis intermissum : cum ad quem omnis meus
labor : omnis actio : omnis institutio uite referebatur : continuo mente
atq̃ animo requisiui . Et heu sepius repetito : ubi est noster parens : ubi
lux nostra : ubi studiorum nostrorum princeps ac concitator : ubi aucto
ritas illa summa : iterum atq̃ iterum exclamaui . Et quanquam antea se
pius nunc mecum ipse : nunc cum necessariis commune omnium incomo
dum detrimentumq̃ defleui : tamen quasi tum de illius obitu mihi primu
esset renuntiatum : nouo quodam dolore uehementer perculsus atq̃ commo
tus : non sine plurimis lacrimis orbitatem communem nostrum omnium ·
acerbissimam deploraui . Subministrabat mihi dolorem partim preteritoru
temporum felicium recordatio inde statim emersa : partim rerum presentiu

magnificence from which he derived his soubriquet, 'The Magnificent'. Some of these translations had originally been dedicated to Lorenzo's father Piero and his grandfather, Cosimo.[43] The 1416–17 translation of the *Ethics* into Latin by Leonardo Bruni, the humanist chancellor of Florence, had already made Aristotle's treatise more widely available, providing a virtuous classical precedent for a contemporary cult of magnificence that might otherwise have been criticized as vainglory.

Magnificence is an attribute of expenditures of the kind which we call honourable, for example those connected with the gods ... and similarly with any form of religious worship, and all those that are proper objects of public-spirited ambition ... A poor man cannot be magnificent ... but great expenditure is becoming to those who have suitable means to start with, acquired by their own efforts or from ancestors or connexions, and to people of high birth and reputation and so on; for all these bring with them greatness and prestige ... A magnificent man will also furnish his house suitably to his wealth (for even a house is a sort of public ornament), and will spend what is becoming.[44]

Following on the authority of Aristotle and of other ancient writers such as Thucydides, Seneca and Cicero, building was seen as the primary expression of magnificence.[45] It also took on a moral dimension, as an expression of individual virtue.[46] As Alberti put it in his

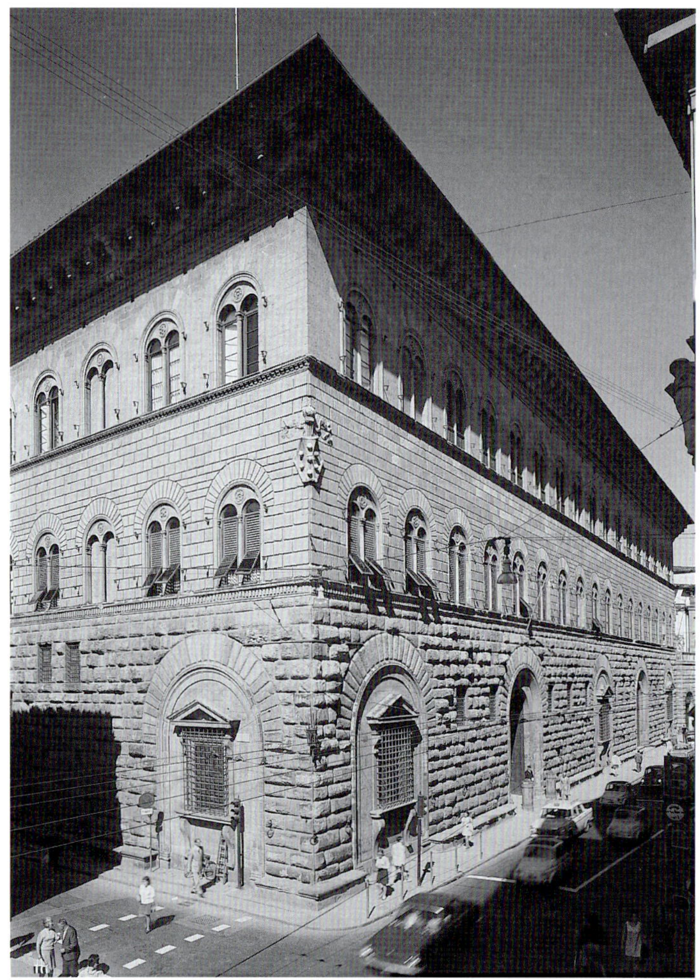

17 Michelozzo di Bartolomeo, Palazzo Medici, 1445–57, Florence

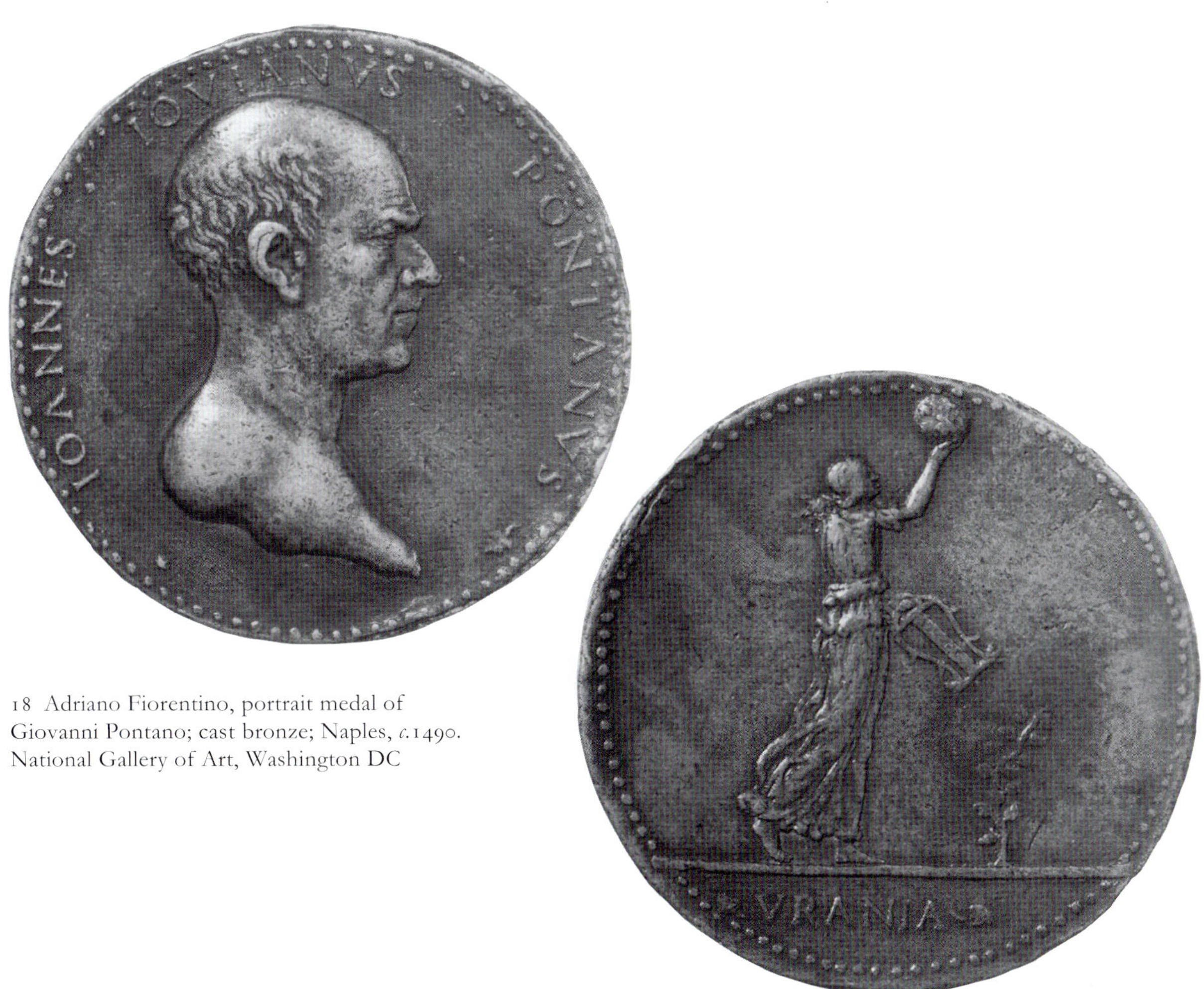

18 Adriano Fiorentino, portrait medal of
Giovanni Pontano; cast bronze; Naples, *c*.1490.
National Gallery of Art, Washington DC

treatise *On Building*: 'Since we all agree that we should endeavour to leave a reputation behind us … for this reason we erect great structures, that our posterity may suppose us to have been great persons.'[47] Magnificence through honourable expenditure on building was seen as an embodiment of personal virtue, as well as a means of enhancing and securing one's public reputation in perpetuity.[48] The aim above all was to re-create the glory of ancient Rome in the modern city. Writing in 1497, Sabadino degli Arienti praised Ercole d'Este, Duke of Ferrara, for his building projects, spreading out from the central ducal palace, through public fountains, churches, and the family's splendid villas at Belfiore and Belruiguardo. Summing up Ercole's magnificence, using a commonplace derived from Suetonius, Sabadino compares the duke with the emperor Augustus, 'who found Rome made of brick and left it built of marble'.[49]

Although the model was not narrowly Florentine, most commentators agreed that Cosimo de' Medici, who transformed the urban scene in Florence through secular and sacred building projects, was the first exemplar of magnificence in modern times (fig. 17).[50] Cosimo was consistently identified as the ideal patron of the arts.[51] In the words of Giovanni Pontano, the Neapolitan court secretary (fig. 18):

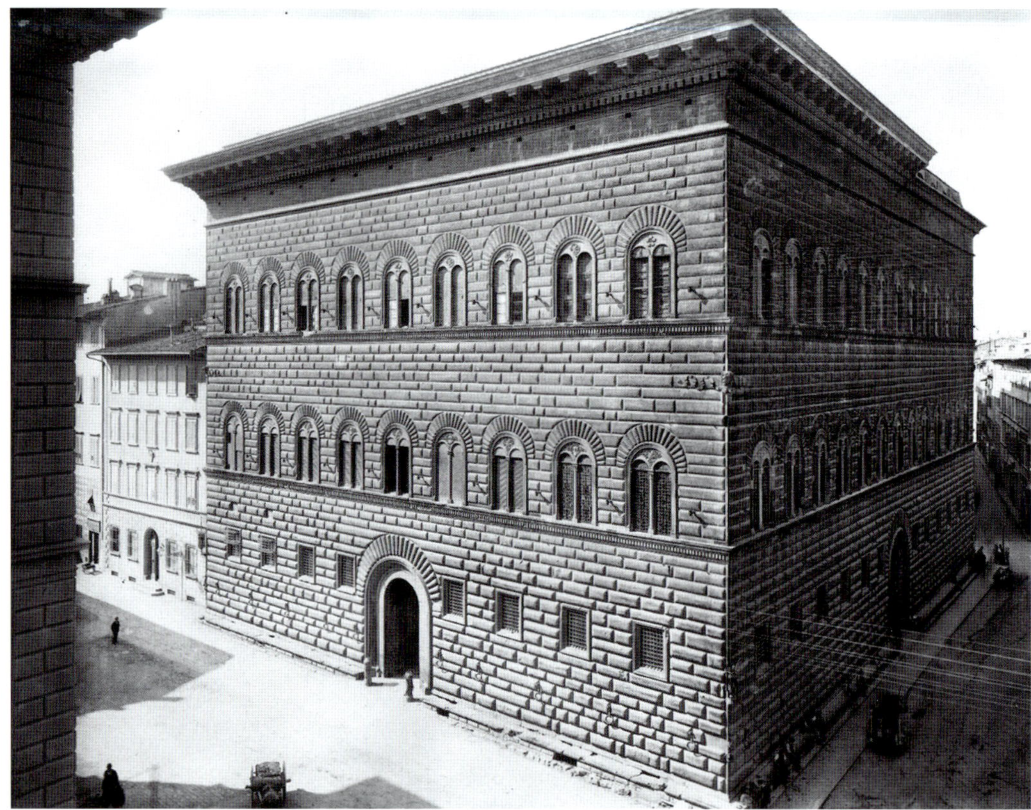

19 Giuliano da Sangallo, Il Cronaca, and Benedetto da Maiano (attributed), Palazzo Strozzi, begun 1489, Florence

In our days Cosimo [de' Medici, ruler] of Florence has renewed the ancient magnificence, both in building temples and villas and in founding libraries … he was the first to renew the custom of turning private money to public good and using it for the embellishment of his country … Cosimo's prestige was greatly enhanced both by the villas he built with extraordinary magnificence … and by the palace whose construction renewed an ancient and almost forgotten style of building.[52]

As Pontano states, style was vital. It could win approval and ensure permanence. It could even, it was thought, prevent destruction by the mob.[53] With ruins all around them as lasting physical reminders of ancient Roman greatness and grandeur, re-creating classical style in form and ornament was a way of ensuring permanence and lasting fame.[54] When the apothecary Luca Landucci looked critically across the street from his shop in Florence, he could see that the large palace being erected by Filippo Strozzi (fig. 19) was designed to last 'almost to eternity', as he recorded in his diary.[55] It was not just a matter of size and solid construction, but also of the rich carving and use of Strozzi insignia all over the building.[56] The fact of building enhanced an individual's magnificence, but it was the detailed attention to planning, materials and ornament that made a palace a public monument for ever associated with that person and his lineage.[57]

Although the emphasis of contemporary writers on the theme of magnificence was generally secular, ecclesiastical building projects were extremely highly regarded. The cathedral in Florence, for example, was the single most important building project in the city throughout the fifteenth century.[58] Individual Renaissance patrons turned to ecclesiastical patronage out of personal piety, local loyalty and a desire to commemorate or enhance their civic standing, and their own records of their expenditure on building projects often open with or include refurbishing the local church.[59] The fifteenth century saw the appropriation of ecclesiastical space through the erection of tombs, altars and family chapels in churches and religious foundations.[60] While there was perceived to be a fine balance between legitimate magnificence and extravagance,[61] between self-aggrandizement and what Machiavelli described as 'civil modesty',[62] spending on personal possessions was now considered to be a legitimate activity that touched every aspect of civic life.[63] Nor was this phenomenon restricted to Florence, although this city has been more thoroughly studied than any other.[64]

Splendour and gentilezza

This emphasis on spending well as an individual reached into the very heart of the household, into what Matteo Palmieri in the mid-1430s called 'the splendid lifestyle of private citizens' (*nello splendido vivere de' privati cittadini*).[65] Splendour was the expression of magnificence in the private sphere in a way that was perceived as being both virtuous and pleasurable. Spending gladly was part of the package.[66] Recording his own expenditure, the patrician Giovanni Rucellai stated that 'I think I have done myself more honour by having spent money well than by having earned it. Spending gave me deeper satisfaction, especially in the money I spent on my house in Florence.'[67] Developing from this new emphasis in contemporary thinking, the proper uses of wealth within the domestic interior became a matter of moral and ethical debate. Giovanni Pontano articulated his sense of the term 'splendour' through a discussion of household furnishings and their proper role in building public reputation:[68]

By household furnishings we mean every domestic item such as dining vessels and plate (*vasa, lances*), hangings, bedsteads and things of this kind, without which it is not possible to live in a fitting manner … we call objects ornamental if we acquire them as much for use as for embellishment and splendour, such as statues, panel paintings, tapestries, benches, seats inlaid with ivory, cloth woven with gemstones, boxes and chests painted with arabesques, crystal vases and other such things with which one adorns one's houses according to the circumstances … The sight of these things is pleasant and brings prestige to the owner of the house as long as many people are able to frequent the house and admire them. But the ornamental objects … should be as varied as possible and so too, each should be in its appropriate place. There is one [type of] object which should be adopted in the hall, another for the women's apartments; some are destined for everyday use; others kept for Holy Days and for solemn feasts.[69]

Palmieri considered that gracious civic life was created by the impression that 'magnificent households' and 'abundant furnishings' made on observers.[70] The moralist and critic Fra Sabba da Castiglione (fig. 20) recommended rich furnishings because they 'argue for talent, polite manners, civility and courtly values' (*ingegno, politezza, civiltà e cortegiania*).[71] Just as the exterior of a palace should express the virtue of the patron who built it, so the art objects and furnishings with which people surrounded themselves in the domestic interior were now seen as the means whereby they could convey their own sense of decorum, refinement and civility.

The prestige of possession extended beyond antiquities, works of art and silver plate to

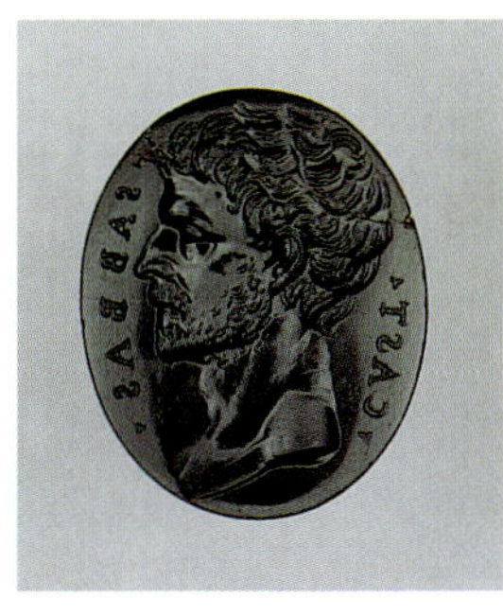

20 Giovanni Bernardi da Castelbolognese (attributed), gem portrait of Fra Sabba da Castiglione; sard intaglio; Rome or Faenza, before 1533. The British Museum, London

a small core group of furnishings by the mid-fifteenth century.[72] These were splendid and ornate pieces of furniture incorporating the family's arms and devices, which confirmed and conferred honour. Ranging from architectonic sets of inlaid or painted furniture, such as bedsteads and daybeds, to painted chests and birth trays of the kind described in Chapter Two, these pieces were retained when others were sold, and individuals made provision for them in their wills.[73] These were all art objects, in which design, invention, artistry and technical skill, were valued components. Giovanni Rucellai, mentioning with pride the number of inlaid pieces of furniture in his house 'by the best masters not only in Florence, but in Italy' was making a considerable claim, for in his own estimation 'there have never before been such master craftsmen in woodwork, in inlay or in marquetry, capable of such great skill in perspective that it cannot be bettered in painting'.[74]

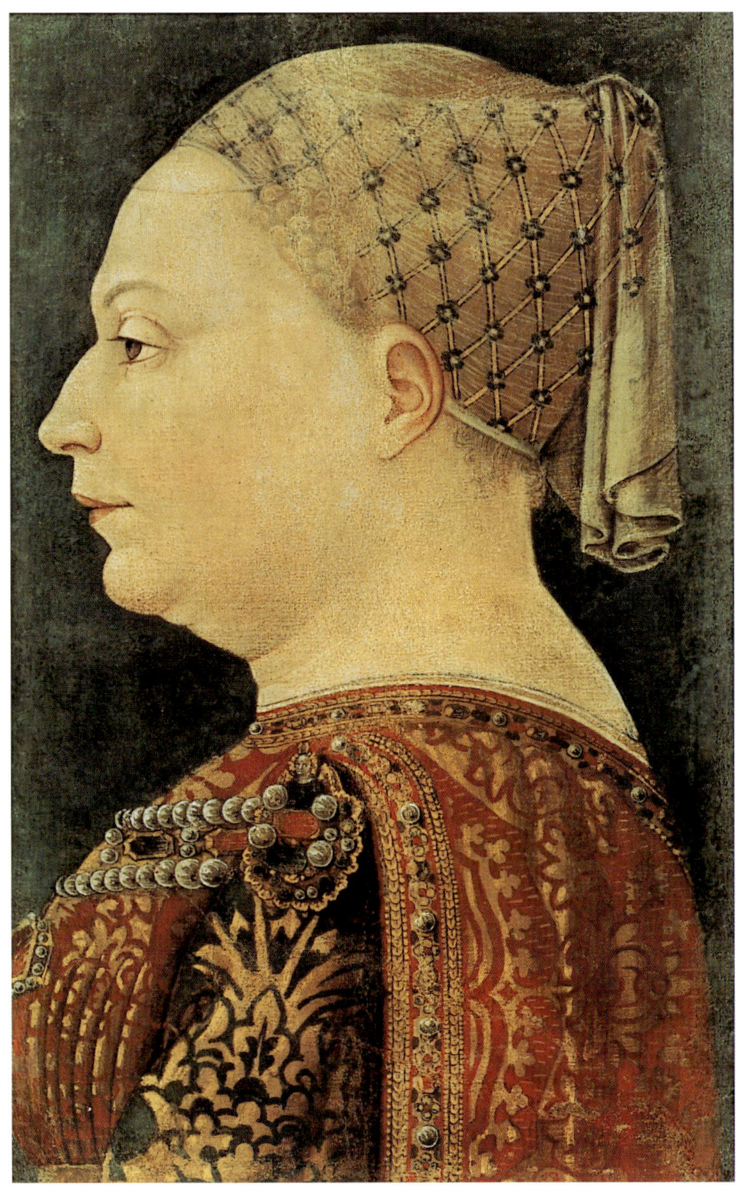

21 *Bianca Maria Visconti, Duchess of Milan*; tempera on canvas; Ferrara or Milan, *c.*1460–70. Pinacoteca di Brera, Milan

The concept of splendour was thus intimately linked with notions of discrimination, decorum and appropriateness: the boundary between magnificence or splendour and ostentation was crucial in contemporary thinking. Sumptuary laws were proclaimed by civil governments, attempts – not usually very successful – to impose decorum by ensuring that men and women dressed according to their rank, and to control and curb lavish expenditure, seen as a moral and financial threat to the established social order.[75] When Nicolosa Castellani composed an oration protesting against sumptuary legislation imposed by papal authority in Bologna in 1453, when all women were denied cloth of gold or silver, she based her arguments on commonly held views of the virtue of outward display. Such an edict removed the proper distinction of rank, depriving noblewomen of the only means they could employ to proclaim their status publicly. In addition, she argued that women such as Battista Sforza, Duchess of Urbino, and Bianca Maria Visconti (fig. 21) should be able to express their personal merit – indeed, their learning – for which they were famed, through their fine attire.[76] If the oration was delivered, the cardinal legate was not persuaded, but neither were the Bolognese citizenry to take much notice of his views. After the wedding of Sante Bentivoglio, first citizen of Bologna, to Ginevra Sforza, the event that had provoked the sumptuary edict in the first place, hundreds of their guests were excommunicated as a result of their lavish clothing.

However, humanist observers demanded that individuals should do more than obey legislation; for men and women to display true splendour they should possess the ability to discriminate, to observe decorum for themselves. According to one contemporary, 'very few Italians in fact live the life of true gentlemen, even if they have the manner and style of a gentleman'.[77] Perceptive commentators distinguished between substance and inappropriate show. Pope Pius II observed of Borso d'Este that: 'He desired to seem rather than to be magnificent and generous … He bought as many precious stones as he could and never appeared in public without jewels. He collected rich household furnishings: even in the country he used gold and silver dishes.'[78] Borso stands condemned for importing overly ostentatious, excessively urbane values into the pastoral context of the villa, where humbler dining vessels would have been more appropriate.

A poem by Antonio Camelli, criticizing Milanese women for their vulgar ostentation in dress and jewellery, makes much the same point:

> Their dresses of silk and rose-colour,
> Their head-dresses of cloth of gold, on the breast a jewel,
> Sleeves embroidered, or made of silk brocade.
> On the shoulder a rich and beautiful balas ruby;
> Interlaced pearls around the neck,
> With an engraved gem or nielloed pendant [hanging from the necklace],
> Every finger wears a ring.

Such is the cumulative impression that, the poet writes, seeing them dining at table, you are reminded of the overcrowded counter of a German shop (*paion tutti botteghe da Tedeschi*).[79]

If Borso and the women of Milan were getting it wrong, how should they have decorously combined magnificence with appropriate modesty? In his mid-fifteenth-century biography of the king of Naples, Vespasiano da Bisticci tells of a joke played by

Alfonso of Aragon that clearly distinguishes between an outsider's flashy ostentation and the king's noble splendour. Such a distinction between sobriety and vulgarity in dress was to be repeated by Baldassare Castiglione in what is now probably the most celebrated prescriptive text of the period, his *Book of the Courtier*.[80] Vespasiano wrote:

Sometimes the king would divert himself … There was once in Naples a Sienese ambassador who, after the way of his people, was very haughty, and as the king mostly wore black clothes, with a buckle to his cap and a chain of gold round his neck, being seldom seen clad in silk or brocade, this ambassador when he had audience with the king would always wear garments of the richest gold brocade. The king often jested with those about him concerning the wearing of this brocade, and one day he said, laughing, to one of his gentlemen,'… I should like to alter the colour of that brocade.' He then arranged an audience in a poor apartment, and commanded that everybody should jostle the Sienese ambassador in his brocaded coat … so that none of those who knew the story could keep from laughing when the court was over at seeing how this brocaded coat, once crimson, trimmed with fur and golden fringe, was marred and spoilt. When the king saw him go out of the room in this plight, he could not refrain from laughing….[81]

Beyond the mere fact of ownership, it was therefore the individual's sense of the aesthetic qualities inherent in art objects, and his sense of decorum in using them and incorporating them into his daily manner of life, that singled him out from his peers. As Pontano himself says, 'The vulgar [*sordidus*] and the splendid [*splendens*] man both use a knife at table. But one of them uses a knife which is sweaty [*immundus*] and has a horn handle; and the other uses a shining knifeblade which has a handle made either of some noble material [*aut e praestanti materia*] or which has been worked with craftsmanship [*aut affabrefacto*].'[82] It was not just cleanliness and good manners that communicated one's social standing, but the variety and perceived quality and style of serving dishes and utensils.[83] This was expressed early on in Vespasiano da Bisticci's famous description of the merchant-humanist Niccolò Niccoli dining:

Of all men [ever born] he was by far the cleanest, in his eating habits as in all else. When he was at table he ate from the most beautiful antique vessels and in the same way his table was full of ceramic vessels [*vasi di porcellana*] and other most ornate vessels, and he drank from cups of rock crystal or some other fine hardstone. To see him at table, as old as he was, gave one a sense of gentility [*era una gentilezza*]. He always insisted that the table cloth before him be of the whitest, like all his other linen. Some may be astonished to hear that he possessed such a vast quantity of table-ware, and to these may be answered that in his day things of this sort were not so much in vogue or so highly prized as they have been since. There was no house in Florence that was more adorned than his or where there were more refined things than in his, so that whoever went there, whatever his interests, found an infinite number of worthy things.[84]

Vespasiano sets up Niccoli as an *exemplum* of splendour as an ancient virtue concerned with decorum, the dignity of an individual and its outward expression. Here was a self-reliant man whose discrimination far outstripped his spending power, who was neverthe-less, by these qualities, able to lead his contemporaries in the revival of ancient art and learning.[85] Tellingly, Vespasiano followed his eulogy of Niccoli with an account of the rediscovery of Pliny the Elder's *Natural History*, the text that was instrumental in shaping contemporary attitudes not only to artists and their particular kinds of skills, but also to collecting and classical learning.[86] His praise of Niccoli is informed by his sense of the value of ancient civilization, and Niccoli's role in revitalizing it in modern Florence.

In addition to his classical sense of gravity and decorum, Vespasiano proposes Niccoli as a model of a more distinctly modern sense of civilized behaviour, *gentilezza*, which he also valued highly. *Gentilezza* carried a range of meanings and associations. It could denote gentle birth and social status. Household lists of the Este court in the last quarter of the fifteenth century rank *zentilhuomini* only just after the five companions (*compagni*), the closest associates of the duke.[87] But the word could also encapsulate gentle manners or nobility of spirit. As with the Renaissance reassessment of nobility and noble behaviour, so with gentility: manner and inner character were a vital element in the equation. In his romance, *Filocco*, Giovanni Boccaccio gave one of his characters a speech in favour of *gentilezza* as a spiritual quality rather than a distinction of birth or status. 'If we rightly consider what gentility truly is, … we shall find it to be solely a quality of the spirit. And whatever may be the social rank of someone who is found to have a virtuous spirit, that person rightly may be, and must be, called gentle.'[88]

Gentilezza qualified magnificence and splendour in that it defined artistic discernment and attuned, educated tastes. It was a quality that distinguished the ruling elite and that could be used, along with satirical wit, to differentiate the ruler from the ruled. The humanist scholar Angelo Poliziano used an anecdote about Cosimo de' Medici to prove the superiority of city culture and Cosimo's place within it. When Cosimo, first citizen of Florence, magnanimously offered a visiting peasant a muscatel pear – a delicacy despite its shrivelled appearance – the peasant exclaimed 'Oh, we give those to the pigs.' Cosimo replied, 'We don't', and motioned to a servant to take the pears away.[89]

The point of the story is to celebrate the superiority of educated urban values. The contemporary concept of *gentilezza* centred on the necessity of perceiving and appraising the right value and aesthetic quality inherent in things as proof of being truly civilized.[90] This is where a passionate concern, shared by patrons and artists alike, for form and style in art objects became significant, as not only conveying, but transmitting moral qualities. Just as art could be *nobile*, so too is it described as *gentile*. The programme provided by Leonardo Bruni in 1424 for what were to be Ghiberti's second set of doors for the Florentine Baptistry stated that the reliefs should be in humanist terms *illustri* (vivid), *significanti* (worthy of memory) and *gentile*.[91] This last term Ghiberti would have recognized, since he described the painters Simone Martini and Lippo Memmi as *gentili maestri*.[92]

Rituals for virtuous display

The social virtues described here were displayed at key moments that were partly designed to show them off. Each rite of passage had its distinct rituals to mark and display social distinctions. Lying-in following birth was a major event in the life of a patrician family, highlighting the importance of family and lineage and, in the case of a dynasty, securing and legitimizing their hold on power (see fig. 164). This was an occasion for special displays of furnishings and art objects in the bedchamber, serving as a reception room. The urban elites of other cities made no less of an event of lying-in, to the extent that sumptuary legislation was introduced to curb conspicuous consumption and public display of wealth. In Milan, the ducal government attempted to limit the use of expensive materials, ultramarine blue, gold and silver leaf, in painting and decorating furniture such as cradles.[93] Nevertheless, the Milanese court put on its own spectacle, as a Ferrarese lady attending the ceremonies associated with the birth of an heir to Lodovico Sforza in 1493 wrote back to her native city. She describes the visitations and the various displays put up in the rooms leading to the birthing chamber:

Firstly, in the great chamber of the treasury, which acted as an antechamber to the illustrious birthing chamber, the tribune of silver vases was opened … From this one entered the birthing chamber … near the fire [was] the bed where the most illustrious lady lay … This bed, with a bench round it, was covered in red velvet brocade and was covered with a hanging of crimson cloth entirely embroidered with letters and massive gold roses. The letters were in one case 'LUD', and in the other, 'BEATRICE' done delicately and both had a white enamelled rosette. And so too, the small headboard above had a golden apple, lovely and delicate. Around the hangings there was a rich golden fringe and they say that it was worth about 8,000 ducats, and they say that the other fittings … came to 7,000 ducats.[94]

The baby Massimiliano had a cradle in an adjoining room, which had been 'made here in Milan, very elegant, and entirely gilded with four columns and a lovely canopy made of gold cords and blue silk with its tiny hangings covered with cloth of gold as high as the tester, truly a rich and elegant object'.[95] The proud father held audience in a reception room where presided the court astrologer, 'without whom nothing is done'.[96] The ceremonies were supervised by the seneschal, who received the guests and ensured that each 'according to their respective dignity' was allowed to visit the different rooms.[97] Special cradle coverlets could also be made of silk taffeta, lined with fur or down or decorated with embroidery, which made a cradle an object for displaying a baby.[98] Such considerations were particularly important for Italy's ruling dynasties, especially in marking the birth of a male heir. The Este rulers of Ferrara seem to have made a speciality of cradles, sending another one 'worthy of an emperor' to Milan in 1493 to mark Massimiliano's birth.[99]

The same stress on family lineage, especially in the interest of male heirs and male bloodlines, marks the pomp and circumstance seen in funeral and mourning rituals.[100] These developed in the course of the fifteenth century as a means of asserting social distinctions. An individual's will could stipulate the sums to be spent on the various expected elements: funeral expenses; the nature of a grave and how it was to be marked or identified or, further up the social scale, the type of tomb and its location within a family chapel; the number of family members who were to wear expensive cloth in their mourning dress; the numbers of clergy, candles and masses.[101] Spending on a grandiose and beautiful tomb, and often on the family chapel around it, was an important element in building magnificence and was generally justified as money well spent.[102] As one Florentine patrician put it, 'After this life, we need somewhere to live.'[103] Moreover, Pontano considered the glory of ancient Roman tombs as having 'the marvellous power of exhorting us to virtue and to glory, especially when they are dedicated to worthy men'.[104] Nevertheless the emphasis on the moral worth of the individual was important, as that is where virtue lay, rather than in the splendour of sculpted marble. As Leonardo Bruni argued: 'In what way can a tomb, a dumb thing, help a wise man?'[105] A man's reputation lay in his good name and in his work, which would speak for him eloquently in a way that no mute monument could.

Bruni may have chosen to emphasize the virtue of the individual, but it is evident that the rituals and monuments in Florence commemorated an individual as a worthy member of a social group – usually, but not exclusively, the family or the wider clan network.[106] Filippo Strozzi stipulated in his will that his funeral should be 'ornate', and so it was, as his son dutifully recorded.[107] The full clergy of the Church of San Lorenzo were employed, and the entire Church of Santa Maria Novella was draped in expensive black cloth as a sign of mourning. Similar cloth was provided for male members of the Strozzi clan, and large numbers of candles were provided. The number and quality of candles was an immediate and understood indicator of social status and a major expense in itself. The finishing touch was the unexpected display of deference provided by the craftsmen who had been employed by Filippo in constructing his great family palace. It was 'a spectacle unknown to our city'.

Although they were evident in other rituals, contemporary attitudes to magnificence, legitimate display and decorum were particularly apparent in the series of events marking betrothal and marriage. As a secular affair, confirmed rather than made by religious ceremony, marriage was regulated by secular unwritten custom, which varied from region to region and according to social status. Marriage was perceived as a way of building a family's power and prestige through alliance that would strengthen its social standing, honour and political influence. It was therefore regarded as a public rather than private matter, for the alliances between families that were made or strengthened by marriage were regarded as the fundamental building block of civil society.[108]

Contemporary commentators were in no doubt that marriage was a legitimate occasion for magnificence. Pontano devoted a special section of his treatise on magnificence to wedding rituals.[109] Man, he explains, distinguishes himself from the animals by the fact that he forms stable relationships for the benefit of children through marriage.[110] Marriage alliances also consolidate the social fabric as all citizens are 'chained together' through these links. 'Rightly then have marriages been held in high esteem by princes and private citizens, both in ancient Rome and in our own time, and rightly should one exhibit a particular splendour and magnificence in celebrating them.'[111] He cites as an example the wedding festivities organized by Alfonso of Aragon to celebrate the marriage of his niece, Eleonora of Portugal, with the Holy Roman Emperor, Frederick III, in 1452. This was marked by hunting before an elaborate dinner 'for over thirty thousand people', served out of doors beneath awnings, with wine fountains. Spectators were rewarded with gifts of food. 'I do not know if the sun had ever seen anything more magnificent of this type of magnificence.'[112] All this was legitimate ostentation in Pontano's eyes, while he cites the examples of the ancient Roman emperors Nero and Heliogabalus as having been merely profligate in their spending.[113] For Pontano, contemporary magnificence expressed through marriage outshone any ancient precedent.

The same feeling of rivalry with ancient Roman culture lies behind the comments made by Leonardo Bruni concerning his own wedding in 1412.[114] As the author of a panegyric to the city of Florence, Bruni regarded the magnificence of the urban scene as evidence that Florentines were 'capable of acquiring dominion and sovereignty over all the world'.[115] The same was true of the high level of expenditure and luxury to be seen at his wedding. His bride, Tomassina di Simone della Fioraia, commanded an extremely high dowry of

1,100 gold florins, indicating her high social rank.[116] Celebrating the marriage therefore demanded an appropriately high level of expenditure and display. Describing the wedding feast in a letter to his friend Poggio Bracciolini, Bruni tells how

I emptied the market, I exhausted the spice dealers, the taverns, the cooks, the makers of stuffings, the poulterers – the famous and unknown ones alike. But while these costs may seem huge, they aren't really, because they bring more fuss than expense and involve more noise than loss. But what is much more intolerable, is that there's no end to the women's clothes and finery. I could wish that those Romans of yours, of whom nothing of their former glory has remained besides empty boasting, could see the gold, the silver, the purple, the pearls, and the rest of the adornments of the women of Florence, so that they would leave off having such an absurdly high opinion of themselves.[117]

The teasingly misogynist tone of Bruni's letter echoes the condemnation of women expressed in sumptuary legislation. The displays of riches in private houses at noble weddings, and the cost of women's clothing and jewellery worn and paraded at these occasions were seen as causes of concern.[118] 'Women have forgotten,' proclaimed a Florentine law,

that it is not in conformity with nature for them to decorate themselves with such expensive ornaments when their men, because of this, avoid the bond of matrimony on account of the unaffordable expenses … For women were made to replenish this free city and to observe chastity in marriage; they were not made to spend money on silver, gold, clothing and gemstones.[119]

Once again such legal impositions were largely ignored and art objects of all kinds were produced as markers for particular events, and had their own distinct roles within the series of rituals that constituted betrothal and marriage. The exchange and traffic of art objects, in private houses, civic spaces and street parades, conferred public legitimacy and recognition on the alliances made by marriage. We know about these customs among the urban elites from a variety of sources: sumptuary legislation, treatises and letters and account books that detail expenditure, gift exchange and negotiations between families. Surviving art objects, of the types produced and circulated at these moments, do not merely commemorate marriage, but embody contemporary concepts of virtue and honour, which were to be put on public display. For this reason, the linked ceremonies associated with marriage best demonstrate the many ways in which particular social and individual virtues were proclaimed in the arena of the Renaissance court and city. A case study of the moral values associated with marriage and the objects that embody them is therefore the basis of the next chapter.

Chapter Two

Betrothal, Marriage and Virtuous Display

In the fourth decade of the fifteenth century Leon Battista Alberti composed a nasty little satire dedicated to marriage – the institution standing condemned largely on account of the manifold failings of women. One of a series of after-dinner literary bon-bons, he dedicated an Italian version of his 'advice' to Piero de' Medici: 'I loved you because I judged that your virtue and breeding clearly merited my love and that of other scholars'. The tone of the dialogue is brutally misogynist throughout (one character echoes the words spoken by Cato the Elder in Livy's *History of Rome*, 'for like an untamed beast, they say, a woman can never be bridled'), and, of the three male interlocutors, one, Trissophus, makes great claims for his bachelor state. In doing so, however, he adumbrates the various reasons that might tempt a young Florentine to take a wife:

But despite your arguments, your urgings, and your pressures, I resolutely thwarted your attempts to make me enter the blight of matrimony. My firm resolve was not shaken by your promises of lavish dowries, of kinship with noble families, of women's beauty, of prestigious matches, of hopes of offices and honours, or of alluring displays of wealth.[1]

All of these, bar one, have a more or less practical foundation. However, all of them could be reconstructed as social virtues: good citizenship, magnificence and nobility. Alberti (or Trissophus) omits, not unexpectedly, the concept of selfless love, which he expounded in his treatise *On the Family* – theories adapted from Aristotelian and Ciceronian common-places of ideal friendship.[2] Alberti held much the same view as the one expressed by Francesco Filelfo in a Latin letter of 1439 celebrating the marriage of a friend; Filelfo argued that the three best qualities of marriage were honour or virtue, usefulness and pleasure.[3] Nor does Alberti's list in this dialogue contain the utilitarian justification for marriage, which was so commonly adduced in the period – the need to produce children.

In Florence, as in Venice, marriages tended to be contracted between the families of fellow citizens, an element within the city's elaborate network of political and commercial patronage and allegiance. In Naples and the northern Italian courts, marriage was similarly viewed as a political and diplomatic tool, but now with a more international out-look. Although the arrangement of local marriages could be used to tie local aristocratic families more closely to the ruling house, unions were also designed to raise the status of ruling families (an oldest son taking a bride from a longer established or more powerful dynasty in Italy or beyond), and to cement alliances between states (in these cases it was often daughters, legitimate and illegitimate, who were ruthlessly exploited as diplomatic tools). Bianca Maria Sforza, for example, the daughter, sister and niece of successive dukes of Milan, was affianced twice before the highly desirable future Holy Roman Emperor Maximilian I was finally landed.

In all these cities art objects had their part in the practical business of arranging a marriage; their value lay in their capacity to translate both tangible wealth and practical function into messages of abstract virtue. Marriage comprised a series of rituals demanding complex social exchanges in which art objects played a key role as symbolic markers, bearing a range of associations and cultural resonances for contemporaries; during the betrothal period, which might last for some months, requisite art objects would be commissioned, purchased, exchanged and assembled. Objects and furnishings, acquired to celebrate and commemorate matrimony, stressed the importance of both individual virtue *and* family and lineage through their narratives, moralizing and symbolic imagery, and the use of arms, emblems and devices to signal ownership and alliance. Art objects are frequently listed among the debits, gifts, loans, exchanges, purchases and sales that accompanied particular moments in the series of events which constituted betrothal and marriage.[4]

In Florence, the city that has been most studied from this point of view, ritual exchanges were often carefully documented by the groom, or by his male relatives, in memoranda books.[5] In recording these transactions, men were concerned above all with property rights, but also by the financial and familial debts they incurred in marking marriage alliances with due ceremony, decorum and magnificence. This was the time when many patrician Florentine men opened their account books, the moment when they entered the art market, buying, trading and commissioning art objects and rich furnishings for what was to be transformed into the marital bedchamber. Such items as fine mirrors with heraldic markers on the frames, painted wall panels (*spalliere*), birth trays (*deschi da parto*) for display on the walls, Virgin and Child paintings and reliefs, and the bedstead with its accompanying chests and matching daybed, painted or with wooden inlaid decoration, incorporating the families' arms, were often put together in the room at this point. The bedstead and wall panels could be designed and made as a set to be built into a specific room, with mottoes, inscriptions and arms. Designed as objects that demonstrated and strengthened a family's sense of its honour and collective virtues, expressed through a set of recorded individual histories, they were made to be treasured over several generations. This special category of fine furnishings was known in fifteenth-century Florence as *masserizie*, a word that, revealingly, covers not only furniture and utensils but also the concept of domestic economy and thrift in managing a household, employed by Alberti in his recipes in Book Three of *On the Family*. *Masserizie* were intended to convey domestic virtue and concomitant familial honour and were not to be sold or alienated.

The court account books of the Este of Ferrara demonstrate similar concern for the buying, commissioning and reconditioning of objects connected with the celebration of weddings. While it remained the case that it was the male head of the family who paid for jewellery, silver and furnishings, these objects were usually manufactured to accompany the bride into her new home, for her own use and to furnish her apartments. The 'provisions' (*fornamenti*) of an Este bride might include a bedframe, carved or painted chests and boxes (*cofani*) and even quite large religious pictures. In 1453 similar objects 'for her profession' accompanied 'the Illustrious Lady, Sister Verde', the sister of the reigning marquis Borso d'Este, when she entered a convent, equipping her for her marriage to Christ, among them an image of the Virgin 'with a triumph of angels' painted by Andrea da Vicenza and containing a donor portrait.[6] Furniture might be new or second-hand.

In 1448, for example, Niccolò Panizato and his associates were paid to repaint eight *cofani* that had come to Ferrara with Margherita Gonzaga, the dead first wife of Marquis Leonello d'Este. The painters were to eliminate the Gonzaga arms and replace them with those of the husbands-to-be of Leonello's sisters, Beatrice and Camilla d'Este (who were also to receive four new boxes, some carved, some history-painted).[7] The tradition continued. During the preparations at the end of 1489 for the marriage of Isabella d'Este to the heir to the marquisate of Mantua in 1489, Francesco Gonzaga, her father paid for the manufacture of eleven carved, gilded and painted chests and for the 200 pieces of gold needed to gild the four spherical knobs of her bedframe. Her younger sister, Beatrice, had to make do with five chests that had been repaired and redecorated.[8] The court artist Ercole de' Roberti was largely responsible for the painting and gilding aspects of all these works and he briefly accompanied Isabella to Mantua after her marriage. Sforza brides of the ruling dynasty of Milan in the fifteenth century are documented as taking with them a whole range of tapestries and cushions made from expensive fabrics, sometimes valued, like silver and jewels, as part of their dowry.[9]

The dowry contract might stipulate the value and nature of gifts associated with marriage.[10] Many of these objects drew their significance from the carefully orchestrated familial and public events at which they were exchanged, messages reinforced by their type and decoration. These events varied, but could include a formal exchange of vows, attendance at Mass as a couple, an exchange of rings at a secular ceremony, a wedding feast and other public celebrations marking the consummation of the match, and the procession by which the husband 'led' the bride to her new home.[11] In pre-Tredentine Italy the timing, order and conjunction of these ritual moments was not fixed. Some of the art objects presented and exchanged during this period, such as wedding chests or presentation boxes, can be identified precisely from documentary and visual evidence. Other surviving pieces can be linked to betrothal and marriage only by their type or iconography, in that, for example, they are decorated with amorous inscriptions or devices: paired arms, the coupled names of men and women or their heads facing one another on the same object. In interpreting these objects, one moves from precise documentation to informed guesses about the status and significance of a given piece.

The cost of magnificence: dowry and jewellery

Apart from the financial penalties involved in arranging marriages, there were social dangers in making what was considered to be an 'inappropriate match' in terms of inequalities in rank. In the view of the historian Francesco Guicciardini, 'Nothing in our civil life is more difficult than properly marrying one's daughters.'[12] What was needed was a clear-sighted assessment of one's family's social rank, which, by its very nature, was rare since men tended to overestimate their own standing and seek ambitious matches that could never be realized. In the interim they rejected suitable matches. Other men – he names one – took the first offer for their daughters, resulting in marrying beneath their rank: 'It is necessary therefore to measure carefully one's own social condition and that of others.'[13]

Nevertheless, as Alberti suggests – and this was true, above all, in mercantile societies – money, its possession and its transfer were at the heart of the business of getting married. As an alliance between families, the bride's dowry represented a share of her father's wealth, which was intended to maintain her in her marriage and then pass intact to her at the death of her husband.[14] The dowry decided the nature of the match, representing as it did the honour and social standing not only of a given woman but also of the family whence she came. Indeed, without it, there would generally be no possibility of marriage.[15] During the late fourteenth and fifteenth centuries dowry inflation did not just increase the financial burden imposed, but drove daughters into convents and could even jeopardize the very survival of family lineages. Hence the wife of a wealthy Tuscan merchant could write in 1398 that daughters 'do not make families, but rather unmake them', a demonstration of the tension between the necessary role of women as childbearers in a society preoccupied with lineage and family survival, and the unwelcome financial penalties involved in marrying off a daughter.[16] Providing poor or orphaned girls with dowries was therefore seen as an act of charity on the part of individuals or confraternities, while in Florence some dowries were financed through a state-administered dowry fund.[17] When Saint Nicholas of Bari, according to his legend, threw money into the window of the house occupied by a man and his three depressed and dowerless daughters, he was ensuring they could marry, a point that was not lost on fifteenth-century viewers of painted panels illustrating the scene (fig. 22).[18]

Highly expensive clothing and jewellery signalled the magnificent spending of money and were therefore important items of display associated with betrothal and wedding rituals among the urban elites.[19] In addition to cash, they could make up part of the dowry itself, or could accompany the bride as part of her trousseau. Indeed, the dowries of dynastic brides were frequently divided between ready money and objects in kind.[20] When Bianca Maria Sforza was betrothed, abortively, in 1487 to John Corvinus, the only son of Matthias, King of Hungary, she was assigned a dowry of 150,000 ducats: 100,000 in cash, 40,000 in jewellery and 10,000 in clothes and other adornments. By the time her marriage to the future emperor Maximilian I was being negotiated in 1493, her dowry had risen to 400,000 ducats. The inventory of her goods included silver both for her *credenza* and for the altar, the pieces all valued by the weight of precious metal they contained.[21] The 1503 dowry of Lucrezia Borgia, the daughter of Pope Alexander VI, at her (third) marriage, to Alfonso I d'Este, was 300,000 ducats, including silver worth 30,000.[22]

Florentine documentary evidence suggests that once a marriage contract had been formally signed, the groom was expected to woo his betrothed with gifts, or sometimes with loans or hired pieces intended for her to wear for a limited period. This practice was not, however, unique to Florence. Clothing, made from expensive textiles, embroidered in gold thread by specialists, trimmed with fur and set with pearls and gemstones, is frequently listed in account books as part of these gifts or exchanges. A letter from Alessandra Macinghi Strozzi, a member of one of the leading patrician families of Florence, to her son, recording the marriage she had arranged for her daughter in 1447, gives a sense of the role played by jewels and clothing in representing the wealth and honour of the two families allied through marriage.[23] Writing from Naples, Alessandra, the

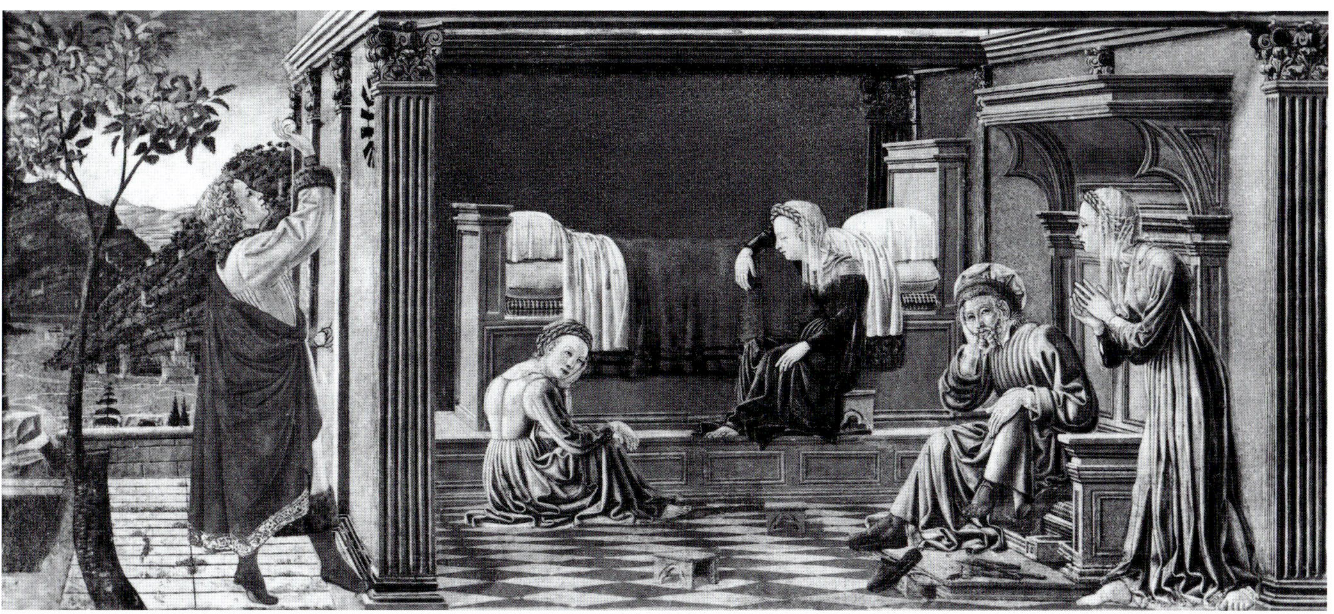

widow of an exile, spelt out the way in which a bride was the focal figure in the transfer of property that marriage represented. She also emphasized the importance of dressing and presenting the bride according to contemporary notions of beauty and splendour; here she was fortunate, since the groom, Marco Parenti, was a wealthy silk merchant. The letter makes clear the role of both the dowry and gifts from the bride's family, and the counter-dowry gifts from the groom. First Alessandra described the groom as 'a young man of good birth and abilities and an only son, rich, and twenty-five years old, and he has a silk manufacturing business'. She then gave details of the dowry and cash gifts:

I am giving him a dowry of 1,000 florins, 500 due to her from the Monte [the state administered Dowry Fund] in May 1448; the remaining 500 I have to give to him, made up of cash and trousseau when she goes to her husband's house ... And we found that to place her in a nobler family with greater political status would have taken 1,400 or 1,500 florins, and this would have been your ruin and mine... .

She expressed approval of the betrothal gifts Caterina had received:

When she was betrothed, he [the groom, Marco Parenti] ordered a gown of crimson silk velvet for her and a surcoat of the same, and it is the most beautiful cloth in Florence, which he had made in his own silk manufactury. And he had a garland of feathers and pearls made [for her] which cost eighty florins. To go under it there is an arrangement of two strands of pearls costing at least sixty florins, so that, when she leaves the house, she will be wearing more than 400 florins on her back. And he is ordering for her some crimson velvet to be made up into long sleeves lined with marten [fur], for her to wear when she goes to her husband's house. And he is having a rose-coloured gown made, embroidered with pearls. He feels he cannot do enough of having things made, because she is beautiful and he wants her to look even more so. There's not a girl in Florence to compare with her and she is beautiful in every way, or so many people think....[24]

Alessandra makes clear that, as a widow and an exile from Florence, she found it difficult to provide the necessary dowry to make her daughter a suitable match. Even when the bride's family could pay a dowry and had been contracted to do so, the groom might be anxious to prevent dowry default by giving his bride a counter dowry as a kind of limited insurance; valuable items that could be sold soon after the wedding once they had served their ceremonial purpose.[25] Again, financial considerations were inextricably linked with family honour. When Alessandra wrote to her son, Filippo, in 1465, advising him of the marriage contracted for him, she wrote: 'Get the jewels ready, and let them be beautiful, for we have found you a wife. As she is beautiful and the wife of Filippo Strozzi, she will need beautiful jewels, for just as you have honour in other things, she does not want to be lacking in this.'[26]

Although the costs of clothes and jewellery could be crippling, borrowing or hiring items was an accepted means of procuring jewellery for a limited period.[27] There seems to have been plenty of incentive for grooms to consider the jewellery that they gave their brides as borrowed finery or, at best, as temporary gifts, and not as their bride's possessions.[28] The sumptuary laws seem to have recognized and even strengthened this perception: a Florentine edict of 1472 stated that married women could wear certain pieces associated with betrothal and marriage for only three years, after which it would be strictly forbidden,[29] evidence, even if the edict was ignored (as sumptuary legislation all over Italy frequently was), that such pieces were visually distinctive. There was little social stigma attached to borrowing in the Quattrocento, judging by contemporary comments, as it seems to have been accepted that there was a limited number of exceptional jewels in circulation at any one moment within a local elite. Magnificence could be hired or borrowed as well as bought.

Apart from saving money, the borrower cemented ties of mutual obligation within his family network by borrowing jewellery such as wedding pendants, pearl necklaces and brooches, which generally seem to have been perceived as a set, or parure. The Florentine patrician Francesco Castellani recorded two loans of the same piece of wedding jewellery in his account book; first, in 1443, he lent a 'necklace', as he described it, to his wife's kinsman Antonio Strozzi. The necklace seems to have comprised strings of pearls with two silver 'brooches' each covered with a rosette of pearls: 'The said Antonio said that he wanted it for Gemma, his contracted bride, my cousin … for a month or two, as if he had bought it for her himself.' As always in these transactions, Francesco had his goldsmith weigh and value the parure, though in this case he broke his customary practice of demanding a written receipt for its loan – a sign of his trust in the borrower.[30] Francesco seems to have altered the necklace on its return for presentation to his second wife in 1450. In the same year, he lent the remodelled piece to a relative of his new wife:

I record that on the 20 day of June in the abovementioned year 1450, I lent to Andrea Allamanni, my wife's relative, my necklace of strung pearls formed into an interlace pattern, with 64 pearls … on a double chain of silver, to which is attached a silver clasp on one end of the collar, and similarly on the other end, where it attaches with a brooch with a sapphire and a little crown above with three fat pendant pearls.[31]

As before, Francesco recorded the weight of the different parts of the jewel and the estimated value of individual pearls. He also noted the return of the parure, and, ominously, that it weighed less than it had done before, though he stated that he was certain that the borrower was not aware of this. A chain had been changed and the pearls replaced with those of lesser value. He explains that the borrower had also written to say that he had made these alterations 'so that it [the parure] would not be recognized'.[32] One receives a sense here of a small elite circle of friends and relatives within which this kind of jewellery circulated, so that an individual piece might have been recognized on its fourth appearance all too easily. Hence the impulse to disguise it.

It is not always easy to picture the types of jewellery associated with marriage ceremonies from contemporary documents. Depictions of the Mystic Marriage of Saint Catherine[33] or of the famously virtuous matrons of classical antiquity are invaluable for the typology of contemporary jewels and the ways in which they were worn. These can be compared to fifteenth-century portraits of women, giving them a different resonance, which alters our reading of them, for the women portrayed are likely to be wearing finery that was purchased (or borrowed or hired) for them for personal display during a particular series of events within a given time limit. In Milan, Mantua and Ferrara portraits were not infrequently executed in connection with the arrangement of marriages. A portrait could be the means of discovering the appearance of a bride-to-be, as when the Milanese court portraitist Zanetto Bugatto was dispatched to Paris in 1468 to paint Bona of Savoy, the sister-in-law of the French king, whom Galeazzo Maria Sforza was considering as a politically desirable bride.[34] Its function was not always so straight-forwardly inquisitive. In 1454 Niccolò d'Alemagna painted the portrait of Beatrice d'Este, natural daughter of Marquis Nicolò III d'Este, shortly before her marriage to Tristano Sforza, a bastard son of Francesco, and such gifts seem to have been common during negotiations of Este marriages.[35] The portraits painted in the 1470s by Cosmè Tura of the children of Ercole I d'Este, Duke of Ferrara, were sent to the families of their betrothed as a form of ritual exchange. The appearance of his daughters Lucrezia, Isabella and Beatrice may have been of some interest to their prospective grooms, but the infant Anna Sforza could have been none the wiser about her future husband by looking at the portrait of a one-year-old Alfonso.[36] Such portraits were not only painted, but could be rendered still more permanent as medals. In August 1484 Isabella d'Este acknowledged receipt of a medallic portrait of her future husband, Francesco Gonzaga.[37] Even after marriage, paired portraits celebrating prestigious alliances were commonly executed. In Florence there is no evidence of such ritual exchange (perhaps the preponderance of local matches played its part). Nevertheless, even there paintings of women (not infrequently also paired with images of their husbands) provide useful evidence, given that jewels of exactly the types described in letters and inventories are frequently depicted, with considerable attention paid to their content and facture, 'likenesses' of items of exceptional significance for the status and identity of the wearer.[38]

In both Florence and at the courts of northern Italy, the value of jewellery as a feature of marriage lay in its combination of highly expensive materials with the beauty and symbolic potential of their fashioning. It would seem from both pictorial and documentary evidence of the second half of the fifteenth century that the head brooch and shoulder brooch or pendant, with its accompanying strings of pearls, may have been conceived of and presented as a set with distinct elements that could be worn as separate pieces. This is implied in the Florentine patrician Giovanni Rucellai's comments on gifts for his son's bride in 1466:

I had one rich necklace with diamonds, rubies and pearls valued at 1,200 large florins. And one shoulder brooch with a big balas ruby and pearls that cost 1,000 large florins, and another for the head valued at 300 large florins, and one chain for the neck of large pearls and with a large pointed diamond, pendant ... of which the diamond alone cost 200 ducats.[39]

In the mid-Quattrocento there was little that was distinctively Italianate about the style of this jewellery. Three jewels surviving in The British Museum and dating to the 1440s appear to be exceptional survivals as part of a set of wedding jewellery, comprising two brooches that feature suspension loops so that they can alternatively be worn as pendants, and a smaller brooch that was probably designed to be pinned to a textile band as a hair ornament (fig. 23). Although they were found as a group in the River Meuse, which runs through the diocese of Liège, they are extremely similar to contemporary Italian descriptions of marriage jewellery, both in style and facture.[40] The largest and most intricate of the three features the half-length figure of a woman wearing a robe with scalloped sleeves. She frames the central rose-cut sapphire with her hands. Her face and hands are keyed for white enamel and traces remain on one of her cheeks. She wears a large table-cut diamond at her neck, and her figure is surrounded by beads of gold set on high stems and three rubies. Originally there would have been two pearls, for which one fitting survives, and beads of white enamel in the pierced settings on the lower edge of the jewel.[41] It is not dissimilar in form and facture to the piece worn by Bianca Maria Visconti in her portrait in the Brera (see fig. 21), one of a pair with another of her husband Francesco Sforza, Duke of Milan, which was executed by (probably) a Ferrarese artist in the early 1460s.[42] She is depicted wearing a double string of large pearls, perhaps similar to Castellani's parure, with a large pendant, attached to her undersleeve by a gold brooch of a type referred to in the Milanese documents as a 'shoulder brooch'.[43] The brooch features an angel of enamelled gold, accompanied by four pearls and two table-cut gemstones. Bianca Maria had two examples of 'large shoulder brooches' (*fermagli grandi da spalla*) similar to the largest of the Meuse group, but neither of the pieces recorded in inventories of 1459 and 1468 is identical to the one in her portrait.[44]

The close similarities between the angel brooch in Bianca Maria's portrait and the

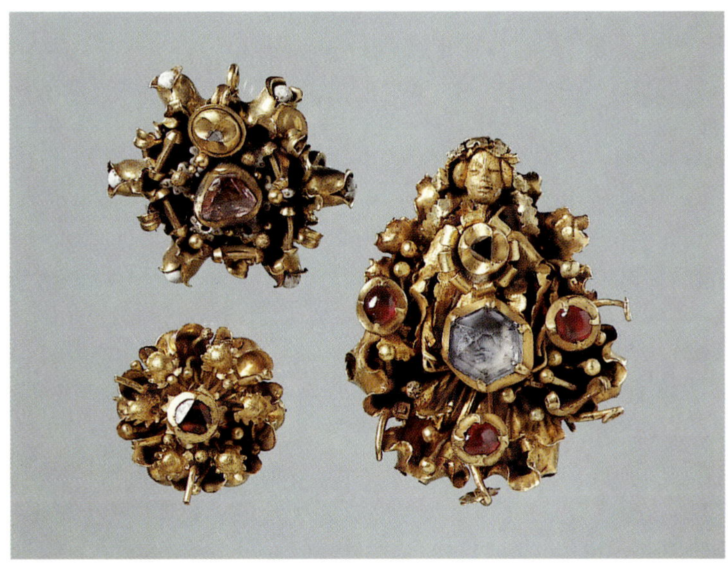

23 Three jewels; gold (the figurative jewel with traces of enamel) and gemstones; probably Franco-Burgundian, mid-fifteenth century. The British Museum, London

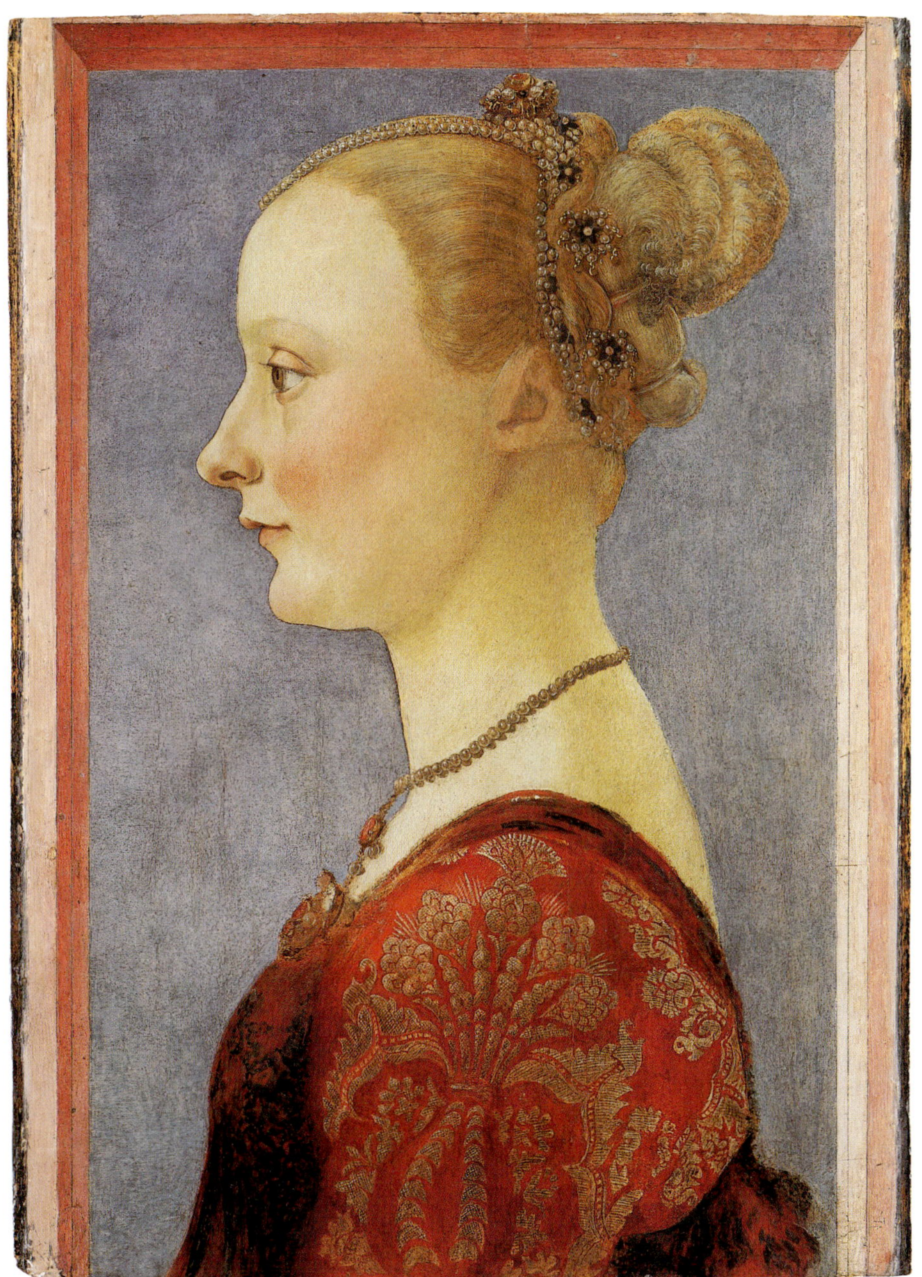

brooch with a woman in The British Museum raise questions about the origins of this type
of jewel. The Meuse group had long been considered to be Flemish or Burgundian,
although it has now been attributed to Germany.[45] If these jewels were indeed made in
northern Europe, as seems likely, the style and technique may have been exported south to
Italy; at any rate, the stylistic connections between Bianca Maria's painted brooch and
the British Museum piece demonstrate a certain communality of elite material culture
across Europe. Similar pieces are described in documents and portrayed in other Italian
paintings, although between twenty and forty years after the proposed dating of the Meuse
jewels. This slippage between the different kinds of evidence for the production and
circulation of this type of jewel may be an accident of survival, or it may point to the
different perceptions of relative wear for textiles and jewellery. Whereas textiles, such as

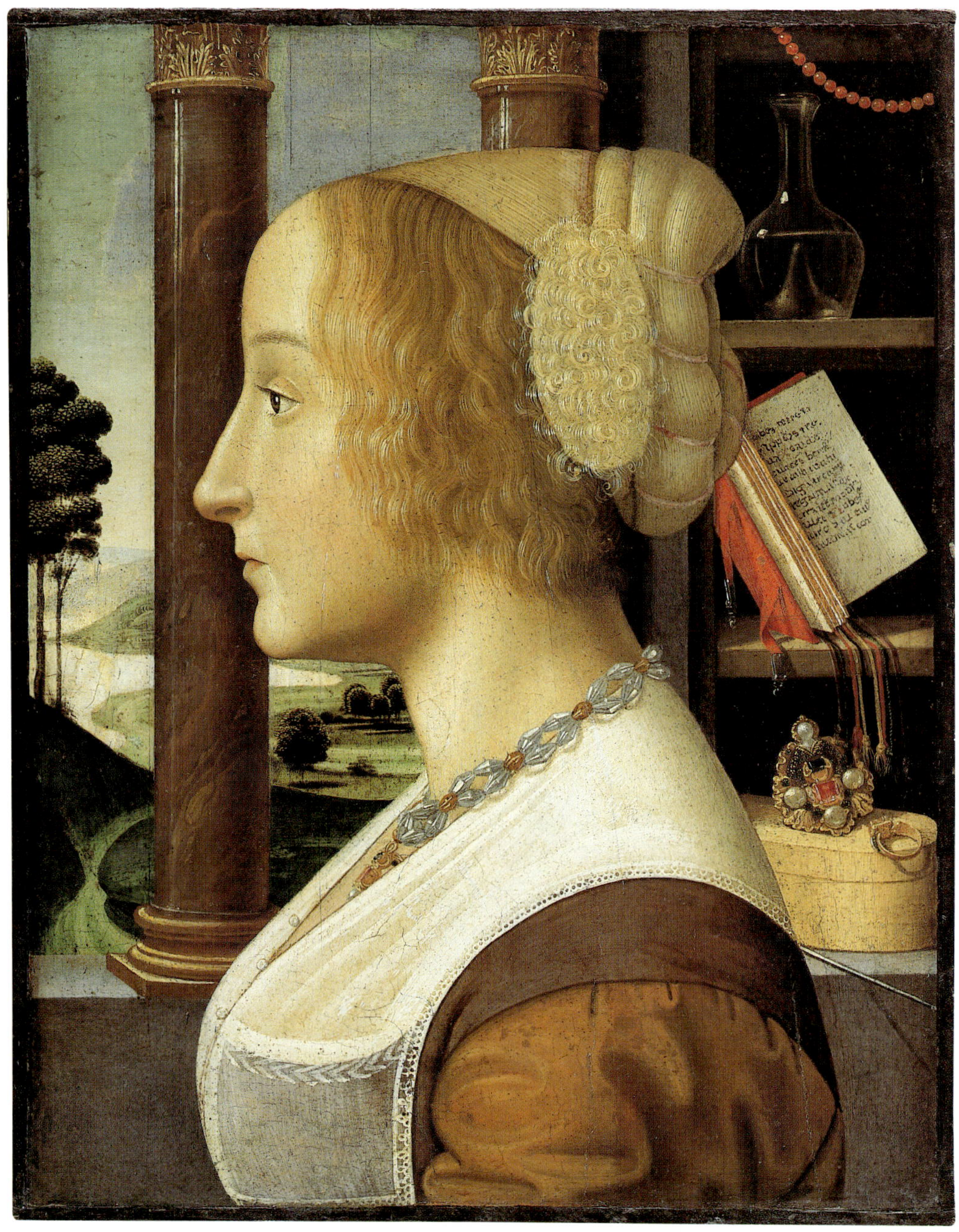

25 Bastiano Mainardi,
Portrait of a Woman;
tempera on panel;
Florence, *c.*1490–1500.
Preußischer Kulturbesitz
Gemäldegalerie, Staatliche
Museen zu Berlin

elaborate brocaded silks, had to be of the latest design and in mint condition to be worn for such important events as betrothal and marriage rituals (although there was a flourishing second-hand market), jewellery seems to have had a longer wearing life.[46]

Contemporary Florentine and Bolognese paintings indicate that the fashion for this type of figurative enamelled gold brooch as a marriage gift was not restricted to Milan. A fine example, featuring an angel, appears in Antonio del Pollaiuolo's damaged panel portrait of an unknown woman, presumably a local Florentine, dating to 1470–80 (fig. 24).[47] She wears the jewel as a pendant from a pearl necklace, according to the adaptation of this kind of marriage jewel in the last two decades of the fifteenth century. Another panel from a pair of male and female portraits in Berlin by Bastiano Mainardi (fig. 25) represents a marriage pendant that is even closer to the British Museum jewel than that shown in the portrait of Bianca Maria Visconti.[48] The white enamelled face and hands of the woman presenting the central gemstone, exactly paralleling the design of the British Museum jewel, can be clearly seen. Shown alongside is a ring, a box made of a single sheet of shaved wood, a coral necklace and a missal: all typical dowry and betrothal items recorded in documents.[49] Another painting executed in about 1470, with the arms of the Loiani family of Bologna, illustrates a jewel similar to the British Museum example. It shows a man and two women (possibly a husband and his first and second wives) kneeling before Saint Catherine of Bologna (fig. 26). The foremost woman, in Italian costume, wears jewellery associated with marriage: a head brooch with an enamelled swan attached to a hair band; a pearl necklace, and another with two hands holding a ring, probably referring to the giving of the woman's hand in the marriage vow; a textile belt with decorated buckle and belt-end; and, finally, a shoulder brooch of the angel type, which is represented almost natural size and in meticulous detail.[50]

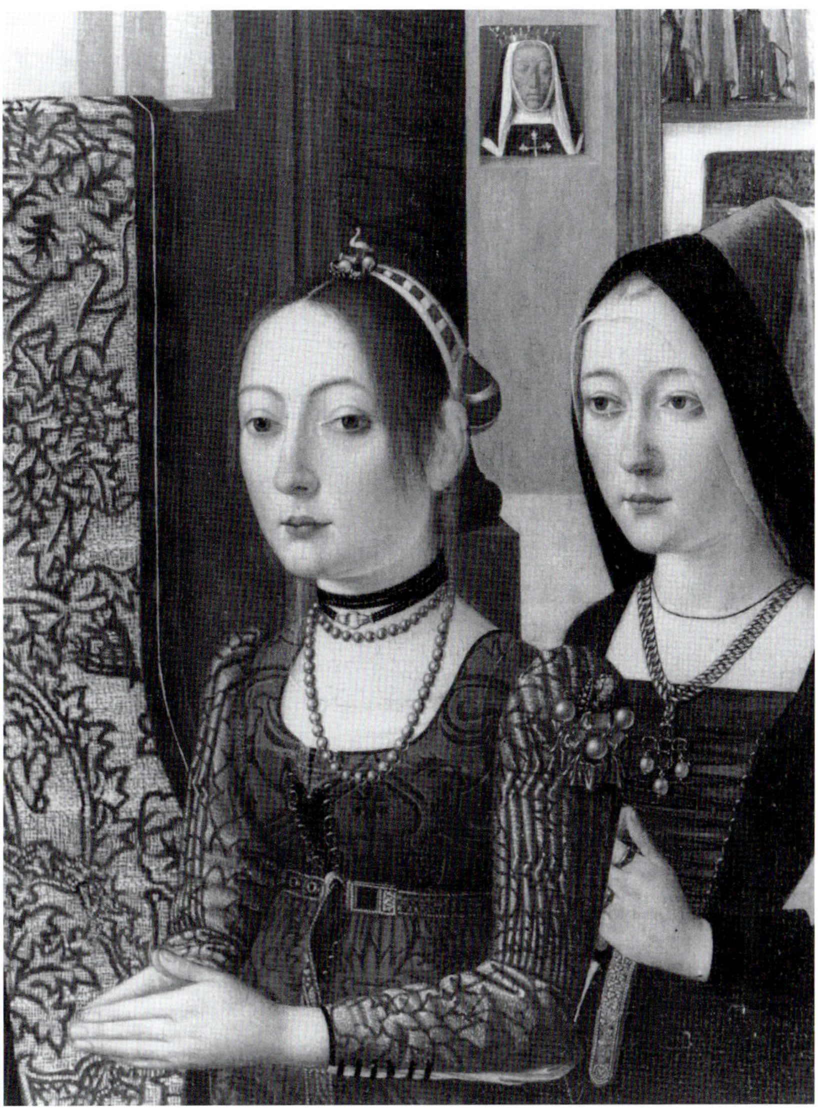

26 The Baroncelli Master, *Saint Catherine of Bologna with Three Donors* (detail); oil on panel; Bruges (?), *c.*1470. Courtauld Gallery, London

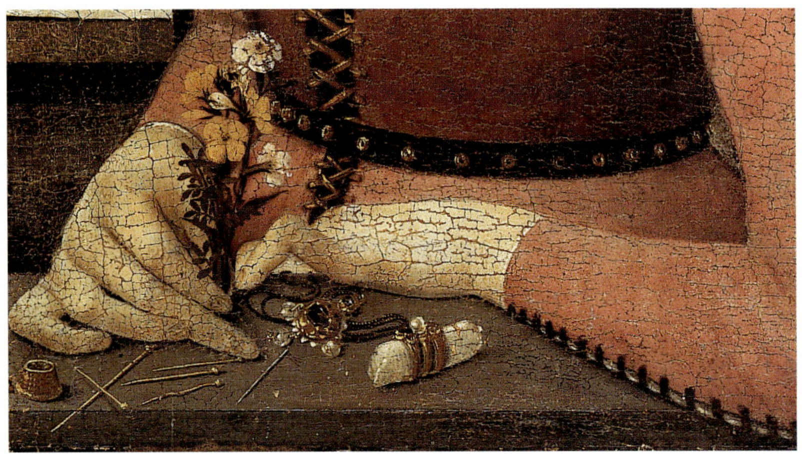

27 Domenico Ghirlandaio (workshop), *Costanza de' Medici Caetani* (detail); tempera on panel; Florence, *c.*1480–90. National Gallery, London

Equally telling in terms of the specific context in which jewellery was intended to be viewed is the Florentine portrait panel of Costanza Caetani, executed in about 1480–90 and attributed to the workshop of Domenico Ghirlandaio (fig. 27).[51] The inscription identifies the subject as Costanza de' Medici, a member of a cadet branch of the banking family and the wife of Franceso Caetani. Not only the inscription but also the details of jewellery proclaim this as a portrait celebrating this prestigious alliance. The three rings on a folded sheet of paper accord with those described in contemporary account books as gifts from a husband-to-be to his betrothed; the pendant is of a type referred to in a document of 1482 as a marriage or 'wifehood' pendant (*pendetta di moglianza*), which was bought or hired for use at weddings.[52] One Florentine recorded renting out a similar pendant set with a diamond and three pearls to a fellow patrician.[53] Although this term appears in a Florentine account book, the phrase seems not to have been used to distinguish marriage jewels in inventories as movable property.

The portrait of Costanza Caetani also includes objects proclaiming the domestic role of the wife. Needles, needle cases and thimbles were also typical marriage gifts: in 1506 one Venetian bride received: 'a small oblong silver basket, skilfully-made; a needle case, likewise of silver, filled with needles from Damascus; and silver tongs and a thimble covered in fine filigree work'. These objects symbolized her new responsibilities following the consummation of her marriage, when they were presented to her along with the traditional sweetmeats.[54] Such gifts assist the interpretation of a surviving nielloed needle case, decorated with putti and a woman with a distaff accompanied by a woman's name, HARIA [MARIA?] DE ARCANZOLI (fig. 28).[55]

A careful reading of slightly later pictorial and documentary evidence enables us to define a type of betrothal jewel in use at the Sforza court of Lodovico il Moro, the future Duke of Milan. This took the form of a massive pendant to be attached to a pearl necklace that, as shown in contemporary portraits, sat tightly on the neck. When Lodovico married Beatrice d'Este in 1491, he gave her as a betrothal gift 'a beautiful necklace of fat pearls strung together with gold flowers and with a beautiful jewel for attaching to the said necklace, comprising a very fine emerald of large dimensions and a mounted balas ruby [*balasso*] and pearl in the shape of a pear'.[56] Such jewels are depicted in the portrait of

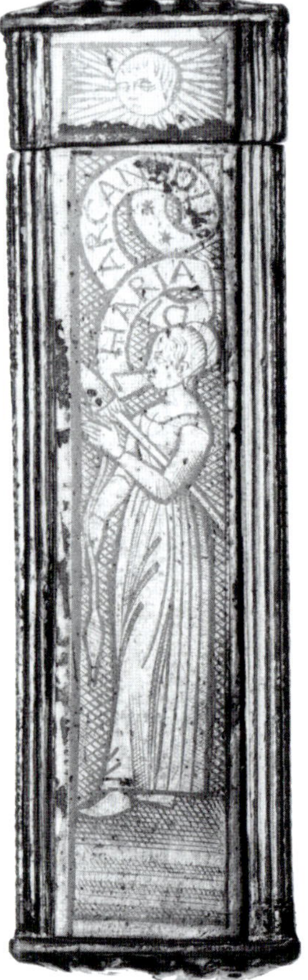

28 Needle case with image of a woman with a distaff; silver with niello inlay; Florence (?), *c.*1500. The British Museum, London

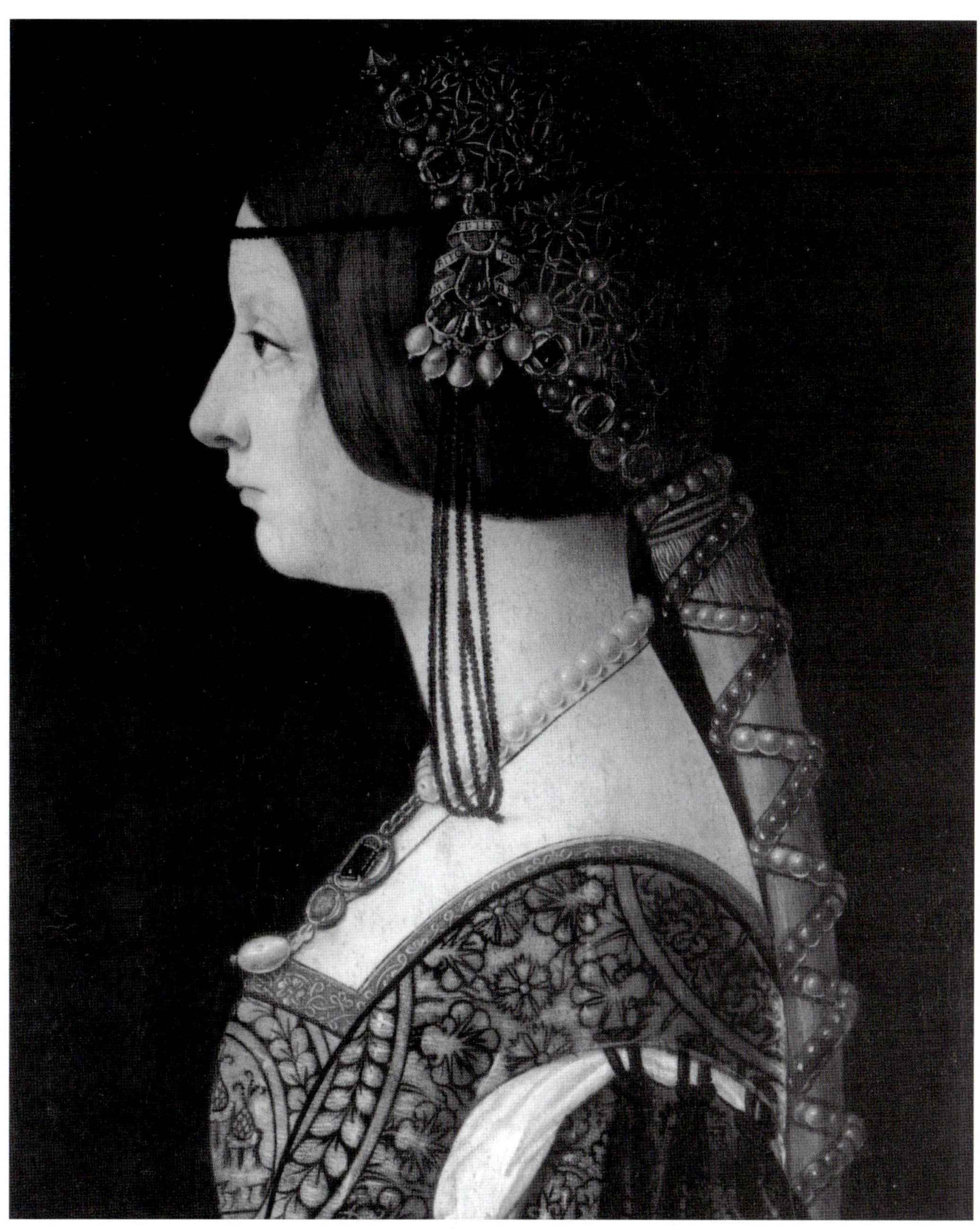

29 Ambrogio Preda,
Bianca Maria Sforza (detail);
painted panel; Milan, 1493.
National Gallery of Art,
Washington DC

Lodovico's niece, Bianca Maria Sforza, executed by Ambrogio Preda during the negotiations of her marriage to Maximilian (fig. 29).[57] Bianca Maria also wears a head brooch (*brochetta di testa*), on one side of her head, attached to a textile band. Also documented as a type of betrothal jewel, it is in the form of Lodovico's device of the brush, or *scopetta*, and enamelled with the Latin legend MERITO ET TEMPORE (With merit and with time).[58]

Another portrait of a young woman, which from its style appears to be Emilian, shows that the individual elements of a jewel were bearers of meaning (fig. 30). In the foreground the woman holds a single cornucopia between her fingers like a flower, in just the way that both men and women sometimes display a pink or carnation as an emblem of betrothal. The motif is reinforced by the jewel she wears – a pendant featuring two flaming cornucopias, emblems of Hymen, goddess of marriage.[59]

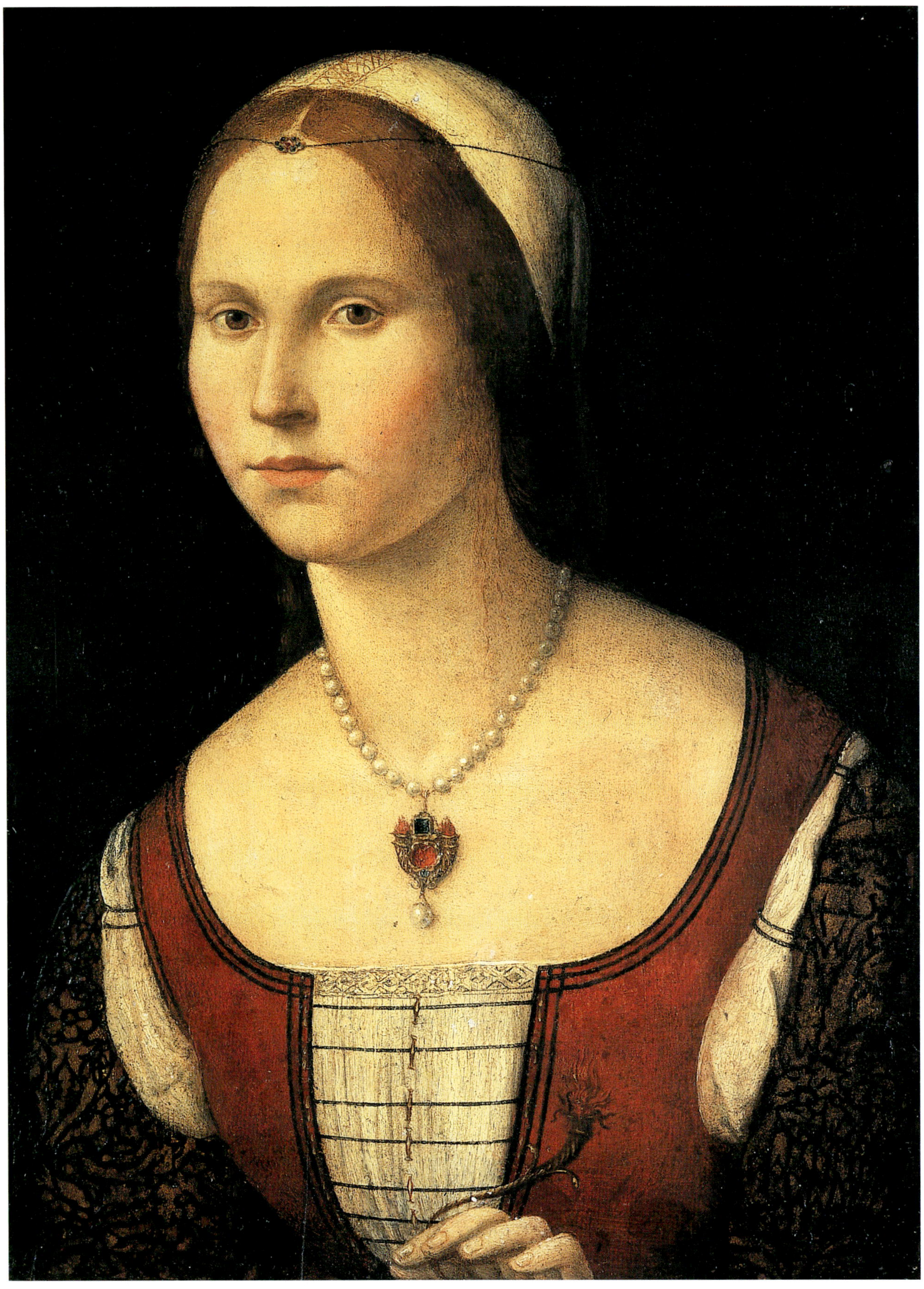

Images of ideal love and beauty

Of all Alberti's possible temptations to enter the married state, the least pragmatic is surely the allure of woman's beauty. This was not a frivolous consideration. Beauty in women during the late fifteenth and early sixteenth centuries was given a moral dimension, being perceived ideally as a mirror or sign of virtue within.[60] Both chivalric and Petrarchan modes of thought emphasized female beauty. And neo-Platonic doctrine, as expounded by the philosopher Marsilio Ficino, stated that:

the internal perfection produces the external. The former we can call goodness, the latter beauty. For this reason, we say that beauty is a certain blossom of goodness, by the charms of which blossom, as by a kind of bait, the hidden internal goodness attracts beholders. But since the cognition of our intellect takes its origin from the senses, we would never be aware of and never desire the goodness itself hidden in the heart of things if we were not attracted to it by the visible signs of external beauty.[61]

The beauty of a woman that compelled love in men could be seen as more or less synonymous with her virtue, and to pay tribute to her beauty was therefore to praise her for the manner in which it rendered her virtue visible. Moral qualities were popularly perceived as literally making beauty: 'Integrity [*onesta*] makes beauty', as one saying accompanying an idealized woman's head on a maiolica plate proclaims.[62] A present of a mirror, in which a woman could view herself, thus suggested the recipient's ideal beauty and her virtue. The message is explicit in the Italian legend of a single-sided medal, thought to be a self-portrait of the artist known as Lysippus the Younger, once polished to function as a looking-glass: 'Admire on one side your beautiful face, and on the other that of your

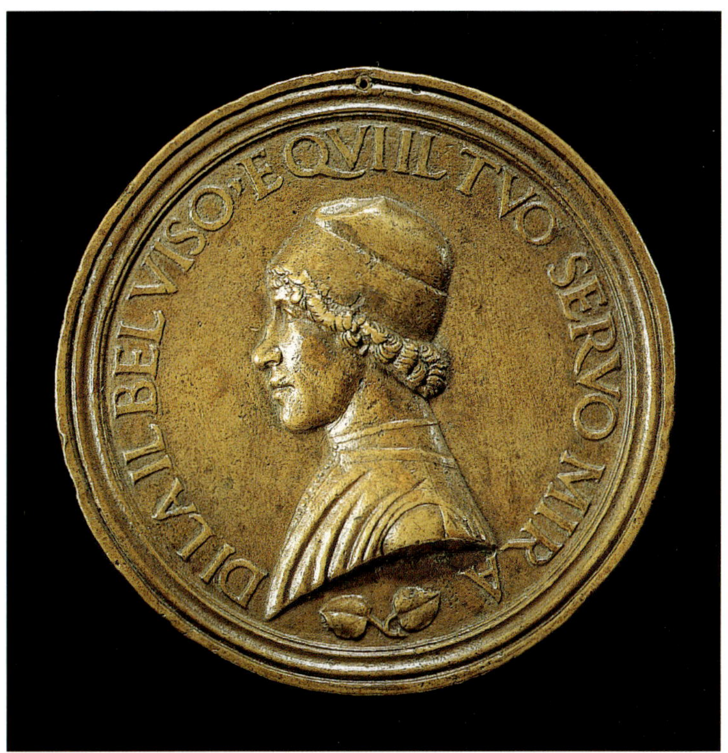

(*Opposite page*)
30 *Portrait of a Young Woman*; oil on panel; Emilian (?), *c.*1500–10. Private collection, Scotland

31 Lysippus the Younger, self-portrait (?) mirror-medal; cast bronze; Rome, *c.*1471–84. The British Museum, London

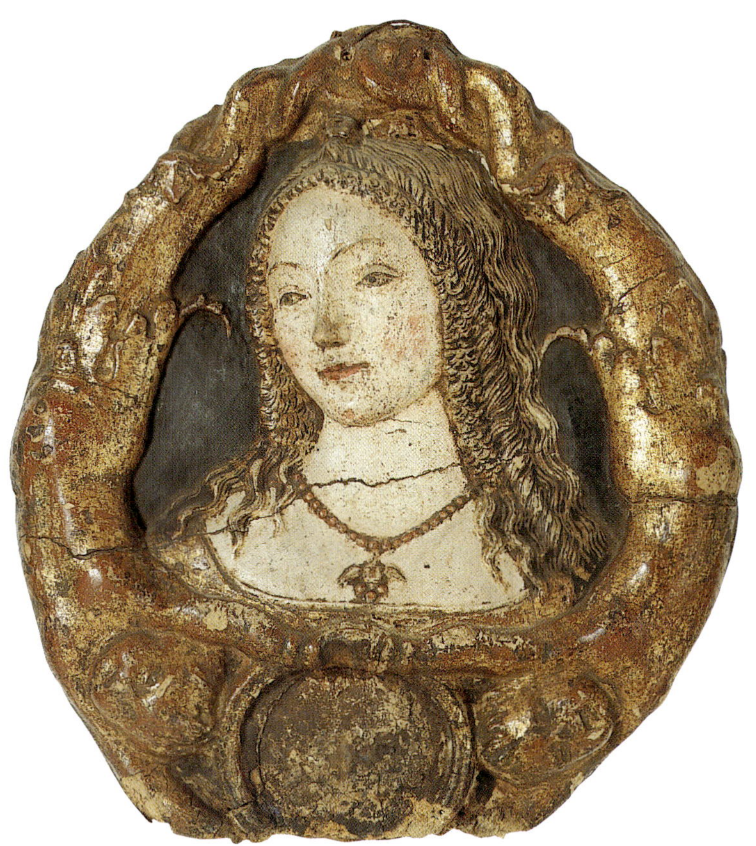

servant' (fig. 31).[63] A mirror was therefore especially appropriate either as a dowry gift or part of a newly appointed marital bedchamber, especially if it incorporated in its frame an image of a woman who conformed to contemporary notions of female beauty, suggesting a likeness between the real woman gazing at herself, and the ideal.[64] The bride's appearance was linked through the medium of the mirror to general conventions and ideals, as in contemporary panel portraits in which the reverses have been found to relate an individual face to moral maxims and claims to high social status.[65] A papier-mâché mirror frame made in Siena late in the Quattrocento builds on these assumptions, showing a young woman in her wedding finery, complete with head brooch, coral necklace and pendant, with putti encircling her head and linking hands under her chin in a gesture recalling the exchange of vows at marriage (fig. 32).[66] The small circular hollow beneath shows where the tiny steel convex mirror would have been set, thus projecting the woman's reflection directly under that of this idealized bride. This juxtaposition is also found on maiolica mirror frames, which develop from the tradition of representing idealized heads on dishes accompanied by tributes to real women, such as the example inscribed 'Divine and beautiful Lucia' (see fig. 1). Such dishes must have served as personalized gifts.[67]

One of the most visually sophisticated uses of male and female heads with an amorous inscription is seen in an opaque green goblet decorated with enamelling and gilding (fig. 33). Made in Venice, this glass is of a type conventionally described as a betrothal goblet, although no documentary reference for this has yet been found.[68] The two roundels, set against a ground densely stippled with touches of white enamel, frame the

heads of a man and a woman, both in specifically Venetian patrician dress of the period
c.1490–1510.[69] Both are viewed in idealizing profile: that of the woman is flanked by
cornucopias, while the man's profile is accompanied by an Italian inscription,
AMOR.VOL.FEE (Love requires faith). The motto was thought to be classical and Latin in
origin, and was taken up in humanist circles in the fifteenth century as 'an ancient saying'
(*un detto antico*), as exemplified by its earlier use in a Florentine print of 1465–70 (fig. 34).[70]
Here one sees an idealized youth wearing the device of Lorenzo de' Medici – a diamond
ring and feathers – embroidered on his sleeve. He receives an armillary sphere from a
nymph wearing a marriage brooch made of pearls and a pointed diamond on her head, to
whom he in turn gives a scroll inscribed in Italian 'Love requires faith, and where there is
no faith, love is powerless.' This motto was associated with Lorenzo's faithful love for his
ideal mistress, Lucrezia Donati, by Luigi Pulci in his poem, *La Giostra* (*The Joust*): her motto
was *Spero* – I hope – on which the sphere (*spera*) included in the print makes a visual pun.[71]

It is known that textile belts with gold or parcel-gilt fittings, which included particular
arms, emblems or inscriptions, served as gifts of friendship. That a nielloed buckle and
belt-end could carry complex meanings designed by the patron is illustrated by Marco
Parenti's commission of belt fittings as a gift for a friend in Naples in 1451.[72] Parenti
provided a detailed interpretation of three symbols and the inscription, 'a fantasy in my
own style' (*una fantasia a mio modo*), and how these were intended to work together.[73]
Indeed, it would have been difficult to reconstruct the intended meaning of these lost belt
fittings without this accompanying letter. The way in which a belt was worn, and the fact

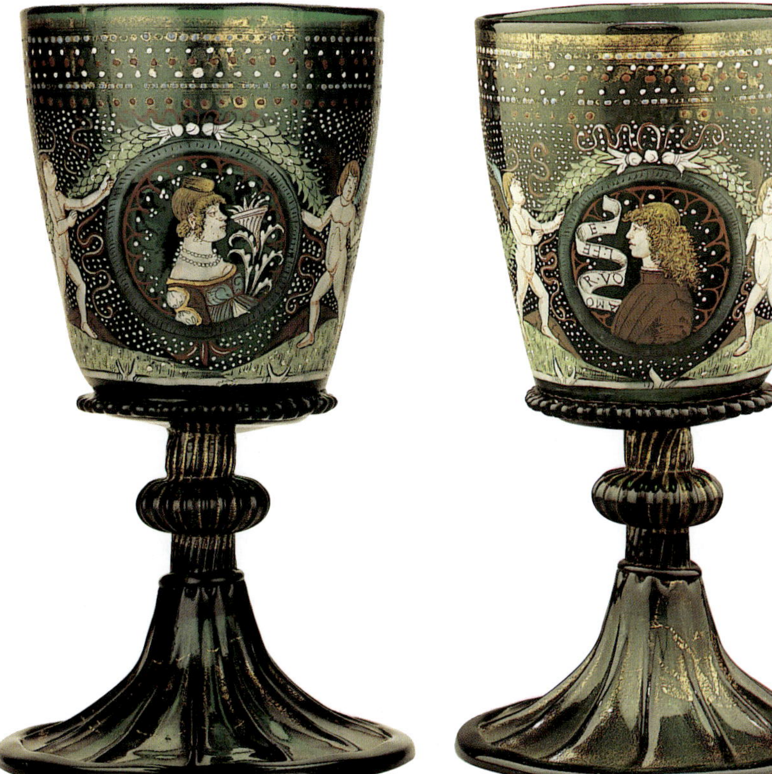

33 Giovanni Maria Obizzo
(attributed), goblet with roundels
of the heads of a woman and
man; green glass, enamelled
and gilded; Venice (Murano),
c.1490–1510. The British Museum,
London

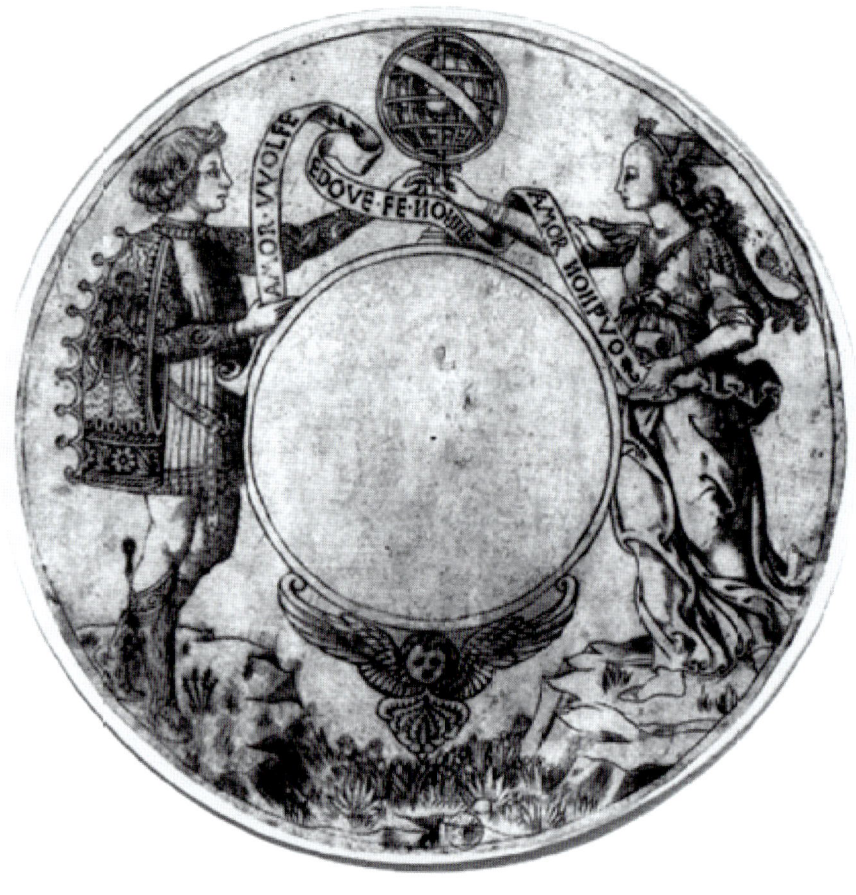

34 Baccio Baldini (attributed),
youth and nymph holding an
armillary sphere; engraving;
Florence, *c.*1470. Bibliothèque
nationale de France, Paris

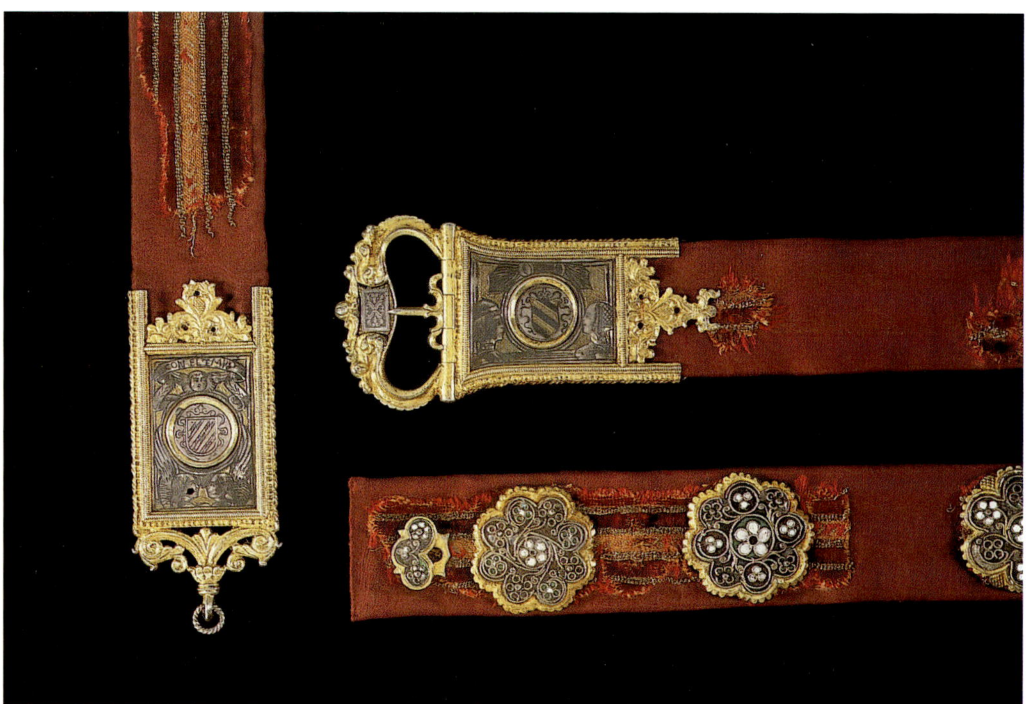

35 Fragments of a belt
with a silver-gilt and niello
belt-end and buckle,
bearing the arms of
Malatesta of Rimini and
Cesena; enamelled
plaques; and fragments of
tablet-woven red velvet
(remounted on modern
textile); north Italy,
mid-fifteenth century.
The British Museum,
London

that the buckle and belt-end provided three visible fields for personalized imagery, made it an attractive gift. Examples with Sforza devices on the buckles or belt-ends are listed in the Milanese documents in the late fifteenth century, and illustrated in portraits.[74]

The iconography of surviving examples is simpler, suggesting that belts were also made as personalized gifts of love, and markers of betrothal. A surviving piece comprises two fragments of a velvet belt with a silver-gilt buckle and belt-end and nine enamelled mounts (fig. 35). The tablet-woven belt has retained some if its deep red colouring, which would have made it a perfect foil for the silver-gilt fittings. The buckle, pierced at the inside edge so that the velvet belt can be sewn into it, is soldered together from silver sheet and cast elements, all heavily gilt. Profile portraits of a man and a woman are cut out of nielloed silver set against a densely hatched ground. They face one another on either side of an inset roundel with a shield of arms and the initials L and B, presumably referring to the couple for whom it was made. The belt-end, which is of similar facture and style, is double-sided and has a loop at its point for hanging small accessories. One side, which is intended to be read vertically, bears the nielloed arms of the Malatesta of Rimini and Cesena on an inset roundel held by the figure of an angel. The reverse is set with a nielloed plaque showing a man's and a woman's head facing one another and the Italian inscription CON EL TEMPO (With time).[75] The motto echoes the meaning of the Latin inscription MERITO ET TEMPORE seen on the head brooch in Preda's portrait of Bianca Maria Sforza (see fig. 29).

The heads facing one another on the buckle of this belt suggest that a surviving Bolognese niello print may derive from a plaque on a betrothal gift. The curved left edge perhaps indicates the placing of the original buckle whence the impression was taken.[76] A mid-Quattrocento Venetian belt fitting engraved 'clara.b[ella]' – 'beautiful

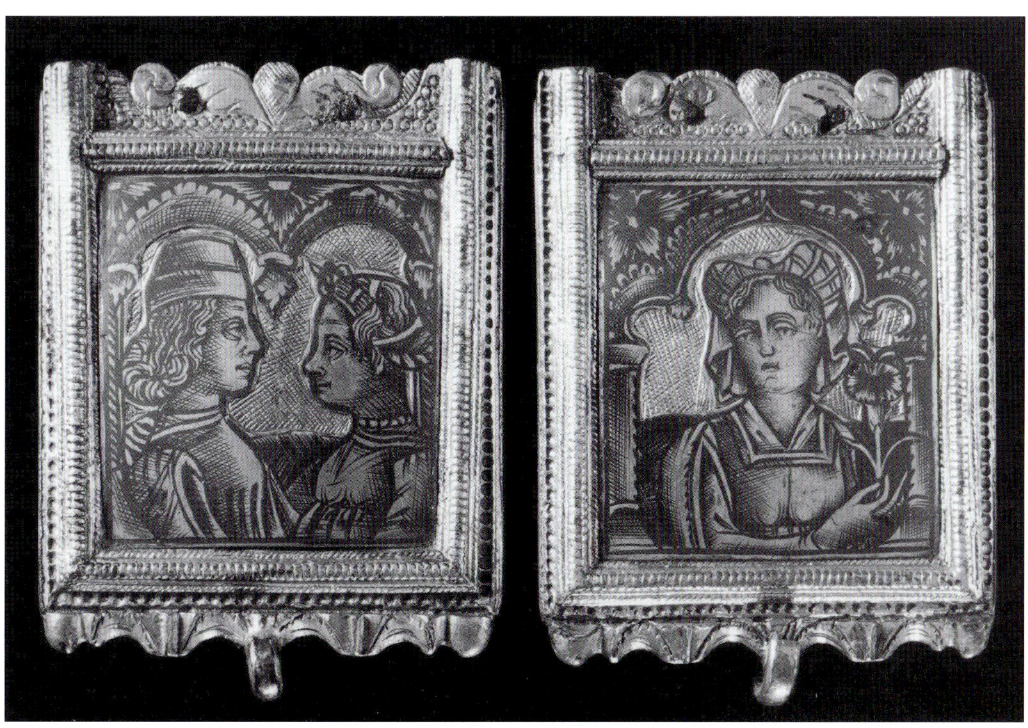

36 Belt-end with image of a woman holding a pink, and an amorous couple; silver-gilt with nielloed plaques; north Italy, mid-fifteenth century. The British Museum, London

Chiara' – must have been intended as a tribute to a woman of that name to whom the belt was given.[77] The conventional iconography of facing heads is developed further on the double-sided belt-end in The British Museum (fig. 36).[78] The couple are shown beneath an arcade, dressed in the costume of the mid-fifteenth century. The connection with marriage or betrothal is demonstrated by the fact that the woman is wearing a head brooch on her elaborately dressed hair and a pearl necklace, all of which, we have now seen, constituted bridal dress. She has boldly placed her hand around her husband's neck. Contemporary beholders would have regarded the iconography of the niello decoration on the reverse in the same way, for it shows a woman beneath an ogee arch holding a pink or carnation, a symbol of love.[79]

Celebrating chastity in marriage

If beauty revealed virtue, there was general agreement as to what female virtue comprised. Baldassare Castiglione summed up much earlier thought in the third book of the *Courtier* when he made Gaspare Pallavicino say:

for from women's incontinence countless evils result that do not from men's. Therefore … it is wisely ordained that women are allowed to fail in all other things without blame, to the end that they might be able to devote all their strength to keeping themselves in this the virtue of chastity; without which their children would be uncertain, and that tie would be dissolved which binds the whole world by blood and by the natural love of each man for what he has produced.[80]

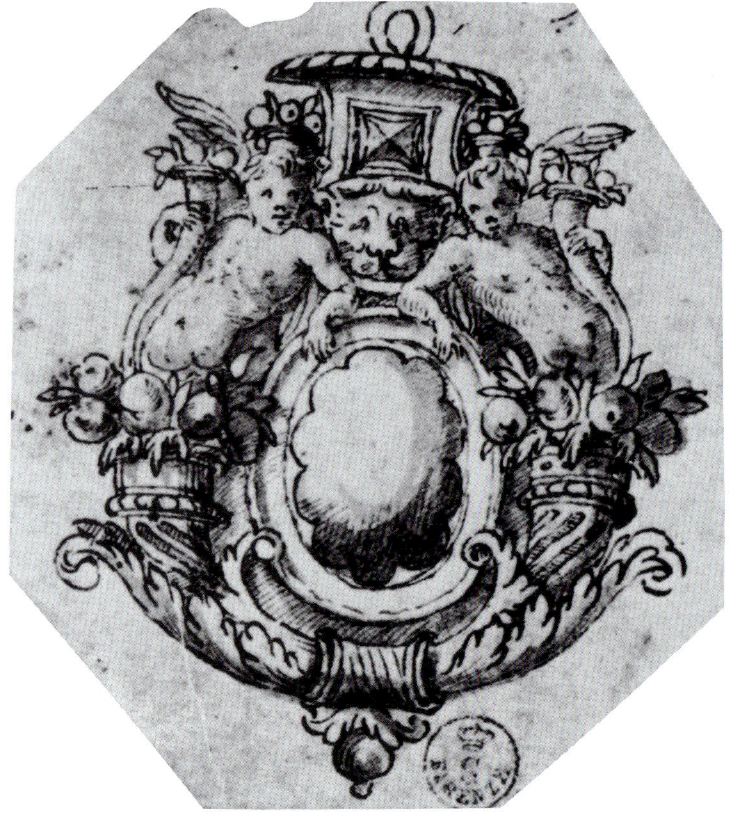

37 Goldsmith's design; pen and ink and wash, Florence, mid- to late sixteenth century. Gabinetto dei Disegni, Uffizi, Florence

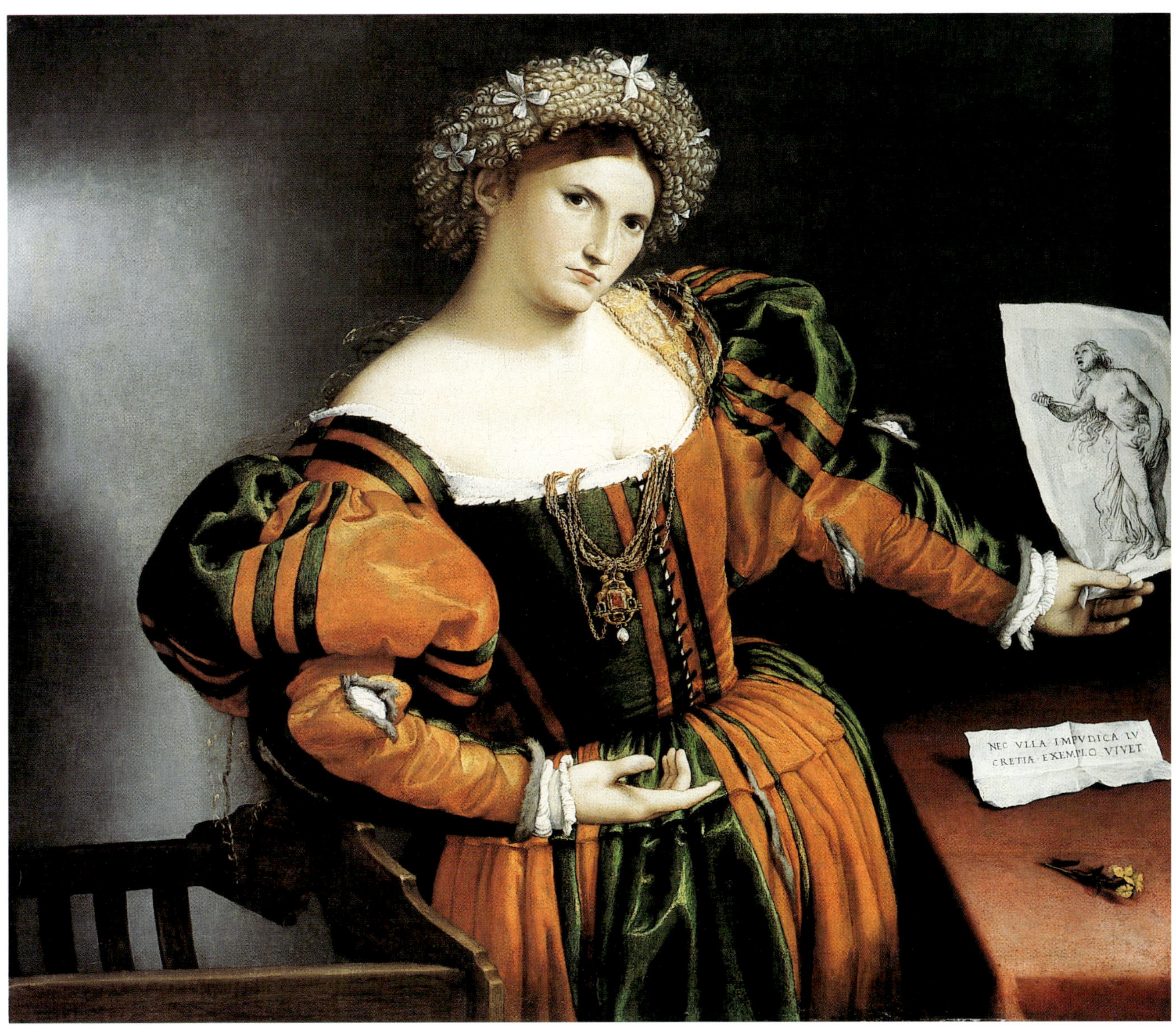

38 Lorenzo Lotto,
*Portrait of a Woman as
Lucretia*; oil on canvas,
Venice, *c.*1530–3.
National Gallery,
London

Vespasiano had earlier gone further: virtue, he claimed was a more valuable dowry than money.[81] At a moment when the bride was so central to events, images pertaining to female chastity were particularly in evidence.

One well-known portrait, Lorenzo Lotto's *Portrait of a Woman as Lucretia* (1530–3), may have been intended to mark the subject's betrothal or marriage (fig. 38).[82] The jewelled pendant on a heavy chain, stuffed into her corsage, is central to this interpretation of the painting, for its form and facture are that of a type associated with marriage pendants. The earlier evidence from Florence and Milan shows that these typically took the form of two or three large gemstones, often in a figurative setting and usually with paired motifs, with one or more pendant pearls. It appears that the typology did not change much in Italy during the sixteenth century. Here, the two figures of putti that frame the central table-cut ruby – often included as fertility symbols in items given and exchanged at betrothal and marriage – are perched atop matching cornucopias, themselves emblems of abundance and fertility, which we have already seen appearing as framing elements on marriage items

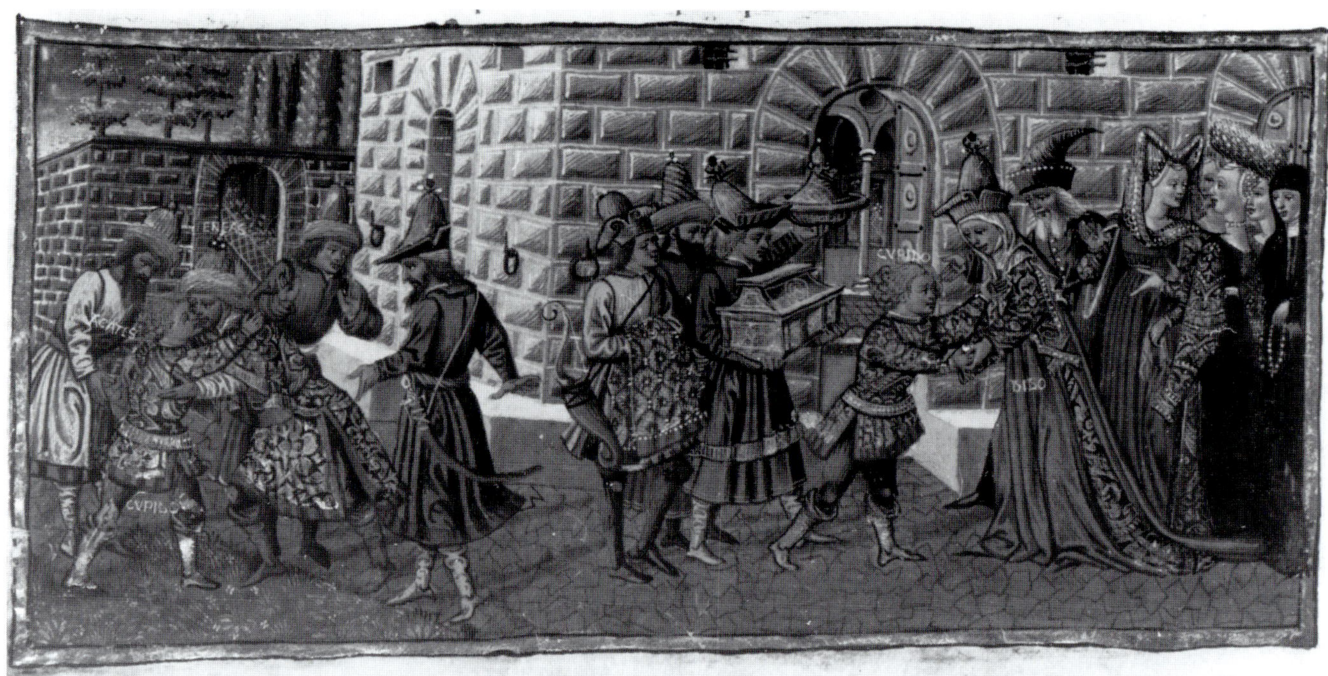

39 Apollonio di Giovanni, manuscript illumination, *The presentation of Aeneas's gifts to Dido*; tempera on parchment, from Virgil's *Aeneid*; MS 492, Biblioteca Riccardiana, Florence

or as integral elements in marriage iconography.[83] The design of this jewel resembles a rare surviving goldsmith's drawing, dating from the later sixteenth century, for what would seem from its iconography to be a marriage jewel, comprising exactly the same elements of putti and cornucopias bursting with fruit (fig. 37).[84] Lotto's interest in (and knowledge of) jewels is documented in his memoranda as well as in his paintings, as is his friendship with goldsmiths such as the Venetian Carpan brothers.[85] This jewel, affirming the status of the subject as a married woman, is at the centre of the picture and should surely be included in any reading of its meaning. It is therefore significant that the unknown young woman holds out and draws the viewer's attention to the drawing in her hand, which depicts Lucretia's suicide following her rape by Tarquin.[86] A note in Latin on the table beside her reads 'Nor shall ever unchaste woman live through the example of Lucretia'. The words, taken from Livy's *History of Rome*, are Lucretia's, indicating that although she herself was guiltless, she would not want to provide any unchaste woman with an excuse for living.[87] Thus the unknown subject of the portrait identifies herself with Lucretia, as an exemplar of chastity in marriage.[88]

Such imagery was commonly applied to objects bought or exchanged as part of marriage ritual. San Bernardino, preaching to women in Siena in 1425, referred to two sizes of box of the type a bride took with her when she left her father's house for her husband's, the larger ones presumably being the marriage chests (*cassoni*) that symbolized the transfer of the woman's dowry and trousseau. The other size was

that little chest: you know, the one in which you keep your ring and pearls and [marriage] jewels, and other similar things; and sometimes you place there the letter which your lover sends you, and you put in it musk … so that when you open the chest, it sends a strong perfume throughout the house, and you lock it with a key, and wish to keep it always with you.[89]

San Bernardino had a keen understanding of women's experience and often championed them, particularly in his critique of contemporary marriage, while condemning feminine indulgence, as he saw it, in matters of dress and fashion.[90] Here he played on his female listeners' proprietorial feelings in likening the contents of this box to a woman's private conscience. He also forged a link between marriage on earth and the mystical marriage of the soul to Christ.[91] Nothing could suggest more clearly the kind of power with which these particular gifts, marking a woman's transition from one state to another, were imbued.

We gain some idea of the appearance of such 'bride's boxes' (*cassette da sposa*) in the work of the Florentine painter and illuminator Apollonio di Giovanni, whose workshop made wedding chests, bride's boxes and birth trays, and who included a depiction of a bride's box in his manuscript illumination *The presentation of Aeneas's gifts to Dido* (fig. 39).[92] And the types of bride's boxes referred to by San Bernardino were not restricted to Tuscany, for references to them appear in centres such as Genoa and Ferrara.[93] A popular form in Tuscany, identifiable from pictorial evidence, seems to have been a long, narrow box with a high stepped lid, with shields of arms painted at either end, or paired on one side, representing the allied families. A box in The British Museum has a crudely joined wooden core covered with linen as a ground for gesso (fig. 40). Some of the gesso elements appear to have been moulded, but the finished effect after painting and gilding imitates more expensive carved prototypes, such as the 'bride's box painted and gilt with figures carved in relief' that is listed in an Este inventory of 1436.[94]

A larger and more elaborate example derives from a Venetian workshop that specialized in boxes illustrating the story of Susanna and the Elders, a story that, like the tale of

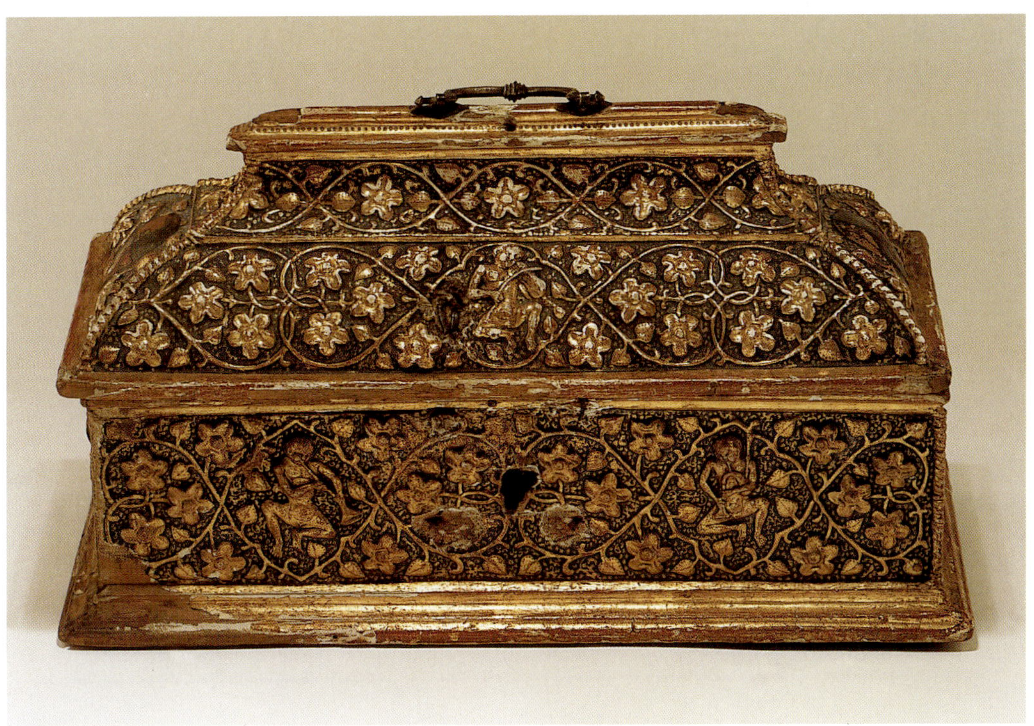

40 Betrothal box; wood with painted and gilded gesso decoration; north Italy, early fifteenth century. The British Museum, London

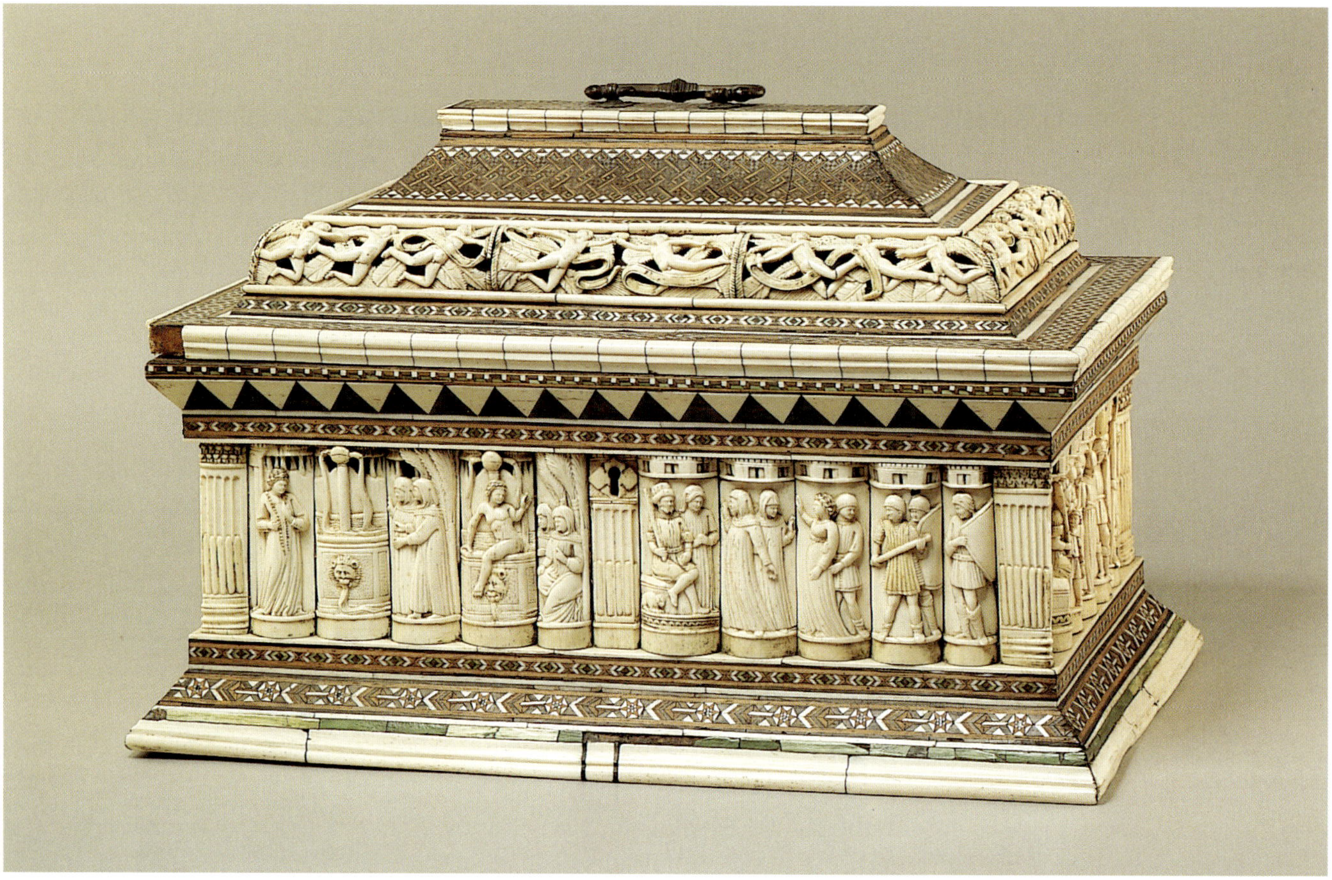

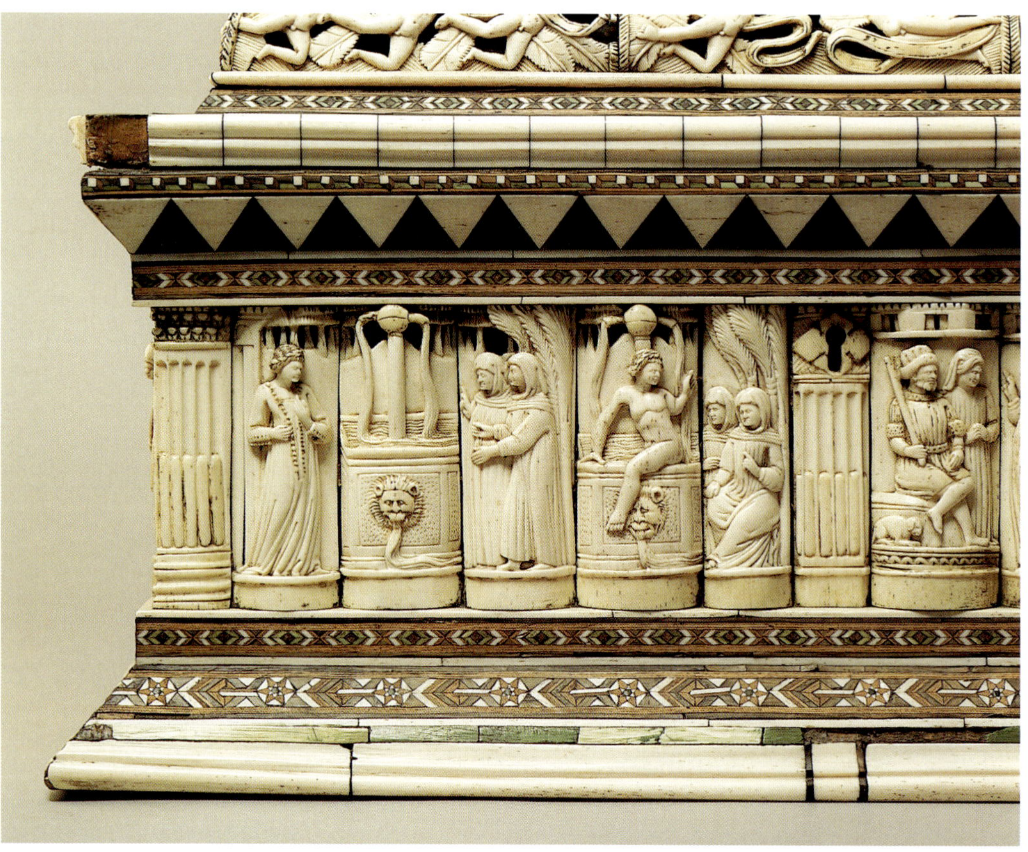

41 The 'Susanna Workshop', betrothal box with the story of Susanna and the Elders; carved bone elements on a wooden core, traces of painted decoration; Venice, early fifteenth century. The British Museum, London

42 'Susanna in her Bath', detail of fig. 41.

Lucretia, deals with chastity in marriage (figs 41, 42).[95] The narrative is conveyed using groups of figures carved in bone, divided by bone frames that punctuate the narrative. At the beginning of the story a clothed Susanna moves towards her bath; she bathes, then attempts to flee the spying Elders, and finally they denounce her in court. Her naked figure in the bathing scene is realized with particular sensuousness, using the whiteness and reflective qualities of the bone (fig. 42). Putti on the lid bear scrolls, which, like those emanating from the mouths of the protagonists in the scenes on the side in cartoon fashion, would presumably have pointed up the narrative with painted inscriptions. Paired arms reinforce the link with marriage and the specific marital virtue of the owners of the box.

We know from memoranda books and from sumptuary laws that attempted to control this kind of public display of wealth that such presentations actually occurred, and that the contents were typically jewellery of the kind that San Bernardino refers to.[96] The print with the idealized figures representing the exemplary Lucrezia and Lorenzo (see fig. 34) was probably intended for use in decorating circular boxes of betrothal gifts.[97] Other round engravings made in Florence, probably mostly in a single workshop, play on chaste themes such as the chastisement of Cupid and the Virgin with the unicorn, the latter featuring a blank pair of arms to be filled in with the arms of a specific couple when the design came to be used.[98] This visual language is echoed on surviving round boxes, which indicate that the prints were intended to provide inexpensive decorative alternatives to the boxes decorated with moulded and carved gesso that were finished with gilding and painting.[99]

'*What she sees, she makes*': *fertility and talismanic properties*

The visual emphasis on chastity in marriage was closely linked with the promotion of childbearing and the celebration of fertility; female chastity was viewed as so crucial chiefly because it ensured the legitimacy of any offspring, of sons in particular. Hence *masserizie* came to include objects with talismanic significance: birth trays painted with emblems, personifications and narratives of fertility or with images of the male children that it was hoped would be born to the couple; or Virgin and Child paintings or reliefs, devotional images that celebrated motherhood.[100] Like the dolls dressed in real swaddling clothes that were given to Florentine women at weddings, these images could be dressed up with costly textiles and hung with jewels to make their presence more real in the bedchamber in which they hung.[101] Jewellery could even be embedded into the medium of a devotional relief to enhance its significance and efficacy as an aid to prayer.[102] Plump figures of little boys in the guise of the Christ Child or St John the Baptist were even given to brides as dolls as part of their trousseaus,[103] while living children played a role in betrothal and wedding ceremonies.[104]

Items given at marriage might include other devotional objects, which also served as charms to aid the wearer in conception and childbirth. Typical gifts in dowries, counter dowries and trousseaus were Agnus Dei: circular medallions of wax made from paschal candles that were stamped with the Lamb of God (*Agnus Dei* in Latin). Distributed by the pope at Easter, these were preserved in metal containers by the recipients.[105] Agnus Dei were traditionally thought to have special talismanic properties; Pope Urban V claimed in 1366: 'This Agnus … destroys sin … and augments virtue. It at once preserves the pregnant woman, and delivers her of her child.'[106] This may have been one reason why, like so many items associated with promoting and commemorating childbirth, Agnus Dei made suitable betrothal and wedding gifts. Gold and silver versions are described among the trousseaus of Anna Sforza and Angela Sforza Visconti in 1491 and 1493,[107] while the Florentine patrician Alamanno Rinuccini had one specially made from gold, with a sapphire and pendant pearl, as a gift for his bride in 1504.[108] Cheaper parcel-gilt, niello and copper alloy pendants survive, with the Agnus Dei on one side and the sacred name of Jesus in the form of the monogram IHS on the other, as do similar cases with openwork, presumably designed to display the wax impression, in one case inscribed with a phrase from the Latin Mass adapted to make its meaning more personal to the wearer: AGNIE DEI MISERERE MEI QUI CRIMINA TOLLIS (Oh Lamb of God, that takest away the sins of the world, have mercy upon me). Other pendants of the same type, which may also have been Agnus Dei cases, survive that bear women's heads on one side or the heads of a couple facing one another, strengthening their association with betrothal and marriage.[109] Since they are often mentioned in wills in conjunction with coral branches as charms for children, Agnus Dei had connotations with fertility, childbirth and sympathetic magic protecting both mothers and babies.

The boxes given at betrothal and marriage could also be decorated with imagery that was thought to provide the right visual messages in promoting and celebrating fertility. A round box in the Ashmolean Museum in Oxford (fig. 43) is decorated with *pastiglia* (gesso) reliefs, with a putto blowing a trumpet at the centre of the lid, and is thought to have been made in Siena in about 1450.[110] Single figures of fat male infants often appear as fertility symbols on items made to encourage or commemorate procreation and childbirth.

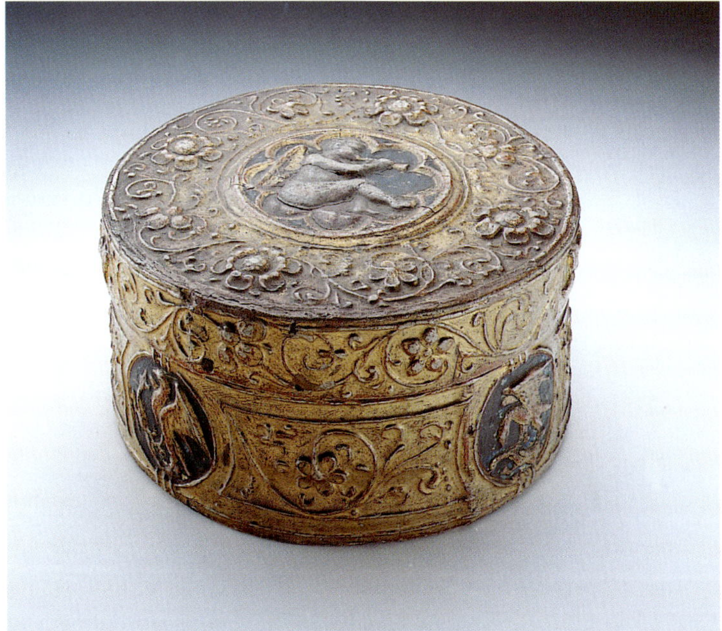

43 Round box with image on lid of a putto blowing a trumpet; wood with painted and gilded gesso decoration; Siena, first half of the fifteenth century. Ashmolean Museum, Oxford

Sometimes a child is shown playing a game or accompanied by an animal; urinating (associated with wealth and good fortune); holding cornucopias (symbols of abundance which often appear on marriage items); or playing an instrument, as in this instance.[111] Some of these iconographies are more explicit in their sexual connotations – images of naked boys playing or gambolling alongside bagpipes;[112] others may refer to popular sayings, now lost, that would have made their meaning clear. The boys in these depictions often wear coral necklaces as amulets, thought to ward off evil influences, as real infants did both at home and when they were sent out to the wet-nurse shortly after birth.[113] Married women were encouraged through visual imagery to identify with the children depicted, according to the long-held belief expressed in the saying that 'what she sees, she makes'.[114]

Tokens of kinship, expressions of will: ring ceremonies

The presentation of the bride's box, occurring about the time of the exchange of vows between the couple in a secular ceremony, brought an end to the betrothal period. Contemporary depictions of the marriage of the Virgin or other biblical couples represent the exchange of vows as taking place in front of a church and in a public space, witnessed by a notary.[115] This could be preceded or followed by attendance at Mass, although marriage was not deemed to be a sacrament.[116] According to Florentine custom, the notary would ask the couple individually if they wished to marry and they would join hands after repeating *volo* (I wish to). They were then declared a married couple by the notary.[117]

The implication of the word *volo* is one of love freely given. Here then was a moment theoretically disassociated from considerations of money and politics, the moment when bride and groom stood together as participants of a marriage ceremony that reflected Ciceronian ideals of intimate trust in a moral contract. The words used and the importance of the gesture of linked hands is recorded on maiolica plates, which can be thus interpreted as commemorating or recalling a marriage.[118] The exchange of vows before the notary was sometimes public (and at lower levels of society such an assertion was all that legal marriage required),[119] but could also take place in private, in a domestic context. We know that the act of signing the contract, which constituted the formal element in marriage, if not the exchange of vows, sometimes took place in the study of the head of the household where notarial documents concerning the family were signed and kept for reference.[120] A maiolica inkstand in Boston (fig. 44), with its facing heads of a man and a woman and the inscription IO TE DO LA MANO, DA ME LA FEDE (I give you my hand, give me your faith) accompanied by joined hands, echoes the exchange of vows and the gestures of a civil marriage.[121] It is not too fanciful to link words and iconography to signing a marriage contract or exchanging vows before a notary, and to suggest that this inkstand may have been designed for use on such an occasion.

In the account of contemporary marriage rituals given by the Roman humanist Marco Antonio Altieri, who wrote a treatise on marriage around 1504,[122] he describes how the exchange of vows between the couple was accompanied by the ring ceremony, as the groom placed a signet ring with the arms of his family engraved upon it on his bride's

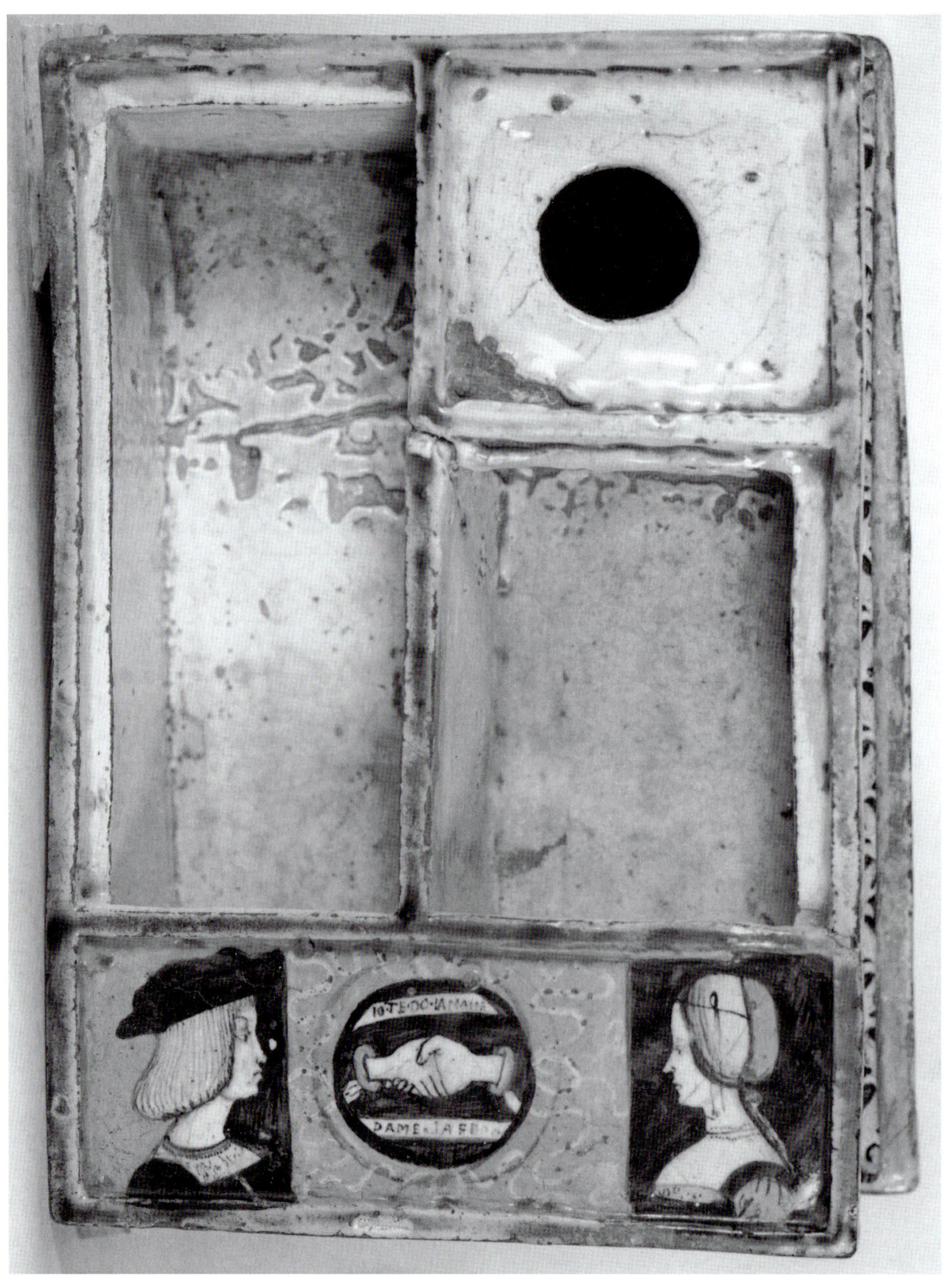

44 Inkstand with
images of a couple
and clasped hands;
tin-glazed ceramic
(maiolica); Faenza (
c.1500. Museum of
Fine Arts, Boston

finger. He also gave her two other rings, one with a sapphire and another with a balas ruby. Other relatives of the groom also presented rings 'in commemoration of the new marriage alliance' between their families (subsequently the mother of the bride gave the groom a silver ewer and basin with his arms impaling those of his wife, and then gave all the wedding guests expensive lengths of cloth).[123] The 'day of the ring' was a key festivity, ending in a ceremonial dinner at the house of the bride symbolizing the end of her time under her father's roof.[124] Rings were exchanged between the couple at various points in courtship, and the groom might give his wife several, limited in some cities by sumptuary legislation, which were set with gemstones, as recorded in memoranda books.[125] We know, for example, that Giuliano de' Medici gave his bride 'two little rings', one with a diamond, the other with an emerald. Ring giving also took place within the husband's family, marking the kin-group into which the bride was marrying, and setting up ties of obligation that would demand future exchanges.[126] Knowing this, it would be difficult to determine the status of any single surviving ring, given the range of the social exchange and the nature of the chivalric ideas that informed ring giving. Explicit links with marriage, as opposed to love, friendship or kinship, are difficult to identify in the absence of specific clues. Nevertheless, some examples can be connected with marriage. A diamond ring in The British Museum is exceptionally rare as one that, to judge from its inscription, was specifically a marriage ring given by a husband to his wife (fig. 45).[127] It is of extremely high quality both in design and workmanship, matching the gemstone to the setting and inscription with perfect judgement. The pyramid-cut diamond is set in a scooped quatrefoil gold setting. Its hoop broadens at the shoulders and is divided into two bands, inscribed in black letter *Lorenso*aLenaLena*.[128] The black-letter inscription is rare on Italian rings; the woman's name is repeated in order to balance the man's, which covers two lines on the hoop on the left. Equally unusual on surviving rings are the words of the inscription: a message of intimate affection between a named couple. Ownership was usually demonstrated by the use of arms and devices or the full name of a single person, rather than of a couple described on first-name terms. It is this feature, and the form of the woman's name, Elena or Madalena, shortened in the manner of a nickname or informal name known only to intimates, which again suggests that this is a marriage ring.

Virtues combined, public display

The dinner that followed the ring ceremony was a highly ritualized and splendid affair, which the sumptuary legislation did little to curb. This was the most public part (albeit for a selected public) of the wedding and here, then, was an opportunity to draw any of these threads together. During celebrations of dynastic (and political) alliances the bride was also the focus of present giving on these occasions, sometimes on an incredible scale. An account of the 1493 *publice spondalizie* of Lucrezia Borgia to Giovanni Sforza, Lord of Pesaro, includes in the description of presents given by the duke of Milan and his brother, Cardinal Ascanio Sforza, a silver 'service for a *credenza*', reputed to be worth 'a thousand ducats or thereabouts', some of the pieces of which are listed in the inventory of her *guardaroba* after her third marriage, to Alfonso d'Este.[129] Magnificent feasting was

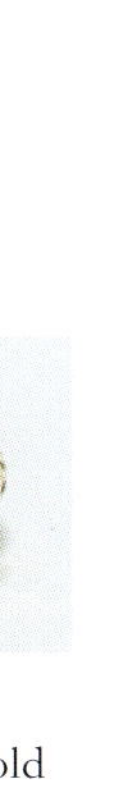

45 Ring inscribed *Lorenso*aLenaLena*; gold set with a faceted diamond, with enamelled black letter script on the hoop; north Italy, fifteenth century. The British Museum, London

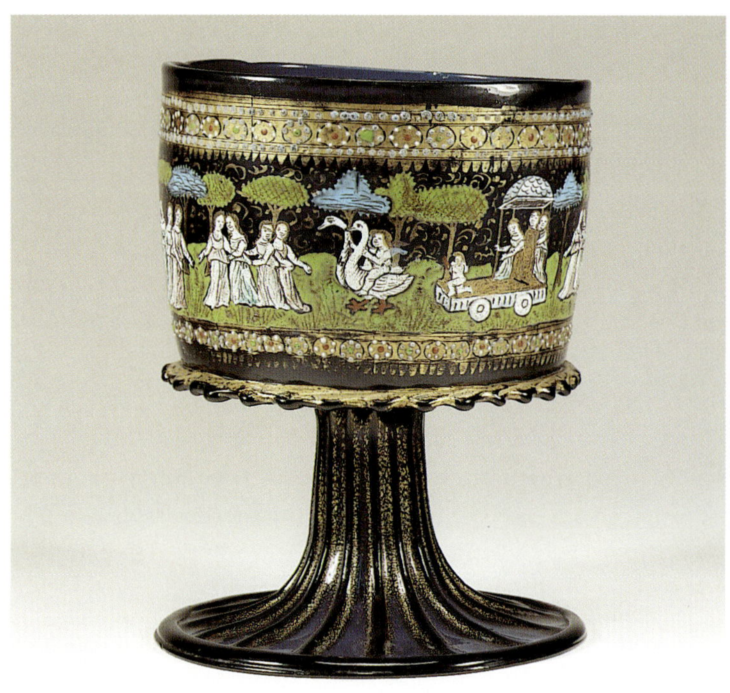

46 Standing cup with *The Triumph of Hymen*; blue glass with enamelled and gilded decoration; Venice (Murano), mid-fifteenth century. The British Museum, London

47 Periphery view of the same glass, showing the enamelled band with *The Triumph of Hymen* as a continuous scene.

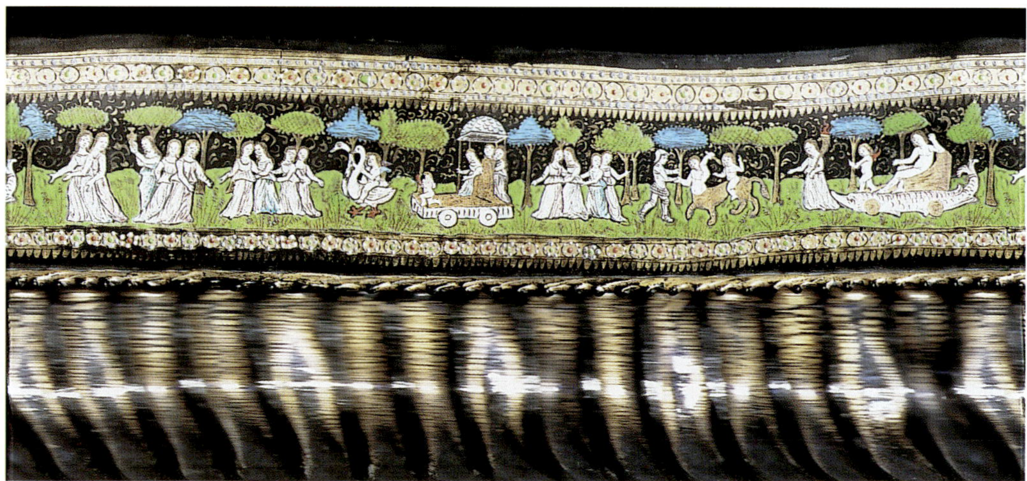

accompanied by other forms of hospitality: music and dancing, and, in the case of marriages between ruling dynasties, by elaborate spectacle, tournaments and allegorical plays; the bride and groom might, for example, make ceremonial entries seated on specially commissioned and decorated triumphal cars. The marriage of Lucrezia d'Este to Annibale Bentivoglio in 1487 was accompanied by the Battle between Chastity and Matrimony.[130] Building on the imagery of Petrarch's *Triumphs*, weddings were often described in triumphal terms.[131] Such stock themes are echoed in an object that was very likely used at such a feast – another glass that one can legitimately connect with marriage or betrothal (fig. 46).[132] The cup, which probably originally had a cover (for use in formal presentation), is decorated with an unbroken band of enamelled decoration, reminiscent of a contemporary woodcut illustration in a printed book. Here we include both the complete glass, and another photograph taken while the glass rotates (fig. 47), which shows the

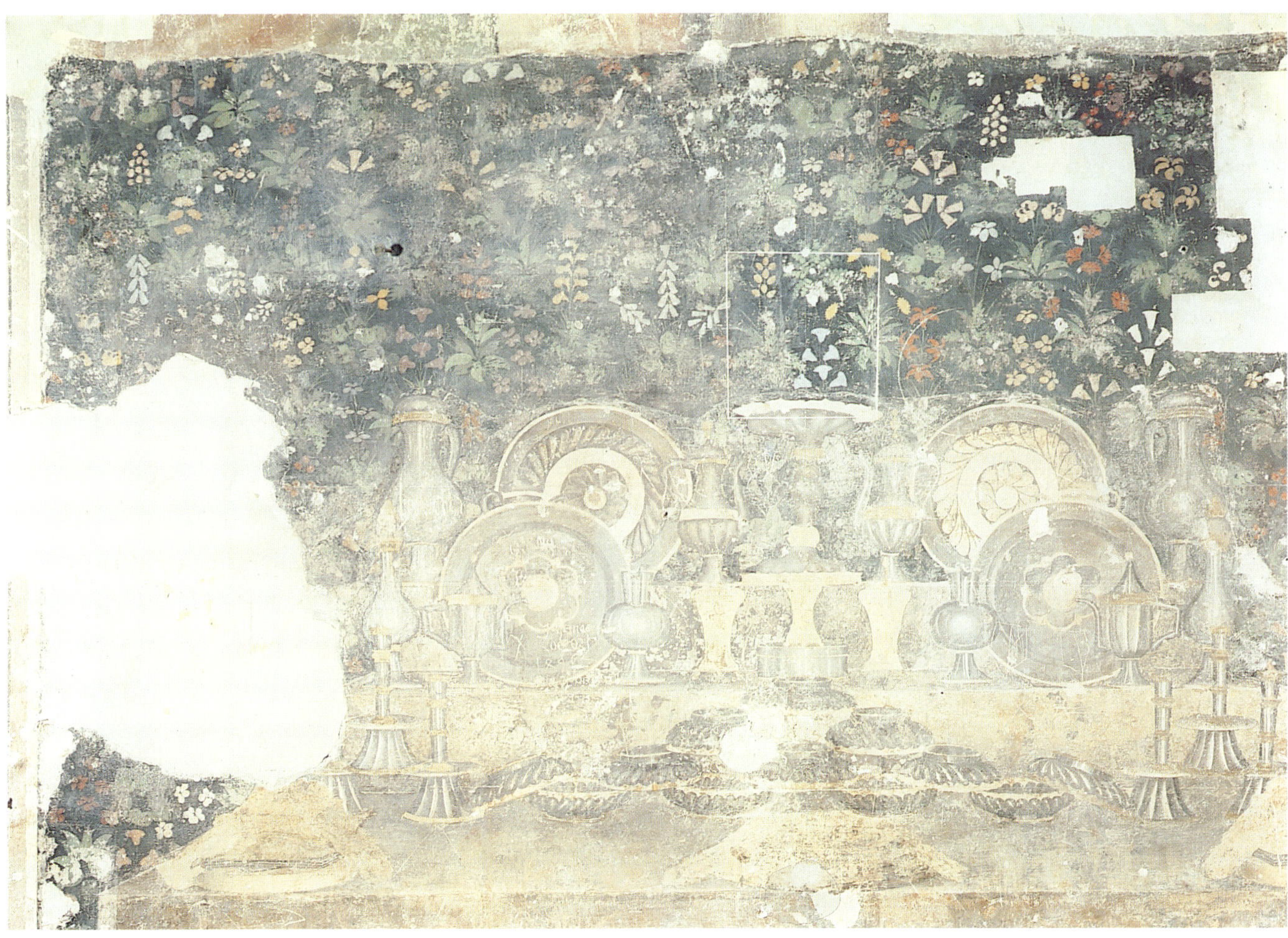

narrative as a single sequence, seen therefore as it might if turned in the hand. On one side the naked figure of Venus reclines on a curious fish-shaped chariot, preceded by a woman with a flaming cornucopia, the attribute of Hymen, goddess of marriage. Ahead of her in the narrative sequence, a centaur – perhaps representing lust – fights with a knight in armour. At the centre can be seen three clothed female figures sitting beneath a canopy on a chariot drawn by swans, with Cupid bound before them. This group represents chaste love. The two triumphal cars are separated by identical groups of four maidens who appear to be dancing. However hazy the significance of particular elements, the general tenor of the narrative representing the triumph of married love over profane love is clear.

Wedding feasts held in or outside palaces by ruling families or patricians are described by chroniclers or in family memoranda. A room, an inner courtyard or even an outside space would be fitted with platforms and benches, hung with tapestries and swags of greenery, with an elaborate 'staged' *credenza* at one side.[133] Plain and parcel-gilt vessels would typically be displayed against an imported tapestry from Syria or Flanders. A fresco in the *sala* of Palazzo Altemps in Rome shows a *credenza* displaying silver plate, laid out on three shelves ('stages') against a Flemish *alla verdura* tapestry, as it might have been at a wedding (fig. 48). The show of silver here is probably similar to the one that was set up in the palace – perhaps in this very room – for the wedding of Girolamo Riario and Caterina Sforza in 1477.[134]

Such splendid items as the vessels massed together in this fresco were limited in number and restricted in circulation in the late fifteenth century. Just as in the case of borrowed jewellery, even wealthy patricians would have had no hesitation in requesting their loan from a wealthier family member, neighbour or friend.[135] Sixteenth-century Italians looked back on these customs with amazement, since by their time such luxuries as plate had become more commonly available to a wider social group. One commentator noted how the Florentine patrician Giovanni Chellini,

since he possessed much silver plate, frequently and almost continually lent pieces of it to Florentine citizens who were taking up office or celebrating a wedding. So we see that he lent six silver dishes to Neri Capponi when he was sent as ambassador to Milan … he also lent plate to Bernardo di Cristoforo Carnasecchi for the wedding of one of his daughters to the son of Gianozzo Manetti, in short, one could fill a book with such loans.[136]

Another Cinquecento writer found nothing admirable in the old practice of lending:

I found that, in the year 1467 at the marriage of Niccolo Martelli, and at a supper which the knight Messer Antonio Ridolfo gave to the Duke of Calabria … at a banquet given by Giovanni Aldobrandini and at others given by men equal to these citizens of mark and by no means of lean purse, as well as on other occasions of sitting down together, the same silver appeared, being lent round by the same circle of friends.[137]

By the time both commentators were writing, in the second half of the sixteenth century, the idea of magnificence that had informed Italian elite behaviour the century before had changed beyond recognition.

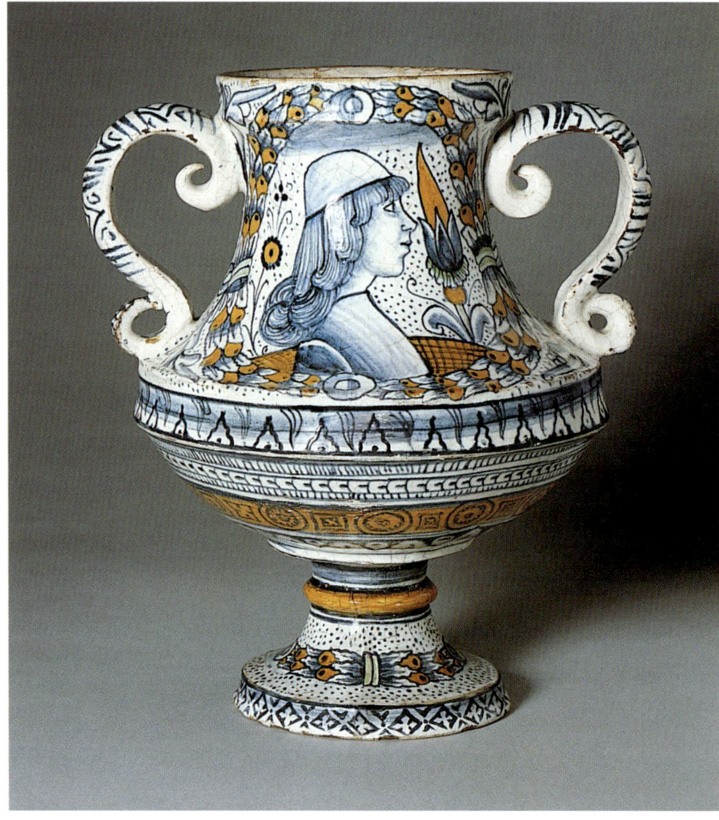

49 Two-handled vase with image of a man in profile; tin-glazed ceramic (maiolica); Deruta, c.1490–1520. Fitzwilliam Museum, Cambridge

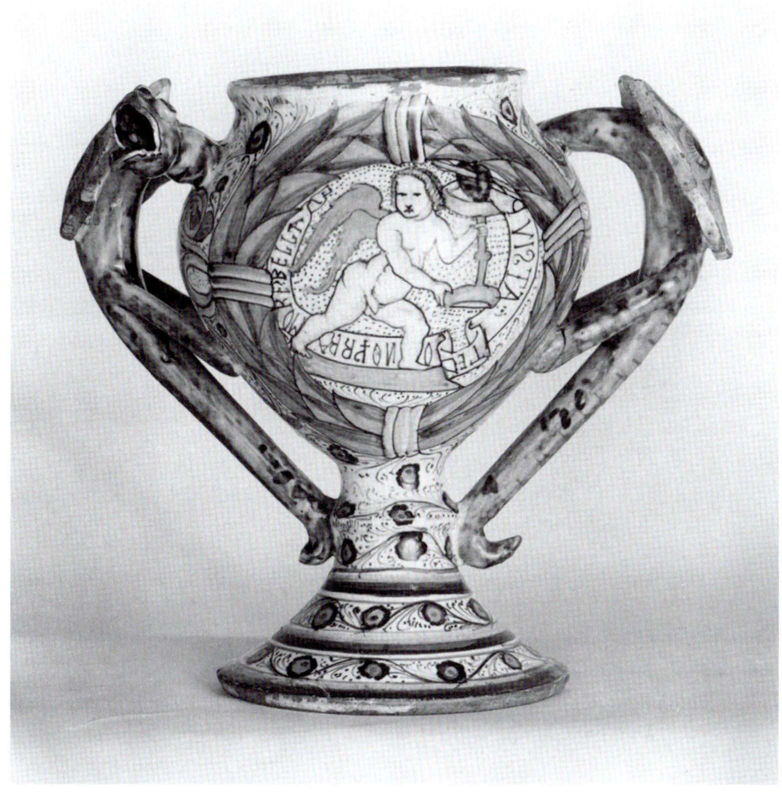

50 Two-handled cup
with Cupid carrying a
goblet containing a
heart pierced by an
arrow; tin-glazed
ceramic (maiolica);
Deruta (?), *c.*1470–80.
Victoria and Albert
Museum, London

For those who could not get their hands on silver, maiolica could be used instead. Two-handled maiolica vases survive of a form known traditionally as a wedding vessel or *coppa amatoria*,[138] and may derive from lost silver prototypes. In one, the delicately painted profiles of a man and a woman on each side (fig. 49) suggest its probable function as a piece connected with betrothal or marriage – perhaps made to decorate a tiered *credenza* set out for a wedding feast as shown in contemporary depictions. Further evidence that vases of this form were used in conjunction with one part or another of a wedding ritual is provided by the imagery and legends on surviving pieces. Deruta pieces often have images of pierced hearts or conjoined hands; one late-fifteenth-century example reads QUISTA TE DONO P[ER]AMORE BELLA (I give you this, beautiful one, as a token of love) and P[ER] AMORE TE PORTO IN QUISSTA COPA BELLA (For the love I bear thee in this fine cup) (fig. 50).[139] Other examples, such as one with the arms of the Baglioni of Perugia, bear what appear to be references to romantic frustration on the part of the male giver: EL NON PODER ME FINE (Not being able to is putting an end to me).[140]

Wedding chests, birth trays and the making of family memory

The feast would generally be followed by the consummation of the marriage in the house of the bride's father, and then at some later stage by the procession of the bride. This procession had in itself the character of a triumph, as San Bernardino made clear in one of his sermons:

Consider for a moment the lady when she goes to her bridegroom. You see that when she goes to her husband, she goes on horseback, all decked out with such music, with such triumph … She is dressed so elaborately, with silver ribbons, with tassels, with her fingers full of rings; her hair is arranged and combed; she has garlands on her head; she has a fillet; and on every side she is dazzling with gold.[141]

The bride was accompanied to her new home by her trousseau in large wedding chests (*cassoni, casse, forziali* or *forzieri*) loaded onto the back of a mule in the procession.[142] In the early fifteenth century the chests tended to be commissioned by the family of the bride on her behalf, and this custom continued in courtly circles. In Ferrara, as we have seen, their manufacture – or even repair – was undertaken, when the bride belonged to the ruling house, by her family.[143] In Florence, at least from the mid-Quattrocento, there was a shift from the bride's family to that of the groom, and wedding chests as monuments to marriage were commissioned in pairs by the groom or by one of his male relatives at betrothal, and took several months to make.[144] Such chests carried complex messages proclaiming family and individual virtue and honour, and the power and the propagation of a given lineage. Florentine *cassoni* were painted with didactic narratives from ancient history and poetry, selected both to instruct and to establish a connection between the exemplary virtues of the ancients and the present virtues of their owners, a link made by the prominent presence of their arms within the decorative scheme.[145] The paired nude (or partially nude) figures of a man and a woman on the undersides of the lids, only visible when the chest was in use, carried connotations of fertility.[146] Once the chests had been unloaded at the bride's new home and set in place in the marital bedchamber, their contents could be shown off to wedding guests. In Rome around 1500, the custom seems to have been for the mother of the bride to open the chests to show off the trousseau and dowry items as being more than sufficient for the couple's needs.[147] The sense of magnificent abundance that characterized all aspects of wedding ritual focused on the marital bedchamber in which the chests were set, and we have seen that the chamber was often redecorated in preparation for marriage, along with the suite of adjoining rooms that made up the groom's apartment in his family palace.[148]

Quattrocento fashion, until the last quarter of the century, when wooden inlay, carving and gilding took over in Florence, favoured the incorporation into *cassoni* of painted narrative scenes, often of classical inspiration. Although we have scattered references to their making by a range of techniques all over Italy, from Calabria to Padua, by far the best evidence for painted examples comes from Florence, and is found in the workshop ledgers of Apollonio di Giovanni and his business partner, Marco del Buono, both of whom were painters.[149] The ledger lists chests made for marriage alliances between the most powerful families among the urban elite. Covering the period 1446 to 1463, the ledger shows that the workshop was both fashionable and productive, and recounts that in one year alone, 1452, the workshop produced twenty-three pairs of chests.[150] Some complete (fig. 51) or restored chests have been attributed to this workshop on the grounds of style, recogniz-able by the use of stock themes and by repeated figures or figural groups. Many other such painted panels have long since been removed from their chests, valued as autonomous painted images in their own right.

Inventories and contemporary literature make the role of great chests in the life of a married couple, particularly in the relative privacy of the bedchamber, very clear.[151] Boccaccio makes several references to the positioning and functions of chests in his

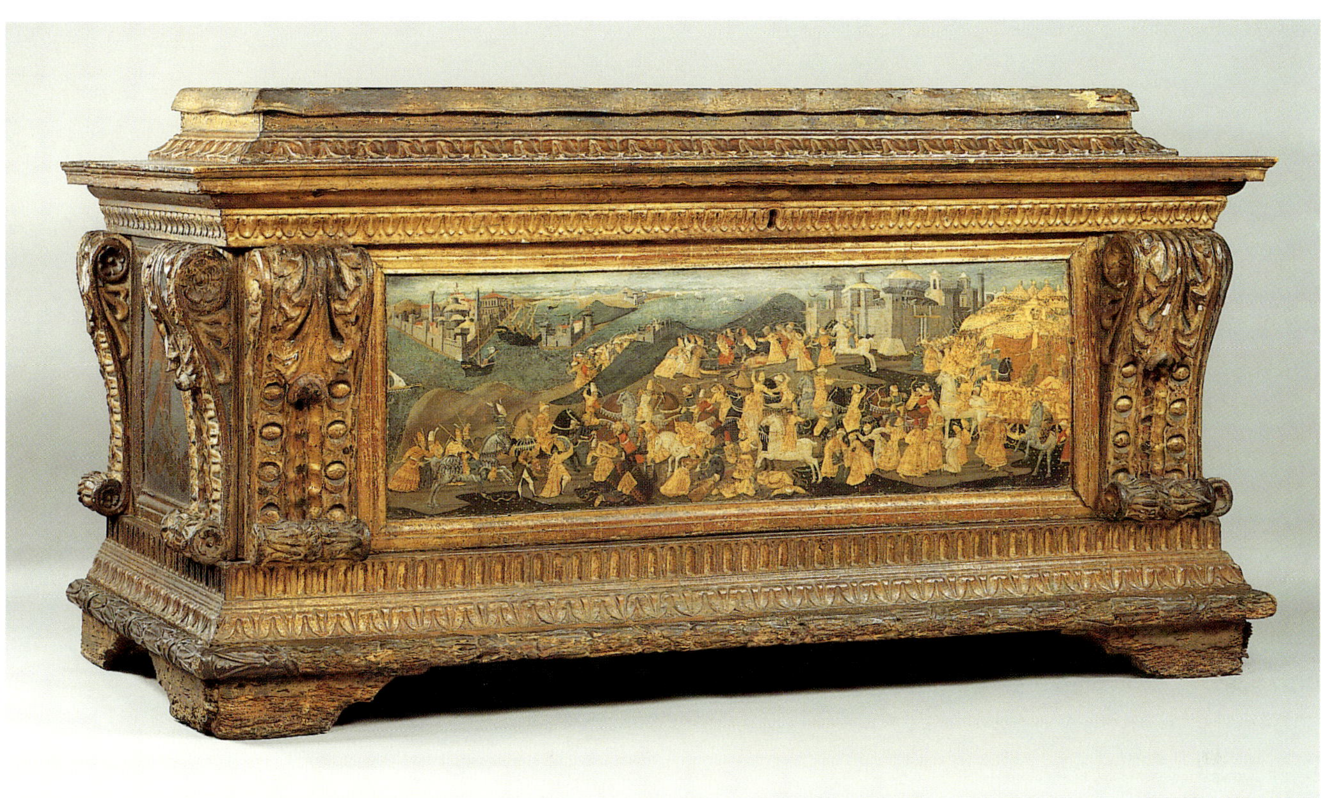

Decameron. In one tale a young man is led into a woman's bedchamber and seated with her 'on an elaborate chest at the bed's foot'.[152] Another racy story puts a large chest of the *cassone* type at the heart of an account of adultery. Two male friends are each married to attractive women; one of the two has an affair with the other's wife. When the cuckolded husband plots with his faithless wife to bundle her lover into the chest in their bedchamber, he is tricked again and finds himself locked up instead. His wife and her lover, Zeppa, then make love on the lid of the chest above him:

He [Zeppa] took her in his arms and started kissing her and, having laid her on the chest in which her husband was safe under lock and key, did there disport himself with her to his heart's content as she with him. Spinellocio in the chest heard all that Zeppa said, and how he was answered by the woman, and the Trevisan [amorous] dance that afterwards went on over his head, whereat his mortification was such that for a great while he scarce hoped to live through it.[153]

Given the role of the bedchamber as the centre of a woman's existence indoors, and that great chests were painted as gifts for women, or as part of their dowry, the painted narratives on these chests have sometimes been considered in terms of their meaning in an intimately feminine ambience. The interpretations of the myths and historical legends that appear on these mid-fifteenth-century chests should certainly be related to the social world that they inhabited; one that saw little disparity between antique or biblical subject matter and the way in which it was rendered in recognizably contemporary terms. Painted mythical and biblical narratives that told of exemplary women – the stories of Susanna and Esther, of patient Griselda, Lucretia or Eurydice – articulated concepts of feminine virtue as perceived by contemporary society.[154] They also emphasized the relative obligations of men and women to each other in marriage, and in society generally. Unravelling the narrative elements in each story, in which scenes are combined in unbroken strips, often with labels to identify the principal protagonists, implies active participation. Women are sometimes depicted, in scenes such as the 'Birth of the Virgin', sitting in groups on floor cushions, benches around bedsteads, or low chests in their bedchambers in a way that would have placed them at the right level to see the painted histories clearly.[155] Generations of children would have known them well as a kind of open storybook, dramatic and colourful, encountered when toddling around on the floor of their parents' bedroom.[156] Indeed, the mystic and reformer Fra Girolamo Savonarola took parents to task for letting their children see 'beds and daybeds [painted] with images of naked women with men in certain indecent acts'.[157]

Not all the subjects for *cassoni* had to relate specifically to female virtues. Many of the stories illustrated seem to relate as much or more to the preoccupations of men – whether fathers or husbands – than especially to women.[158] The fact that women were encouraged to live strictly indoors rather than loitering at windows or doorways, or in the street, is likely to have made them the principal users of the *camera*. For them it became a reception room, where they could surround themselves with female friends, family, servants and children over about two years old (when they got home from being farmed out to the wet-nurse),[159] as well as a place to sleep. This must have affected their experience of pieces of decorated furniture associated with their arrival at the house or apartment. However, the Florentine bedchamber was not an exclusively female space. All the patrician decorative schemes we read about are for 'my' room in the family palace where a father or both parents were living, which was to become the marital chamber, and inventories often open with the principal chamber (first item, a Virgin and Child image), which frequently contains the main items that are connected to marriage exchange and commissioning. Although alliances between dynastic ruling families elsewhere in Italy[160] (and perhaps the very grandest of the Florentine social elite) demanded separate apartments for husbands and wives, equal in status, who, following Alberti's recommendations,[161] would meet up in one or other chamber at will, there can be no doubt that, for the most part, married couples slept together in a single bedchamber. Men may have been the primary occupiers of other parts of the house – the study, for example, rather than the bedchamber – but men as well as women needed somewhere to sleep and to store their clothes and possessions. Inventories record the mess and confusion of bedchambers occupied by named individuals rather than by couples, but they document them as lived-in spaces where both men and women kept their clothes in chests round the bed or in the next-door *anticamera*, where one often finds all kinds of useful things jumbled together (objects for the hunt, olive oil, window fittings, cloaks indicating membership of a confraternity and so on).

Moreover, there were some male authors who believed that while women's essential inferiority was a *sine qua non*, they could achieve a little more than virginal or marital chastity. The humanist Agostino Nifo enumerated the desirable virtues for women in his treatise *On the Prince* of 1520–1. They ranged from chastity (again), modesty and silence to moderation, temperance, abstinence and sobriety. However, he noted that ancient *noble* women were praised not just for chastity and fidelity, but for patience, patriotism, learning and eloquence, political skills and liberality. In sum, therefore, the proscriptions for elite men and women did not differ substantially, and women could do worse than simply

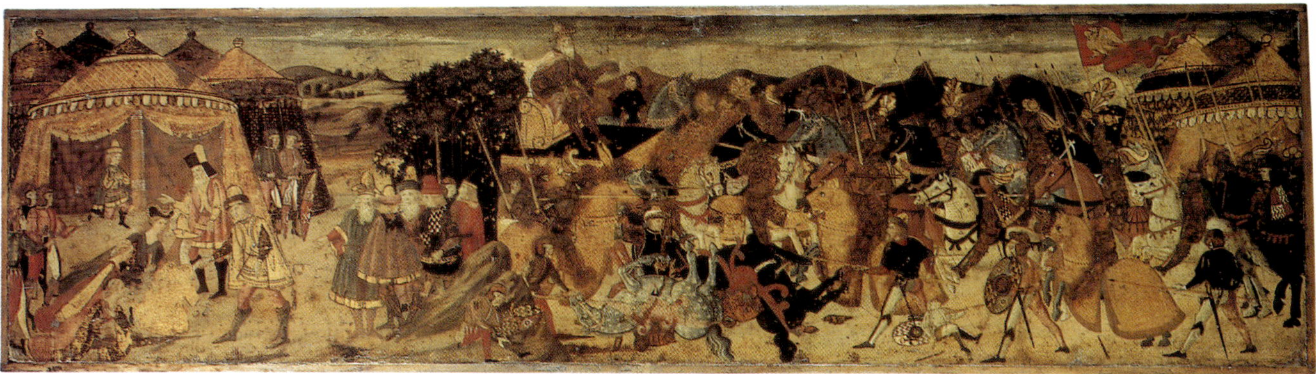

52 Apollonio di Giovanni
and Marco del Buono
(attributed to workshop),
*Alexander the Great and the
Battle of Issus*; *cassone* panel
painted with tempera;
Florence, *c.*1440.
The British Museum,
London

emulate their husbands.[162] The *cassone* narrative could therefore revolve around the actions of an exemplary man while still being usefully addressed to a woman.

Thus, the justly famous chest, stuccoed and painted almost certainly after a design by the Mantuan court artist Andrea Mantegna, that accompanied the fourteen-year-old Paola Gonzaga to Austria in 1477, when she married the Count of Gorizia, takes as its subject the story of the Justice of Trajan (which we will see in Chapter Five may have had particular significance for Gonzaga women).[163] And a very ordinary panel from the front of a wedding chest in The British Museum (fig. 52) depicts two scenes from the life of Alexander the Great. On the right is the Battle of Issus, in which Alexander defeated Darius III, King of Persia; Darius is shown in a chariot riding in the midst of the battle. Darius fled the battle, and on the left, Darius's abandoned mother, wife and daughter are treated kindly by the victorious Alexander. The clemency of Alexander here demonstrates his virtue and magnanimity as victor, as well as his valour. The story is probably taken from the moralizing account in Plutarch's *Life*, although it also appears in the work of other late classical authors. The panel, painted in Florence about 1440, has been attributed to the workshop of Apollonio di Giovanni and Marco del Buono. In addition to the tempera paint, it is decorated with gilding and punching, and incorporates figure groups, such as that of Alexander and the women, that are typical of the standard figure types reproduced so often by Apollonio and his collaborators. Similarly schematic is the way in which the battle is treated. However, its poor quality and condition make it impossible to attribute it precisely to a specific Florentine workshop. Given the success of Apollonio's shop and Marco's partnerships with other painters, there must have been lesser rivals for what was such a fashionable trade in mid-fifteenth-century Florence.

Painted birth trays (*deschi da parto*) were often made by the same workshops and painters who made great chests, and could be bought or commissioned at the same time in anticipation of the birth of an heir.[164] These objects were a key part of the ritual celebrations that followed the birth of a child, paintings that could then be arranged around the walls of the bedchamber. The imagery on birth trays pertains as often to themes of marriage or love as to birth, though scenes of, for example, the birth of the Virgin identify the female recipient in her prescribed role as wife and mother. These were the kinds of object that could be given by parents to their children and children-in-law when they married as

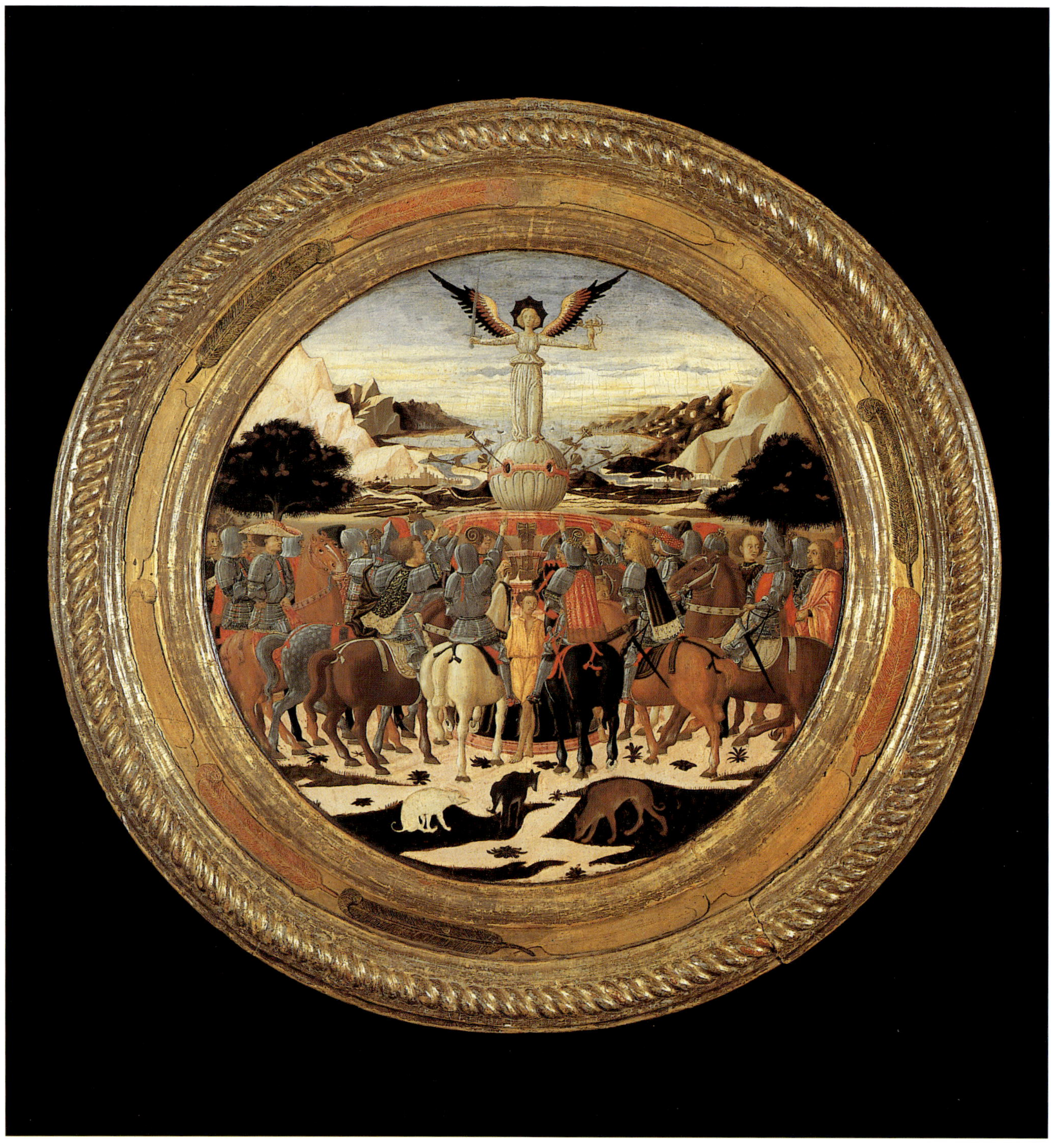

53 Giovanni di Ser Giovanni (called Lo Scheggia), birth tray (*desco da parto*) with *The Triumph of Fame*, front, made to commemorate the birth of Lorenzo de' Medici; tempera on panel; Florence, 1448–9. The Metropolitan Museum of Art, New York

presents for setting up house together. When, for instance, the Florentine Tommaso Minerbetti married in 1521, his father gave him and his wife (who was not pregnant at the time) a birth tray, which may originally have been given to him on his marriage in 1494.[165] Birth trays certainly had proud familial associations and were displayed in the household, often in the study of the head of the household. One Florentine goldsmith kept two in his study, inventoried in 1424, and Lorenzo de' Medici kept the tray made in commemoration of his birth in the small room adjoining his study in his private apartments (fig. 53).[166] Owning birth trays was not just an elite phenomenon, since it is estimated that around half of Florentine households owned at least one between 1400 and 1500. Given their status, they could be used more than once in the rituals of a single family, or sold and reused with new arms painted on them. One tray from the workshop of Apollonio di Giovanni and Marco del Buono, showing Petrarch's *Triumph of Love* and clearly dating from around 1460–70, is painted with arms on the reverse, indicating that it was used at the marriage of Costanza Gianfigliazzi to Francesco Samminiato, who were married in 1537. Nothing could indicate more clearly the long life and continuing high status of these objects in Renaissance society.[167]

By the mid-sixteenth century these practices were history. Vasari's biography of the painter and sculptor Dello Delli, which appeared in the second edition of his *Lives of the Painters, Sculptors and Architects* in 1568, explained the artistic potential of *cassoni* and the pattern of social demand that had brought them into being – a demand that no longer existed. According to Vasari, Dello found that working in terracotta did not pay sufficiently well, and so, 'having good drawing skills', he turned to painting, where he discovered a talent for small figures

which served him well, since in those days they used to use for the bedchambers of citizens large wooden chests in the shape of tombs with the lids variously decorated. Everyone had these chests painted. The front and ends were decorated with various narrative subjects, and the corners and other parts were enriched with the arms and devices of the house. As for the stories which used to be painted on the front of the body of the chests, they were for the most part fables taken from Ovid or other poets, or else histories told by Greek or Roman historians; and similarly scenes of hunting, jousting, or romances, according to what each person loved best. The inside was then lined with linen or cloth, according to the rank and means of the people who had them made, so as better to conserve the clothes of fine cloth and other precious things inside. What is more, they painted in such a manner not only the chests, but the wall panels, the cornices which ran round the room, and other ornaments for the room, which in those times one used to use magnificently, as one can see in infinite examples throughout the city. And this kind of thing was in use for many years, so that even the most exccllent painters employed themselves on such things, without being ashamed, as many would be today, at painting or gilding similar things. And that this was the case can be seen up into our own times, apart from many other examples, in some chests, wall panels and cornices in the apartments of Lorenzo the Magnificent, which were painted by the hands of artists of no mean talent, but excellent masters, with all the jousts, tournaments, hunts, feasts and other spectacles painted with judgement, with inventiveness and with marvellous skill. One sees the remains of such things not only in the Medici Palace, but in all the noblest palaces in Florence. And there are those who, keeping faith with those old customs, have not removed such things to give place to modern ornaments and ways.[168]

Vasari's ambivalence about these painted pieces has been picked up by modern commentators. He admired the magnificence of the ornamentation but at the same time condemned the artisanal nature of the work: artists, he implied, had moved on, scorning mere decorative work and placing a new emphasis on the dignity of *disegno*.[169] Nevertheless, his ideological programme does not prevent a tinge of nostalgia from appearing in his account. These objects were still possessed by the heirs of their original commissioners as prompts to family memory. Vasari could still see them in the possession of longer established families (as opposed to the *parvenus*). Indeed, his observations are borne out by the presence of old painted chests in Florentine inventories of the mid- to late Cinquecento, and this practice does not seem to have been confined to Florence.[170] In the Courtauld Gallery in London there survives a pair of chests that were commissioned by the Florentine patrician Lorenzo Morelli for his marriage to Vaggia di Tanai Nerli in 1472 (fig. 54). They were the product of no fewer than three craftsmen: the woodcarver Zanobi di Domenico, and the painters Jacopo del Sellaio and Biagio di Antonio. The chests originally stood on a high base, which raised the painted panels off the floor to become more visible. Above them on the wall was a gilded carved cornice with two painted panels (*spalliere*). When Lorenzo Morelli's son got married in 1472 the chests were among his wedding presents, and they stayed in the family for at least 200 years, featuring in an inventory of 1680 as 'two great chests painted and gilded and history-painted with back-rests and the arms of Morelli and Nerli', a part of the Morelli patrimony.[171]

This inventory reference gives some sense of how such chests comprised part of a family's memory of its own ancestral past, and how that history became absorbed into the present. That a large chest of this type could be a spark to the nostalgic remembrance of family events is clear from a description given by Palla Strozzi, in his will, of a momentous meeting concerning a sale of beloved family property which had taken place thirteen years before. He called his feelings to mind by remembering the room in which the meeting took place and the chest (*cassone*) next to which he had stood while speaking. 'Marietta [Palla's wife], Giovanni and I commiserated with each other over the lost house … And standing in that room [the chamber next to his own bedchamber] beside a chest, I told Giovanni everything and he was deeply sorrowful on my account.' Fixing his memories on an actual space and a significant object, both well known to him, gave authority to the agreement, serving as a kind of proof.[172] Such a chest could make family memory.

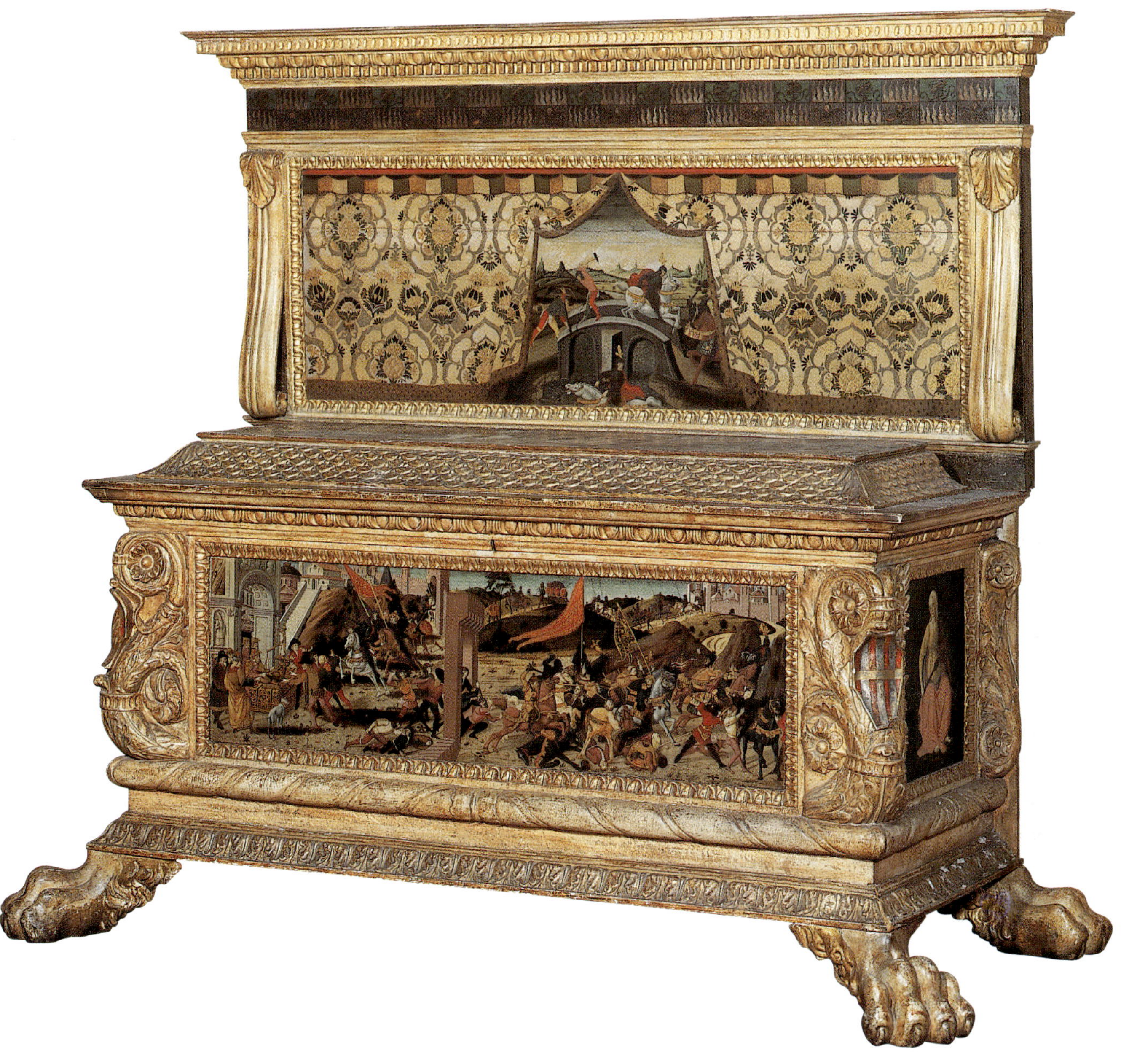

54 Biagio di Antonio, Jacopo del Sellaio (painters) and Zanobi di Domenico (woodcarver), one of a pair of Morelli–Nerli wedding chests (*cassoni*) with Morelli arms and scenes of Roman history derived from Livy: *Episodes from the Lives of Marcus Furius Camillus and Horatius Cocles*; tempera on poplar with gilding; Florence, 1472. Courtauld Gallery, London

Chapter Three

All'antica Style

The meaning of art objects of all kinds did not depend only on their imagery and iconography. Moral messages could be reinforced by the specific connotations of the visual language employed. Makers and patrons made deliberate choices.

Pan, sexually voracious and master of nameless terrors, is not, for example, the most obviously virtuous of figures. We have seen in the first two chapters that classical subject matter was used, in conjunction with narratives drawn from other traditions, to transmit messages of virtue. Pan, however, was no Alexander or Lucretia. Nevertheless, the demigod is depicted at the centre of a maiolica plate of about 1510, perched on a tree stump, playing his syrinx, and standing for the first syllable of the name of the plate's commissioner, Pandolfo Petrucci, first citizen of Siena, whose arms float above Pan's head (fig. 55). Two idealized shepherds, bearing arms of lesser families, kneel in homage.[1] Around the Pan roundel are two major bands of ornament. The first is a sober pattern of so-called anthemion ornament. More striking is the outer border, an ordered arrangement of the fantastic and phantasmagorical, where paired griffin-like beasts, with a superfluity of scrolling limbs, prance to either side of volute-handled urns, while acanthus fronds transmogrify into curly-tongued dolphins. At first sight this seems too decorative, too light-hearted an object to convey the tyrannical leadership of the wealthy Sienese merchant or his elevated cultural ambitions.

However, the painting of this plate derives virtuous meaning less by its iconography than by the referential style in which it was rendered. Although he still has his identifying horns (and rather hairy thighs), this Petrucci Pan has lost most of his libidinous, goaty excrescences, the satyr's phallus and haunches that one might expect in the personification of lust. This aspect of his mythology is reduced, and his meaning is altered by his metamorphosis into a beautiful, classically proportioned youth, whose appearance depends on recognizable allusions to ancient sculpture. He bears, in fact, a striking resemblance to a well-known Hellenistic statue, of which there survived many Roman copies, of the (hornless) shepherd-boy Daphnis, part of a group depicting the youth's instruction on the pipes by Pan.[2] Daphnis benefited from his teaching to become the inventor of bucolic poetry,[3] and the image on the plate seems deliberately to make Pan/Daphnis both master and pupil, his own disciples flanking him like acolytes. In addition to this poetic metaphor of obeisance, this blending of forms and iconologies may, in part, have been intended to illustrate a philosophical theory of the human condition, to communicate the notion of man's mutability, his glorious qualities of transformation, which the philosopher Pico della Mirandola expressed by urging his reader to seek the Pan in himself, to identify one aspect of his behaviour of the many that made up his uniquely protean whole.[4] The image may have still another layer of meaning. In this more heroic image Pan's muscled legs have been moved into a different position from those in the Daphnis

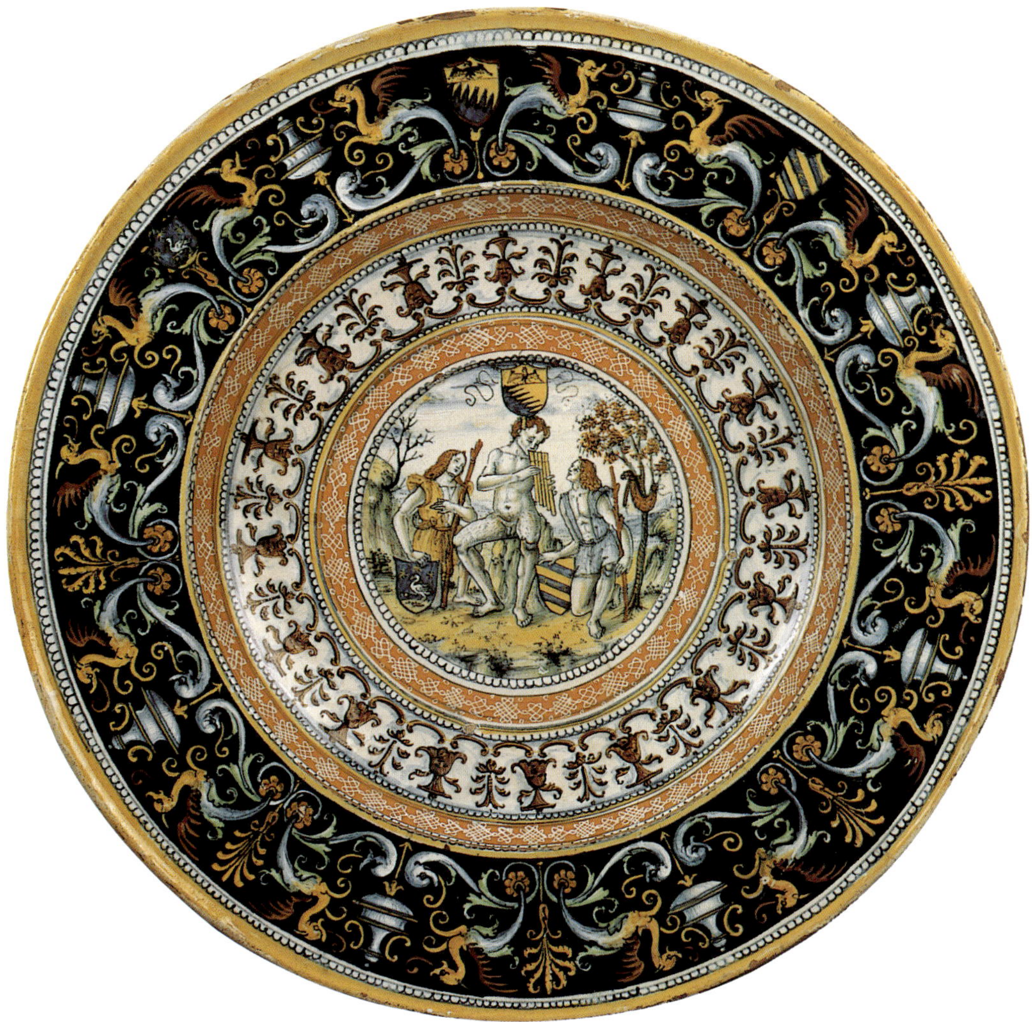

sculpture – he is less effete – suggesting the painter or designer of the plate had studied one of the several small sculpted copies made of the famous and fragmentary ancient sculpture of a seated Hercules, the *Belvedere Torso*, in which the missing limbs are replaced.[5] Thus Petrucci's Pan is a significant combination of (more or less) accurately derived ancient sources.

The decorative elements are similarly combined to convey meaning. The inner border takes its form from ancient architectural ornament. The outer, for all its exuberance, is a somewhat restrained example of the system of ornament dubbed grotesque – *grottesche*. This is a term first encountered in 1502 (in the contract for the decoration of the Piccolomini library in Siena by Pinturicchio), in reference, as Benvenuto Cellini was later to explain, to the underground grottoes in Rome where the painted originals had been found, the rediscovered chambers of the Golden House of Nero.[6] That these were to be read as a worthy art, even the kind of pictorial poetry worthy of Daphnis, can be divined from an anonymous verse accompanying a print engraved by the so-called Master of the Die after a design by Perino del Vaga and issued in 1530 (fig. 56):

Poet and painter as companions meet
Because their strivings have a common passion
As you can see expressed in this sheet
Adorned with friezes in this worthy fashion.
Of this, Rome can the best examples give,
Rome towards which all bright talents are heading,
Whence now, from grottoes where no people live,
So much new light on this fine art is spreading.[7]

Although initially it appears somewhat frivolous in its imagery, this plate therefore sets out, through its style and visual references, to embody the particular virtues of a powerful individual. After all, magnificence and nobility, talent, even modesty, and the ability to combine these virtues were not to be hidden; and to be properly expressed and to be appreciated they had to be public – and publicized. We have seen that patrons used art objects as the accoutrements and tangible attributes of virtuous living and ceremonial. In selecting them, the buyers and commissioners of art were faced with various stylistic options, all of which had particular connotations. The courtly style of northern Europe could be associated with chivalric values, a theme of abiding importance. Hence the difficulty of locating the origin of the few surviving pieces of fifteenth-century jewellery. Other stylistic distinctions were also made, referring to the sometimes distant origins of an object or the technique used by an Italian craftsman to manufacture it. The 'Greco' – meaning Byzantine – was a category that, at least in Venice, was not despised, and there was a variety of words for Ottoman and other Islamic styles. Some art objects seem to have been designed and decorated in such a way as to reinforce local identity, made as expressions of civic, courtly or commercial pride. Above all, however, there developed a conceptual sense of the house as an antique space in which ancient virtues could be re-enacted, reinforced by carefully chosen styles of architecture and by the objects contained within it. Since, as we have seen in Chapter One, the Renaissance lexicon of virtue was largely quarried from ancient texts, so its visual expressions gained weight by a similarly referential attitude to the antique, a move to express classical ideas in classical forms.

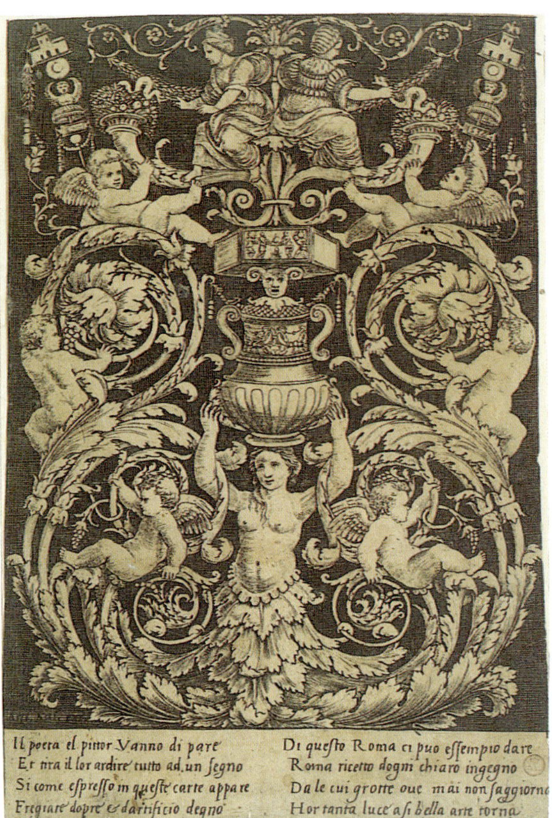

56 Master of the Die after Perino del Vaga, *Grotesques*; engraving; Rome, *c.*1530. Victoria and Albert Museum, London

Messages of the antique: wealth, nobility and discrimination

To make their point, art objects had to be visible and visitable in the home.[8] Possession of objects demonstrated possession of virtues – at least to those sections of society deemed capable of appreciating their messages (and the domestic arts were therefore subtly different from public monuments). Thus, although access to different parts of a house or palace might sometimes be carefully controlled, especially when its owners were in residence, it is evident that few spaces were completely private, and that carefully monitored tours of ostensibly private spaces were given to the privileged few. The Sforza dukes of

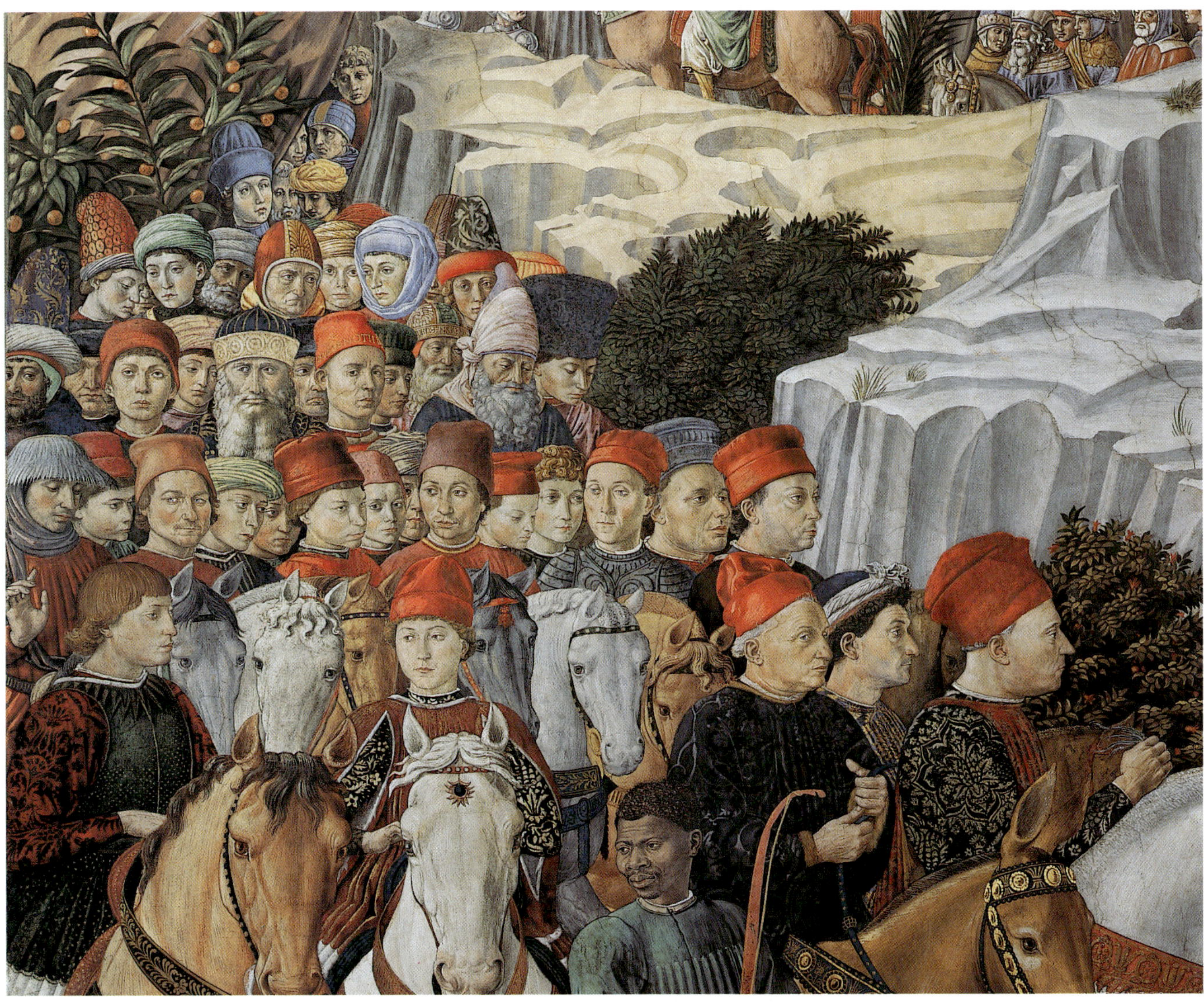

Milan went straight for the jugular, conducting ceremonial tours for ambassadors to their treasury in the 1490s, where their guests were greeted by the sight of hundreds of coins strewn on carpets and of gold portrait medals depicting their hosts, worth 10,000 ducats apiece.[9] The contents of the Palazzo Medici were also ritually shown off. Although its visitors were certainly supposed to get the equivalent basic message – to be astonished by Medici expenditure – here they were also expected to understand that money had been spent discriminatingly and virtuously. In August 1480 Cardinal Giovanni of Aragon was led through the palace by Lorenzo de' Medici, perusing the garden behind it and another Medici garden close to the convent of San Marco, both containing antique statuary, and pausing to admire the chapel frescoed by Benozzo Gozzoli (fig. 57). The visit was reported in breathless detail by Antonio da Montecatini to Ercole I d'Este:

Then he entered the *studio*, the chamber that had belonged to Piero, and there he examined the said *studio* with copious quantities of books, all worthy, written with a pen – a stupendous thing. Then we returned to the little loggia opening off the study. And there on a table, he had brought his jewels … vases, cups, hard-stone coffers mounted with gold, of various stones, jasper and others. There was there a crystal beaker mounted with a lid and a silver foot, which was studded with pearls, rubies, diamonds and other stones. [He also showed] a dish carved inside with diverse figures, which was a worthy thing, reputed to be worth 4,000 ducats. Then he had brought two large bowls full of ancient coins, one of gold coins and the other full of silver, then a little case with many jewels, rings and engraved stones … then Monsignor went to see San Marco and the library, and then Lorenzo's garden there.…[10]

These 'worthy' highlights – the chapel, the study (often called the *scrittoio*) and the gardens – were the most regularly celebrated Medici spaces.[11] The lavishly decorated chapel represented, in miniature, the family's pious expenditure; the study and the gardens were places where other virtues could be precisely enacted.

Since the possession of ancient virtues was thought to depend to a great extent on the knowledge of ancient precedent, the scholarly investigation of the classical world became a virtue in itself. The *studiolo* was the place where virtuous scholarship was performed, intellectually but also physically. Niccolò Machiavelli wrote of going into his *studiolo* at his villa at San Casciano gravely dressed in 'the robes of court and palace' as an entry into 'the antique courts of the ancients';[12] the room had become a journey and a metaphor. The study has sometimes been presented as an especially sequestered, secure place for solitary contemplation. This it may have been, but it was also the intellectual heart of the house, where business and legal transactions were undertaken and, especially, where virtue was generated through reading and research. Scholars less exalted than the Medici might choose to make a *studiolo* from a corner of their bedchamber; a portrait drawing by

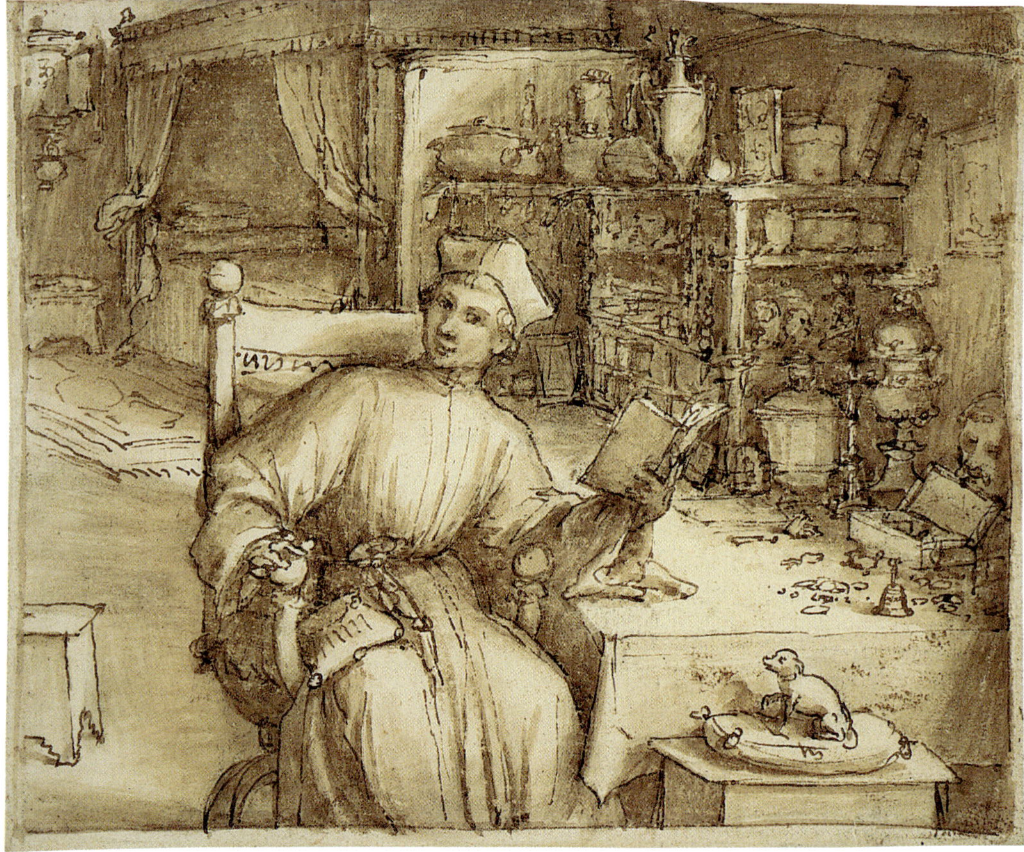

58 Lorenzo Lotto, *Cleric in his Study-Bedchamber*; brush and brown ink over black chalk; Venice, *c.*1530. The British Museum, London

Lorenzo Lotto of a young cleric, surrounded by his collection of antiquities and other precious objects in just such a carved-out space, demonstrates that objects could become the intellectual attributes of a whole range of individuals (fig. 58). For its owner's merits, worldly and scholarly, to be appreciated, for the metaphor to be understood, the place had to be visible and visitors had to be able to find in it the signs and attributes of virtue. Isabella d'Este, for example, was tediously keen to publicize her collection as the adjunct of her much vaunted scholarship, even ensuring that distinguished visitors were given access in her absence. She was immensely proud of the room in which she housed her objects, ancient and modern, the archaeologically termed *grotta* (connected to her *studiolo*), and, in November 1514, she wrote that 'concerning the key of the *grotta*, we instruct that on occasions when certain gentlemen wish to view, you should give the key to Zoan Jacomo *castellano*, ensuring that it is then returned'.[13] Cardinal Pietro Bembo made similar provision, leaving a key with his custodian Gerolamo, enabling scholars to visit his study when he was away from Padua.[14]

If objects in the study were intended to transmit messages of their owner's scholarship (in the pursuit of virtue), no objects better encapsulated ancient virtues, and their investigation, than antiquities themselves. Coins, gems, sculptures and other artefacts could be studied – employed as the material evidence, as the artistic manifestation of a glorious past. As the investigation of antique notions of virtue became ever more profound, and prescriptions on their modern application more developed and available, so modern-day men and women increasingly sought a visual vocabulary for modern objects, their own attributes of virtue, that was properly and accurately derived from antiquity. Stylistic choices became narrower as discriminating owners recognized that the 'ancient' appearance, variously understood, of an object might have particular meaning. This trend started, understandably enough, in the study. Men and women increasingly purchased and commissioned revived forms of ancient artefacts – bronze statuettes, commemorative medals or portrait cameos and intaglios – objects usually kept in the *studiolo*. Moreover, the very tools and utensils of scholarship – inkstands, lamps, cabinets, books themselves – employed the languages of antiquity, their forms and ornament dependent on close observation of the antique. And just as many of the virtues investigated in the study were actually performed elsewhere (magnificent hospitality in the *sala*, male continence and female chastity in the bedchamber), so the aesthetic of the study generated a visual response in other rooms in the house. Antiquities were displayed elsewhere, especially in gardens and courtyards, and many other domestic objects adopted ornamental languages, which were seen as and called *all'antica*.[15] Jewellery, fabrics, picture frames, and precious metal vessels used for dining can all be found described in this way. From reading inventories, however, it is not always clear what the term conveyed. Sometimes clues are provided in other parts of descriptions. In the Este collections in 1494 there was, for example, 'a wooden panel painted with an Our Lady, framed with friezes and an architrave *all'antica*'.[16] In this instance the *all'antica* appearance of the frame evidently depended on architectural elements. Other objects were more superficially 'antique'. Mid-Quattrocento *cassone* paintings, for instance, might be set into chests that imitated, rather approximately, the shapes of Roman sarcophagi, but in which figures optimistically labelled Alexander or

Aeneas wore contemporary or exotic Burgundian or Byzantine costumes rather than classical draperies (or nothing), not a jot different from figures identified as David or Griselda (see figs 51, 52, 163, 190 and 191). During the course of the fifteenth century such efforts increasingly gave way to others that displayed a more profound understanding (even if it was often second-hand) of the technical accomplishments and aesthetic aims of the Greeks and Romans (see fig. 54).

To gain a clearer picture of what virtues *all'antica* languages for objects were thought to convey, one must turn to humanist descriptions of antiquities and the less elevated responses of other contemporary viewers and owners, which echo them. Humanists, and those influenced by them, wrote revealingly of the surviving remains of Greece and Rome, and many patrons matched Isabella d'Este's self-declared 'insatiable desire for things antique'.[17] Increasingly ruthless collectors scrambled over one another to grab valued items as they competed to form ever larger, ever more lavish and ever more self-consciously representative bodies of archaeological material; by the mid-Quattrocento a species of collectomania had taken hold. A letter of October 1455 from Carlo de' Medici in Rome to his brother Giovanni in Florence gives an evocative picture of the skulduggery of fanatical collectors:

In recent days, I have bought around thirty very good ancient silver coins from a garzone of [the painter] Pisanello, who died recently. I do not know how, but Monsignor di San Marco [the Venetian Cardinal Pietro Barbo, later Pope Paul II] learnt of this and, finding me one day in Santo Apostolo, took me by the hand and would not let me go until he had led me into his chamber, and there he took rings and seals and money that I had in my purse from me, to the value of twenty florins, and would not return them until I handed over the above-mentioned coins....[18]

The reasons for this enthusiasm were many and nuanced, and the proper 'delight in antiquities' was thought to derive from the acquisition of various kinds of knowledge, as well as the gentlemanly possession of innate powers of connoisseurship. The terms of approbation were derived, to no small degree, from reading ancient literature. Copies of Vitruvius's treatise on architecture could be found in many libraries. Pliny the Elder's *Natural History*, with its abundance of 'facts' concerning ancient art and artists, patrons and collectors was much consulted. This famous text not only influenced much of the discussion of surviving and rediscovered antiquities, it, and other ancient writings, also had a profound impact on Renaissance artistic practice, as patrons and artists sought to re-enact events, images and relationships they found described.[19] Pliny and other ancient authors were sometimes critical of over-expenditure on luxury goods, including art, and of overly ostentatious display. Set against this distaste, however, were powerful examples of ancient rulers who collected and commissioned works of art. Pliny's description of the emperor Nero's fondness for Myrrhine vessels, tableware carved from agate or a similar semi-precious stone, finds an echo in the extortionate prices paid for hard-stone vases and ancient engraved gems in the Renaissance:

When T. Petronius, a man of consular rank, was about to die owing to the enmity of Nero, he broke a Myrrhine ladle, which he had bought for 300,000 sesterces, in order to cheat the emperor's table of its inheritance. But Nero, as was proper for an emperor, outdid everyone by paying one million sesterces for a single bowl. That it cost so much for one who was an emperor and father of his country to have a drink is a fact that must be recorded.[20]

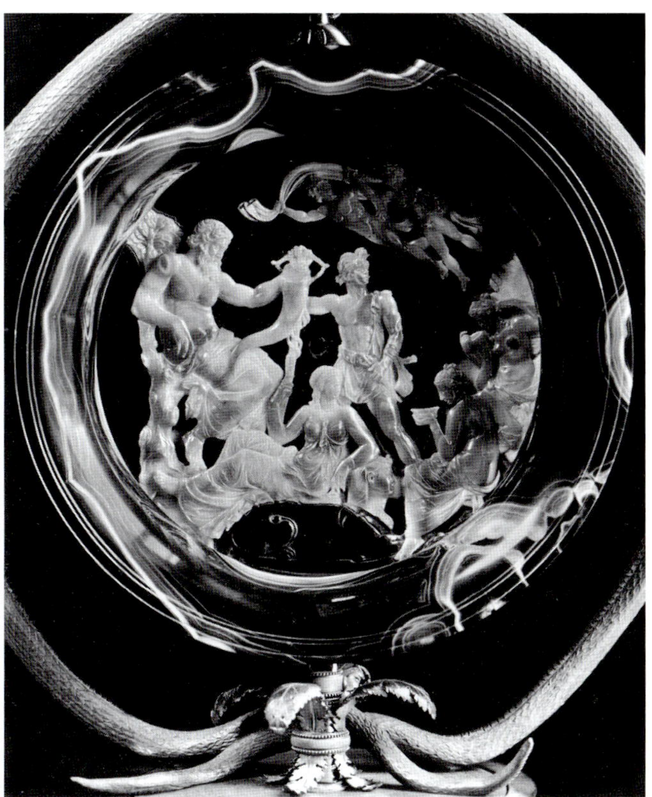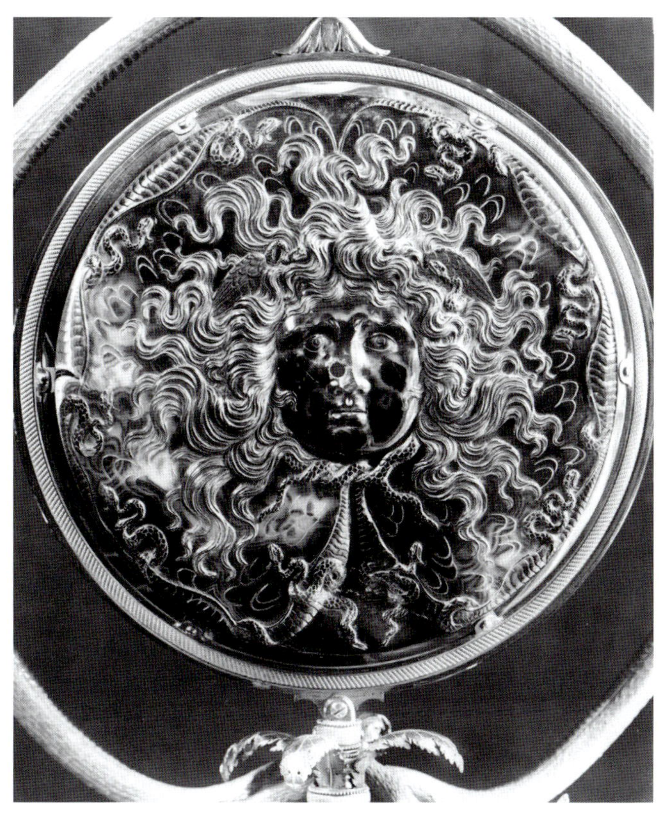

The emperor Nero was not an obvious role-model, regularly condemned for his over-weening arrogance. Yet even he could be taken as an exemplar of magnificence, of virtuous spending. This was a model that could be imitated precisely. Ancient gems and hard-stone vessels were always among the most highly valued objects in a family's possession. We have seen that, when inspected by Cardinal Giovanni of Aragon, the widely celebrated cameo now known as the Tazza Farnese (fig. 59) was reputedly valued at 4,000 ducats, and that this was worthy of note. It had previously formed the centrepiece of another great collection, that of Cardinal Lodovico Trevisan, Patriarch of Aquileia.[21] By 1492, in the post-mortem inventory of the goods of Lorenzo de' Medici, the 'dish of sardonyx and chalcedony and agate, in which there are several figures and on the outside a head of Medusa' had attained a value of an astonishing 10,000 florins.[22]

The prices for modern engraved gems never reached such extraordinary heights. Nevertheless, the Sforza dukes of Milan typically sought to unite the intrinsic value of precious stones with the revived art of gem engraving. As early as 1454 Piero de' Medici owned 'a head of the Duke of Milan, mounted in silver' among his gems, and in 1479 a large cameo of dukes Francesco and Galeazzo Maria Sforza, framed in gold, was listed in the inventory of the goods of their chancellor, Cicco Simonetta.[23] That the modern could be seen as the symbolic equivalent or even desirable substitute for the ancient is demonstrated by the fact that in January 1497 Lodovico il Moro displaced an intaglio depicting Caesar with a portrait of his recently deceased consort, Beatrice d'Este, as his private seal for particularly important documents.[24] And even if they did not match the ancient, exceptionally high valuations were indeed given to engraved portrait gems if the stones were precious: in an undated inventory of the Sforza treasury is listed a ruby – *balasso* – worth 1,000 ducats with 'the effigy of the Most Illustrious Lord Lodovico', probably the same piece that Vasari in the 1568 edition of his *Lives* says was executed by the much-praised Milanese engraver Domenico de' Cammei (of the Cameos), 'a rare thing and among the best intaglios by modern masters that can be seen'.[25] The quality of Milanese gem-engraving can be seen in an exquisite cameo in The British Museum, the portrait of Lodovico's nephew Duke Gian Galeazzo Sforza, perhaps by Domenico de' Cammei himself (fig. 60).

Although pride in ownership of ancient artefacts carved from semi-precious stones was clearly connected to the considerable sums of money spent on them, conspicuous expenditure for its own sake was not the only message. Ancient precedent provides a partial explanation of their high valuation: money had to be spent well, and financial outlay could be focused precisely on the objects that had signalled magnificence in the past. However, although gold and silver coins were often priced solely according to their precious metal content, the Tazza and other engraved semi-precious stones were not intrinsically very valuable.

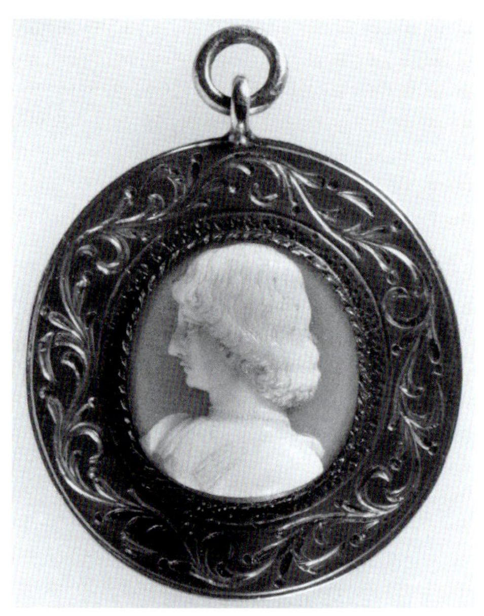

60 Domenico de' Cammei (attributed), portrait gem of Gian Galeazzo Sforza; onyx cameo; Milan, *c.*1490. The British Museum, London

The value of such antiquities (which was truly economic as well as theoretical)[26] lay as much in the fact that antiquarian collecting was interpreted as an adjunct of other virtuous activity. In 1505, for example, the sculptor-courtier Gian Cristoforo Romano wrote to Isabella d'Este of 'Madonna Felice, the daughter of the Pope, who is a gentlewoman of noble talent and kindness, and who is dedicated to literature and to antiquities and all the virtuous deeds, and who is your slave…'.[27] Thus, when Lorenzo had his name carved on many of his gems and vases (see fig. 74) (though not the Tazza Farnese) and the Este marked their ancient coins with the family eagle, they were signalling not merely their physical possession but their intellectual ownership of the concepts their antiquities transmitted, their appreciation of the difficulty of their manufacture and the artistry of the result.[28]

Objects, in the first place, were appreciated as a means of adding information to surviving ancient texts, as documents of the events and personalities described, or empirical demonstrations of textual falsehood or veracity.[29] Indeed, they were used as tools for the understanding of the languages in which these texts were written. The humanist scholars who promoted literary study were frequently philologists and ortho-graphers who sought to trace the development and chronology of the Latin language, as well as to ensure that the Latin in which they wrote themselves was appropriately used and correctly ancient, unadulterated by medieval corruptions. Since the manuscript transcriptions from which they worked could not always be trusted, other evidence was required of ancient Latin usage – its vocabulary, style, grammar and spelling – evidence that could be garnered from archaeological remains, above all from carved inscriptions and coins.[30] At the same time scholars turned their attention to the shape of the letters in the inscriptions they read, pioneers of the discipline of epigraphy.

Collectors were clearly understood as sharing these erudite concerns. A career humanist, Pandolfo Collenuccio of Pesaro, wrote to Lorenzo de' Medici from Bologna in June 1491. His offer of coins is couched in notably orthographical and historicist terms:

There have come into my hands about fifty ancient coins. Among them, I have found five which I think Your Magnificence does not have, and which therefore I send to you. The first is Marcus Aurelius Severus Macrinus, he who had Antoninus Caracalla killed, and was emperor after him with his son Diadumenian. It is notable for its beautiful reverse and it says OPELIVS, rather than OPILIVS, as it is written in all the books. The second is that Philip, the first Christian emperor, who ruled with his son and died in Verona. I send it on account of the reverse, which I do not remember seeing among your others. There are also three that I think are of Alexander [the Molossian] of Epirus, uncle of Alexander the Great, who was captain of the Tarentines in Italy and who defeated the Brutii. Therefore the reverse is inscribed VRECTION [ΒΡΕΤΤΙΩΝ in the original Greek], that is 'of the Brutii'. Livy writes about him in Book VIII of *ab Urbe condita*....[31]

Antiquarianism was not, however, a matter of neutral positivist research; it was about inspiration and emulation. In about 1440 Poggio Bracciolini wrote a famously witty self-portrait of himself as collector in his book *On Nobility*. In one passage he explored the concept of virtuous ownership, seeking to demonstrate that the possession of antiquities conferred on him an intellectual ancestry that rendered him noble:

I have often heard the [nature of true nobility] discussed by two most learned men, tied to me by close friendship. Some time ago, when I retreated from Rome to my own country for a change of air, Niccolò Niccoli and Lorenzo de' Medici [the brother of Cosimo il Vecchio], both learned men and my best friends, joined me at my request. I had tempted them there especially by the display of some sculptures I had brought from Rome. When they were in the little garden, which, with my few curious marbles, I was longing to make famous by the show of some small household stuff, Lorenzo, laughing as he looked around, remarked, 'Our host here has read that it was the custom among those ancient men of early times to adorn their houses, villas, gardens, courtyards and study rooms with various images and paintings of their ancestors, indeed with statues, for the fame and ennobling of their lineage, and since images of his own ancestors were lacking, he sought to make this place, and himself too, noble with these puny and broken remains of marble, so that because of the novelty of the thing, some of his glory might, through these, survive to posterity.'[32]

The humanist Niccolò Niccoli begged to differ, claiming that the foundation of nobility was not to be sought in things, but in the mind, through the striving for wisdom and virtue. The banker agreed, but countered,

'Yet we do see nobility being conferred with the aid of paintings and various images … and it is hungered and sought after by outstanding talents [*ingeniis*], for it is well known that the most learned men have devoted much labour and study to buying statues and paintings….'[33]

Confirmation of the ennobling role of objects, and the search for ancient models of virtue, can be found in the humanist biography of Alfonso of Aragon, another former owner of the Tazza Farnese,[34] in which Antonio Beccadelli cites the King's declaration that his favourite coins, of Julius Caesar, which he carried around with him, 'did marvellously delight him and in a manner inflame him with a passion for virtue and glory'.[35]

Certain ancient art objects therefore encapsulated particular virtues: the images of ancient rulers praised as just, wise, or magnanimous were seen as physically and physiognomically encapsulating their justice, wisdom or magnanimity. Thus the study of ancient art objects was seen as an element in the pursuit of equivalent nobility, glory and wisdom, and ownership could be taken as the outward expression of those virtues. However, the powerful did not restrict their affiliations to past rulers. The desperation of both Lorenzo de' Medici and Isabella d'Este to own portraits of Plato overrode the dubious authenticity of the objects on offer to them. Lorenzo's biographer states that he 'had long desired the image of Plato', but when a bust, claimed to have come from the ruins of the Academy, was tracked down in Pistoia, it was a modern concoction combining a seemingly ancient bust or perhaps a knocked about modern piece (not anyway of Plato) with a base on which the philosopher's name was falsely inscribed (fig. 61). Lorenzo nevertheless held the portrait in great veneration, and the philosopher Marsilio Ficino owned a copy of it, in front of which 'he always had a lamp lit … so dear was it to him'.[36] Isabella's bust was at least certainly ancient, with some humanist affirmation of its identity: it had been taken as the subject of an epigram by Pietro Valeriano.[37] It belonged to the Venetian painters Jacopo and his son Gentile Bellini, and was offered to Isabella in 1512 by Gentile's brothers, Giovanni and Niccolò, who, so as to justify the price (actually knock-down at 15 ducats), falsely claimed that it belonged to an anonymous Venetian lady for whom they were acting – disinterestedly. Isabella's agents in Venice, Taddeo Albano and Lorenzo da Pavia, both had severe doubts over its subject and some reservations about its condition: it was

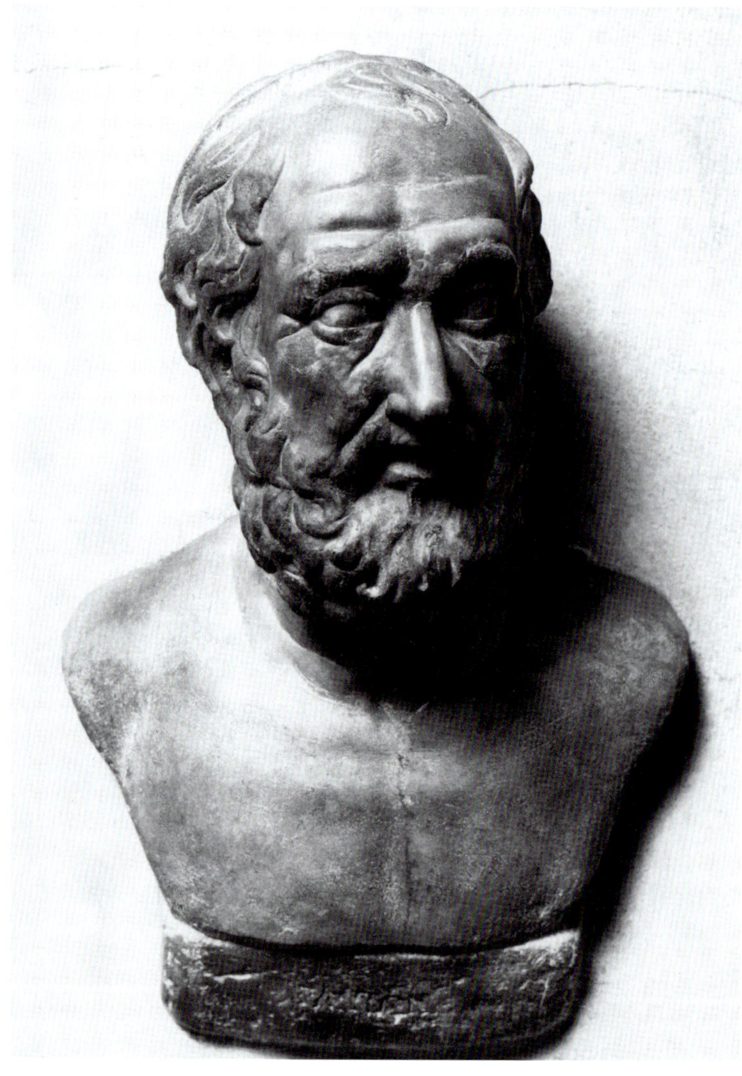

61 'Plato'; carved marble, 'restored' state; first or second century AD (or fifteenth century). Palazzo Medici-Riccardi, Florence

missing an ear and most of its neck and shoulders, and its nose had been replaced, bizarrely, in wax. But, although they advised against the purchase, Isabella could not resist.[38] If the aspirations and qualities of the modern owners were considered to be conditioned and reflected by the objects they were viewing, then the celebrated virtues of the historical figure could be connected with their own. Moreover, the artistic strategies employed for the representation of ancient heroes, understood as a combination of veristic accuracy and the subtly idealizing elimination of unsightly blemishes, were seen as a key element for the efficacy of such works. No wonder they applied the same stylistic criteria to their own portraits.[39]

That the style of ancient works was considered important is not open to doubt. The verbal portrait of Piero de' Medici ensconced in his *scrittoio* in the treatise by the Florentine goldsmith, architect and sculptor Antonio Averlino moves from the academic and inspirational to the aesthetically pleasurable and shows the connection between these related concepts. Piero had

effigies and images of all the emperors and worthies that there ever were, some [made] of gold, some of silver, some of bronze, of precious stones [*pietre fine*] and of marble or other materials that are marvellous things to behold. Their worth [*dignità*] is such that to look at these portraits carved in bronze alone … is enough [to appreciate] their excellence, which fills his soul with delight and pleasure at their sight. These give pleasure in two ways to those who understand and enjoy them as he does; first for the excellence of the image represented; secondly for the worthy mastery of ancient and angelic spirits who, through their sublime talent, have made such base things as bronze, marble and suchlike prized so greatly. And other things of price, such as gold and silver, become much greater through their mastery … [Gold] they have made worth more than gold by means of their skill and [similarly] they have made those materials more base than gold worth more than gold itself. He takes pleasure first from one thing and then from another, praising one for the dignity of the image because it was made [by the hand of man] and another that reveals greater skill [*tanta arte*] because it seems to have been done by nature rather than man. When we see things made by the hand of Phidias or Praxiteles, we say that they do not appear to have been fabricated but to have come from heaven.[40]

Piero's ability to appreciate the artistic quality and importance of an object was deemed significant, perceived as a mark of the owner–beholder's own innate talents and status. Baldassare Castiglione, in his *Book of the Courtier*, turned discrimination into a prerequisite for *gentilezza*. Lodovico Canossa of Verona was credited with the view that a gentleman 'should be able to judge the excellence of statues both ancient and modern, of vases, buildings, medals, cornices, intaglios and the like'.[41] It was therefore tempting to feign nobility and gentlemanly status through ownership. Fra Sabba da Castiglione wrote:

I have known many great men; great men, I say, in riches and dignity, but for the rest, ignorant, gross and stupid … these men, in order to demonstrate their talent and spirit to the common people, used to make great show of delighting in antiquities, especially in the medals of men who have been worthy and famous in the world, though their taste and understanding in these matters was like that of an ass faced with music played on the lyre.[42]

What, then, was the excellence that a discriminating viewer was supposed to divine? What had Sabba's donkey-eared Midas figure missed? We have seen words like 'good', 'worthy' and 'marvellous' employed to describe objects, all terms that impart their viewer's ability to judge and, indirectly, the qualities of their owners. Beauty had its own meaning

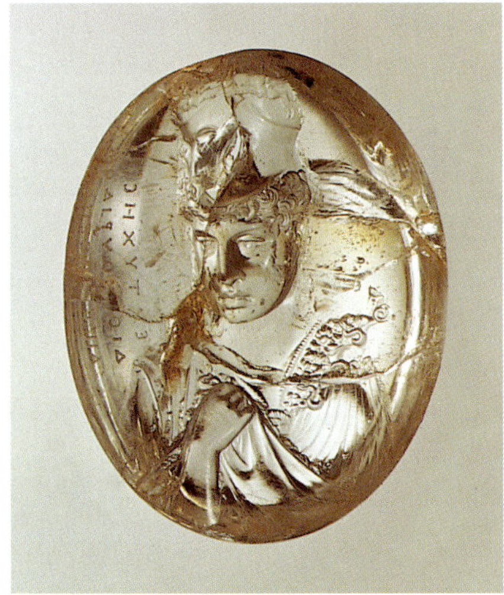

62 *Pallas Athena*; rock-crystal intaglio;
Italy (?); end first century BC.
Antikensammlung, Preußischer
Kulturbesitz, Staatliche Museen
zu Berlin

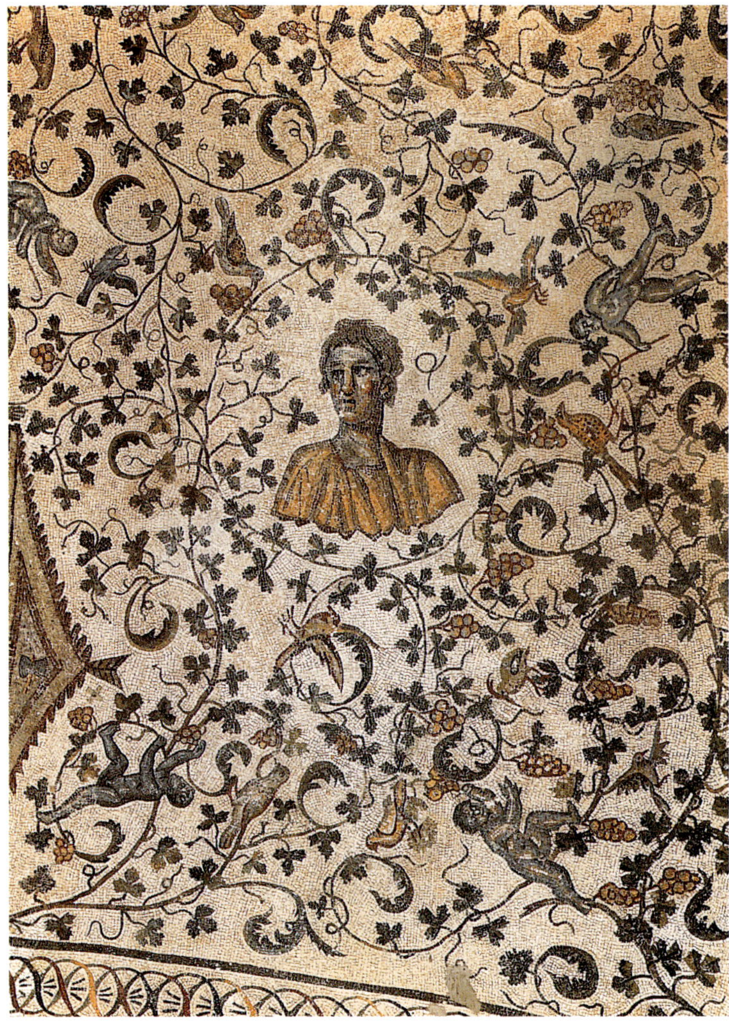

63 Ornamental mosaics; mid-fourth
century AD. Church of Santa Costanza,
Rome

and was assessed through processes of comparison, even in scholarly tools like coins.
Ambrogio Traversari, writing from Venice in 1433 to his antiquarian peer, Niccolò Niccoli
in Florence, stated that some gold coins of Constantine and Constans, which he had
studied, were beautiful indeed but in no way equal in artistic merit to one of Berenice, a
Ptolemaic queen of Egypt, that he had also examined.[43] The technical virtuosity to achieve
beauty was also admired. In 1445 the humanist scholar Cyriacus of Ancona described in
detail an antique intaglio seal engraved in rock crystal 'the size of one's thumb', thought by
him (mistakenly) to represent the figure of Alexander the Great (it is actually Athena):
'When you hold up the gem towards the light … the breathing limbs are seen to shine out
with complete solidity, and with luminous crystal shadows in the hollows …' (fig. 62).[44]
Ornamental motifs also received loaded descriptions. The late antique mosaics in the
Roman Church of Santa Constanza were assessed by Giovanni Rucellai in 1450. His
terminology is enormously revealing. He thought the mosaics in the vaults of the
ambulatory 'very pleasing with animals, birds and leaves and other *gentileze*', the physical
manifestation of Vespasiano da Bisticci's behavioural concept. And he lavished paeons of
praise on the dome mosaic 'with perfectly formed little figures and with leaves and trees
and with many *spiritelli* [little putti] who disport themselves in diverse ways, that is the most
graceful, gratious and *gentile* mosaic not only in Rome, but in the whole world' (fig. 63).[45]

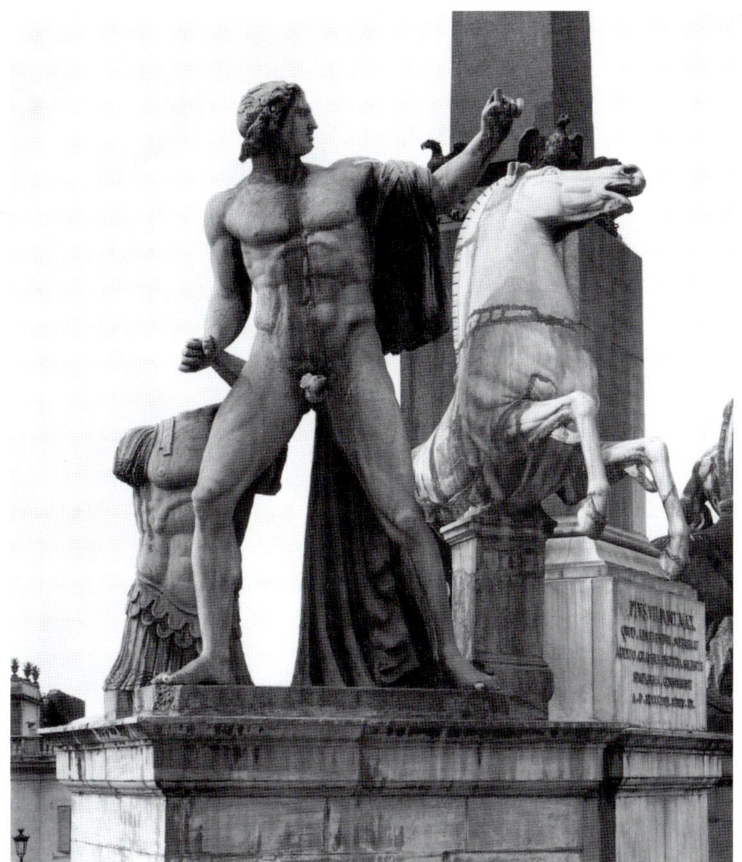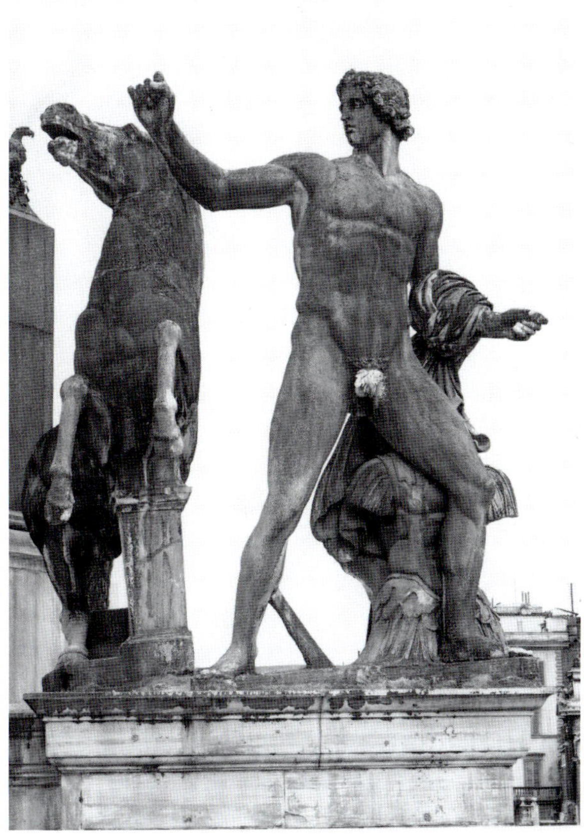

64 and 65 The *Dioscuri* (the Horse-Tamers of Montecavallo); marble; Roman, second century AD after Greek fifth century BC prototypes. Piazza del Quirinale, Rome

Finally, it was widely acknowledged that the attainment of beauty or grace depended on the individual talents – the *ingegno* – of artists, those very artists whose names collectors could read in Pliny's *Natural History*. The marble *Dioscuri* on Montecavallo in Rome were much celebrated as great works of art in their own right, independent of their subject matter (figs 64, 65). This appreciation was partly due to the fact that the pair of youths, then unidentified, struggling to control the horses in their charge have erroneous inscriptions on their bases: OPVS FIDIAE (the work of Phidias), OPVS PRAXITELIS (the work of Praxiteles). They were therefore assessed as works by great artists, whose talents and careers were described in detail in the *Natural History*; it was common in the period to attribute all sorts of antiquities to sculptors whose names were known through Pliny. The scholar Francesco Filelfo wrote of the *Dioscuri* in 1470:

Even now one can see in Rome those two marble horses and the two young men next to them made out of marble, and each of them has a wonderful beauty and exceptional greatness, which Praxiteles and Phidias achieved through their noble art. For in making the horses, they did not have the horses Cyllarus and Arion before their eyes nor, in executing the young men, any Hercules or Jason. They did not leave such famous works to be admired as portraits; rather they used the brilliance of their innate talent [*ingenium*] and their own thought instead of a model.[46]

The *ingenium* or *ingegno* of the artist could be recognized only thanks to the viewer's own native talent. Lodovico Sforza, *il Moro*, wrote in March 1495 to Giovanni Giacomo Schlafinato, Cardinal of Parma, regarding a gift of antique sculpture: '… it is not reputed alien to the desires of talented minds [*animi ingenui*] to have some testament of the virtue of the ancients in this art of carving and founding'.[47]

Learning the languages of virtue

These, then, were the concepts and qualities that owners and buyers wished to be conveyed through their possession of their modern *all'antica* art objects, objects that could bear a scholarly and connoisseurial scrutiny. For an object to succeed in speaking its message, it had to use one of the visual languages of antiquity accurately. Artists needed to learn these idioms and how to use them appropriately. And it is evident that during the course of the fifteenth and early sixteenth centuries a certain breed of artist – some painters, more sculptors and, especially at the outset, artists practising or trained as gold-smiths – adopted the model of philological and orthographical research that humanists had applied to texts to use in their own investigations of the visual languages of antiquity. These artists applied their expertise to the manufacture of new art objects, the physical equivalents of modern humanist texts in which ancient writing styles and established topoi were appropriately and inventively combined.

As one might expect, owners did not restrict their expectations purely to the figurative, to painting and sculpture. Descriptions of particular categories of ostensibly functional art objects show the level of learned reference to be contained within them. This is exemplified by a sequence of three accounts of inkstands. In 1430 the Ferrarese court humanist Guarino da Verona used a thank-you letter as the occasion for an ekphrasis – a deliberately evocative account written in emulation of ancient authors – of the appearance of one modelled or moulded in clay:

… how could I find the words and style worthy of the inkstand you sent me? Though certainly its form is most beautiful, elegant and apt, this is overshadowed by the truly Phidian skill and workmanship I feast my eyes on. If I fix my gaze on the leaves and little branches and look at them attentively, shall I think I am looking at real leaves and real branches and that they could be safely bent this way and that? So does the diligence of Art seem to rival the ease of nature. Often I cannot have enough of the pleasure I find in examining the little figures and the living faces in the clay….[48]

This inkstand sounds rather unlikely, but the description, even if invented, highlights the need for objects to live up to this kind of cultural expectation. That they did so is demonstrated by the humanist Pietro Summonte's 1524 description of a tooled leather inkstand and a leather cabinet in the shape of a triumphal arch, executed some years earlier by the Neapolitan Masone di Mais, himself the brother of a humanist scholar, 'in the construction of which … there was so much imitation of antiquity and such quality of the intaglio decoration, customary in work of this sort, as to amaze anyone who saw such novel objects'.[49] Here, novelty is seen as deriving from a conflation of antique sources. That artists working for particular rich and educated patrons came to be very aware that these ornamental elements might be invested with appropriate meaning is demonstrated by a letter of October 1546 from the sculptor-founder Vincenzo de' Grandi (Vicentino) in Padua in which he attempted an explanation of the iconography – 'the subject and meaning' (*il soggietto et significato*) – of an inkstand he had made for Cristoforo Madruzzo, Cardinal of Trent.[50] At the top it was decorated with *bucrania* ('*teste secche di vaca*') and festoons or swags, the kind used by ancient architects for 'Doric works, of the kind shown by Leon Battista Alberti and Vitruvius in their books, and that nowadays one sees in Rome on ancient constructions – arches and other Doric buildings', appropriate:

because the inkstand is an instrument that serves gentle spirits in the writing of things important and worthy of memory, through which, by labouring with one's talents one can gain perpetual glory and immortal fame, dedicating one's name to the temple of Divinity. Thus the *bucrania* signify the hardship on which glory depends, and they are hung with garlands which stand for no less than the triumph of virtue and the honour of glory. So nowadays we use them in the palaces of princes and we put garlands of leaves, flowers and fruit in the temples of God when we have some great triumph.[51]

He then goes on to explain the multiple meanings of the eagle that was placed on the top. The rather vague antique resonances described by Guarino had taken concrete form by the mid-sixteenth century.

This letter shows the extent to which objects created by artists had become their texts, and how their accurate and appropriate usages of the grammar, vocabulary and phraseology of ancient visual languages became ingredients in the meaning of a whole range of modern works of art. To guarantee the intellectual and stylistic messages of these culturally loaded art objects, their authors' knowledge of the proper sources had to be absolute and recognized. The artists had to become antiquarians. Many of the descriptions of ancient artefacts cited so far in this chapter have come from the writings of humanist scholars: Poggio Bracciolini, Cyriacus of Ancona, Ambrogio Traversari, Francesco Filelfo and so on. However, even at the beginning of the fifteenth century it was widely accepted that the judgement of artists, of makers, on the quality and authenticity of a piece carried especial weight. It was a point that both the Florentine goldsmith-sculptors Lorenzo Ghiberti and Antonio Averlino (who tellingly called himself Filarete, 'lover of virtue' in Greek), made in the treatises or commentaries they had written in imitation of their humanist peers. Ghiberti, for example, in his *Commentaries* (composed in 1448–9) establishes an explicit link between 'painters, sculptors and experts' (*pictori … statuarij et … quelli erano periti*), summing up a problem thrown up in the *Natural History* by stoutly claiming 'I speak as a sculptor and assuredly believe it has to be so.'[52] Poggio Bracciolini was certainly pleased to have the sculptor Donatello's stamp of approval on a sculpture he was in the process of acquiring in Rome in about 1430.[53] In the mid-Quattrocento the attitude of other humanists to artists might be somewhat patronizing. When the humanist scribe Felice Feliciano dedicated two parts of his sylloge of ancient inscriptions to Andrea Mantegna in 1463 he praised Mantegna as a man 'ever most prompt and partial to the investigation of antiquities of this sort'.[54] Nevertheless, he lorded it over the painter, asserting his own superior scholarly status: 'There is no desire in me that is dearer and more ancient than that you should become as learned as possible, and be a man of consummate knowledge in all worthy subjects....'[55] Feliciano was probably conscious of his own scholastic deficiencies in making this statement, but even if his doubts about Mantegna's scholarly credentials were legitimate there was no gainsaying his discriminating eye. In an account of Mantegna's visit to Florence three years later Giovanni Aldobrandini wrote, 'Andrea has great *ingegno* not in painting but also other things [presumably including antiquities], and a superb eye [*optimo vedere*] and it seems to me that he deserves great commendation.'[56]

By the beginning of the sixteenth century the triumph of the antiquarian artist was complete, his authority unquestioned. On 14 January 1506 the famous marble sculptural

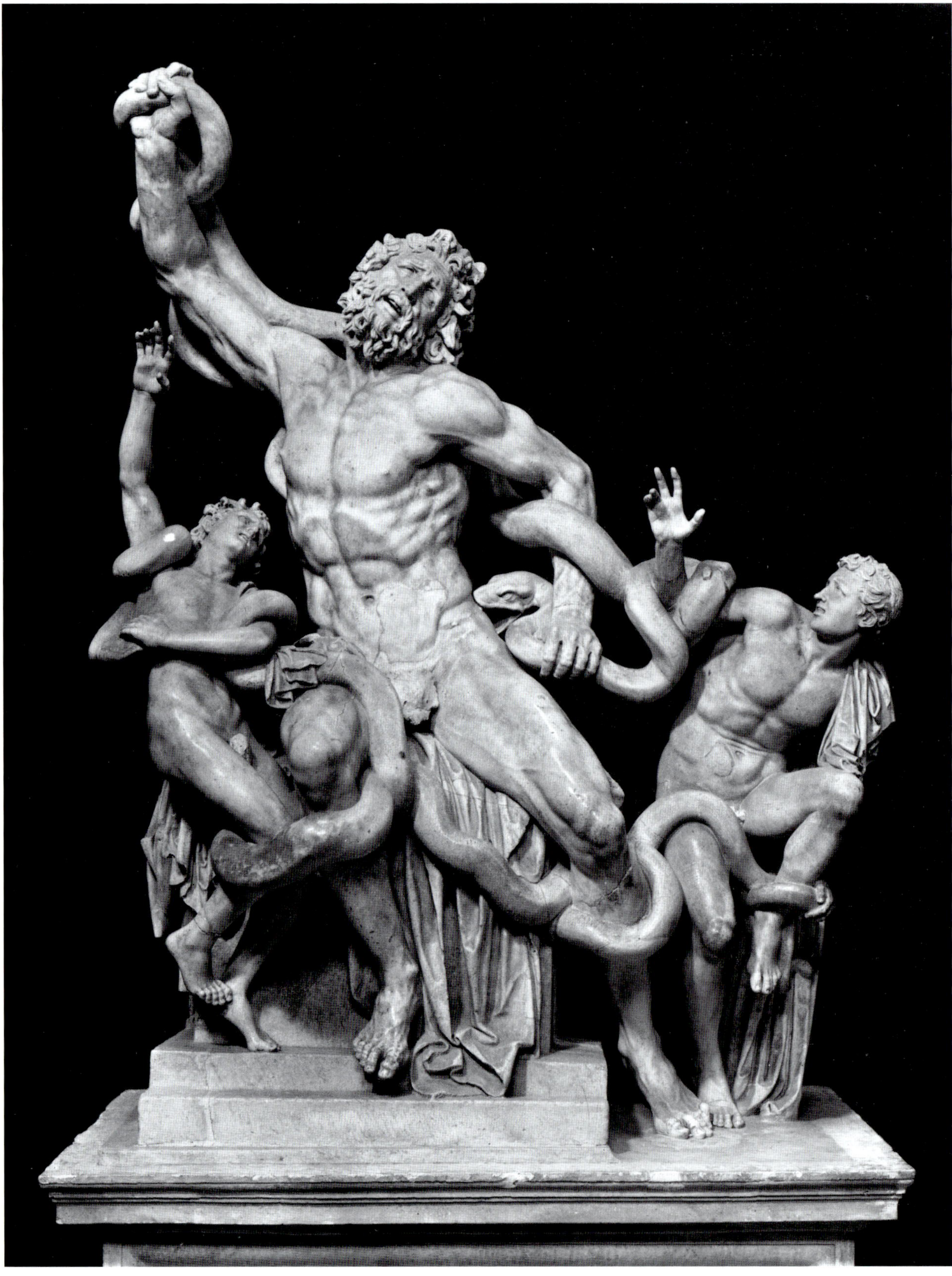

group of Laocoön and his sons was discovered in a vineyard in Rome on the Esquiline (fig. 66). At its discovery Pope Julius II dispatched the artists Michelangelo and Giuliano da Sangallo to see it in the ground. Sangallo is said by his son to have made the revelatory and self-consciously educated statement: 'This is the *Laocoön* of which Pliny writes.'[57] The opinion expressed the following year by Michelangelo and his fellow sculptor Gian Cristoforo Romano that it had actually been carved from four pieces of marble rather than from the single block Pliny had claimed in his *Natural History* was approvingly cited as authoritative by Cesare Trivulzio (though it was actually constructed from seven or eight): 'The authority of Pliny is great, but our artists can also be right. Nor should one undervalue the ancient saying: "How fortunate the arts would be if they were judged solely by artists."'[58] The painter Raphael was given the title of *commissario delle antichità* in 1515 by Pope Leo X, and charged, according to the rhetoric of his appointment letter, with protecting 'ancient pieces of marble and stone that bear inscriptions and other remains which often contain things memorable, and which deserve to be preserved for the progress of classical studies and the elegance of the Latin tongue' from the vandalous attentions of the quarry-men of Rome.[59] The previous year Raphael was said to have acted as guide and companion to the antiquarian Andrea Fulvio in exploring the ruins of Rome. Certainly Fulvio gained authority for his own observations by citing this joint exploration with the artist in the preface of his 1527 *The Antiquities of the City of Rome*.[60] The authority of Cinquecento artists, and the esteem in which their antiquarian connoisseurship was held, had derived both from their imitation of theoretical humanist investigations and from the cumulative kinds of practical expertise demanded of them by patrons who accumulated and collected antiquities and their modern equivalents: not only making but dealing, appraising, valuating, restoring and reproducing.

Ties of friendship between, for example, Leon Battista Alberti and Donatello, or between the antiquarian scribe Felice Feliciano, the painter Andrea Mantegna, the goldsmiths Daniele da Venezia and Cristoforo di Geremia, and the gem-engraver Francesco Anichini da Ferrara ensured that scholarly, antiquarian methods might be easily passed on.[61] Some artists read, and learned Latin to do so. Ghiberti's account of the history of ancient art in his *Commentaries* is based almost entirely on Pliny's. But literature gave insufficient clues to the artist bent on re-creating ancient art. Raphael famously lamented, 'I should like to find [i.e., to revive] the beautiful forms of the buildings of the ancients, but I don't know if mine might not be the flight of Icarus. Vitruvius affords me much light, but not enough …'.[62] His experience must have been typical and it was acknowledged that textual accounts of ancient sculpture or architecture made little sense without studying the material remains of the cultures of Greece and Rome.

Some artists, including Ghiberti, his fellow Florentine Donatello, and Andrea Mantegna, built up small collections of antiquities in imitation of their humanist peers.[63] Humanists also made record drawings of less available or transportable remains, drawings that were used as scholarly resources. Cyriacus of Ancona gave copies of his touchingly amateur studies of buildings and monuments in Italy, Greece and Asia Minor to Pietro Donato, Bishop of Padua.[64] Collections of antiquarian drawings, their authorship unknown, were owned by Piero de' Medici and Lodovico Gonzaga, 'the greater part [of

(*Opposite page*)
66 *Laocoön*; marble; Roman copy after Hellenistic original, first century A.D. Vatican Museums, Vatican City

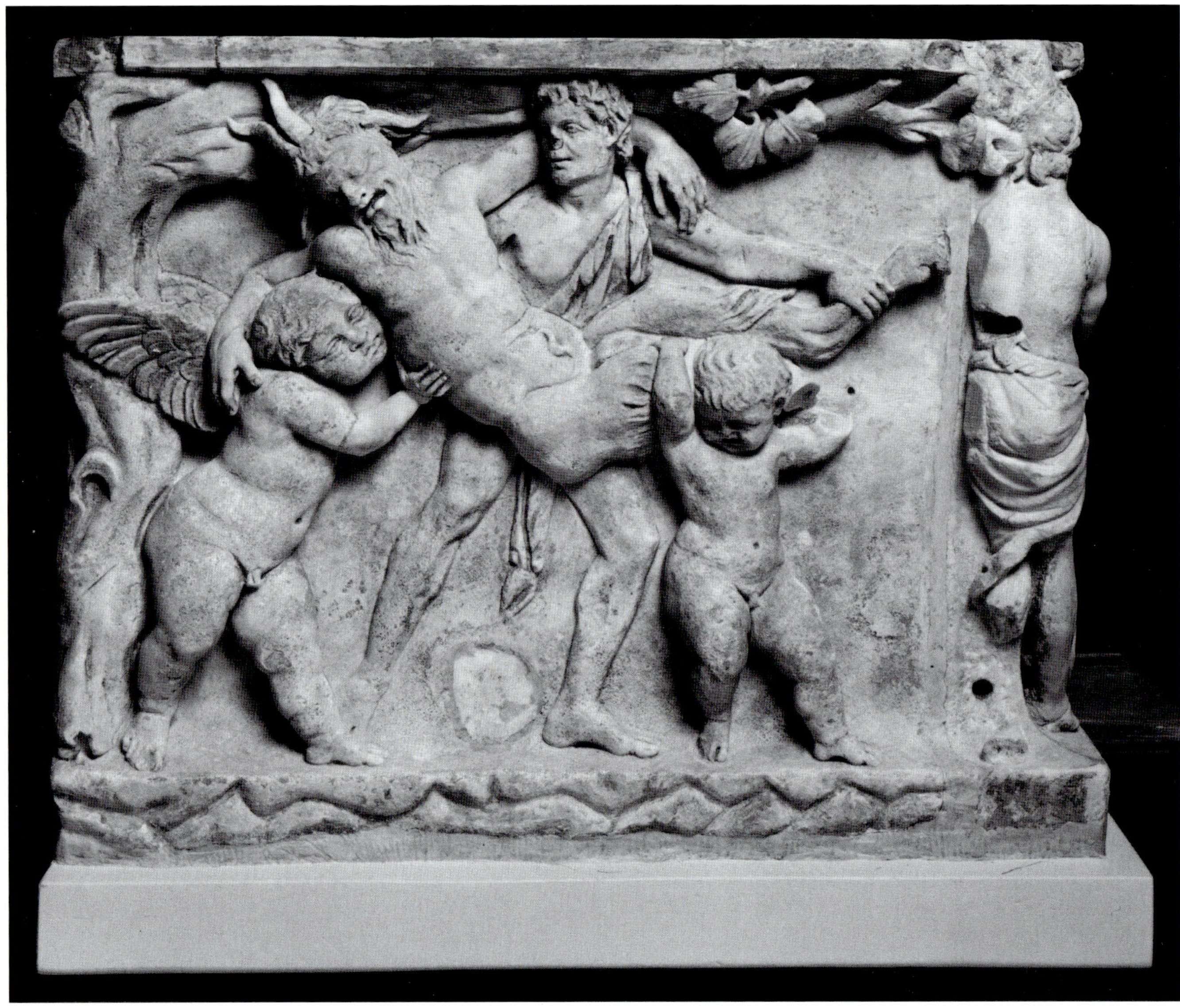

the latter] are battles of centaurs, fauns and satyrs'.[65] Some, if not most, of these are likely to have been executed by professional artists, and many survive, such as the albums by the Bolognese painter Amico Aspertini, which may have been executed primarily in the spirit of antiquarian research.[66] Even for him, these drawings were a repertoire of visual sources for his own paintings. Filarete appears to have consulted sketches by his friend Cyriacus.[67] However, like many others, he may also have made his own. Of the many drawings made in the first half of the Quattrocento, the largest group are attributed to the painter (and medallist) Pisanello and his shop.[68] These generally depict single figures or small groups taken from Roman sarcophagi, evidence that Alberti's advice to draw ancient sculpture, even if it were mediocre, was a reflection of current practice. Certain objects were drawn over and over again, to such an extent that they must have formed a recognizable main-stream of the visual culture of the time. A sarcophagus with reliefs of the *Triumphal*

67–9 Sarcophagus with reliefs showing *Triumphal Procession of Bacchus and Ariadne* (*above*, left end; *opposite top*, right end; *opposite bottom*, lateral relief); Rome, mid-second century AD. Townley Collection, The British Museum, London

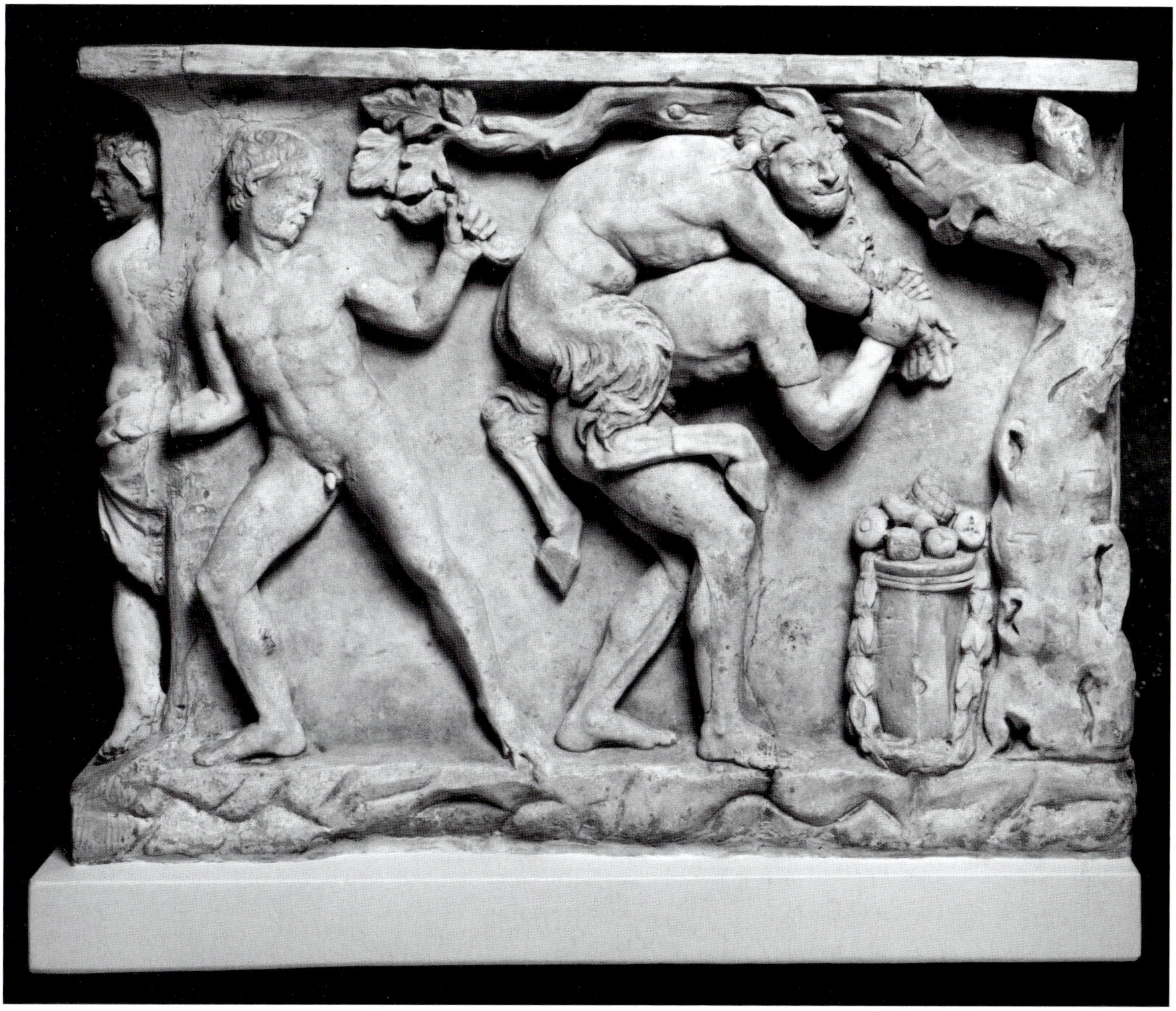

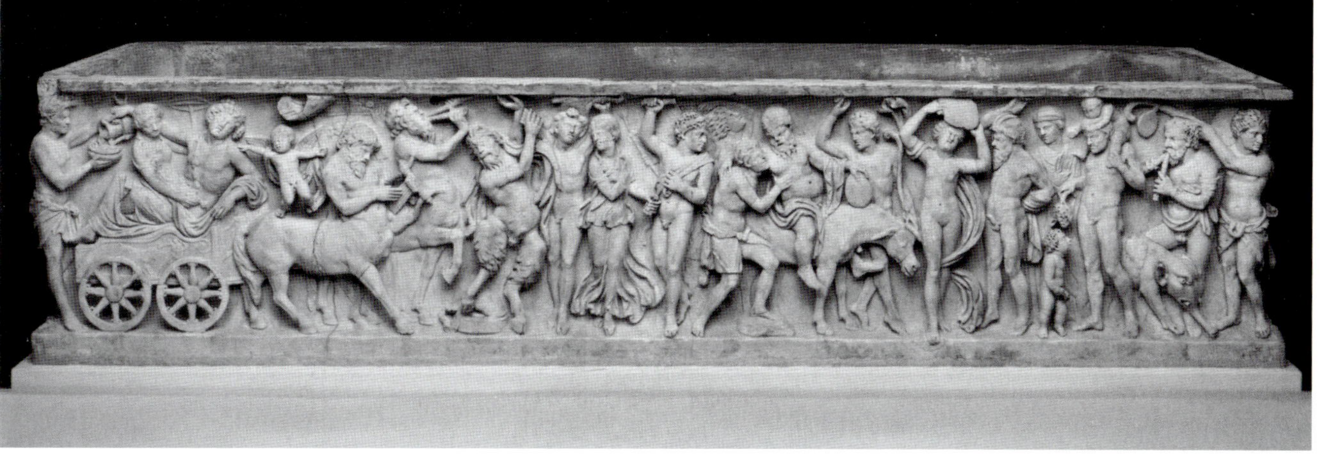

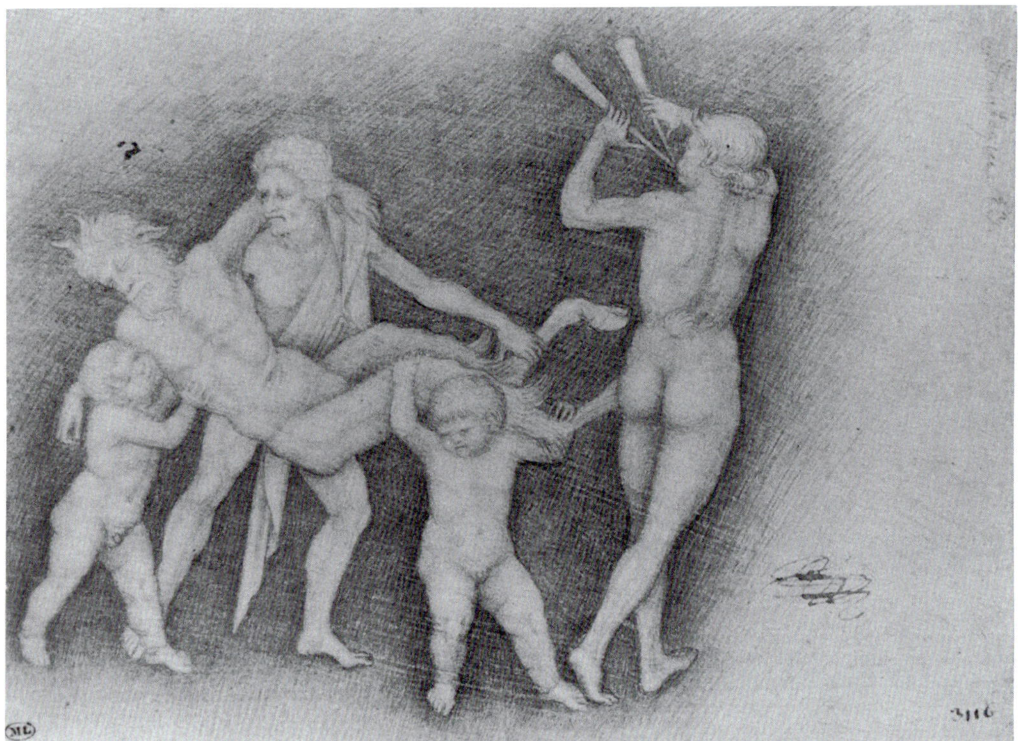

70 *Drunken Pan*, after left end of Bacchus and Ariadne sarcophagus; silverpoint on parchment; central Italy, *c.*1420–40. Musée de Louvre, Paris

Procession of Bacchus and Ariadne, first recorded near the Church of Santa Maria Maggiore in Rome and now in The British Museum (figs 67–9), provoked a series of drawings beginning in the 1420s (figs 70, 71).[69] Misunderstandings of pose and costume in some individual drawings in these sequences show that many artists copied existing drawings rather than dutifully sitting down in front of the sculpture itself. Indeed, as humanist records, they were regarded as status-enhancing teaching tools. In the autobiography, now lost, of the Paduan painter Francesco Squarcione, he boasted that he had travelled (like Cyriacus and others) in Greece, making drawings of 'many things of note that seemed likely to promote skill in art', and setting his many pupils in his humanistically termed 'studium' to copy statuary and reliefs.[70] His most successful pupil, Andrea Mantegna, was the artist most fully to absorb his lessons. However, only one drawing after the antique by him survives, sketched in Rome in 1488–90: on its verso is a copy of warriors on a Trajanic frieze set into the Arch of Constantine, and his attitude to his source – a blend of the artistic and the antiquarian – can be determined by the fact that details of hair and facial expression have been 'restored', though larger missing limbs are left as stumps (fig. 72).[71] Testimony of such an approach can be found in the figurative quotations of countless Renaissance painters. Some of these citations are, as we will see, deliberately disguised. Others were more explicitly antiquarian, perhaps never more so than in Mantegna's nine canvases of the *Triumphs of Caesar* (fig. 73), painted for Francesco Gonzaga in the last two decades of the Quattrocento and eventually set up in the palace of San Sebastiano.[72]

Artists undertook similar investigations of ancient ornament. Many drawings of architectural fragments survive. For painters, the unearthing of the grottoes, only later identified as the Golden House of Nero, the Domus Aurea, was of particular importance. The rubbish-filled labyrinth was packed with ancient Roman paintings – 'grotesques'. This archaeological discovery coincided fatefully with the coming together of groups of mostly foreign painters from Tuscany, Umbria and the Marches to work at the Vatican in the 1480s.[73] The penetration of the grottoes by artists (and others) is documented by their names scratched rudely into the paintings; the names of the painters Bernardo Pinturicchio and Domenico Ghirlandaio, and many others, can still be seen.[74] It is unlikely that these graffiti were purely acts of casual vandalism; rather, they were statements of intellectual and cultural appropriation, an equivalent to Lorenzo de' Medici's defacement of his gems. These 'we were here' also make explicit the fact that artists had undertaken antiquarian investigations at first hand. Here was the long-awaited equivalent

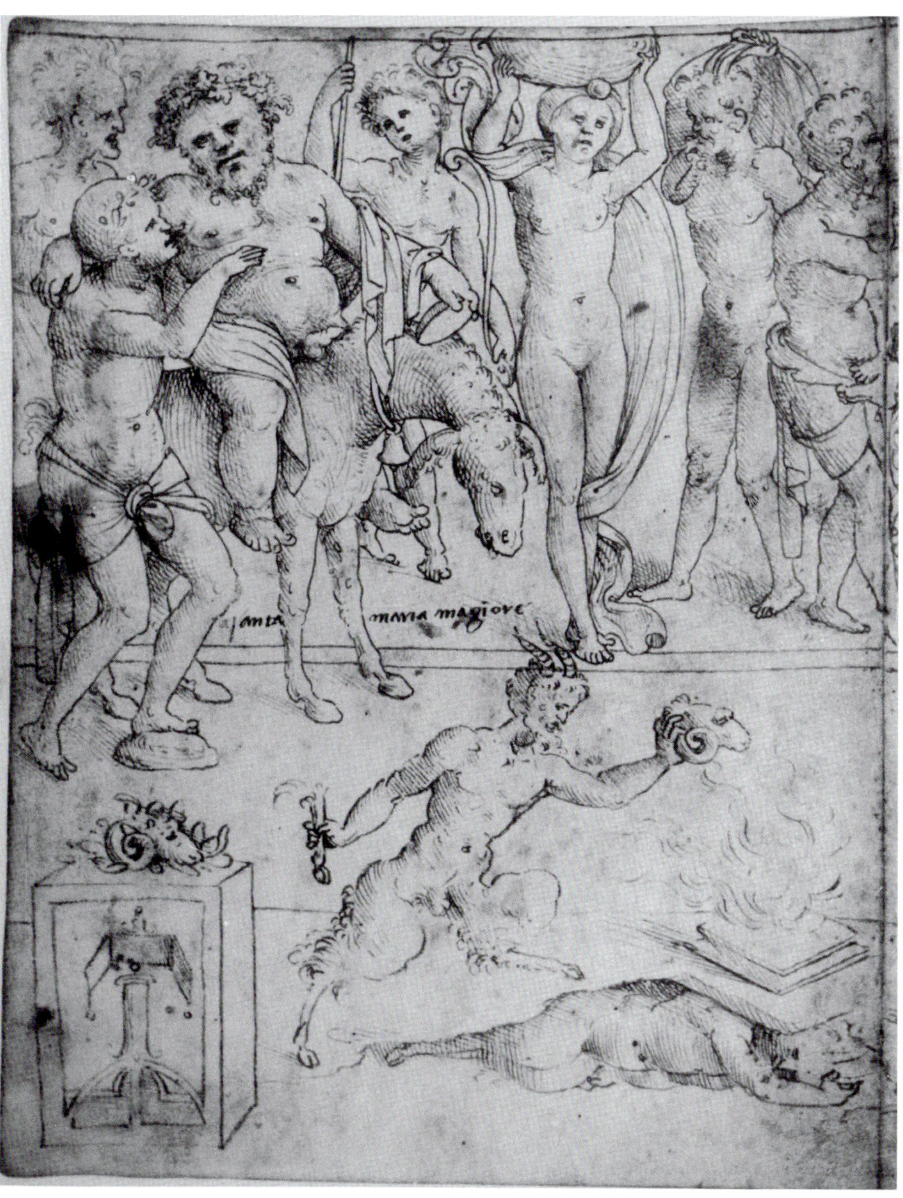

71 Amico Aspertini, figures from Bacchus and Ariadne sarcophagus; pen and ink; from 'Wolfegg Codex', fols 31v–32; Rome, *c.*1500–3. Schloss Wolfegg, Germany

of the rediscovery of ancient texts by humanist scholars. The pictures contained much the same combination of elements as in the list of *gentile* ingredients in Giovanni Rucellai's Santa Costanza mosaics.

Like those of sarcophagus reliefs, drawings by these painters were intended as both specimens of artistic antiquarianism *and* models for their own works and those of their workshop. And once again they were copied by colleagues and assistants.[75] The styles and motifs of the Domus Aurea grotesques were thus quickly exported through much of Italy. As authentic survivals of ancient painting, reproduced or reinvented grotesques took on particular importance in the decorative schemes of both chapels and secular interiors. They were employed by Pinturicchio as early as 1483–5 in the Bufalini chapel in Santa Maria in Aracoeli in Rome.[76] He used them again in the Piccolomini Library, abutting Siena

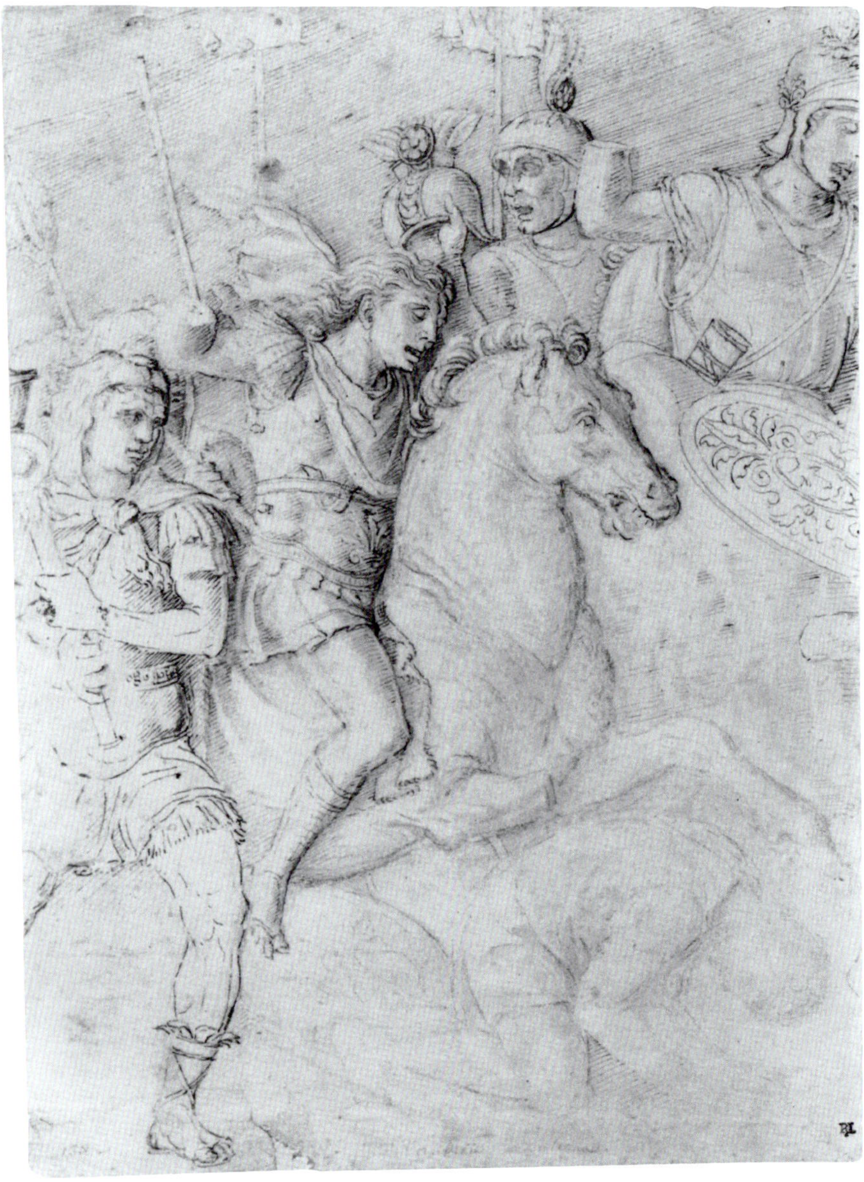

72 Andrea Mantegna, drawing after Trajanic frieze; pen and ink on paper; Rome, 1488–90. Graphische Sammlung Albertina, Vienna

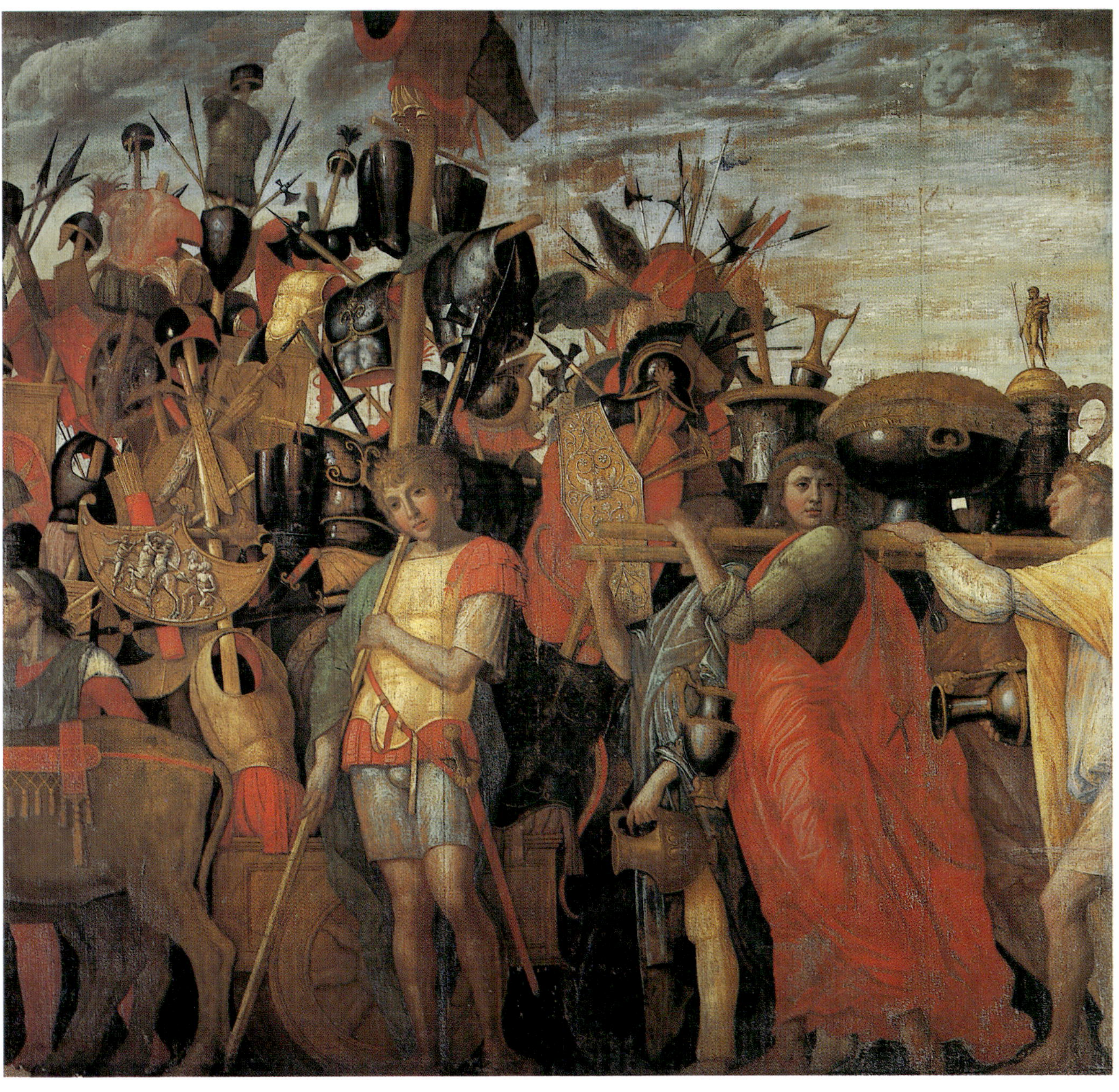

73 Andrea Mantegna, *The Triumphs of Caesar: Trophies and Bearers of Coin and Vases*; distemper (?) on canvas; Mantua, *c.*1486–1506. Her Majesty the Queen, Hampton Court

cathedral. As a form of architectural decoration, they could be properly appropriated for other architectural elements. The decoration of the principal chamber of the palace of Pandolfo Petrucci was undertaken by Pinturicchio, Luca Signorelli and Girolamo Genga. Surviving maiolica floor tiles from this room with black-ground grotesques and the dates 1509–13 suggest that one of these painters, probably Pinturicchio, provided ceramic painters with their designs for tiles.[77] He or one of his companions may even have been responsible for the design of the Petrucci Pan plate. Its roundel figures certainly recall works by both Pinturicchio and Signorelli.[78]

The Petrucci plate is an early example of the many pieces made in Italy in the second two decades of the sixteenth century, where the grotesque had become an antiquarian *lingua franca*. It supplemented ornamental motifs less appropriately derived from sculpted architectural reliefs and entirely supplanted another ornament style erroneously believed, perhaps, to have ancient origins. The elegantly twisting plant scroll seen on ceramics made in Florence in the third quarter of the fifteenth century was copied from imported Hispano-Moresque lustreware (see figs 164–6). It is interesting to note, however, that book illuminators in the mid-Quattrocento used a not dissimilar form of ornament for page borders, one now termed 'white vine-stem decoration' but often called by contemporaries *all'antica*.[79] This stylized interlacing pattern of stems and leaves silhouetted against dark grounds was not, in fact, derived from actually ancient sources, but probably instead from more recent Tuscan models, and it disappeared with the arrival of the grotesque, when it was perhaps realized that any belief in its ancient origins was ill-founded. Ceramic painters followed suit and such interlace was rejected in favour of the grotesque, the sole ancient painting style sanctioned by antiquarian authority.

Agents, dealers and appraisers: the humanist goldsmith

Drawing antiquities was not the only way in which artists worked in imitation of, or in parallel with, their scholarly peers. In March 1505 Isabella d'Este returned an ivory head sent to her by Giovanni Gonzaga in Rome. She had turned it down because in the judgement of her two artists, Gian Cristoforo Romano and Andrea Mantegna, the latter exercising his renowned eye, it was 'neither ancient nor good'.[80] In December that year Gian Cristoforo wrote one of the many, often somewhat gossipy letters he exchanged with Isabella d'Este, as she sought treasures for her *grotta*: 'I will be alert, and I have already warned several of those who excavate, and others who would like to excavate, to show me antiquities before the others. I will lack no diligence....'[81]

These are two of many instances when Gian Cristoforo can be found working as an assessor or authenticator of antiquities and as an agent (and a dealer, if his rake-offs, unrecorded, were substantial enough to earn him an income on top of his own sculptural commissions). He was called upon by his Sforza and Gonzaga patrons to examine extremely various ancient artefacts: coins, gems and sculpture, large and small. He was by no means the only artist who was employed in this way. With so much money and credibility at stake, it was extremely important that the antiquities purchased by men and women of standing should be of optimum quality, in the best possible condition and, of course, truly antique. Members of the Medici and Gonzaga families could rarely go shopping themselves for ancient works of art, but they and their peers compensated for their own lack of mobility by exploiting elaborate networks of agents, dealers and representatives across Italy and the Mediterranean world. Initially, many of those collecting ancient works of art on behalf of the Medici, Este or Gonzaga were the same humanist scholars who had pioneered the antiquarian studies that had made them so desirable in the first place. Sculpture from Greece and Asia Minor was acquired with the assistance of Poggio Bracciolini by Cosimo de' Medici, who later inherited three antique heads with a Rhodes provenance from Poggio.[82] They had come originally from Cyriacus, a merchant of mercantile stock, working as an agent for the dealer-governor of Chios, Andreolo Giustiniani.[83] Sabba da Castiglione acted in Rhodes on behalf of Isabella d'Este, smuggling pieces out despite the known strictures of the authorities. In a world without illustrated sales catalogues, collectors perforce relied on experts whose expertise was such that they could be trusted to pass informed judgement on objects for sale.

It is true that some small objects could be purchased directly from finders or from traders in the market set up in the Campo dei Fiori in Rome. However, patrons often chose to deal with more expert middlemen rather than buy directly from finders and stall-holders. The merchant Giovanni Ciampolini in Rome became the chief source of antiquities for Lorenzo de' Medici. Ciampolini was a collector himself, owning a much-studied group of inscriptions, and he was believed to possess very real facility. Between 1484 and 1487 protracted negotiations were conducted between Ciampolini and a trio of Florentines employed by the Medici bank in Rome – Antonio Tornabuoni, Luigi da Barberino and Nofri Tornabuoni – acting for Lorenzo in the purchase of a carnelian intaglio of *The Chariot of Phaeton*. When it was finally acquired for 200 ducats, Ciampolini explained the qualities of the gem to Luigi da Barberino: 'After the owner, who is most expert and upon whose judgement everyone relies for such things, showed me the singular artistry and difficulty of each detail, it seemed to me even more wonderful.'[84] Luigi had been taught the qualities of the gem by an expert. After Giovanni's death, his business was inherited by his son Michele. It is known that, in addition to dealing in antiquities, Michele, on at least one occasion, supplied Pope Alexander IV with cut rubies for the papal tiara.[85] Although there is no evidence that Giovanni himself dealt in precious stones, this double-dealing – in both precious stones and antiquities – had a long tradition, one that was to have considerable impact on the works the artists themselves produced.

That goldsmiths and gem merchants dealt in this way is not, perhaps, surprising. Their livelihoods depended on their recognized abilities to assess the qualities of faceted and unworked precious and semi-precious stones, so closely linked to their judgement of the quality and authenticity of ancient cameos and intaglios. These abilities were acknowledged by the employment of goldsmiths to assess the accumulations of modern objects made from gold and silver, cut precious stones and small antiquities after the death of their owners: the estate of Cardinal Lodovico Trevisan, for example, was itemized in Florence in April 1465, the inventory witnessed by two goldsmiths, Rainaldo de' Ghini and Antonio di Jacopo, who can almost certainly be identified as the multifaceted Antonio del Pollaiuolo.[86] The Milanese goldsmith Caradosso was probably the most active of all his generation as an evaluator of both gems and antiquities. With a flourishing trade in diamonds, rubies, pearls and other precious jewels, his works in precious metal were enormously famous during his lifetime, and his knowledge of gems was practically demonstrated by his renowned manufacture of the papal tiara and morse for Julius II. He was consulted by many of the most active collectors of his day, including Isabella d'Este and Lodovico il Moro. In 1495 the Sforza duke went so far as to define Caradosso's 'profession', not by his works but by his knowledge of 'things antique'.[87] Caradosso deliberately developed his antiquarian expertise: in July 1489, while struggling with the Florentine authorities to allow the free passage of pearls and carnelians, he reported that he hoped 'to see the things of Lorenzo', the famous Medici antiquities collection.

Goldsmiths were naturally also expected to manufacture the mounts and settings for gemstones, not merely for precious emeralds or rubies but also for antique cameos and intaglios. A passage in Ghiberti's *Commentaries* demonstrates how such activities could be exploited for humanist ends. He wrote an extended account of mounting a hugely famous intaglio, the *Apollo, Marsyas and Olympos* that was then believed to have been the gem used by Nero for stamping seals (fig. 74). The intaglio may have been discovered by Niccolò Niccoli, and when Ghiberti worked on it, it was probably before it was presented by the *signori* of Florence to Cardinal Lodovico Trevisan. It passed later into the Barbo and Medici collections. Ghiberti's narrative is fashioned to show off his own technical mastery, but also his antiquarian knowledge (although his interpretation of the subject matter was actually misguided):

74 Dioscourides (attributed), *Apollo, Marsyas and Olympos*: 'Seal of Nero'; cornelian intaglio; Roman, first century BC to first century AD. Museo Archeologico Nazionale, Naples

At that time [in 1428] I made a gold mount for a carnelian, the size of a nut in its shell, into which a most excellent ancient master had carved three extremely well executed figures. I made a dragon with wings a little apart and with its head lowered as its handle, its neck raised in the middle and the wings making the mount for the seal … Engraved around these figures, by my hand, were antique letters spelling the name of Nero, which I executed with great care. The figures in this carnelian were an old man sitting on a lion skin and tied to a dead tree with his hands behind his back; at his feet there was a child kneeling on one leg and looking at a youth who had a scroll in his right hand and a lyre in his left. The infant appears to be asking the youth to teach him; these three figures were made to show our [three] ages. They are certainly by the hand of Pyrgotoles or Policleites [names known from Pliny and the signature on a surviving gem]. They were more perfect than anything I have ever seen engraved in intaglio.[88]

Ancient gold and silver coins might also find their way naturally to goldsmiths' shops, perhaps in the first instance as bullion to be melted down and turned into something else, but later finding their own market amid the burgeoning field of humanist studies. In June 1494, the humanist poet Matteo Maria Boiardo wrote from Reggio of a group of ancient gold coins then in the hands of a goldsmith, one Filippo Corino, that was offered to Ercole d'Este.[89] Moreover, since goldsmiths had to be trusted to assess the value of a precious stone and not to adulterate the preciousness of gold and silver with base metals, it might be argued that they could be trusted on other fronts: the antiquities they had on offer could be assumed to be genuine. In the later fifteenth century Venetian goldsmiths built up considerable stock. Domenico di Piero was dubbed 'jeweller and singular antiquarian'.[90] When he died in 1497 Isabella d'Este sought detailed information on the contents of his considerable estate, a greatly prized and envied collection of antiquities. The pieces were then in the hands of another Venetian jeweller, Gian Andrea de Fiore, and in October 1498 Isabella's agent informed her that there were available

certain small panels [*tavolette*] into which are inserted gold coins, thirty-six per panel, all very beautiful. Their price was half a ducat for each coin plus the value of the gold. He also showed me certain other little panels with several cameos, so that each panel contains about eight, among which there was one which had two of the best engraved gems, one of Hercules strangling a three-headed Cerberus, the other of a nude man who fans a badly wounded leg with a wing: the Cerberus is very beautiful and Signor Gian [Andrea] is thinking of buying it, but I believe he will have to buy the whole panel … All these things belonged to the late Domenico di Piero, who stipulated in his will the way in which everything would be sold and for what price.[91]

In fact, collectors could purchase antiquities from goldsmiths and gem-dealers (often one and the same) from the mid-Trecento, and from coins and engraved gems it was only a short step to dealing in bronzes and larger-scale sculpture. As early as 1335 a wealthy and erudite notary from Treviso, Oliviero Forzetta, on a shopping expedition in the Serenissima looked to goldsmiths like Simone da Venezia and others to supply him not only with fifty ancient coins but with heads of bronze or marble.[92] Thus it is not remarkable to find that in 1495 Caradosso was responsible, for example, for the purchase of a marble Leda on behalf of Lodovico Sforza, and its subsequent (not very legal) export from Rome. Earlier, the Mantua-born goldsmith Cristoforo di Geremia supplied Lodovico Gonzaga, Marquis of Mantua, with mounted and unmounted pearls and gems. He too handled sculpture. He dispatched four antique heads from Rome to Lodovico Gonzaga in April 1462 and offered to obtain more although he risked the 'punishment of excommunication by sending similar things beyond Rome'.[93] As a way of both currying favour with his long-distance patron and advertising his stock, he made a gift of one of them. The Mantuan ambassador in Rome wrote: 'I send … by the muleteer Nani four antique heads among which is that of the emperor Hadrian, of which in particular Cristoforo di Geremia makes a present to you …'.[94] Cristoforo himself wrote 'I also send four ancient busts or heads … which are considered good by experts',[95] these experts including, by implication, himself.

This was another humanist skill properly appropriated by artists – the ability to distinguish between not only the good and the bad but also the authentic and the fake. When Traversari, for example, was inspecting numismatic and antiquarian collections in Venice in 1432–5, he met Cyriacus, who showed him gold and silver coins among which were portraits of Lysimachus, Philip of Macedonia and Alexander the Great, pieces Traversari doubted were genuine Macedonian issues.[96] That Cristoforo di Geremia was casting himself in this role is indicated by another letter written by the Mantuan ambassador in Rome. In November 1462 Cristoforo's warning against counterfeit gems was relayed to Marquis Lodovico Gonzaga: he had said

that if someone should come to you to sell little cameos, your Highness should be careful when you buy not to be fooled, because there is someone here who makes fakes [*contrafacti*], by gluing the white part [onto dark stones], pieces of such perfection that if there is no-one there who knows

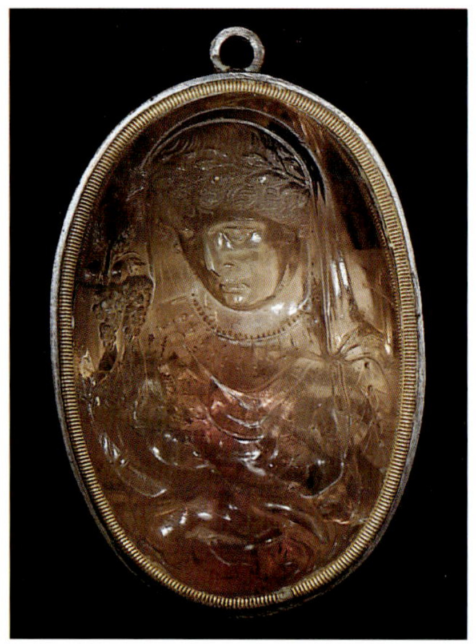

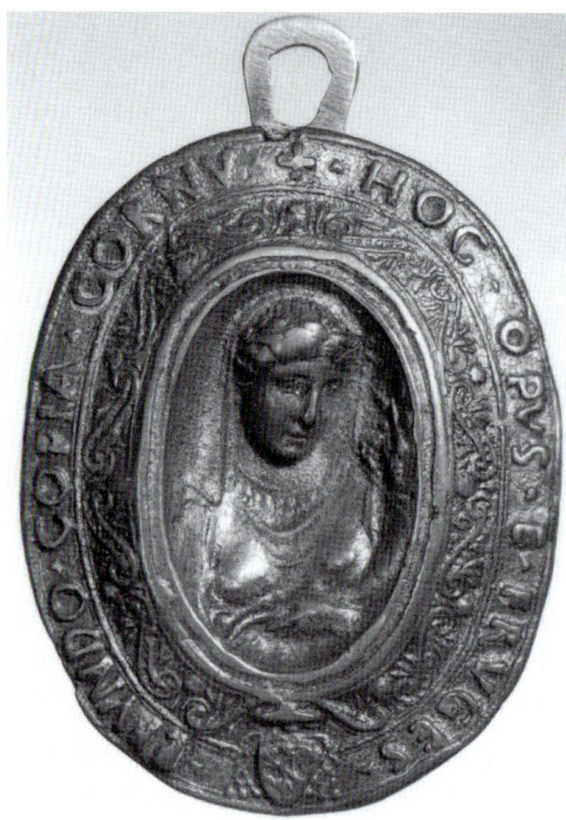

75 (*Left*) *Abundance*; amethyst intaglio; first century BC. Bibliothèque nationale de France, Paris

76 (*Right*) Cristoforo di Geremia (attributed); cast bronze plaquette after antique *Abundance* gem; before 1464. National Gallery of Art, Washington DC

cameos well, the only way to recognize them is to touch the sides of the whites with a file, because they are soft.[97]

Caradosso's ability to spot fakes was so esteemed that he could queer the pitch of a dealer as much-frequented as Giovanni Ciampolini. This trust in his judgement is revealed most explicitly by a letter written to Lorenzo de' Medici from Rome in February 1489. The previous summer Caradosso had been in Florence, where he had examined an engraved carnelian that Ciampolini had offered to Lorenzo. The dealer, it was reported, was now nervous about contacting Lorenzo on new business, scared off by the thumbs-down Caradosso had given the gem:

… as far as I understand, he [Ciampolini] is worried in case your Magnificence is still disposed towards him as you were because, I believe, you were told by a certain Caradosso and other goldsmiths, who were there [in Florence] last summer, that the carnelian they saw … and which Your Magnificence believed antique, seems dubious to them, and that [Ciampolini] wanted to take you for a ride.[98]

It is not surprising that it was sometimes difficult to distinguish between the old and the new, or that Caradosso and his fellow goldsmiths were thought to have the best eye. Goldsmith-dealers were not above a little improving of antiquities to make them more marketable. Cellini described the activities of goldsmiths in Rome in 1523, their 'many labours on ancient gems' undertaken 'to increase the value'.[99] Patrons may have expected a certain level of informed restoration. In a letter of May 1507 to Isabella d'Este, Giorgio de Negroponte, one of her agents in Rome, expressed no shock at the chasing of the surfaces of corroded ancient coins to make them more attractive (only quibbling at the extortionate mark-ups):

I hear that some people buy ancient coins that are beautiful in form but are weighed down by rust [*ma carche di rugine*] for eight or ten ducats to gain twenty-five or thirty, and sometimes they lose from them and sometimes they get a good deal. Not four days have passed since someone who bought one of Nero for six ducats and having cleaned it up [*netata*] was offered twelve, but he wanted no less than twenty-five.[100]

Goldsmiths also regularly took impressions from gems engraved in intaglio; these, like cameos in relief, could be used as the basis for casts made of sulphur or, surviving more commonly today, lead or bronze. These metal reliefs, now valued independently of their gem origins, are today termed 'plaquettes' and were then called *piastre* or *rilievi*. Goldsmiths made casts of gems for sale as a way of advertising their wares, sending them to potential buyers.[101] However, they seem also to have made casts as records, three-dimensional equivalents to their drawings of ancient sculpture and ornament. (Ghiberti's description of the Seal of Nero shows by its confusion of left and right that he was describing a cast that had reversed the image.)[102] These were circulated by scholars when original material was unavailable or unaffordable, a method of spreading information among the humanist community. In 1442 Cyriacus of Ancona cast an edition 'for the knowledge and understanding of men' of one particular gem representing, he believed, one of the mythical creatures who menaced Odysseus during his voyage; he was thanked for 'the lead reproduction [*simulacrum*] of the monster Scylla, taken from a sardonyx or agate gem, made with your most noble casting skills'.[103] Other casts were made to signal ownership, material and intellectual. These, however, seem to have been executed by goldsmiths. One of the earliest such bronze reliefs can be securely dated between 1440 and 1464, an intaglio impression cast to communicate the fact that the gem from which it was taken was in the possession of Pietro Barbo (figs 75, 76). The 1457 inventory of Barbo's gems includes an intaglio: 'a large head, laureate, with its torso, holding in the left hand a horn full of grapes and it is the head of a woman – of the goddess Plenty or Abundance – in white amethyst … a truly excellent thing, worth eighty ducats' (most others were valued at only one or two).[104] The method and style of facture of this bronze are very close to a group of cast impressions taken from the *Apollo, Marsyas and Olympos* mounted by Ghiberti – the so-called Seal of Nero (see fig. 74)– which had passed from the Trevisan to the Barbo collection. As well as existing independently, a cast impression from this intaglio was employed as the reverse of an oval medal of Barbo after he had become Pope Paul II in

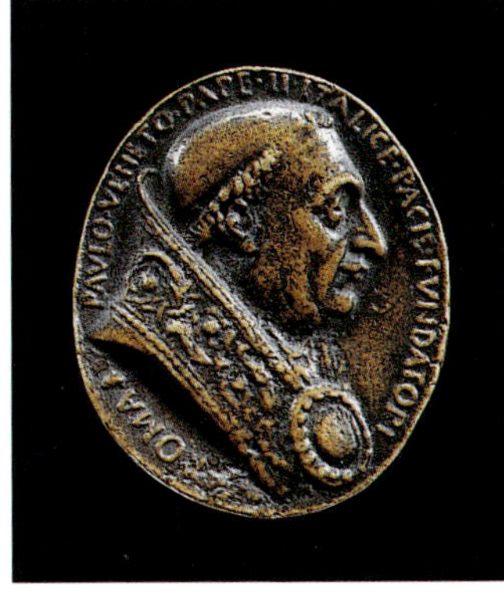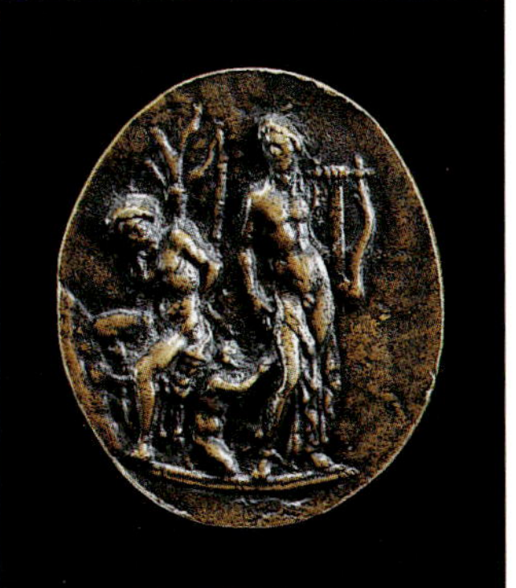

77 Cristoforo di Geremia, portrait medal of Pope Paul II with 'Seal of Nero' reverse; cast bronze; Rome, 1464–71. The British Museum, London

1464, the work of Cristoforo di Geremia (fig. 77).[105] Impressions of a large number of other gems in the Barbo collection were also cast in bronze. Their appearance and quality are consistent with both the 'Nero' *Apollo, Marsyas and Olympos* on the medal and the *Abundance* relief, and archaeological evidence suggests that they too were made in workshops attached to the Barbo Palace of San Marco.[106] Cristoforo's authorship of the medal lends authority to the theory that he may have been responsible for the production, under the Pope's auspices, of many of these little bronze reliefs.

Manufacturing all'antica *art objects: the philology of ancient art*

Casts of gems were used as an element in the ornament of inkstands, pen and sand boxes, bells and mortars. This was one of the ways to make the paraphernalia of study look antique, a strategy that was paralleled by the many painted manuscript borders that incorporate representations of ancient gems into ornamental schemes of different kinds. Some modellers and founders of such objects had a supply of moulds taken of ancient gems; it appears that the casts made from these moulds, applied to these utensils, were not always issued separately as independent reliefs, and thus lost their primarily scholarly function, becoming purely ornamental.[107] This technique had the advantage of incorporating reproductions of genuine antiquities into modern objects. It cannot, however, necessarily be interpreted as a demonstration of the thorough investigation of antique form and ornament of the kind that could be called philological.

Given these multifarious contacts with ancient artefacts, however, it is not surprising that it was particularly among goldsmiths that a philological approach to making new objects was pioneered. Caradosso, for example, was known for his ability to translate ancient sculptural images into another medium. Choices were sometimes made in consultation with their patrons. In 1512, for instance, reference is made to Federico II Gonzaga's wish that Caradosso should make a hat-badge representing the Laocoön group (see fig. 66), 'a gold Laocoön all in relief with his sons and the serpents, made by embossing and not cast'.[108] Isabella, informed of it by her son, said she longed for such a piece but she was strapped for cash. She called such emblematic hat-badges *imprese virtuose*, a phrase which translates as both 'virtuous devices', 'devices' being the term applied to such images, and, more abstractly, 'virtuous enterprises'.[109]

Goldsmiths extended their approach beyond the merely figurative to embrace form and ornament. In 1468 Carlo de' Medici commissioned a bronze candelabrum from the goldsmith-trained sculptor Andrea del Verrocchio (fig. 78) for the chapel of the Audience Chamber of the Florentine Palazzo della Signoria, to mark his two-month period as Gonfaloniere in May and June of that year, specifying that it should be 'worked to resemble a

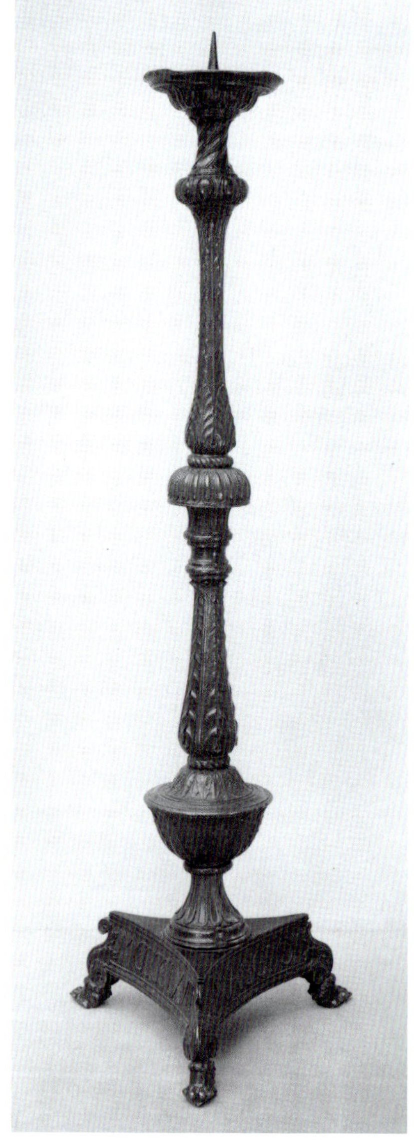

78 Andrea del Verrocchio, candelabrum; cast 'bell metal' bronze; Florence, 1468–9. Rijksmuseum, Amsterdam

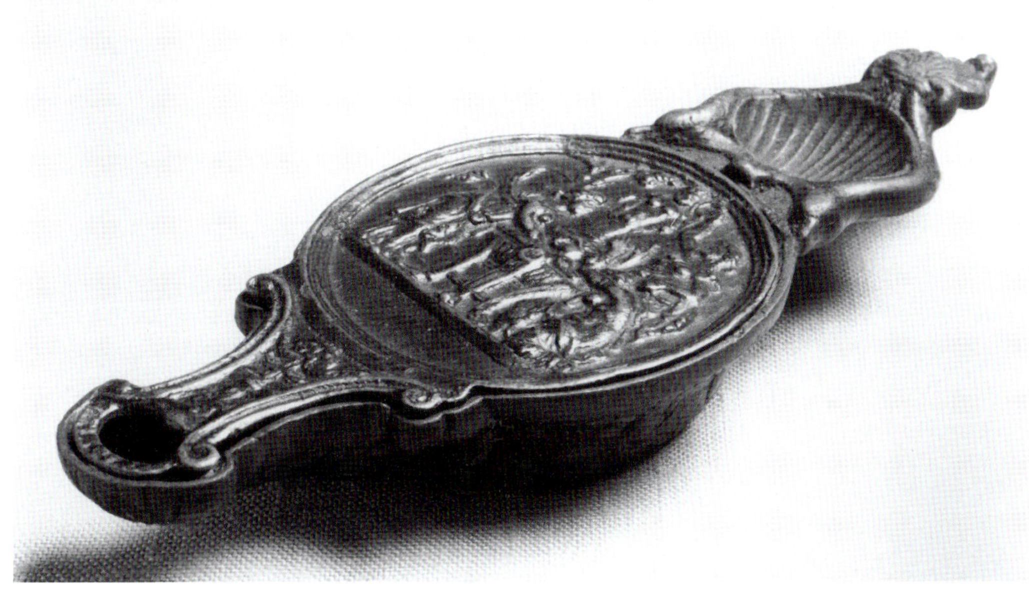

79 Cristoforo di Geremia, oil lamp with relief of *Sacrifice to Priapus*; cast bronze; Rome, before 1480. Victoria and Albert Museum, London

certain vase', an ancient stone (or hard-stone) urn.[110] Such artists might also be more actively involved in selecting their sources. An exchange of letters concerning a crystal salt to be finished and mounted by Cristoforo di Geremia for Lodovico Gonzaga reveals the initiative shifting from patron to artist. In 1461 Lodovico sent to Rome a piece of rock-crystal that his engineer, Giampietro da Figino, had started to carve, the work interrupted by the latter's unfortunate demise. He requested that Cristoforo should 'carve it and reduce it to the proportion of that basin which can be found in Santa Maria Rotonda' – a porphyry bath urn then at the Pantheon – its cover, feet and 'frame' to be made of gold. Cristoforo furnished a lead model showing the proposed 'adornments', but Lodovico had reservations, worrying that the feet were too spindly, out of proportion with the crystal, and suggesting they should be 'more stable and substantial' (*più fermi e massici*). The quantity of gold required was of no account, 'as long as they are beautiful'. The correspondence continued. Cristoforo seems to have added a little column to the feet and he went on to make a 'polished cover', based on the lid of another antique basin at Santa Maria Maggiore, which was to be set with rubies. The piece finished, the last letter, accompanying its dispatch, furnishes final proof that the salt was intended by the artist to look as correctly *all'antica* as possible, even if it meant omitting materials that would add to its material (but not aesthetic) value: 'I also return the rubies, because they did not see how to incorporate them without ruining the arrangement of the antique' (*l'ordine del anticho*).[111] Cristoforo's ability to appropriately combine antique elements in this way can be assessed in two bronze oil lamps, adorned with reliefs of *Sacrifice to Priapus* (fig. 79) and *Sacrifice to Cupid*. They copy the form and style of Roman lamps almost exactly and both were published as antiques in the seventeenth century.[112]

Cristoforo was not the only goldsmith who taught himself to use these ancient sources appropriately, with complete stylistic and technical fidelity. It was sometimes even a point of pride that the goldsmiths' work should be indistinguishable from their models. Pier Maria Serbaldi da Pescia was an engraver in the Medici circle, a specialist carver of porphyry. He has been fingered as a forger, the author of a porphyry vase noted by Marcantonio Michiel in a collection in Venice, 'which has been sold as an ancient work at great price'.[113] But the activities of this *grandissimo imitatore delle cose antiche*, in Vasari's words, are less clearly categorized, and it is possible that he did not initially intend the vase to be taken as an antique. In 1491 Serbaldi engraved an intaglio, which he made 'to experiment if it could pass as ancient',[114] a test for dealers and collectors as to whether they truly possessed antiquarian expertise, one dependent for its success on his properly applied artistic and antiquarian skills. He launched the piece on the open market, passing it to a man who sold it on to an equerry of the Cardinal of Naples. He, in turn, tried to sell it to Nofri Tornabuoni, who reported the joke to Lorenzo:

Then it came into the hands of those connoisseurs, and some believed it ancient and some had their doubts. Ciampolini, as soon as he saw it, said he thought it was modern, or, even if ancient, that it had been retouched. This equerry who came there to show it to me is Franco Sabette and he was counting on reselling it to me and making a profit of ten ducats, asking me twenty-five for it. Having already been warned by Pier Maria about his caprice … I pretended that I liked it but that I would not take it without Ciampolini's advice, and in this way I got rid of him.[115]

Although his key clients were informed, Serbaldi must have been pleased by the failure of (some) others to recognize his intaglio as antique, proof of his successful assimilation of *all'antica* style and method.

His attempt to achieve absolute authenticity appears to have been common and many Renaissance gems remain difficult to distinguish from their antique prototypes to this day (fig. 80). The subjects of many of the signed engraved gems of Valerio Belli, the leading gem-engraver of his day, are classical, scenes such as the crystal *Sacrifice to Hygeia* in

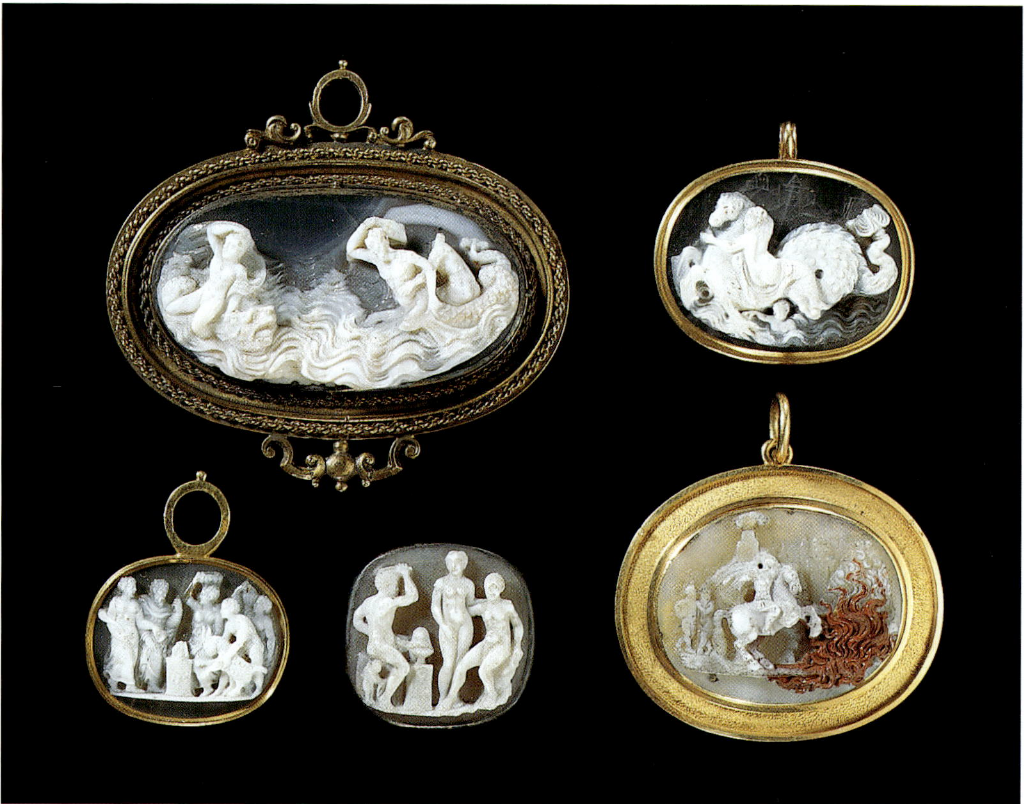

80 Gems with mythological scenes: *Nereid and Hippocamp*; *Triton and Nereids*; *Venus in Vulcan's Forge*; *Sacrifice*; *Marcus Curtius leaping into fiery gulf*; onyx cameos; Italy, second half of fifteenth century to first half of sixteenth century. The British Museum, London

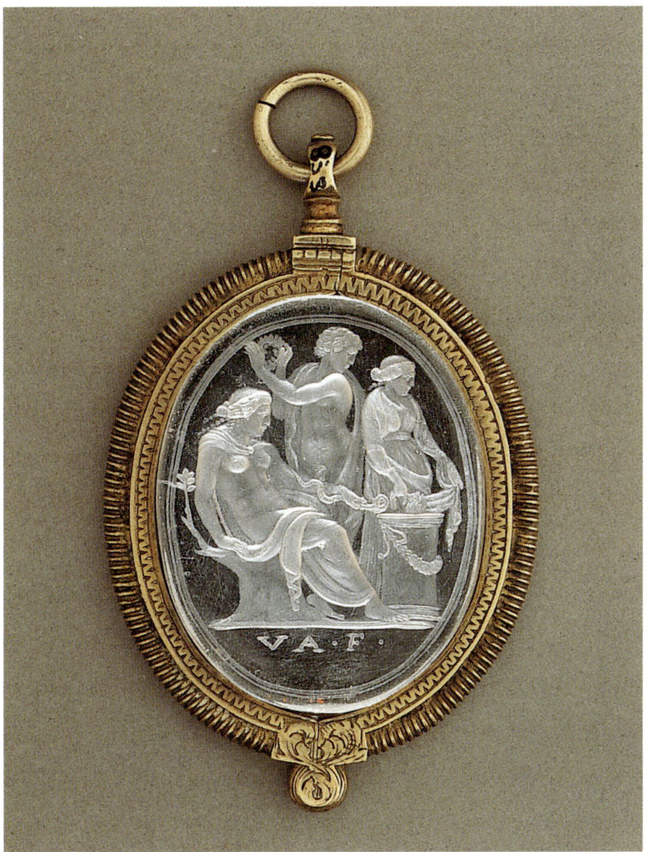

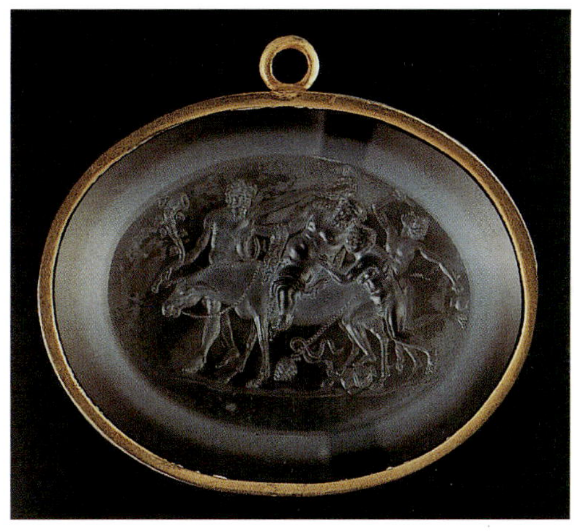

81 Valerio Belli, *Sacrifice to Hygeia*; rock-crystal intaglio; Rome or Vicenza, 1521–46. The British Museum, London

82 Valerio Belli (attributed), *Drunken Silenus supported on a Donkey* (after Townley sarcophagus, see figs 67–9); onyx intaglio; Rome or Vicenza, *c.*1521–46. Museo Archeologico, Florence

The British Museum (fig. 81). However, not all his works have his signature, and his and other unsigned pieces of the period seem intended to challenge perceptions of the boundaries between ancient and modern – some designed to stress continuity, others originality and superiority. The point is made by the relationship between an unsigned intaglio sensibly attributed to Belli and the much-drawn Bacchic sarcophagus in The British Museum (see figs 67–9). In the Museo Archeologico in Florence this beautiful onyx intaglio, formerly catalogued as ancient, must in fact be the work of a Renaissance engraver, perhaps Valerio Belli (fig. 82).[116] It copies, almost exactly, part of the lateral relief on the sarcophagus, the detail of the drunken Silenus supported on a donkey. Here, then, the engraver chose to exercise his modern (though anciently derived) technical skills at the service of a well-known image that was authentically antique.

It is perhaps easiest to follow the process by which artists, goldsmiths above all, learned uncorrupted ancient idioms and their appropriate application by looking at the relationship between ancient coins and modern portrait medals, which are more precisely datable than many other *all'antica* works produced in this period. Benvenuto Cellini's instructions on how to strike medals show how his modern pieces were intended to impart his knowledge of ancient working methods, the result of close, specialist observation:

From what we can gather by reason of what the [surviving] coins show us, one sees immediately that when the art of making medals began to flourish in Egypt, Greece and Rome, the emperors put the impression of their heads on one side and, on the other, an *impresa*, according to the great deeds they had … we who come from the profession, who look deeper into the matter, notice the quantity of medals struck for a single emperor by many different masters.

There follows an account of his own method, put into practice for his medal of Pope Clement VII and in his lost medal of Cardinal Pietro Bembo:

The first thing to be done is to make a model in white wax of the head, the reverse and whatever there may be, to the exact size and relief of the final work; this we know was how the ancients did it….[117]

By these means, medals might come to look increasingly like ancient Roman bronze coins. By asking to what extent medallists felt the need to reproduce faithfully the styles and techniques of their prototypes in their modern works, one can assess how truly philologically derived was their approach to the languages of antiquity.

Just as copies were cast of ancient gems, so too were coins reproduced. Sabba wrote that while it was desirable to adorn one's house 'with ancient gold, silver and bronze coins … those that cannot manage the antique, adorn them with modern ones cast [*tragettate*] by the Venetian Giovanni Corona, very diligent and precise in such work'.[118] The identity of Corona remains a mystery – perhaps he was a member of the Veneto painting family – but we know that one of the brothers of the painter Sandro Botticelli, was employed in the same way in Florence.[119] Since they were cast, with a concomitant loss of crispness and detail in the relief, numismatically aware collectors would have found it a relatively simple matter to spot them as reproductions (rather than fakes). Indeed, some lead copies were identified in the 1457 inventory of Pietro Barbo's coin collection, probably by the Cardinal himself. However, because they were struck, other copies, made for much the same purpose as Serbaldi's gem, were less easily distinguished from out-and-out forgeries.

Enea Vico made an attempt to classify the works of 'imitators' in his 1555 *Discourses on the coins of the ancients*. However, by treating all copies of ancient coins as forgeries his thinking may have been anachronistic.[120] In his chapter 'On the frauds [*fraudi*] which are perpetrated on modern coins to make them look antique' he identified three principal ways of making forgeries: the 'completely ancient', the 'partly ancient' and the 'completely modern'. The 'completely ancient', for example, could be made by 'the false joining together of two sides of coins of different emperors' using solder and filing the edges to conceal the join, or by re-engraving an ancient coin with an engraving tool or jeweller's wheel.[121] We have already seen that even this latter activity was found acceptable by collectors.

According to Vico, other modern 'forgeries' were made by engraving entirely new dies for striking them. He uses the same word as Michiel, listing 'the imitators' who 'have been best at making new iron dies in my time': first on his list are the goldsmiths and die-engravers Vettor Gambello (Camelio) of Venice, Giovanni Cavino of Padua and his son, and Benvenuto Cellini.[122] Such pieces can be attributed on stylistic grounds to Gambello and Cesati, and there is no doubt that Cavino, whose dies survive, actually executed new 'ancient' coins. But, even if their productions fooled some later collectors, were they really intended as forgeries in the first instance? Other examples show that numismatic 'forgeries' were made as demonstrations of antiquarian knowledge and technical

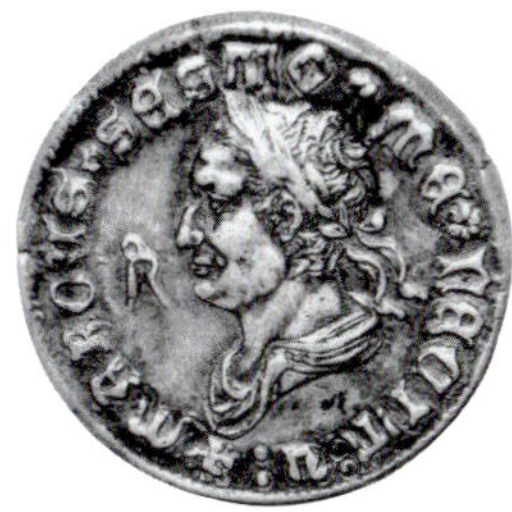

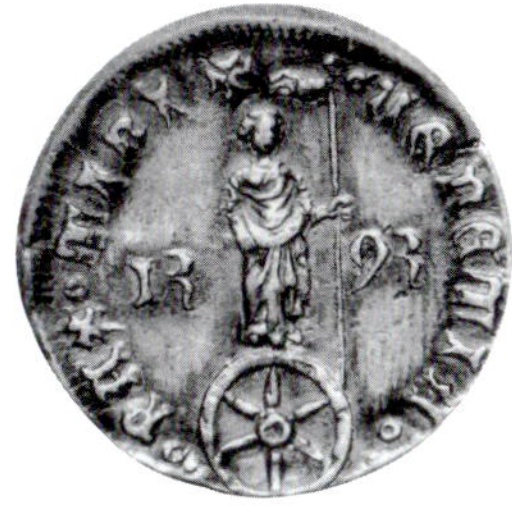

83 Marco Sesto, portrait medal of Emperor Galba; struck bronze; Venice, 1393. American Numismatic Society, New York

virtuosity, and it is often difficult to distinguish between these and intentional counterfeits. Some, indeed, may have been both, depending on the maker's level of knowledge and the discrimination of his audience.

Therefore, when Lorenzo Ghiberti, who, according to Vasari, was 'very fond of copying [*contraffare*] the dies of antique medals', did so, what was he actually doing?[123] Was he a forger? Or was he, like Serbaldi, making demonstrations of his own mastery, as he did in mosaic? A goldsmith might take pride in adapting the skills needed to engrave intaglio gems to fashion the steel dies with which 'ancient coins' could be struck. The tools needed were much the same. None of the fruits of Ghiberti's engraving activities can now be identified, but a parallel instance can be adduced in the 'coins' engraved and struck by the Venetians Lorenzo, Marco and Alessandro Sesto. All three were members of a family who executed traditional goldsmiths' works but who were also employed at the Venetian mint from 1390. Both Marco, in 1393, and Lorenzo, at much the same time, engraved dies for *all'antica* 'coins', both with the portrait of the emperor Galba, and both signed by their makers (fig. 83). Alessandro's effort of 1417 is the more self-consciously *all'antica*, the portrait derived from a Greek coin, with a reverse that seems to depict a scene of the Rape of Proserpine or of Perseus rescuing Andromeda. The goldsmiths not only made a point of their individual parity with the engravers of ancient coins, they also drew a parallel between their state employers and the regimes that had issued their ancient prototypes. Both images of Galba have reverses with the female personification of Venice, Marco's piece with an inscription that translates as 'Peace be with you, Venice'.[124] Neither was intended to fool anyone. Between these and the productions of Gambello and Cavino a range of goldsmith medallists executed portrait medals with ancient subjects and, like those of Gambello and Cavino, some were considered genuine antiques by those who were not in the know. Whatever their original purpose, the *all'antica* medals of Filarete, Cristoforo di Geremia and Valerio Belli have much to tell us on what was thought to look properly ancient at different periods during the Renaissance. The similarity of these pieces to their medallic portraits of the moderns demonstrates an increasing emphasis on a correctly numismatic idiom. This is a message reinforced by how other artists, such as Pisanello, Antico, and Gian Cristoforo Romano, used ancient source material.

Commemorative portrait medals of contemporary figures were not made in any quantity until the 1430s and 1440s. They were revivalist, humanist objects *par excellence*. Their function was believed to be consistent with the perceived commemorative role of ancient bronze coins: the same word, *medaglia*, was used, in fact, of both ancient and modern pieces and, although portrait medals were occasionally cast and struck in gold and silver, bronze remained the medium of choice.[125] A letter of 1446 from the humanist-scholar Flavio Biondo to Leonello d'Este, Marquis of Ferrara, makes this explicit: 'Malatesta has told me that you have ordered about ten thousand bronze coins to be struck after the fashion of the ancient Roman emperors, with on one side your name inscribed next to the representation of your head …'.[126] No such coins were possible at a time when coinage, even small change, was expected to have a precious metal content, and this is likely to be a reading of Leonello's copious medal production. If so, it suggests that Biondo thought of these medals as the modern successors to ancient coins. Another letter makes this link equally explicit. In 1461 Sigismondo Malatesta, Lord of Rimini, wrote (or rather the humanist Roberto Valturio wrote on his behalf) to the Sultan of Turkey, Mehmed II, to introduce the Veronese medallist Matteo de' Pasti, from whom Sigismondo had commissioned many medals from about 1450, and who was then on his way, abortively, to enter Mehmed's service. This letter provides a rare insight into a patron's motives, adding up to a kind of manifesto for medal-making in the Quattrocento. Firstly, the antiquarian context is stated: the fascination engendered by the portraits of past princes, generals and notables. Then the primary interest is outlined: the capacity of the portrait to bestow immortality on its subject. Thirdly and lastly, a parallel is drawn between Mehmed's potential employment of Matteo and the use made of the painter Apelles and the sculptor Lysippus by Alexander the Great to execute his portraits, the only artists permitted so to do.[127]

During this period medal production was focused in Italy's dynastic courts, in Mantua, Rimini, Milan, Naples and, above all, Ferrara. Lodovico Gonzaga, Sigismondo Malatesta, Filippo Maria Visconti, Alfonso of Aragon (see fig. 14) and, especially, the numismatically knowledgeable Leonello d'Este recognized that, by commissioning medals, they could preserve not only their own name, fame and appearance, but that of members of their family and of their courts (usually humanist writers and teachers).[128] The reverses of these medals bore emblems and allegories that stood for one or other of the personal virtues they wished to project. Their tool was the painter Pisanello. He may not have been the 'inventor' of the medal, as is often claimed, but he was certainly its great popularizer. By identifying the paradigm in his work, we discover the ingredients that were supposed to convey their antique conceptual heritage at the moment of their revival. Pisanello was numismatically literate. He had been the owner, it should be remembered, of the ancient coins hijacked in Rome by Pietro Barbo from Carlo de' Medici and in 1435 he made a

84 Pisanello, *Coin Portraits of Julius Caesar, Augustus, 'Alexander the Great' and Hercules*; pen and ink and wash with black chalk underdrawing on prepared paper; Ferrara or Verona, *c.*1435–41. Musée de Louvre, Paris

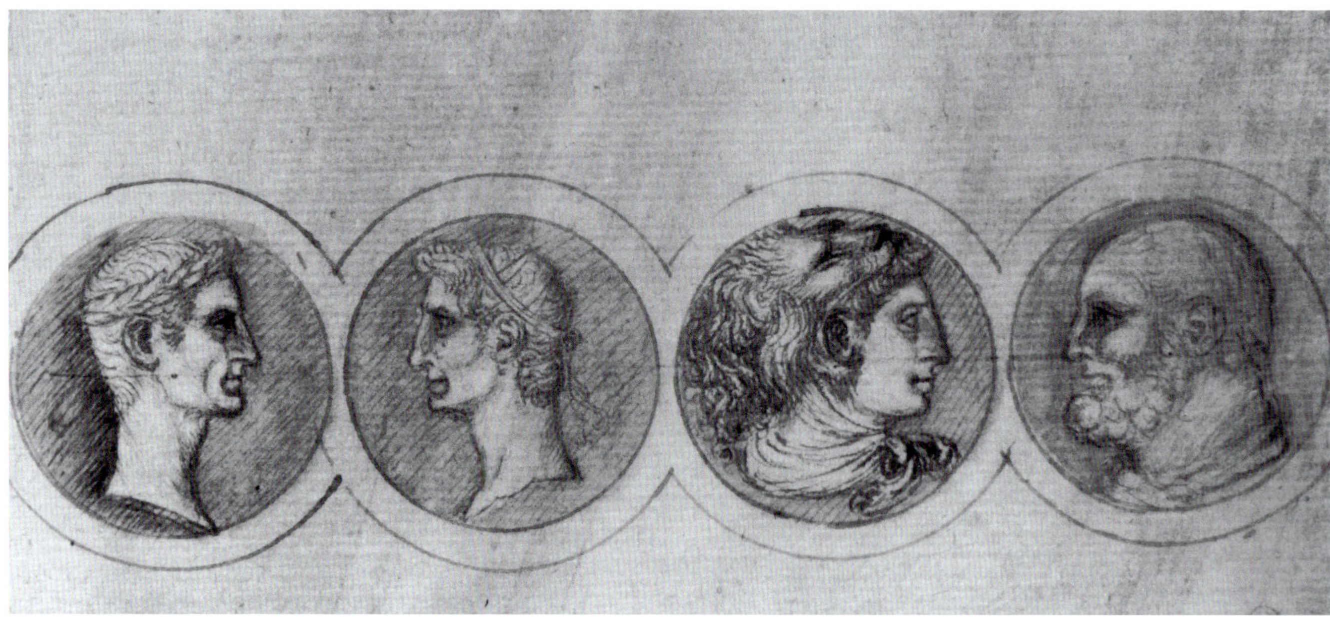

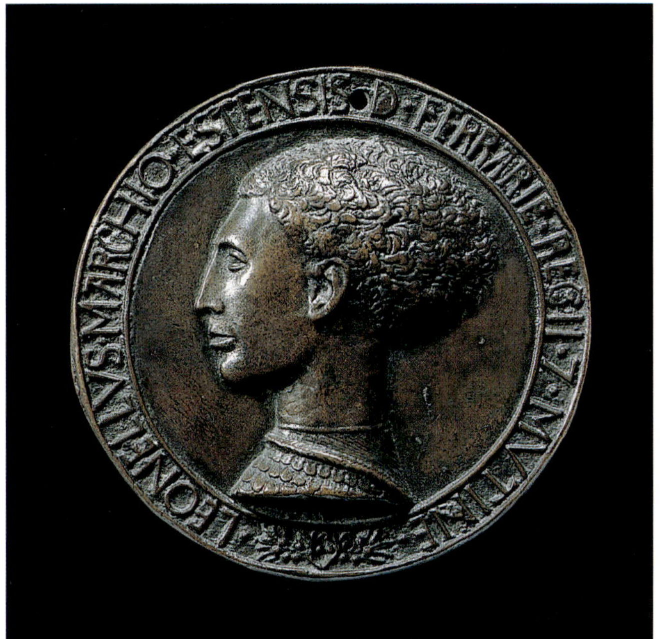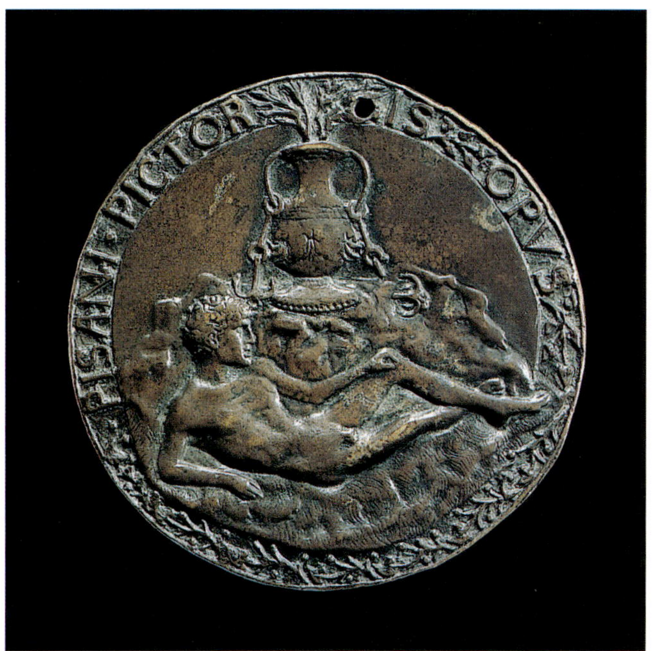

85 Pisanello, portrait medal of Leonello d'Este; cast bronze, Ferrara, *c*.1442. The British Museum, London

birthday present of an 'effigy' of Julius Caesar, a painted or medallic copy of an ancient coin, or perhaps the coin itself, to Leonello.[129] An indication of its appearance is provided by his Louvre drawing of the features of Caesar, one of four little sketches of three ancient coins and an ancient gem portrait of Hercules (fig. 84).[130]

On the same sheet he copied a coin of Alexander the Great, believing that the lion-skinned head of Hercules on its obverse was the ruler's portrait. This image informed his six portrait medals of Leonello. Pisanello was clearly making a point about his patron Leonello's style of rule by transforming his bony, angular features into an elegantly proportioned head which closely resembles his Alexander (fig. 85).[131] The proper interpretation of the portrait depended on knowledge of both ancient texts and artefacts. Valturio's source for his parallel between Mehmed and Alexander, Matteo and Lysippus was the account by Plutarch:

Alexander decreed that only Lysippus should make his portrait. For only Lysippus, it seems, brought out his real character in the bronze and gave form to his essential excellence. Others, in their eagerness to imitate the turn of his neck and the expressive, liquid glance of his eyes, failed to preserve his manly and leonine quality.[132]

So, as well as rearranging his features, Pisanello turned Leonello's stringy mop of hair into a leonine mane. The image of the leonine Leonello/Alexander therefore worked on four levels. It is a play on his name (which translates as 'Little Lion') and it is a physiognomical allusion to his virtues as ruler. His hair was also intended to stand for the lion skin worn by the 'Alexander' of the Greek coin and, lastly, to refer to Plutarch's description of Alexander's own leonine appearance. Thus, as Leonello becomes Alexander, Pisanello claims parity with Lysippus (as the young Michelangelo was to with Phidias, as we shall see).

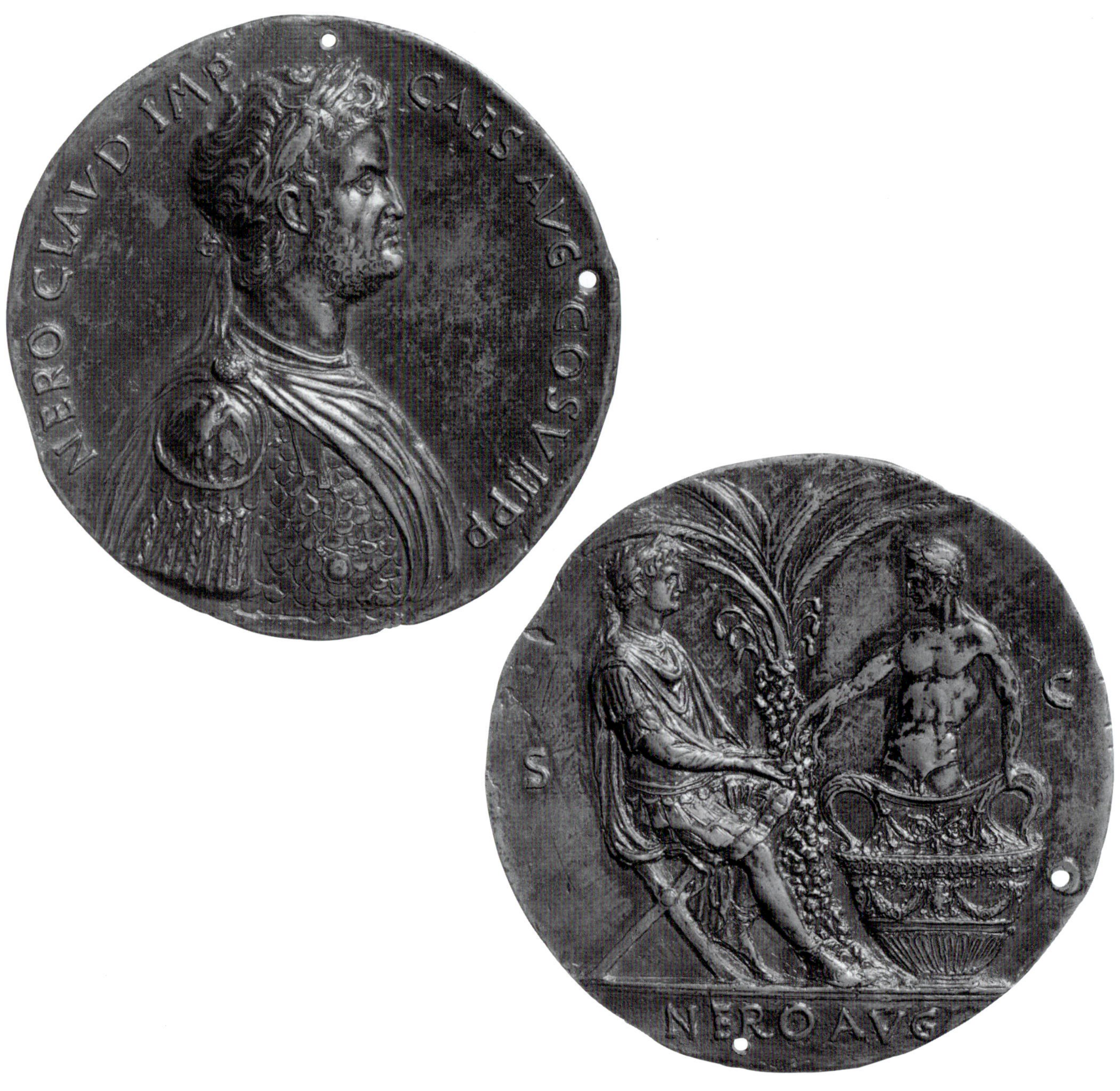

Despite the proper use of bronze, the profile format, the interdependent relationship between the two sides, the Latin inscriptions and the occasional pertinent antique trope, taken from antique statuary as often as from ancient coins, in many important ways Pisanello's medals do not look very antique at all. Their method of manufacture was different for a start: cast from wax models rather than struck like ancient coins. They are also all significantly larger. And it is now apparent that a large part of their vocabulary is derived from the manuscript illumination and metal-work of France and Burgundy. However, it seems that these were not regarded as disqualifying ingredients in the reading of these medals as *all'antica* and it is possible that these aspects of Pisanello's medals may be explained by their relationship to copies of medals portraying the emperors Constantine and Heraclius.[133] The originals had been purchased by Jean, Duke of Berry, in

86 Antonio Averlino, called Filarete (or workshop), portrait medal of Emperor Nero; cast bronze; Rome, *c.*1435–45. National Gallery of Art, Washington DC

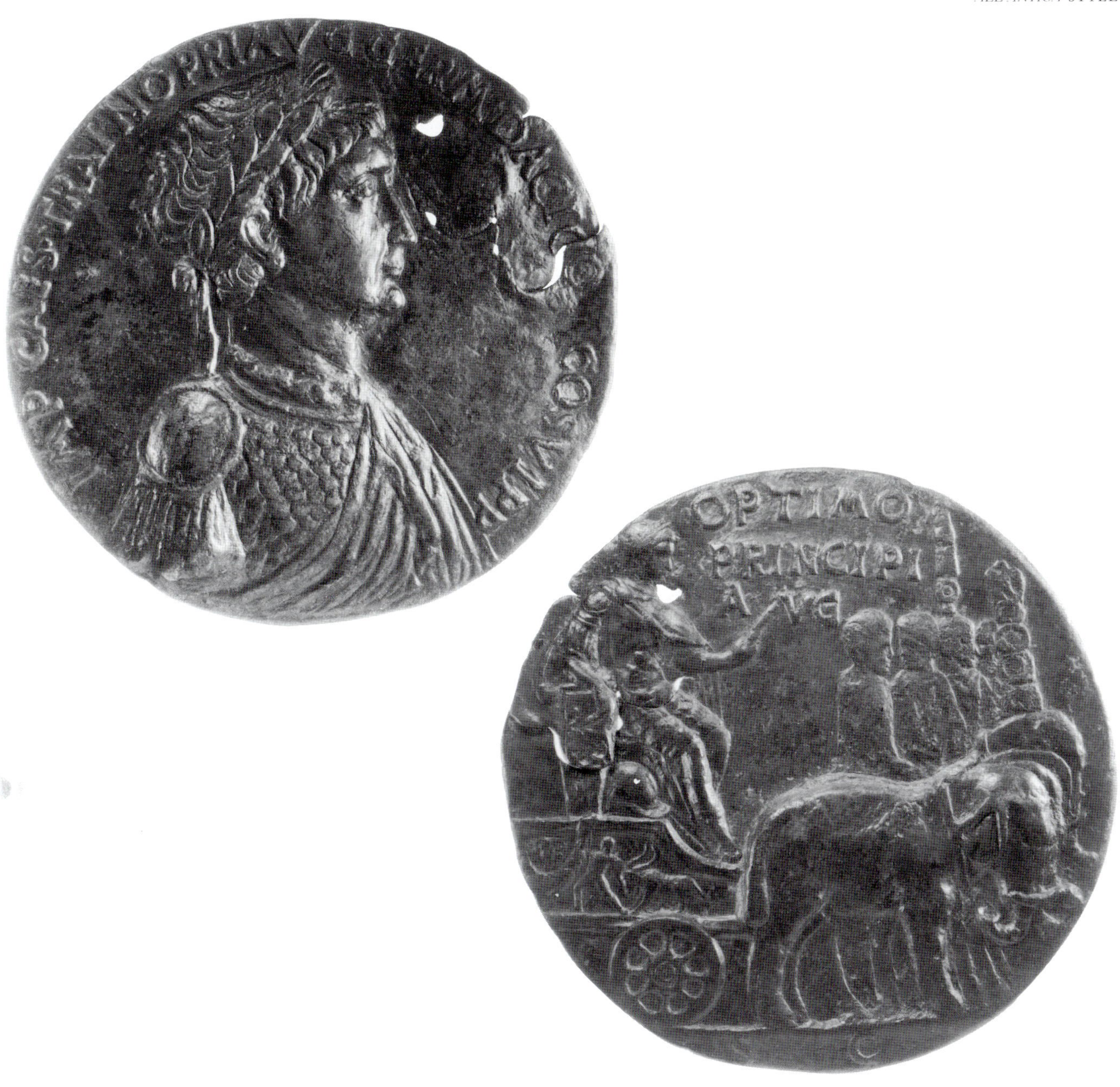

87 Antonio Averlino, called Filarete (or workshop), portrait medal of Emperor Trajan; cast bronze; Rome, *c.*1435–45, Bibliothèque nationale de France, Paris

Paris in 1402 from a Florentine merchant. The appearance of two specimens of Heraclius in a 1432 inventory of the goods of Marquis Nicolò d'Este shows that casts circulated in Italy from an early date, by which time they may have considered authentically ancient. With these in mind, then, Pisanello's medals might have looked *all'antica* to the satisfaction of his contemporaries.

The medals depicting ancient emperors modelled during Pisanello's lifetime and just after his death by Filarete (and his workshop) and Cristoforo di Geremia are similarly large and cast. By virtue of their subject matter, however, they are significantly iconographically closer to ancient coin prototypes than Pisanello's. Filarete, trained by Ghiberti, made medals of four Roman emperors and of the empress Faustina the Elder, based on portrait roundels he had inserted into the frame of the doors to St Peter's.[134] They may be used as

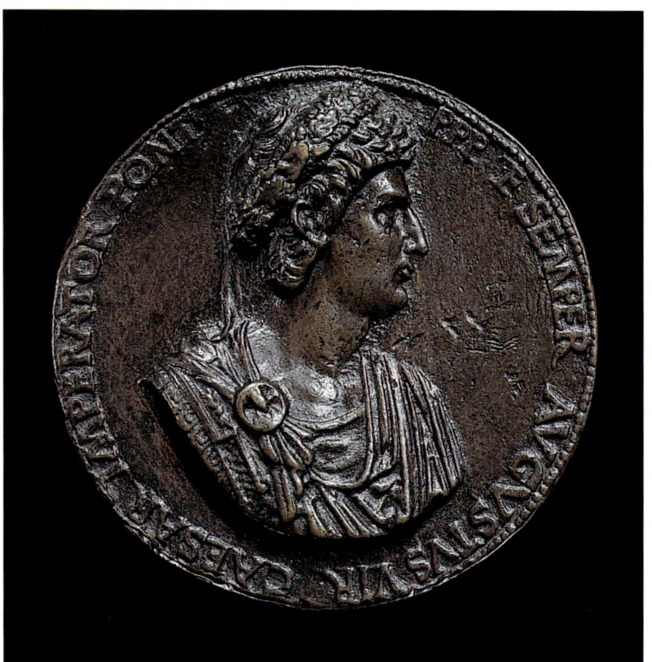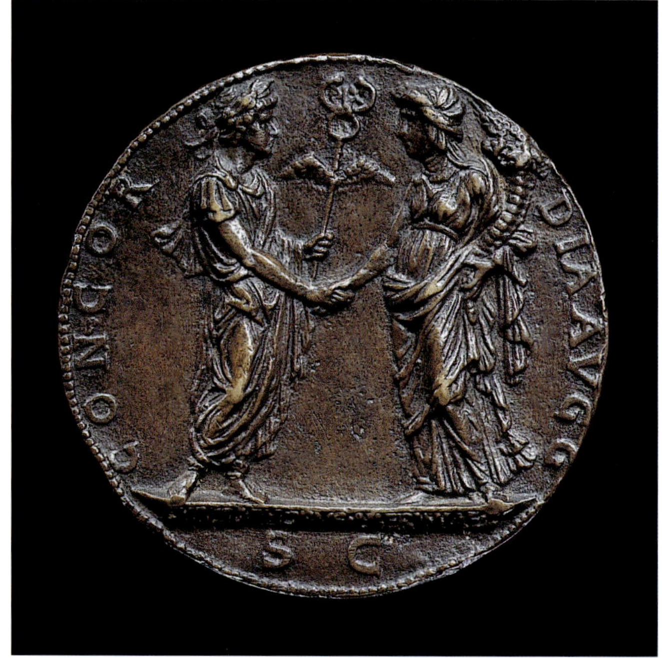

a measure of the degree of philological accuracy achieved by this first generation of goldsmith-antiquarians. Many of the Latin legends are blundered. And, as with Pisanello's medals, the sources for their reverse imagery are an eclectic mix of the sculptural and the numismatic. On his medal of Nero, for example, Filarete illustrated an episode in the life of the emperor of a kind that would never have been commemorated by an ancient coin: the suicide of Seneca (fig. 86).[135] The reverse shows the emperor calmly contemplating a naked Seneca standing in an elaborately *all'antica* vase, the bath in which he cut his wrists. While the figure of Nero is taken from a coin image, the Seneca has a well-known sculptural source. Filarete's references sometimes appear more learned. The portrait of Trajan is close to that on his coinage (fig. 87). One cannot, however, find the reverse, a chariot drawn by elephants, among the coins of Trajan, but it cannot be a coincidence that he took as his model a coin of the emperor's sister, Marciana.[136] Cristoforo di Geremia made a single medal of Constantine, whose exact date cannot be determined and in which the proportions of the figures are closer to their numismatic sources (fig. 88). However, although it has a reverse illustrating Concordia, more or less precisely copying coin types, the portrait was derived from an ancient sculpture found in the Baths of Constantine and sited on the Capitol.[137]

Both Filarete and Cristoforo also made commemorative medals of their contemporaries. Filarete's medal of his intimate friend Francesco Filelfo can probably be dated to 1447 (see fig. 5).[138] On its reverse is a Mercury in much the same pose as the little nude youth pulling at a goat on the triumphal car on the reverse of Filarete's medal of Trajan. A motif derived from ancient gems, this is one of the least authentically numismatic parts of the Trajan, but nevertheless it was a motif that Filarete had used in an *all'antica* object, giving it a legitimacy in this more modern context. Cristoforo's large cast portrait medal of Alfonso of Aragon (fig. 89) is particularly close in the arrangement of head and shoulders to his medal of Constantine.[139] The Bellona on the reverse has almost the same draperies and posture as the Mercury on the Constantine Concordia reverse. Another medal of his

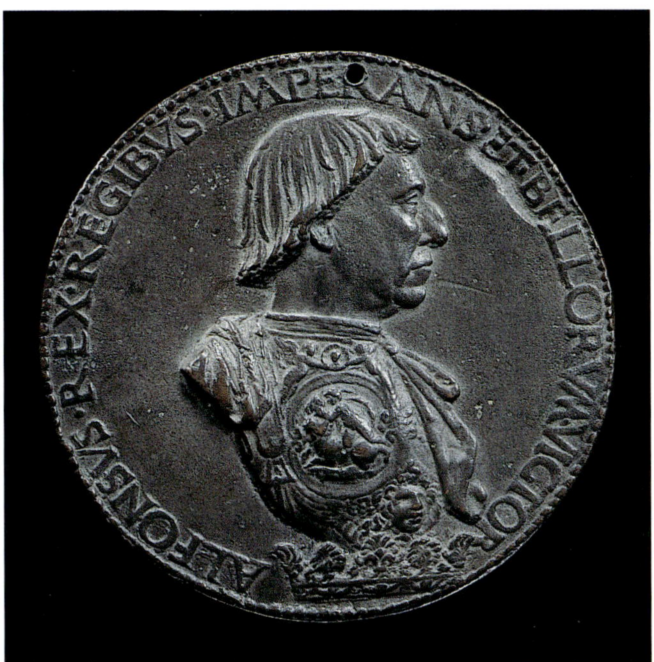
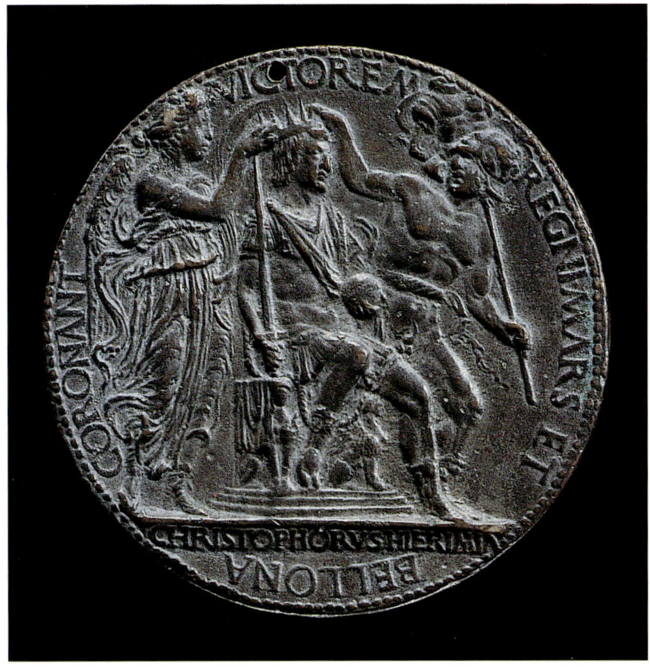

89 Cristoforo di Geremia,
portrait medal of Alfonso
of Aragon; cast bronze;
Naples or Rome, 1456–8.
The British Museum,
London

employer, Lodovico Trevisan, has a sculptural triumphal procession on the reverse, which
Mantegna must have known (fig. 90, see fig. 73);[140] and his various portraits of Paul II,
from whom Cristoforo received payment for foundation medals in 1469, get closer in size
to the coins on which they are based.[141] Cristoforo was the uncle of another maker of cast
medals, who – revealing his ambitions – called himself Lysippus the Younger (see fig. 31),
and whose range of antiquarian references included funerary sculpture, inscriptions, and
elegant lapidary epigraphy, as well as coins themselves.[142]

In the Gonzaga territories of Mantua and Sabbionetta, from the 1480s onwards, the
forms and styles of medals by the goldsmith-trained sculptor Pier Jacopo Alari Bonacolsi
(who always signed himself, self-consciously, Antico) and Gian Cristoforo Romano
became ever more linguistically correct. Their medals were still cast but were much crisper,
imitating the struck appearance; and were smaller, much closer in size to ancient bronze
coins than many of their predecessors. It is true that Antico, famous more for his bronze
statuettes than his medals, which he made only at the beginning of his career, continued to
employ non-numismatic, primarily sculptural, sources.[143] Gian Cristoforo, however,
became one of the first to develop a truly *all'antica*, properly derived numismatic language

90 Cristoforo di Geremia,
portrait medal of Cardinal
Lodovico Trevisan (also
called Scarampi or
Mezzarotta); cast bronze;
Rome, 1461–5.
The British Museum,
London

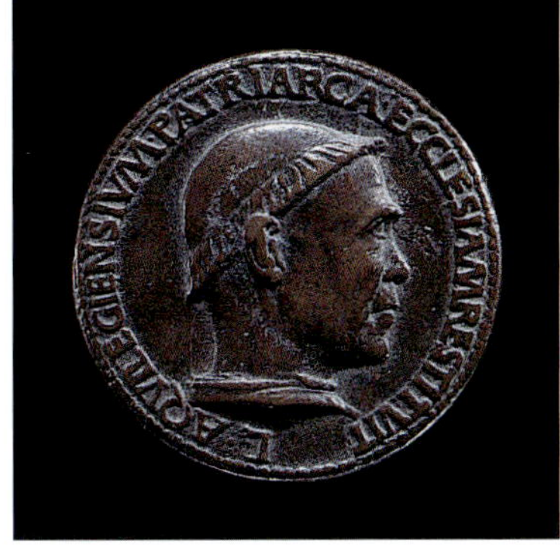
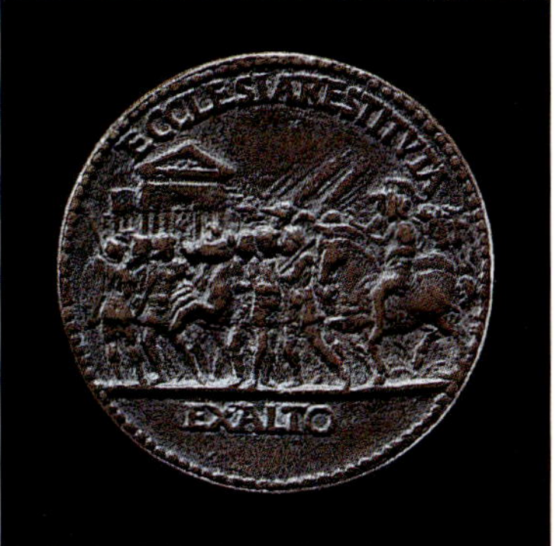

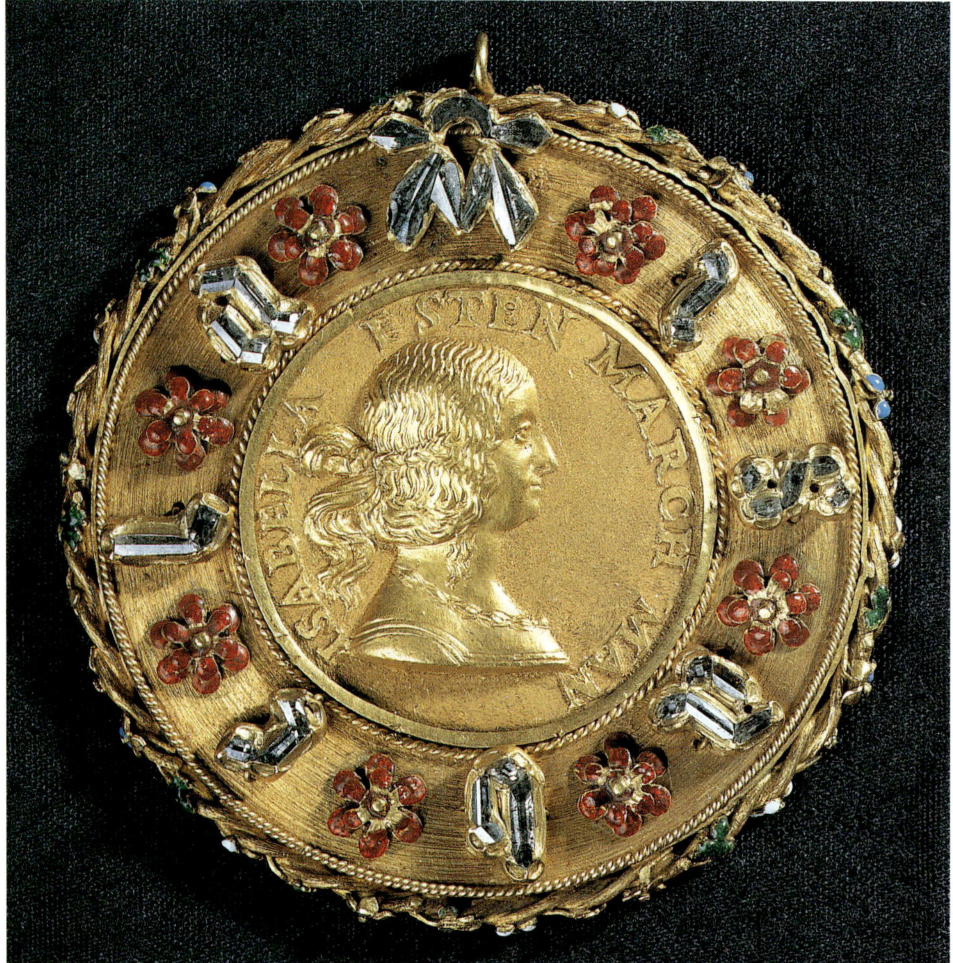

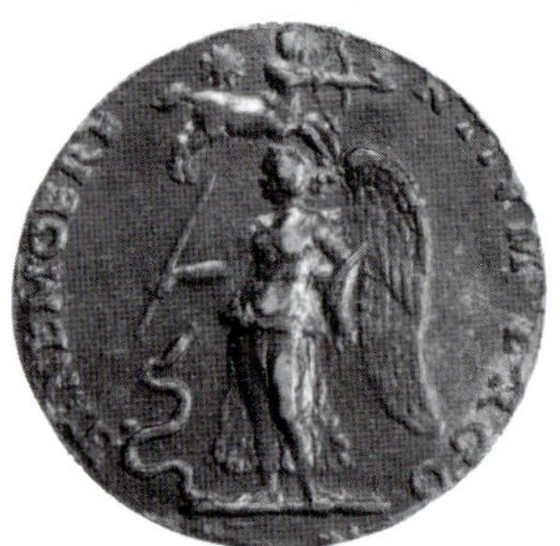

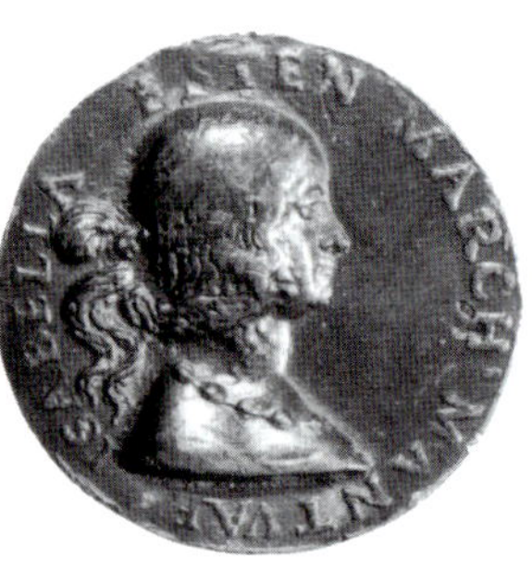

91 Gian Cristoforo Romano, portrait medal of Isabella d'Este (obverse); cast and chased gold, in enamelled frame set with precious stones; Mantua, 1498–*c.*1507. Kunsthistorisches Museum, Vienna

92 Gian Cristoforo Romano, portrait medal of Isabella d'Este; cast lead; Mantua, 1498. The British Museum, London

for the Renaissance medal. He was an artist of some range, commissioned to carve large works in stone, including tombs and portrait busts, but also to model and cast smaller objects – commemorative medals – in both jeweller's gold and *all'antica* bronze. His eclecticism of genre, type and medium is directly paralleled by his activities as agent and appraiser. Gian Cristoforo cast a medal of Isabella d'Este in 1498 (fig. 92). The piece was widely distributed, especially among appreciative scholars and poets, and a spelling mistake in the Latin of the first generation of casts was quickly corrected. Isabella's own elaborately chased gold specimen was displayed in her *grotta* next to an ancient cameo of Augustus and Livia, mounted in the same kind of jewelled and nielloed frame (fig. 91). The piece was praised as revealing its subject's *ingegno*. Her *ingegno* was signalled by Gian Cristoforo's ingenious and unusual combination of various personifications (Peace, Nemesis and Victory) and astrological motifs from coins of Augustus, Claudius, Vespasian and Antoninus Pius.[144]

Caradosso is said by later sources to have engraved dies for striking medals, but though he is known to have worked at the papal mint in Rome (and therefore must have engraved dies for striking coins) none of his productions can now be identified.[145] Serbaldi, too, employed the technology for hardening the tools required to shape exceptionally hard porphyry stone and applied it to the iron or steel dies used to strike medals.[146] By doing so, they were probably able to combine the correctly ancient technique with *all'antica* numismatic style and motifs. This is certainly what the goldsmith Vettor di Antonio Gambello (Camelio), employed at the Venice mint from 1484, set out to do.[147] Identified by Vico as the first of his 'imitators', here was another jeweller with a knowledge of ancient coins and gems. In an inventory drawn up in January 1527 of the goods of Bernardino di Redaldi, dogal secretary, one finds numismatic material stored in three bags, including 'eighteen medals and three coins [*monede*] with certain accounts, the pawn of master Vettor, engraver [*intaiador*]'.[148] Nevertheless, his adopted soubriquet suggests that Camelio translated the Italian word for 'camel' into a rather inaccurate Latin word indicating his activities as a gem-engraver, the maker of cameos, and his style is as informed by gems as it is by (especially Greek) coinage. Certainly his impossibly youthful, *all'antica* self-portrait of 1508 has a 'Sacrifice' reverse that is strongly reminiscent of an intaglio design (fig. 93).[149]

The description by the Portuguese painter Francisco da Hollanda of his encounter in Rome with Valerio Belli in 1537 gives further clues as to the contemporary function of Vico's 'frauds':

Valerio da Vicenza was an old man, in good health and spirits, and a gentleman of fine culture; he was, moreover, the one man in the present time in Christendom who could rival the ancients in the art of carving medals in high or fairly high relief … Valerio … produced from beneath his velvet dress fifty medallions of purest gold, fashioned by his hand after the manner of ancient coins and so admirably done that they seemed to increase my respect for antiquity. They were struck from dies with marvellous skill. Among these medallions he showed one of Artemisia in the Greek manner, with the Mausoleum on the reverse side, and a Virgil in the Latin style, with pastoral scenes carved on the reverse, which took my fancy above all the rest. And thenceforth I esteemed Master Valerio a greater man than I had thought….[150]

The coins were deemed proof of his technical mastery. Belli's series of medals was started a decade at least before Francisco saw them. The majority represented personalities from ancient history and myth who could never have had coins struck in their name and image: poets and poetesses, generals and military heroes and the three philosophers Socrates, Plato and Aristotle (fig. 94).[151] Although many make learned reference to coin prototypes, they were not intended as forgeries. Indeed, the sophisticated audience who could afford Belli's precious metal product would surely have recognized that the source for his reverse of a medal of Aeneas (fig. 97) was Raphael's Vatican fresco *The Fire in the Borgo*, mediated through a print by Gian Jacopo Caraglio (fig. 96). But these coins were intended to look ancient, and Belli carried over his approach to his sole portrait of a contemporary. The dies for Belli's struck medal of Pietro Bembo were prepared in 1532. A letter survives revealing Bembo's concern that rather than being depicted nude on

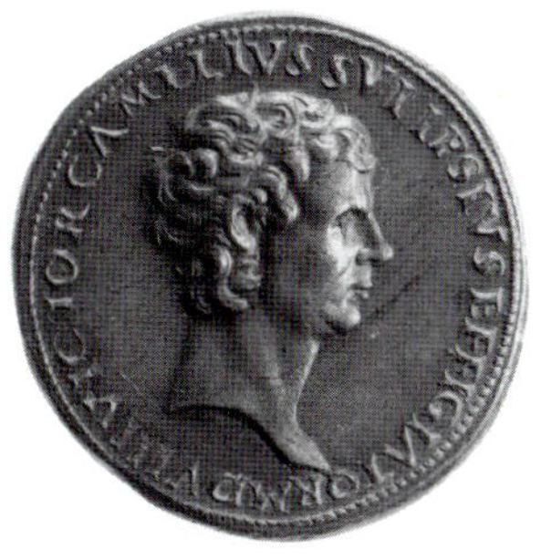
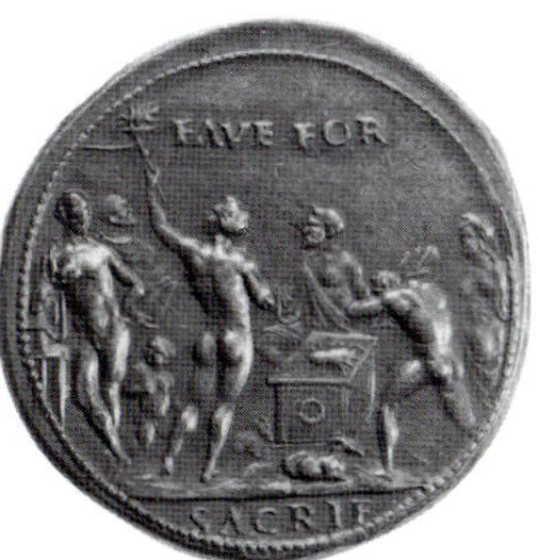

93 Vettor Gambello, called Camelio, self-portrait medal *all'antica*; struck bronze; Venice, 1508. The British Museum, London

the reverse, he should be given a little discreet drapery (fig. 95). On the front, Bembo, truncated at the neck, is depicted as an Augustus (albeit one with a rather curious bob).[152] On the reverse he is shown reclining on the ground in the pose of a river god, indulging, according to a famous description by Horace, in poetic thoughts. The stylistic journey the medal has undergone in slightly less than a century is demonstrated by a comparison of this figure – derived almost certainly from a coin – to the awkwardly proportioned reclining figure on the reverse of Pisanello's Leonello d'Este, which copies the pose of a statue, now on the Capitoline, converted into the personification of the River Tiber.

And here we return to Giovanni Cavino, whose 'forging' activities are so celebrated that modern numismatists have taken to calling all Renaissance Roman coin forgeries, cast or struck, 'Paduans' in his honour. Indeed, many of Cavino's 'coins' copy almost exactly their

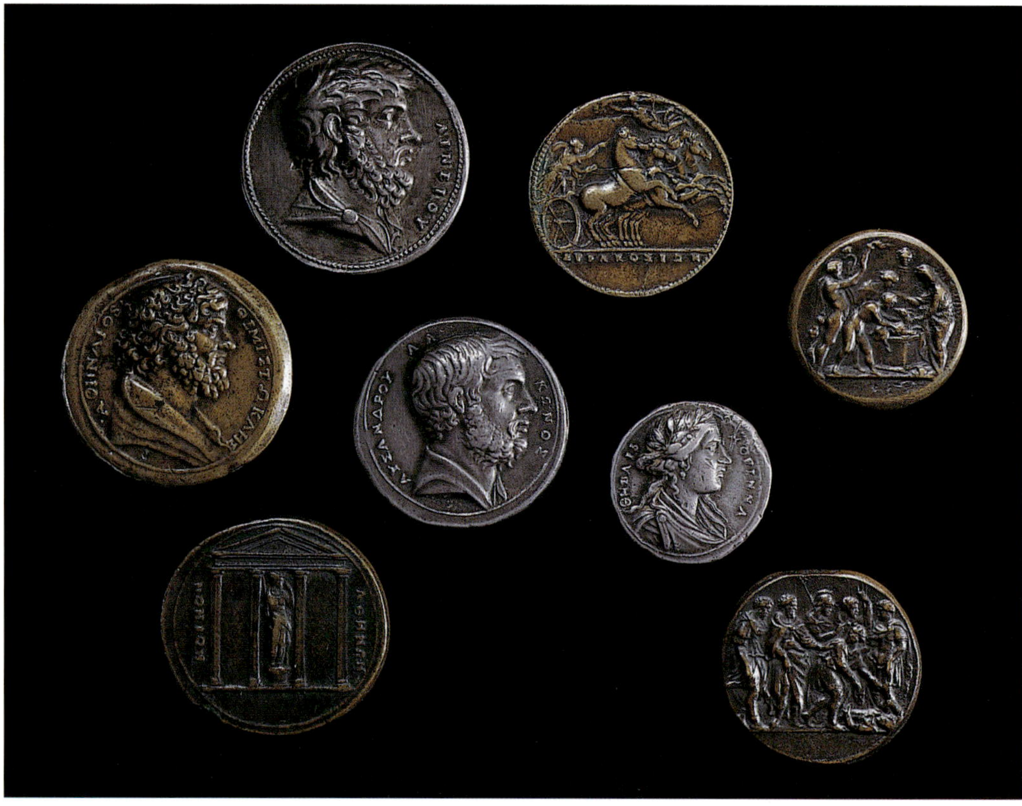

94 Valerio Belli, *all'antica* portrait medals: (clockwise from left) Themistocles, Arethusa (reverse), Iphigenia (reverse), Pompey (reverse), Corinna, Lysander, Solon (reverse); struck silver and cast bronze and silver after struck originals; Rome and Vicenza, *c.*1521–37. The British Museum, London

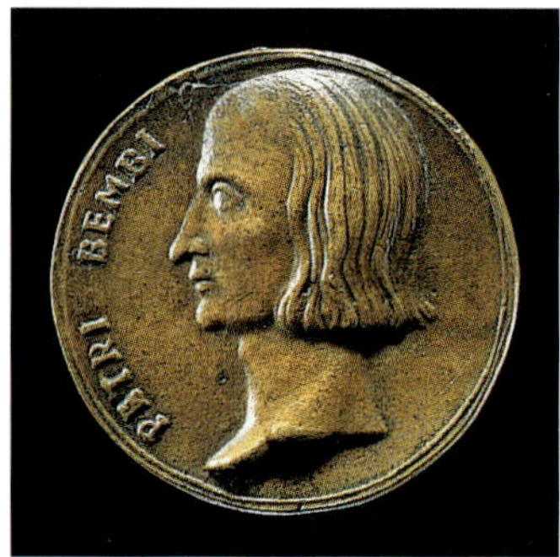
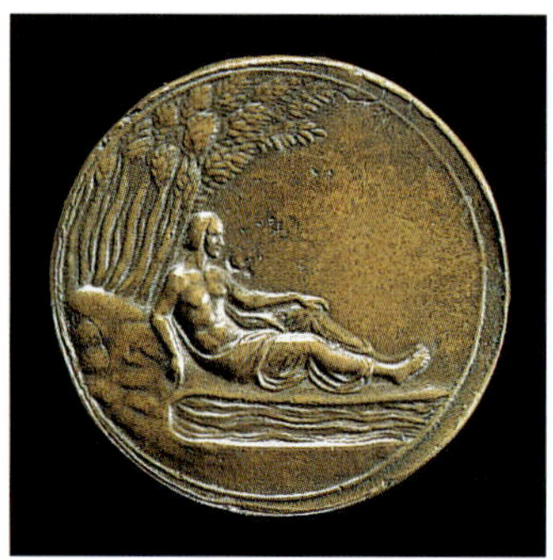

95 Valerio Belli, portrait medal of Pietro Bembo; struck bronze; Vicenza, 1532. The British Museum, London

96 Gian Jacopo Caraglio after
Raphael, *Aeneas and Anchises*;
engraving; Rome, *c.*1525.
The British Museum, London

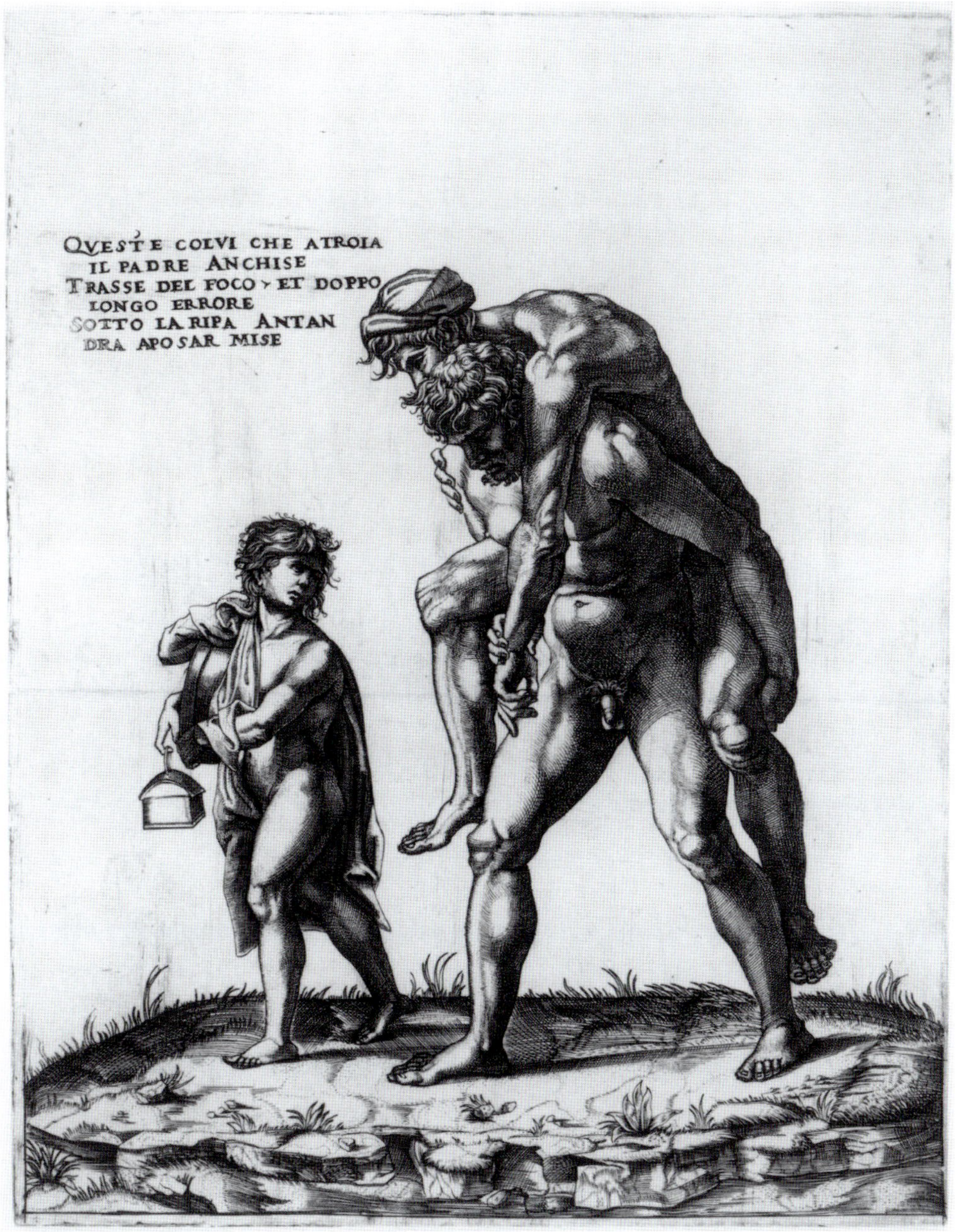

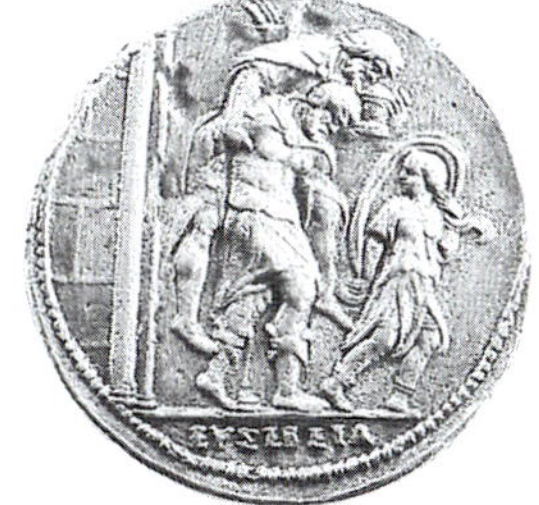

97 Valerio Belli, *all'antica* portrait medal of Aeneas (reverse);
cast silver after struck original; Rome, *c.*1525–37.
The British Museum, London

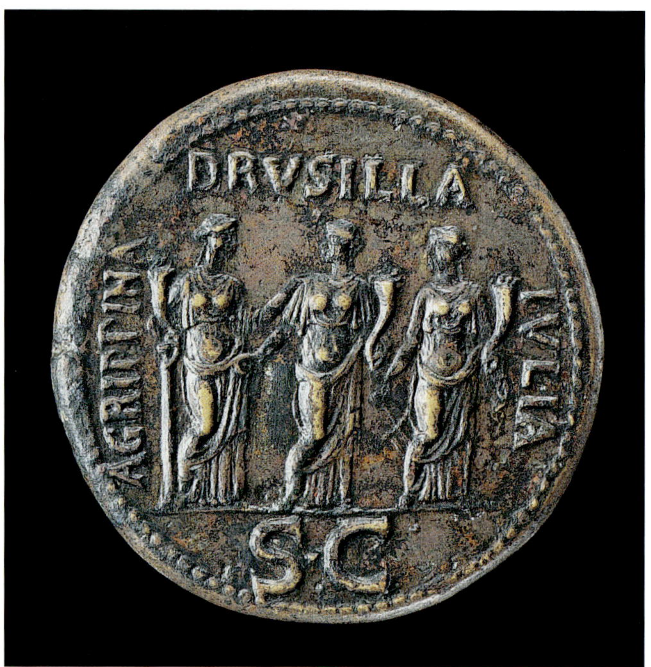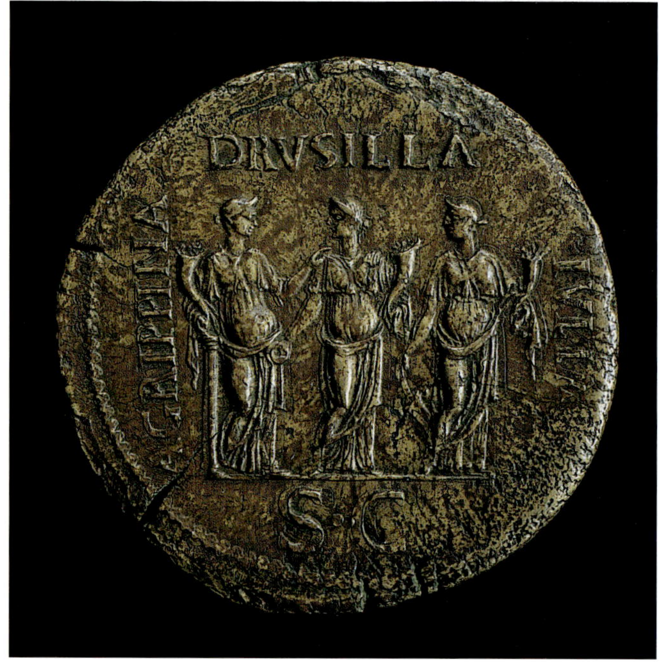

antique prototypes and were struck in bronze in such a way that their fabric is very close to that of ancient Roman coins. Thus pieces such as his faithful copies of the bronze coins of, for example, Augustus and Caligula (figs 98, 99) are problematic.[153] But his copies may not have been intended to deceive in the first instance. It is not clear if the differences between original and copy are deliberate or subliminal; certainly Cavino's depiction of the ill-fated sisters of Caligula on the reverse conform to the Renaissance ideal of female beauty – small breasts and a gently swelling abdomen – rather than the ancient Roman preference for large breasts and a small belly. Cavino was at the heart of the learned humanist community of Padua. It is inconceivable that scholarly collectors like the jurist Marco Mantova Benavides or the antiquarian and numismatist Alessandro Bassiano, both of whom commissioned commemorative medals from Cavino, would not have known that he had engraved dies for ancient coins. Cavino's technically more advanced die-struck 'frauds' would have been harder to recognize once they had left his hands but one must assume that he sold directly to his first clients and that, since they must have been fore-warned, his coins performed the same function as reproductions, his own skills assessed by their nearness to their prototypes.

However, any of Cavino's 'coins' struck in gold or silver of a size significantly larger than Roman *aurei* and *denarii* would have looked immediately wrong. Take, for example, his silver piece depicting Antinous with a reverse showing Bellerophon taming Pegasus (fig. 100), larger than any genuine silver Roman coin.[154] It is true that the portrait is very like those on coins struck in the second century by Hadrian to commemorate the death of his lover, but its reverse, an image derived from the 'Praxiteles' *Dioscurus* (see fig. 65), cannot be found among authentic issue. The fact that, in addition, the portrait of Antinous has a distinct resemblance to the head of the Montecavallo sculpture suggests that Cavino may have been using this piece to make an antiquarian point about the date or identity of the sculpture. Here again is an amalgam of learned references, the equivalent of a piece of humanist prose, to be deconstructed by a learned collector rather like a text. It was

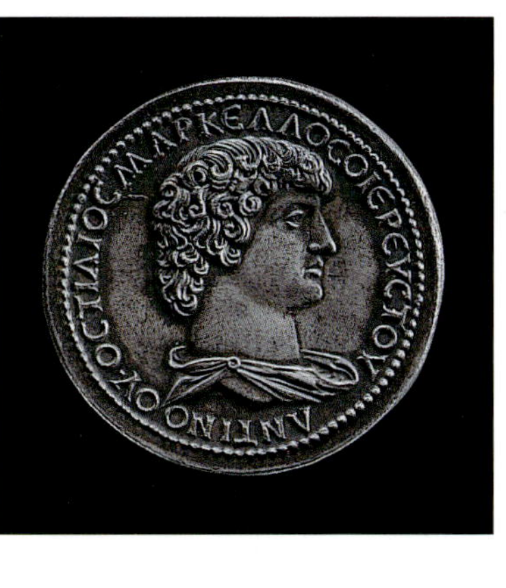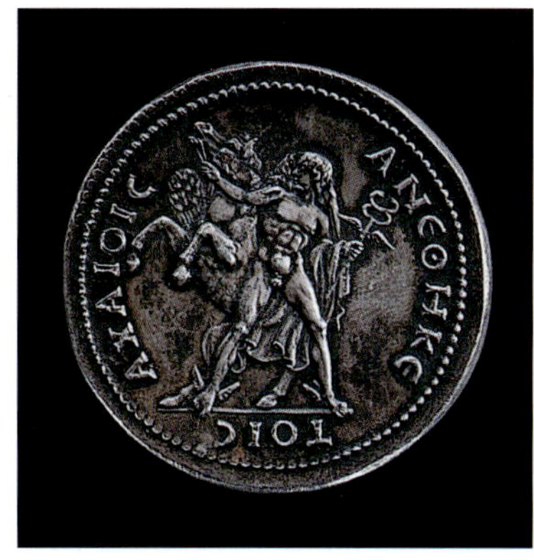

100 Giovanni Cavino, medal of Antinous; struck silver; Padua, *c.*1530–40. The British Museum, London

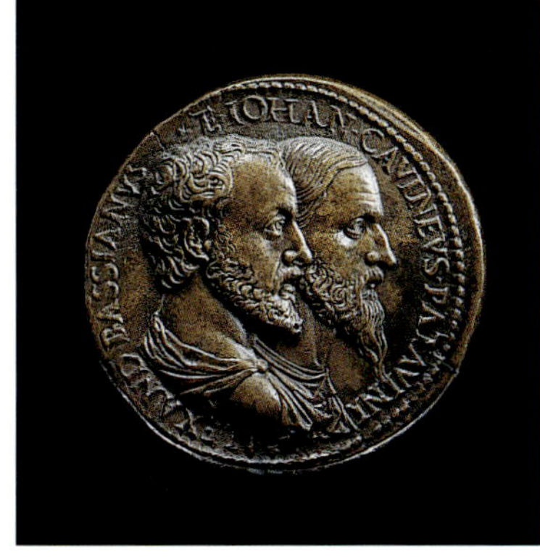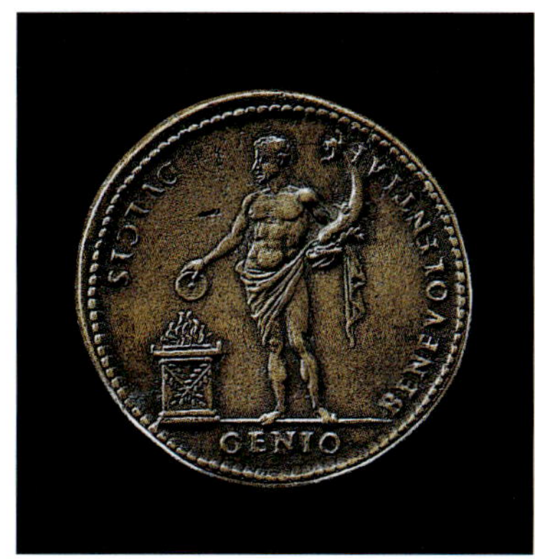

101 Giovanni Cavino, portrait medal with self-portrait and portrait of Alessandro Bassiano; struck bronze; Padua, *c.*1535–40. The British Museum, London

designed to transmit not only its author's consummate technical skills as an engraver but also his scholarly credentials.

Cavino engraved dies of many of his scholarly contemporaries in Padua, and of visitors to the university town, some of whom must have been among the buyers of his 'ancient' coins. The reverses are frequently adapted from the dies he used for ancient coins. Cavino portrayed himself with his Paduan friend and adviser, the pioneering numismatist Alessandro Bassiano, and this self-portrait medal advertises his approach to the medals of contemporaries.[155] They both wear *all'antica* tunics, and the Genius figure – the 'spirit of benevolence' – on the reverse comes probably from a coin of Nero (although the dolphin is an odd addition to the prototype). But, more than that, the medal was often struck without using the customary restraining collar, so that the metal disc (the same size as a Roman bronze coin) on which the jugate portraits are struck has splayed and cracked in the manner of a Roman coin (fig. 101). Their hair and beards are cut with the dry precision that Cavino employed on his 'Roman' coins. At last we encounter a proper combination of ancient technique, and ancient numismatic language, accurately applied to the type of objects from which they were derived.

Sculpture in bronze and marble: authenticity and invention

The imitation of the antique could take different forms. Medals and engraved gems remained so closely tied to their intellectual roots that it is scarcely surprising if their authors felt the need to pursue ever-increasing philological purity. But this literalism was not desired of every kind of object. In his book *On Painting* Alberti made a distinction between the finicky techniques of gem-engravers and the greater artistic ambition of painters: 'Galen, the doctor, writes that in his time he saw carved on a ring Phaeton drawn by four horses whose reins, breasts and feet were distinctly seen. Our painters leave this sort of fame to the sculptors of gems, for they are engaged in greater fields of praise….'[156] Indeed, Vasari reported Francesco Squarcione's condemnation of the St Christopher frescoes in the Ovetari chapel by his former pupil Mantegna, 'because in making them he had studied antique sculpture from which it is impossible to learn to paint perfectly because stones always retain their hardness.'[157] This may, though, have been a fiction designed to sustain a later view, and, notwithstanding the *Triumphs*, in many of his pictures, portraits and religious subjects, Mantegna made every effort to transform his sources. It is clear that while some patrons may have expected antiquarian fidelity, others wanted works in which the artist had assimilated but reinvented his sources, pictures and sculptures that remained identifiably rooted in the proper study of the antique but which were inventively modern. These were intended as pieces that followed Seneca's oft-repeated precepts of *imitatio*: works in which visual *exempla* had been transformed, as bees turn nectar into honey.[158]

Thus when Cristoforo Landino, writing in about 1480, identified the Florentine sculptor Donatello as a 'great imitator [*imitatore*] of the ancients', this does not turn him into a literal copyist.[159] For Sabba da Castiglione the modern was, by definition, less desirable than the ancient, but certain modern works were more than acceptable if they lived up to the standards set by ancient artists. In 1518–19 he described 'the adornments of the house', stating that some

people adorn their houses with antiquities, such as heads, torsos, busts and antique statues – of marble or of bronze. But because good ancient [works] are not only rare but also unobtainable without the greatest difficulty and expense, they therefore adorn them with the works of Donatello, who in both carving and casting can be compared with any ancient Greek sculptor, as if he were Phidias or Praxiteles, or he may even have been a better master than them, of greater talent [*di più alto ingegno*] as his divine works in stone and bronze in Florence prove … or with the works of Michelangelo, the glory of our time in both carving and painting … These two, even though they are modern, can be deservedly mentioned among the most important ancient Greeks.[160]

The praise directed at these two sculptors shows that they were thought to have moved beyond mere imitation, to have absorbed prescriptions for literary *inventio*, and applied them to the visual. Only through talented invention, through thought, could they match Filelfo's description of the *Dioscuri*.

This tension between the sometimes conflicting desires for antiquarian authenticity and artistic inventiveness is best illustrated in the field of sculpture. Here, unlike figurative painting, artists had precise models, small bronzes and larger marbles, to follow. Once again, sculptors could learn the sculptural language of antiquity as agents, restorers and copyists. Many collectors wanted their antique sculpture whole, ordering the replacement of missing heads and limbs. Stone-carvers were the obvious candidates for such work.[161] However, since dealers in coins and gems were often goldsmiths and since they handled other antiquities, it was natural that they might extend their restoration activities to larger-scale objects. Goldsmiths certainly were asked on occasion to 'finish' very large sculptures.

In June 1468 Cristoforo di Geremia, 'familiar [member of the household] of our father, the pope [Paul II]', received the considerable sum of 300 gold florins for his restoration of the bronze equestrian statue of Marcus Aurelius (fig. 102).[162] Vasari tells of the restoration of two marble figures of Marsyas, one white, the other red, placed in the Medici Palace garden by Cosimo de' Medici and his grandson Lorenzo. One was by a specialist in sculpture, the other by a goldsmith who turned to sculpture some time into his career. The white marble was thought to have been restored by Donatello. Although it is not unlikely that the sculptor undertook such tasks, it has been suggested that the restoration of what might be 'his' Marsyas, a piece with a Medici provenance in a pinkish marble, 'white' perhaps in comparison to its red companion, may in fact have been the work of another sculptor, Mino da Fiesole.[163] Andrea del Verrocchio, on the other hand, was certainly responsible for the restoration of the other, red stone Marsyas; the Medici were billed for his work on 'the red nude' by his brother after the sculptor's death. It is suggestive, given the dealing activities of so many goldsmiths, that there has been no agreement as to how, when or from whom Verrocchio learned how to carve stone. Trained as a goldsmith in the late

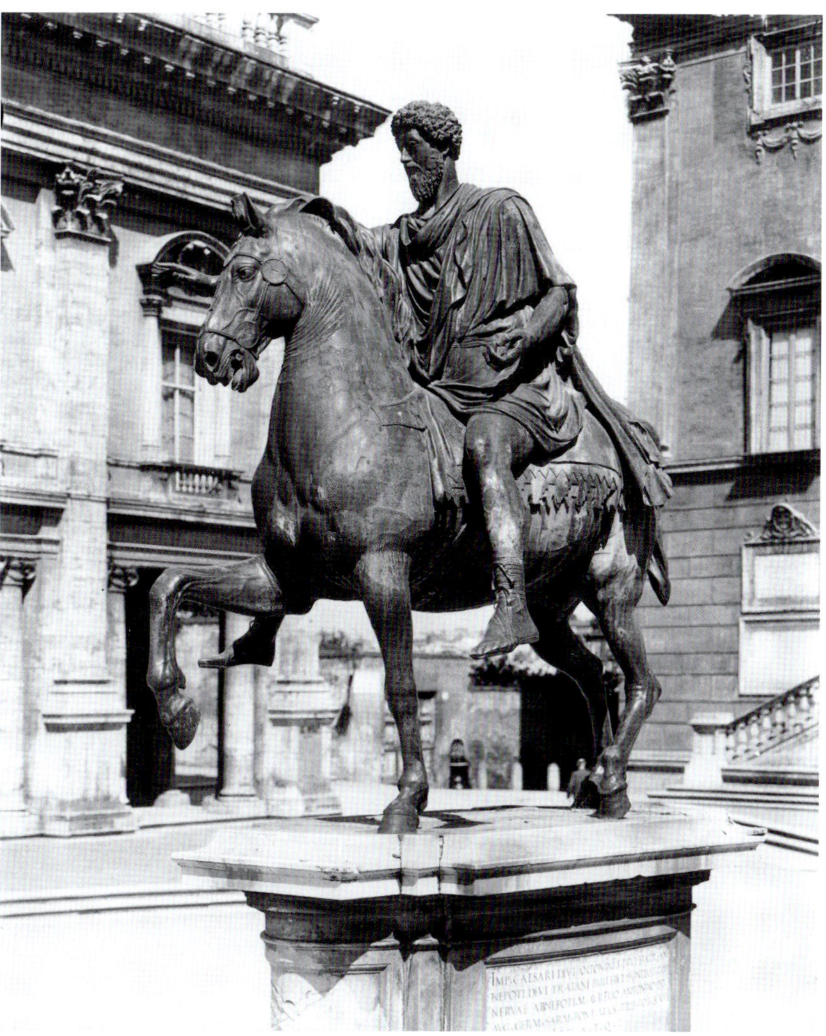

102 Equestrian portrait of Emperor Marcus Aurelius; bronze; Roman, *c.*176 AD. Musei Capitolini, Rome

1450s and early 1460s, successively by Antonio Dei and Francesco di Luca Verrocchio (from whom he took his name), there is no record of any time spent in mature apprenticeship to a practising sculptor. Perhaps restoration was part of the goldsmith-dealer's armoury and perhaps, as was to be the case with Benvenuto Cellini, Verrocchio learned how to carve stone by learning to restore.

It is certainly the case that at least one other goldsmith-sculptor, who worked primarily in metal, restored marble sculpture. Antico was chiefly celebrated as the sculptor of bronze statuettes, and the techniques he employed to cast and part-gild these bronzes shows that he had a goldsmith's training.[164] Nevertheless, a large part of his job in the Gonzaga service was the restoration of ancient works in stone, particularly for Isabella d'Este. He was another who acted as agent and assessor for the Gonzaga in the purchase of antiquities and he proved his capability as a restorer on one of several trips to Rome after 1495 by his work on the *Dioscuri* of Montecavallo (see figs 64, 65). He was not the first to attempt their restoration – one or both had been tackled in 1470 by Leonardo Guidotius on the orders of Paul II[165] – but Antico's later intervention is indicated by the signature carved on the back of the supporting pier of the 'Praxiteles' *Dioscurus* (see fig. 65), now partly worn away and reading 'ANTICVS MAN[T]VANVS R[E]F[ECIT]' (remade it).[166] Although it is not visible from the ground, this signature shows how significant, symbolically and practically, such work was in the eyes of both the artist and his contemporaries. The particular contribution of the restorer was indeed recognized as a crucial ingredient in the 'improvement' of a damaged antiquity. The style of additions had to be visually consistent with the presumed original appearance of the ancient work, but a certain licence was granted to make it better even than when new. In May 1506 Antico wrote to Isabella:

I send the two heads to your Ladyship, which I restored [*conzai*] several days ago, and again I remind your Ladyship that you should ensure that those who handle them should do so with diligence ... To the first I added the nose of marble and also an eye and some parts of the drapery. To the other I added [those parts] which you see, with a compound [*una compositione*] that will last for a thousand years....

Isabella's reply shows how much she believed the works to have been improved:

We have received the heads, which you have restored so well that we believe that the original sculptor did not shape and carve them as well in the first place. In this one recognizes the perfection of your art....[167]

When Antico made bronzes he made them with all the attention to philological accuracy we have come to expect from the goldsmith. The genesis of the independent bronze statuette was another manifestation of the desire to reproduce antiquities. Some of the earliest copy famous statues. Not even Isabella d'Este wielded sufficient power to obtain antiquities of the symbolic importance of the *Dioscuri*, the portrait of Marcus Aurelius or the *Laocoön*, and artists were quick to spot an opportunity that might be not merely lucrative but also further bolster their reputations as antiquarians. Filarete is usually thought to have modelled, in about 1440–5, the first bronze reduction of a famous ancient sculpture, the Marcus Aurelius, to which, when he presented it some twenty years later to Piero de' Medici, he appended a self-consciously antiquarian dedicatory inscription, identifying the subject (wrongly) as the emperor Commodus Antoninus.[168]

Copies of celebrated ancient sculptures continued to be made in large numbers at the end of the fifteenth century. In the 1496 inventory of the goods of Gianfrancesco Gonzaga, it is discovered that the lord of Sabbionetta kept in his study at least three bronzes that were recognized as copying antiquities: a Marcus Aurelius ('the horse of San Giovanni [Laterano] with Antonius upon it') and, separately listed, 'a Giant from Montecavallo' and its companion, 'a horse of Montecavallo made of bronze' – one of the *Dioscuri*.[169] That these bronze statuettes were viewed primarily as methods of bringing great works of sculpture into the home is indicated by the Venetian Marcantonio Michiel's description of the bronzes in the collection of Marco Mantova Benavides at Padua: 'The little figures of bronze are modern by various masters and they derive from the antique, such as the seated Jove.'[170] In March 1517 it was suggested in a letter to Alfonso I d'Este, Duke of Ferrara, that Antonio Elia, who was in the employ of his brother Cardinal Ippolito in Rome, should be commissioned to fabricate wax models for reproduction in bronze, stating that Elia was already famous for his reproduction of the *Laocoön* as well as of 'other antique objects considered good by Caradosso and other good masters'.[171] Similarly, the energies of Antico were almost entirely directed at 'completing' replicas of ancient statuary in ways that demonstrated his antiquarian know-how by reference

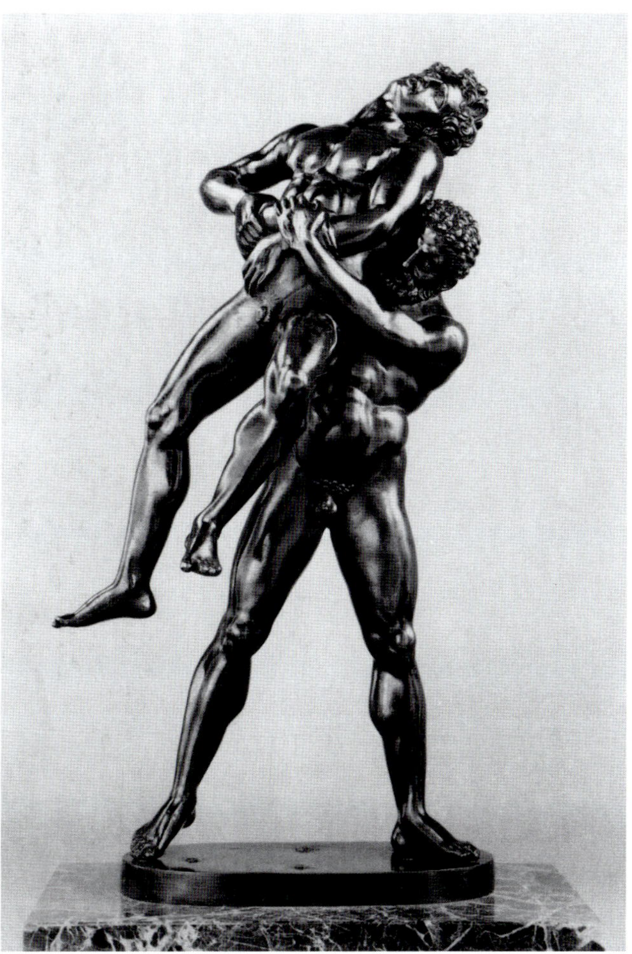

103 Pier Jacopo Alari Bonacolsi, called Antico, *Hercules and Antaeus*; cast bronze with silvered eyes; Mantua, *c.*1500–11. Victoria and Albert Museum, London

to other surviving antiquities (fig. 103).[172] Antico's own creative interpolations are deliberately reduced, and Isabella termed his works *antichità*.[173] His approach was very similar in his bronze bust portraits, mostly of Roman emperors; the head, thought to represent the young Marcus Aurelius, now in the Getty Museum in Los Angeles (see the frontispiece), is, for instance, based on an ancient marble bust-type of the emperor in his youth, although the sculptor has added the rather peculiar moustache and sideburns.

Bronzes might also be made and seen as the modern equivalents of the many small bronze sculptures – those termed 'Corinthian' by Pliny – that survived from antiquity. Artists and owners were fired by the description by Statius of the artistry contained in a statuette of a resting *Hercules*, supposedly by Lysippus and owned by Alexander the Great: '… such dignity had the work, such majesty, despite its narrow limits. A god was he … small to the eye, yet a giant to the mind! … What precision of touch, what daring imagination the cunning master had, at once to model an ornament for the table and to conceive in his mind mighty colossal forms!'[174]

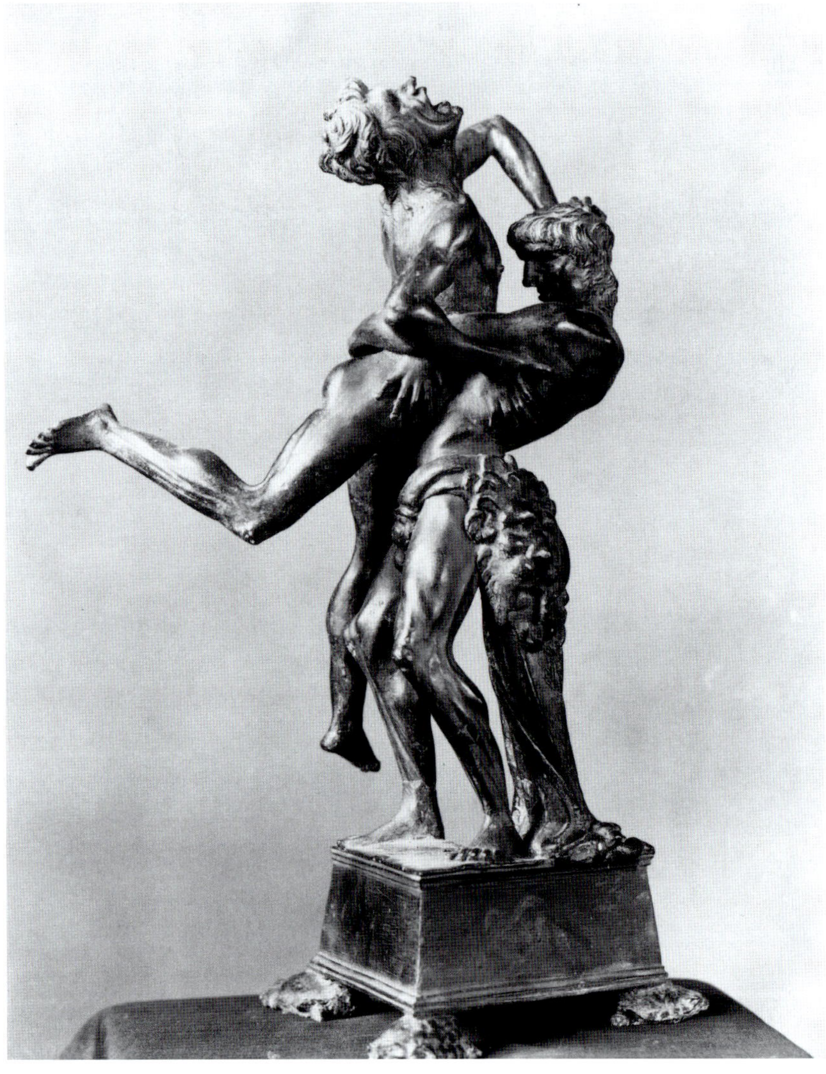

104 Antonio del Pollaiuolo, *Hercules and Antaeus*; cast bronze; Florence, *c.*1470–80. Bargello, Florence

105 Bertoldo di Giovanni (cast by Adriano Fiorentino), *Bellerophon Taming Pegasus*; cast bronze; Florence or Padua, *c.*1480–6. Kunsthistorisches Museum, Vienna

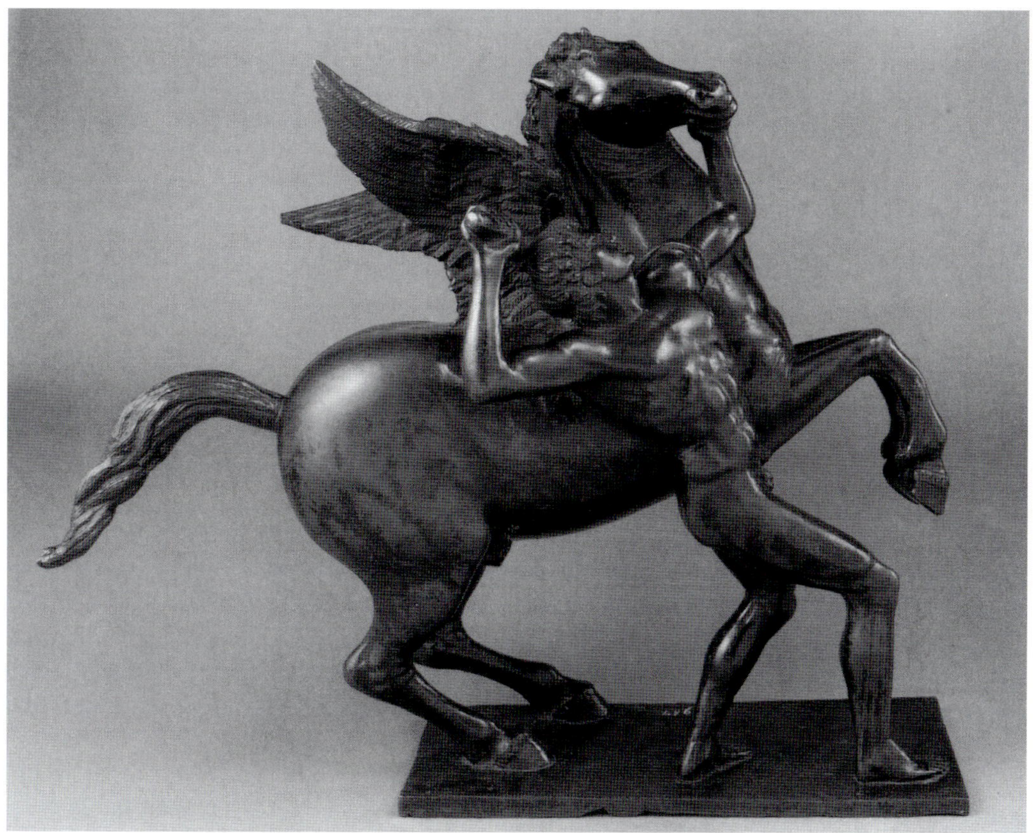

The Florentine practice was different. Although Lorenzo de' Medici is known to have owned ancient bronzes, including a *Hercules* excavated at Luni,[175] the antique was only a starting point for the bronzes by modern Florentines that he bought or commissioned, exercises in competitive artistry. The bronze sculptures made, from the mid-1470s, by the goldsmith Antonio del Pollaiuolo and the sculptor Bertoldo di Giovanni are radically different from Antico's exercises in antiquarian 'restoration'. Pollaiuolo, as a goldsmith and appraiser, was properly conversant with the antique and may have been responsible for the late-Quattrocento addition of the bronze figures of Romulus and Remus to the Etruscan bronze *She-Wolf* on the Capitol in Rome.[176] Even these, however, look more Donatellan than ancient and his own bronzes display an extraordinary inventive capacity. His *Hercules and Antaeus*, for example, shows the moment when the mythical hero overcame Antaeus, hitherto protected by his mother, Earth, by lifting him off the ground and squeezing him to death (fig. 104).[177] This is a free reworking of a subject known from antique sculptural representations. However, in a departure from type, Antaeus is turned belly to belly with Hercules in a murderous embrace. Their unclassical grimaces of pain and effort and their knotted musculature give the piece a feral, frenetic quality.

Bertoldo di Giovanni, the household artist of Lorenzo de' Medici, was used by his master as an appraiser of antiquities and a keeper of the Medici sculpture garden at San Marco. Some of his bronzes are deliberate attempts to achieve antiquarian accuracy. His *Battle* relief, one of the most highly valued modern objects owned by Lorenzo, sets out to

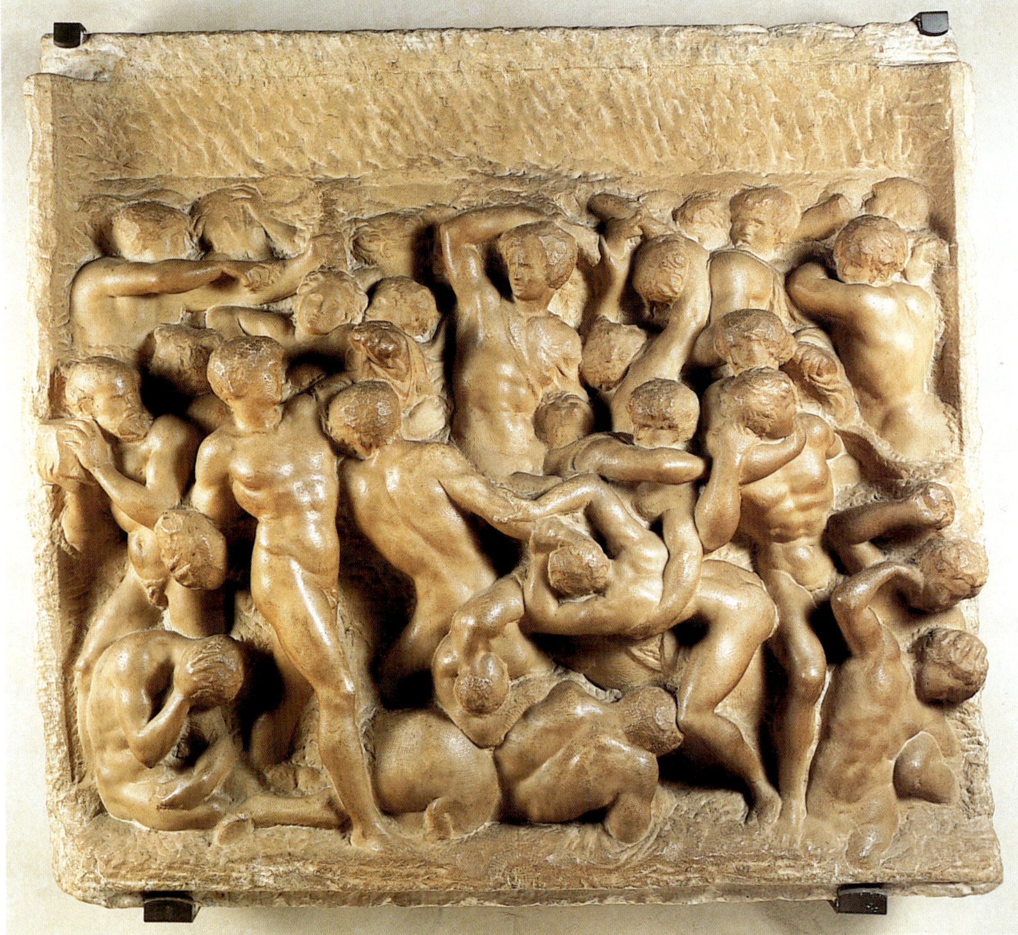

106 Michelangelo, *Battle of the Centaurs*; marble; Florence, *c.*1490–2. Casa Buonarroti, Florence

complete a badly damaged sarcophagus then, as now, in the Camposanto at Pisa. His *Bellerophon Taming Pegasus* (fig. 105) may not have been owned by the Medici (it was in Padua by 1521–43). As in the Pegasus reverse of Cavino's Antinous (see fig. 100), Bertoldo's starting point was the 'Praxiteles' *Dioscurus*. He also referred to ancient coins and gems, probably including a *Pegasus* belonging to Domenico di Piero that he had perhaps been able to inspect in Venice.[178] In other works, such as a mounted Hercules he executed for Ercole d'Este, the emphasis seems to have been placed on his own poetic powers. The work is *all'antica*, but there are no references to particular objects to dominate its overall impact as a modern, inventive work of art.

Bertoldo, therefore, could switch between idioms, depending on the nature of his commission. It was a skill he was to pass on to his most famous pupil, Michelangelo. Trained in the sculpture garden at San Marco, perhaps itself the site for Medici sculptural restoration, Michelangelo's precocious skills were immediately recognized, drawing him to the attention of Lorenzo de' Medici and Angelo Poliziano, a considerable antiquarian and the humanist tutor of Lorenzo's sons. Ascanio Condivi, Michelangelo's pupil and biographer, informs us that it was the latter who advised Michelangelo on the iconography for his powerful *Battle of the Centaurs* relief of about 1490–2 (fig. 106), an object intended both as an imitation of a sarcophagus relief and as a re-creation of Plutarch's description of the shield of Phidias's *Athena Parthenos*.[179]

Marble sculpture with classical subject matter was another revived medium for art objects, and Michelangelo's pioneering involvement in its production shows his rejection of antiquarian literalism to make pieces designed chiefly to show off his own artistic powers. After the *Battle of the Centaurs*, he went on to carve a *Sleeping Cupid*, now lost, fully in the round.[180] Its story parallels the episode of Serbaldi's gem. Michelangelo's sculpture, perfectly rendered in an antique idiom, became a 'fake', only to be reclaimed later as a modern masterpiece. Condivi dated the piece to late 1495 or early the following year: Michelangelo made 'a God of Love of marble, at the age of six, who lies in the pose of a man sleeping'.[181] It was then purchased for 30 ducats by a Florentine merchant resident in

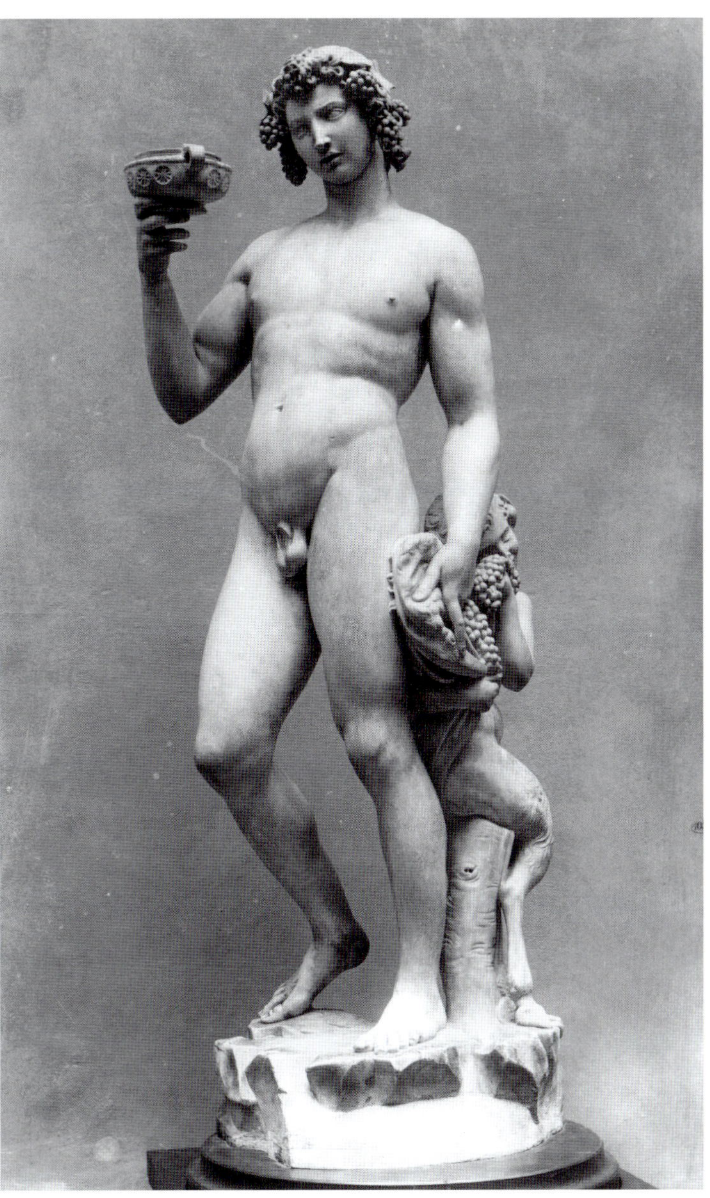

107 Michelangelo, *Bacchus*; marble; Rome, 1496–7. Bargello, Florence

Rome, Baldassare del Milanese, who dirtied the surface by burying it in a vineyard and then sold it on in Rome for 200 ducats as an antique 'of great price'. Different accounts impute greater or lesser degree of dishonesty to Michelangelo himself. Vasari, in the second edition of his *Lives*, followed Condivi, nominating Lorenzo di Pierfrancesco de' Medici, cousin of *Il Magnifico*, as the plot's instigator. The victim was Raffaele Riario, Cardinal of San Giorgio, who owned important antique statues. The fraud unmasked, the money returned, the piece was put back on the market. One of Isabella d'Este's correspondents in Rome described it as '… a little boy, specifically a Cupid, recumbent and asleep, resting on one hand … It is held by some to be antique and by others to be modern. Whichever is the case it is absolutely perfect.' A month later the same correspondent wrote:

That Cupid is modern and the master who made it has come here, although it is so perfect that everyone thought it antique. Now that it has been clearly established as modern, I believe that he will sell it at a lower price, but if your Ladyship does not want it, since it is not antique, I will say no more about it.[182]

Although Isabella did not pursue it then, she obtained the piece in 1502 and chose to set it up in her *grotta* as the modern counterpoint to an antique *Sleeping Cupid*, supposedly by Praxiteles, purchased on the advice of Gian Cristoforo Romano and restored by Antico.[183]

Vasari wrote that 'the Cardinal … did not escape blame for not recognizing the merit of the work'.[184] As a discriminating gentleman, he was clearly supposed to be able to distinguish between an ancient work and one created a matter of months before. Although neither Vasari nor Condivi suggest that Michelangelo set out deliberately to carve a counterfeit, the *Cupid* must nevertheless also have looked sufficiently authentic to suggest the deceit to Baldassare del Milanese or Lorenzo di Pierfrancesco, and its capacity to deceive was clearly seen as a mark of Michelangelo's success. Once the truth was out, the piece was reinterpreted in the way that it had been intended: as the demonstration piece of a modern artist showing he could rival an ancient sculptor. Riario took the point and, swallowing his pride, immediately employed the twenty-one-year-old artist – who had arrived in Rome to recover the *Cupid*, armed with letters of introduction from Lorenzo di Pierfrancesco – commissioning a marble *Bacchus* (fig. 107). This was a notably early example of revivalist classical statuary. It was made, according to the later, rather extreme statement of Francisco da Hollanda, 'for the purpose of fooling the Romans and the pope with its antique style'.[185] But it is more likely that Condivi, parroting the artist himself, is more accurate in his account of the artist's aims: to create a piece 'the form and aspect of which corresponds in every part to the intention of the ancient writers'.[186] Writers, not sculptors. Filelfo's description of the *Dioscuri* uses terms derived from Pliny; Phidias and Praxiteles had *ingenium* – innate talent, the personal ability to transform and create. It was a word that came up over and over again in connection with works of art. Thus, although the marble garden sculpture was an ancient medium, Michelangelo's own subjective and *ingegnoso* observation of fleshy insobriety is made very apparent. The extent to which *ingenium*, or *ingegno*, was perceived as a valuable and separately quantifiable element in works of art of all kinds will be seen in the next chapter.

Chapter Four

The Value of *Disegno*

Ingegno – derived from the Latin, *ingenium* – was a term (and a concept) that was frequently employed in the many humanist paeans of praise to artists and their works. For Filelfo, echoing earlier commentators, it was the transforming factor that raised the sculpted *Dioscuri* above the level of mere portrait records. The word is sometimes translated as 'intelligence' or 'intellect'. When applied to the beholder of a work of art, it often implies the ability to discern, to judge quality. It certainly contains all these notions. But *ingegno*, above all, was a virtue that could not be learned, a quality that could only be developed and exploited. As the etymology of the word suggests, it was something its possessor had to be born with, talent that was natural, innate and therefore entirely individual.

It was a virtue desirable not only for artists, but for their patrons. The social and intellectual elite, who used the term, were also expected to exhibit *ingegno* in their own political or scholarly activities. We have already seen that their possession of this particularly important virtue, as with so many others, could be displayed through the objects they acquired. Lodovico il Moro believed that the proper, educated appreciation of ancient sculpture signalled its owner's *ingegno*. The works of famous and heroicized artists could send the same message. Patrons needed employees whose talents would transmit their own; the Ferrarese poet Lodovico Carbone wrote, for example, that 'the merits of princes are reflected in the talents of their subjects'.[1] Thus mutually rewarding pacts were developed between artists and patrons. These were usually temporary, covering the purchase or commission of single works of art. Salaried artists at the courts of Naples and northern Italy were, however, expected to produce a series of 'masterpieces', of which could be said, as Francesco Gonzaga, Marquis of Mantua, did of Andrea Mantegna's *Triumphs of Caesar*, 'While they are the work of your hand and your *ingegno*, we nonetheless take glory in having them in the house.'[2] Some years earlier, in May 1478, Mantegna himself had written to Francesco's grandfather, Lodovico, demonstrating, not only his high regard for his own talents, but the manner in which he perceived them to be of use to a patron: 'When I decided to enter your service, I made it possible for you to say of yourself that you were in possession of something no other prince in Italy could boast of.'[3] Even in republican Florence, an individual as powerful as Lorenzo de' Medici required the services of an artist who would not only bolster his magnificence but would perform as his *ingegnoso* artistic mouthpiece. When Bartolomeo Dei reported the death of Lorenzo's household sculptor in 1491, he stated that 'Bertoldo, most worthy sculptor and the best maker of medals, who always with the magnificent Lorenzo did worthy things, died at Poggio two days ago', a clear indication of how Bertoldo di Giovanni's works were seen as essentially connected with Lorenzo. The letter continues: 'The loss is very great and [Lorenzo] is very much grieved, because there is not another in Tuscany, nor perhaps in Italy, of such noble talent and skill [*ingegno e arte*] in such things.'[4]

These twinned contrasts of inventive, intellectual gifts with their practical, skilful application (*ars* or *arte*) were derived from Petrarch's much-quoted pairing of Giotto's 'hand and talent' (*manus et ingenium*).[5] Once again it was a division that artists recognized and promoted themselves. Ercole de' Roberti, court artist in Ferrara under Ercole I d'Este, in a letter pleading his poverty, listed his only assets as 'my arm and the little virtue given me by God' (*le braxa, et quella pocho de vertù me ha dato dio*).[6] Indeed, painters, sculptors and goldsmiths, in raising their own status, adopted a range of social and intellectual strategies (including, as we have seen, their proclaimed antiquarianism), but it was most important that it could be demonstrated that their own work was predicated on the intellectual and inventive, as distinct from solely manual dexterity.

How was this factor to be recognized? The intellectual and the artisanal had in the first place to be made distinct from one another; *ingegno* had to be discernible from *arte*. The feature of the work that fulfilled these demands was *disegno*, for, if an artist's *ingegno* dictated his capacity to invent, *disegno* was its visible manifestation. This is, yet again, a word with a broad spectrum of meanings. It is often translated as 'design', but our modern word, used generally in an industrial context, is considerably narrower than the Renaissance term. During the fifteenth and sixteenth centuries *disegno* encompassed a wide range of meanings, covering a spectrum from intention or plan via design to drawing. The term's very fluidity implies that these three concepts or processes were understood as absolutely interdependent: drawing was an intellectual activity as much as (or sometimes more than) a physical act of putting pen, chalk or metalpoint to paper; here again we have a multiple meaning that embraces both thought and product.[7] It is true that the Sienese Francesco di Giorgio, equally adept as an engineer and architect, painter and sculptor, adapted a famous phrase of Vitruvius to identify *disegno* as an ingredient in artistry that he perceived as separate from *ingegno*: '… just as we see many who have doctrine [*dottrina*] and do not have *ingegno* and many who are endowed with *ingegno* and not doctrine, so many have doctrine and *ingegno* but do not have *disegno*'.[8] It is not absolutely clear from this passage whether he believed that *disegno* was something that could be learned, but for most of his contemporaries drawing represented the planning, the thinking stage of art production. This is the meaning of the word in the 1488 poem by Bettin da Trezzo, dedicated to the embroiderers of Milan:

> Those who choose silver and gold [threads], others who spin,
> Those who make embroideries and tapestries …
> And some [who make] table-covers for joyous people,
> And they who design with a tranquil mind [*chi designa cum mente tranquilla*].[9]

Here *disegno* was the cerebral element within a manufacturing process. This combination of the intellectual and the practical is found elsewhere. In the 1440s, when the goldsmith-sculptor Lorenzo Ghiberti wrote his *Commentaries*, he called *disegno* the 'foundation and theory' of painting and sculpture.[10] Thus he lays the ground for Vasari's statement that *disegno* was 'the father of our three arts, architecture, painting and sculpture, deriving from the intellect'.[11] It is revealing that Vasari places architecture first in the list, since the functional division between the roles of architect and builder had been long appreciated. However, there was no training for architecture as such. It was recognized that its successful practice was dependent on the architect's knowledge of the rules of classical ornament, orders and proportion, and his understanding of the principles of harmony, perspective, mathematics and engineering. The lengthy list of painters, sculptors, goldsmiths and wood-workers who turned to architecture is headed by Giotto.

Just as important to the development of the notion of artistic *ingegno* were the divisions of labour common to the various manufacturing processes for certain categories of magnificent art object: tapestries and other hangings, wooden inlay (*intarsia*) and, in particular, objects made of gold, silver and precious or semi-precious stones. We have seen that contemporary diarists, chroniclers and letter-writers took almost as much account of tapestries, gold and silver as they did of churches and palaces, and more than they did, for example, of paintings; one *litterato*, Gasparo Visconti, even addressed a sonnet to a *balasso* – a ruby mounted in an ear-ring – belonging to Beatrice d'Este, Duchess of Milan.[12] These art forms were, after all, by far the more expensive. Tapestry manufacture, for example, was highly labour-intensive, but the greatest costs derived from the prices of the raw materials: silk and gold and silver threads. And while the very grandest palaces cost a great deal of money (the Strozzi in Florence spent about 200,000 lire on their *palazzo* up to 1506), most others were more modest. In Ferrara the smaller and less ambitious palaces built in the 1490s by its duke, Ercole I d'Este, for favoured courtiers cost between 2,200 and 3,200 lire compared to the 25,000 lire (9,000 ducats) spent by his predecessor, Borso, on a set of five embroidered hangings. In contrast, a fresco cycle executed by one of Ercole's court painters, the portrait specialist Baldassare d'Este, in the Chapel of San Domenico in Ferrara, with its twelve narrative scenes, a *Maestà* and five donor portraits, cost a mere 130 ducats.[13] The costs of building resided mainly in raw materials and the skilled labour demanded to work them; contemporary beholders were therefore often made aware of the virtuous sums of money involved by the frequent accentuation of particularly expensive materials. It was also increasingly held that the building's value depended on the creativity of its talented design – which would, once again, be seen to mirror the patron's.

Even more than buildings, the primary (financial) value of, for example, a gold chain or silver ewer remained intrinsic. Hence the rules of many goldsmiths' guilds stipulated that the quality of precious metal used for such objects had to match the local coinage. However, when gold or silver coins or bullion were made into something else, still enormously valuable, other messages could be communicated, obviating the need for the kind of vulgar display that we have seen the Sforza dukes of Milan favoured, or, at least, modifying it. Just as the impact of a palace did not rely merely on the quality and quantity of stone, bricks and mortar, but on the end to which these elements were arranged, so it was recognized that the form of an object made of gold or silver was significant. Isabella d'Este added to the already intricate meaning of her medal by Gian Cristoforo Romano by turning it into a precious jewel, having a specimen cast in gold and set in a frame with her name studded in diamonds (see fig. 91).[14] And arriviste though the Sforza may have been, they were also keen enough to link their wealth to their religious devotions so that, in addition to piles of coins, visiting ambassadors could admire sixty-six silver figures of saints, whose cost and pious intention were not markedly different from those of a chapel. Other people made a similar show of magnificent piety. In his will of October 1483

Cardinal Francesco Gonzaga bequeathed to the Cathedral Church of Mantua 'my large candelabrum, made in the manner of a tree with the images of Adam and Eve', a piece apparently taken from his palace.[15]

More crucial than their iconography, however, was the level of invention (and concomitant fashion) in the combination of figurative and ornamental elements – the quality of *disegno* in these highly expensive objects. Certain categories of gold and silver objects became additionally valuable for their design (and for the craftsman's technical ability in realizing it). This was a more abstract, more intellectual measure of worth than their mere cost, and a sign that catering for guests took not just wealth, but effort and thought. Almost all of these secular Quattrocento pieces are lost: one of the few important exceptions is a pair of rock-crystal flasks mounted in gilt and enamelled silver which may have been commissioned by the Este family from a Venetian workshop in the second half of the fifteenth century (although their origin is far from certain)(fig. 108).[16] As fashion moved on, gold and silver were commodities too valuable to preserve as monuments or relics of bygone styles. Such objects were all too liable to be melted down when their owners were faced by financial crisis, especially in times of war, or simply because they had become too unfashionable to continue functioning properly as the signifiers of *ingegno* married to

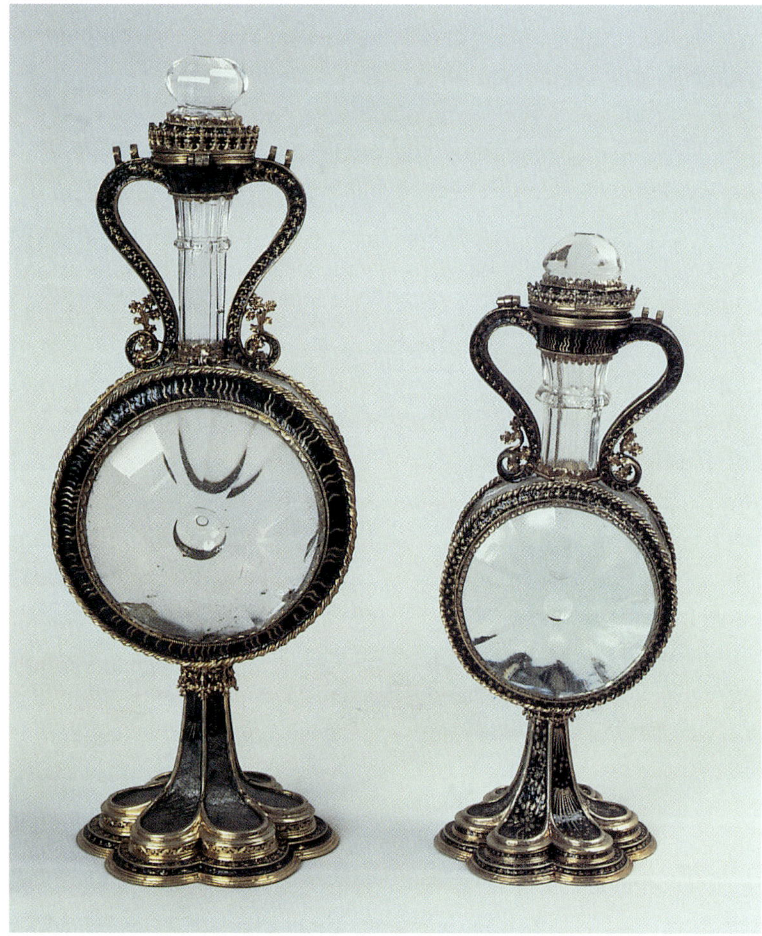

108 Pair of flasks; rock-crystal in silver gilt and enamelled mounts; Venice (?), second half of fifteenth century. Galleria Estense, Modena

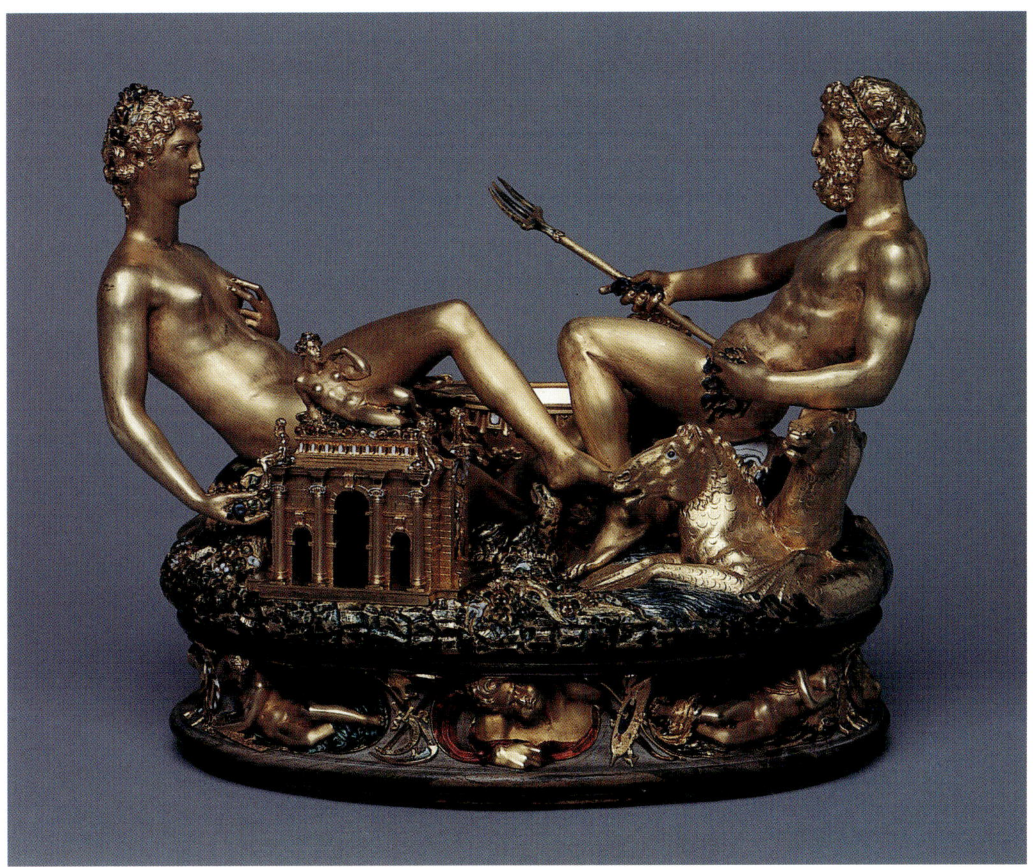

wealth. Ercole d'Este, Duke of Ferrara, for example, ordered the destruction of the silver service commissioned by his predecessor, partly because it was damaged, but also 'because the fashion of it has not pleased him',[17] and Ghiberti mourned the effort of design demanded by goldsmiths' work when it was so prone to destruction.[18] Even Benvenuto Cellini's famous salt, begun for Cardinal Ippolito d'Este and finished for the French king Francis I in 1543, was rescued only at the last moment from the melting pot that accounted for the rest of Charles IX's outdated service as early as 1562 (fig. 109).[19]

Thus we depend on descriptions, and from them it is clear that the design of many of these pieces was very ambitious indeed. A 1473 inventory of the silver belonging to Ercole d'Este furnishes the first detailed account of a silver service, with elements gilded and enamelled, mostly designed by the court artist Cosmè Tura: the elaborately decorated contents of the ducal *credenza*, made in Venice the year before by the goldsmith Giorgio de Allegretto, which had cost a total of 2,714 ducats, or just over 7,736 lire.[20] Some, but not all, of the thirty-eight individual pieces are described as *facti alantiqua*. Among them were the three large flasks – *fiaschi* – probably the most elaborate pieces, bearing enamelled ducal arms, each originally supported by two 'wild men … who with their shoulders and hands support the bodies of the … flasks', like caryatids, and with lids on which were posed pairs of griffins. The decorative features on the other pieces in the service *(vasi, bacili* and *confettiere)* are taken from a now familiar menu: *spiritelli*, cornucopias brimming with flowers, Este eagles, dolphin handles and swags *(feste alantiqua)*, of which some were enamelled; much the same lists of ingredients as we encountered in the previous chapter.[21] Interestingly, these individual elements are sometimes individually termed *all'antica*, while the whole is not so described. Other, simpler pieces omit the phrase. And it is important to distinguish even this less ambitious plate from the many more workaday items by the Ferrarese court goldsmith, Amadio da Milano. The Este account books attest that he and others, working without a designer, were commissioned to make relatively cheap, primarily functional objects for sometimes less than 100 lire.[22] It is true that the Tura service must have been used for dining, if only on rare occasions. Indeed, the lids of these *certi vasi grandi alantiqua* designed by Tura were modified to make them more practical, to prevent them being dropped and broken when in use (*per che li cuperchii ne lo operarli non cascasse e rompese*).[23] But that the function of this service was primarily for magnificent display is indicated by its permanent association with Ercole d'Este's *credenza*, as described by local diarists who chronicled ceremonial events.[24]

Such distinctions were clearly made and practical daily use was secondary in other instances. In 1523–4 Lucagnolo di Jesi, Cellini's second employer in Rome, made a large coverless vase with two handles for Clement VII. Cellini described its purpose: 'Lucagnolo's was a rather large silver vessel, which served on the table of Pope Clement, into which he flung away bits of bone and the rind of various fruits while eating....' Despite this seemingly rather useful function, the goldsmith goes on to categorize it as 'an object of display rather than necessity [*fatto più presto a pompa che a necessità*]. The vase was adorned with two fine handles, together with many masks, both large and small, and masses of foliage, of such beautiful grace and design [*tanta bella grazia e disegno*] as could be imagined....'[25] Later, Cellini himself, still in Rome worked on 'one of those great water-vessels called *acquareccie*, which are used as ornaments to place on *credenze*' for the bishop of Salamanca. Another passage in his *Autobiography* shows one such vase to have been a very substantial 87 centimetres tall.[26] Silver could, indeed, be classified by its level of functionality. On the title page of an album of copies of designs for goldsmiths' work from the first half of the sixteenth century, now in the Fitzwilliam Museum in Cambridge, is listed a two-handled covered *tazza* with a figure on its cover 'for the *credenza*'. This is the grandest piece and it is followed in a kind of hierarchy by two types of cup for drinking wine, and then by much simpler goblets for drinking water.[27] Goldsmiths evidently needed to know the purpose of a commission in advance of its manufacture. A much later source makes this division still more explicit. In 1575 the Milanese Jacopo da Trezzo wrote to Grandduke Francesco I de' Medici, asking if the cup he had commissioned was 'a vessel to drink from or only to look beautiful' (*un vaso per bever o per sol bel vedere*).[28]

In asking this question Jacopo was almost certainly trying to discover how complicated the design was to be. The ornament for these most expensive display pieces had, so as to observe the proper decorum, to be appropriate for the object being made, the quality of design of a precious object equivalent to the preciousness of its medium. Several passages in the *Hypnerotomachia Poliphili*, published in Venice in 1497, give clues as to what was required. In his prolonged fantasy, the narrator gives meticulous descriptions of the architecture and the many valuable objects he encounters. Although the ostensible scale of these fictive palaces and their contents is huge, many of them seem to be descriptions of monstrously enlarged specimens of the art of the goldsmith, an impression confirmed by the illustrative woodcuts accompanying the text (fig. 110). The preciousness of materials is continually stressed and linked to its workmanship. Words like *egregio* and *ingegnioso* are often used. This passage, for example, describes the gold walls of a palace, apparently imagined as blown-up versions of objects like the embossed silver plaquettes that were attached to a famous inkstand by the leading goldsmith Caradosso:[29] 'You admire the splendid lining of the encircling walls, of the purest beaten gold plates, with appropriate carving [or engraving], most suitable [*condecentissime*] to that precious material.'[30] This is the description of a fountain: '[a] most rare work erected with such keen talent [*cum tanto acuto ingegno*], principally that extraordinary vase [*insolente vaso*], the four most perfect harpies, which were of the most rare and carefully chosen lapis that I have seen, [and] where are placed three figures of brightly shining gold, and containing such

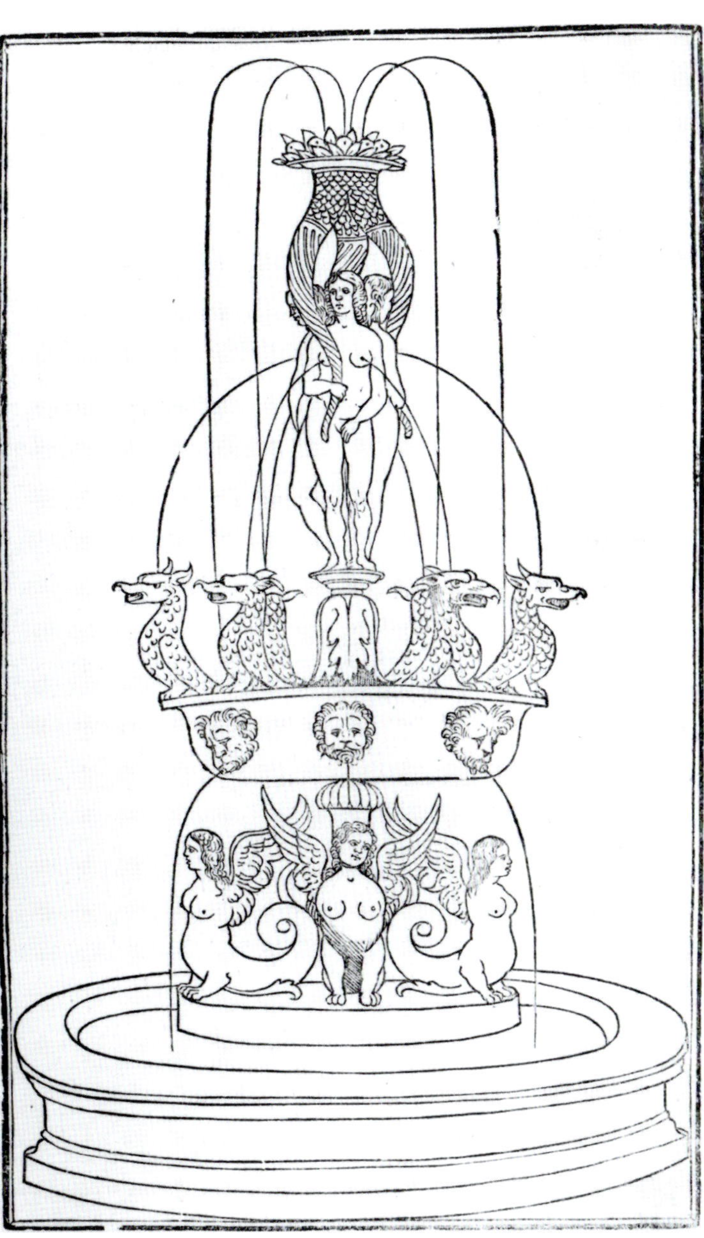

110 *Fountain*; woodcut illustration from the *Hypnerotomachia Poliphili*; Venice, 1499. The British Museum, London

artifice and polish …'. The author goes on to marvel that things made of a material as intractable as lapis could be worked as if the material were as soft as wax.[31]

Such inventiveness was important for the reception of objects like the dishes and vases in the Este service largely because it was clearly seen as deriving from or, at the very least, reflecting that of its commissioner. This concept is revealed, for instance, in the characteristically sycophantic communication from the humanist-scholar Giovanni Sabadino degli Arienti to Isabella d'Este in August 1505 lauding her newly engraved seal, another example of goldsmiths' work: '… certainly the hands of him who made the seal are not a little masterly [*maestrevole*], nor yet of little talent [*di poco ingegno*] the person who has put the master to such a delicate and industrious work'.[32] Sabadino implies that the *ingegno* of the seal belonged to Isabella; it signalled *her* talent. Since it was in the design of the object more than in the manufacture that the *ingegno* resided, Isabella, in common with her predecessors and peers, needed artists skilled in *disegno* who could mediate this much vaunted genius. To gain such employment it was important, then, that a particular artist should be identified as a designer (the 'architect' of an object). The *disegno* of an object was therefore viewed as a distinct element, albeit appropriate or complementary, within the overall meaning of a piece of gold or silver. That such a division was made is revealed in a phrase in the awestruck letter that the fifteen-year-old Galeazzo Maria Sforza wrote to his father, the duke of Milan, after he had visited the Palazzo Medici in Florence in 1459. He was, he said, able to admire 'designs of infinite kinds and of priceless silver'.[33]

If Renaissance owners and beholders believed that the *disegno* contained in an object should be discernible, their ability to identify it may have been determined partly by their knowledge of the divisions of labour inherent in many manufacturing practices, and partly by their recognition that design was often a separate stage from the actual fabrication of an object. Here was the same distinction that was made between architecture and building. Indeed, *disegno* could be regarded as an optional element. In September 1537 Federico Gonzaga, Duke of Mantua, was considering the case he wished to have made for a clock from the workshop of Maestro Cherubino, one of the leading clock-makers of his day. In this instance he decided that the impact of an already precious object (valuable for its technical *ingegno*) should not be diminished by intrusive decorative furbelows. He ordered a plain case, 'a simple thing, without those ornaments [*ornamenti*] designed by Giulio Romano'.[34]

In the first place, there may have been purely practical reasons for these divisions of design and labour. Before enormous sums were spent, patrons must have wanted to see how the objects they had commissioned would turn out. Moreover, if an art object was ordered from any distance, a patron's wishes could most conveniently be conveyed by sending a cheap three-dimensional model or, more usually, a drawing (architects frequently sent designs from one city to another). At their simplest, these drawings might consist of the emblems or coats-of-arms to be woven into tapestries in Brussels or painted on dishes and vases in Valencia (see figs 164, 165). However, as different centres in Italy became more identified with particular types of art production, such practices became more frequent, and often more complicated. The correspondence between Rome and Mantua discussing the mount designed by the goldsmith Cristoforo di Geremia for

Lodovico Gonzaga's *all'antica* crystal salt furnishes details of this procedure. Lodovico's Roman ambassador gave the marquis an update on Cristoforo's progress:

> Now he has made a model [*uno modello*] of the adornments of those dimensions and proportions with which he was furnished. It will be a beautiful thing. And he says that here, in the shop of Maestro Simone [di Giovanni, a Florentine, who was one of the leading goldsmiths in Rome] is one whom he believes will make it better than any man in Italy … He believes that the expenses will be between seven and eight ounces of gold.[35]

The model was lead. It had been fashioned by Cristoforo, but he was not intending to execute it in gold himself. A hierarchy had already been set up. Once again the patron had pole position, receiving credit from the artist himself for the object's pleasingly inventive appearance. The work completed, Cristoforo called it '… your salt, which I sent to you mounted according to Your Lordship's design' (*secundo el desegno de Vostra S[ignoria]*.).[36]

The correspondence of the arch-interventionist Isabella d'Este shows what might happen if no such drawing was provided. In the first years of her marriage to the heir to the marquisate of Mantua, she often employed one Michele, a leading goldsmith at her father's court in Ferrara, to make her jewellery. In 1491 she rejected a gold enamelled *stringa*, probably a thin chain, ordered from Michele 'because it is not sufficiently graceful' (*per non havere bona gratia*). She requested another 'also of gold and enamelled like this one, but he should put all his industry into giving it good grace and such gesture [*gesto*] that you know it for a looped *stringa* and capable of being worn as a pendant round the neck'. Because of the goldsmith's understandable uncertainty as to what exactly was intended she at last sent a drawing.[37] By doing so, it can be argued, she would no longer have identified Michele as the author of the chain; instead she had shifted that responsibility to the draughtsman and, as the patron directing him, to herself. This applied equally when she sent drawings and three-dimensional models to glass-makers in Venice, and to the drawing and little bits of string dispatched to Perugino in Florence to let him know the desired size and appearance of the participants in his painting the *Battle between Love and Chastity*, which she had ordered for her *studiolo*.[38]

Mainly because of its great intrinsic value, goldsmiths' work was one of the key fields in the establishment of the concept of the *disegnatore*, whereby craftsmen of different kinds sought to demonstrate their artistic status. In Florence in the first three-quarters of the Quattrocento goldsmiths were certainly regarded as highly as (if not more highly than) most painters or sculptors. Certainly as members of the Arte della Seta, the Silk Guild, they had access to political office and thus some influence on the civic life of the city,[39] and, as in many other cities in Italy, greater importance than members of the usually more recently established painters' guilds (where they existed). In the middle of the next century Vasari could write that 'at that time [in the Quattrocento] it was the custom, and no man was considered to be a good goldsmith unless he was a good designer [*disegnatore*]…'.[40] Supporting Vasari's statement are the several instances of goldsmith-trained painters, sculptors and architects. Brunelleschi started in this way, and the goldsmith-sculptor Lorenzo Ghiberti's shop was said to have included Donatello and Luca della Robbia (thus four of the five heroes of the artistic revival celebrated by Alberti in the Italian text of his treatise *On Painting* had goldsmith connections), as well as

Paolo Uccello, the Rossellino brothers, Desiderio da Settignano, Andrea del Verrocchio, Antonio del Pollaiuolo and Maso Finiguerra, and, while these may not be accurate claims in all instances, the message comes across clearly that Ghiberti's shop was viewed as a 'school' of *disegno*.[41] It is interesting to note a parallel situation in Milan, where goldsmiths made a major contribution to the economic success of the city, and where the painters Bramantino and, probably, Cesare da Sesto received their first schooling from gold-smiths.[42] A drawing in the Uffizi by the Florentine goldsmith Maso Finiguerra or a member of his shop, one of several of its kind showing *garzoni* in his workshop learning or practising draughtsmanship, shows the system in operation. Inscribed below the figure is a legend that is almost a manifesto: 'I want to be a good designer and to become a good architect' (*Vo essere uno buono disegnatore e do/ventare uno buono archittetore*)(fig. 111).[43] The fact

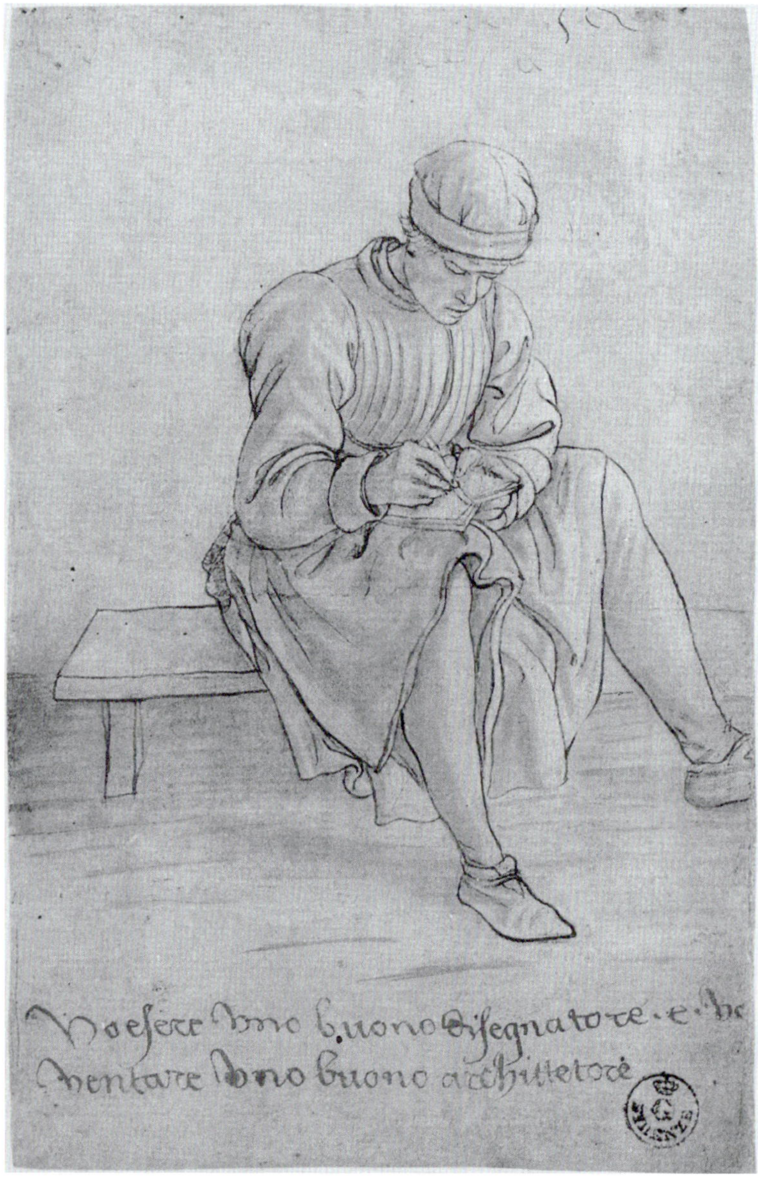

111 Maso Finiguerra (or workshop), *Apprentice or assistant* [garzone] *practising disegno*; pen and brown ink and wash; Florence, *c.*1456–64. Gabinetto dei Disegni, Uffizi, Florence

that so many painters (and architects) in Florence trained as and proclaimed themselves goldsmiths might have been partly dictated by the importance of their guild. However, the statement on the drawing from Maso's shop shows that the thorough grounding in draughtsmanship during his apprenticeship was thought to prove that the self-identified goldsmith was a designer whose skills could be turned to any appropriate use.

In 1471 the Florentine patrician Giovanni Rucellai, listing artists whose works he possessed, applied the term *maestro di disegno* to both Maso and Antonio del Pollaiuolo.[44] That these two artists should be so described is telling. The term had already been used by the Paduan humanist-scribe Felice Feliciano in his 1466 will, in which he bequeathed 'drawings and pictures on paper by many excellent masters of design'.[45] Maso was a specialist in niello work, engraved silver into the lines of which black nigellum – an alloy of

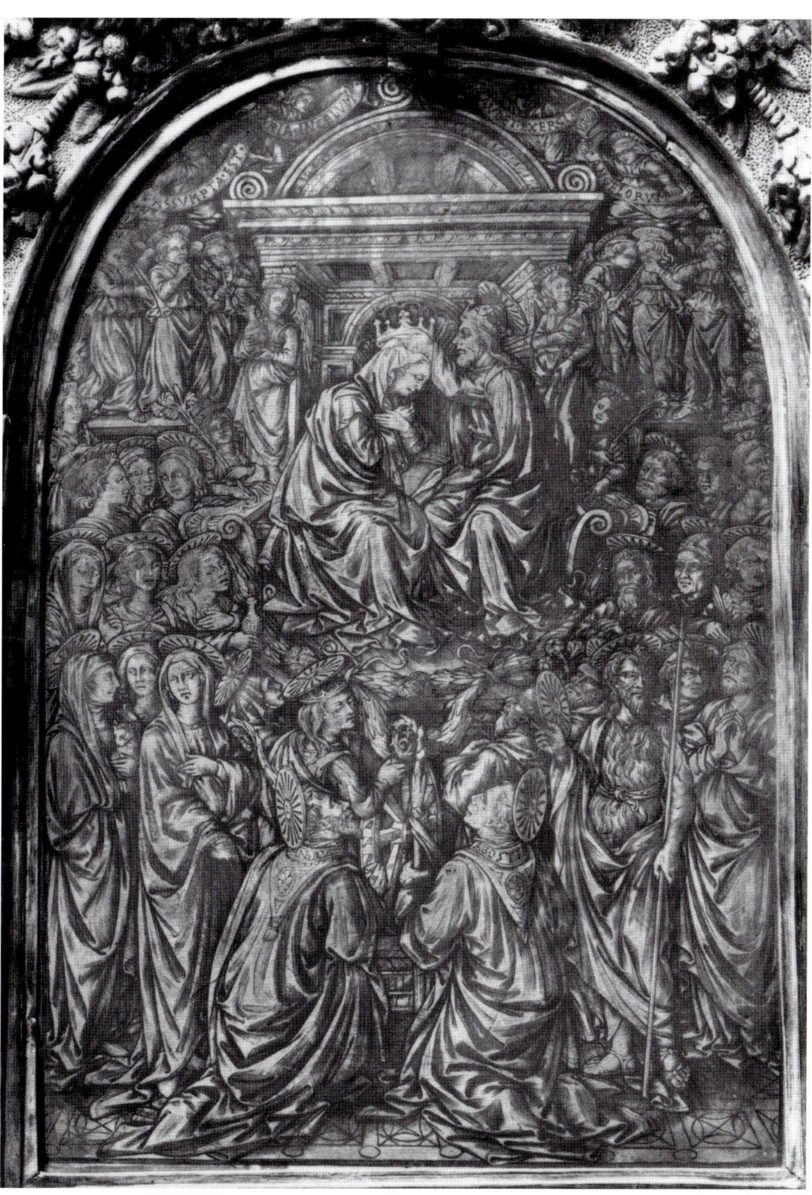

112 Maso Finiguerra, pax with *Coronation of the Virgin*; silver with niello inlay; Florence, 1452–5, sixteenth-century embossed frame. Bargello, Florence

silver, lead, copper and sulphur – is fused. His extraordinary mastery of this technique is best demonstrated on the pax depicting the *Coronation of the Virgin* paid for by the Arte di Calimala – the Merchants' Guild – for the Florence Baptistry in 1452–5 (fig. 112). This rare survival is stylistically closely linked to his drawings, the nigellum so treated as to stand for the ink washes.[46] Antonio del Pollaiuolo, too, was trained and continued to practise as a goldsmith. He also received commissions for chalices and crosses, candelabra and reliquary busts. He was often given work by the powerful Florentine guilds, and was paid just over 2,006 florins for his share of the work on the silver cross of the Baptistry of San Giovanni. His secular work included silver basins and the gilded silver helmet presented to Federigo da Montefeltro, Duke of Urbino, by the city of Florence, which had Hercules and a griffin on its crest and was said to be worth 500 ducats.[47] Although he is not recorded as a niellist, his six enamels of the holy family and saints for 'a large silvered and enamelled

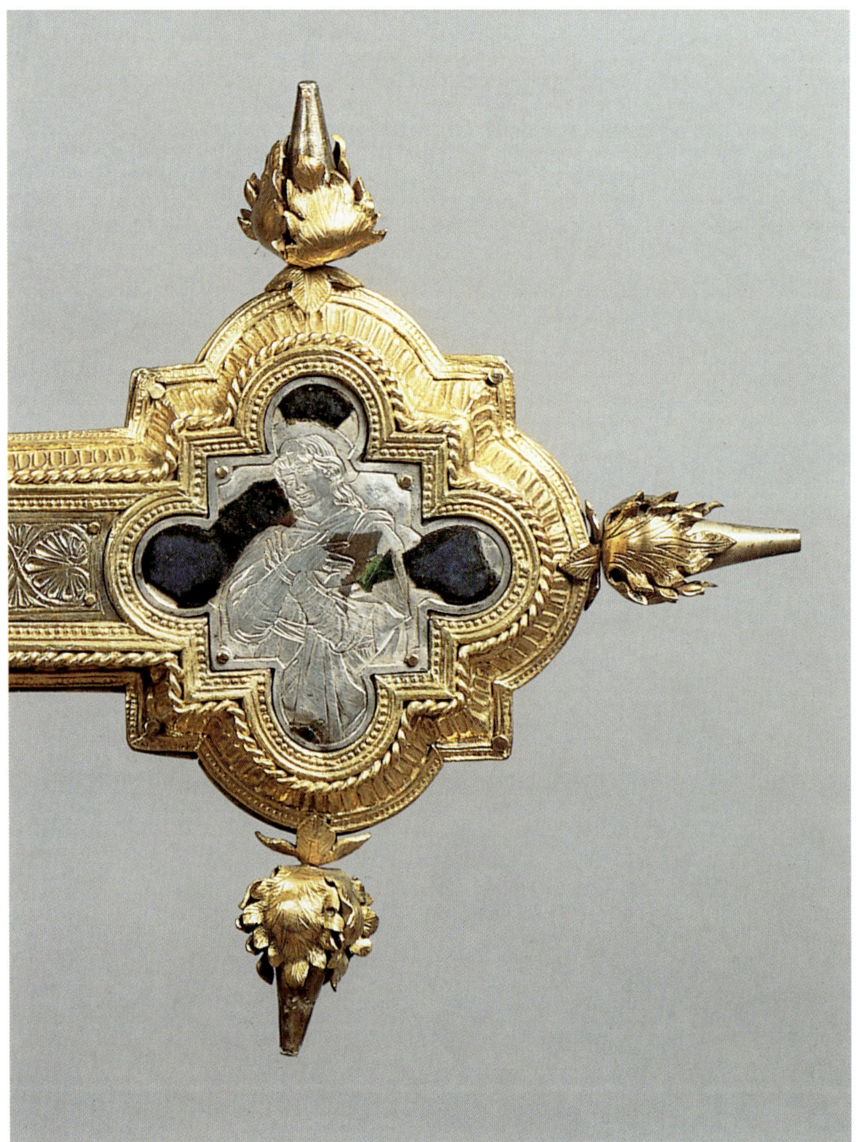

113 Antonio del Pollaiuolo, crucifix (detail with plaque of Saint John the Evangelist); engraved, partially silvered brass and enamel; Florence, 1476–83. Bargello, Florence

(*Opposite page*)
114 Giuliano da Maiano after Maso Finiguerra, *Circumcision of Christ*; wood with *intarsia* inlay; Florence, 1463. Sacrestia delle Messe, Duomo, Florence

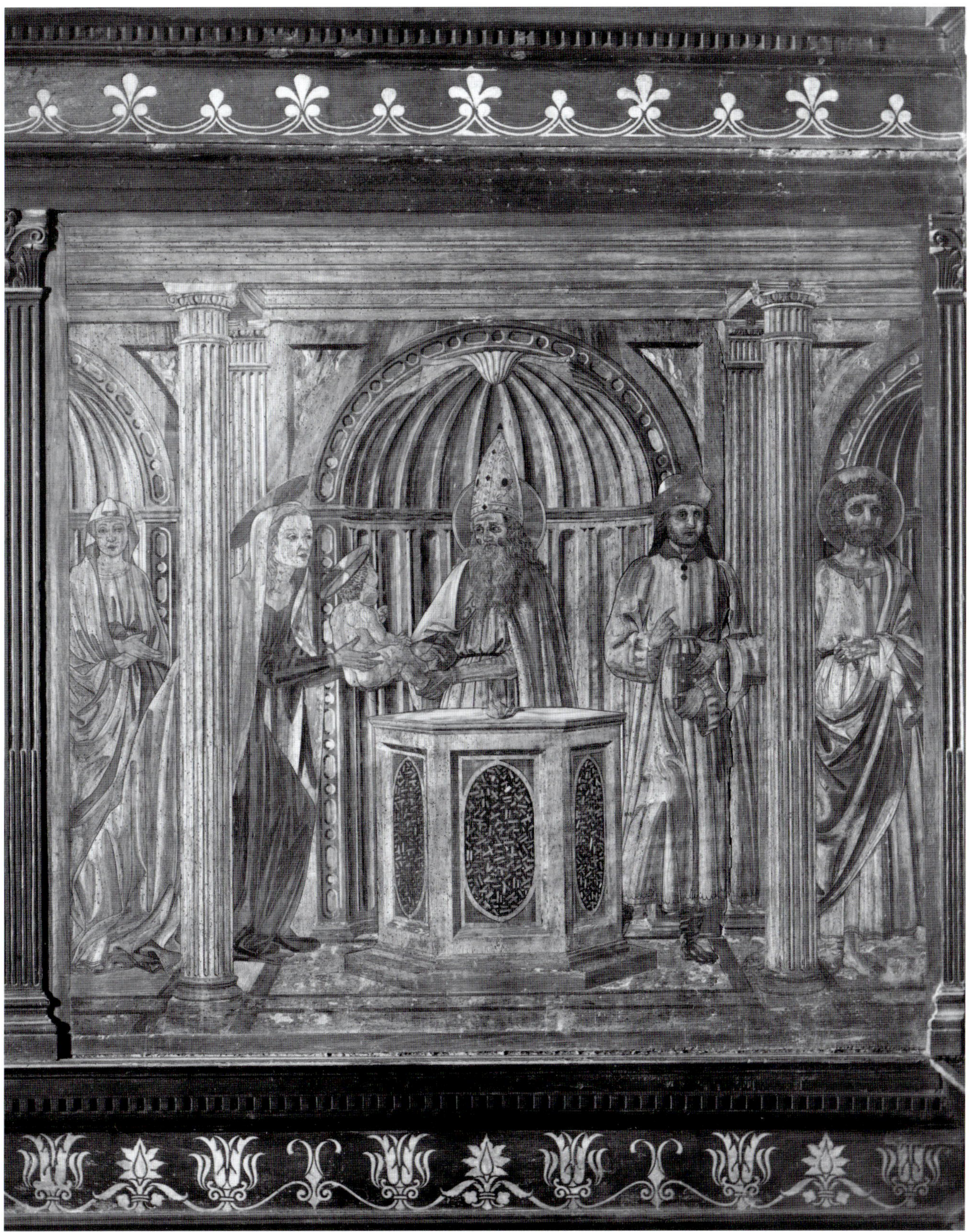

brass cross' made in 1478 for the monastery of San Gaggio near Florence show a similar reliance on *disegno* (fig. 113).[48] These plaques, reinserted into a later crucifix, which is now in the Bargello, are exceptionally skilful examples of a common goldsmith's technique, one that had been employed by Ghiberti. The engraved contours of the figures show through the translucent enamels to describe the forms and sometimes the decorative detail of costume, face and hair, a linear effect that speaks immediately of their origins as drawings.

Thus the finished products of both of these fifteenth-century goldsmiths depended on their capacity to produce an inventive, figurative *disegno*, and signalled those abilities through a precious, difficult and highly regarded medium. (It is not surprising in this context that Landino was later to claim that the humanist amateur Leon Battista Alberti worked with an engraver's burin: proof of the intellectual connotations of the medium.)[49] With their capacity for designing established, both Maso and Antonio were frequently called upon to apply their *disegno* to make figurative designs for other media, justifying Rucellai's description of them. They had a model in Lorenzo Ghiberti, who provided drawings for the stained-glass roundels in the drum of the dome of Florence cathedral and who boasted in his *Commentaries* that 'few things of importance were made in our city which were not designed and devised by my hand'.[50] Although *intarsia* specialists were seen as experts in the use of architectural perspective, they were sometimes assisted with the figurative elements. Thus Maso drew 'five figures' for *intarsia* panels set up in the sacristy of the Florentine Duomo (fig. 114). Pollaiuolo was paid at least 90 florins for drawings for the embroideries of the ceremonial vestments of the Florence Baptistry and also designed an altar frontal for Pope Sixtus IV for the Basilica of San Francesco in Assisi.[51] Both may have been asked by Rucellai himself to design *intarsia* panels for the interior of his palace.

The goldsmith's skill as a draughtsman was highlighted in a well-known Florentine engraved print of about 1460–5 depicting Mercury, protector of merchants, who flies above a goldsmith's shop; while his assistants are busily engaged in the sale of elaborate plate, the master himself is wielding a metalpoint, or burin, drawing a (possibly female) nude (fig. 115).[52] This engraving, one of a series showing the planets, may even have been an act of self-promotion, since, because the intaglio engraving of a plate demanded essentially the same skills as the engraving of silver for enamel or nielli, print-making in Florence had become the preserve of the goldsmith. The planets series has been attributed to the goldsmith Baccio Baldini. Thus the technique and, more crucially in this context, the design that lay behind it could be singled out as a property of the goldsmith. Even if Vasari's identification of Maso Finiguerra as the print's inventor might be an over-simplification, it is true that some of the earliest autonomous prints to be executed in Italy (precursors of those prints made to be coloured as playing cards or box lids) were taken from sulphur casts made, starting in 1447 at the latest, from Maso's nielli (figs 116, 117).[53] This practice may have been inspired in the first place by the desire to preserve examples of his output, as both the equivalent of a stock of workshop drawings and as examples of his engraving talents, a necessary precaution given the propensity of its owners to melt down the finished product. But it was quickly realized that, as multiples (therefore unlike drawings), these prints could be circulated to an ever-more appreciative

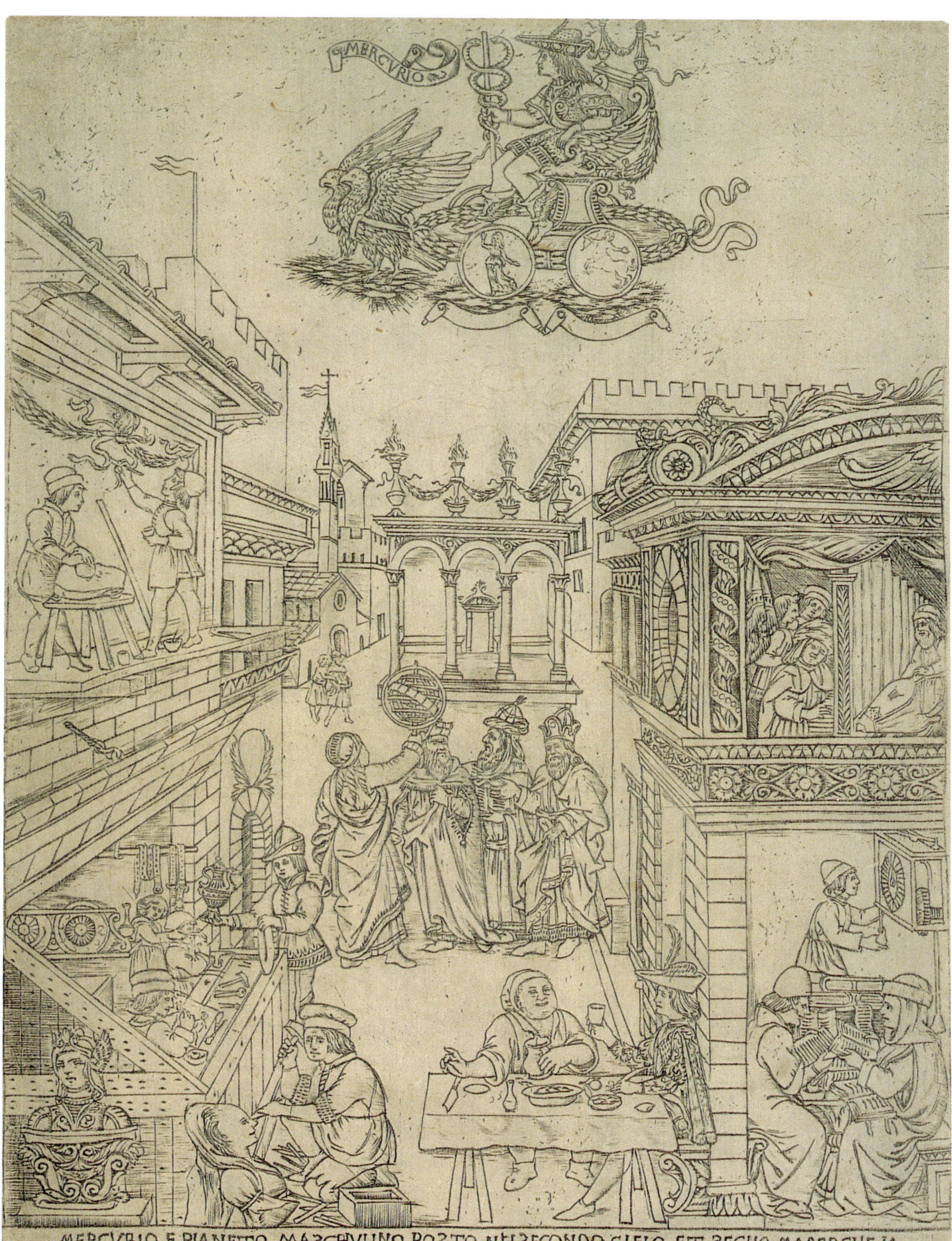
MERCVRIO
MERCVRIO E PIANETO MASCHVLINO POSTO NELSECONDO CIELO ET SECHO MAPERCHE LA
SVA SICITA EMOLTO PASSIVA LVI EFREDO CONQVEGLI SENGNI CH SONO FREDDI EVMIDO COG
LI VMIDI E LOQVENTE INGENGNIOSO AMA LESCIENSIE MATEMATICA ESTIVDIA NELLE DIVI
NASIONE A ILCORPO GRACILE COE SCHIETTO ELBRI SOTTILI ISTATVRA CHONPIVTA DE
METALLI A LARGIENTO VIVO ELDI SVO E MERCOLEDI COLLA PRIMA ORA E IS EZZ
LANOTTE SVA E DELPI DELLA DOMENICHA A PERAMICO ILSOLE PER NIMICO AVENE
RE LASVA VITA OVERO ESALTATIONE EVIRGO LASV MORTE OVERO NVMILIASIONE
E PISCE HA HABITASIONE GEMNI DI DI VIRGO DINOTTE VA E IZ SENGNI IN 38
DI COMINCIANDO DA VIRGO IN ZO DI EZ ORE VA VN SENGNO

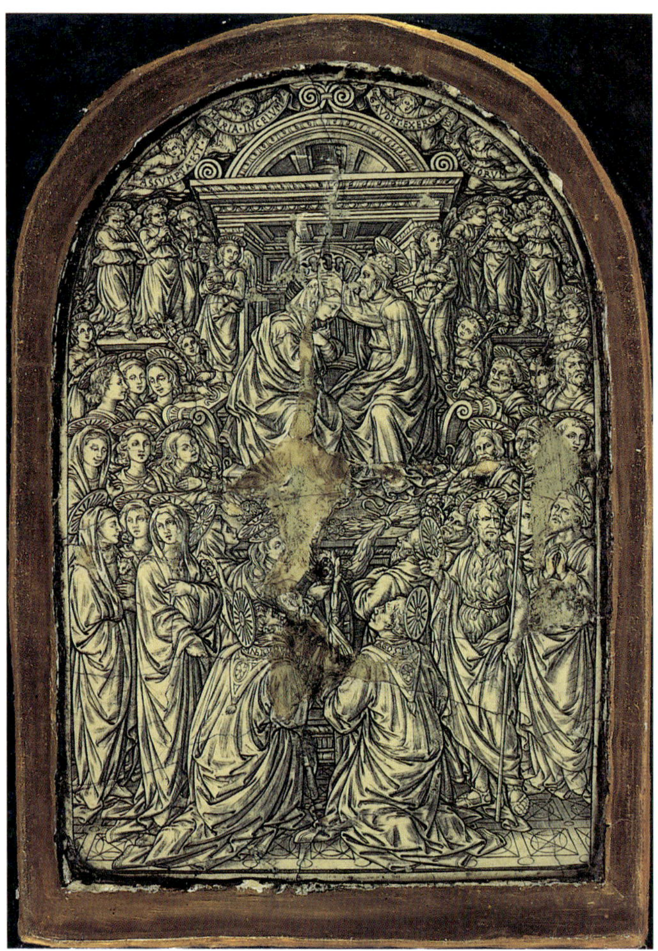

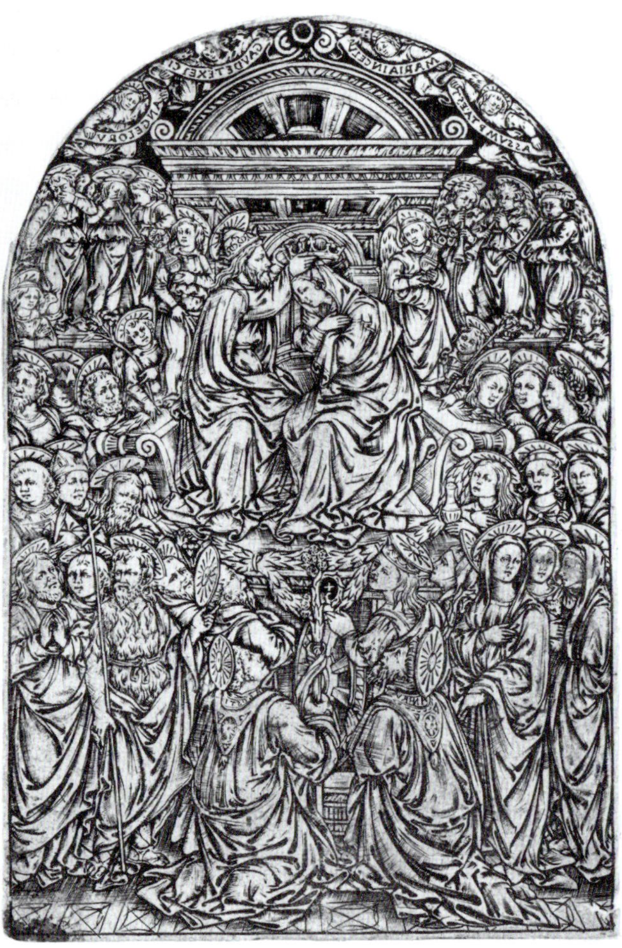

audience, that they could be strategically used to promote their authors as intellectual designers.

Antonio del Pollaiuolo was to build on Maso's example. In 1468–70 he signed his justly famous engraved print *The Battle of Nude Men*.[54] This engraving was perhaps reproductive, or assumed to be. Sabba da Castiglione, in discussing Pollaiuolo's special talents, wrote: '… and in researching the nude [he was] very diligent and practical, as one can see by a picture in low relief of the *ignudi* of the chain', a distinguishing feature of Pollaiuolo's print.[55] In its first state this survives in only one impression, now in Cleveland, and its rarity and technique suggest that the plate was not suitable for issuing a large edition. Shortly afterwards, however, the plate was reworked, and the prints taken from it are much more common (fig. 118). The design therefore became more widely available. Because engraving was a goldsmith's technique, the medium itself demonstrated the goldsmith's claim to be viewed as a *disegnatore*. Indeed, some later prints make deliberate reference to the birth of the medium in the goldsmith's *bottega*; the scale and technique of a group of late fifteenth-century small 'niello-manner' prints, many signed O.P.D.C. (Opus of Peregrino da Cesena), are intended to recall the preciousness of silver niello plaques themselves.[56]

116 Maso Finiguerra, *Coronation of the Virgin*; sulphur cast after pax; Florence, *c*.1455. The British Museum, London

117 Maso Finiguerra, *Coronation of the Virgin*; niello print; Florence, *c*.1455. The British Museum, London

Although the art of *disegno* may have been seen as a specialism of these spectacularly successful Florentine goldsmiths, even in Florence they were not the only artists to be entrusted with designing responsibilities. So many others were painters that by the end of the Quattrocento the perception of goldsmiths as designers *par excellence* had changed. Paolo Uccello and Donatello had also provided drawings for the stained glass in the Florence Duomo *oculi*,[57] and the painter Alesso Baldovinetti joined Maso in providing Giuliano da Maiano with a design for the Sacristy *intarsie*.[58] When Pollaiuolo took up painting, executing pictures for some of the most prestigious sites in Florence, he may have been prompted by the notion that, although less lucrative, such work increased the chances of his being perceived as an *ingegnoso* designer. The Bolognese goldsmith Francesco Francia later followed the same route (figs 119, 120). Even Ghiberti, acutely conscious of his status, may have joined the Painters' Guild in Florence in 1423 for a similar reason. Patrons were, perhaps, more likely to see figurative drawings by painters (*modelli* showing them what altarpieces or frescoes would look like) than by goldsmiths, whose works, notwithstanding Maso or Pollaiuolo, were mostly less dependent on describing the human form, the task for which the most *disegno* was deemed to be required. It was, moreover, chiefly the paintings of antiquity that were so often and lovingly

118 Antonio del Pollaiuolo, *The Battle of Nude Men*; engraving (second state); Florence, *c.*1470. The British Museum, London

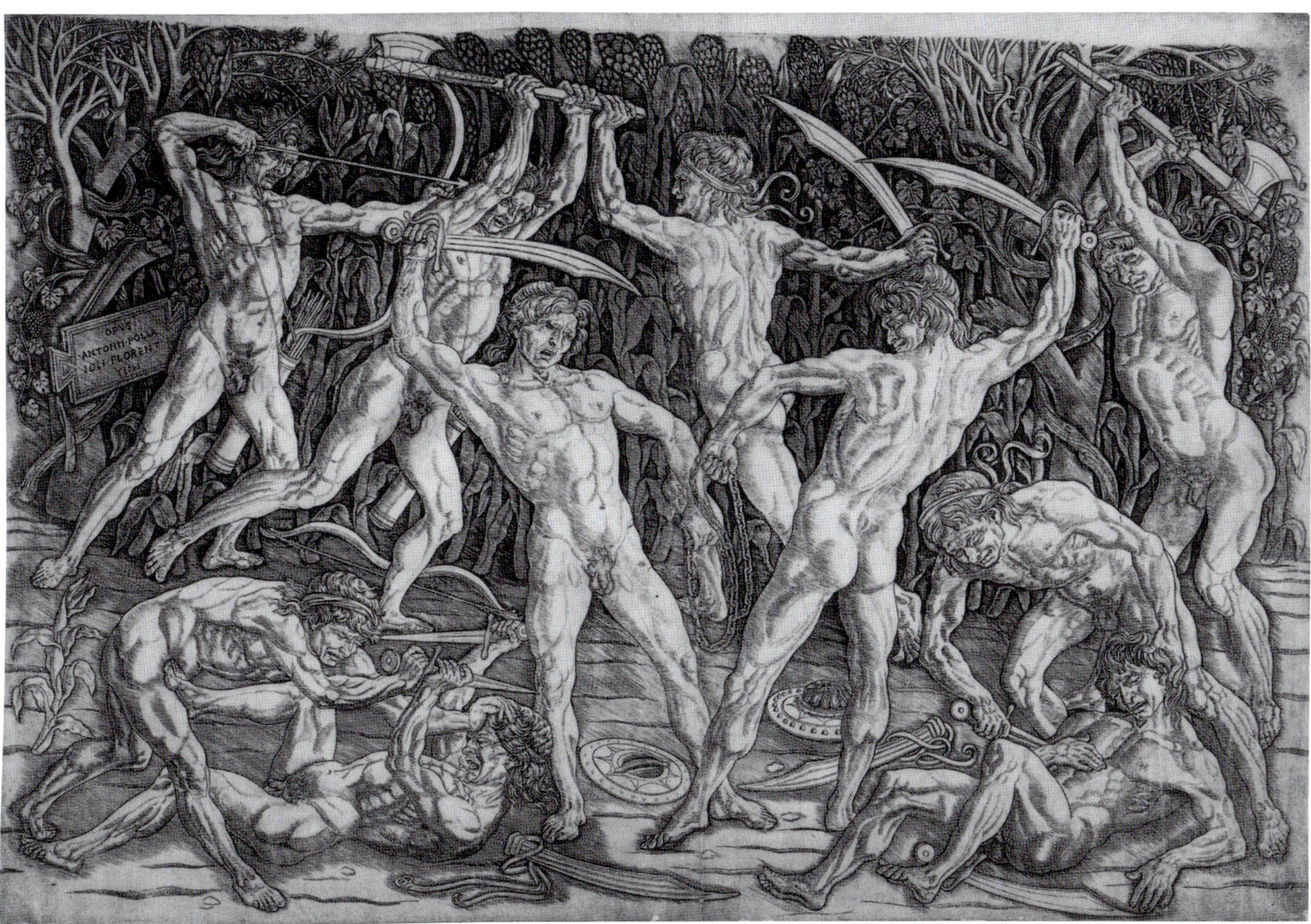

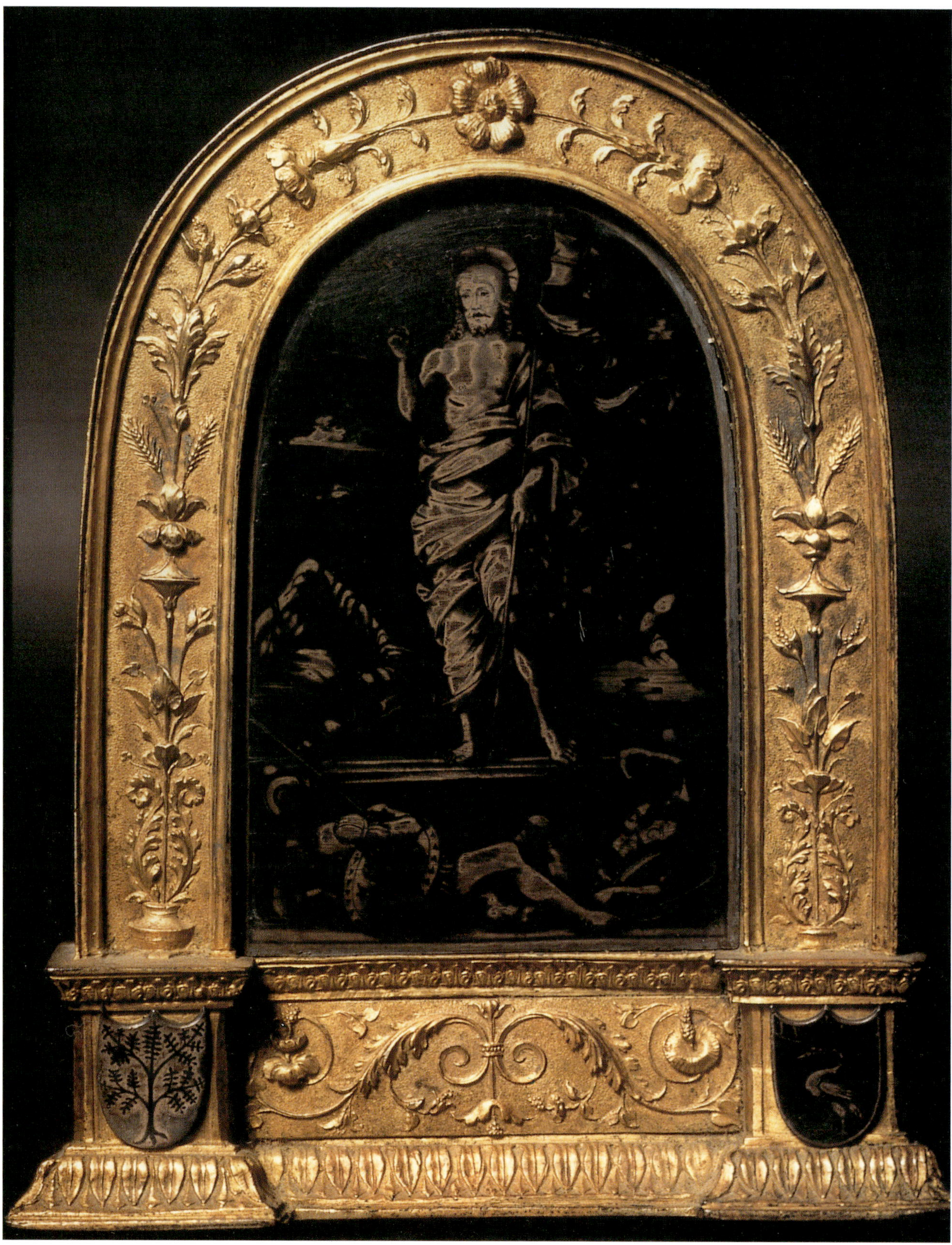

described in ancient texts. Above all, by the turn of the century 'drawn' figurative motifs were appearing less and less frequently in objects made by goldsmiths. Sculpted and embossed figures, in relief and in the round, remained important but as objects became ever more consciously *all'antica*, with an increased emphasis on using classical stone and hard-stone vases as models, there was a gradual abandonment of flat figurative enamels and nielli in the Cinquecento.

The model for such painter-designers can be found in Pisanello, whose employment in 1449 by Alfonso of Aragon helped establish a pattern to which later court artists were expected to conform. The most celebrated painter of his day, who had worked for the Este in Ferrara, the Gonzaga in Mantua and many other powerful rulers, Pisanello capitalized on this position to become a designer, to make drawings that he himself would not (and

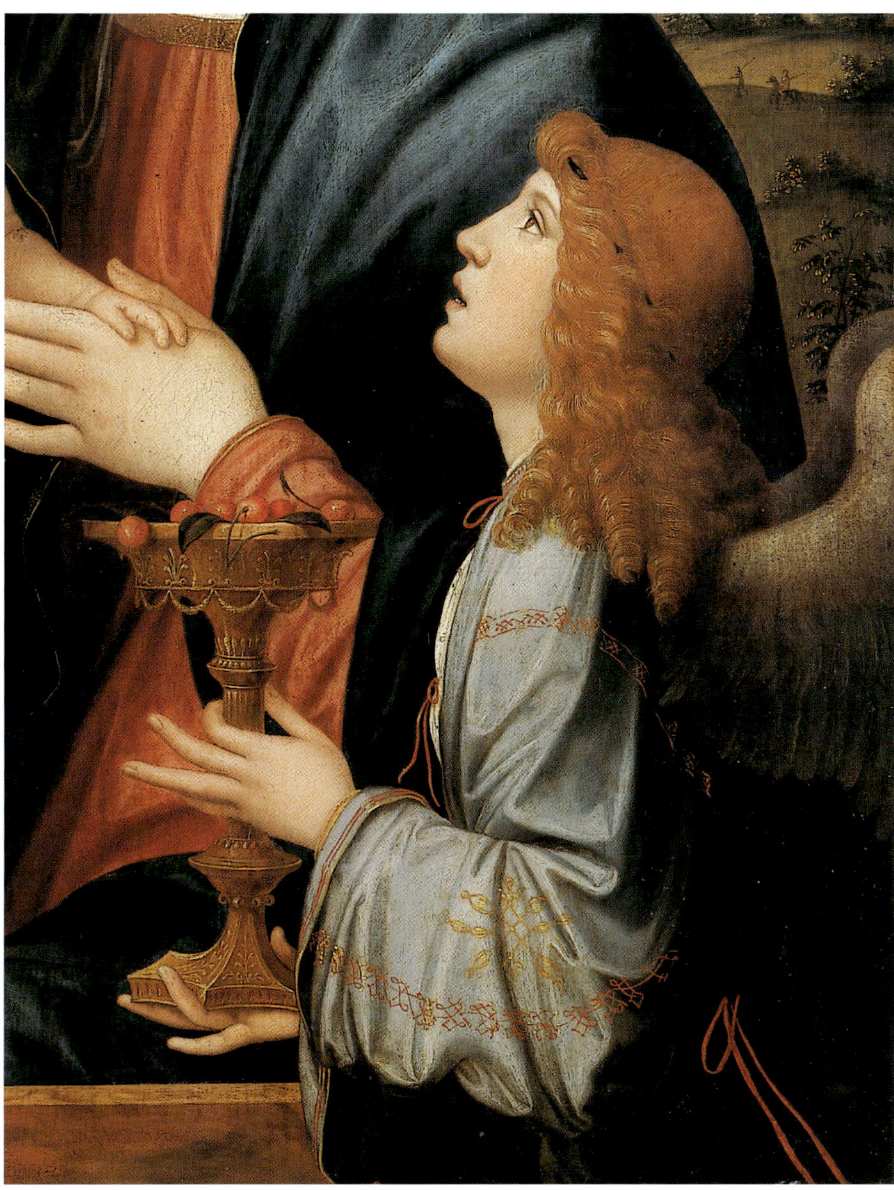

(*Opposite page*)
119 Francesco Francia, pax with *The Resurrection of Christ*; silver plaque with niello inlay in silver-gilt frame; Bologna, *c.*1481. Pinacoteca Nazionale, Bologna

120 Francesco Francia, *Virgin and Child with an Angel* (detail of goldsmiths' work); oil on panel; Bologna, 1490. National Gallery, London

could not) translate into finished works. In Naples he was paid an enormous salary (400 ducats a year) to design embroideries and goldsmiths' work, among other things. Alfonso's letter of appointment to Pisanello reminds us of a patron's motives in receiving into his household a craftsman (*opifice*) of Pisanello's natural talent and skill (*ingenium atque artem*): 'There is nothing more becoming to a prince than to pursue with honour, dignity and rewards men of virtue [*virtute*] and endowed with elegant and outstanding talent [*ingenio*], and to embrace them with benevolence and love; for thus it comes about that the minds of others are roused to virtue if they see the rewards bestowed on virtue.'[59] Despite, or because of, Alfonso's admiration of Pisanello's painting talents, none of the drawings made by Pisanello and his shop in Naples are directly related to paintings (fig. 121).[60] Alfonso seems to have realized that he could use the huge talent of Italy's most famous artist more broadly – to promote a high level of inventiveness for *all* the art objects made for his court. Freed by his court employment from restrictive guild regulations, Pisanello could turn his attention to the design of non-painted works (including, it appears, the architecture of the Castel Nuovo), thus reinforcing the intellectually satisfying separation between creative inception and mechanical execution.

Moreover, it seems that such design work was as, if not more, lucrative than painting

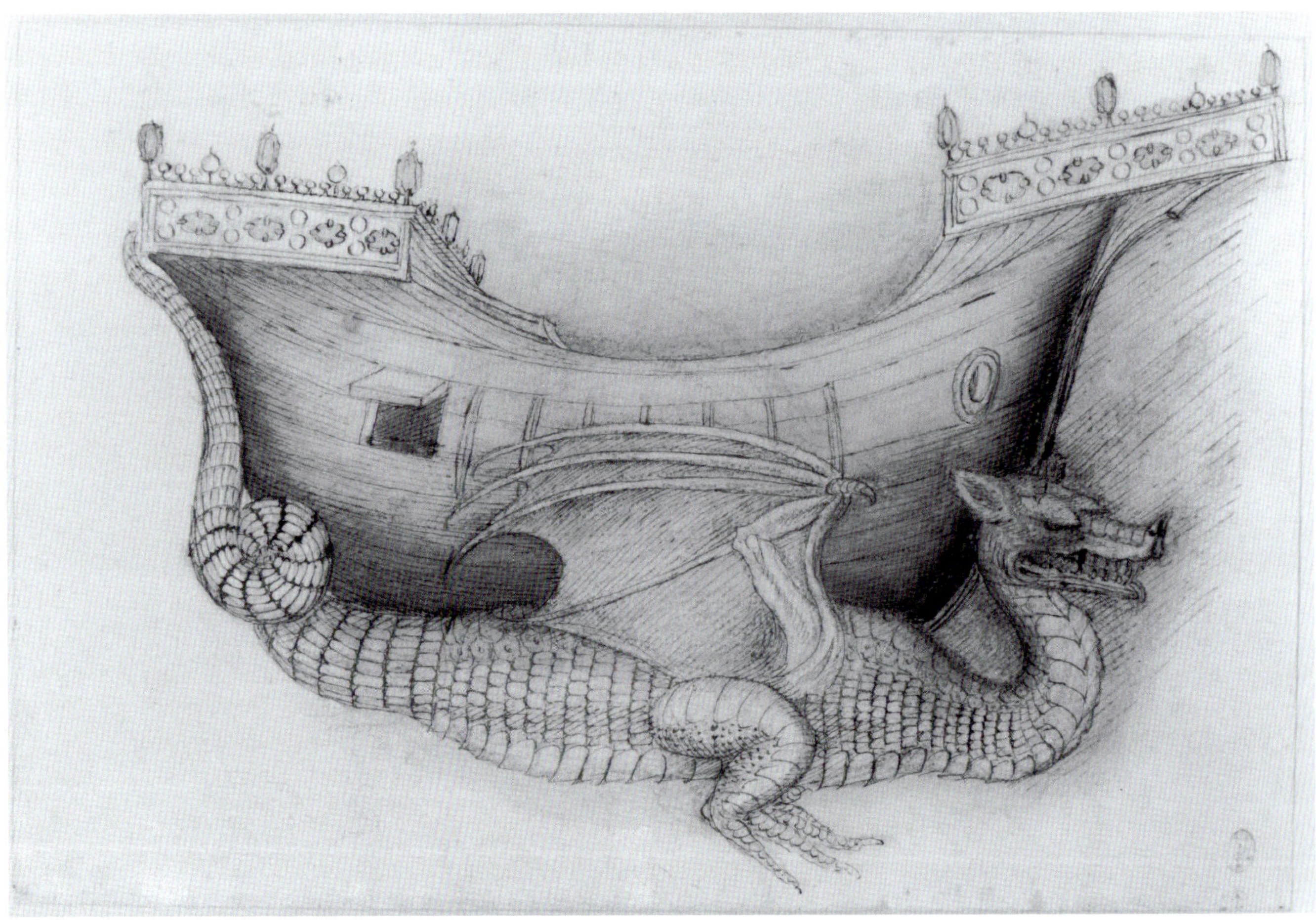

121 Pisanello (or workshop), design for a dragon salt-cellar; pen and ink over black chalk; Naples, 1448–50. Musée du Louvre, Paris

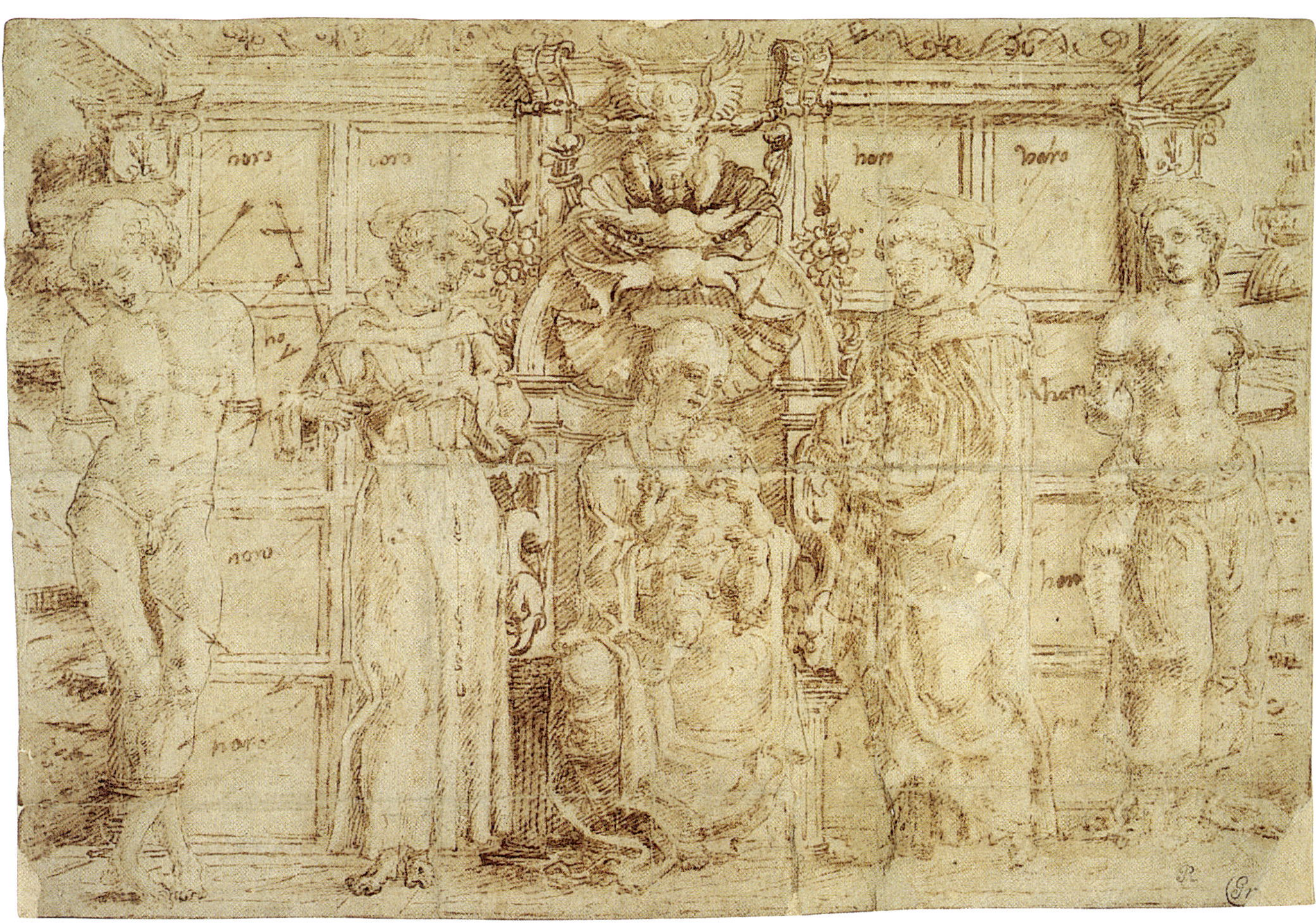

122 Cosmè Tura, *modello* drawing for an altarpiece of the Virgin and Child, and four saints; pen and ink; Ferrara, *c.*1470–5. The British Museum, London

itself. Beyond their retaining salaries, court artists were sometimes paid substantially for special projects. Cosmè Tura, the practitioner of the '*ingeniosem artem picture*', was taken on in Ferrara in 1456. Although some of his extraordinary panel paintings may have been executed for his Este employers, there is no documentary record of them. Instead, surviving records show that he was employed to make designs for tapestries and, as we have seen, for the silver service on Ercole d'Este's *credenza*. His drawing style is revealed in a sketch made for the potential patron of an altarpiece, a composition that includes elements such as the dolphins on the Virgin's throne, which were to appear in his lost designs for silver, as the inventory description has shown (fig. 122). Tura travelled to Venice to 'give the style' (*dar modo*), making drawings for the larger pieces and, presumably, to supervise Giorgio de Allegretto in his complicated task. Tura was rewarded for this work with a payment of 45 lire.[61] This may seem a small sum when the total cost of the service is considered, but it compares favourably to the 70 lire paid in the following year for an altarpiece with the Virgin and Child, and four saints on two small wings, a sum that included the cost of pigments.[62]

No wonder that practitioners of the visual arts sought such work so eagerly. Tura's artistic domination of the Ferrarese court thwarted the ambitions of another painter born

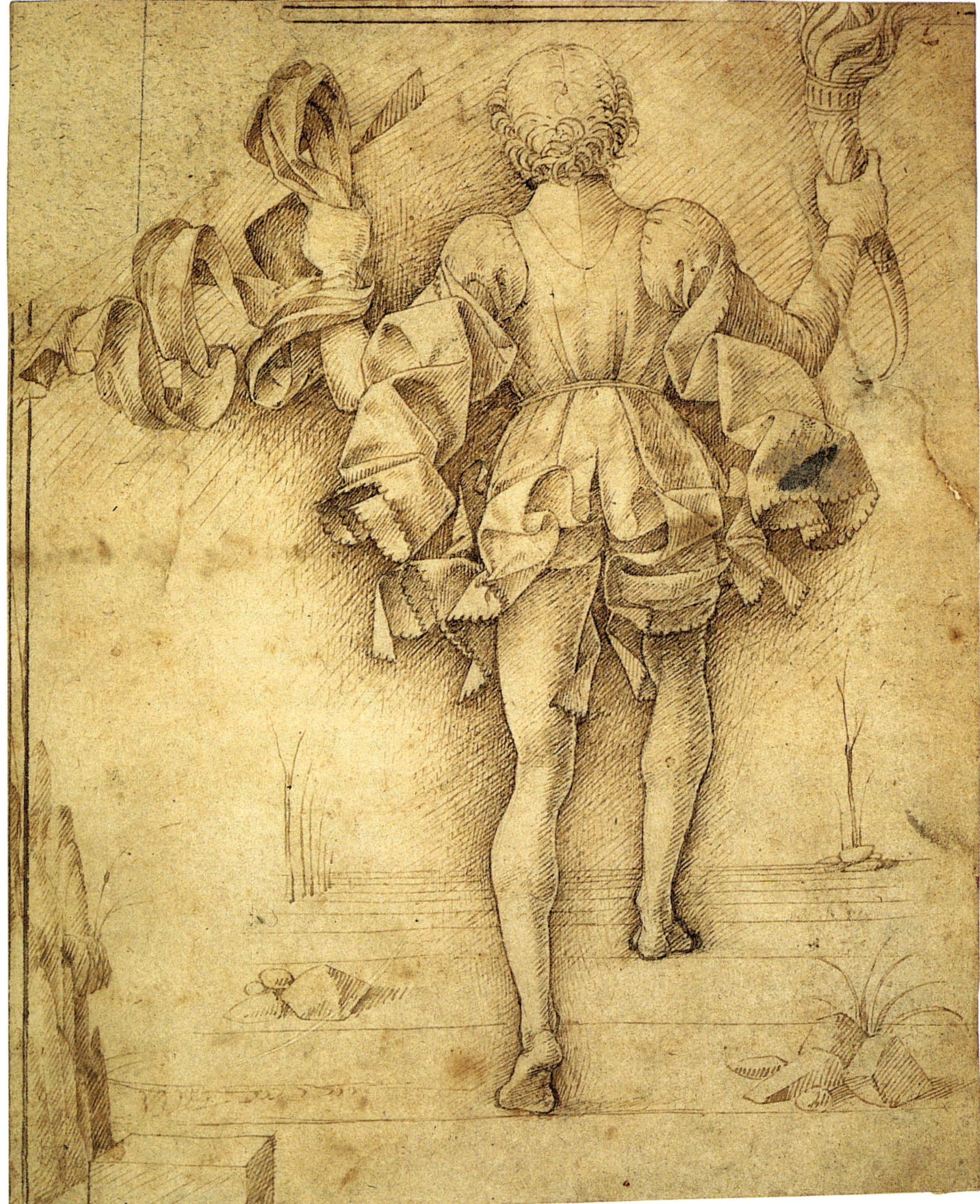

in the city, Francesco del Cossa. A remarkable draughtsman (fig. 123), Cossa felt slighted
when Borso d'Este paid him a journeyman rate for his 1470 wall-paintings in the Palazzo
Schifanoia in Ferrara,[63] and left the city to pursue his career in Bologna, where he met with
immediate success. He continued to paint, but he also worked as a designer. There is no
record of him designing goldsmiths' work (though it is not impossible), but he repeatedly
executed drawings for *intarsia* panels, stained glass and, possibly, embroideries.[64] He
became the object of clamorous praise by the scholarly community of the city and when he
died in 1476–7, the poet, Sebastiano Aldrovandi, echoed Giovanni Rucellai by calling him
a *gran mastro al disegno*, suggesting that this term was now readily understood.[65]

The growing supremacy in most cities of the painter-designer in the Quattrocento can
be documented again and again (and the situations in Florence and, to a lesser extent,

Milan seem exceptional). Francesco d'Antonio, for example, was a successful goldsmith in in mid-fifteenth-century Siena. He is recorded working on his own but when he was faced with a prestigious commission for the reliquary bust of Santa Caterina in the chapel dedicated to her in the Church of San Domenico, he modelled the head after designs by the painter Giovanni di Stefano Sassetta.[66] Francesco Squarcione, in Padua, also made drawings for the *intarsie* in the sacristy of the Santo.[67] Zanetto Bugatto, the Sforza court portraitist in Milan, provided the designs for ten gigantic gold medals of Galeazzo Maria Sforza and his consort, each piece worth 10,000 ducats.[68] Gentile Bellini was made responsible for designing a relief for the Scuola Grande di San Marco in Venice.[69] When the Milanese Ambrogio Preda, the portraitist of Bianca Maria Sforza (see fig. 29) entered the service of Emperor Maximilian he was called upon to design coins, tapestries and even the costume of the emperor's guard. He had already made designs for vases for Archbishop Varad of Hungary.[70] These are only a few examples among many.

Above all the rest, however, there was Andrea Mantegna, Gonzaga court artist in Mantua from 1460. In 1469 he also executed a drawing of a peacock and peahen to be woven into a tapestry.[71] A set of drawings survive in Frankfurt that are evidently designs for engraved plaques to be attached to the terminals of a crucifix.[72] The design of various Gonzaga medals and of Francesco Gonzaga's 1495 coinage has also been attributed to Mantegna.[73] The coin dies were engraved by Gian Marco Cavalli, who had earlier, in February 1483, been charged with the execution of a silver service designed by Mantegna, which, like the Este service, contained elaborate vases.[74] It would be unwise to pretend that these designing tasks accrued more acclaim than Mantegna received for his learned and beautiful paintings. This was the painter, after all, who was allowed nine years to complete his famous *Camera Picta*. Nevertheless, Mantegna, always avidly engaged in the enhancement of his status,[75] attempted to isolate his mastery of *disegno* as a part of his aspirations to the status of artist. Although his paintings achieve so satisfactorily the effect of relief, like those of Tura, Pollaiuolo and other *disegnatori* of their generation, they are notably linear, seemingly intended to make their *disegno* obvious to the beholder.[76]

Moreover, in the early 1470s, he took up the challenge thrown down by Florentine goldsmith-designers (perhaps, in particular, the famous Antonio del Pollaiuolo), when he started to make prints. Although it has been generally argued that Mantegna executed his prints himself, the technical demands and time required might be thought to preclude his direct participation in engraving the plate. In fact, it now appears that he entered into some kind of business arrangement with Gian Marco Cavalli, who was to engrave plates after the painter's highly valued drawings.[77] By collaborating with a goldsmith – providing *him* with designs – Mantegna was surely attempting to fashion himself as a universal *ingegnoso* artist; he made at least two sculptures (including his self-portrait) and took up architecture, designing his own palace and funerary chapel.[78] Just as importantly, he produced these works as exercises in inventive *disegno*. He ensured a market for some of his early engravings by sticking to religious themes – works that therefore could be purchased as highly sophisticated specimens of the many printed devotional images that had long circulated in Italy. He was also more adventurous, choosing subjects that emulated that of Pollaiuolo's print – two *Bacchanals* and the *Battle of the Sea Gods*

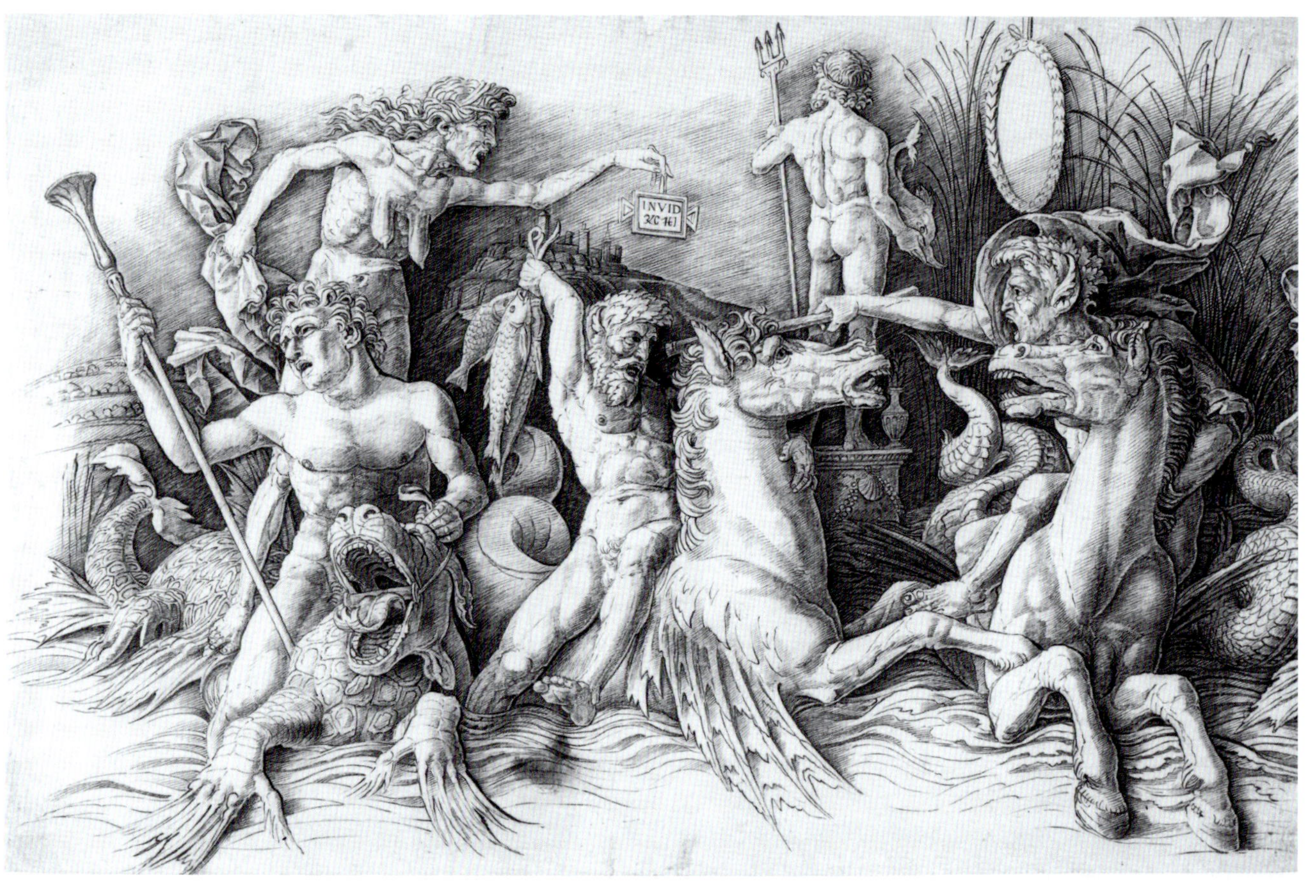

(fig. 124), which offered more scope for untramelled invention.[79] It cannot be coincidence that the protagonists of these *poesie*, all variations on antique models – satyrs, nereids, tritons, putti and hippocamps – so closely recall the decorative vocabulary employed by Tura, for example, in designs for the Este service. These were the characters in which the most bizarre and wonderful feats of nature could be excitingly combined by an artist of natural 'genius'.

During the first three-quarters of the fifteenth century painters and goldsmiths probably enjoyed approximately equivalent status, one or other group favoured depending on the city in which they worked. But that painters prevailed in the last two decades is demonstrated by a set of instances. For example, from about 1475 Mantegna's drawings were engraved by a second group of print specialists.[80] At this stage the name of the engraver was usually the only one to appear, the goldsmith's technical skills still constituting authorship (though the educated elite were probably in no doubt as to who was the designer of the image – the lack of Mantegna's own signature on his earlier prints is perhaps an indication of his extraordinary fame, rather than of any uncharacteristically modest self-effacement). This division of labour was to establish the pattern whereby Donato Bramante's signed 1481 architectural *fantasia* was engraved by Bernardino Prevedari (fig. 125), who had trained as a goldsmith in the Milanese shop of Giovanni Antonio Zaffaroni.[81] Prevedari had been commissioned by the painter Matteo Fedeli 'to

124 Gian Marco Cavalli after Andrea Mantegna, *Battle of the Sea Gods*; engraving; Mantua, *c*.1475. The British Museum, London

(*Opposite page*)
125 Bernardino Prevedari after Donato Bramante, *Architectural Fantasy*; engraving; Milan, 1481. The British Museum, London

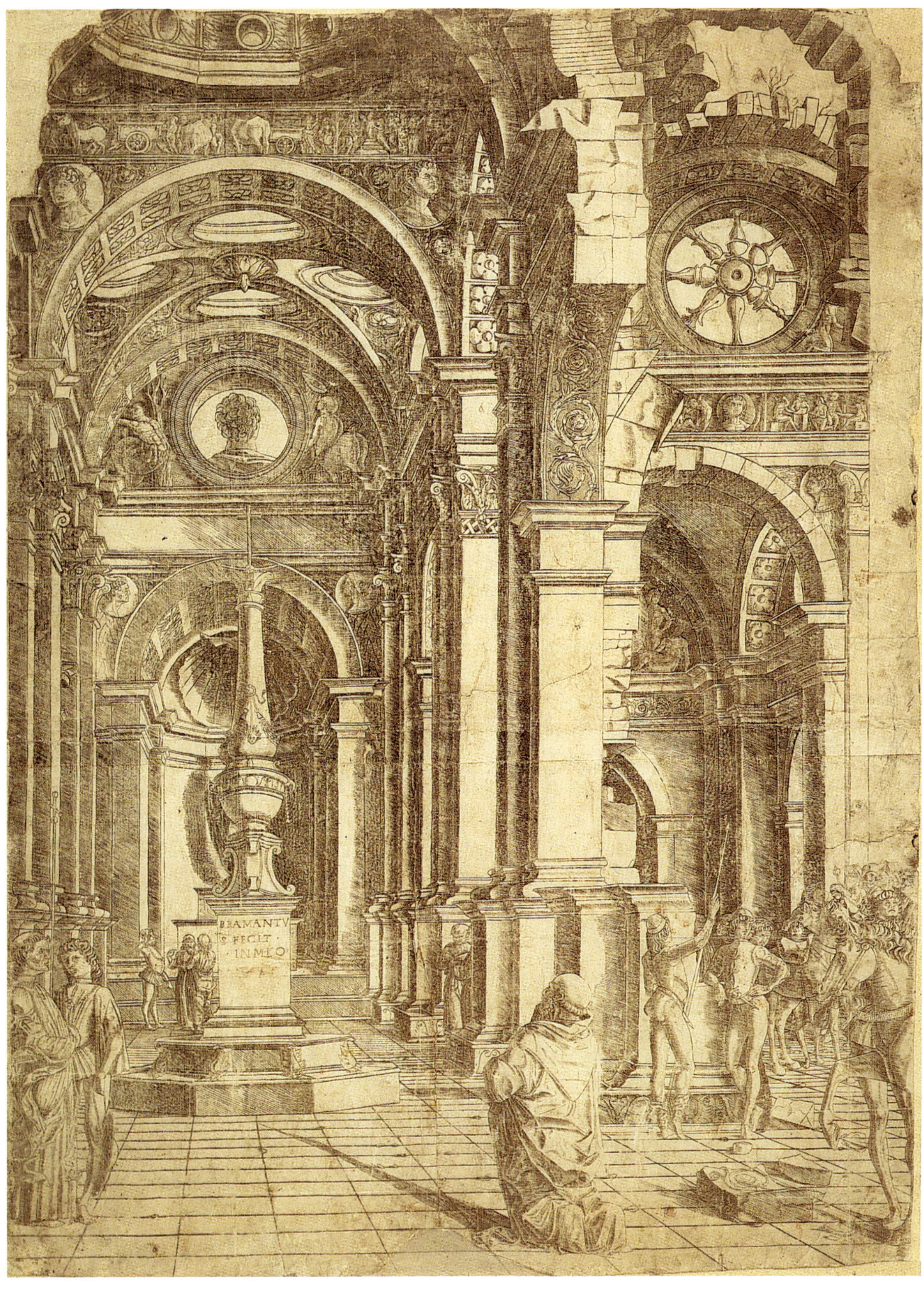

make … a print with buildings and figures, according to the design on paper made by Master Bramante of Urbino'. The very fact that these goldsmiths were not creating their own designs is significant. In the first and second decades of the sixteenth century drawings by Raphael were made into prints by Marcantonio Raimondi, who had learned his trade in Bologna with Francesco Francia, perhaps the most lavishly praised goldsmith of his day (see figs 119, 120). By this date the name of the inventor of a composition appeared in prints more often.[82] Like Pollaiuolo, Francia himself, although he continued to advertise his parallel career through his signature as a goldsmith on his many altarpieces, seems to have increasingly turned his talents towards his painting, which was in enormous demand.[83] Of course, many goldsmiths continued to design routine works themselves, just as Amadio da Milano had done in the Quattrocento. Some, like Caradosso, designed and executed works of extraordinary complexity and aesthetic ambition, and were famous for doing so.[84] But whereas painters continued to provide designs for goldsmiths' work (including many reproductive prints), after 1500 or thereabouts there appear to be no examples of goldsmiths performing as designers for media other than their own.

With the ascendancy of the painter in the last years of the fifteenth century there developed another potential tactic for raising the status of art objects: their acknowledged authorship by famous men. Although making designs for goldsmiths' work (and for other media) and the related activity of printmaking were so crucial in achieving an artistic position for painters, one cannot be sure that the spectator who admired the *credenza* of the Este or Gonzaga also knew that its contents were designed by Tura or Mantegna (though Pisanello's prominent signature as PICTOR – painter – on his medals might suggest that the contribution of great artists was already known and celebrated). However, given the enormous demands now made upon painters of the very highest calibre and the salaries they could command, the recognition of their designs became more crucial in conveying the influence and wealth of their patrons. Design authorship had never mattered more to the reception of goldsmiths' work.

Raphael's designs were certainly acclaimed, his drawings avidly collected and carefully preserved. His cartoons for the Sistine Chapel tapestries of the *Acts of the Apostles* were renowned throughout Europe.[85] He seems to have worked with Marcantonio and Baviero de' Carrocci (il Baviera) to exploit his drawings commercially as engravings – works purchased because they were by Raphael.[86] In 1510 the goldsmith Cesarino Rossetti da Perugia, then based in Rome, acknowledged receipt of 25 gold ducats for 'the composition and making of two bronze salvers', for the Sienese banker Agostino Chigi, from floral designs by Raphael.[87] And, when he provided goldsmiths with designs for metalwork, there was no question but that his was the more important contribution. When Francesco Maria della Rovere, Duke of Urbino, was defeated in battle by the forces of Pope Leo X, and was faced with the need to melt down his silver, his wife and mother attempted to rescue from the melting pot 'two basins with two bronze handles, very beautiful in their design [*molto belli de designo*] and [in] the antique mode, designed [*designati*] by Raphael' by offering to give them to Isabella d'Este, presumably in expectation of some financial compensation, sooner than throw away such beautiful work.[88] Although it is not abso-lutely certain that Raphael provided designs for the pieces as a whole, as one might expect,

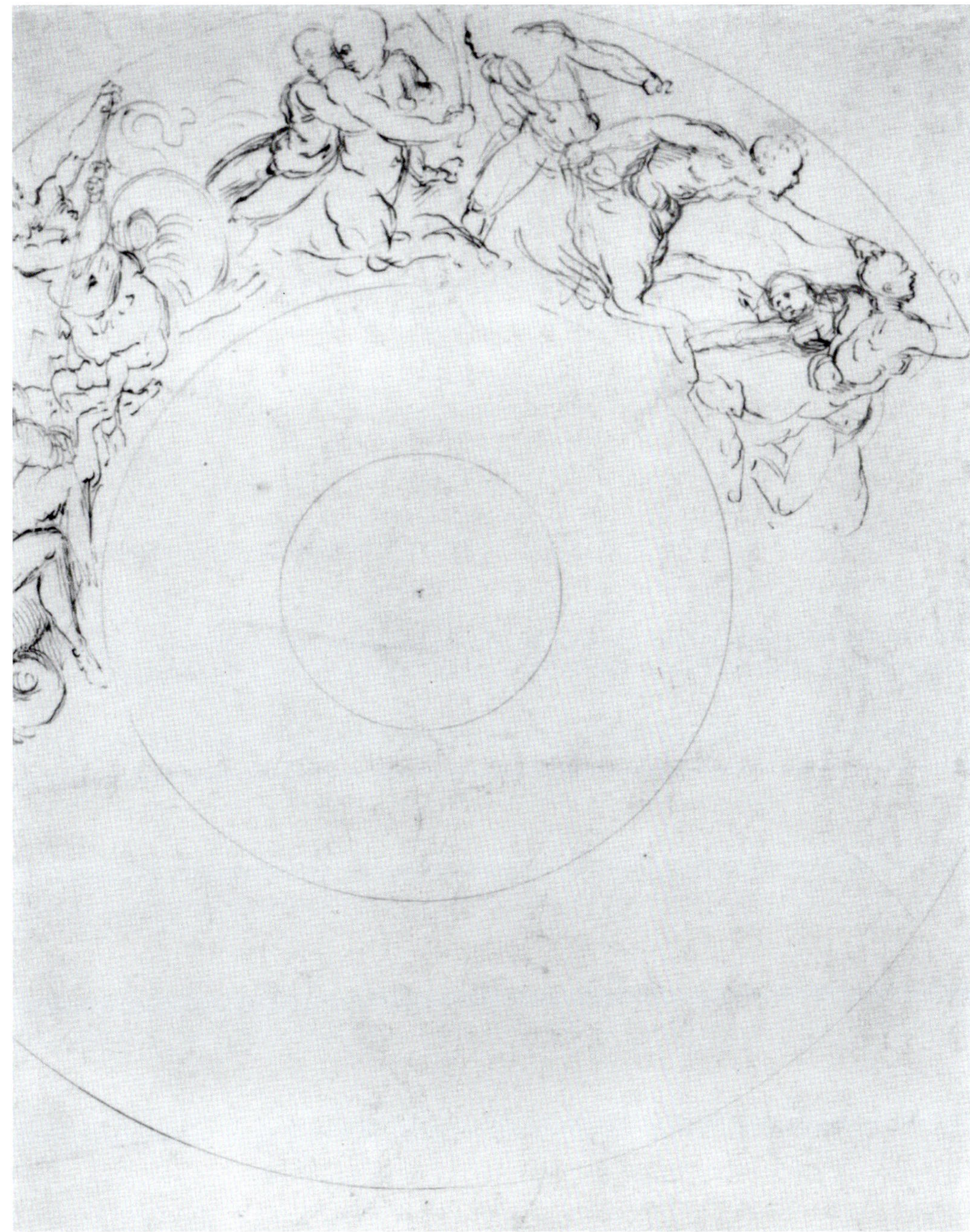

or merely for their handles, it is evident they were singled out because they were 'by' Raphael. It is noticeable that the goldsmith's name is nowhere mentioned. A drawing by Raphael for the border of a vessel now at Windsor, a rapidly sketched design of nymphs and tritons (recalling the design tropes of Mantegna's print), may be related to this project (fig. 126).[89]

Similarly, Perugino, Raphael's teacher, was dubbed *pictor excellentissimus* when he provided two groups of Perugian goldsmiths (Giovanni Battista di Mariotti de Marco and Filippo Giovanni Battista Mattei, and Federico Rossetti assisted by his more skilled younger brother Cesarino, who had earlier worked the Raphael drawings on the Chigi salvers) with the designs for a pair of elaborate nefs – boat-shaped salts or centrepieces – ordered in December 1512 by the prior of the Community of San Giuseppe in Perugia. The nefs were both unusually ambitious in design; the first (to weigh between 32 and 35 pounds) would have nineteen figures, two horses, foliage decoration, and other ornament. It is hard to imagine that, as effective overseer of two separate executive groups, Perugino would not have been thought the most important contributor to the projects.[90]

Given Raphael's activity in this area, it is not surprising that painters emerging from his large workshop also made designs for the decorative arts on the same basis, artists like Perino del Vaga and Polidoro da Caravaggio, both of whom benefited in particular from the patronage of the magnificent Farnese family.[91] Cellini seems to have been exceptional in this period in possessing sufficient skills to design his works in gold and silver himself. He attributed his success to his ability to draw, writing in his autobiography that 'when, among the jewels, there are placed figures, that [the jeweller] should know how to design [*disegniare*], otherwise he will not come to make anything good'.[92] But even he started by following designs by others. In Rome he obtained the commission for an *acquereccia* – a large two-handled vase – through the painter Gian Francesco Penni, *il Fattore* who also provided him with the design. He made other large silver vases after designs by Penni.[93] Indeed, his later artistic independence had to be demonstrated through the episode in his *Autobiography* when he reported his studied rejection of a drawing by Giulio Romano offered to him by Federico Gonzaga, and cited Giulio's opinion that he had no need of it.

That Cellini chose Giulio Romano, the leading pupil of Raphael, as his judge is nevertheless telling. Giulio, another artist of 'noble *ingenium*',[94] was perhaps the most complete painter-designer of them all.[95] In 1524 he became court artist to Federico Gonzaga, Marquis, then Duke, of Mantua. His talents as a designer were so esteemed that he was given the task of creating the entire 'look' of the Mantuan court: the architecture of the Palazzo Te and numerous other buildings, the design of many frescoes (some of which he executed himself) and tapestries.[96] He also produced a quantity of drawings for silver. A letter mourning his demise in 1546, written by Cardinal Ercole Gonzaga to Ferrante

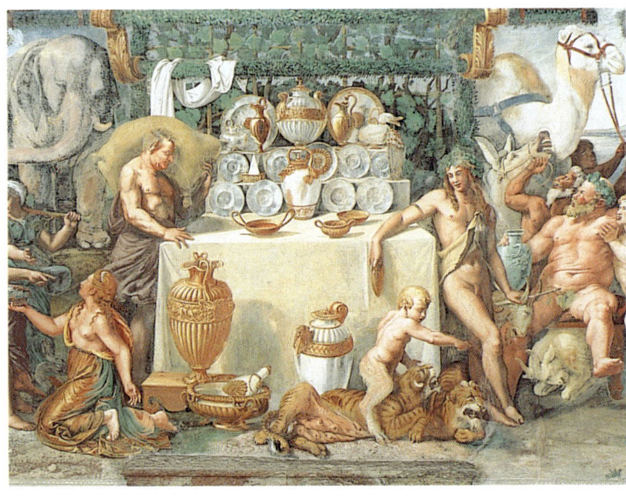

127 Giulio Romano
(with assistance),
The Marriage of Psyche (detail);
fresco; Mantua, 1528.
Palazzo Te, Mantua

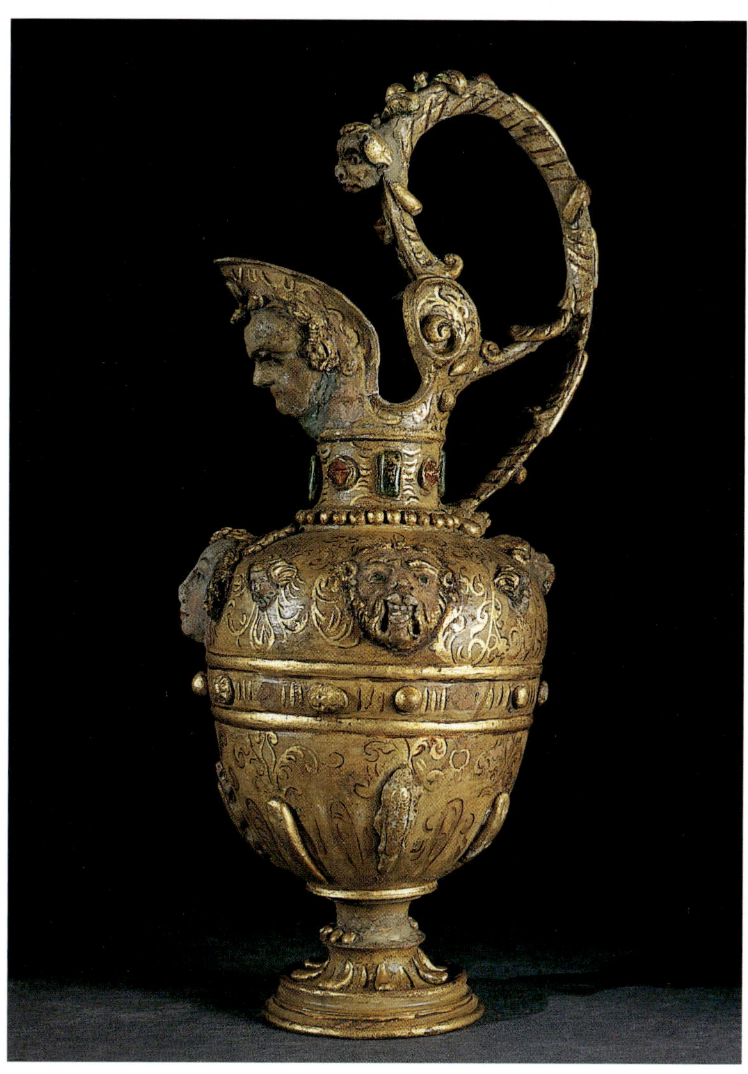

128 Terracotta model
for silver ewer;
Italy, *c*.1550–75,
Gilbert Collection,
London

Gonzaga, demonstrates that such work was considered even above his painting. The Cardinal wrote that

the death of this rare man has … acted upon me to spoil my appetite for the fabrication of silver, of painting and so on, because in fact I lack the will to make anything without the design of that beautiful talent [*senza il disegno di quello bello ingegno*], wherefore these little things finished, the designs for which I have before me, I think that buried with him will be all my desires.[97]

Here is explicit confirmation that *disegno* in the service of silver design was perceived as a symptom of *ingegno*. Vasari's account reflects the probable interpretation of Giulio's designs for silver by the artist's noble patrons. He extolled the fresco *The Marriage of Psyche* at the Palazzo Te (fig. 127): '[There] are three tiers of bizarre vases, basins, cups and such things fashioned in various forms and fantastic styles … an instance of Giulio's talents and ability, which was rich, varied and copious in invention and artifice.'[98]

Other Gonzaga documents give further indications that a gulf between the painter and the goldsmith had now opened. Goldsmiths could not always be trusted to carry out designs correctly, and Giulio preferred to have silver made locally so that he could act as supervisor. In February 1542 he wrote to Ferrante Gonzaga, then in Sicily, enclosing the designs for a pitcher and ewer (*boccale e bacino*), both with marine motifs. He was, however, anxious about consigning the execution to Sicilian goldsmiths, recommending instead two tried and tested locals (one of them probably his friend Ettore Donati): 'In truth the design needs careful working because there is nourishment for the eye in the variety of fish, which are hard to distinguish from real ones.'[99] In another revealing letter to Ferrante written in September 1546 Giulio complained:

One of Your Excellency's servants has brought me a vase, which does not correspond in any way to my design and even when it did agree with it, it does not surprise me that it did not turn out well since I was not present, because when one wants to make an unusual form, it is always necessary to make a model of wood or some other material, and test it first so that any defect emerges, and many times results can be achieved with an effort....[100]

A terracotta *modello* for a ewer from the second half of the sixteenth century now in the Gilbert Collection in London appears to be a unique survival of this practice (fig. 128).

Moreover, the value placed on his designs for goldsmiths' work is demonstrated by the fact that they were preserved and reproduced in exactly the same way as his purely figurative efforts (figs 129, 130). More than 200 drawings by Giulio or his workshop for the decorative arts are scattered through collections in Europe and America, slightly less than half of them for metalwork.[101] Some have instructions to the executive goldsmith. Others are inscribed in Giulio's hand with the function and patron of the piece. In the Victoria and Albert Museum, there is, for example, a drawing of a ewer inscribed 'For his lordship, the Cardinal of Mantua with all these ornaments' (*S[r] Cardinale di ma[n]toa co[n] tuti questi or[na]mi[n]ti*).[102] Another drawing of a covered salt is annotated: 'This I made for his Lordship Don Ferrante Gonzaga' (*Questo feci alo S[r] do[n] ferante gonzaga*) (fig. 131).[103] Many of these drawings were purchased in 1555 from Giulio's son by the enterprising scholar-dealer Jacopo Strada, who had already bought all of the architect Sebastiano Serlio's graphic works in Lyons, and Perino's drawings from his widow, Caterina Penni, in Rome. It seems likely that they were bought with the intention to copy them.[104] Copies of both Giulio's and Perino's designs were probably bound together in albums. A book of such copies, from the end of the Cinquecento, containing 100 drawings for silver made in the first half and entitled 'Drawings [*disegni*] for making gold and silver vessels to serve

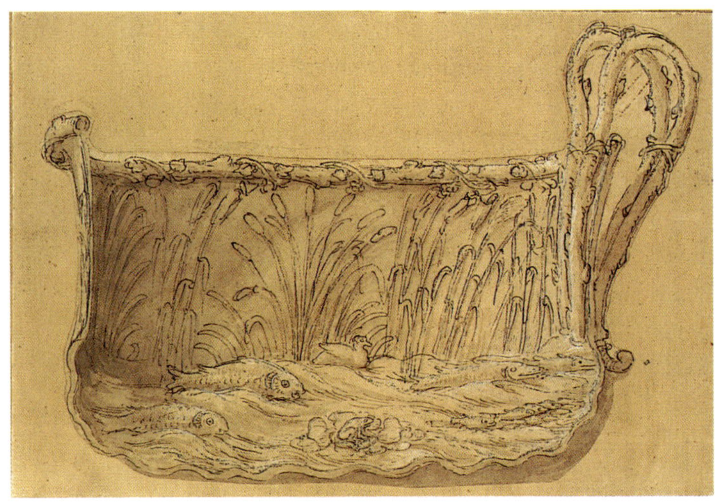

129 Giulio Romano, design for the interior of a basin; pen and ink and wash; Mantua, *c.*1525–45. The British Museum, London

130 Giulio Romano, design for a
double-spouted ewer; pen and
ink and wash; Mantua, *c*.1525–45.
The British Museum, London

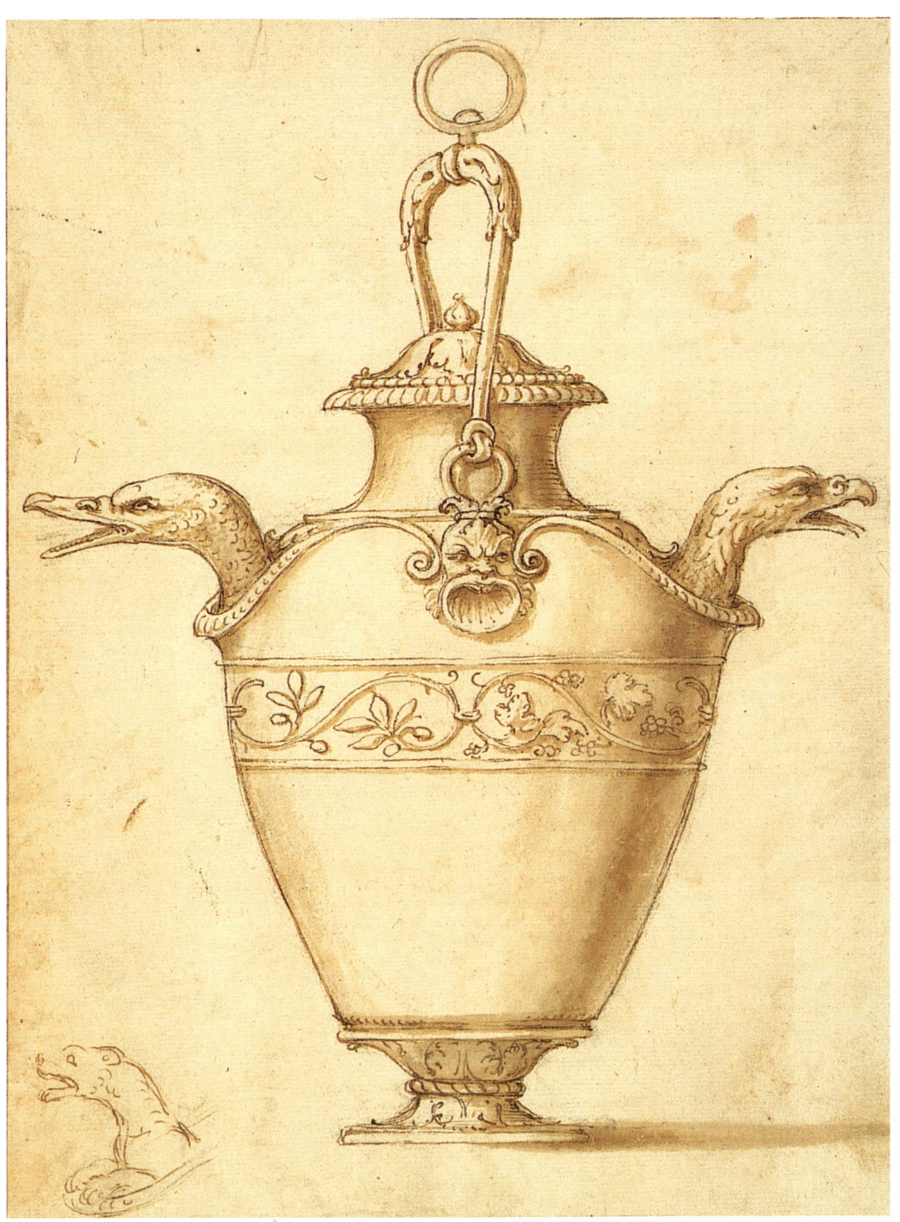

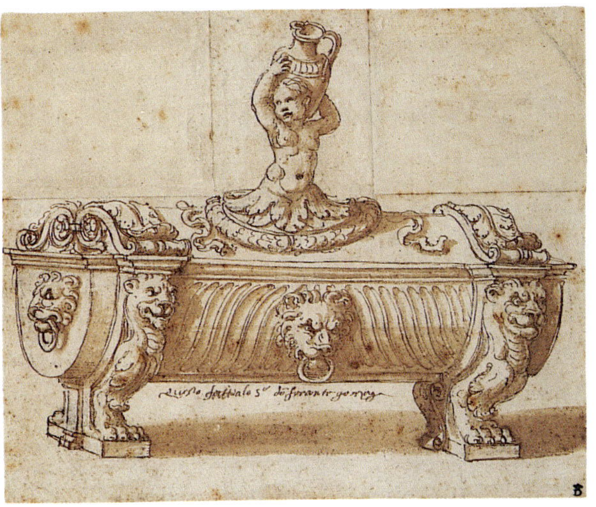

131 Giulio Romano, design for
a covered salt-cellar for Ferrante
Gonzaga; pen and ink and wash;
Mantua, after 1540 (?).
Chatsworth House, Derbyshire

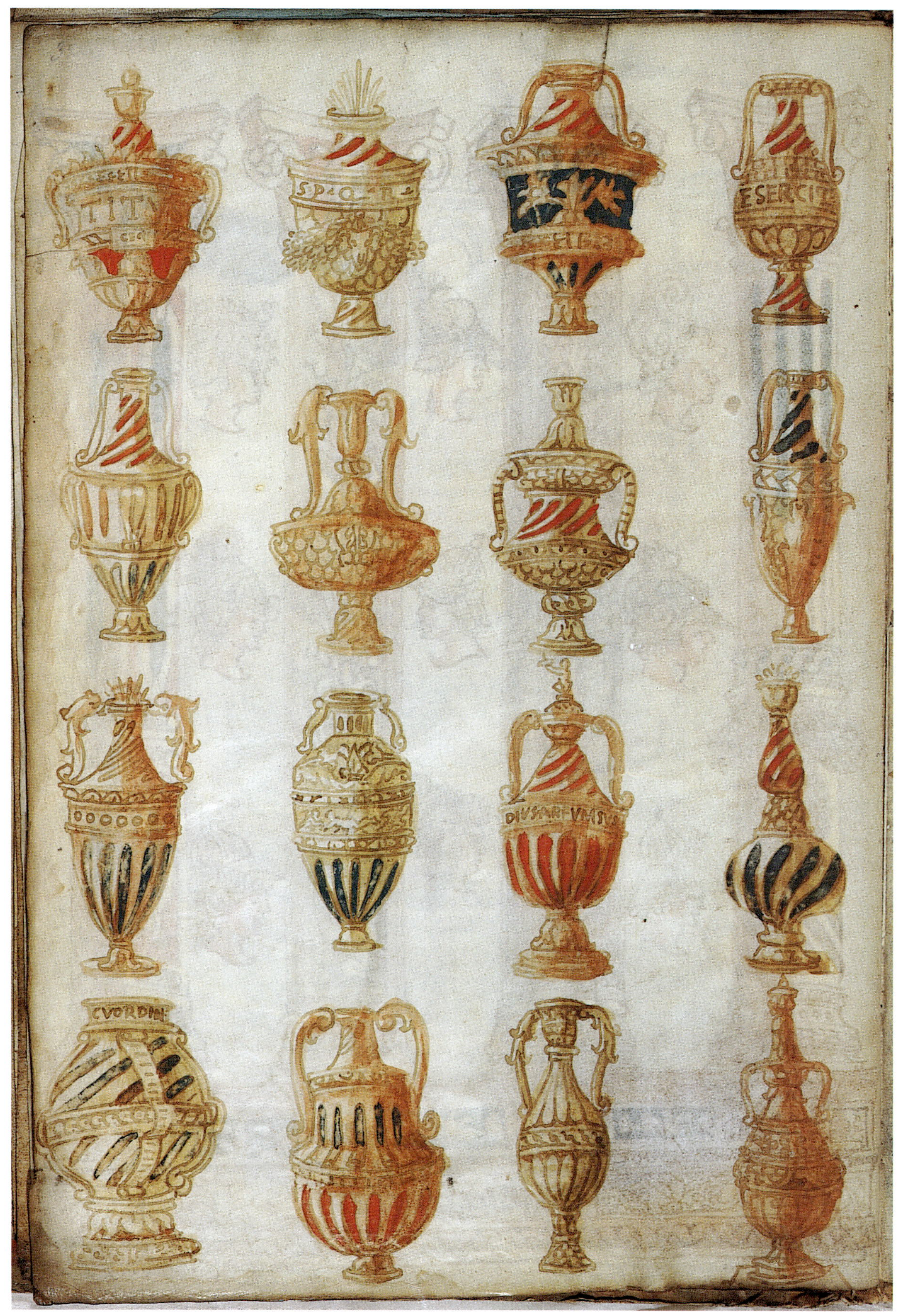

TIT
SP·Q·R·
ESERCIT
DIVSAREVMSVS
CVORDINI

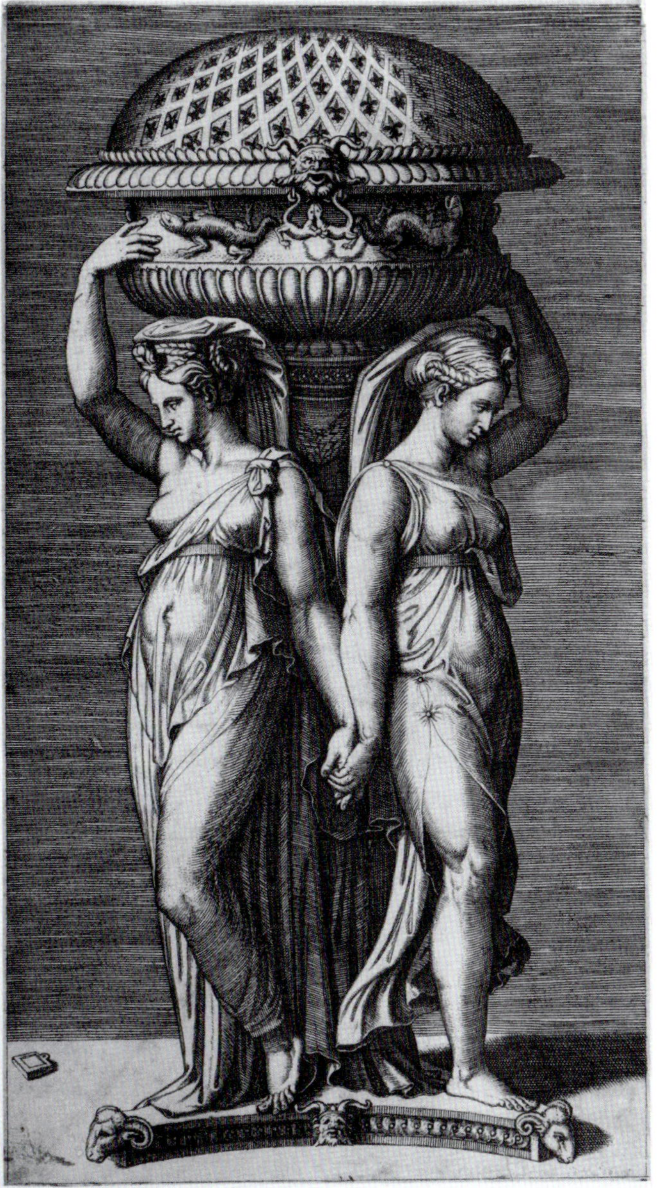

on the *credenza* or table of a great prince, all made in the antique mode and as are used today in Rome at the table of the Pope, cardinals and great lords' has survived in the Fitzwilliam Museum in Cambridge.[105]

Such practices were already current in the fifteenth century. In August 1485 Cosmè Tura earned 12 lire 'for the manufacture of making a drawing of the *credenza* with the silverware of the *sala grande* of Excellency to be sent to Milan to Signore Lodovico [il Moro]'.[106] A page from an album of architectural design and ornament, now in the Soane Museum, executed in northern Italy probably in the last quarter of the fifteenth century, is filled with coloured designs for gilt and enamelled *all'antica* vases (fig. 132).[107] The interest of patrons and collectors in these drawings gives a clue as to the function of the many so-called large-scale, high-quality 'ornament prints' (a nineteenth-century term that, revealingly, embraces engravings of architectural motifs) executed after 1500 or there-abouts. They could be and certainly were used as design sources by other artists (and,

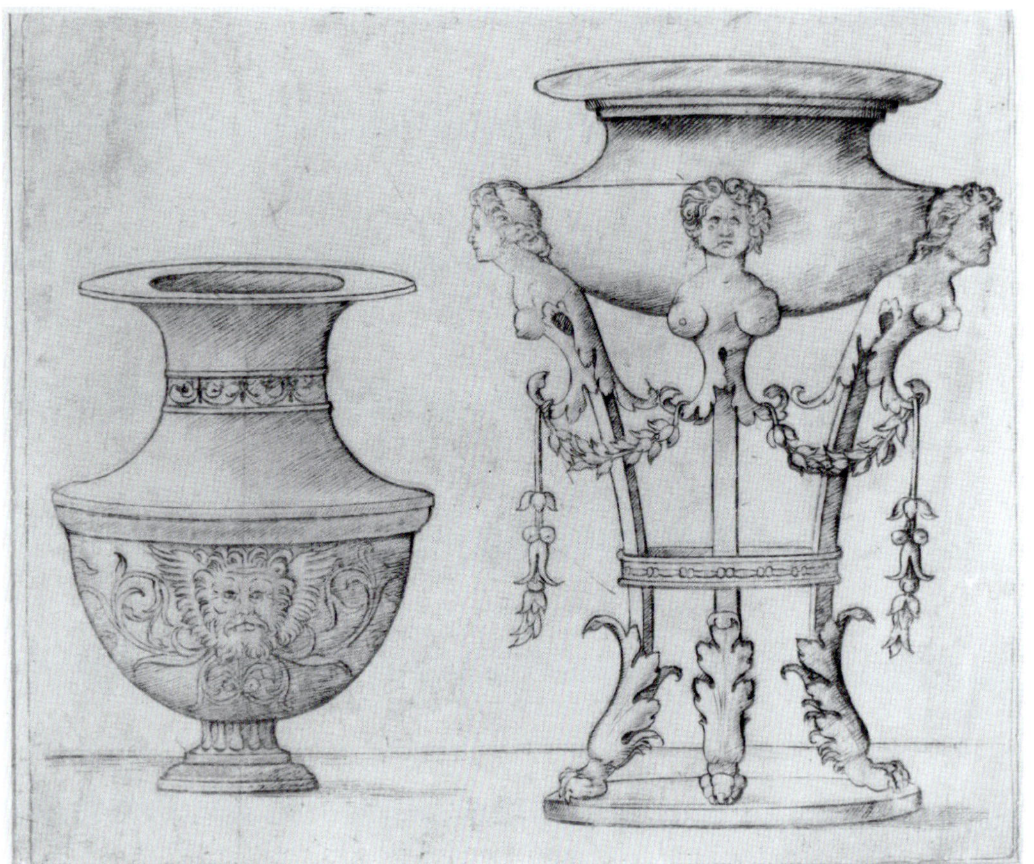

134 Giovanni Antonio da Brescia (attributed) after Andrea Mantegna (?), *all'antica* vessels; engraving; Mantua, *c.*1510–20. Victoria and Albert Museum, London

because some such prints were executed in Italy with this sole function in mind from probably the 1520s, this is how they are usually discussed today), but that is not necessarily how they were first intended. Like the pioneering figurative *disegni stampati* by Mantegna and Pollaiuolo, ornament prints were often produced as models of great design. A few were clearly reproductive. Marcantonio Raimondi, for instance, engraved a print after a design by Raphael for a bronze perfume burner that had been sent to Francis I of France (fig. 133).[108] Zoan Andrea and Giovanni Antonio da Brescia, both of whom made prints after Mantegna's figurative designs, also made prints of ornament and of *all'antica* art objects (fig. 134).[109] It is by no means impossible that some of these might also have been based on Mantegna's inventions.

Two prints were engraved by Cherubino Alberti in 1583 after knife designs executed earlier in the century by Francesco Salviati (fig. 135), the celebrated painter who had trained as a goldsmith (with Francesco di Girolamo dal Prato, said to be the best draughtsman among the goldsmiths of his day) but who never practised the art.[110] Salviati's role as inventor of these designs is signalled and the original drawings may also have contained signatures or had, at least, a traditional attribution attached to them. One of the prints reproduces a design that was actually translated, albeit in a somewhat simplified form, into a knife that is today in the Bargello (fig. 136).[111] The knife is undated but it may actually

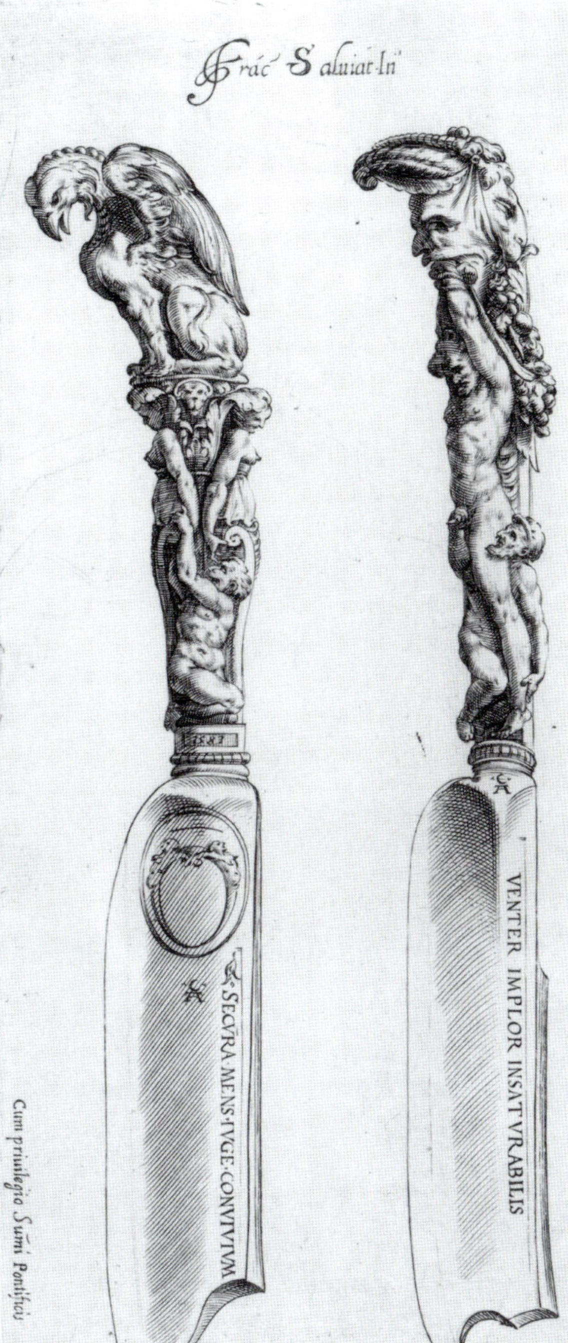
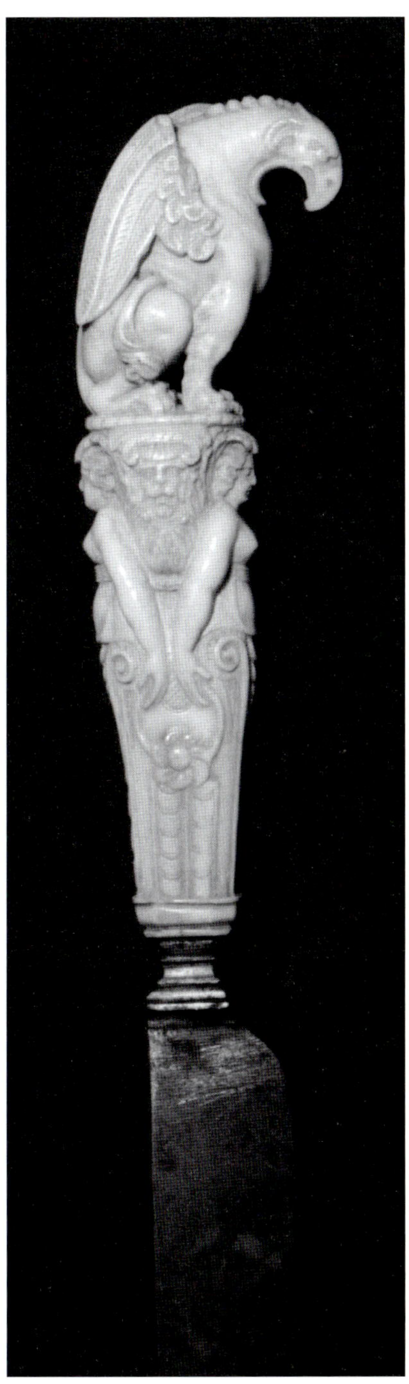

135 Cherubino Alberti after Francesco Salviati, designs for knife handles; engraving; Rome, 1583. The British Museum, London

136 After Francesco Salviati, knife handle; carved ivory; Italy, mid-sixteenth century. Bargello, Florence

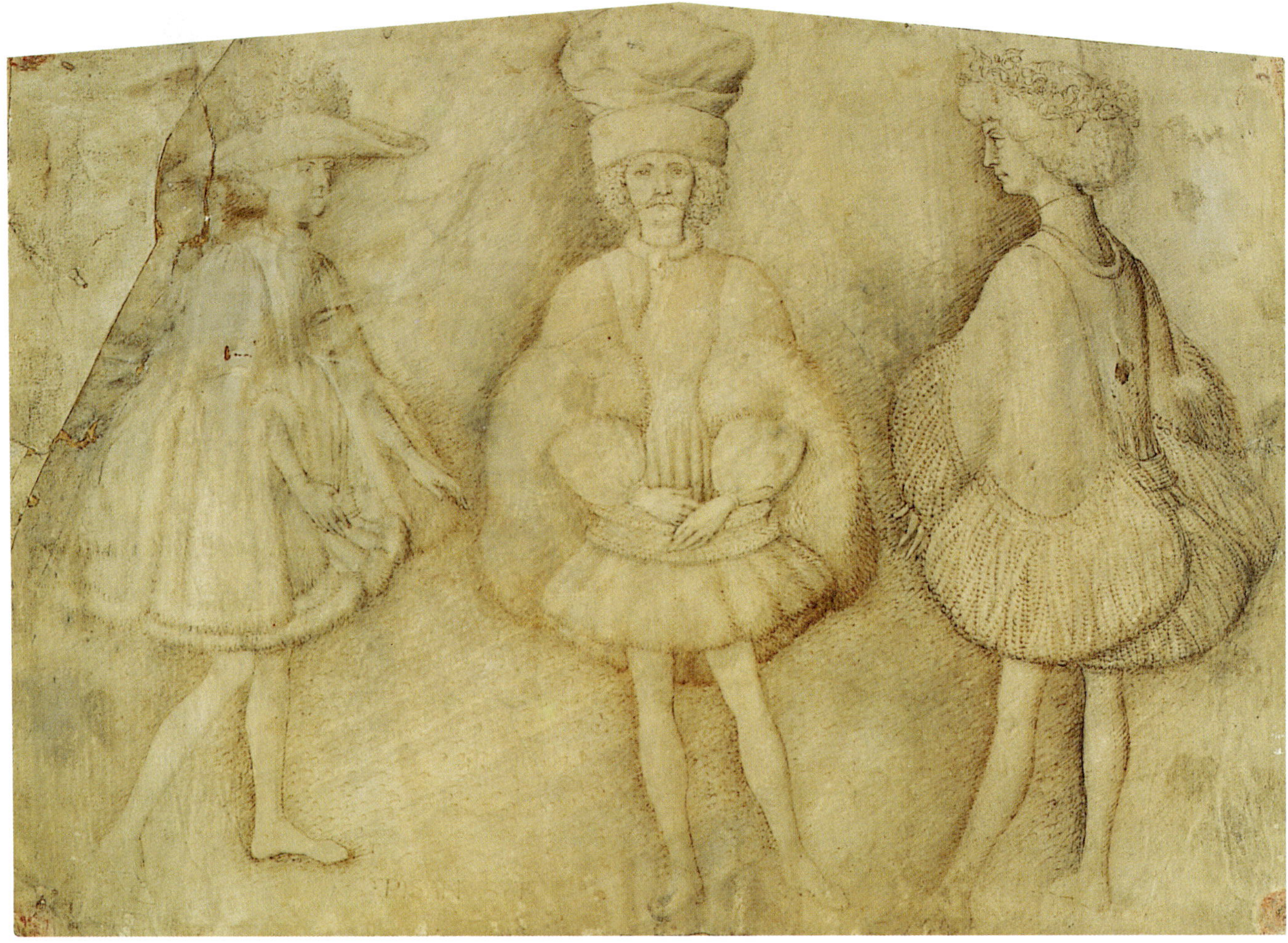

137 Pisanello, *Three Men in Court Dress*; pen and ink and wash with black chalk on parchment; Mantua or Ferrara, *c*.1432. The British Museum, London

predate the print rather than copy it, as is generally assumed. However, it is also possible that Salviati executed these designs as wonderful exercises in *disegno*. This is the way that one should understand many other ornament prints and in this respect they differ little from figurative prints made by Marcantonio and Agostino Veneziano after the drawings of Raphael and Giulio Romano, or by Gian Jacopo Caraglio after Perino, Parmigianino and Rosso Fiorentino. Engravings of vessels and ornament were printed alongside these figurative works from a very early date. The generally excellent condition of surviving examples points to their careful storage; they were not left floating about in a workshop or tacked to walls above workbenches. If prints of *vasi di pompa* such as those made by Agostino after designs by Polidoro da Caravaggio were indeed used as *modelli* by craftsmen, this was not their primary function.[112]

At more or less exactly the same time as such works on paper began to be prized by collectors, artists started making drawings as completed works of art in their own right. The engraving of prints discussed was paralleled by the execution of presentation drawings – highly finished works of art made as examples of pure *disegno* – so called today because some of their best-known authors gave them to their friends. In fact, as many of them may have been sold as given away. Offshoots of the *modello*, the tradition can probably be traced back to Pisanello, our first painter-designer. In the early 1430s Pisanello signed a drawing in pen and brown ink on parchment, showing three young men seen from different angles in magnificent court dress, PISANVS F[ECIT] – Pisano made this (fig. 137).[113] While there is no reason that this drawing should not have been used later as a design source, its level of finish and, in particular, the inclusion of a carefully lettered signature suggests that it was an end in itself. Some of Mantegna's most finished drawings have also been characterized in this way. He included an elaborate signature on a drawing of *Judith and her Maid-Servant*, now in the Uffizi.[114] Two early drawings for silver were clearly prized as *invenzioni* beyond the fact that they could be translated into actual objects: Pollaiuolo exceptionally appended his signature (as an *horafo*, a goldsmith) to two designs on a single sheet of the 1460s in the Uffizi, for a censer and a salt (fig. 138); Salviati's beautifully complex drawing in the Ashmolean of a vase (fig. 139) can certainly be classified as a presentation drawing or even a drawing for sale, much more finished than its use as a source for a goldsmith would demand.[115] Although the enjoyment of such drawings by Francesco de' Medici, Grandduke of Tuscany, falls outside the chronological scope of this book, it is likely that he inherited his pleasure from his princely forebears. In October 1572 Giorgio Vasari wrote that 'every evening the Prince has wished me to be present until three o'clock in the morning to draw vases as long as I live'.[116]

Michelangelo, sculptor, painter and architect, was commonly dubbed the 'prince', or even the 'god' of *disegno*, not just on account of his own works but because he not

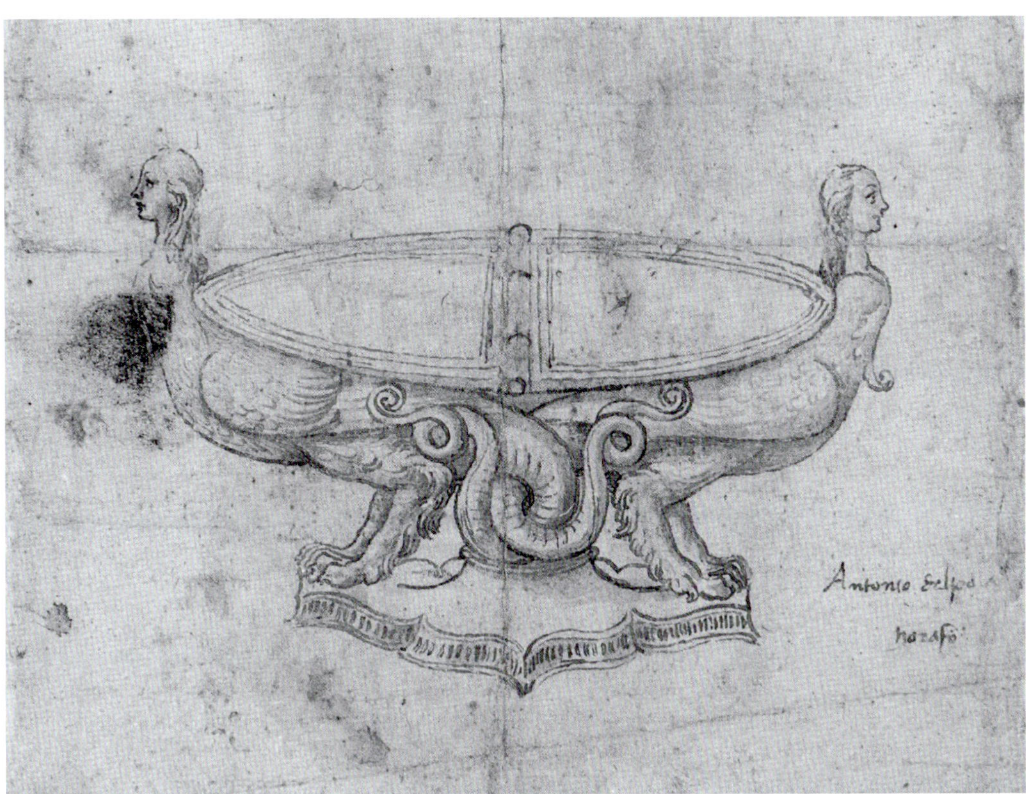

138 Antonio del Pollaiuolo, design for a salt-cellar; pen and ink and wash; Florence, *c.*1460. Gabinetto dei Disegni, Uffizi, Florence

infrequently made drawings and cartoons for others to follow. He attained his extraordinary position by extending the division between design and execution in the production of gold and silver to a recognized distinction between himself and other painters and sculptors, making a series of designs for Sebastiano del Piombo, Jacopo Pontormo (both successful in their own right), his biographer Ascanio Condivi, and 'Minighella, a clumsy painter of Valdarno but a very amusing man', among others.[117] When the designs were translated into finished paintings, Michelangelo's designing role was certainly known, and these drawings were usually treasured and copied. His only surviving drawing for a goldsmith (fig. 140), now in The British Museum, was also copied by other artists. Despite this lack of graphic evidence, however, it seems that his collaborations with goldsmiths were not infrequent. He often assisted his friend Piloto[118] and made models for a salt-cellar

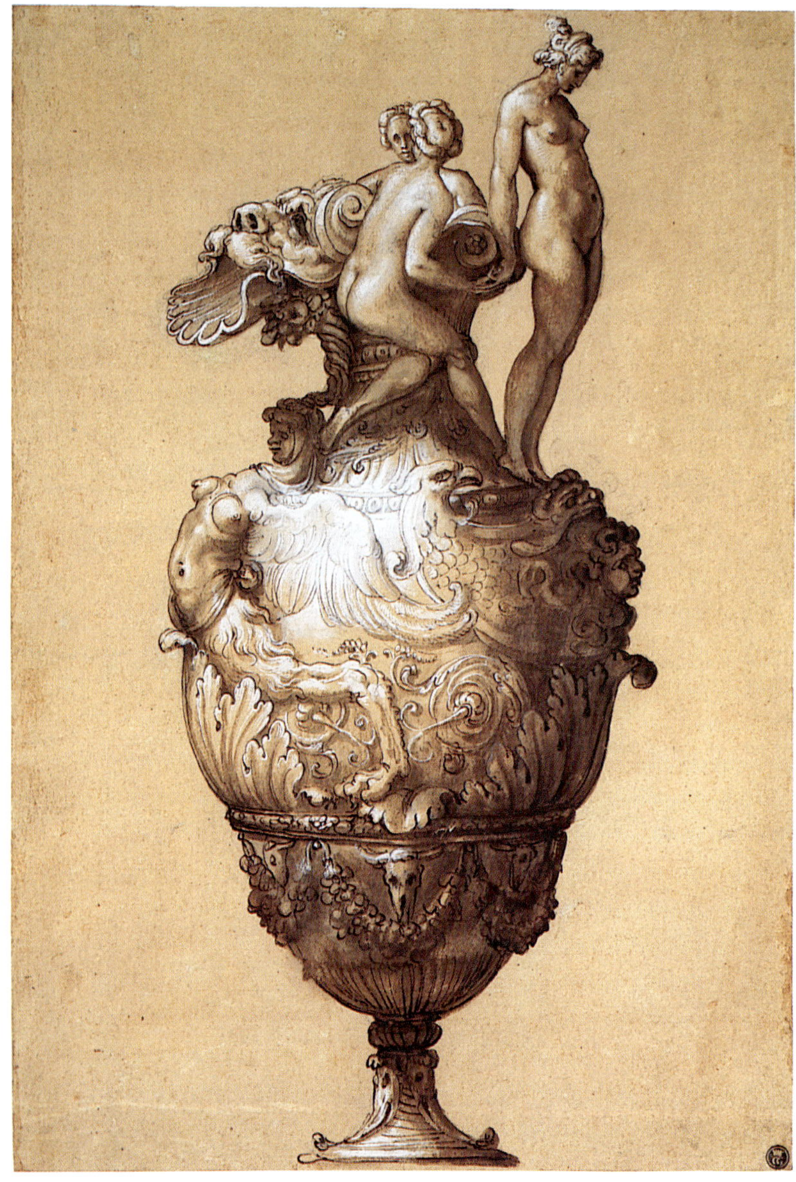

139 Francesco Salviati,
presentation drawing of a vase;
pen and ink and wash over black
chalk with white heightening;
Florence (?), c.1545–50.
The Ashmolean Museum, Oxford

commissioned by Cardinal Alessandro Farnese from the Roman goldsmith Manno di Sbarri. The cardinal was presented with alternative designs – a drawing and a terracotta – and a letter from Tommaso de' Cavalieri, friend to both artist and patron, who brokered the deal, shows that Michelangelo prepared the model himself: a vessel supported by four tortoises with a lid surmounted by single sculpted nude.[119] The attribution of the British Museum drawing for a salt with a Cupid on its cover to Michelangelo is confirmed by a letter written to Francesco Maria della Rovere, Duke of Urbino, in July 1537 by his Roman agent, Girolamo Staccoli:

… the model of the salt-cellar with relief decoration was finished a few months ago and some of the animals' legs, on which the vessel of the salt will be placed, are begun in silver, and around this vessel there run certain festoons with some masks, and on the cover a figure in the round with other

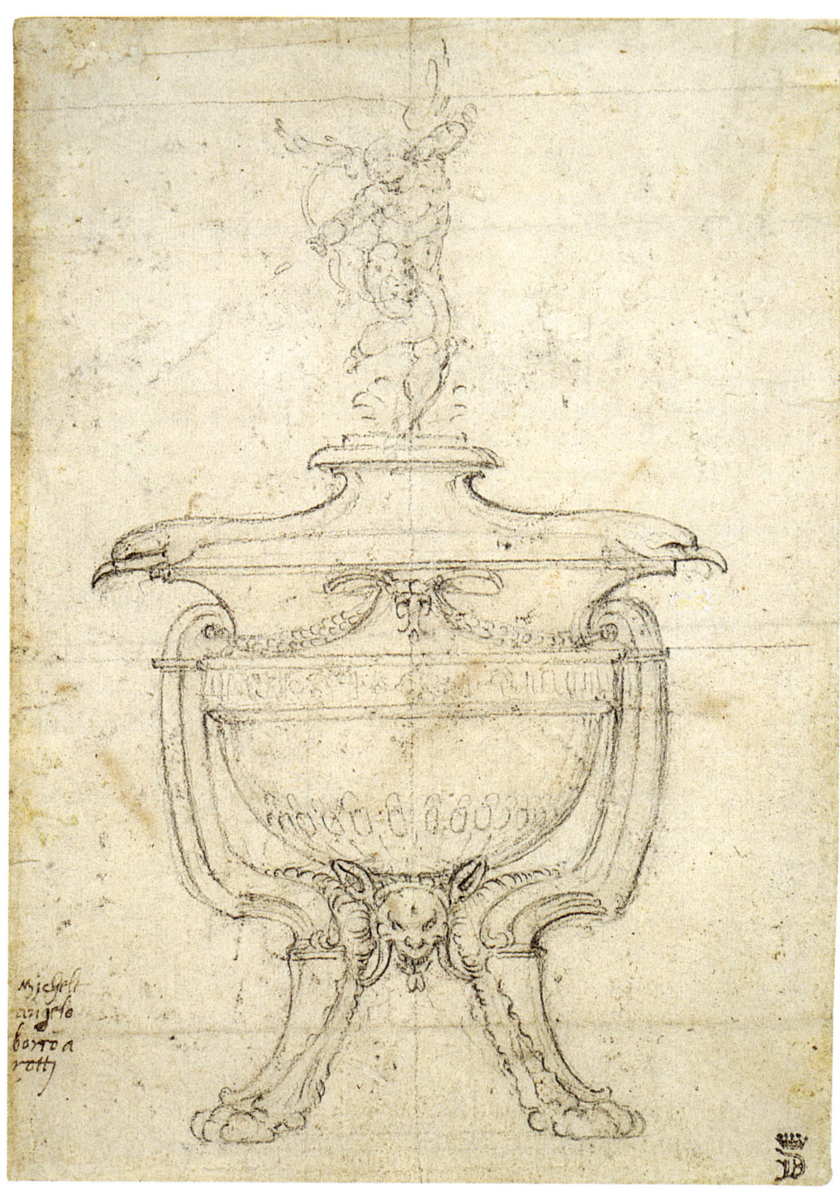

140 Michelangelo, design for a
salt-cellar; black chalk; Rome, 1537.
The British Museum, London

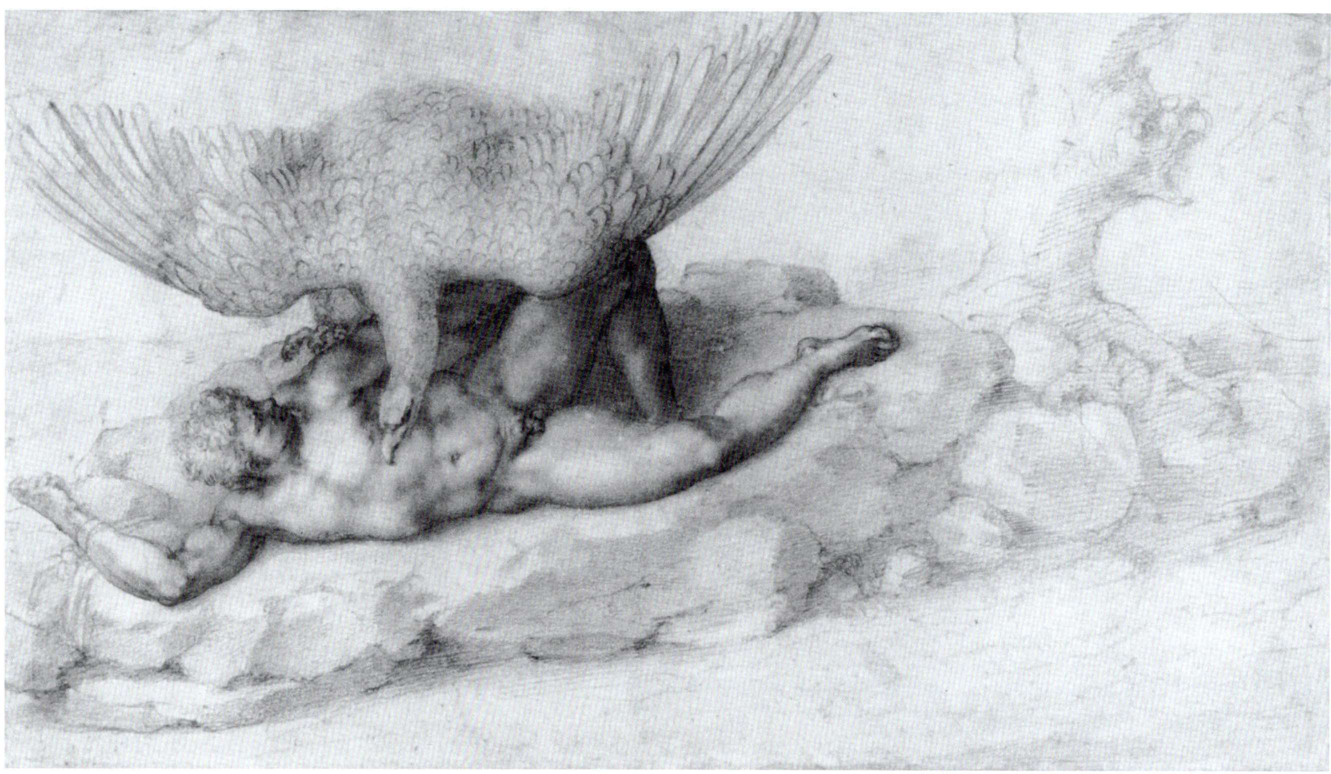

141 Michelangelo, *Tityus Devoured by a Vulture*; black chalk; Rome, 1532. Her Majesty the Queen, Windsor

foliage, according to how Michelangelo prescribed and according to the abovesaid finished model. Considering that he has spent over eighteen ducats in its manufacture, and as it is going to cost more than this, I did not wish to proceed further without the knowledge and approval of your Majesty….[120]

Michelangelo was also one of the first artists whose *invenzione* was acknowledged on a print by another hand: Marcantonio made a print, naming Michelangelo, after one of the male nudes in his cartoon for the unexecuted fresco of the Battle of Cascina, of which Cellini said 'nothing survives of ancient or modern art that touches the same lofty point of excellence'.[121] It was perhaps the fact that his drawings were so valued that inspired him to execute in the early 1530s the largest group of presentation drawings seen up to that time. He gave the first pair, black chalk drawings of *Tityus Devoured by a Vulture* (fig. 141) and the *Rape of Ganymede*, to Tommaso de' Cavalieri in 1532. As the visual equivalent of the many loving sonnets dedicated to Cavalieri, the choice of subjects was deliberately literary. The next year he added a *Fall of Phaeton* to the group, the composition 'improving' a renowned sarcophagus then to be seen outside the church of Santa Maria Aracoeli in Rome. There now survive three autograph versions of this narrative; the earliest, in The British Museum (fig. 142), was sent to Cavalieri with a message offering to draw another version the next evening if he disliked it, or to finish it if he was pleased. Although Cavalieri retained this drawing, Michelangelo executed two more, one now in the Venice Accademia (fig. 143) and the other – the most finished of the three, which was sent to Cavalieri probably in late August 1533 – in Windsor (fig. 144).[122] Their arrival was a public event, and Cavalieri received visits from the Pope, Cardinal Ippolito de' Medici and 'everyone'.[123] It is likely that the drawings were made with the expectation that they could be copied; indeed, Vasari compares them to the drawings made by Michelangelo for the painter Sebastiano del Piombo. In this way they could profit Cavalieri, who seems sometimes to have acted as Michelangelo's go-between or agent, as well as functioning as propaganda for the 'genius' of the artist.[124] Drawn and painted copies were made by artists in Michelangelo's circle, Giulio Clovio and Salviati, and all three were engraved as prints in the 1540s by Nicolas Beatrizet.[125] Most tellingly, Ippolito de' Medici immediately took them away to have them cut into rock-crystals by the noted gem-engraver Giovanni Bernardi da Castelbolognese, a commission he probably completed before his patron's death in 1536.

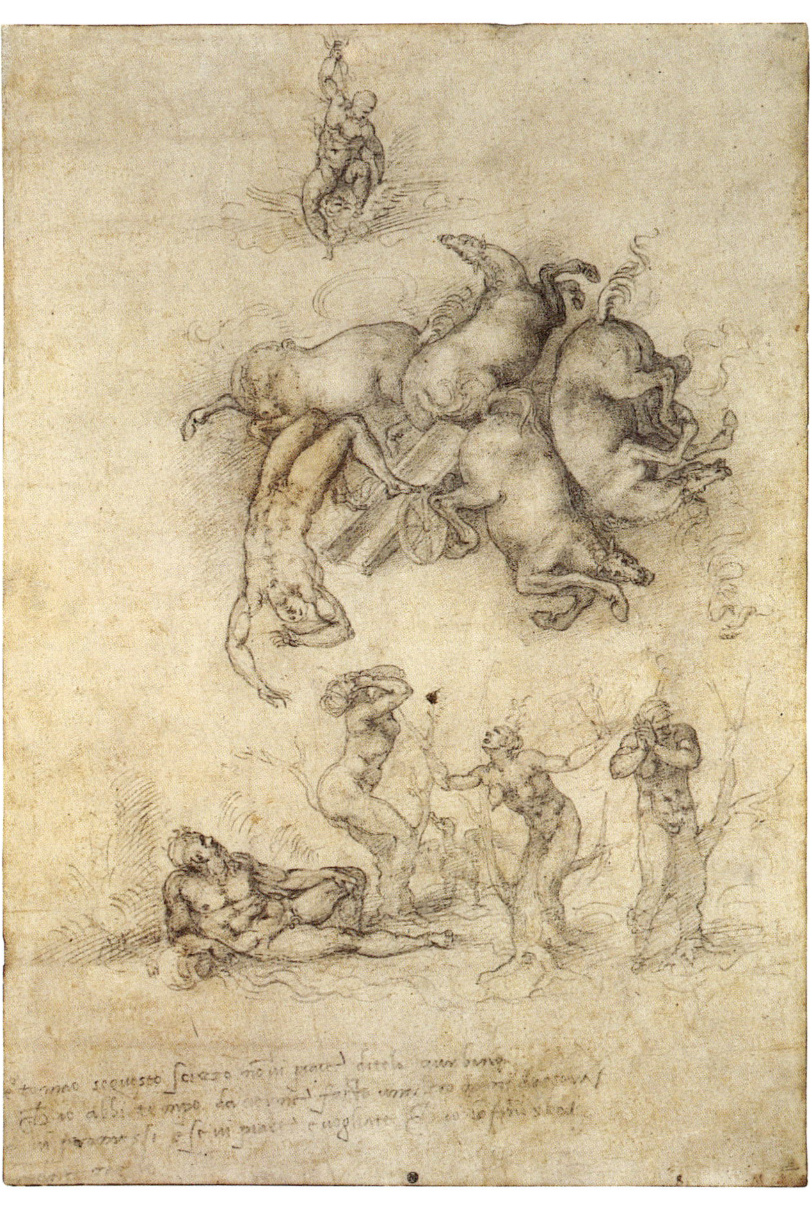

142 Michelangelo, *The Fall of Phaeton*; black chalk; Rome, 1533. The British Museum, London

For these drawings to be rendered in crystal they had to be regarded as compositions displaying remarkable *ingegno* – a step beyond the simpler concept of design quality matching the preciousness of the medium. Gold and silver might be costly but gemstones were considered valuable in another way: it was thought that they might contain designs composed by Nature herself. Engravers were expected to release or realize Nature's art; they could, for instance, exploit the coloured layers contained in a stone to give appropriate hues to the image on a cameo; the genius of Nature guiding the hand of the natural genius of man.[126] Collectors adored the transparency of rock-crystal and its engravers were considered the carvers of light itself. Thus for a painter to have his designs reproduced in this medium was recognition of his *ingegno*. The list of painters so considered is not unexpected. Polidoro, Perino and Salviati all made designs for gems in Rome, many of

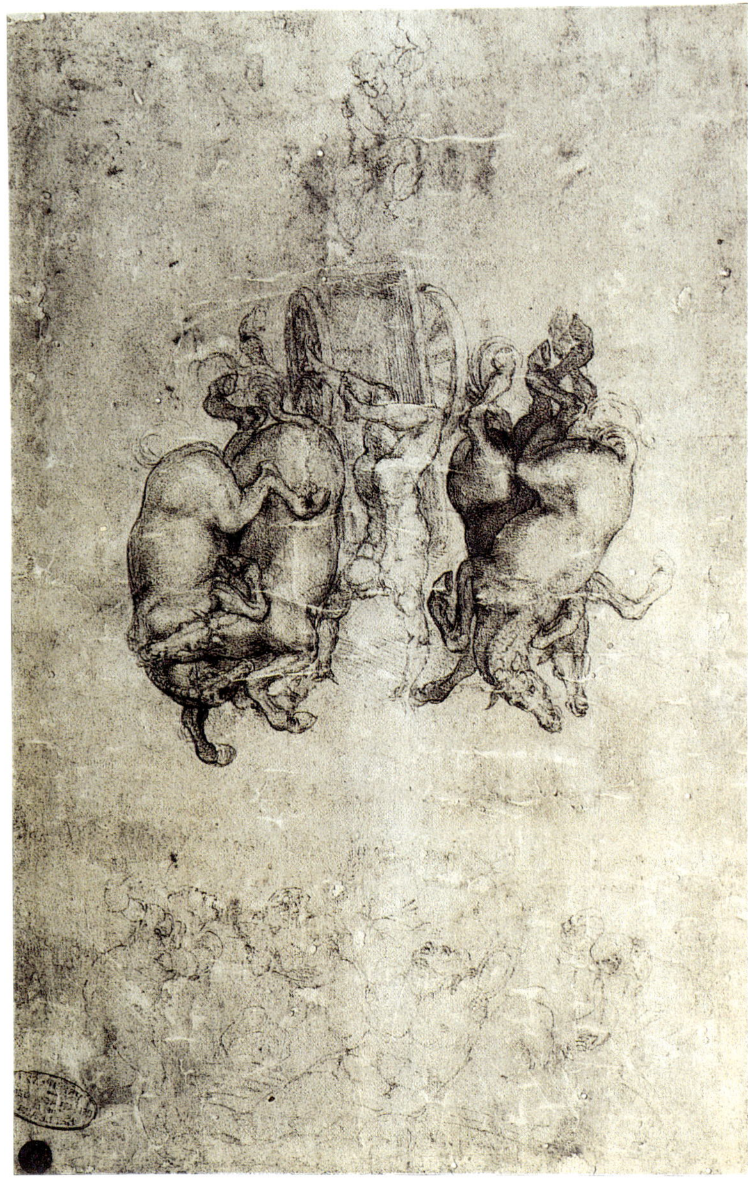

143 Michelangelo,
The Fall of Phaeton;
black chalk;
Rome, 1533.
Accademia, Venice

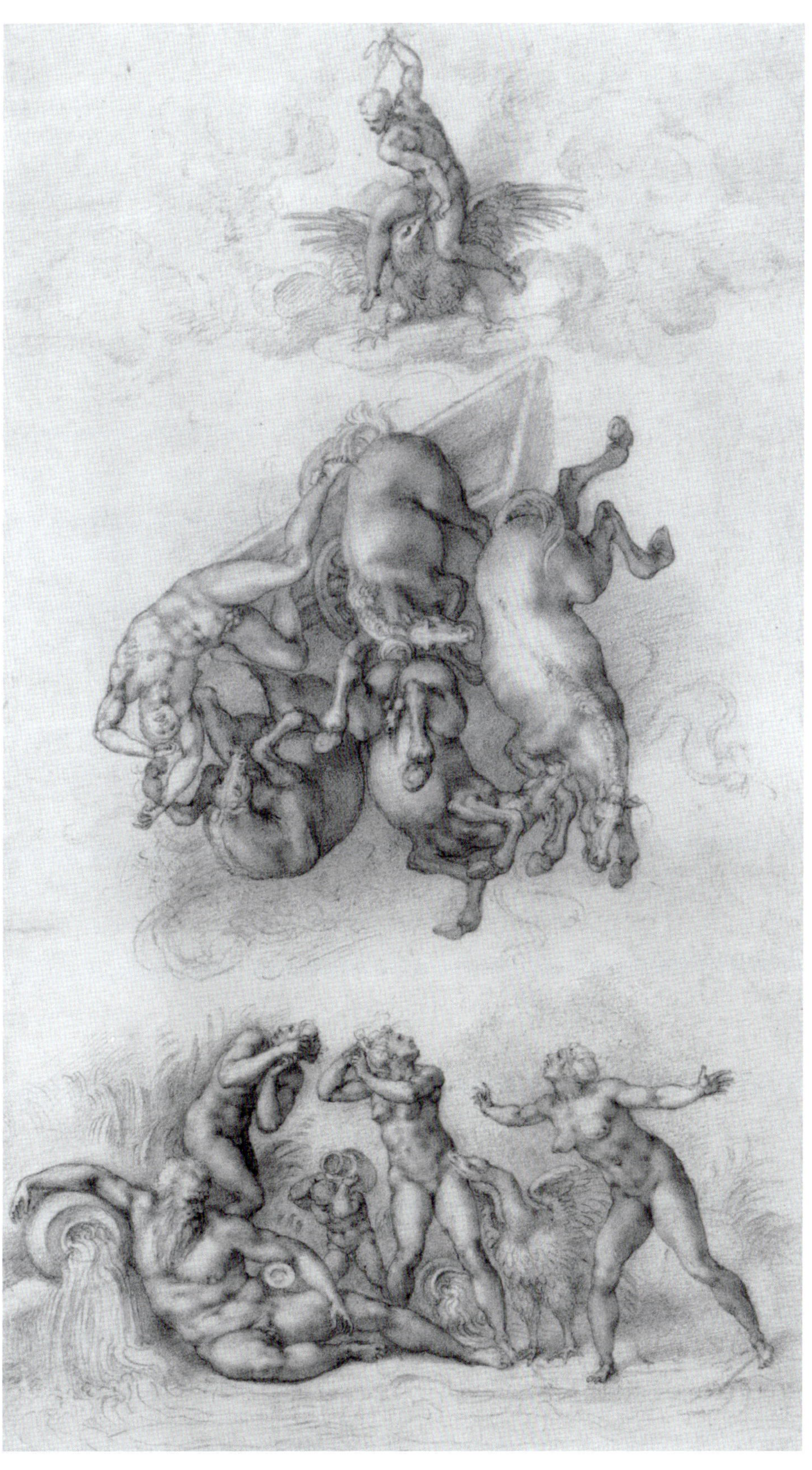

144 Michelangelo,
The Fall of Phaeton;
black chalk; Rome, 1533.
Her Majesty the Queen,
Windsor

them for the Farnese.[127] Giulio also made drawings specifically for gems; one, for a second casket commissioned by a member of the Farnese family, Cardinal Alessandro, was later turned into a print.[128] In 1521 the Vicentine Valerio Belli, praised by Vasari as an engraver but condemned by him as an inadequate draughtsman, repeatedly petitioned Michelangelo for a drawing. His subject was to be 'a sacrifice'. There is no evidence that Michelangelo complied (though a signed rock-crystal in The British Museum (see fig. 81) shows Belli's debt to the great Florentine), but the lack of specificity of Belli's request indicates that the iconography of the proposed crystal intaglio was unimportant. In his last, direct plea to Michelangelo, Belli states that he has a beautiful piece of stone waiting and that the finished work would 'do honour to your *concetto* and not bring you shame'.[129]

Although gem-engravers might sometimes simplify a composition for technical reasons, they seem to have been expected to follow the designs provided for them relatively faithfully. The leading engraver in Italy in the last decade of the Quattrocento was Francesco Anichini. In March 1496 Isabella d'Este ordered a turquoise intaglio gem of Orpheus from him. It would cost 10 ducats and the engraver had been provided with a drawing. Giorgio Brognolo, one of Isabella's agents in Venice wrote to his mistress: 'I have received the drawing of Orpheus and given it to Francesco Anichini, who says that it is not possible to make in that way, that is with his legs bent, but that he will make it well [with Orpheus] standing, saying that in such a little thing he cannot render it otherwise.' Isabella insisted on Orpheus remaining seated and got her way, the engraver now enthusiastically reporting that 'the turquoise could not be better suited to the purpose, since it has a certain black vein that will seem like the rock on which he sits'.[130] Isabella later allowed Anichini to select his own subjects.

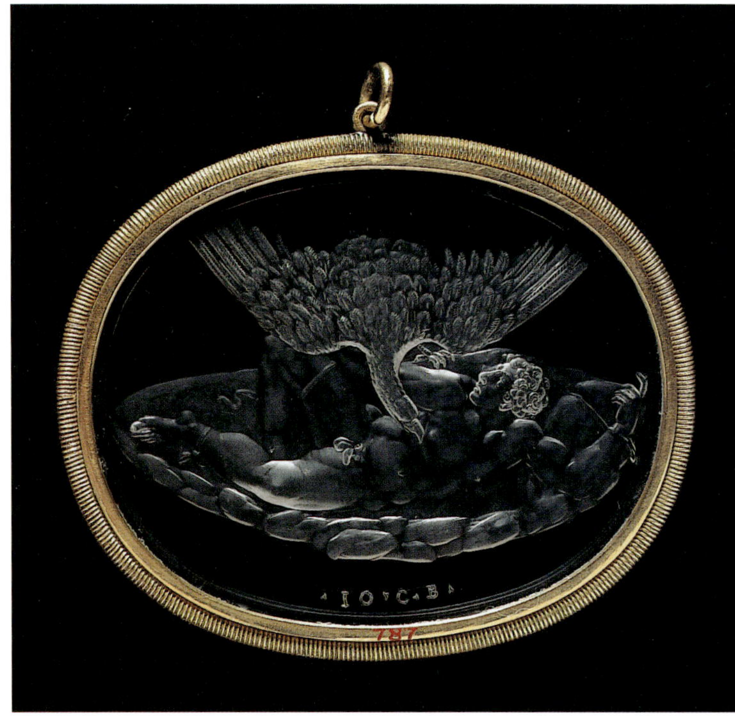

145 Giovanni Bernardi da Castelbolognese after Michelangelo, *Tityus*; rock-crystal intaglio; Rome, *c.*1533–5. The British Museum, London

After the death of Cardinal Ippolito in 1535 Bernardi's rock-crystal intaglios fell into the hands of Pier Luigi Farnese, son of Pope Paul III and later Duke of Parma and Piacenza. In the early 1540s Pier Luigi commissioned Bernardi to make a *second* set of crystals (a fact that has caused much confusion among recent scholars), to be mounted in a precious metal casket he was planning at the same time, the design of which is perhaps related to a drawing by Salviati in the Uffizi.[131] Of these six gems, only two survive, sharing a provenance and of approximately the same size: a *Tityus* in The British Museum (fig. 145) and a *Phaeton* in the Walters Art Museum, Baltimore (fig. 146). Plaquettes were cast from impressions from three others – another *Tityus*, another *Fall of Phaeton* (fig. 147) and a *Ganymede* – which differ slightly in their use of Michelangelo's prototypes and are bigger, all about 68–70 × 91–92.5 millimetres.[132] It is known that in planning the second casket Farnese looked to Perino del Vaga to make designs for three further crystals. When first approached and on learning that Michelangelo was the author of earlier designs, Perino had refused, not wanting to offend the 'god of *disegno*' and unwilling to invite comparison lest he should suffer the fate of Phaeton. Eventually he agreed to provide sketches but not finished drawings. In Perino's implicit recognition that his rapid sketches would not be valued and preserved in the same way as Michelangelo's very finished drawings, we have a by now rare instance of a famous painter deliberately making his contribution anonymous.[133] His prediction was well-founded and his designs are lost, but the crystals are reasonably thought to be the *Rape of Deianira*, *Venus and Adonis* and the *Fall of Icarus*

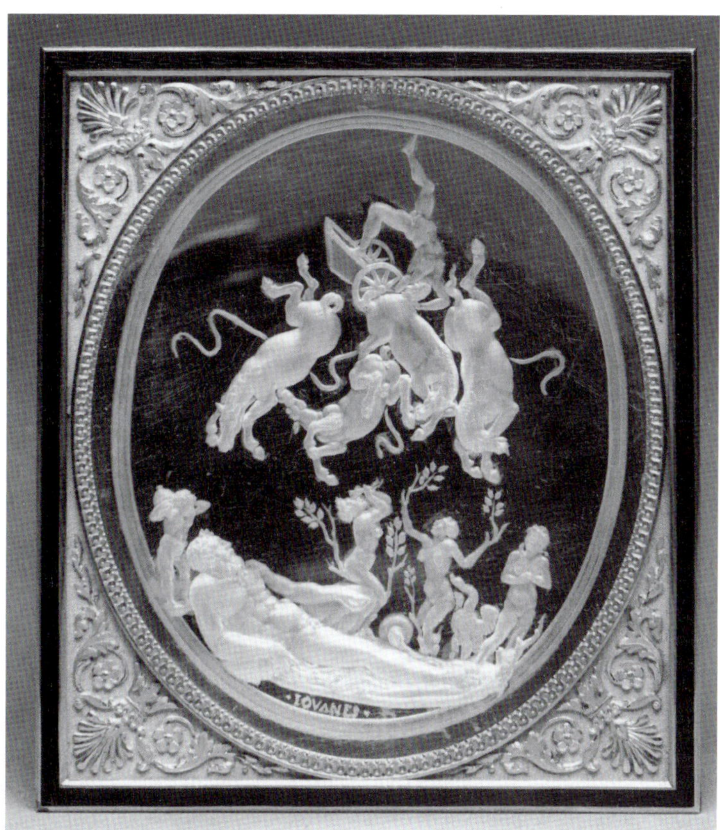

146 Giovanni Bernardi da Castelbolognese after Michelangelo, *The Fall of Phaeton*; rock-crystal intaglio; Rome, *c.*1533–5. The Walters Art Museum, Baltimore

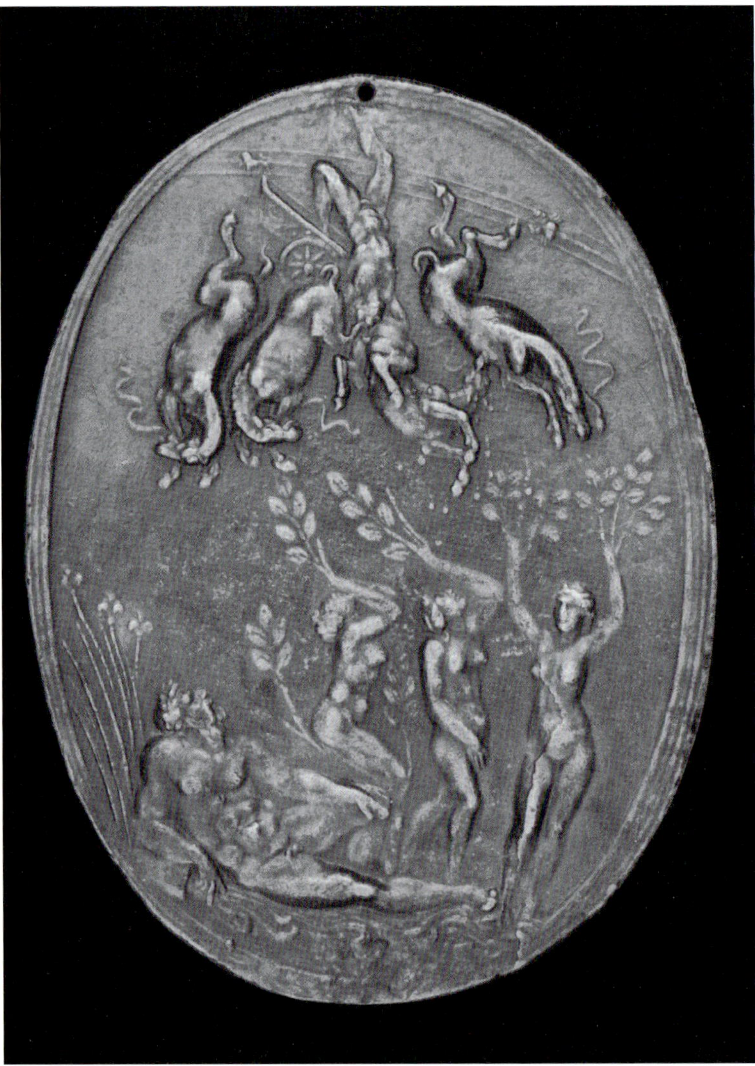

147 After Giovanni
Bernardi da
Castelbolognese
after Michelangelo
plaquette with
The Fall of Phaeton;
cast bronze; Rome (?),
after *c*.1440–50.
The British Museum,
London

by Bernardi which survive unmounted in the Hermitage in St Petersburg (the casket may never have been made). Since these are about the same size (all 70 × 94 millimetres) as the plaquettes taken from impressions of Bernardi's lost rock-crystals, it can be surmised that the two crystals after Michelangelo that *do* still exist are both from the first set made for Cardinal Ippolito and that the companions to the Perino-inspired gems are lost.

The surviving Michelangelo designs and Bernardi rock-crystals are revealing of the relationship between designer and executor in the mid-Cinquecento. Both Bernardi's versions of the Tityus gem copy Michelangelo's drawing as faithfully as any patron might reasonably demand, omitting from the original only a damned soul trapped in a tree. However, because there were three alternatives for the Phaeton design, Bernardi had more room for manoeuvre. The gem in Baltimore combines elements from both the Windsor and the British Museum drawings, suggesting therefore that Cavalieri retained both. The river god and left-most Heliade at the bottom are derived from the British Museum drawing. The three horses on the right reverse the Windsor drawing. Jupiter has been eliminated and Phaeton moved to a position above the chariot. The swan also comes from the Windsor drawing, as does the little putto, although he has been moved and reversed. The plaquette after the lost crystal from the second set is less faithful to the Windsor drawing and closer to the British Museum sketch. Only the two horses on the right are derived from the Windsor version. The horse on the far left is related, for once, to the Accademia drawing, indicating that Cavalieri had managed to keep hold of this sheet as well. The river god and Heliade are still copied from the British Museum example, but the other Heliades are simplified versions of Bernardi's own inventions for the Baltimore gem. Phaeton himself, seemingly derived from another Michelangelesque source in the Baltimore crystal, is now a little closer to the British Museum model – only excepting the position of his left leg. The putto and swan have been eliminated.

Thus, although the finished Phaeton gems were still to be closely related to *concetti* by Michelangelo, Bernardi could assert his own creativity in his approach to his models. Through an inventive combination of Michelangelo's designs, he was perhaps attempting to present himself as an artist with skills beyond his glyptic expertise. Such efforts were perhaps a last-ditch attempt by a goldsmith-technician to regain the lost status of goldsmith-designer. It is unlikely, however, that his patrons were convinced. For the owner of objects like the Bernardi crystals, their worth could be assessed by their design by *ingegniosi* artists and their 'difficult' execution by a hugely celebrated master craftsman. Bernardi's signature was therefore an important ingredient, the equivalent to that of the skilful engravers of Mantegna's designs, given that Michelangelo's authorship of the drawings he was copying was already so well known. The combined contribution of two or more men of great reputation was higher than if the gems had been designed and fabricated by Bernardi alone. However little they might like their reduced status, there was therefore little reason left, in the eyes of their patrons, for gem-engravers or goldsmiths to be masters of design.

Chapter Five

Glass and Maiolica: Art and Technology

In the previous chapters we examined ways in which the value of celebrated designs could be enhanced by their conversion into precious media. Here we look at how certain raw materials, not themselves inherently valuable, could be transformed by new technologies into art objects of perceived worth – intellectual if not financial. Ever-increasing technological refinements had their own appeal, raising the status of particular categories of art object to a level that was sometimes perceived as approaching that of goldsmiths' work. Pottery and glass, potentially valuable on account of the ways in which they could be worked, could, like gold and silver, be further dignified by the contribution of a 'designer'.

In his biography of Alfonso I d'Este, Duke of Ferrara, the historian Paolo Giovio, wrote that the duke sought the company of 'the most excellent craftsman of the various arts' rather than of more obviously important men.[1] His passion for the processes of manufacturing art objects started early. He was felt to have an inappropriately intimate relationship with the Ferrarese court artist Ercole de' Roberti, who was censured by his employer, Duke Ercole I, in 1494 for the childish pranks he had committed in the company of Alfonso, the son and heir of the duke.[2] As early as 1493 Alfonso ordered pigments from Venice so that he could experiment with painting.[3] But his interest in materials was not confined to the 'noble' art of painting, an interest that might be legitimized by the list of ancient aristocratic amateurs cited by Alberti (who was one himself). He also turned his hand to metal founding, woodcarving and pottery. Giovio claimed, for example, that Alfonso 'applied himself to the founding of metals, much as a smith; and he was so successful at these arts that he went beyond all the best craftsmen with his inventiveness in the mixing of metals at high temperatures … '. From wood he made 'flutes, tables, and chess pieces, beautiful and ingenious boxes, and many other similar objects'. And 'he also sometimes made the most beautiful ceramic vessels, which could be used as household utensils'.[4]

That the duke of Ferrara occupied himself with such technological experimentation indicates the importance attached to medium during this period. The value of an art object rested not only in its design but, sometimes, in the level of technical difficulty needed to carry out that design. An additional element, played up in artistic biographies, was the manner in which such challenges were solved. Much account was taken of the technological breakthrough required to harden the tools used for striking medals or carving porphyry. This is hardly surprising, for although Italian patrons, collectors and scholars looked to Pliny's *Natural History* for information on ancient art and the biographies of ancient artists, the books on art are arranged by medium, and its fashioning into objects. Renaissance Italians took note of Pliny's oft-repeated remarks on the appropriate union between material and design. The ingenuity required to produce a metal alloy might make it more valuable, in his eyes, than a medium that had greater intrinsic financial value.

'Corinthian bronze', he wrote, 'is valued before gold and almost before silver.' Later he added, 'Formerly copper used to be blended with a mixture of gold and silver, and nevertheless artistry was valued more highly than the metal.'[5]

We have seen that this kind of remark was echoed in Filarete's report of Piero de' Medici's pleasure in antique engraved gemstones – 'worth more than gold itself' – because of both the virtuous artistry contained within them and the extraordinary technical skill and effort required to realize it. Even semi-precious stone, however, had an intrinsic value, which the raw materials needed for ceramic and glass production did not. The histories of glass- and maiolica-making illustrate the very real technical challenges they presented; ones that provided plenty of scope for rivalling and even outdoing the ancients.

In 1468 the Venetian Signoria presented, instead of a more usual gift of silver plate, a glass vase to Emperor Frederick III on his visit to Venice. The emperor, a northerner after all, was insufficiently conversant with Italian humanist readings of such an object's aesthetic worth. Since it was not fashioned from the expected precious metal, he is said to have deliberately let it drop and break to show that it was, despite its beauty and technical finesse, of insufficient financial value.[6] However, many native Italians assessed glass art objects in very much the same ways as they treated semi-precious stone and bronze. These words in praise of glass appear in the treatise on metals and metallurgy by the Sienese metalworker Vanuccio Biringuccio, written not for craftsmen but as part of the process of educating patrons, and printed in Venice shortly after his death in 1540;[7] they seem to sum up the set of concepts that, taken together, imbued glass with its value:

… a material whose body, as we see, is transparent and lustrous, and it is coloured with substances or traces of metal to any desired colour, in such a way that with the beauty of gems it deceives the judgement of the eyes of very experienced men. Certainly, in glass Art surpasses Nature; for although she has produced [rock] crystal and all the other kinds of gems that are much more beautiful than this, no way has yet been found for working these as is done with glass … The best glasswork that is made in our times and that which is of greater beauty, more varied colouring, and more admirable skill than that of any other place is made at Murano. In addition to colouring them all possible tints, they make them very clear and transparent like true and natural crystal, and ornament them with paintings and other very fine enamels. Thus it seems to me that all the metals must give way to glass in beauty.[8]

Biringuccio identifies the properties and potential of glass, ones that made it appeal to Renaissance patrons as much as, or more than, gold and silver. He emphasizes the skill and sophisticated technology required to make it. In the first place, the transparency of glass rivalled the clarity of rock-crystal, which had been valued since classical antiquity, and, once transparent, glass could be coloured to imitate or counterfeit precious and semi-precious stones. In addition, glass could be blown, moulded and manipulated into a greater variety of forms than any other material available to the Renaissance craftsman. Lastly, it could be gilded, painted with enamels, or engraved; all techniques fully exploited by fifteenth-century Venetian glassmakers. These qualities, intrinsic to the medium, therefore put it on a par with the finest goldsmiths' work in precious metals.

But only if, like gold and silver, it were not just made but also decorated or designed with sufficient artistry.[9] From the early Cinquecento, just as with goldsmiths' work, painters became important as designers, for, although Venetian glassworkers were renowned for their skill and technological invention as craftsmen, they were considered lacking in artistic invention – *poveri d'invencione* – requiring designs by others to work from. Discerning patrons provided their own models in the form of drawings commissioned from artists, or sent goldsmiths' work or existing glass vessels to the Venetian workshops as patterns. Isabella d'Este frequently returned glasses that were not to her liking and beleaguered her agent in Venice with instructions as to how to improve her commissions. Her letters, written over a thirty-year period, indicate not only her awareness of the latest technological fashions, but also her regard for glass as a new and distinctly modern art form.[10]

Antiquity and precious stones: competition and revival

Much of what we know about the development of Venetian glass and the introduction of new techniques and materials comes from archival evidence.[11] The first written rules (*capitolare*) for the glassmakers' guild in Murano was approved by the mayor (*podestà*) in 1271, while the guild register (*mariegola*) was approved in 1441.[12] Later documents demonstrate that glassmaking was tightly controlled, for the civic government of Murano, not to mention the Venetian Republic itself, was keen to regulate the production of a prestigious and lucrative export. It sought to control not only the trade in raw materials needed to make luxury glassware, but also the movements of master producers. Legislation therefore varied from protective measures safeguarding the exclusive use of imported materials, or giving special privileges to those perfecting a new product, to draconian punishments for those who left the Republic to set up workshops elsewhere. Production and export was limited to seven months of the year, culminating in the Ascension Day Fair (La Sensa) at St Mark's in early June, at which the latest products were displayed and sold.[13] During the recess glass was not to be made or exported without a special licence from the authorities, and glassmakers, desperate for employment, were prohibited from seeking work outside Murano.[14] Although there is some evidence that Venetian craftsmen set up glasshouses in Austria from the beginning of the fifteenth century,[15] it was mainly from the 1540s that, despite the opposition of the Venetian Council of Ten, Muranese glassworkers were to set up glasshouses abroad, in Antwerp from 1541 and London by 1548.[16] By 1550 Muranese glasshouses numbered thirty-six, and were able to dominate the northern European luxury market and the export trade to the Near East.[17]

The glassmaking fraternity was close-knit, competitive and highly litigious, quick to denounce to the Podestà of Murano anyone who broke the rules of the guild. We therefore know the names of many of the leading craftsmen, and of the painters (including two women) whom they contracted as enamellers for their glasses. Unfortunately, however, these names can rarely, if ever, be matched up with surviving wares with any certainty, since fifteenth-century Muranese craftsmen did not sign their enamelled pieces, unlike 'Master Aldrevandin' and 'Master Bartolomeus', who famously signed beakers in the fourteenth century: a clear sign of their sense of achievement in creating an artistic commodity (fig. 148).[18] Trecento products had reached as far west as Cornwall and as far east as Estonia within a few years of production, indicating the scale of the market for luxury glass even before the technological advances of the fifteenth century.[19]

The best account of working molten glass (and one that was to be lifted in its entirety by Georg Agricola fifteen years later) is contained in Biringuccio's treatise, which makes clear that he had observed the process closely (fig. 149). Having described the construction of the furnace and the manner by which the glass is made molten and purified in clay crucibles, he explains:

I remind you that it [glass] is a thing which is worked while hot and that it is worked with great facility … by being blown by men's breath with certain iron tubes. Every worker possesses two of these tubes, which are slender and about one and a half *braccia* long. With one of these they take the glass from the pot by attaching it to the point and then wrapping it around little by little like a

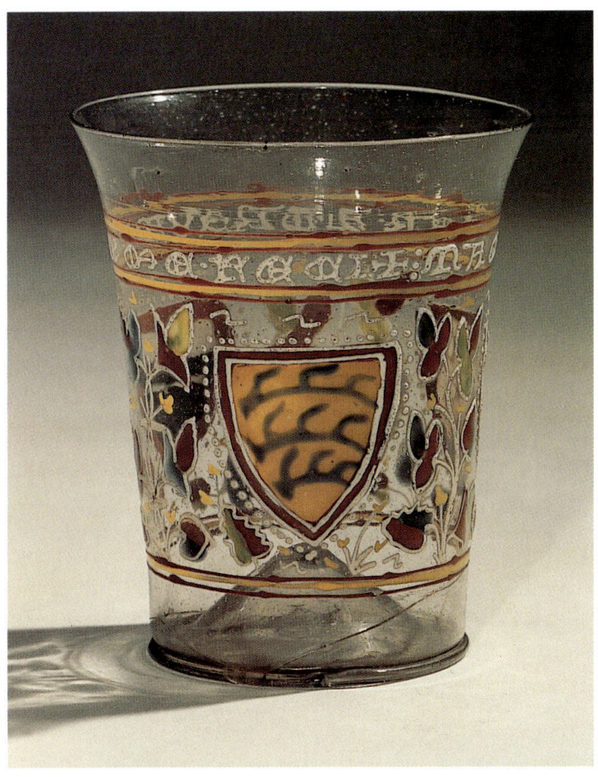

148 Master Aldrevandin, beaker; enamelled glass; Venice (Murano), early fourteenth century. The British Museum, London

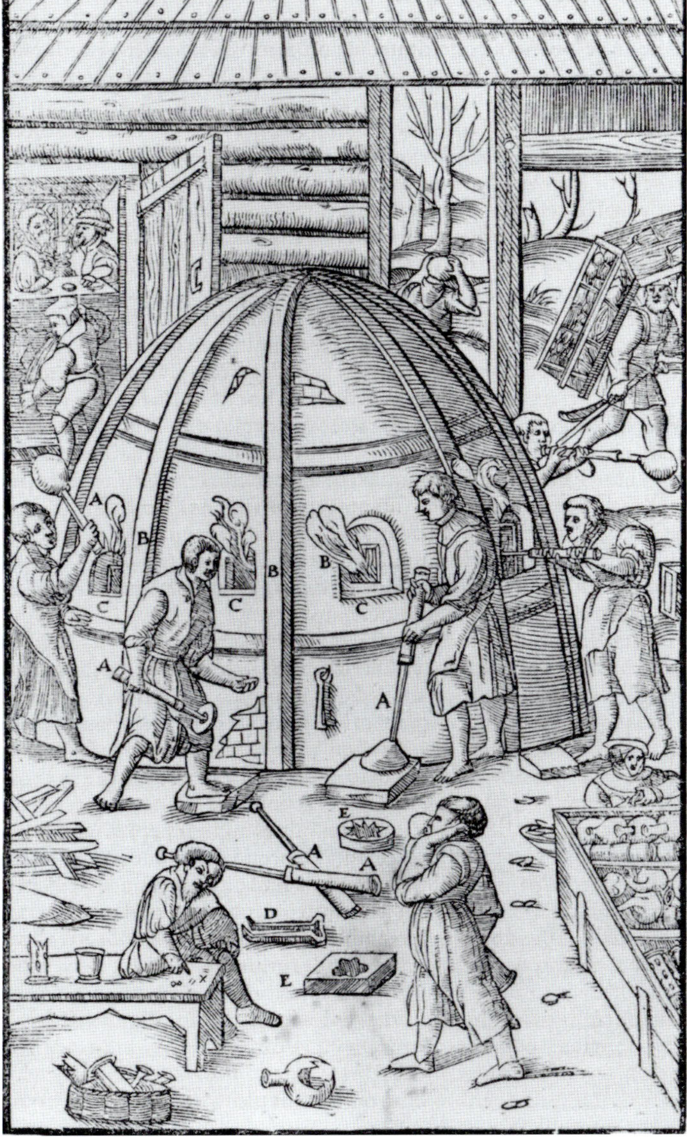

149 *A Venetian glass furnace*; woodcut illustration from Georg Agricola's *De re metallica*, book 12, p. 510; Basel, 1556. The British Library, London

viscous thing, taking the quantity they wish and giving it the form of a large ball. The first thing they do after withdrawing it is to press it on the marble, turning it over and over so that it unites. Then blowing … through the opening of the tube they make it a bubble and they elongate it by swinging it about over their heads, or they mould it in a hollow of bronze … They give it the form of the vessel which they wish by warming and blowing, by pressing [into a mould] and enlarging. Then, separating it from the first tube, they take hold of it again at the bottom with the other tube [the pontil] and improve it, cutting its mouth with a pair of shears; and they finish it by attaching feet or handles or other parts of different glasses or even by gilding it with pure gold.[20]

The glass medium had several, sometimes overlapping, cultural values. Like so many other producers of art objects of the period, Muranese craftsmen made conscious attempts to imitate and surpass ancient Roman techniques. During the fifteenth century they perfected a type of glass known as *cristallo,* a fine colourless glass that gained its name by its all-important resemblance to natural rock-crystal. *Cristallo* was therefore significant as an artificial material that rivalled one of the most coveted natural materials, rock-crystal, long valued for making drinking vessels, reliquaries, and optical lenses. Moreover, there were ancient Roman precedents for Renaissance *cristallo*; Pliny had described the ancient Roman equivalent as the finest of all glass types in his *Natural History* and stated that glassware 'has now come to resemble rock crystal in a remarkable manner, but the effect has been to flout the laws of Nature and actually increase the value of the former without diminishing that of the latter'.[21] The lightness, transparency and clarity of Renaissance *cristallo* represented a technological breakthrough that could be glossed as a glorious revival.

Although Angelo Barovier, a famous glassmaker from a leading dynasty of master glass-makers, has traditionally been credited with the perfection of *cristallo*, recent research indicates that the technique was not the achievement of one man, but rather a development that stretched over nearly two centuries.[22] It resulted from the use of particular raw materials and the skills developed in purifying them: soda from imported Levantine ash, which was used exclusively from the 1280s; silica from pulverized quartzite pebbles from the River Ticino; and manganese imported from Germany as a decolourizing agent. All these essential ingredients were in use in Murano before 1400, although the process of purifying the soda from the imported ashes and the discovery of a stabilizing agent seems to have been developed only around 1450, and is first recorded in writing in a Florentine recipe book of about 1460.[23] This is perhaps where Angelo Barovier came in, for he was certainly making *cristallo* by 1455, when he and his son Marino were invited to Milan by Duke Francesco Sforza – with the rare approval of the Venetian authorities – to introduce the new technique there.[24] He was back in Venice by 1457, when, along with two other owners of glass workshops, Jacopo d'Anzelo and Niccolò Mozetto, he was given the special privilege of keeping his furnaces operating to make *cristallo* during the annual recess.[25] Clearly, the Venetian government saw the development and success of *cristallo* both as a mark of prestige and a potentially extremely valuable export, and documents show that there were at least four workshops with the same privileges in making this new product by 1460.[26]

Using the *cristallo* composition as a base, other new types were developed. Some of these must also have been inspired by ancient Roman practice. *Millefiori* glass (*rosette* in the

150 Two bottles and a goblet; *millefiori* glass (bottles moulded, with silver mounts); Venice (Murano), *c.*1500. The British Museum, London

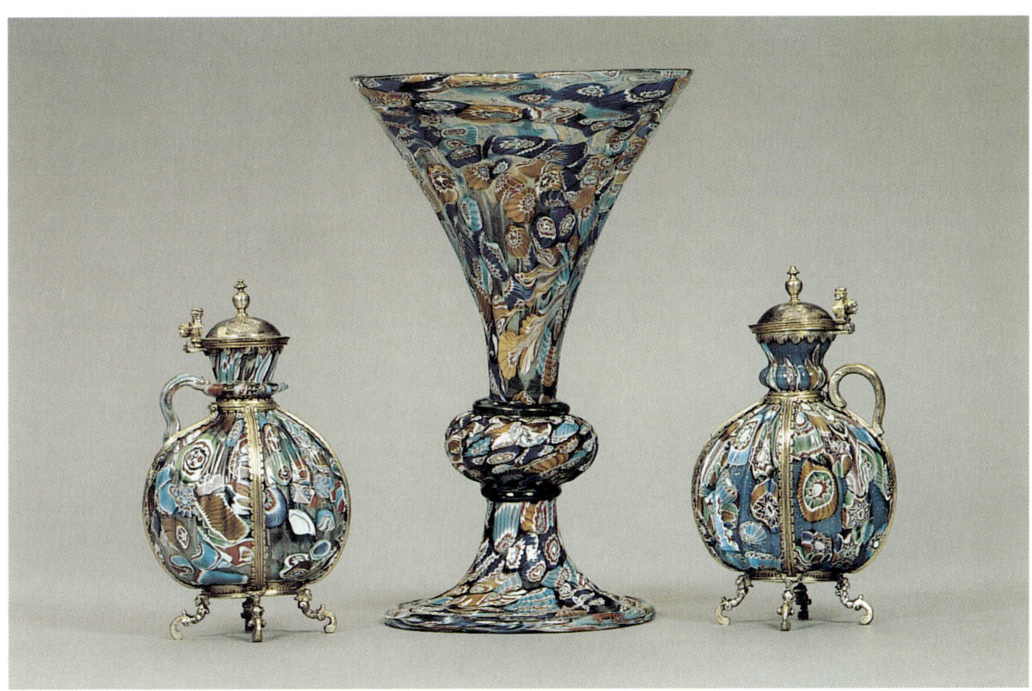

documents) was certainly developed to imitate a Roman technique, though the method and results were different. *Millefiori* was made from multicoloured canes sliced into thin sections that resembled flowers. The ancient Romans had laid out a single layer of sections on a circular ceramic plate, heated and compressed them, then formed them by slumping them over a mould. However, the fifteenth-century technique was to incorporate the sections into a gather of clear glass that then could be moulded, blown and manipulated to arrive at an artistic result, which, though imitating an ancient Roman glass type, looked completely different (fig. 150).[27]

Vessels might also be coloured to imitate gemstones: dark green, sapphire blue (first documented as a colour in 1446)[28] and aubergine purple glass.[29] Glass had long been used to counterfeit cut gemstones for use in jewellery and embroidery: Cellini regarded Milan as the centre for the making of glass, foil-backed gems, although city statutes expressly (though theoretically, perhaps) forbade the practice.[30] But Venice was also a centre, and there again perpetrators could expect to be punished; the Senate issued a decree in 1487 to forbid 'the multiplication of false stones of every sort' under heavy penalties, including permanent exclusion of guilty craftsmen from the Goldsmiths' Guild.[31] Such counterfeit stones were permitted for use only in ecclesiastical vestments, and for setting in so-called papal rings, large copper alloy, gilt rings set with false stones and engraved or enamelled with the arms of popes, perhaps as emblems of investiture. Cardinal Francesco Gonzaga owned 'a ring of gilt bronze with one counterfeit ruby and the arms of Pope Paul [II]', similar to a surviving ring in The British Museum.[32] Since Cardinal Francesco had assisted in the election of the Pope, his ring may commemorate the latter's investiture.[33]

The chalcedony technique, imitating, like *cristallo*, a semi-precious stone, is first documented in 1460: two examples in The British Museum are probably early experiments

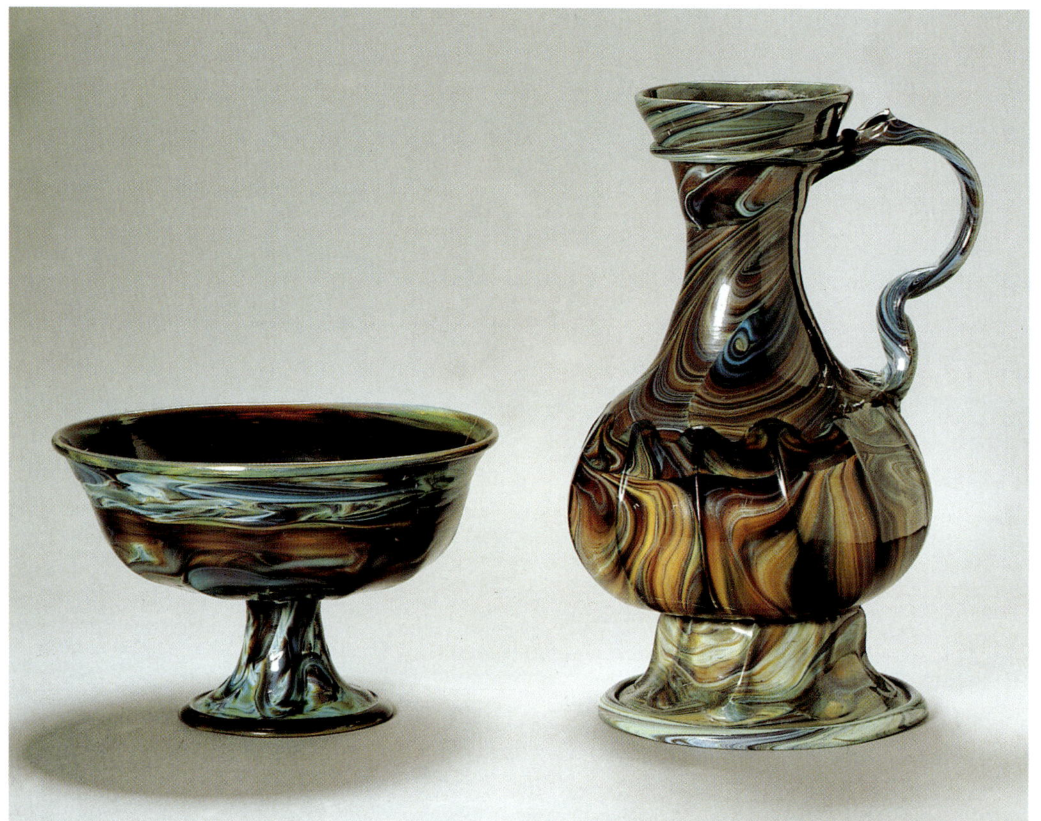

151 A jug and footed bowl; 'chalcedony' glass, the jug moulded and with applied handle; Venice (Murano), *c.*1500. The British Museum, London.

152 Giovanni Maria Obizzo (attributed), betrothal goblet with two roundels with pairs of lovers; opaque turquoise glass with trails of white glass and dark blue glass knop, gilded and enamelled; Venice (Murano), *c.*1490–1500. The Waddesdon Bequest, The British Museum, London

judging by their form (fig. 151).[34] The Florentine Filippo Strozzi sent an agent to Venice in 1475 to take delivery of 'eleven chalcedony vessels of various forms bought at Murano from Maestro Bono' (Jacopo Bon d'Anzelo at the sign of the Cock).[35] Like *cristallo*, *calcidonio* represented what one humanist commentator, Marcantonio Sabellico, described in 1500 as 'a sweet contest between man and Nature' in imitating hard-stones.[36]

More exclusive still was a brilliant turquoise body, developed by the end of the fifteenth century, when a single archival reference mentions 'four little jugs of turquoise glass' in the inventory of glass in dispute between Marietta Barovier and her brother Giovanni in 1496 (fig. 152).[37] The technique sought to imitate the semi-precious stone imported from Khurasan. Turquoise glass had been made in ancient Egypt. It was later made there (though not in a continuous tradition) under Islamic rule, a famous example being the tenth-century glass bowl in the Treasury of San Marco in Venice, which may well have been known to Venetian glassmakers in the fifteenth century, stimulating their interest in manufacturing it themselves.[38] Opaque cobalt-coloured glass had also been made in north-east Italy in the first century, judging by archaeological evidence; pieces may have turned up in Venetian collections as models, along with later Islamic examples.[39] Whatever the prototypes, turquoise glass seems to have been extremely rare and very few pieces survive.

Oriental and Islamic techniques provided inspiration, as did surviving glass from the ancient world. A milky glass, known, appropriately, as *lattimo* (see fig. 156), imitated the opaque white body of Chinese porcelain, which in the fifteenth century was arriving in Venice in the form of diplomatic gifts and luxury imports.[40] The very whiteness of this new body was evidently celebrated as a very special material quality. An indication of this new aesthetic appears in the *Hynerotomachia Poliphili*, where a stone wall is described as having a pellucid whiteness excelling that even of *lattimo* from Murano.[41]

Ornament: adding material value

The prestige and value of the glass body might be enhanced by its decoration with enamels and gold leaf, or with the application of circular blobs of coloured glass (prunts) once again imitating precious gems.[42] Gold could be added to glass vessels in one of two ways. Hot gilding consisted of cutting a strip of gold leaf and laying it onto the 'gather' of

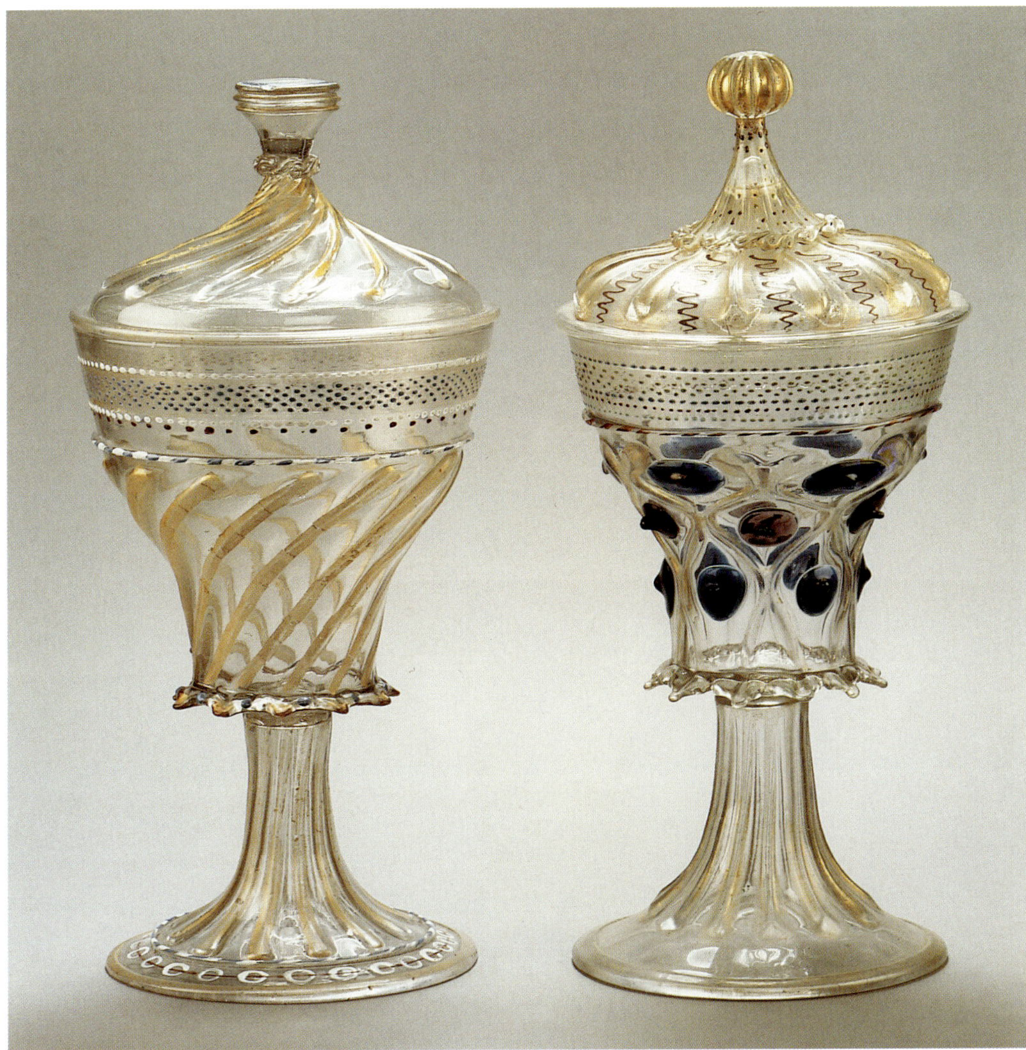

153 Two covered cups; *cristallo* glass, moulded, enamelled and gilded with raised gilded ribs, one with applied prunts of coloured glass; Venice (Murano), fifteenth century.
The British Museum, London

warm glass so that it melted on contact. This is the method by which the *millefiori* bottles in The British Museum were gilded. A vessel could then be moulded and blown, attached to the pontil (leaving a visible mark on the finished glass), opened out and shaped, stretching the gold into a thin layer with a granular appearance. Gilding could also be applied to a blown vessel that had been cooled. Gold leaf would be applied using gum arabic and water as an adhesive. The points at which the gold leaf overlapped can usually be seen on even the finest finished glasses. The gold layer could be incised with decoration, frequently a scale or leaf pattern, or with an inscription.[43] Mid-fifteenth-century glasses are heavily decorated with gilding, especially on raised ribs (*a coste dorate* in the documents)[44] and on the stems, covers, knops (moulded elements on stem or cover) and feet (fig. 153).

Gold around the rim of drinking cups was a refinement that was prized by discriminating patrons: Isabella d'Este, writing to her agent in Venice in 1496, criticized the form of some drinking cups that he had ordered for her, and stipulated the relative proportions and decoration of the ones he was to have made in their place:

We have received the twenty glasses which you wrote of having sent in your letter, which are pleasing as to their height, but not in their profile, since the foot is as broad as the cup. Therefore we desire you to have made another twenty of this size, but that they should be made smaller at the foot, and that the cup should not be larger than it is on the ones you sent ... and have the little gold border [around the cup] made so that it covers the lip, and so that there remains no plain glass above the gold border, seeing to it however that the gold band is no broader than it is on these ones. Have the others made plain, without gold, ensuring that the *cristallo* glass be white [i.e. transparent, colourless and without impurities] and beautiful....[45]

Finally, blobs of enamel could be applied over the gold, to add small touches of brilliant colour over etched gold. Enamel could also be used on its own to paint a patron's arms, or could be employed figuratively to depict heads, complete figures in narrative scenes or grotesque designs (fig. 154). A fifteenth-century manuscript gives the best account of the enamelling process, which was closely derived from Islamic techniques. The delicate and difficult art of refiring the decorated glasses is emphasized:

To paint glass, that is to say, cups or any other works in glass with enamels [*smalti*], take the *smalti* you wish to use, and let them be soft and fusible, and pound them upon marble ... in the same way

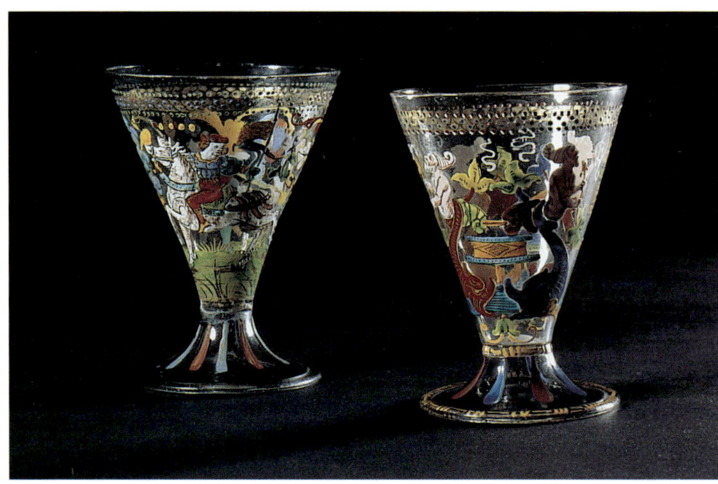

154 Two goblets; *cristallo* glass, enamelled and gilded; Venice, Murano, mid- to late fifteenth century. The British Museum, London.

155 Footed dish scene of a man slaying a water monster; moulded *cristallo* glass, enamelled and gilded; Venice (Murano), early sixteenth century. The British Museum, London

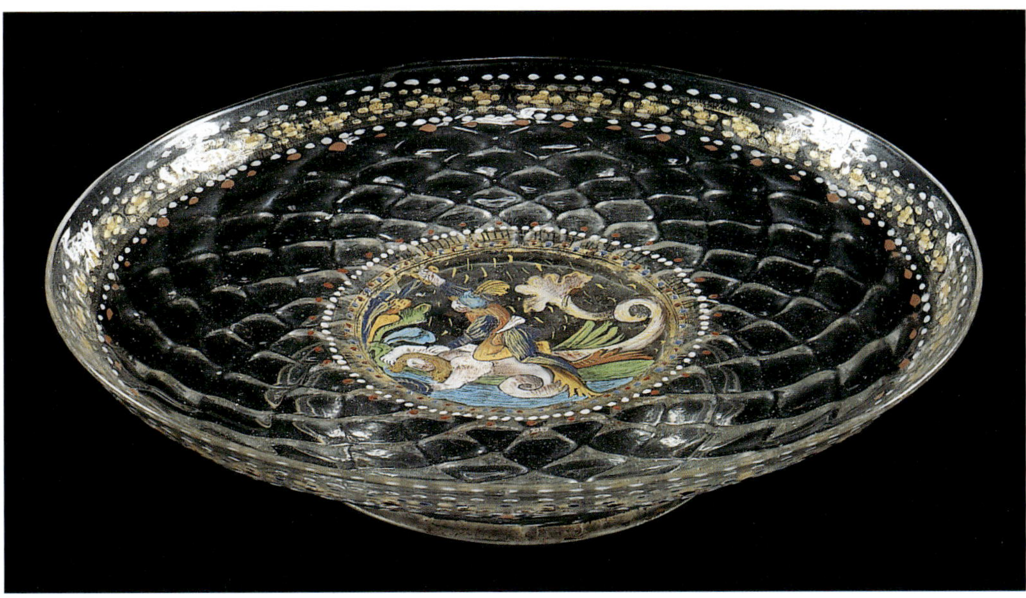

that goldsmiths do. Then wash the powder and apply it upon your glass as you please and let the colour dry thoroughly; then put the glass upon the rim of the [annealing] chamber in which the glasses are cooled … and gradually introduce it into the chamber towards the fire which comes out of the furnace and take care you do not push too fast lest the heat should split it, and when you see that it is thoroughly heated, take it up with the pontil and put it in the mouth of the furnace, heating it and introducing it gradually. When you see the enamels shine and they have flowed well, take the glass out and put it in the chamber to cool, and it is done.[46]

Enamelled figurative decoration added considerably to the financial as well as artistic value of glass (fig. 155). A dispute between two glassmakers in 1474 reveals that a gilded beaker was priced at 4½ soldi, while the same form enamelled with two figures was priced at 9. A glass with a complex narrative scene, such as one sees on 'betrothal' glasses, was priced much higher, at 40 soldi (see fig. 152).[47]

References to specialist glass painters working in enamel – to be distinguished from glassmakers – appear in the documents from the 1440s onwards. Painters were often named in disputes that came before the courts, revealing that tensions were high between furnace proprietors and the painters whom they employed. The glassmakers always sought to retain control of the delicate firing process and of the finished product, although one painter managed to set up his own furnace in 1470–1 against considerable vested interests.[48]

Painters mentioned in the earliest documents must have worked largely on the strongly tinted glasses then being produced: the sapphire blue and, much more rarely, emerald green or aubergine purple. Of the fourteen specialist painters (*pictori*) mentioned from 1443 to 1517, two were women. Indeed, one of the earliest references is to one Elena de Laudo of Murano, who is mentioned as working between 1443 and 1445 on blanks provided for her by the workshop of Salvatore Barovier. Blanks were delivered to her for painting and then collected to be taken back, presumably, to the furnace to be fired.[49] Elena came from a glass-painting dynasty: another member of the family painted a window in

Santi Giovanni e Paolo in Venice, and two others are named as 'painters of Murano'.[50] A second woman, Marietta Barovier, who inherited her family workshop from Angelo in 1460, along with her brother Giovanni, is mentioned in a document of 1487 as being given the privilege of constructing a special kiln (*sua fornace parvula*) for making 'her beautiful, unusual and not blown works'.[51]

Neither woman's work can be identified, whereas that of another painter, Giovanni Maria Obizzo, is thought to be capable of identification. He seems to have specialized in decorating *lattimo*.[52] The glass was whitened by the addition of lead and tin-oxides, much like those used to make tin-glaze as a white ground for maiolica at the same date, and the result in both crafts was the same: to stimulate the use of figurative, pictorial decoration. Obizzo is named in a legal dispute of 1490, when Bernardino Ferro was charged with having fired illegally 'more than a thousand pieces of *lattimo* and other colours, all gilt and enamelled', which had been painted by Obizzo.[53] Only about fifteen *lattimo* pieces survive; among them are six standing cups, bowls and a ring-handled flask, each with painted decoration of a single male head or those of a man and a woman shown separately (and, significantly, the single documentary reference to a representation of a named individual on glass appears in 1496, when a *lattimo* glass 'with Dante on' is named in the group of enamelled glasses in dispute between Marietta Barovier and her brother).[54] All these surviving pieces bear such close stylistic similarities that there is good reason to attribute them to one specialist painter. This is more than likely to have been Obizzo, given both that he is specifically recorded as a painter on *lattimo* and that the fashion for this glass type was extremely short-lived. His male and female busts are highly reminiscent of the figure

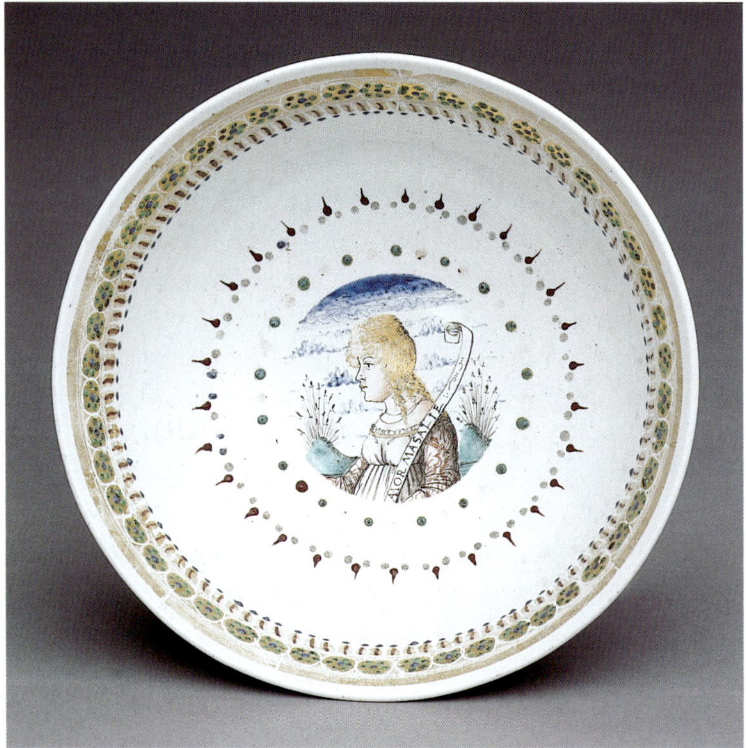

156 Giovanni Maria Obizzo (attributed), bowl, interior showing woman's head and inscription; opaque white (*lattimo*) glass, enamelled and gilded; Venice (Murano), *c.*1500–10. Kunsthistorisches Museum, Vienna

types employed by the Venetian painter Vittore Carpaccio, and are dressed in the Venetian fashions as recorded in the painter's dated works between 1495 and 1508. On three pieces attributed to him, an inscription in Venetianized Latin or Italian, written apparently in the same script by the same hand, appears on a banderole. On one *lattimo* bowl a male bust is accompanied by EGO VOBIS SERVO SON (I am your servant). In another case, a female bust is flanked by the legend AMORE MASALIE (Love assails me) (fig. 156).[55] Another work by Obizzo may have been an equally exceptional glass, elegantly flaring out at the lip, this time of opaque turquoise glass (see fig. 152). Decorated with three trails of *lattimo* and a knop of lapis lazuli-coloured glass, the cup is gilded and enamelled with two pairs of lovers, shown in what appear to be intended as daytime and night-time scenes.[56] But perhaps the most visually sophisticated use of male and female heads with an amorous inscription appears on an opaque green goblet, also attributed to Obizzo (see fig. 33).[57] Here, the male bust is accompanied by AMOR.VOL.FEE (Love requires faith). The busts are framed in two roundels, supported by naked putti standing on a pale green sward and accompanied by flying ribbons and green swags. However, for all the visual ambition of the design, there is a slight awkwardness in the join between the swags on one side of the glass, which may imply that the enameller was working from a drawn design and found it difficult to dispose the composition across the rounded surface of the glass. The band of gold leaf used in the gilding seems to join at exactly the same spot, showing that this is where the design was conceived as beginning and ending when it was translated onto the field of the glass.

The reputation of glassmakers

The prestige of glass as a luxury commodity among Europe's elites extended to master craftsmen in the art. Angelo Barovier, a member of the leading glassmaking dynasty of Murano, was a man of considerable status in Venice and beyond, one of the few master craftsmen allowed to leave Murano and work elsewhere. As we have seen, he has been credited with a number of technological breakthroughs of the mid-fifteenth century, including the perfection of *cristallo*, but his greatest achievement was perhaps that of promoting glass not only as a luxury product but as a Renaissance art form outside his native Venice.[58] He had a reputation akin to that of court artist to a succession of famous patrons, including Francesco Sforza and Alfonso of Aragon in Naples. Filarete, who knew Angelo at the Sforza court in the 1450s, praised him in his treatise as his 'very good friend … Maestro Angelo of Murano, the man who makes those beautiful objects of *vetri cristallini*'.[59] Partly due to this friendship, Filarete became familiar with the latest glass technology and its potential, and enjoined other architects to do the same.[60] He wished to exploit its figurative potential in his imaginary city, Sforzinda, through wall tiles 'which will be flat, and inside one will see sculpted figures, animals, and various things, in such a way that it will be a worthy thing to set eyes upon'.[61] The sense Filarete gives of the dignity of glass, even in the noblest court settings (and their inclusion was briefly planned as an element in Mantegna's *Camera Picta* in the Gonzaga *castello* in Mantua),[62] is heightened by contemporary references to Angelo as a leading glassmaker. He was certainly the only glassworker to have an epitaph, bolstering his reputation as 'the greatest craftsman in crystalline glass vessels', composed by the eminent humanist Lodovico Carbone. The poet further addressed Barovier as 'he who knew the whole art of glass, Angelo who was endowed with angelic powers of *ingegno*' (*Angelus angelico praeditus ingenio*).[63] This must be one of the earliest tributes to a maker, regardless of the medium in which he worked, as a model of *ingegno*, a good measure of the status of glass technology, its products and its makers in the late fifteenth century.[64]

Indeed, all the evidence suggests that Venetian enamelled glass quickly became an elite taste throughout Italy, and beyond. *Cristallo* – either glass or rock-crystal – is listed as exemplifying the virtue of splendour in the life of an individual in Giovanni Pontano's treatise on social virtues of the 1490s.[65] Collections were formed by rulers: that created by Ferdinand and Isabella of Spain was so remarkable that the queen left it to Granada cathedral in 1516.[66] Armorial pieces can sometimes be precisely dated, like the two surviving pilgrim flasks with the arms of Giovanni Bentivoglio impaling those of Ginevra Sforza, apparently made for their wedding in Bologna in 1464.[67] Other glasses can be dated by documents, such as fragments from the site of the royal palace in Buda with the arms of Beatrice of Aragon, consort of King Matthias Corvinus of Hungary, who is known to have received Venetian glass as diplomatic gifts from Ferrara in 1486.[68] Earlier inventory references to glass in the possession of two cardinals known for their artistic discrimination and fine taste indicate that Venetian glass early became highly rated enough to be included along with rock-crystal, hard-stone, and the silver and gold dining vessels cited by Biringuccio. Two blue glass salts, set like hard-stone vessels in silver-gilt mounts, are listed among the luxury items belonging to Cardinal Lodovico Trevisan in 1465. These were obviously splendid objects, as they were enamelled with three coats of arms on their bases and had special leather travelling cases tooled with the cardinal's arms.[69] Venetian glass and rock-crystal vessels coexist in the inventory of Cardinal Francesco Gonzaga.[70] The cardinal, who, like Trevisan, had a substantial collection of gems, had a blue glass dish described in some detail in the inventory of his estate in 1483: 'A basin of gilded blue glass, with in the middle two figures of jousting men' (*Uno cadinello de vetro azuro lavorato ad oro, et in mezo due figure de homini giostranti*).[71] The description echoes the kinds of chivalric scenes enamelled on surviving glasses, with knights on horseback or encountering mythical beasts (figs 154, 155).[72]

They were not the only powerful patrons in whose collections one finds valued specimens of glass. Aubergine-coloured pieces are listed among the contents of the bed-chamber of Lorenzo de' Medici, finding its place among paintings by Pesellino, Paolo Uccello, and Pollaiuolo: on the chimney breast of the room were 'two little jugs of purple glass' (*Dua orciuoli di vreto paghonazo sopra il chammino*).[73] Further down the social scale, references to crystalline glass (*cristallino* as opposed to *cristallo* for rock-crystal) sometimes appear in inventories of members of the urban elites in the last two decades of the fifteenth century. A good example is the inventory of a Sienese doctor and civic official, Bartolo da Tura, who owned Venetian crystalline drinking glasses, kept on display with pieces of armorial silver in his study in his town house in 1483.[74]

Leading artists, as well as their patrons, were interested in glass as an art form.

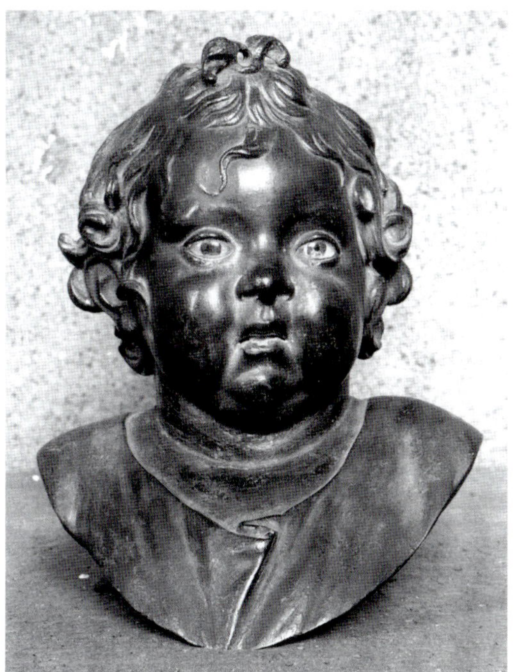

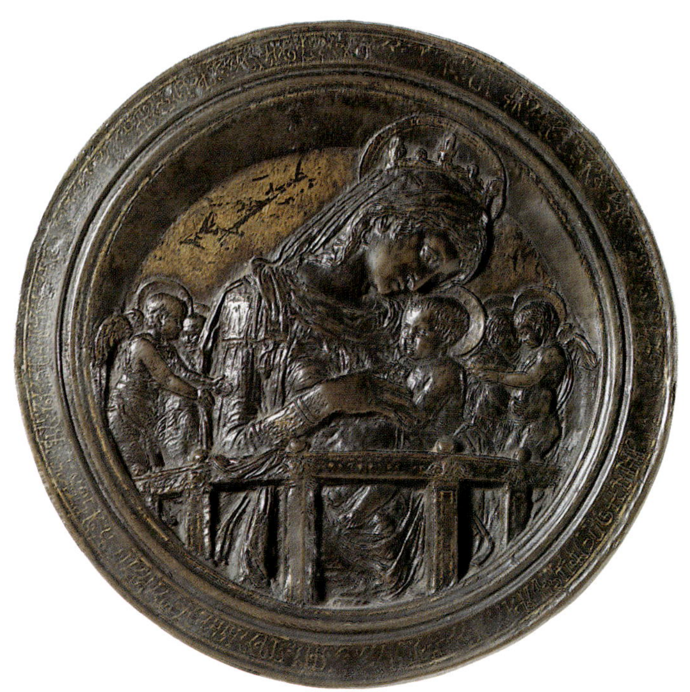

157 Bust of a boy; cast bronze with inset glass eyes; Venice (the eyes made in Murano), *c*.1500. Galleria 'Giorgio Franchetti' alla Ca d'Oro, Venice

158 Donatello, *Virgin and Child* (*Chellini Madonna*); cast bronze; Florence, *c*.1456. Victoria and Albert Museum, London

The example of rare turquoise glass listed in the inventory of Andrea Mantegna's son's possessions in Mantua in 1510 is all the more significant as an indicator of the painter's social pretensions and sense of his own rising status as the artist employed not only by the Gonzaga, but earlier by Lodovico Trevisan. Described as 'a little flask of turquoise glass with the device of the sun upon it', it had 'on top of it [stored up-ended on the neck] a little beaker of glass, painted with leaf designs'.[75] This flask must certainly have been a special commission, since it was enamelled with his personal *impresa* of the sun, a former Gonzaga device that had been awarded to him by his patron, Marquis Lodovico. Andrea was extremely proud of his ownership of this device; it also featured on his gold livery collar and his dining silver, and was worked on the coverlets of his bed.[76] Other painters enjoyed representing the translucency of *cristallo* and may therefore have owned it; it may be no coincidence that the Venetian painter Carlo Crivelli often included examples in his paintings executed in the 1490s. There is, however, only one contemporary representation of enamelled glass,[77] and depictions of glass decorated with canes is similarly rare.

Artists benefited indirectly from glassmaking by incorporating glass eyes in bronze busts, another supposedly *all'antica* use of the medium: Pomponius Gauricus stated in his 1504 treatise on sculpture that 'so far as the colours of the eyes and pupils [of bronzes and marbles] are concerned, these must be obtained from the Indies or from Murano; Phidias took them from the Indies for his Minerva, whilst we go to Murano, where they are more easily accessible and perhaps of better quality too'.[78]A bronze bust in the Ca d'Oro, a rare survival documenting this practice, retains its contemporary glass eyes, giving it a curiously blank expression (fig. 157). Among leading artists, however, Donatello seems to have been the only one actually to have experimented with the glass medium itself: a bronze roundel that he gave to his doctor, Giovanni Chellini, in 1456 was apparently designed so as to be used as a mould to make glass impressions from the reverse (fig. 158).[79] Chellini recorded the transaction in his memoranda:

I record that on the 27 day of August 1456 I gave medical treatment to Donato, known as Donatello, singular and pre-eminent master in making figures of bronze, wood and terracotta … through his courtesy and as payment for the medicinal treatment that he had received and which I had given him for his illness, he gave me a large tondo the size of a trencher [*tagliere*] in which is sculpted the Virgin Mary with the Child at her neck and two angels at the sides, all in bronze, and on the outer side it was hollowed out so that molten glass could be cast from it, and it would make the same figures as those on the other side.[80]

The importance of form : all'antica *glassware*

The first two decades of the sixteenth century saw a move away from pictorial decoration to a new emphasis on form and the incorporation of coloured canes in filigree glass. Once again the inspiration for both form and technique came from the ancient world.[81] In 1527 the brothers Filippo and Bernardo Catanei, working at the sign of the Serena, applied for a patent to produce canes for making what they called 'glass with threads' (*vetro a fili*), 'glass with twists' (*vetro a retorti*) and 'glass with a fine net' (*vetro a reticello*); they were granted the sole right to make these types of filigree glass for forty years from 1537.[82] Isabella d'Este was quick off the mark in ordering glass decorated with vertical white canes: she wrote to her agent in 1529:

Thinking that at the glassworkers' stalls at the Ascension Day Fair there will appear those beautiful new glasses, you are to buy between ten and twelve drinking glasses of various forms, footed cups and beakers, and they should have white cane decoration [*fili bianchi*], and should be plain, without gilding.[83]

The more complex cane techniques were generally mastered by 1540, when Biringuccio describes *vetro a retorti* and *a reticello* in all but name:

Look at the rosaries, saltcellars and drinking vessels in which one actually sees twisted designs [*a reticello*] of thorn branches and other crisscross inlays which appear to be in relief but actually are plane. Look at the large things, as well as the small, which they make of white or coloured glass and that seem to be woven of osier twigs equally spaced with the greatest uniformity and exactness … I must tell you that I have seen glass the colour of pearl or tinted green or blue or formed in various spirals [*vetro a retorti*] made entirely of a single very slender fibre like a thread, more than thirty *braccia* long, all in one piece like gold or silver drawn through the drawplate.[84]

What Biringuccio describes better than any other authority is the way in which the embedded canes appear three dimensional. Few early examples of these glass techniques survive, among the earliest being the two jugs blown by Venetian craftsmen and set in silver-gilt mounts hallmarked for London 1548–9 (fig. 159).[85] These jugs prove that both striped and twisted decoration using glass canes, white *and* coloured, was in use by this date. The technique by which they are made could have been practised only by Venetians at this early date, while the bulbous form is uncompromisingly English and demonstrates an attempt to cater to local demand. It may be that these two glasses represent the work of the eight Muranese glassworkers who petitioned the Council of Ten in Venice in 1549 as to why they had not obeyed an edict commanding them – and others working in

Antwerp – to return to Murano. Their petition claims that they were unable to leave because they were working on contract in London, and had two and a half years to go.[86]

It was not only the use of coloured canes in complex patterns embedded into clear glass that typified Venetian glass from the 1520s, but also the manipulation of *cristallo* into ever more fantastic forms. Novelties were first displayed at the Ascension Day Fair, which, like visits to the glasshouses in Murano itself, was firmly on the tourist map by about 1500. The Venetian diarist Marino Sanudo mentions the work displayed at three booths at the fair in 1525, those of the Barovier, Serena and Ballarin workshops: 'among other things, a galley and a very beautiful ship' were to be seen.[87] In 1521 Ermonia Vivarini, was allowed a special patent to produce vessels in the form of ships: the splendid ewer of *cristallo* and blue glass is an example of this kind of elaborate vessel dating to around 1525–50 (fig. 160).[88] Leandro Alberti singled out just this kind of glass in his famous description of the marvels of Murano in his *Description of All Italy* of 1550: 'I saw there (among other things made of glass) a scaled-down model of a galley, one *braccia* long and with all its rigging and equipment, so perfectly in scale that it seemed impossible to model such things accurately in such a medium.'[89]

With the rise of such complex forms, realized in a transparent and almost weightless medium, painters were more likely to be employed as designers of the forms of vessels

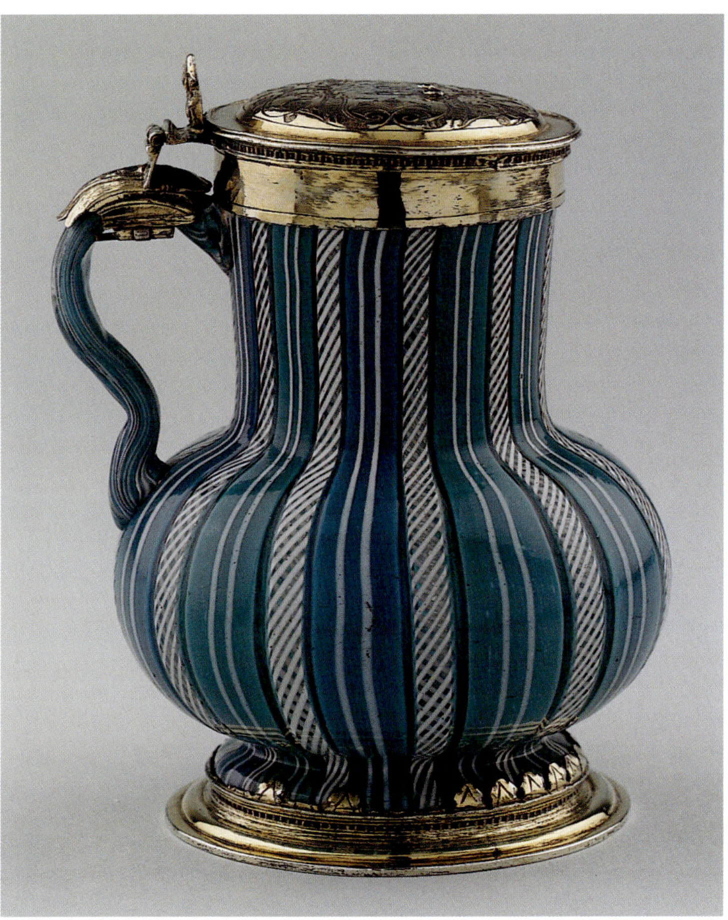

159 Tankard; glass of *vetro a reticello* technique with silver-gilt mounts; London, before 1548–9. The British Museum, London

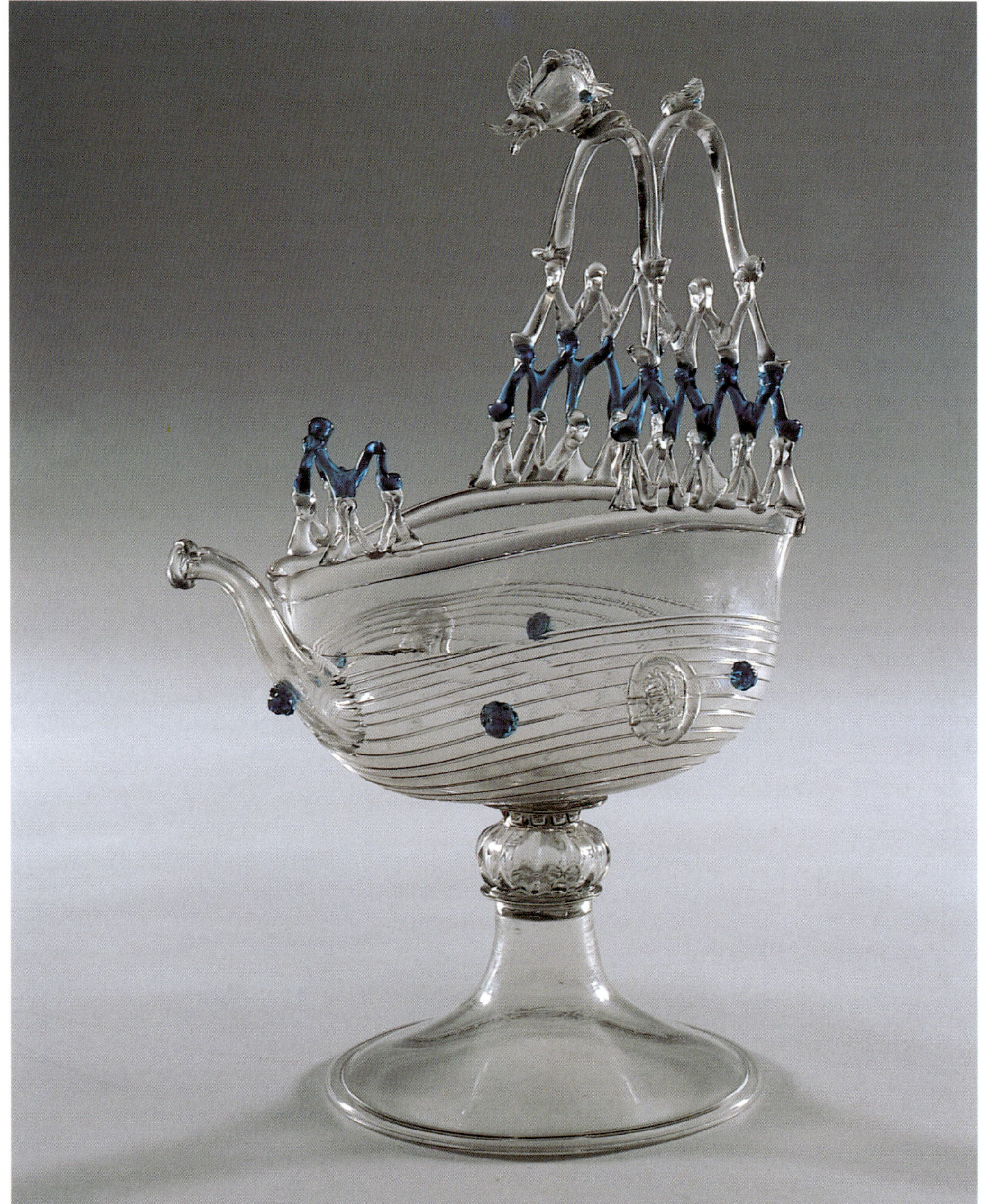

than in decorating them. This shift away from painted decoration in favour of fantastic or bizarre forms seems to have occurred around 1530, judging from written sources and from the decline in fashion of enamelled glass in Venice by this date.[90] Glassworkers looked to dining silver for inspiration; the forms of their pieces also show how they intended their best wares to rival silver-gilt vessels for luxury consumption. Perhaps the best examples of this aesthetic are the two magnificent covered cups in The British Museum (see fig. 153). A letter written by Pietro Aretino to Federico Gonzaga in 1531 exemplifies this new aesthetic on the part of discerning patrons. Since the Gonzaga controlled the marquisate of Monferrato, in which Altare, the only Italian rival glassmaking centre to Murano was situated, Aretino may have intended his letter to spur competition and emulation.[91] He explains that he is sending a box full of glass vessels:

only so that you can see the antique form designed by Giovanni da Udine. Which novelty has so much delighted the owners of the glasshouse of the Serena that they call the various things which I had made there 'Aretine wares'. Monsignor di Vasone, *maestro di casa* to Pope Clement VII, took some of them to Rome for His Holiness, who in my opinion will enjoy them greatly. And I am amazed at it, since I thought that at the papal court they only valued gold….[92]

Aretino was clearly delighted at the play on his name and the underlying belief that his glass commissions were of such perfectly antique style that they might be considered modern equivalents of the ancient terracottas from Arezzo, known as Aretine wares, which Pliny the Elder had praised so much.[93] This comparison seems to have been something of a contemporary topos, since Leandro Alberti says of Muranese glass in 1550, 'I believe that if Pliny were to come to life, and saw such ingenious vessels, marvelling at them, he would have praised them much more than those terracotta wares known as Aretine….'[94] The comparison depended on the way in which glass was being moulded with lion masks, with figures or entire friezes reminiscent of Aretine wares (fig. 161).[95] The letter also reveals that Aretino saw himself as a leader – even an educator – in matters of taste. A letter written ten years later to the painter Giovanni da Udine, who had famously worked with Raphael, asking for some more glass designs makes it clear that Aretino was keen to use the expertise of the best Muranese craftsmen in realizing the latest *all'antica* designs in order to create a quite new kind of glassware for elite tastes. Artists, and enlightened patrons such as himself, were to educate the glassmakers in this new art form. Passing on a request from Domenico Ballarin, 'idol in the art of glass' for a sheet full of 'those designs to be executed in glass', he flatters Giovanni da Udine: 'Seeing that you possess the essence of that ancient facility of design with such perfect taste … and since I

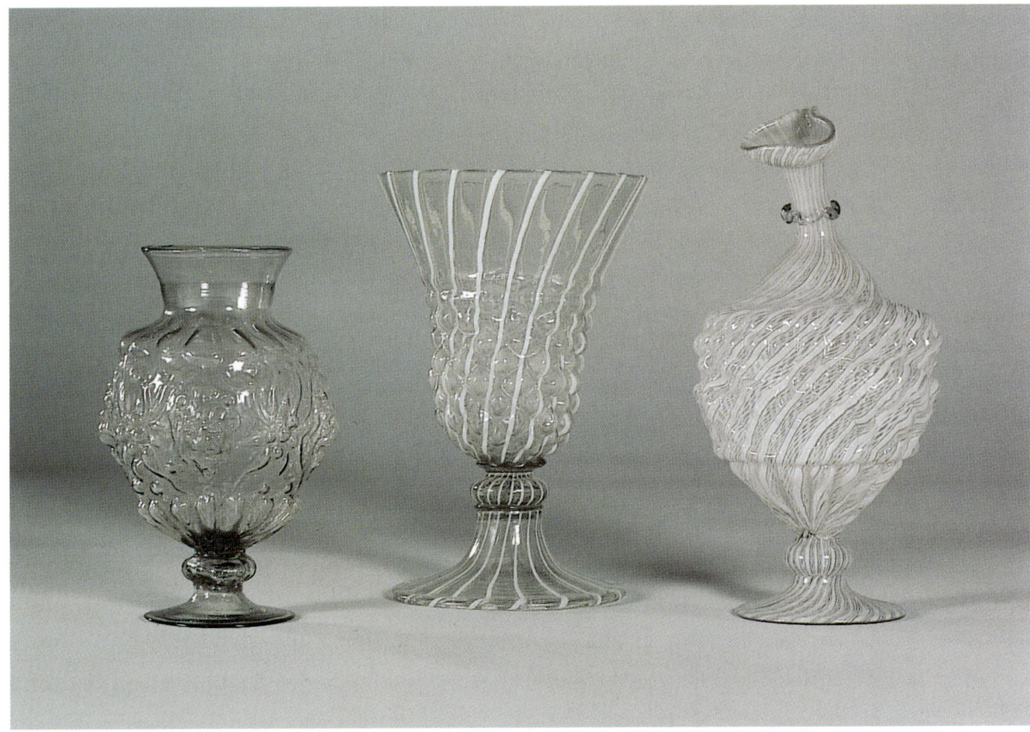

161 Three vessels: (left to right) vase with lion's heads; drinking glass of *vetro a fili* technique; sprinkler of *vetro a retorti* technique with frieze of lions and eagles; mould-blown glass; Venice (Murano), second half of sixteenth century. The British Museum, London

have such a great master of Murano in mind, I pray that you may make me such a great gift.'[96]

Unfortunately, no design specifically intended for glass has been identified among the mid-sixteenth-century designs that survive (although there survive some late Cinquecento examples by Jacopo Ligozzi).[97] However, the designs for silver and for carved and mounted hard-stone vessels examined in Chapter Four, although they may not necessarily have been easy to translate into glass, give some sense of this 'ancient facility of design'. It is clear that there was a permanent shift away from surface decoration, and the pictorial enamelling of the late fifteenth and very early sixteenth centuries, towards an emphasis on ever more elaborate or bizarre forms into which glass could be moulded, blown and manipulated. By virtue of its ancient connotations and its capacity to imitate hard-stone, the medium was thought worthy of the message transmitted by such *all'antica* designs, all the more since they had been developed for other, more intrinsically precious media.

Italian maiolica: surpassing the ancients

If glass was valued because its manufacturers were thought to have equalled the ancients in their technical ingenuity, one ceramic medium appealed because its makers and decorators were believed actually to have surpassed the ancients. During the fifty-year period 1475–1525 Italian potters developed a revolutionary new ceramic: a kind of tin-glazed pottery – maiolica – which astonished contemporaries for its fineness and lightness, and its white, clean surface. Italians celebrated its technical finesse: the acknowledged difficulties and demands of throwing, firing, glazing and lustring. Moreover, the value of these technological qualities was raised still further by their marriage with the 'noble' art of painting.[98] The brightly coloured narratives of *istoriato* (history-painted) maiolica were something not even the Greeks and Romans had achieved.

Even at the short-lived peak of *istoriato* production in the 1520s, ceramics were never valued financially as highly as silver. Objects manufactured in silver retained not only their bullion value but also, as we have seen, potentially an additional prestige through their design by leading artists. We know, for example, that in 1525 a silver-gilt salt designed by Giulio Romano for Federico Gonzaga, Duke of Mantua, cost 31 ducats for the silver and 20 ducats for the workmanship of the goldsmith who made it.[99] In 1530 Federico could buy 100 pieces of *istoriato* maiolica for a mere 25 scudi. Given that a silver scudo was nearly equivalent to a gold ducat in value, one silver salt was therefore the financial equivalent of 200 pieces of maiolica.[100] The letter from Federico's artistic agent in Urbino who gives us this information, the poet Gian Jacopo Calandra, provides a good indication of relative prices of different elements in an *istoriato* service and how these were valued 'according to the workmanship, because they are worth more or less depending on the greater and lesser amount of work', and he made it clear that he was talking about the very best Urbino *istoriato*, a *credenza* of 'really excellent ware painted with landscapes, fables and histories, to my eyes of surpassing beauty'.[101]

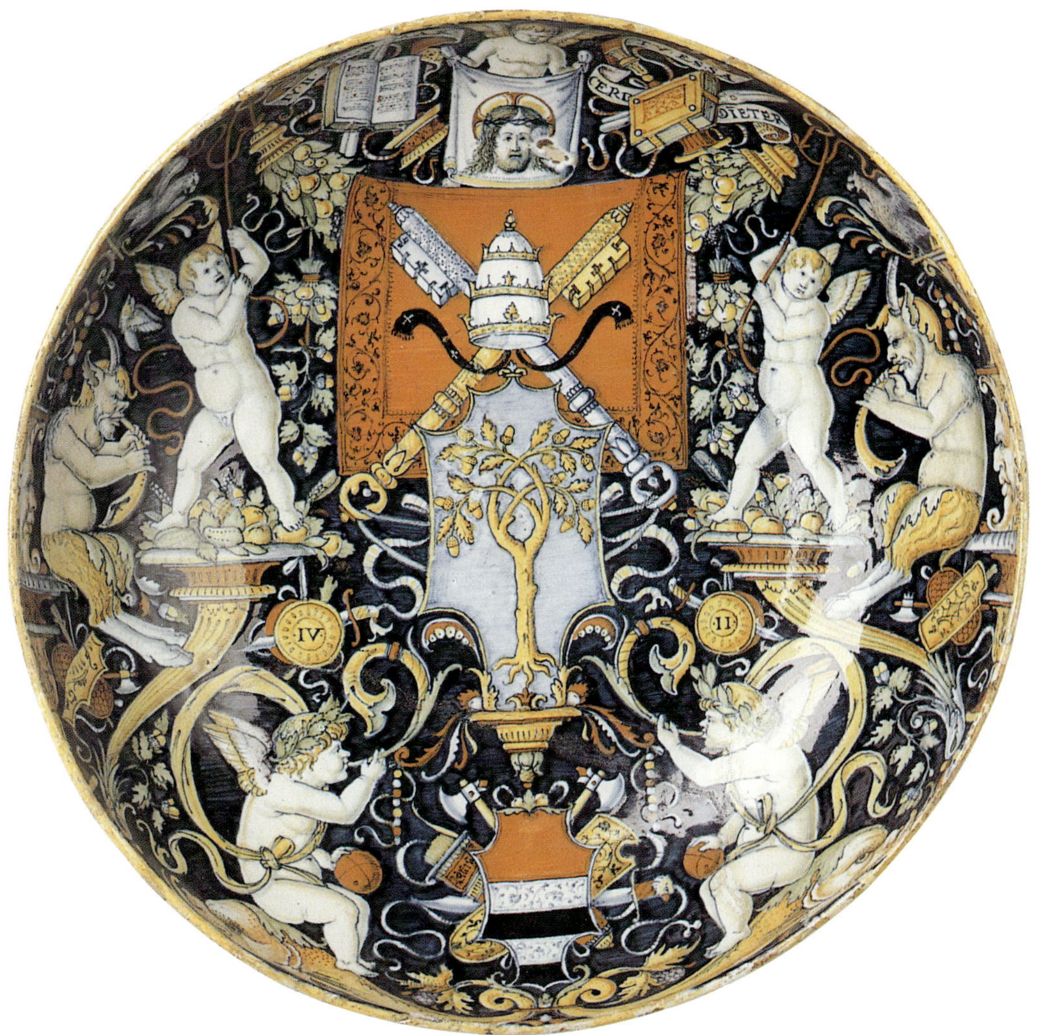

162 'Giovanni Maria',
dish with the arms of Pope
Julius II and the papal keys;
tin-glazed ceramic (maiolica);
Casteldurante, 1508.
The Metropolitan Museum
of Art, New York

Nevertheless, whatever its actual economic worth, its aesthetic value (admittedly within a very restricted elite) was disproportionately high (fig. 162). The terms used for its praise are familiar. When the humanist Niccolò Perotti wrote to a friend thanking him for two gifts of maiolica, he stressed the dignity of the subjects of Jupiter and Diana painted on the pieces, which made them 'glorious to the sacred powers': 'You would not prefer any silver or gold to these clay vessels; they excel all mastery.' He himself preferred them not only to silver but to 'sardonyxes, diamonds, jaspers, crystal or onyxes'.[102] This comparison between maiolica and work in precious stone and metals was also made by leading patrons, and became something of a commonplace in contemporary letters. In 1486, for example, the Ferrarese ambassador advised Eleonora of Aragon, Duchess of Ferrara, to send maiolica tablewares from Faenza to Beatrice of Aragon, Queen of Hungary, 'for she would rejoice in them more than if they were of silver'.[103]

The initial meaning of the word 'maiolica' reveals much about this development, for until the 1490s it was used almost exclusively to denote lustred pottery imported from southern Spain, rather than native Italian products.[104] It was commercial competition with Spanish imports that spurred Italian potters first to imitation and then to rivalry, with such success that they pushed Spanish imports out of their local markets by about 1500.

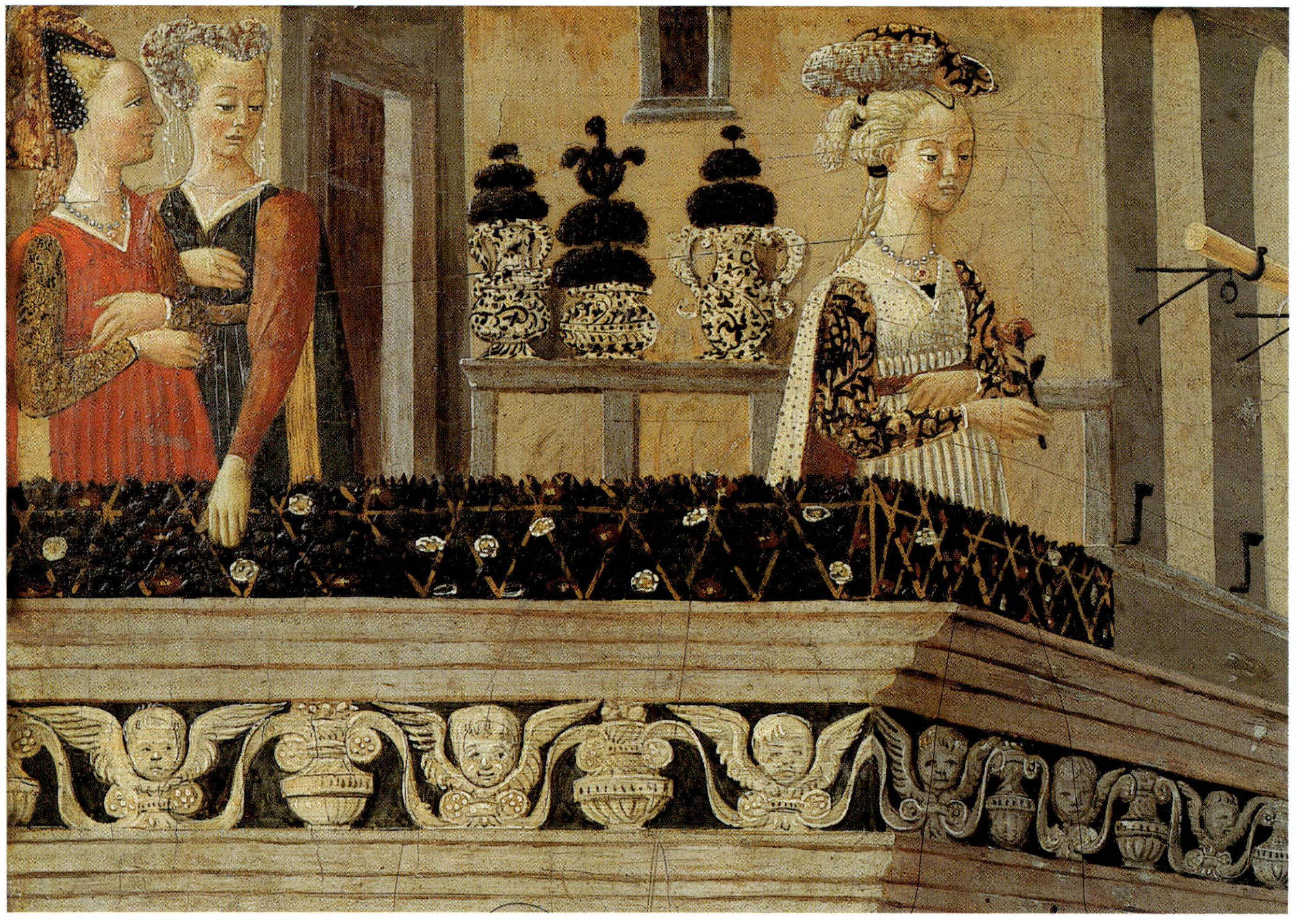

Specialist pottery centres developed, with the help of urban merchants and ruling patrons, before this date: towns such as Deruta, Siena, Montelupo, Pesaro and Faenza. The first decade of the sixteenth century saw the rise of Urbino, Casteldurante, Venice and Castelli as producers of high-quality maiolica. With the evolution of *istoriato* maiolica, which extended the range of pictorial invention to include a new medium, maiolica commanded the attention of some of the greatest and most discriminating artistic patrons.

Thus, the idea that maiolica could have aesthetic and financial value derived from Islamic cultures, where the finest pottery, including oriental imports, had always enjoyed high status. Fifteenth-century Italians imported their luxury pottery through banking houses active in the western Mediterranean. Muslim and Christian potters working in and around the southern Spanish port of Valencia produced pottery in a modified Islamic tradition for special commissions, including complete dining services, as well as standard pieces for the export market.[105] Valencian lustred pottery was admired for its brilliant metallic sheen, with highlights ranging in tone from pale silvery gold to deep red. Firing the vessels to achieve this spectacular effect was a difficult and expensive procedure demanding consummate craftsmanship. The delicate painted decoration in lustre alone or in lustre with cobalt blue, often incorporating arms or devices, won Valencian pottery prestige as a highly valued product among Italian consumers, not least in Florence, throughout the fifteenth century. Many different sources, especially archaeological finds,

202

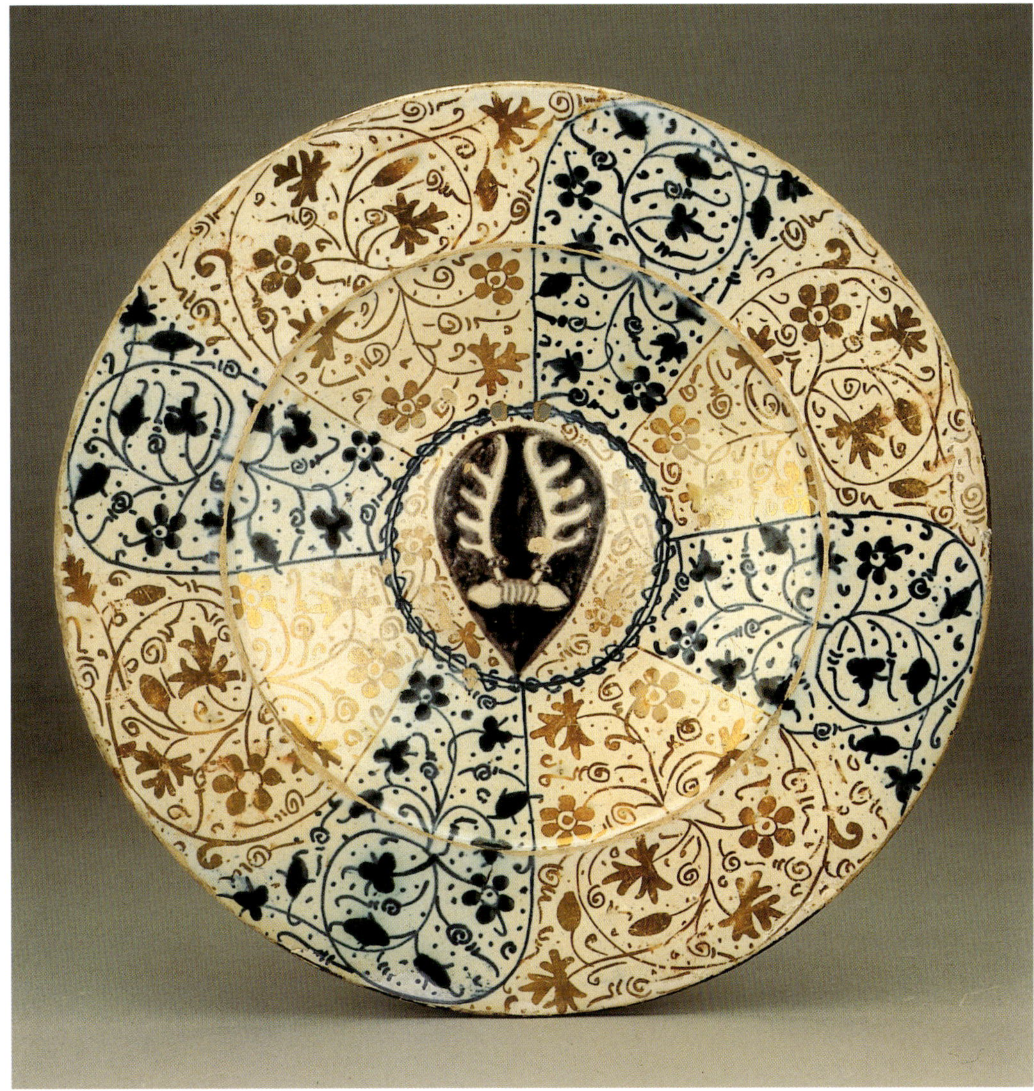

point to the status of Valencian pottery in Tuscany.[106] Paintings depict examples as display pieces used on *credenze*, or as vases, or even as flowerpots, while inventories record their placing in the domestic interior and occasionally estimate their financial value. We know from surviving Valencian pieces that some forms were carefully designed for use as plant pots, for growing basil for example.[107] A sophisticated *cassone* panel, perhaps painted in the mid-fifteenth century for the marriage of Lucrezia Tornabuoni to Piero de' Medici, shows Valencian vases on a balcony, painted with fleur-de-lis designs in blue (fig. 163). They are being used to grow evergreens, which have been pruned into elaborate shapes, the central one taking the form of the Medici *impresa* of the diamond ring and feathers. Such a detail may not be entirely fanciful, given what we know from literary sources about flowers and greenery teased into elaborate arrangements for festivals.

Letters and account books document the commissioning or arrival of Valencian wares.[108] These sources, and the surviving pieces themselves, are valuable indicators of mid-fifteenth-century demand, particularly among the Florentine urban elite. An excellent example commissioned by one of Florence's ruling families, the Soderini, is a small plate with the family's arms at the centre (fig. 164). Valencian potters rarely used manganese purple and seem to have done so only to indicate heraldic tinctures on pieces featuring the arms of foreign clients; this perhaps implies that the pieces were special commissions, controlled by drawings of the arms with their heraldic tinctures to be copied on the ceramic wares. Radiating out from the arms are panels of blue stylized flowers and leaves intertwined with tendrils and stalks alternating in cobalt blue and golden-coloured lustre.[109] This delicate design was typical of Valencian pottery and was much admired by Tuscans. A fascinating inventory of 1480 of pottery accumulated by a Pisan merchant lists a number of pieces painted with what must have been this type of pattern: *fioralixi* (a word derived from the French fleur-de-lis).[110] The inventory of the estate of Giovanni Soderini, which is dated 1421, mentions Valencian pottery among the contents of his study, which perhaps included this beautiful plate as a display piece (possibly used occasionally for formal

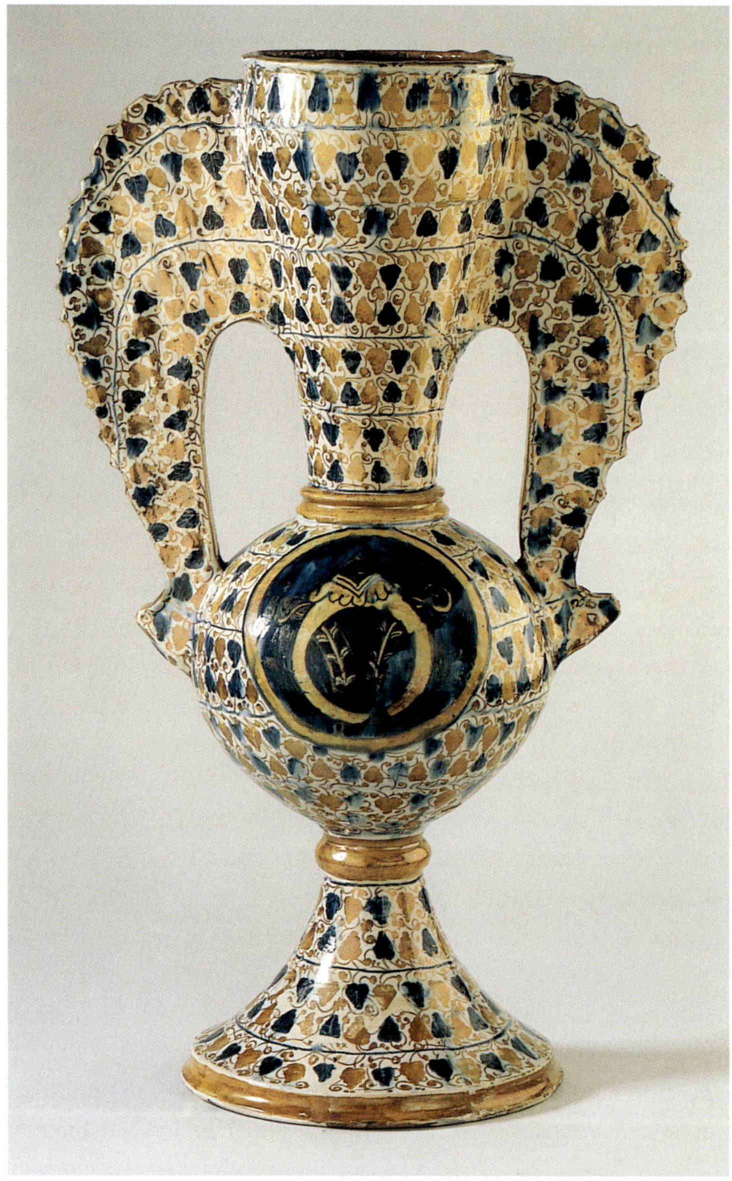

165 Two-handled vase with the arms of Piero or Lorenzo de' Medici with leaf design in lustre and blue; tin-glazed ceramic (maiolica) with lustre decoration; Valencia, Spain, *c.*1465–92, The British Museum, London

dining).[111] The pieces listed in the Soderini inventory included a large deep-sided dish (*rinfrescatoio*) and small dishes, though none of the pieces is described as being painted with the Soderini arms. Their status is indicated by the fact that they shared Giovanni's study with brass candlesticks, pewter dishes imported from Flanders, two manuscript books written in Italian, and a small panel painting of the Virgin.[112] In addition, like silver, Valencian lustred pottery was not merely displayed, as we know from the 1480 inventory, annotated six years later to indicate which items had been broken through use and which had been sold off since the original list had been drawn up.[113]

Piero de' Medici is known to have taken an interest in the latest ceramic technology, not least in commissioning Luca della Robbia to line his study with enamelled earthenware.[114] The aesthetic sensibility of either Piero or his son Lorenzo is documented by a vase in The British Museum, which must have been specially commissioned from Valencia through the Medici bank (fig. 165).[115] The form of the Medici arms painted on the front of the vase and the *impresa* of the diamond ring with three feathers on the reverse date the piece to between 1465 and 1492, since both were used by Piero after 1465 and by his son Lorenzo. The Medici *palle* are painted in manganese purple as a substitute for red, and the uppermost *palla* is painted blue with three fleur-de-lis; an augmentation granted to Piero and his descendants by Louis XI of France in 1465.[116] The vase takes a typically Islamic form, with a long funnel neck, globular body and large wing handles. It is divided into bands of decoration of leaf patterns alternating in cobalt blue and golden-coloured lustre, making it a striking display piece. Whoever ordered it, Lorenzo certainly owned it, and it may be one of two vases (*2 orcioloni grandi con dua manichi da Maiolicha, con l'arme*) that are listed among the contents of the principal reception room in his villa at Careggi in an inventory compiled after his death in 1492.[117]

Such was the demand for Valencian pottery that, from about 1450, Italian potters were keen to imitate it in making fine pottery of their own. A vase with Medici connections can be dated early and signals the beginning of the move to capture the Italian home market (fig. 166). The arms on it document a marriage between the Medici and Orsini families; possibly between Lorenzo himself and Clarice Orsini, who were married in 1469.[118] The form of the vase, with its *fioralixi* decoration in blue bands (fleurs-de-lis were emblems of particular significance for Florentines), closely imitates Valencian prototypes. Significantly, this piece, too, is described in the inventory of a Medici villa at Poggio a Caiano (*uno vaso con dua manichi dipinto coll'arme de' Medici e Orsina*), which indicates its perceived importance.[119]

Evidence for the increased production, diversification and technological advance of Italian maiolica from around 1450 is provided by surviving pieces that, for the first time in post-classical Europe, bear potters' marks, dates, and other written information about their manufacture.[120] The earliest recorded date is 1466, but the custom of inscribing pottery picked up considerably from 1500.[121] By the 1530s names of makers and places of production appear with greater frequency in the inscriptions on reverses of flat tablewares, and it becomes possible to trace the fortunes of workshops, of individual artisans, and the migrations of potters.[122] In addition to the surviving pieces, both collected and excavated, a wide range of documents demonstrates the growth of the maiolica industry, including notarial acts, contracts, tax returns, guild records, business agreements, account books and protective legislation.[123] Technical details of manufacture are provided by an illustrated treatise written around 1557 by Cipriano Piccolpasso, *The Three Books of the Potter's Art*, which is the principal source for this account.[124] Piccolpasso is keen to stress the skill, complexity and difficulty of maiolica production. The treatise was commissioned by a French patron, the Cardinal de Tournon, as a practical design source for French potters.[125] Piccolpasso, however, pronounces that his work is intended 'to show forth all the secrets of the potter', so that the art of maiolica 'will pass to courts among elevated spirits and speculative minds'.[126] By this phrase he makes considerable claims for the dignity of the potter's practice, and it is surely intentional that he structures his work in three books like the classic humanist treatise on art, Alberti's *On Painting*.[127] Piccolpasso was not a potter but a courtier, and he is keen to describe maiolica as a virtuous art worthy of the attention of great princes. He even confirms Giovio's account of the interests of Alfonso d'Este; in giving the invention of a thick white glaze to him, he stated that 'the making of earthen pots … will not diminish the greatness and worth of so excellent a prince'.[128]

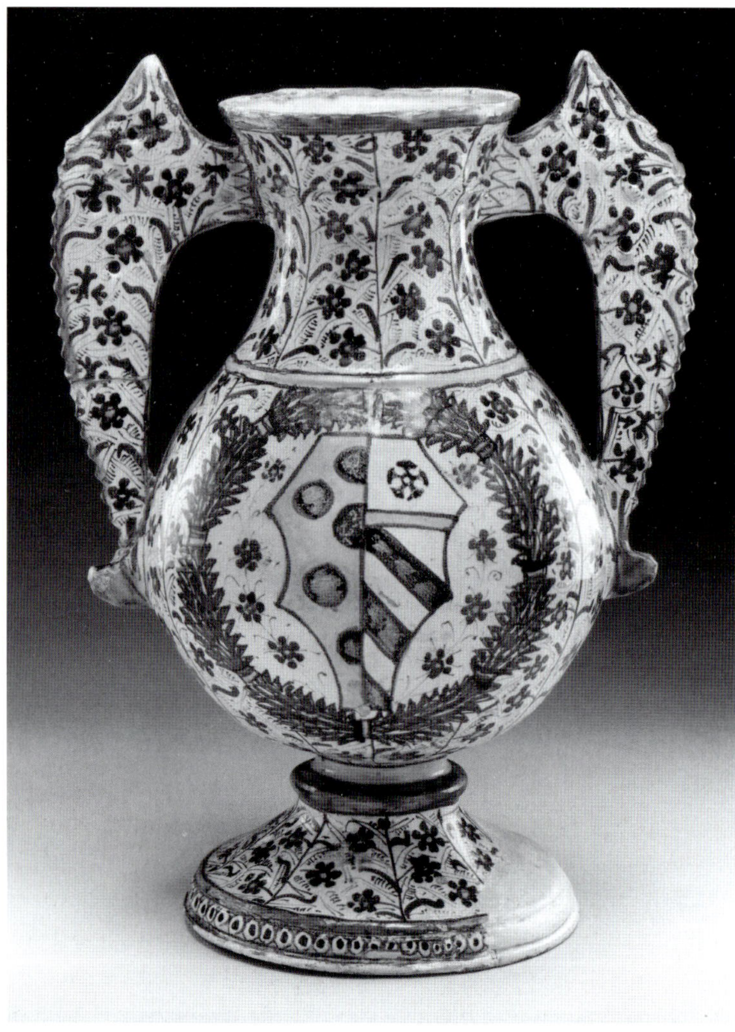

166 Vase with the arms of Medici and Orsini; tin-glazed ceramic (maiolica); Florence or environs, *c*.1470–80. Institute of Arts, Detroit

Clays and raw materials

Piccolpasso was a native of one of the many production centres of fine maiolica, Casteldurante (Urbania), a natural pottery centre owing to clays deposited there by the River Metauro. He describes how chalky clays silted 'to a depth of a foot or two' above the banks. The clay was checked for inclusions of chalk, which, in firing, would turn to quicklime and eventually spall off, damaging the glaze in finished wares. Chalky clay was also dug in sloping ground, in pits with channels for rainwater between them. Clays were flung into heaps to be weathered and broken down, then processed by sieving and straining through cloth, beating to break down impurities, and kneading until smooth.[129] Not all pottery centres used local clays; Piccolpasso explains that Venetian potters (many of whom were migrants from other pottery towns) used clays from Ravenna, Rimini, Pesaro, Ferrara, as well as nearby Padua.[130]

The principal ingredients of the tin-opacified lead glaze used for fine maiolica included both local and more-expensive imported elements, the most important of which was tin. Particles of tin oxide, suspended in the glaze layer, produced the characteristic whiteness of the ground for the painted decoration of maiolica.[131] Tin used by Italian potters travelled considerable distances in what must have been a profitable and highly organized trade.[132] Vannuccio Biringuccio noted in his treatise: 'I have heard from people who know that the largest quantities and best tin found in Europe is what is mined in England [presumably he meant Devon and Cornwall]; I have heard that it is also found in parts of Flanders, and in Bohemia and the Duchy of Bavaria, but the bizarre placenames are too difficult for me.'[133] Ground tin and lead oxides were stirred with a flux or silicate of potash (*marzacotto*) in water to make the tin-glaze suspension.[134] Potash was derived from burning the lees on the inside of wine barrels, and then combined with white, quartz sand.[135]

Dried wood for firing was also required; a fifteenth-century potter's account book records payments for transport by the cartload from up to eight kilometres away.[136] Brushwood and broom were also used in specialist workshops for the third, low-temperature firing needed to produce lustred pottery. Hence the edict of 1465 prohibiting the introduction of these highly inflammable materials into the maiolica town, Deruta, except on the day preceding kiln firings may document an early date for lustre production in the town.[137]

Throwing, forming, moulding and relief decoration glazes

Piccolpasso describes the construction of a foot-driven potter's wheel with heavy flywheel (fig. 167): one is painted on a Deruta maiolica plate of about 1525.[138] An inverted wooden bowl fixed onto the wheelhead with clay made it easier to work the underside of bowls and dishes, with up to five distinct iron tools being used to finish footrings.[139] Considerable care was taken to make the body as thin as possible, not only through expert throwing but also by paring the 'leather-hard' body on the wheel with iron tools before firing.[140] The finest maiolica is astonishingly light to hold and slender to the touch; a revolutionary quality in European ceramics which appealed to discerning patrons. A light

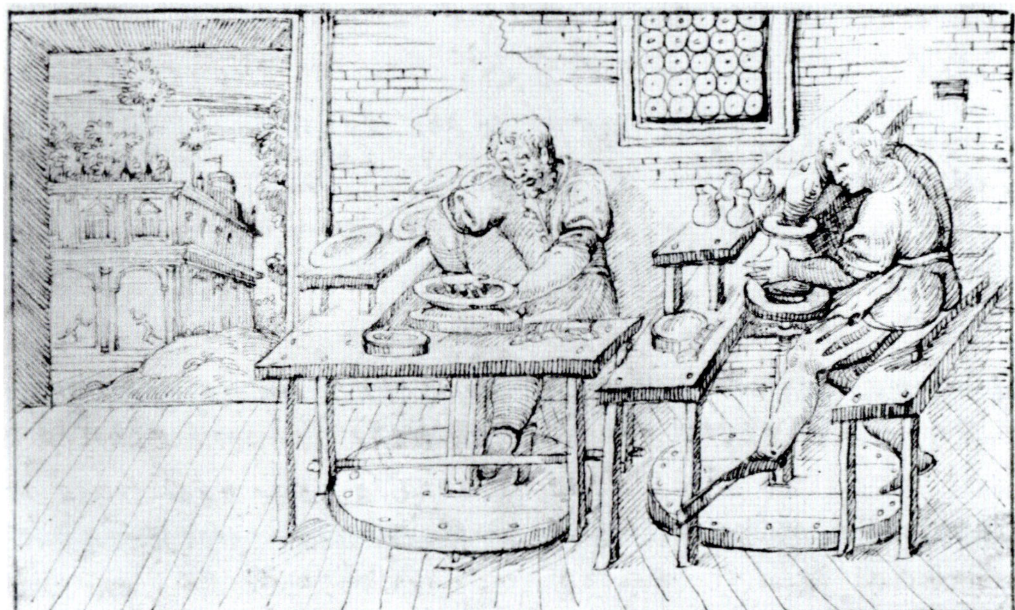

167 Cipriano Piccolpasso, *Throwing pots*, illustration from his manuscript *The Three Books of the Potter's Art*, fol. 16r; pen and ink; Casteldurante, 1557. National Art Library, Victoria and Albert Museum, London

body, along with the white, opaque tin-glaze, was primarily a means of rivalling imported oriental porcelain. However, its very physical state could be seen as embodying social virtues. Isabella d'Este was told that ware being made for her was 'more gallant, thinner and lighter [than the norm] … and they will be very noble'.[141] One of the words is *sottile*, another Plinian umbrella term covering a range of possibilities and one that linked the physical quality in objects – that of delicacy or precision – to an acuteness and subtlety of thought of both artist and owner.[142]

The introduction of moulding diversified maiolica forms, as well as increasing the volume and speed of production while reducing costs.[143] Half moulds of plaster were used in the sixteenth century for open forms: convex for basket-type wares, concave for pieces with relief decoration imitating embossed metalwork.[144] Complex closed forms such as pilgrim flasks, once again based on sculptural table silver, were piece-moulded, with cast handles attached with slip.[145] Applied relief ornament, such as floral scrolls on the undersides of flasks and basins, and serpent handles, were also moulded; Piccolpasso's illustration of four types of handle current in the 1550s is precisely matched by the remains of plaster moulds excavated at a pottery in Rome documented as that of Andrea della Superchina, who had come originally from Piccolpasso's home town, Casteldurante.[146]

Pierced containers known as saggars were used to protect the biscuit ware and enable it to be stacked in the kiln, where it was given a first firing at about 1,000°C.[147] Given that firing temperatures were uneven in the up-draft kiln that Piccolpasso illustrates, painted wares were given pride of place.[148]

Pigments and firing

Wares were dipped in tin-glaze, which, when dry, provided a powdery white, absorbent surface for painting (fig. 168), one that could be tinted by adding cobalt.[149] Indeed, from the mid-fifteenth century a wide range of pigments was developed in addition to cobalt blue, which was used for outlining figurative designs. Green was derived from copper, tin was used for white highlights, yellow was derived from antimony, orange from blending antimony with iron, and purple-brown from manganese.[150] Piccolpasso said of the difficulties of obtaining red that 'as yet this art has no colour that comes out red', but mentions Virgiliotto Calamelli of Faenza's recipe using the earth pigment, Armenian bole: his comments on its unreliability are borne out by the way in which areas of red fired as raised, granular patches on surviving pieces from Faenza and Tuscany.[151]

The technology of preparing pigments, including recipes, local variations in their preparation, and methods of grinding, takes up the whole second book of Piccolpasso's

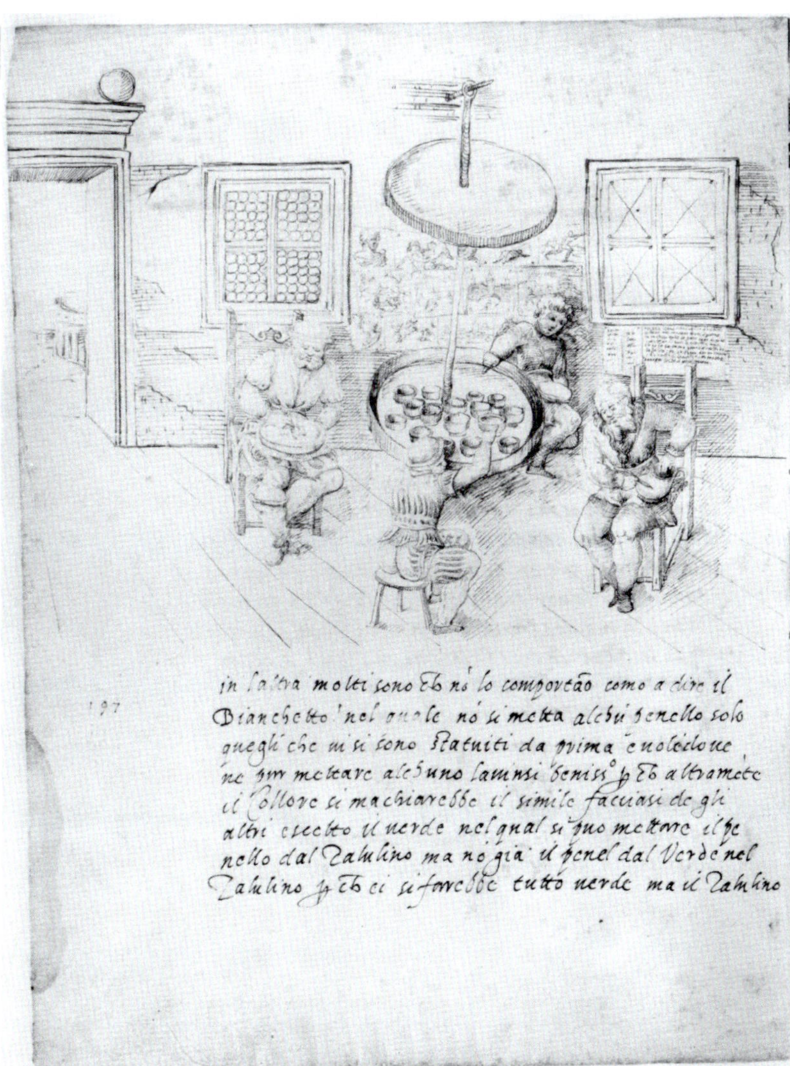

168 Cipriano Piccolpasso, *Maiolica painters at work*, illustration from his manuscript *The Three Books of the Potter's Art*, fol. 57v; pen and ink; Casteldurante, 1557. National Art Library, Victoria and Albert Museum, London

treatise. After painting (see fig. 168), some wares were sprinkled with a clear finishing glaze to give surface gloss and saturate the colours.[152] Given the time and labour spent on painting fine wares, it seems surprising that they were often laid face down on pointed spurs or pegs within saggars for firing: the marks of these may be clearly seen on finished pieces, while surviving kiln failures show them stuck to the surface of the wares.[153] Piccolpasso's illustrations of pierced saggars are again matched by excavated examples.[154]

The kiln had to be swept to prevent dust particles adhering to painted surfaces, then carefully set so that the wares did not touch one another, and so fuse in the firing (fig. 169) or block the fire vents.[155] Finally, the kiln was sealed with mortar; fragments, bearing potters' fingerprints, have been found in potters' waste heaps in Montelupo.[156] A second firing at about 950°C completed the ware – unless metallic lustre was to be applied, in which case a third firing was required to reduce the metal oxide pigments, leaving a metallic coating on the surface.[157] Lustre techniques were jealously guarded by the potters

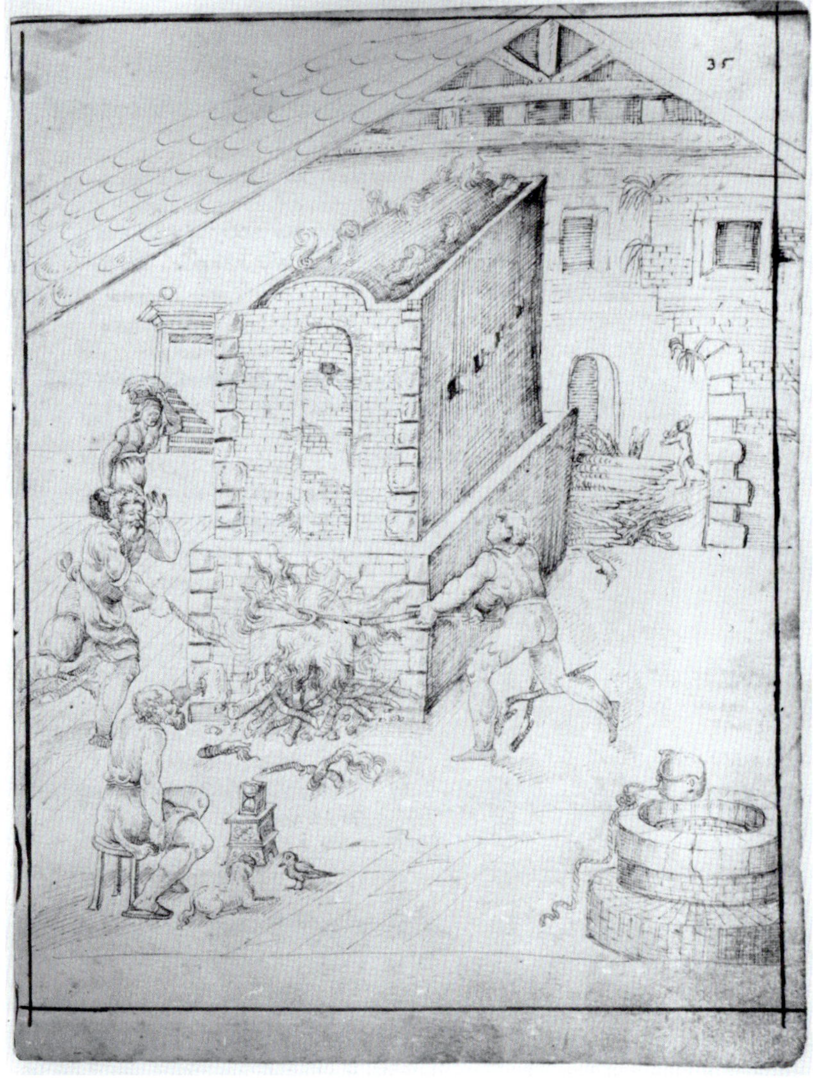

169 Cipriano Piccolpasso, *Kiln firing*, illustration from his manuscript *The Three Books of the Potter's Art*, fol. 35r; pen and brown ink; Casteldurante, 1557. National Art Library, Victoria and Albert Museum, London

170 Maestro Giorgio
Andreoli (workshop),
bowl, *The Expulsion from
Paradise*; tin-glazed
ceramic (maiolica) with
lustre decoration;
Gubbio, 1531.
The British Museum,
London

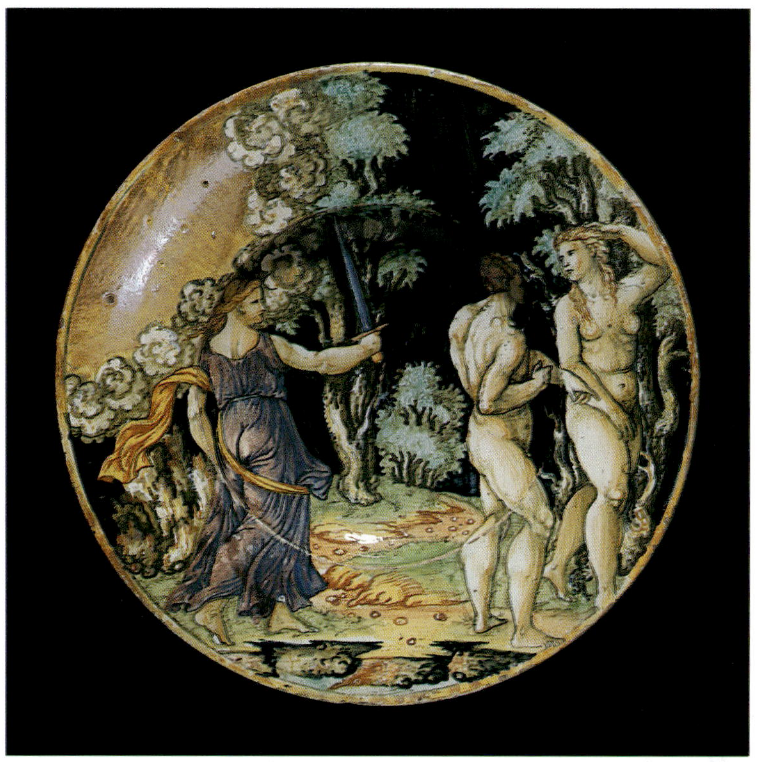

who knew them,[158] but since there was a strong commercial incentive to rival imported
lustreware from Spain, fifteenth-century Italian potters can be shown (from local finds and
analyses of potters' waste heaps) to have made their own short-lived experiments in
Faenza, Pesaro, Montelupo and Caffagiolo.[159] Lustre production was expensive in
materials and had a high failure rate; Piccolpasso, extraordinarily, estimated that only six in
every hundred pieces succeeded.[160] Therefore, it is perhaps not very surprising that it came
to be practised only on a large, almost industrial scale in Gubbio (fig. 171) and Deruta by
specialized workshops in the sixteenth century.[161]

History-painting

Above all, it was the combination of technical and pictorial qualities that placed the best
maiolica at the top of the market. Indeed, Biringuccio emphasizes this very blend of
ingredients: 'The principal basis [of pottery] is derived from two things – the art of *disegno*
and various secrets and alchemical mixtures.'[162] Painting on maiolica is a demanding and
precise art, as Piccolpasso explains. Painters, he says, tended to sit down (a mark of
non-artisanal distinction), unlike fresco painters, and cradle the unpainted pottery – the
blanks – on their laps, painting with the finest brushes, which might be made from the
whiskers of mice (see fig. 168).[163] Unfired tin glaze is an unforgiving medium. It is powdery
and absorbs pigments like blotting paper, demanding a fluent, sure touch. Add to this the
small scale and complexity of *istoriato*, and the fact that the pigments used develop their
final colour only in the firing, and one gets a sense of the difficulties of controlling both line

and colour. Lustre finishes were even harder to control and master in a way that served the narrative (fig. 170), rather than merely adding distracting highlights. When a seventeenth-century historian of Faenza considered maiolica painting to be 'much more difficult than painting on canvas or panel', he had a point.[164]

Piccolpasso provides a special section in his treatise on 'the mixtures [of pigments] with which the *istoriati* are done and how they are laid on in their places so that the art may not be lacking in perfection … for drawing figures and sketching histories on vessels … is done with light and shade'.[165] He gives recipes for two shades of blue, one for outlines and shadows, the lighter shade for working up. He goes on to prescribe the correct pigments for painting rocks and timber; sky, sea and weapons; earth, 'antique remains' and stones; meadows and bushes 'struck by sunlight'; and for human hair.[166]

This listing of the pictorial ingredients of *istoriati* matches surviving pieces and the ways in which painters tackled complex subjects and placed them in landscapes. The use of the word *istoriato* to denote narrative painting on pots is telling, in that Piccolpasso sees no need to explain his meaning. Yet the word, derived from the Latin *historia*, is not commonly used in documents or letters to describe pottery painting. Calandra's 1530 reference to wares with *fabulae* and *istorie* is rare.[167] But Piccolpasso's reference to *istoriati* is vital for what it tells us about both the practice and pretensions of the owners and painters of maiolica. The word *istoriato*, or the practice of decorating ceramics with *istorie*, may refer back to Alberti's treatise *On Painting*, in which he describes how narrative compositions should be put together: 'That which first gives pleasure in the *istoria* comes from copiousness and variety of things … When we have an *istoria* to paint, we will first think out

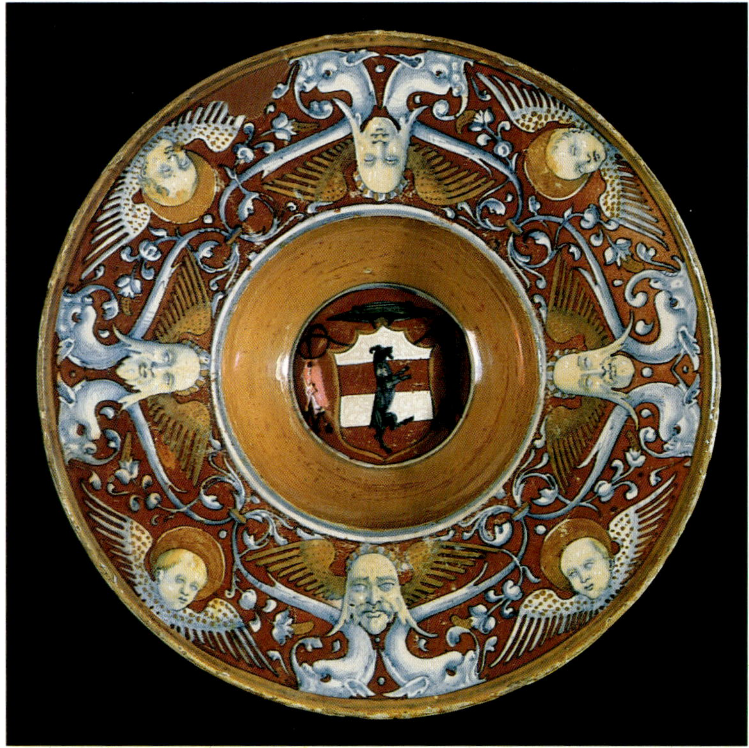

171 Maestro Giorgio Andreoli (workshop), dish with the arms of an unidentified prelate and grotesque decoration; tin-glazed ceramic (maiolica), with red lustre decoration; Gubbio, *c*.1515–20. The British Museum, London

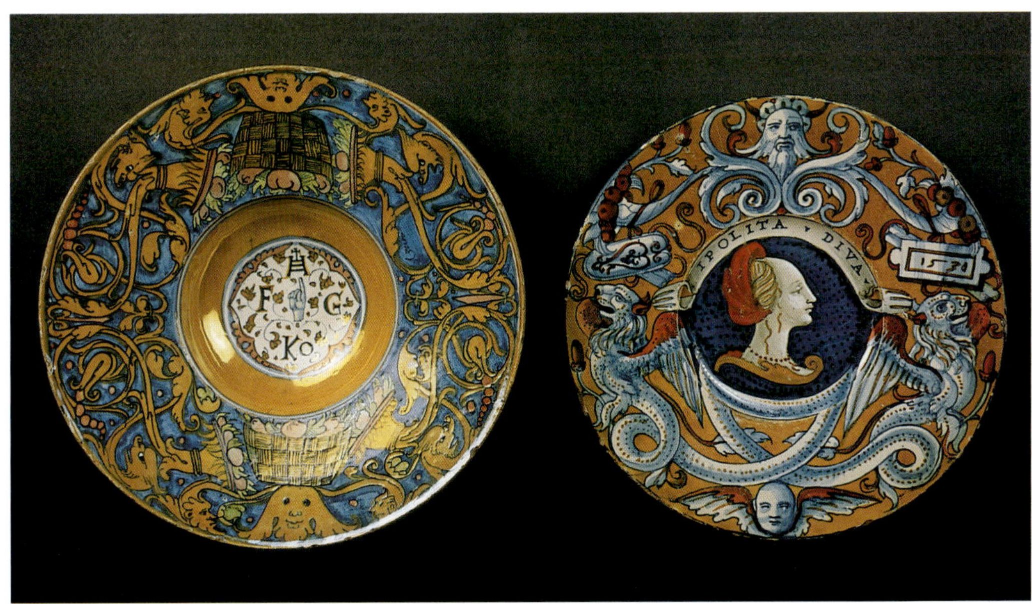

172 Maestro Giorgio Andreoli (workshop), two dishes: left, with grotesques; right, with woman's head and grotesque border; tin-glazed ceramic (maiolica) with lustred decoration; Gubbio, 1518 (left) and 1531 (right). The British Museum, London

the method and the order to make it most beautiful; we will make our model drawings of all the *istoria* and every one of its parts first of all.'[168] By employing this Albertian terminology, Piccolpasso was putting pottery painters on a par with artists occupied with pictures on panel and great fresco cycles.[169]

One surviving plate (fig. 172 left) suggests a degree of collaboration between painters who may have had specialized functions and have worked according to series production methods. The elaborate design on it was laid out by a specialist, who left his instructions to a lesser painter to fill in the ground of his design in blue at the two o'clock position on the dish.[170] Many other pieces document workshop collaboration, making it difficult to interpret inscriptions on the reverse of a given piece as the signature of an individual artist or the imprimatur of a workshop. Some pieces produced in larger workshops are, for instance, inscribed in more than one hand.[171] Until more is known of workshop organization, it will be difficult to generalize about what was typical working practice, since all the evidence – both archival and archaeological – points to a huge variety in the nature, size and organization of maiolica workshops.[172] What is certain is that prestige pieces were produced in the largest ateliers, employing specialist painters on contract, and highly skilled kiln operators to ensure maximum success in firing finished pieces.

The most successful workshops, therefore, were those that controlled the entire process of production: the 1489 tax returns for Deruta reveal that the Masci family of potters owned three workshops, a kiln, clay pits, and woods. This represented considerable capital investment and, not surprisingly, the Masci had the highest tax assessment.[173] Some pottery painters, working in a succession of partnerships with other potters, never achieved such independence: one Faenza pottery painter may have felt forced to diversify, painting not only maiolica but also religious images and *cassoni*.[174] Individual potters sometimes appear to have operated as painters employed on contract at one moment, and then as workshop owners the next – like Francesco Durantino, who worked in the Urbino *bottega* of Guido di Merlino in 1543 and then set up on his own, taking over a kiln in 1547.[175] There was, however, a huge gap between entrepreneurial family dynasties, such as the Masci of Deruta, the Andreoli of Gubbio, the Fontana of Urbino, and the Calamelli of Faenza, and dependent workers, many of them painters, who relied on piecework and sub-contracts.[176] And it is clear that only workshop owners ever attained any social recognition from their trade, whatever the claims other participants in the process may have made for their art.

In the second, 1568, edition of his *Lives,* Vasari singles out *istoriato* for unambiguous praise. By this date *istoriato* had attained a dignity and aesthetic value of its own. Such was its status that it had earned a place on the *credenze* of leading art patrons. From the 1540s the della Rovere dukes of Urbino – the leading pottery centre for *istoriato* – promoted their local industry, not least by commissioning sets of dining ware to the designs of leading artists as diplomatic gifts. Thus Battista Franco was employed by Duke Guidobaldo II to make a series of drawings on the subject of the Trojan War for this purpose around 1545.[177] As Vasari comments:

The Duke thought that Franco's designs would be a success if executed by those who made excellent pottery at Castel Durante, who had made use of prints of Raphael and other worthy artists. He had Battista do numerous designs, which, made into that most elegant form of pottery produced anywhere in Italy, were a rare success. From them were made so many different sorts of pottery vessels as would have sufficed for and done honour to the royal service; and the painting could not have been done better if done in oils by the finest masters ... Duke Guidobaldo sent a double service of this ware to the Holy Roman Emperor Charles V and a service to Cardinal Alessandro Farnese, brother of Signora Vittoria, his [Guidobaldo's] wife. And we should recognize that, insofar as we can tell, the [ancient] Romans were not aware of this type of painting on pottery. The vessels from those days that have been found filled with the ashes of their dead are covered with figures incised and washed in with one colour in any given area, sometimes in black, red or white, but never with the brilliance of glaze nor the charm and variety of painting which has been seen in our day.[178]

Greek figured vases, to which Vasari is referring here, were rare but not unknown; one 'extremely beautiful and ancient earthenware vase ... newly arrived from Greece' was sent to Lorenzo de' Medici from Venice in 1491, much praised by Angelo Poliziano for its exquisite quality.[179] Others must have been excavated in southern Italy.

Vasari himself could claim some knowledge of other ancient vases, for he had something of a hereditary interest in ceramic technology. His surname derived from the trade of *vasaio* (potter), which his grandfather, also Giorgio, had famously practised in Arezzo.[180] This Tuscan city had been a famous centre in the early Roman Imperial period for the production of so-called *terra sigillata*: a type of relief-decorated ware with a glossy black or red surface. Stamps were used to identify a particular workshop's production. From the time of Pliny onward, this kind of ceramic was so strongly identified with Arezzo that it was called 'Aretine ware'.[181] The local historian Marco Attilio Alessi (born in 1470) gives a detailed account of it, based on an analysis of ancient sources and direct observation from excavated pieces. His description reveals the interest of the Medici in collecting examples of this ancient fine tableware, and that pieces entered their family collections is confirmed by inventory evidence.[182] Alessi wrote:

I found an example on the bank of the Castro river … in the form of a beaker, subtle and resplendent so that it surpassed any kind of glass. When the river bank was destroyed in flooding large numbers of fragments were found with letters [workshop stamps] on the base of each vase. And sometimes when the floodbanks were dug, Messer Giovanni de' Medici was present, who was later Pope, and called Leo X when he worthily occupied the throne of Saint Peter. And in some of these fragments, one saw a battle between angels, a hunt with hounds, lions, horses, or chariots; also gods like Bacchus, Jupiter Ammon and others, stamped and moulded with wonderful industry and art.We record here below some of the names which are formed and stamped on these vases which were found on the bank of the said river, near the Ponte delle Caciarelle in the year of Our Lord 1492, in the presence of Giovanni de' Medici, then Cardinal….[183]

According to Vasari, his grandfather continued in this local tradition, but went further in rivalling the ancient ware:

Giorgio … continually occupied himself with ancient Aretine vases. At the time of Messer Gentile Urbinate, Bishop of Arezzo, he discovered the old method of colouring earthenware vessels in red and black, which had been employed by the old Aretines until the days of the King Porsena. As he was an industrious person, he made great vases a *braccia* and a half high, which may still be seen in his house. It is said that one day, as he was looking for vases in a place where he thought the ancients had worked, he found a clay field [by a river] at the Ponte alla Caciarella, in a place of the same name, at a depth of three *braccia*, three arches of ancient kilns, and about them a quantity of fragments and of broken vessels with four complete ones. These he gave to Lorenzo the Magnificent when on a visit to Arezzo [in April 1483], having been presented by the Bishop, a matter which gave rise to the subsequent relations between him and that most illustrious house. Giorgio worked extremely well in relief….[184]

The fact that Vasari the Elder was so intimate with ancient Roman technology and practice that he could not only locate buried kilns, but imitate ancient Aretine vases as display pieces in the family house indicates the status that ancient pottery, and by extension, modern maiolica, could now attain.[185] Admittedly, maiolica had a very different, painterly aesthetic from Aretine ware, which was considered to be a kind of sculpture more than ceramic, and we have seen that moulded glass was more likely to have been influenced by Aretine relief, and by its vitreous glazes. Nevertheless, it seems certain that Renaissance Italians were aware of the ancient status of Aretine pottery as artistically respectable tablewares, the foundation of their sense that maiolica was more than a suitable modern equivalent.

The ingredients of novelty

It was also new. Lorenzo de' Medici, the recipient of Vasari's gift, seems to have regarded the ownership of painted ceramics as a signal of modernity, as suggested in an undated letter to a member of the Malatesta family thanking him for a gift of armorial pottery. He not only employed the standard comparison with silver, he viewed the gift as novel:

I am very grateful for these, on account of their perfect quality and the fact that they are much to my mind [*secondo l'animo mio*]. Nor do I know how to render suitable thanks, for whereas things which are more rare [i.e. made of rarer materials] should be more valued [than pottery vessels], I value these as if they were made of silver, on account of their excellence and rarity, as I say, and the fact that they are a novelty to us here.

In this artfully constructed letter, full of references to ideal friendship, Lorenzo made a virtue out of the fact that these ceramics would be used daily at table. He added that

it was scarcely necessary to have placed your arms on these vases to bring yourself more continually into remembrance and consideration, for my filial affection and observance towards you is such that it needs no such spur, nor will it ever need one. So I hold most welcome and dear these vases which you have sent to me, and I will retain them diligently for my own use, out of love for Your Highness, so that the present esteem in which I hold you may continue day by day.[186]

Another document of 1501 gives a detailed account of a maiolica service as an example of this elite taste. An Urbino potter, Francesco Garducci, is charged with making ninety-one pieces of complex form, decorated with arms, for a cardinal.[187] The patron was Lodovico Podocataro, Bishop of Capaccio and Secretary to Pope Alexander VI. He had been made cardinal in 1500, only a year before this commission.[188] Perhaps ordering this maiolica service was intended as a sign of his social arrival in the papal court. Certainly it indicates an enthusiasm among the papal entourage. This large and complicated order, which may have involved several different craftsmen, was to be completed within two months.[189] This contract proves that Urbino pottery painters were producing *istoriato* pottery by 1501 (when it is generally thought that the Emilian town of Faenza still took the initiative in producing narrative designs). Although the appearance of Urbino products made for the top of the market is well known for the period after 1522, when named painters began to sign their wares, it is not easy to visualize this cardinal's maiolica dishes and vessels. The listing is detailed but includes forms that have not survived: wine coolers with 'spoon-shaped feet'; fruit dishes 'with feet in the form of columns and horses *al'antiqua*'; two large basins '*subtili depincti*' with coats of arms; and water jugs with lions on their lids. In each case the designs to be painted were specified, and a number of drawings and measurements were provided showing forms, profiles and the arms and devices to be included.

The particular qualities that were to distinguish the pieces in this service, however, resided in their painted decoration, for they were to be 'beautiful and well painted and of good colours with the arms of the said cardinal and other paintings to earn the praise and approval of one skilled in the art'.[190] For this cardinal-patron, as for Vasari writing on pottery painting some fifty years later, it was the artistic ingenuity, variety of invention and brilliance of colour that were paramount.

In stipulating a variety of vessels and serving dishes, each with their different functions, this important document exemplifies the way in which dining rituals were becoming more complex and codified, requiring a profusion of specialized serving dishes and table settings from wine coolers to fruit dishes, salad plates and jugs designated for water rather than wine. The forms of the pieces specified may be difficult to interpret – what were spoon feet, and how did columns and horses support the two fruit dishes, for example? – but, since they seem to have been intended to recall *all'antica* goldsmiths' work, it appears, once again, that they were expected to gain extra dignity by their association with silver. Certainly, the small bowls with wide rims copied silver prototypes, as can be seen in a manuscript miniature from a Book of Hours illuminated around 1490–4 by Giovan Pietro Birago for Bona of Savoy, the widowed Duchess of Milan (fig. 173). Here, diners are being

173 Giovan Pietro
Birago, *The Last Supper*,
illumination from
The Hours of Bona of Savoy;
tempera and gilding on
parchment; Milan, *c.*1490,
Add. Ms 34294, fol. 138v.
The British Library,
London

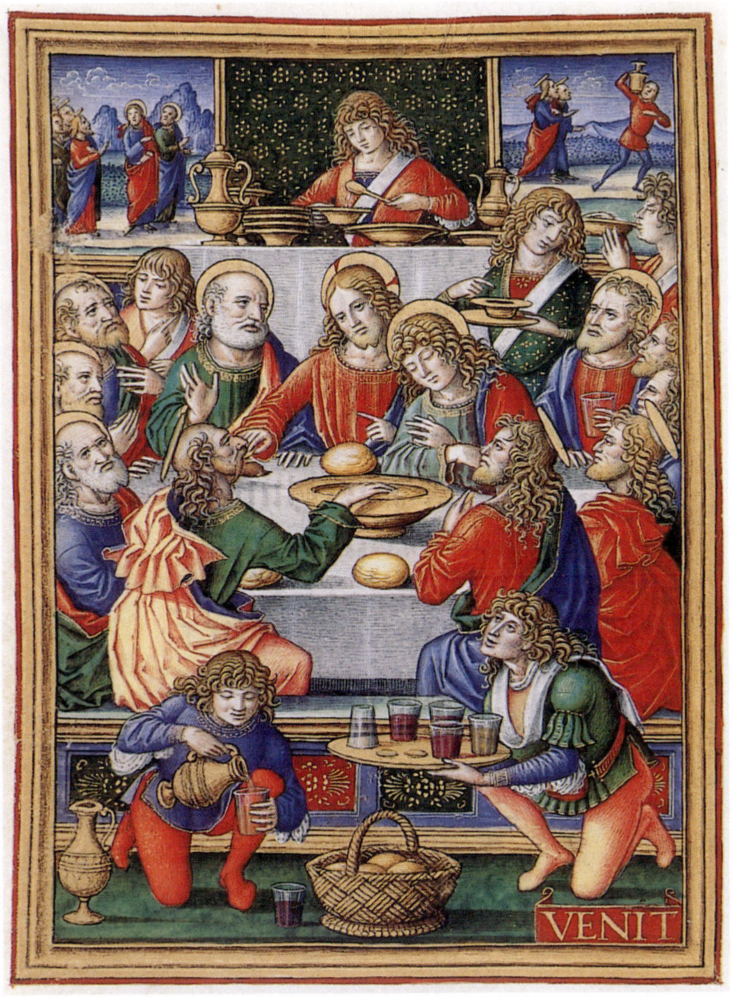

served from silver-gilt bowls stacked upon a table; the form of these bowls is indeed very
common in surviving *istoriato* maiolica of the early sixteenth century, when maiolica was
beginning to find its way onto the *credenze* and dining tables of the ruling elites on
certain occasions. Cardinals may have set the fashion in this regard, and it is indicative that
this cardinal regarded tin-glazed earthenware as eminently fitting.

Maiolica was deemed a medium worthy of taking a central part in another ritual dining
moment. Pottery workshops were quick to profit from the demand for particular wares to
celebrate births. By the second decade of the sixteenth century complex sets of stacking
dishes, made for presentation to a mother and painted with suitable scenes and with arms,
were being produced by many leading workshops. Piccolpasso gave a famous description
of such a set, his only detailed account of the function of the individual pieces that made
up a service, albeit a very specialized function:

You must know then that the five pieces that make up the birth dishes for women, all five have their
function and all five are put together to make a vessel. But to be better understood we will look at
the drawing. These are all five pieces of the set. The way to make a complete vessel is this: the plate
is turned upside down on the footed dish, that is the flat piece where the number 2 is, goes turned

on the hollow of the footed dish marked number 1, the hollow of the bowl goes turned on the feet of the plate, the salt is put thus on the foot of the bowl, above which goes its cover, as can be seen here. See how all together they make one vessel like this, a thing of no small ingenuity. There are others who make them of 9 pieces, keeping always the same order.[191]

For all its apparent impracticality, the set was designed for use and each piece had its specific function: the bowl and footed dish held liquids such as soups, kept warm by their covers, while the flat plate was for chicken – recommended as being essential for new mothers – and the salt provided a condiment. No more than three pieces survive from any one set. Surviving elements range in quality, while a small group are among the most skilfully painted of all Renaissance maiolica. These images are often couched in surprisingly intimate detail, showing a wealthy woman's bedchamber, with the mother about to give birth, surrounded by attendant women who minister to her in her labour (fig. 174). Other pieces treat themes from classical mythology in playful, highly decorative ways, pieces like the double-sided saucer in The British Museum, attributed to Francesco Xanto, showing on one side a nude Venus and her husband Vulcan, who is forging arrows as weapons for three plump putti (fig. 175). The other side depicts Saturn and Apollo driving two chariots across a dramatically stormy sky, with the date 1539 in Roman numerals at the centre.[192] The latter scene would have been encountered first by the recipient as she lifted

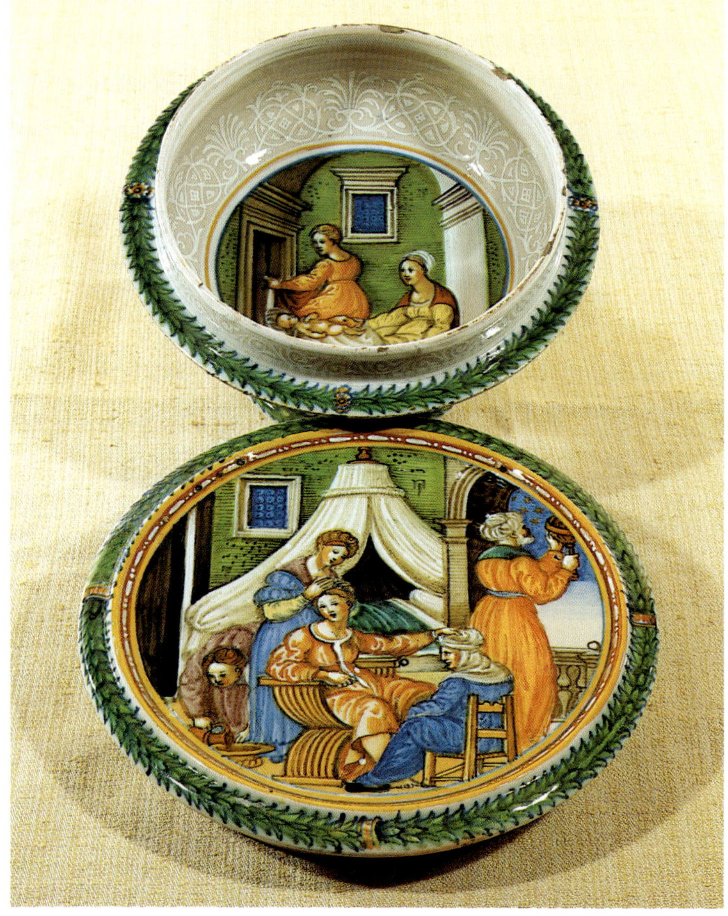

174 Lid (*tagliere*) and bowl (*scodella)* from a birth set, with birth scenes; tin-glazed ceramic (maiolica); Casteldurante, *c.*1525–30. The Victoria and Albert Museum, London

175 Francesco Xanto Avelli da Rovigo (attributed), front of plate from a birth set, *Venus and Cupids in Vulcan's Forge*; tin-glazed ceramic (maiolica); Urbino, 1539. The British Museum, London

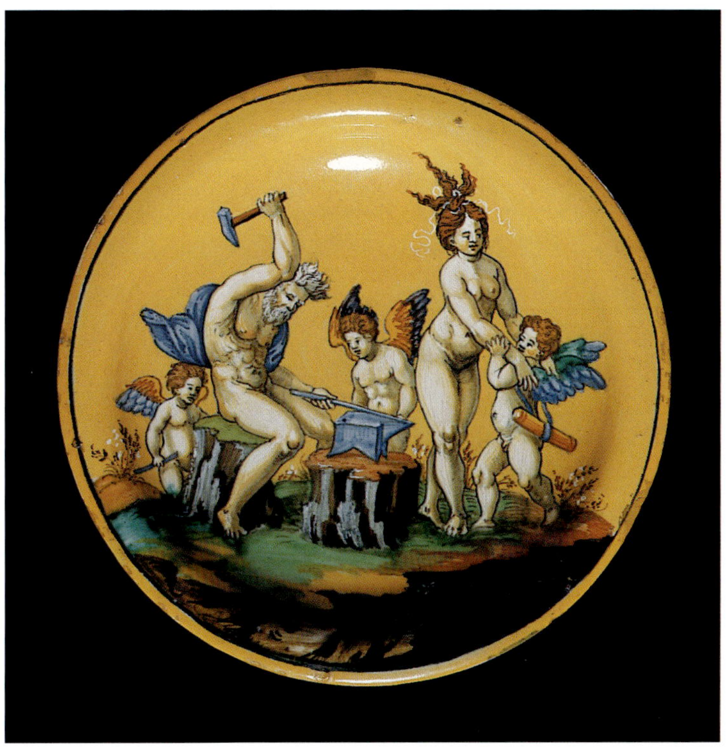

the dish to reveal the intimate familial scene within. In addition to their high quality, other birth pieces are exceptional for the fact that they often represent contemporary birth scenes in the depth of the bowl (*ongaresca*), in such a way that they could be seen only when uncovered by the mother who received the gift.

It is known, however, that maiolica painted with narrative scenes was only occasionally used for dining. A letter of 1528 mentions that Pope Clement VII used *piatti di terra … dipinti a figure* only when dining with his cardinals. Writing to Eleonora Gonzaga, Duchess of Urbino, about the customs of the Medici pope, the writer notes that Clement dined from elegantly decorated white plates rather than from *istoriato* maiolica. He found this curious:

Seeing His Holiness eating off earthenware painted with white on white, I asked his seneschal why His Holiness did not eat from plates with figurative decoration. He told me that His Holiness did not eat from those, reserving them for the use of his Cardinals.[193]

No gift could therefore be of a higher status and the writer recommended that Eleonora should send the Pope an *istoriato* credenza of the finest Urbino maiolica to replace one from Faenza that he was then using:

And the seneschal told me particularly that His Holiness did not care for basins or bowls or candlesticks, nor does he care much for flasks. He very much values having a quantity of plates of the measurements included here and two smaller sizes; only two large platters; two ewers and basins, salts, and other plates such as our Genga [by then, court artist at Urbino] will decide. Above all, the set should be made as quickly as possible, so as to seize the moment, and to speed the work even more one should give the commission to two master potters [i.e. two workshops] who should work on it at the same time.[194]

The writer is suggesting, therefore, that the duchess should take this opportunity of advertising Urbino luxury pottery by commissioning a set of maiolica for the Pope's use. This was her opportunity to ensure that the Pope used Urbino products in place of the remains of a set made in the rival pottery town of Faenza. If she were to act quickly, she could cut out any competition in replacing this set. Eleonora was a keen patron of the Urbino potters; four years before, she had commissioned a superb maiolica service for her mother, the discriminating Isabella d'Este. The idea that the painter Girolamo Genga should design the service, and preside over its making, emphasizes the perceived artistic status of the medium in Urbino.

Use and display

Surviving pieces confirm that fine *istoriato* was designed for occasional use. An example of the humorous, though still sophisticated, inclusion of a functional element, the spout for draining excess juices from cooked food when it was presented at table, appears on a large dish from a dining set made for Cardinal Duprat in 1535 in the workshop of Guido Durantino (fig. 176).[195] Each piece proudly records the subject matter and production place on the reverse. This particular dish is painted with the story of David and Goliath.

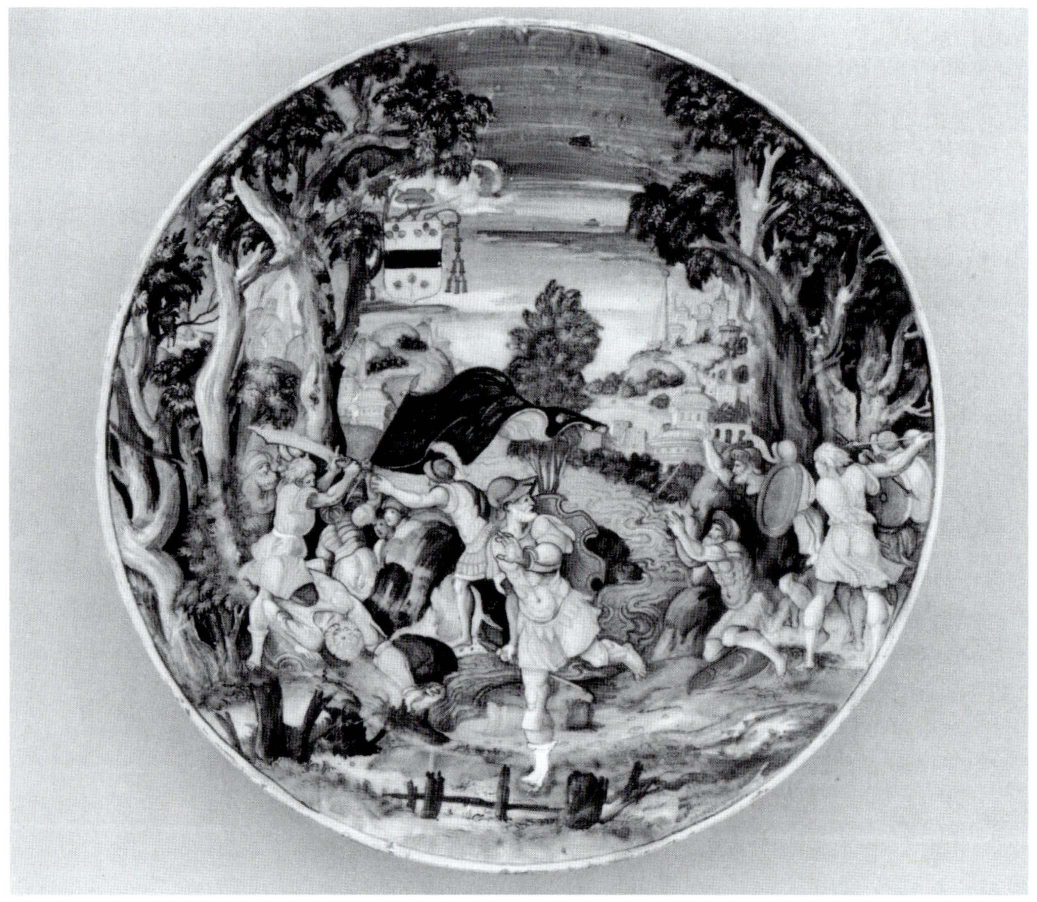

176 Maestro Guido Durantino (workshop), dish with *David and Goliath,* arms of Cardinal Duprat; tin-glazed ceramic (maiolica); Urbino, 1535. Musée du Louvre, Paris

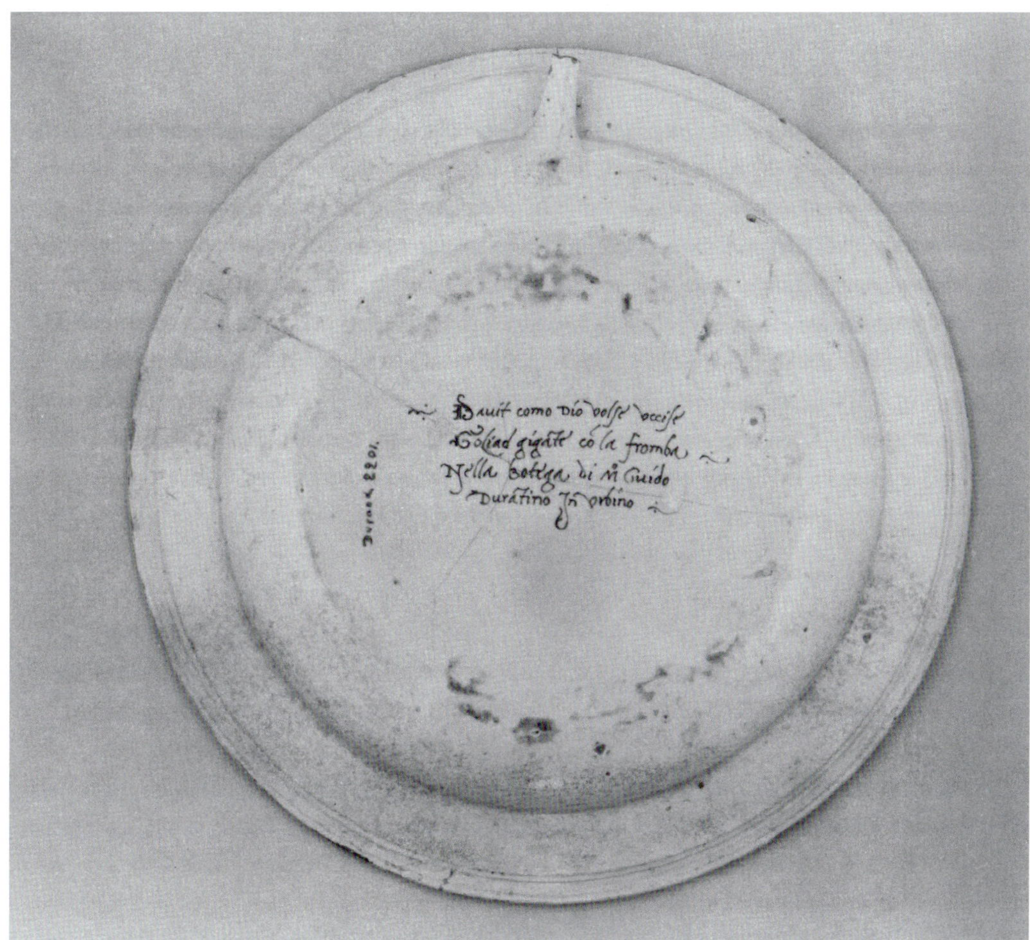

A stream runs away to the left of the well of the dish, indicating the outlet point of a small spout on the underside where any juices settling in the shallow well of the dish would have run out (fig. 177). If they had done so, they would have appeared as an extension of the stream painted on the front in a way that would have made a witty talking point whenever the spout was used at the dining table. This small detail corroborates what we know from the documentary evidence: that such services were used, but always in select social circles in which the artistic and intellectual status of *istoriato* would have been understood. In the right context this type of maiolica could have been regarded as complimenting one's guests for their erudition, classical learning and artistic discernment.

Surely this is what is implied by Clement VII's use of *istoriato* when dining with his cardinals. Use and display were not, however, contradictory functions. Maiolica vessels and dishes could be displayed, with glass, on a *credenza* in the manner of dining silver, as we know it was from the evidence of documents and paintings. The 1483 will of a Ferrarese woman, the widow of a glazier, mentions her *credenza* with twenty-four maiolica dishes of two sizes, and drinking vessels of gilded Venetian glass.[196] Visual references are extremely rare, although a late sixteenth-century painting from Forlì confirms the continuing practice of displaying and using maiolica in showing a set or *credenza* in use at the Last Supper, with other elements of the same service displayed on the *credenza* itself.[197] Plates manufactured in Deruta sometimes have footrings pierced for suspension before the first firing, showing that display – probably on walls – was intrinsic to their function (even if the painters of such pieces altered the image-axis so that they required additional piercings after the object was completed).[198] Nevertheless, however rarely earthenware was actually used for formal dining, the fact that it was used at all was a radical change in itself; one that was not lost on contemporaries. A Neapolitan commentator, Benedetto di Falco, noted in a guidebook to his city in 1535 that 'not many years back, the princes and barons of the Kingdom [of Naples] were accustomed to eat from silver dishes and drink from gold vessels ... but now, in place of the goldsmiths are the potters, who fill the stores [*riposti*] with earthenware vessels'.[199] He deplored this development, seeing maiolica as 'unfitting for great persons', now constrained in their old dining customs by fears of arousing envy through the use of gold and silver.[200] But there was no doubting the arrival of a new dining aesthetic among the intellectual and social elite.

Pottery and humanism: the palace and the villa

The virtuous combination of ancient and modern elements, technological and material, made *istoriato* an art form worthy of humanist attention, a fact confirmed by dining sets bearing the arms either of scholarly patrons, or of those who received them as gifts. A dish, with the arms of the historian Francesco Guicciardini and his wife, Maria Salviati, is dated 1525 on the front and on the reverse, and depicts the Ovidian *Battle of the Lapiths and Centaurs* (fig. 178), a well-known locus for artistic invention replete with learned references, already encountered in Michelangelo's marble relief of the early 1490s (see fig. 106). The set to which it belongs was made in Faenza when Guicciardini was President of the Romagna in the service of Clement, and may therefore have been a diplomatic gift. Beyond his classical education and his experience of ruling a rebellious region only recently subjugated by military force, this scene of a fight breaking out at a wedding feast between the half-human centaurs and the Lapiths may have had allegorical significance for Guicciardini himself. His *History of Italy* (printed in 1561) reveals his interest in the shaping of contemporary history through the interaction of the passions, licence and ambition of individuals, and it is tempting to see this scene as a visual equivalent to his preoccupations as a writer. If so, the subject matter may have been a personal choice or that of someone close to him, and it has been suggested that Machiavelli, who was sent to Faenza by the Pope in 1526, along with Guicciardini himself, may have been the intellectual mover behind the commissioning of this set.[201]

The nature of the most famous of all surviving sets of dining maiolica gives further clues about the social world in which *istoriato*, as a courtly art, was enjoyed in the 1520s. Urbane values were extended into the countryside through the medium of the villa, and here, too, maiolica played an important role as a cultural indicator. Some villas were essentially small palaces made for the urban elite for their pleasure and relaxation. It was thought important to retain close links with the city and its culture. Alberti even stipulated that the villa should be within walking distance of one's urban residence.[202] But if the atmosphere and pattern of life there was freer and less formal than in the urban palaces, it was no less sophisticated. The villa focused a certain literary nostalgia about agricultural pursuits and continuity from the ancient world, and it was seen as the perfect environment for

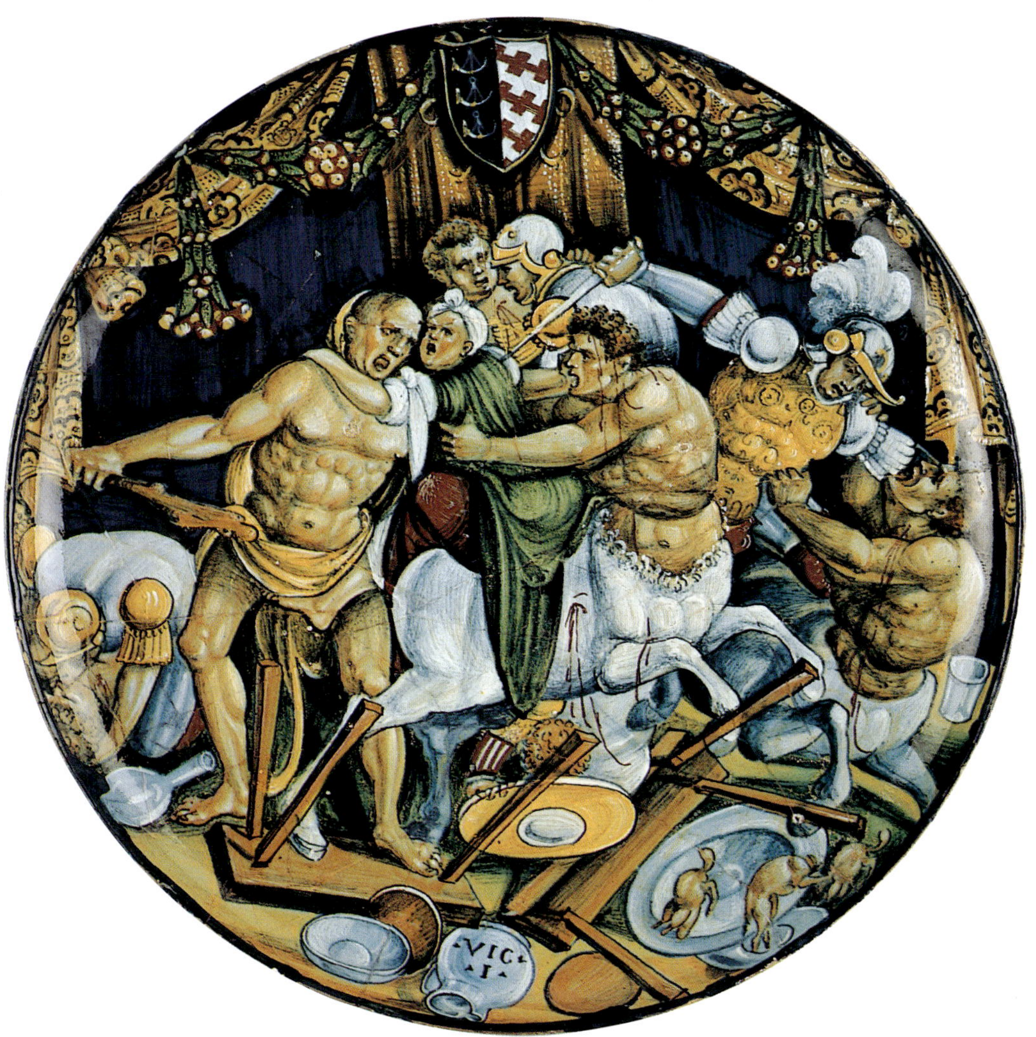

178 Master of the Bergantini
Bowl (attributed), dish with
Battle of the Lapiths and Centaurs,
arms of Guicciardini impaling
Salviati; tin-glazed ceramic
(maiolica); Urbino, 1525.
The British Museum, London

stimulating intellectual company and learned leisure. When Pontano issued a dinner invitation to a humanist friend in the form of a Latin poem, he boasted that there would be nothing crudely rustic about the entertainment, which would show a certain appropriate elegance: 'The table glows with pottery and so does the maplewood *credenza*.'[203]

Fine maiolica at the villa was thus seen as a proof of *gentilezza* and sophistication. The two Medici vases discussed above were listed among the contents of the family villas. Moreover, one of the finest sets of *istoriato* maiolica of the whole period was commissioned and designed to be used at a villa. This beautiful set was ordered from the pottery painter Nicola da Urbino in November 1524 by Eleonora Gonzaga as a gift for her mother, Isabella d'Este. Eleonora mentions the present and its intended function in a letter to her mother of 15 November 1524: 'I have had made a service [*credenza*] of earthenware pottery … since the master craftsmen of this region of ours have some reputation for good workmanship.[204] I shall be pleased if Your Excellency likes it and if you will make use of it at Porto, since it is something suitable for a villa' (*per essere cosa da villa*).[205]

'Nicola da Urbino' has been identified as a master potter referred to in Urbino documents as Nicolò di Gabriele Sbraga. First mentioned in 1520 as a potter (*figulus* in notarial Latin),[206] later documents reveal him only as a workshop owner or *maestro*.

His own artistic career as a painter can be put together on the basis of five signed pieces, two of which identify him as a painter and not just as the manager of a workshop.[207] Three major *istoriato* services of about 1520–5 can be attributed to him on the basis of style alone,[208] of which Isabella's is the second.

The choice of subject matter for the twenty-two surviving components in the credenza, far from being carefully tailored to Isabella's requirements, seems to have been decided by the somewhat random workshop process by which services were typically assembled. Consequently, only two of the pieces may have been specified as being particularly suitable for presentation to Isabella in terms of the messages they bore. The first, *The Justice of Trajan*, is derived from Valerius Maximus, who tells how Trajan was approached by a widow demanding justice in retribution for the killing of her only son (fig. 179). The emperor ordered his own son to be executed when he realized that he was responsible for the death. The story is usually interpreted as a straightforward illustration of just govern- ment that was intended to serve as a moral *exemplum*, particularly suited for a ruler and, used on Paola Gonzaga's *cassone*, was already associated with women of the Gonzaga

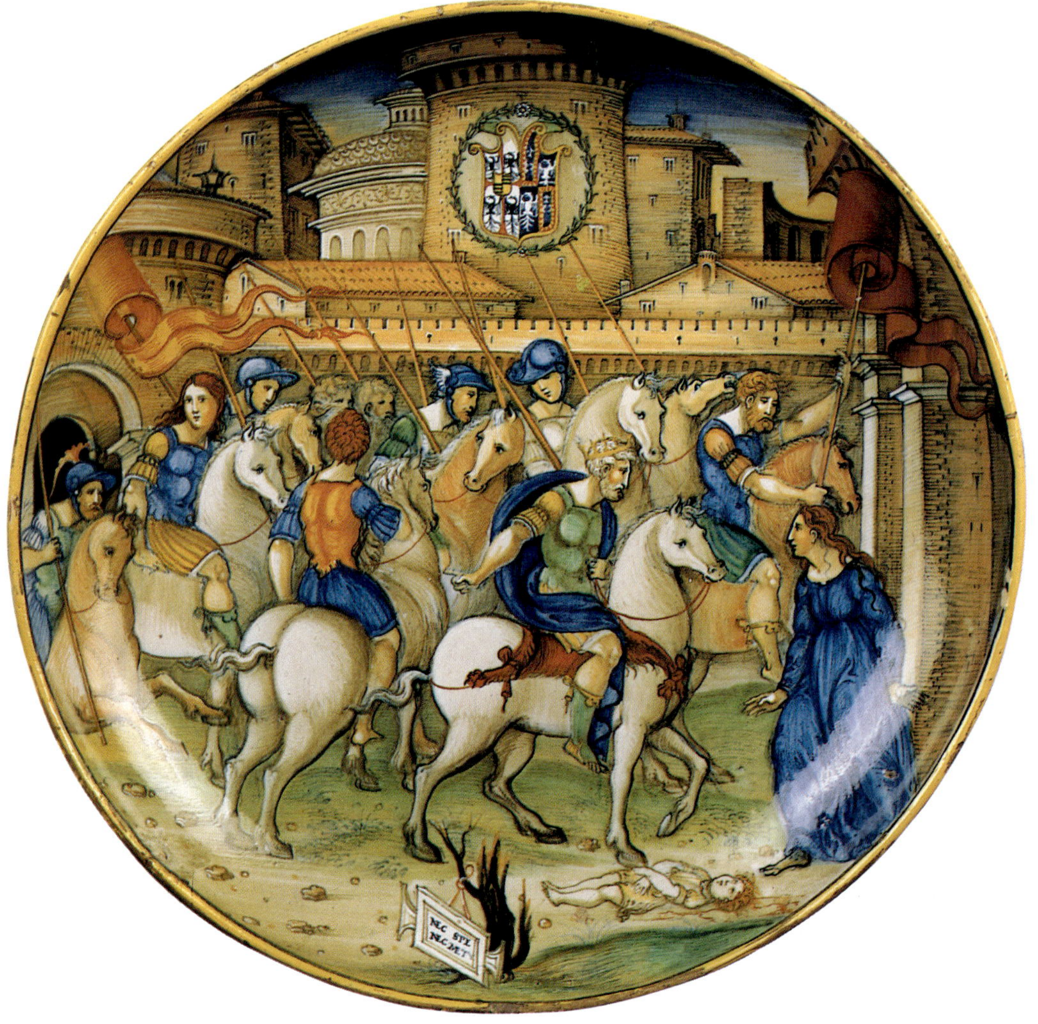

179 Nicola da Urbino, dish with *The Justice of Trajan*, arms and devices of Isabella d'Este; tin-glazed ceramic (maiolica); Urbino *c.*1524–5. The British Museum, London

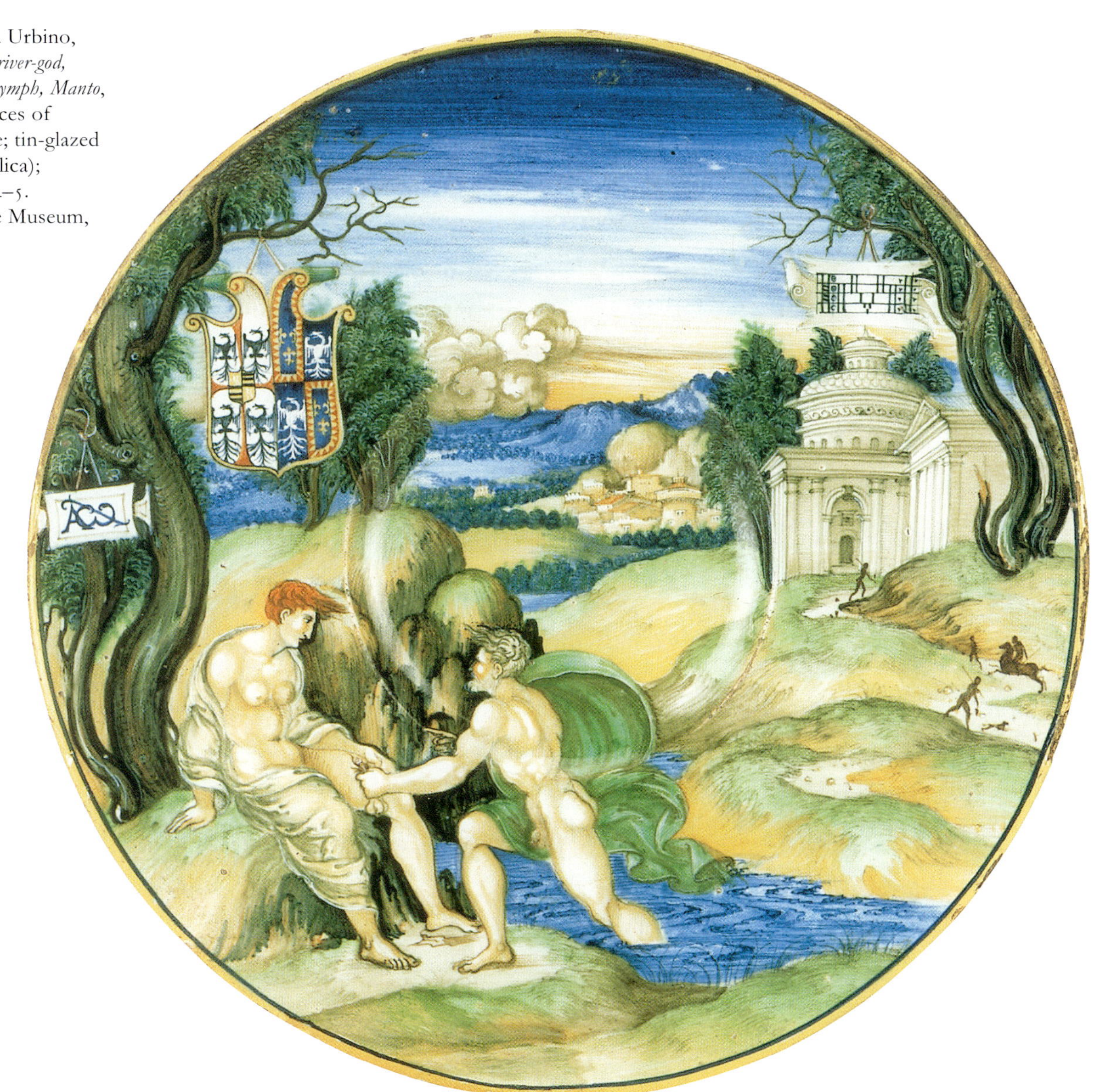

family.[209] According to the tactics of 'antiquarian' painters, Nicola derived his figure of Trajan from the Marcus Aurelius on the Capitol, and the scene is set against classically inspired architecture – seen in the domed temple – of just the style that was being created in Rome in the 1520s by his contemporary Donato Bramante.[210] The second piece made for Isabella's *credenza*, for which the subject seems to have been specially selected for her, illustrates the foundation myth of Mantua (fig. 180).[211] The story is told by Mantua's native poet, Virgil, in both the *Eclogues* and the *Aeneid*. The river-god, Tiber, advanced out of his river to offer an onion, symbol of fertility, to the nymph Manto. Their liaison produced a son, Oenus, who founded a city named after his mother.[212] The subject thus had particular significance for Isabella as marchioness of that city. It also linked her with her daughter, the commissioner of the service. Eleonora Gonzaga and her spouse, Francesco Maria I della Rovere, had taken refuge in Mantua for five years from political troubles in Urbino.[213] The story of Tiber and Manto therefore linked the patron and the recipient of the service in a politically resonant manner that made it even more suitable as a gift.

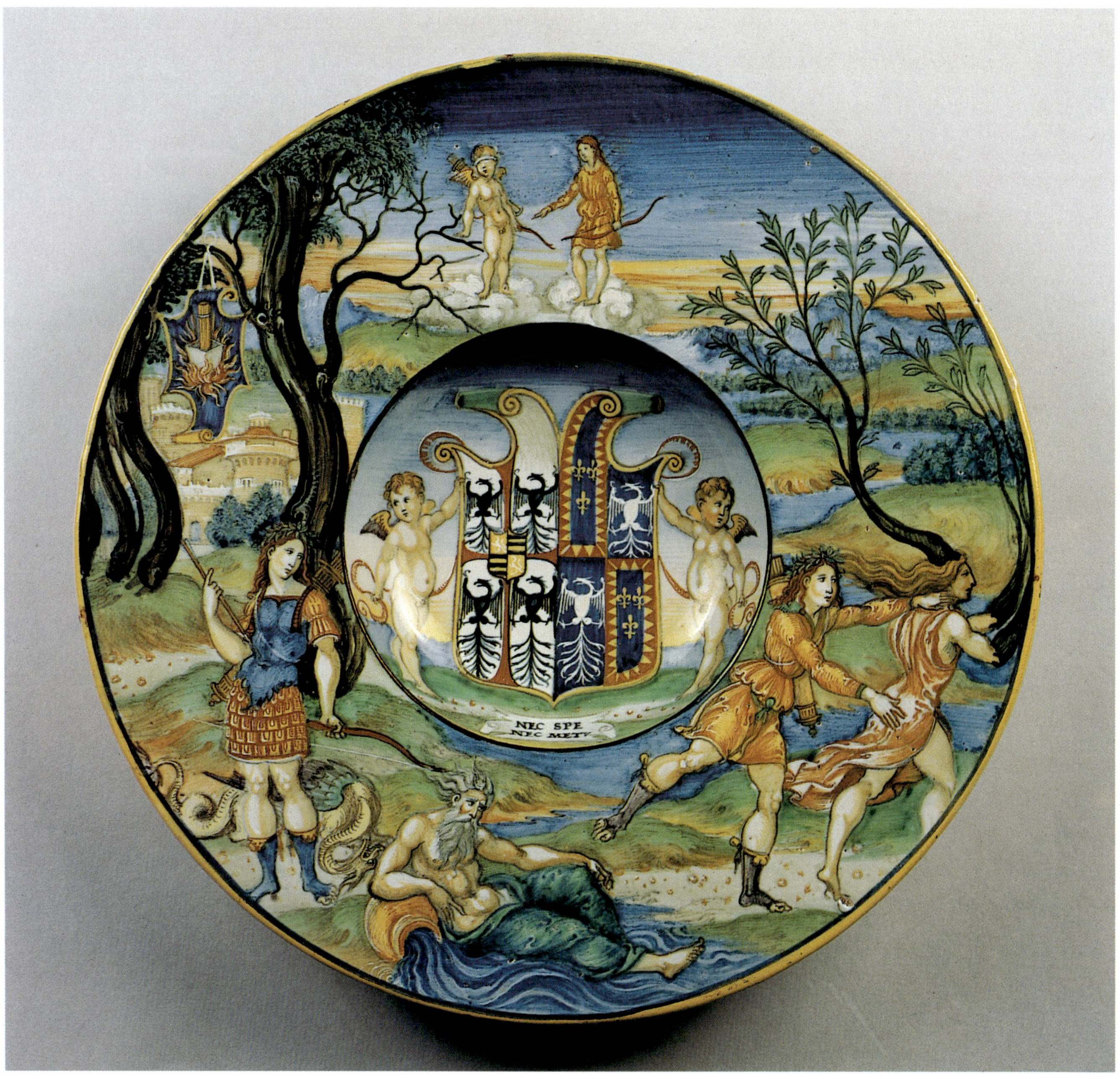

Another plate has the *fabula* of Apollo and Daphne (fig. 181). Like the landscape with its fresh and transparent colouring, the figure of the river-god Peneus is an original contribution of Nicola's. He presumably incorporated this recumbent figure to fill in the lower rim of the plate, a kind of exergue as in gem or medal design – always an awkward space for maiolica painters to fill and a test of their skill in composition. Nicola took the figure from the ancient Roman statue known as Marforio. By identifying this well-known Roman landmark as a river-god he jumped ahead of Andrea Fulvio, who is usually credited with this identification, by three years.[214] The arms at the centre of the plate are those of Isabella's late husband, Francesco Gonzaga, impaling her own and accompanied by her motto NEC SPE NEC METU (without hope and without fear).[215] Francesco's device of the crucible containing gold bars, referring to tried integrity, is shown on a shield.

181 Nicola da Urbino, dish with *The Legend of Apollo and Daphne*, arms and devices of Isabella d'Este; tin-glazed ceramic (maiolica); Urbino, *c.*1524–5. The British Museum, London

Indeed, its harmonious inclusion into the composition is indicative of Nicola's skill as a designer. Since Isabella's service incorporates seven of her devices and mottoes in different combinations, Nicola had to use considerable ingenuity in fitting the required elements into each of his compositions. In *The Justice of Trajan*, the arms are enclosed within a wreath on the wall of a tower, while a tablet inscribed with a motto appears tied to a tree stump in the foreground.[216] Another outstanding feature of the service is its almost cinematic sense of movement. In the *Justice of Trajan* plate, Nicola shows the widow with her hands open at her sides in supplication and grief, open-mouthed as if calling out to Trajan, while an equestrian figure advances on the scene at the left. On the British Museum's plate Daphne runs literally over the edge of the dish, adding spontaneity and a sense of speed to the narrative.

Isabella herself considered her villa at Porto as an amenity for her successors as Marchioness of Mantua. She left it to them in her will – perhaps with its credenza of *istoriato* – 'for their delight and leisure' (*per lor apiacer e diporto*).[217] What was it, though, that made this set so appropriate to the villa? One element may have been the question of its relatively modest medium. Borso d'Este, it will be remembered, was censured for dining off silver in his villas. Surviving pieces of Isabella's service – there are twenty-two of them – give further clues. All but two of the pieces are painted with scenes of classical mythology, or with the history and legends of ancient Rome.[218] Many pieces in the service share a poetic, pastoral air, exemplified by the *Apollo and Daphne* plate.[219] The two scenes from Ovid's *Metamorphoses* are set in a verdant river landscape seen at sunset – an invention of Nicola. Thus he was evolving his own sense of arcadian landscape just as contemporary artists and printmakers were exploring ways in which to translate an essentially literary concept into pictorial form.[220]

A handful of surviving poems laud specific early examples for their narrative and iconographic ambition, demonstrating that humanists appreciated the intellectual potential of *istoriato* pieces.[221] With their complex illustrations of poetry, history and mythology, or conceptualizations of particular virtues, these pieces offered challenges of interpretation that humanists enjoyed. This much is suggested in an early Cinquecento poem by Fausto Andrelini entitled 'He violently rebukes Livia because she broke a cup decorated with various scenes, then he consoles her'.[222] Andrelini described the cup (perhaps fictional) as his special gift, 'brought from the Venetian city', which was 'painted by the skill of an Apelles'. He went on to enumerate the scenes painted on the cup in detail:

… Apollo sang, to the wavering music of the lyre, of the fall of the profane bodies of the Giants.
On another part, Vulcan's chains showed Venus caught with naked Mars to the other gods.
Nearby stood Paris the judge on Phrygian Ida, and gave the apple to Venus;
There also stood indignant Athena with cast down eyes, and there too was the scorned wife of the great thunderer.

Such was its quality that the cup would have made a suitable gift between heroes and heroines in classical antiquity 'if the cup had been made in that time'. She had broken the cup, but then, 'no one else was worthy of such a gift'.[223]

Additional layers of meaning could be added to the subject of an *istoriato* piece by the nature of the visual sources used to construct the iconography: an ancient sarcophagus or marble statue; or motifs from well-known prints by celebrated contemporary artists. Ancient and modern visual references could be combined in one composition. The legend on the back, either a direct quotation from a vernacular text or translation or an allusive description of the subject matter, was another element in the appeal of *istoriato*. By turning a piece in one's hand, one could move from literary inscription to visual representation and analyse the ways in which these informed one another. Thus they were stimulants to erudite discussion, an aspect making them eminently suitable as gifts from one humanist to another. The posthumous inventory of goods belonging to Andrea Mantegna's son, Lorenzo, who died in 1510, four years after his father in Mantua, also indicates the elevated intellectual and artistic circles in which *istoriato* was prized. His maiolica bowl must have been an imposing piece since, very rarely in an inventory, its subject matter is identified. His was a large dish with a figure of the goddess of Fortune and others in a seascape (*uno vaso tondo de maiolica cum la Fortuna depinta suso e altre figure, done dentro una marina*). Mantegna's *istoriato* plate was, like his turquoise glass flask, a possession that pointed to his high social status.[224]

Occasionally we have evidence of exactly how complex iconographies on maiolica were intended to be viewed, rather in the manner of contemporary programmes for cycles of frescoes compiled by artistic advisers for their patrons. When Giovanni Guidiccioni took up office as papal governor of Romagna in 1540, he received a carefully calculated gift of two *istoriato* plates made in Faenza. The donor was a Faventine lawyer, Giovanni Battista Macchi, and he accompanied his present with a sixteen-page Latin letter, dated 19 February 1540, in which the iconography of both plates was outlined in considerable detail.[225] One plate showed Justice as a seated queen with her pair of balances, served by two handmaidens, Clemency and Severity. The four enemies of Justice were shown as captives; Hatred and Avarice were the prisoners of Clemency, Love and Fear those of Severity. The allegory illustrated the virtues a judge required to exercise and safeguard Justice, so that he should not be distracted by any particular affection in punishing or pardoning anyone, able to judge men and issues with an even hand.[226] The fact that maiolica was chosen as the medium for this particular message obviously went beyond advertising a new technology and leading local product: it demonstrates an appreciation of *istoriato* as an art form that could be charged with meaning and could carry specific messages in the same way as the more established arts of panel and fresco painting.

Chapter Six

Art Objects?

In the preceding chapters we have seen that certain commentators made considerable claims for the intellectual, technological and aesthetic status of particular categories of utensil made of glass and ceramic, bronze or silver. They wrote occasionally in similar vein about jewellery made of gold and precious stones, or about furniture with painted, carved and inlaid decoration. Their readings depended on a widely admitted notion that the combination of form and iconography in such objects raised them above both the drably utilitarian *and* the flashily ostentatious. Patrician and aristocratic owners certainly needed to mark social distinctions between themselves and their social inferiors, and here a 'noble' medium might play a part. Only a very few could afford gold, hard-stones or silver for drinking cups, serving dishes and eating utensils. Many – though perhaps not all – of the richest men and women of Italy were equally concerned that such pieces, even if they were made of precious metal, should demonstrate discernment. In an age when 'luxury' (*lussuria*) had profoundly negative connotations, their belongings had, in effect, to modify or disguise their luxuriousness in order to add up to more than just conspicuous consumption. However, even if we agree that 'luxury goods', a term that is often applied to such pieces, is not an adequate classification, are we entitled to dignify them (as we have done throughout this book) with the grandiose term 'art objects'?

Neither phrase would have been recognized in Renaissance Italy. Nevertheless, this was a period when, as we have seen, various attempts were made to define different forms of production and to distinguish between them; some were to be categorized on the same intellectual level as literature, others were to become essentially mechanical. There was no single consistent or clear-cut position and boundaries could be blurred. It is true that it was painting which was most regularly singled out by humanists as an intellectual pursuit. In his treatise *On Painting* Alberti hazarded a rather confused (and confusing) distinction between the artisanal maker and the non-maker – the *faber* and the non-*faber*. 'Painting was honoured by our ancestors with this special distinction that, whereas all other craftsmen [*omnes artifices*] were called makers [*fabri*], the painter alone was not counted among their number [*in fabrorum numero*].'[1] By diminishing the manual, the making aspect of the profession (although he could not deny it altogether), Alberti makes a case for the painter as what would now be recognized as an 'artist'.

It has been rightly realized that this term is anachronistic, that there was no single word in Italian or Latin in the fifteenth and early sixteenth centuries that translates unequivocally as 'artist'. Practitioners were almost always precisely defined by their trades: painters, sculptors and goldsmiths, as well as weavers, potters, embroiderers and woodworkers. Nevertheless, it has been generally accepted that the makers of particular kinds of product – chiefly pictures and sculptures – were increasingly viewed in such a way that they conform approximately to the modern concept of the artist: creators with innate

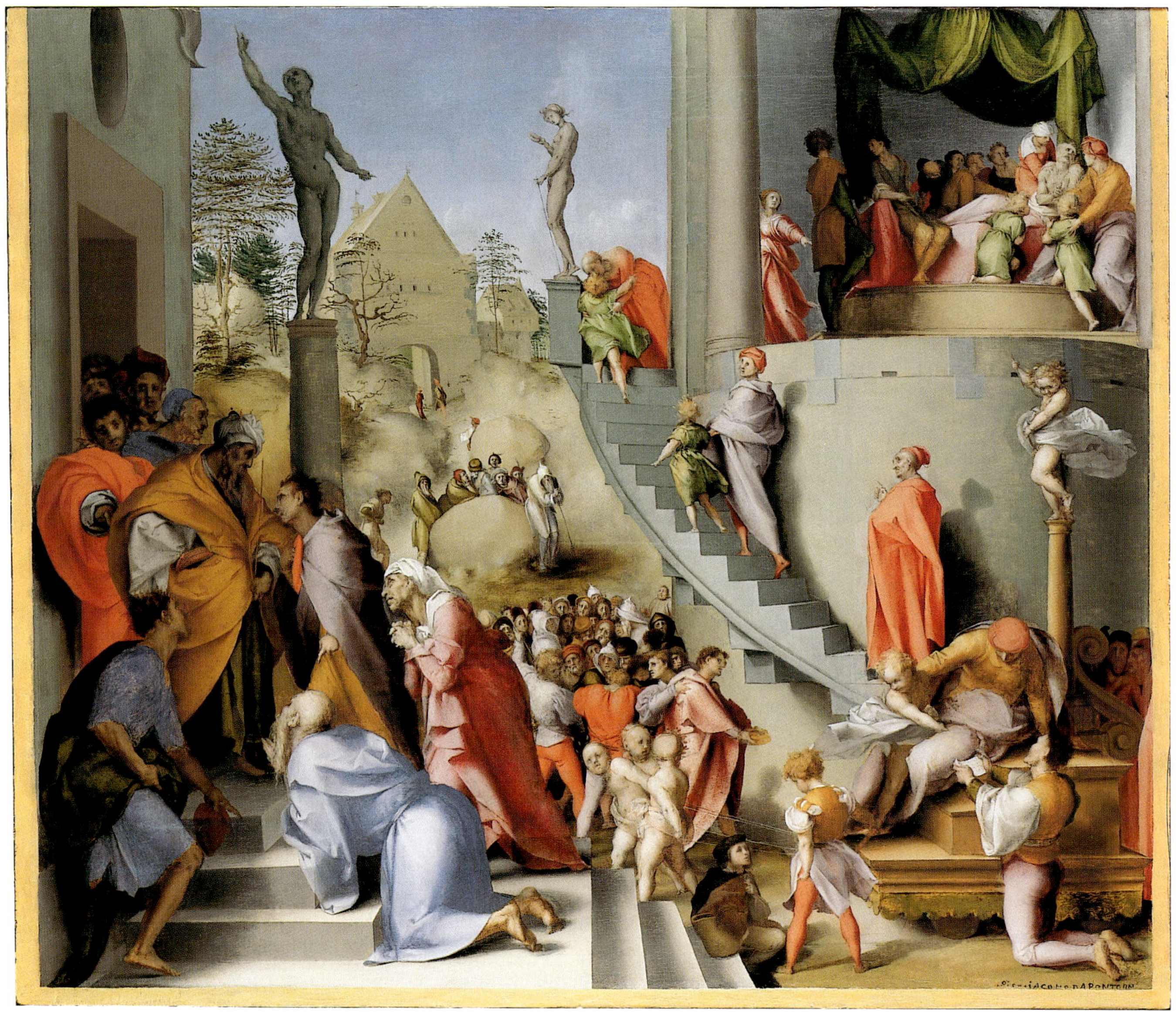

182 Jacopo Pontormo, *Joseph in Egypt*, panel from the bed-chamber of Pier Francesco Borgherini; oil on panel; Florence, 1518. National Gallery, London

imaginative talent.[2] We have seen that members of this select group (who initially included some goldsmiths and one glass-maker) were celebrated as the possessors of inventive *ingegno*, and concomitant *disegno*. Indeed, the classically aggrandizing claims that such-and-such a painter was the new Apelles or that one or another sculptor had surpassed Phidias and Praxiteles quickly became tired clichés. The praise for the individual skills of these artists, however, certainly had an effect on the commissioning activities of a patron like Isabella d'Este, who exhibited a sometimes obsessive desire at the turn of the fifteenth and sixteenth centuries to obtain works by particularly famous artists, such as Giovanni Bellini, Giorgione and Leonardo da Vinci,[3] with the pictures' subject matter being less important than the person who painted them. Perhaps it would therefore be correct to categorize as 'art objects' only those items for which such artists could be identified as the authors.

Such a classification would include the many items of furniture and bed-chamber decoration with *istorie* executed by painters whose reputations for *ingegno* were founded primarily on their large-scale public works: Paolo Uccello, Sandro Botticelli and Jacopo Pontormo (fig. 182), among others, in Florence; Marco Zoppo in Bologna; Francesco di Giorgio and Domenico Beccafumi in Siena; the Venetian Giovanni Bellini; and the Ferrarese court artist Ercole de' Roberti.[4] The prices paid for these domestic works did not differ very substantially from those charged by leading painters for more publicly sited altarpieces in the same period. In an account, for example, of the expenses involved in making two painted and gilded chests prior to the Florentine wedding of Marco Parenti and Caterina Strozzi in 1448, Domenico Veneziano, already supplied with the unpainted *cassoni*, was paid a healthy total of about 33½ florins, of which more than 11 were designated as 'for the part of painting upon the said chests'.[5] This compares very favourably to the 25 florins Andrea Castagno realized for an *Assumption of the Virgin* altarpiece the following year. Moreover, it appears that the participation of an artist famous in the main for his frescoes and religious paintings may have added something to the expenses of such furniture. The cost of Parenti's chest (a total of 50 florins) was somewhat higher than the average price (between 30 and 35 florins) charged by the specialist workshop of Apollonio di Giovanni and Marco del Buono.[6]

This category would also include those objects for which a well-known artist had provided the designs. In this case such a definition might justify the distinction, which, as we have seen, seems to have been developing at this time, between those designing and those making objects to the designs of others; between, in other words, artists and artisans. But, even though such a division was made (and in the Cinquecento especially was progressively important), this definition of the art object is too narrow. It was clearly not always necessary for an object to display an individual authorial voice to be seen as exhibiting art, to raise the object above the luxurious. Indeed, the Renaissance definition of the word '*arte*' was both more specific and more embracing, with a broad meaning that suggests that the division between artist and artisan was by no means as clearly drawn as Alberti's words might imply. It is worth noting that even Alberti was forced to define the painter as an artist by default; the painter is not described as a 'something', he is defined by *not* being a 'something else'. And he has no word for that something else. The word *artista* is not used in the Italian text and when it did appear, mostly in the sixteenth century, it seems to have been used synonymously with another – *artefice*, the Italian translation of the Latin *artifex*. Thus Alberti is already in difficulties. If the *faber* is regarded as of a lower rank than the painter, both are nonetheless *artifices* or *artefici*, 'craftsmen'. Even for Alberti *artifex* was evidently a catch-all term, and painters could be no different from makers in other media; as the etymology of the word suggests, all of them were people who 'made art'.

What was the 'art' they were making? This question needs to be addressed before one can go on to analyse the terms on which art was to be assessed. The precise meaning of the Latin *ars* is elusive: in classical Latin, the word was used to straddle skill, craft, trade, profession, workmanship and knowledge. It was frequently set up in opposition or as the complement to *ingenium*. During this period Horace's *The Art of Poetry* was much cited as the text that established painting as the equivalent of poetry. This famous poem was intended as instructive, apparently written to teach a younger disciple the rules and essential ingredients of a play. In it Horace codified the difference between art and nature: 'Often it is asked whether a praiseworthy poem be due to Nature or to Art. For my part I do not see of what avail is … study, when not enriched by Nature's vein, or native talent [*ingenium*] if untrained; so truly does each claim the other's aid, and makes with it friendly league.'[7] *Ars* or, in Italian, *arte* was thus something that could be taught and learned through imitation from models provided by others. As such, though it was not natural, it could encompass or shape other elements that were so defined, of which *ingenium* was the most important. It was therefore just as crucial an element in a practitioner's armoury as *ingenium*.

This definition of art is consequently less dependent on notions of inspiration than our modern one. It was not a concept that was restricted to the 'intellectual' arts of painting and sculpture, and it appeared, in notably less rarefied contexts than Alberti's puff for the painter, to betoken 'trade' or 'skill'. It is a standard term found in apprenticeship documents; the 1507 agreement between the would-be sculptor Giammaria Mosca and his future masters, the Paduans Giovanni and Antonio Minello, for example, committed the young man to learn 'the art of stone-cutting' (*arte lapicide*) over a period of six years.[8] Benvenuto Cellini, in his treatise on goldsmiths' work, praised Amerigo Amerighi as the outstanding figure of his day in 'the art of working in enamel' (*l'arte del lavorare di smalto*). Amerighi's art was not diminished in Cellini's eyes by his belief that his goldsmith predecessor had 'made use of the beautiful designs by Pollaiuolo'.[9] Amerighi's *arte* was principally technical.

This fact affects our understanding of another word that has recurred in the praise of the different kinds of object discussed in this book: *artificio*. Here is another bridging term. It can be related to *arte* and *artefice* to denote 'craftsmanship'. But since *arte* is defined in relation to the notion of a learnable skill, *artificio* seems to have been used as the antithesis to, sometimes even an improvement upon the natural, the application of technique. The word embraces a desirable quality of human artifice. The modern division between 'craftsmanship' and 'artistry' is eliminated.

Collective style and local identity

Wealthy owners could, therefore, choose to purchase objects whose innovatory design was key to their intended reception, in conjunction with other pieces that displayed *arte* more prominently, in which the demonstration of acquired skills was more important to their meaning than individual, innate talents. It is probable that some of these divisions may have been partly functional and economic. It could be argued that the massive expenditure involved in the construction of a building or the manufacture of a silver service or suite of tapestries justified or demanded special care taken over their design, and encouraged the employment of painter-designers. The sums of money spent on other categories of art object that adorned the interiors of Renaissance palaces were, by the same token, considerably lower and, despite some of the notable exceptions listed above, it was more common for men and women buying such objects – birth trays, *cassoni*, for example, or glass and ceramic tablewares – to order them from specialist workshops.

Such objects could often be purchased on the open market. Even at the top of the market, standardized designs might be personalized only by the addition of names, devices or coats-of-arms.

This might not be the only explanation. These were works in which the *arte,* that quality that raised an object above the merely luxurious, depended on levels of skill rather than aesthetic novelty; in which it could be demonstrated that the maker had taken full and proper account of available models, technical, ornamental and figurative. Although individual innovation was prized in certain contexts, many masters were therefore expected to do no more than conform to communal modes. In this way there would evolve a unified aesthetic for a particular city or region, one that would allow or encourage the identification of local 'schools'. Stylistic consistency ensured appeal to a generally conservative local constituency and, then as now, allowed art objects to be identified as the product of a particular place. In cities where specific trades were especially prominent (goldsmiths' work in Milan and Venice, textile production – and perhaps painting and sculpture – in Florence, as well as the pottery and glass centres identified in the previous chapter), such homogeneities of style might, in addition, reinforce the perception from outside the region that particular art products were local specialities, ones that strengthened messages of civic and commercial pride. Such an attitude shaped the statement made in the tax return of the Masci family, 'who carry out the art [*artem*] of making maiolica pottery and vessels in the said town of Deruta, and their works, beautiful and unprecedented [*inaudita*], are sold throughout the whole world and therefore the city of Perugia glories and grows in fame and everyone wonders to see these maiolica works'.[10] A similar sentiment lay behind the act of March 1513 by Cardinal San Vitale exempting inhabitants of Deruta from paying taxes on the basis that the city produced maiolica renowned throughout Italy. It is likely that the commercial sphere of influence was sometimes smaller than was claimed (though it was indeed the case that Deruta wares were exported in large quantity at least as far as Rome).[11] Similar claims made for Faenza are more credible, not least because of the export of potters as well as their products. Faenza's fame was also due to the perceived quality of the *istoriati* produced there. In a poem published in 1527 Merlin Coccaio wrote: 'Beautiful vases are made at the city of Faenza, / and the fame of the painters seems beyond that [which one would expect from] maiolica' (*Pulcra Faventinum finguntur vasa per urbem, / Supraque majolicam pictorum fama videtur*).[12] The humanist Giovanni Antonio Flaminio made the same point in a letter written before 1536 on the potters and merchants of the city:

… by their vases manufactured with admirable artifice and painting [*miro artificio et pictura*], celebrated throughout Italy, they have not only produced what is always a huge profit, but also a very great name for the city. And certainly those who know, from ancient history, how much fame vases brought to Corinth would not rate this among the least of the ornaments of the city.[13]

The conservative reiteration of stylized motifs, allied once again with a particular technique of applying golden-coloured lustre, makes the task of identifying Deruta products relatively straightforward, even though individual pieces are rarely marked or dated (figs 183, 184). It is likely that both specific techniques and visually defined local idioms were recognized at the time. Leandro Alberti, in his *Description of All Italy,* wrote of the city's product in terms of technique: 'The earthenwares [*vasi di terra cotta*] made here

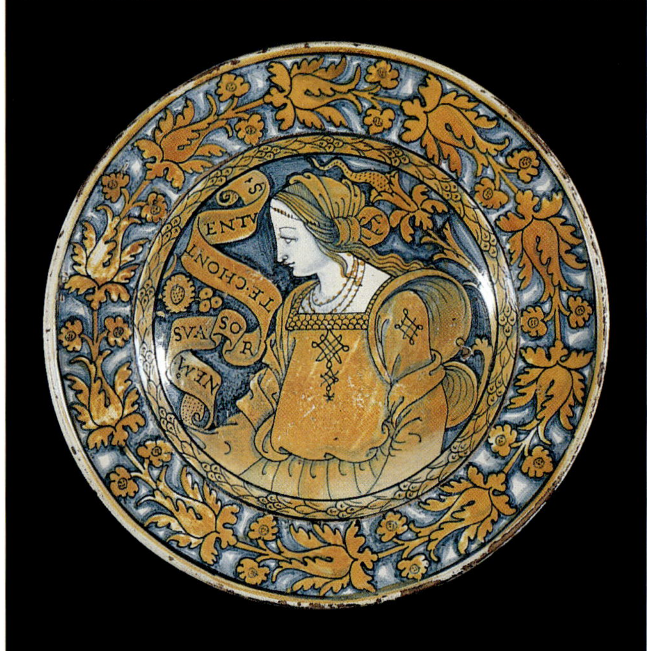

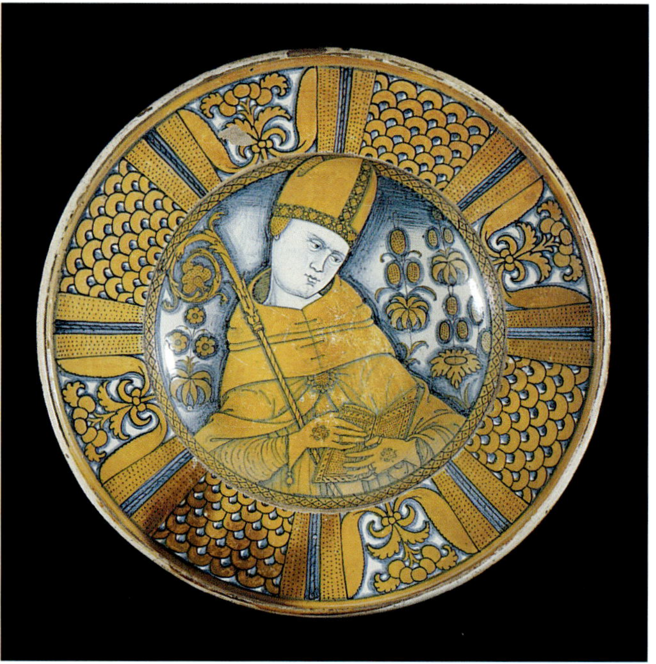

are renowned for being made to look as if they were gilded. And they are made so subtly [*tanto sottilmente*] that up to now no other craftsman [*artefice*] in Italy has been found to equal them, although experiments and attempts … have often been made.'[14] Such assessments could be reinforced by a certain communality of style and ornament. Piccolpasso discussed various ornamental motifs, locating them specifically in Venice, Genoa and Urbino. Of trophies (*trofei*) he said, 'These are in use everywhere, though it is true that trophies are made more often in the state of Urbino than elsewhere … Arabesques [*rubesche*] are more in use at Venice and Genoa than elsewhere.' He claimed that fruit and flower patterns 'are truly Venetian, very graceful things' (*cose molte vaghe*). And he linked 'oak designs' to political imagery (fig. 185): 'These are much used among us from the veneration and duty we owe to the oak tree (*Rovere*) in the shade of which we live happily, so much that it can be said that this is the Urbino style of painting' (*pittura al Urbinata*).[15] Rovere was the surname of the dukes of Urbino and the oak tree was on their arms.

There is evidence therefore that ceramic vessels could often be characterized by their place of production, by the fact that a particular set of visual ingredients were repeated – imitated – by a local group of *artefici*. But they were not the only art objects to be so regarded. Surviving inventories demonstrate that fabrics and goldsmiths' work were also sometimes described specifically as made in the style of a particular city. Unfortunately, it is almost always impossible to discover what special aspect of an object's appearance or technique signalled its origins. In 1463, for example, an inventory of dowry goods of Drusiana Sforza, an illegitimate daughter of Duke Francesco, was drawn up on the occasion of her marriage to Jacopo Piccinino of Perugia. What was it that made the compiler of the list write of one pair of little cloth covers (*fodrete*) that it was worked in

183 Dish with woman's head with legend 'No-one is happy with their destiny' within foliate border; tin-glazed ceramic (maiolica) with lustred decoration and lead-glazed reverses; Deruta, *c.*1500–40. The British Museum, London

184 Dish with head of bishop with book and crozier within foliate and scale-pattern border; tin-glazed ceramic (maiolica) with lustred decoration and lead-glazed reverses; Deruta, *c.*1500–40. The British Museum, London

the style of Ferrara (*a la ferarexe*) and of another that it was Venetian in style (*a la vinitiana*)? How did he distinguish between two embroideries (*brustie*) — one *a la fiorentina*, the other Venetian?[16] Descriptions of silver-plate vessels might afford a few more clues since they are sometimes described more fully (to the extent perhaps that a piece made using a style and technique associated with a particular city may not actually have been manufactured in the city itself). Silver and jewellery were most regularly described as 'Venetian in style'.[17] An *alla Veneziana* piece appears in a list of the silver that accompanied Nicolò III d'Este to Monferrato where he went to take the waters just before his death in 1441: a vessel 'with flowers in relief and animals and a wild man in the middle'.[18] In 1493 – also in Este possession, listed in the ducal *guardaroba* – was a 'large silver basin worked *a la venetiana*' with some gilded elements and other parts left 'white, with a Saint George in a niello tondo in the middle …'.[19] In her dowry in 1474 Caterina Pico had a silver fork and spoon '*alla vinetiana*'; these contrasted with her twenty spoons (*aguchiaroli*) of various kinds with

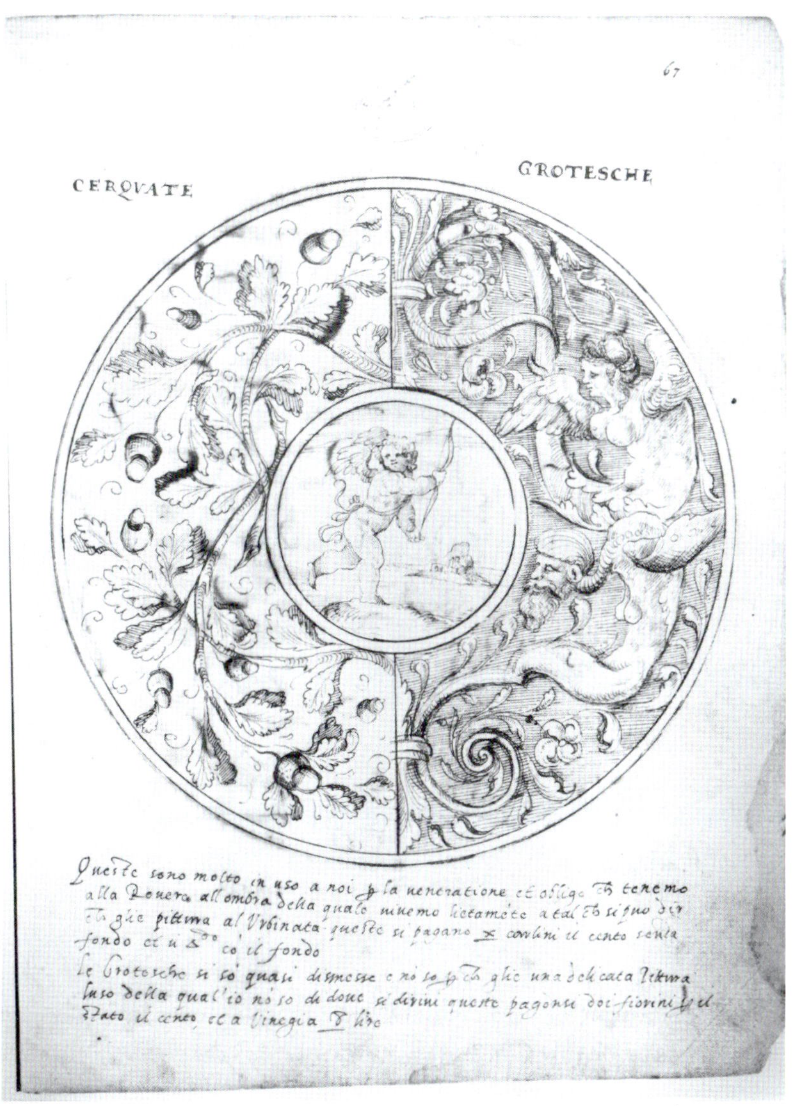

185 Cipriano Piccolpasso,
Oak leaf and grotesque ornament,
illustration from his manuscript
*The Three Books of the Potter's
Art*, fol. 67r; pen and ink;
Casteldurante, 1557.
National Art Library, Victoria
and Albert Museum, London

handles made in the style of Milan (*fornidi alla milanexe*).[20] The metalwork styles of other cities could therefore be identified: Milan and also Rome. Ascanio Sforza's gift of credenza silver to Lucrezia Borgia in 1493 included 'a vessel for sweetmeats, gilded [and] flat [*piana*] *a la romanesca*' that is called *uno mapo*.[21]

Powerful patrons, and in particular rulers, encouraged various forms of local art production as methods of attracting income and as expressions of civic or dynastic pride. If individual *ingegno* could be linked with the virtuous aims of particular powerful men and women, collective styles in which elements were learned and repeated might stand for a whole city. In 1420 Gian Francesco Gonzaga, Marquis of Mantua, had offered half a ducat a month to any 'master of art' (*magistro de arte*), whether absent citizen or allied foreigner, for the rent of his premises in the city for five years.[22] His son, Lodovico Gonzaga, took an even more active role in nurturing talent, looking to Rome and his antiquarian contacts there to give a collectively *all'antica* appearance to the works produced in his domain. In 1476 he wrote to the goldsmith Cristoforo di Geremia in Rome:

There has moved to those parts this *garzone* called Gian Carlo Gentilisia, our citizen, who has a little *disegno* and goes there to learn … We would certainly like to see both him and our other Mantuans make themselves *virtuosi* and good. Thus we would be very pleased if you could see if you could place him with some good master with whom he can learn and make himself skilful [*valente*]….[23]

Gentilisia became a specialist painter of boxes (*cofani*); his little natural *disegno* had been tutored to turn him into a painter of furnishings.

In Florence Lorenzo de' Medici arranged for one Pietro di Neri Razzanti to be exempted from taxation for a decade on condition that he taught the lost art of gem-engraving to the youth of the city.[24] Lorenzo was not, of course, the hereditary ruler of Florence but his power was such that he was apparently held in some measure responsible for the collective aesthetic of the city. In the account by Lorenzo di Filippo Strozzi of his father's canny manipulation of Lorenzo in his role as arbiter, to ensure the magnificence of the Strozzi palace, he uses a telling phrase; Strozzi was told 'that he who ruled desired the city to be adorned and exalted in every way, for just as the good and the bad depended on him, so the beautiful and the ugly would also be attributed to him'.[25] This acknowledged stewardship finds an intriguing echo in a current political metaphor used for Lorenzo. In *c.*1470 Benedetto Dei called him the 'master of the shop' (*maestro della bottega*), a phrase used in connection not only with Lorenzo but also with the dynastic rulers of other cities, such as Galeazzo Maria Sforza, by Dei and members of his circle in the 1470s and 1480s, and which reappears in the works of Machiavelli.[26] The *bottega* was, of course, Florence and the image refers to Lorenzo's political position in relation to the governance of the city. However, Dei, a merchant from a family of goldsmiths, was more alert than most to the fact that *botteghe* have products, not just ideological or systematic but tangible. He consistently linked Florentine pride to both its artists and its consumer goods, listing the painters and other *artefici* of the city, and noting in his *Chronicle*, with some satisfaction, the scale of export of Florentine silks and brocades.[27] It may be no coincidence therefore that in the early 1490s Lorenzo converted the Medici sculpture garden at San Marco into a school for painters (and sculptors), under the tutelage of Bertoldo di Giovanni, specifically to improve local artistic standards.[28]

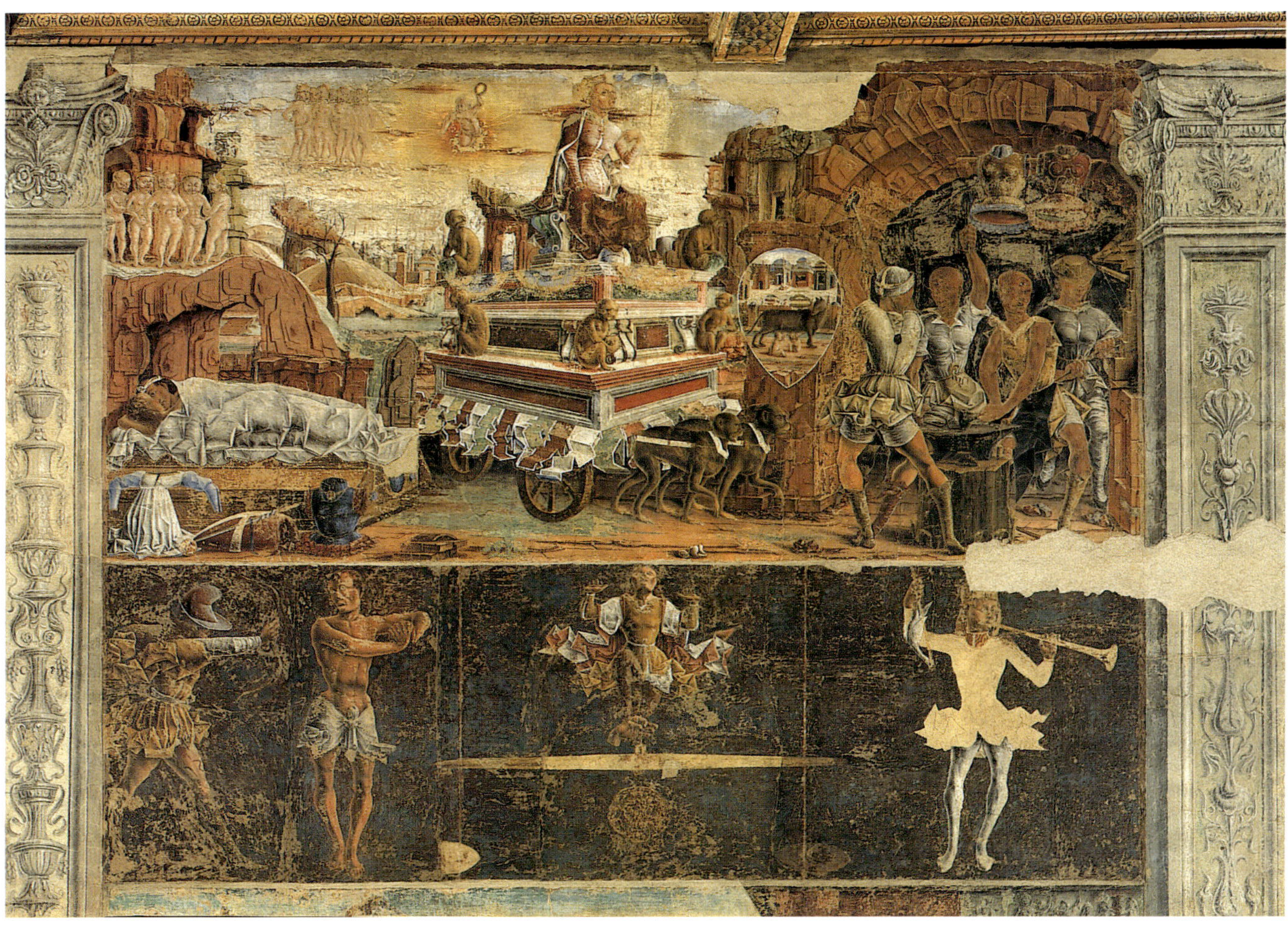

The singling out of a star pupil – Michelangelo – shows that Lorenzo wished his school to strike a balance between the encouragement of individual talent and the establishment of a skilled Laurentian collectivity. This balance of artistic *ingegno* and communal styles was achieved at Mantua and Ferrara by the expectation that the *artefici* of the city would conform, more or less, to the idiom established by the court artist. Not only did Andrea Mantegna and Cosmè Tura provide designs for objects they themselves were not expected to manufacture, they also made drawings for large-scale painting projects that would be executed by others. Thus their individual styles became to some extent standardized and might translate into other media over which they might have exerted no direct influence. In Ferrara, for example, the painters employed by Borso d'Este to paint the Sala dei Mesi at Palazzo Schifanoia seem to been expected to comply with a collective aesthetic for the room (fig. 186). The style is essentially Tura's and includes some direct quotations.[29] Here was painting therefore that, even if it was not so described, was *alla ferrarese*. Moreover, Tura's tensile linearity became a primary stylistic source for the specialist potters of incised slipware, whose workshops were situated within the *castello* at Ferrara (fig. 187).[30] A vast quantity of incised slipware dishes were produced in Ferrara during the last three decades of the Quattrocento, in a period when other centres had turned to the production of maiolica. It was a medium that seems deliberately to emphasize line; earthenware was covered with a pale creamy slip of liquid clay; a design was then scratched or scraped out of the slip to reveal the darker clay beneath, before being heightened with blobs of colour – usually yellows and greens – and given a transparent glaze. The proportions and poses of the youths and young women, with their elegant or energetic dislocations, shoulders raised and heads turned to one side, are the key factor in making them 'Ferrarese'. Their subjects – once again the Muses, virtues, planets, liberal arts – link them to favoured Este iconographies.[31] Thus an established local craft tradition was elaborated and elevated by the introduction of inventions from outside the potter's workshop.

Stylistic collectivity in other centres depended less on following individual examples. Until the last two decades of the Quattrocento (before the advent of Leonardo), there seems, for instance, to have been little interest in Milan, Pavia and the other towns and cities of Lombardy in the identifiable styles of particular artists. Painters, goldsmiths and others employed by the Visconti and Sforza rulers, by their courtiers and by the Church traditionally formed *ad hoc* consortia to undertake specific tasks.

A project would be advertised and a team would get together to bid for it. That it was usually the lowest tender that won these masters the commission shows that stylistic criteria were by no means paramount.[32] It is true that some artists were identified as having particular skills, like the portraitist Zanetto Bugatto (who had been sent by Bianca Maria Visconti to train with Rogier van der Weyden in Brussels) and, especially, the extremely talented Vincenzo Foppa, but even they were expected to execute works that would form visually harmonious wholes; the painter's individuality was suppressed to create a magnificent 'no-style', exemplified by the blue and gold of the wall-paintings of the chapel in the Milanese Castello Sforzesco (fig. 188) or by the frescoes executed by Ambrogio da Fossano (Bergognone) and his *équipe* at the Certosa of Pavia.[33] Thus many of the artists employed on such projects survive only as names in documents, their works remaining stubbornly (but entirely properly from the point of view of their original beholders) unidentified. A situation that is paralleled in other cities. The style of these Lombard painters is characterized by the strong, simplified contours and the often large heads and flattened features of their figures, and by the rich combinations of gilding and bright colour. It may be the case that in this instance the dominant aesthetic was dictated by the commercial supremacy of a particular medium. The execution of small enamelled silver plaques and miniature tabernacles with devotional scenes was a lucrative Milanese speciality (fig. 189).[34] As enamels, their impact depends on a combination of emphatic contours and blocks of strong colour. Surviving pieces vary in quality and ambition and none can be precisely attributed. However, they seem to have set the norm for the stylistic and typological features that came to be perceived as typical of Lombard painting.

The Ferrarese and Lombard models are useful in that, in contrast to Florence, they are

187 Dish with man and woman accompanied by Este and Sforza devices; lead-glazed ceramic; Ferrara, *c.*1480–1500. The British Museum, London

(*Opposite page*)
189 *The Holy Family*; enamel on engraved silver; Milan, *c.*1490–1500. The Metropolitan Museum of Art, New York

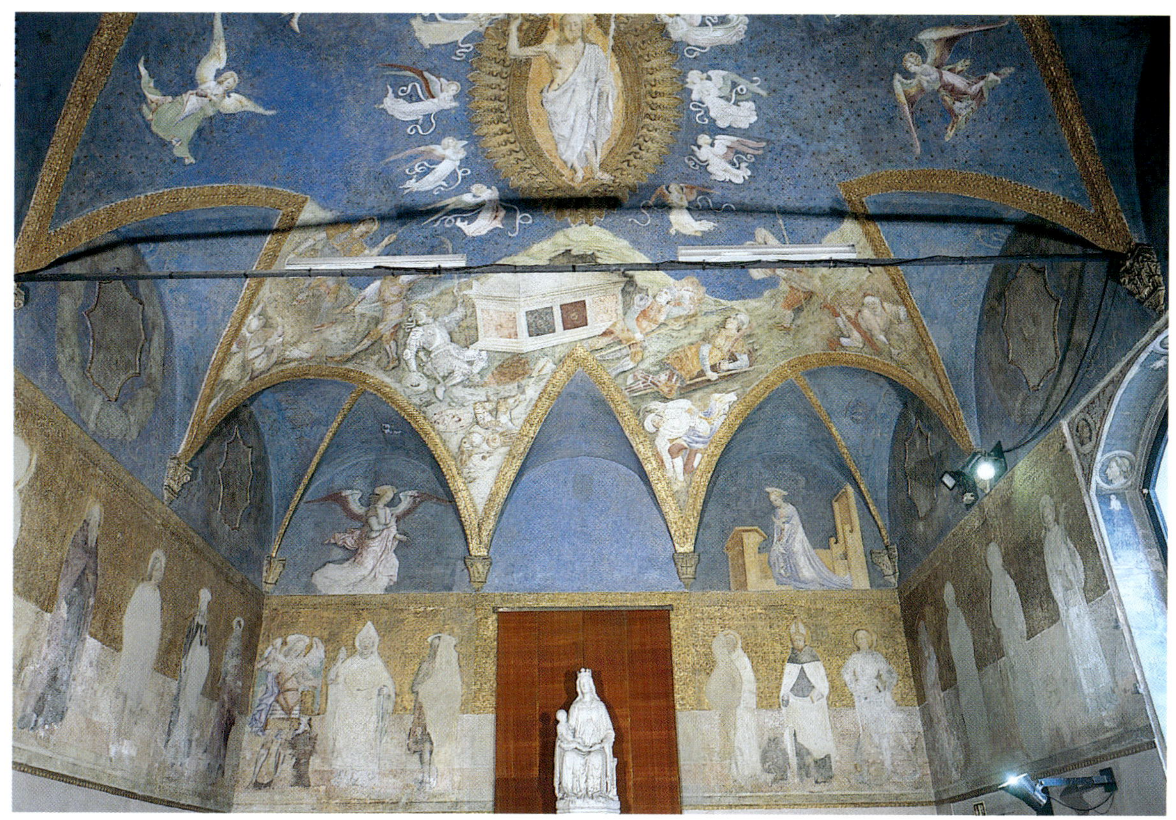

188 Bonifacio
Bembo,
Zanetto Bugato,
Costantino
Vaprio and
others, chapel
decoration;
fresco; Milan,
1470s. Castello
Sforzesco,
Milan

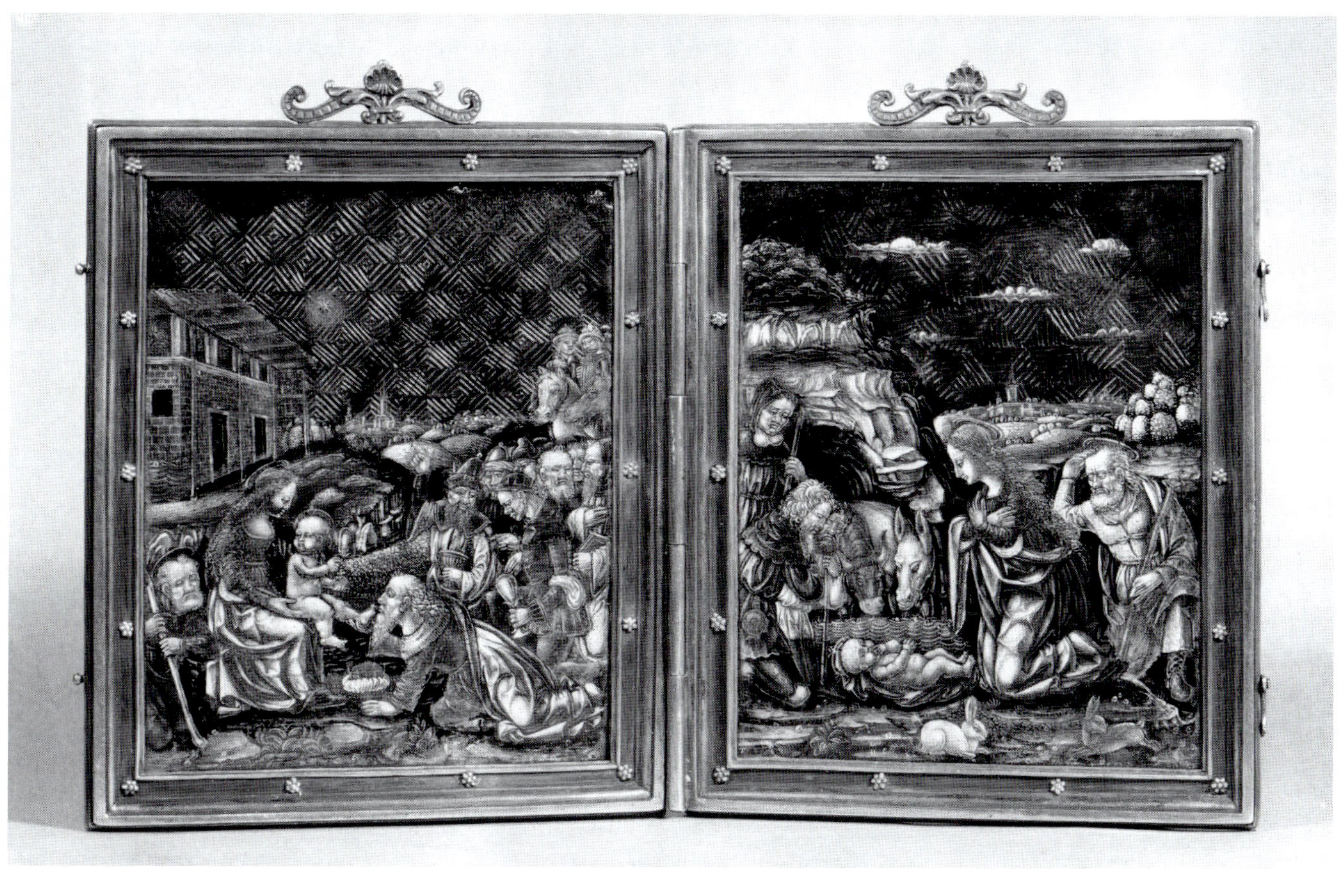

239

relatively clear-cut. A stylistic norm was set by particularly prestigious works of art. Works might become iconic because they were the most precious or important for a local economy. With the advent, at a particular moment, of the star artist, the kind identified in Chapter Four, the collective appearance of a regional school might stem from his celebrated inventions. In Florence the situation was more complicated.

Imitation and the canon

In certain instances works by artists even of some individual renown seem to have derived their aesthetic value precisely from the fact that they did not stray from established models. A case in point is the manufacture and decoration of the *cassoni* and *deschi da parto* that marked marriages and births in Florentine families, where consistency rather than difference seems to have been the aim.

It is unlikely that Apollonio di Giovanni, the specialist painter of marriage chests, was prized for his inventive *ingegno* (figs 190, 191; see also figs 51, 52). Nevertheless, his art was esteemed, considered worthy of the plaudit of a humanist poem in his honour – an epigram written by Ugolino Verino between 1458 and 1464 that laid stress on his *arte*:

Once Homer sang of the walls of Apollo's Troy burned on Greek pyres, and again Virgil's great work proclaimed the wiles of the Greeks and the ruins of Troy. But certainly the Tuscan Apelles Apollonius now painted Troy better for us. And he also painted with wondrous skill [*arte*] the flight of Aeneas and the wrath of iniquitous Juno, with the rafts tossed about; no less the threats of Neptune, as he rides across the high seas and bridles and stills the swift winds. He painted Aeneas, accompanied by his faithful Achates, entering Carthage in disguise: also his departure and the funeral of unhappy Dido are to be seen on the painted panel by the hand of Apollonius.[35]

Apollonio may have been more celebrated than his fellow painters of marriage chests and birth trays but there is little to distinguish him in his technique from his anonymous colleagues working in the 1440s and in the two following decades. *Cassoni* and *deschi* tend to resemble one another closely and it has been extremely difficult for art historians concerned with attribution to systematize them, let alone to allot artists' names to the resultant groupings. None of the objects is signed. Certain subjects and figures frequently recur, some of them obviously appropriate for objects connected with birth and marriage. The exotic Byzantine and 'Burgundian' costumes of the protagonists reappear over and

190 Apollonio di Giovanni and Marco del Buono (workshop), *Scenes from the* Aeneid; *cassone* panel painted in tempera; Florence, *c.*1460–5. Niedersächsisches Landesgalerie, Hannover

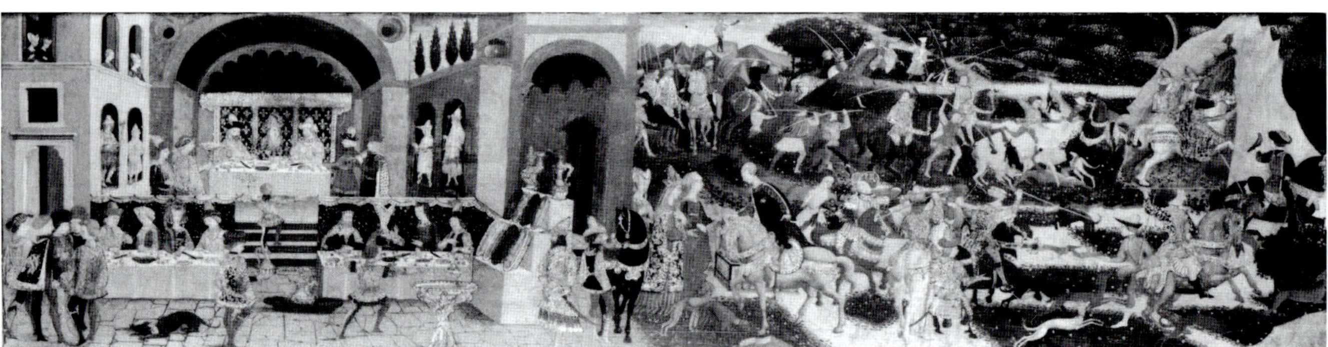

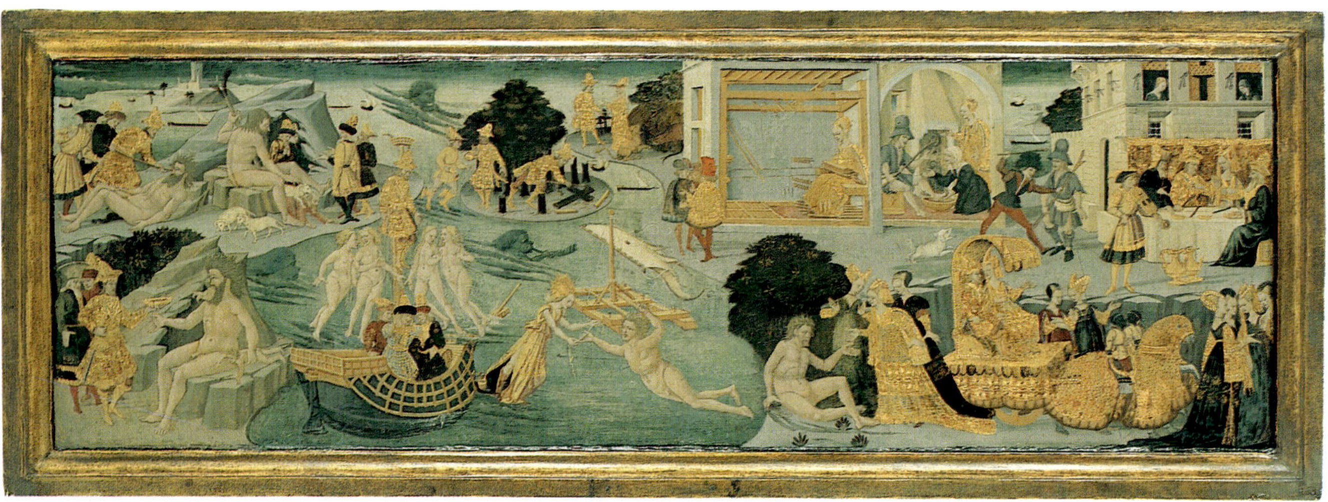

191 Apollonio di Giovanni and Marco del Buono (workshop), *Scenes from the* Odyssey; *cassone* panel painted in tempera; Florence, *c*.1435–45. The Art Institute of Chicago, Chicago

over again. Other stock types, designed to look vaguely antique, are notably reiterated. The origins of these repeated motifs are worth examining.

Apollonio's work has been identified by the fact that paired coats-of-arms on two *cassoni* (one now destroyed) correspond to the families documented by his workshop account book. As Verino suggests, he was a specialist in Aeneas subjects, which he also painted in a manuscript by Virgil now in the Biblioteca Riccardiana (see fig. 39). Nevertheless, the exact make-up of his oeuvre remains controversial. Although he may well have been a pioneering figure in developing the communal visual language for these objects, motifs that might be assumed to have been his turn up in works that are clearly executed by different hands. Moreover, he was able to reuse these motifs, more or less unaltered, over a considerable period of time. One cannot, therefore, expect the kind of logical, linear stylistic development that scholars have traced within the oeuvres of more self-consciously inventive artists.

The repetition of figures and compositions from the Aeneas legend in both panels and manuscript shows that Apollonio must have utilized model drawings. Masters had long ensured a consistent appearance for their products through the use of pattern drawings, often collected and bound together in so-called model books.[36] In the late Middle Ages craftsmen of all kinds (including painters) were content to build up sets of pattern drawings in which the original source of an invention was unknown and unimportant. Certain motifs – especially birds, beasts, flowers and other ornamental features, but also figures – were regularly transposed and included in finished works over considerable periods of time, the types remaining fixed and frozen. Whatever their origins, these drawings would become the design stock of the master and his shop; apprentices and assistants were instructed in a style by copying them. It may even be that patrons were able to consult the volumes into which the motifs were bound to request combinations of particular ingredients. It is usually assumed that, as artists sought to make the products of their shop unmistakably theirs, the designs incorporated by their assistants had to be immediately identifiable as their inventions. This was certainly part of the story. It was not, after all, expected that all the pictures emanating from a master's workshop would have been executed by its head. It is true that contracts might sometimes stipulate that the master in question should execute the work on his own,[37] but, in practice, authorship was judged by who had invented the figure types and ornamental motifs included in a work. Hence the failure of a lawsuit brought against Fra Filippo Lippi by Antonio del Branca in 1451 because, in executing an altarpiece for the Church of San Domenico in Perugia, Lippi had subcontracted the work and the patron felt aggrieved at the consequent loss of quality.[38] That authorship could be extended to the whole workshop is also attested by the appearance of an artist's signature on works that are not of a sufficiently high quality to have been executed by the master himself, but which were painted in a style and contained motifs that were identifiably his. It is unlikely that the purchasers of small devotional shop works signed by Giovanni Bellini (who used cartoons to create workshop replicas) or Francesco Francia would therefore have been unduly disturbed by the fact that they were not from the hand of the master.[39] Thus pattern drawings became valuable commodities and for artists like Maso Finiguerra and Cosmè Tura to make special provision in their wills for the disposal of their precious *concetti* was not at all unusual.[40]

It was also the case, however, that patterns by certain masters were circulated *outside* their *botteghe*. Given that the workshop stock of drawings is thought to have determined the stylistic homogeneity for a particular shop, this is perhaps surprising. Some minor masters were evidently so desperate for good source material that they stooped to larceny: Vasari recounts the theft of all of the drawings executed by Ercole de' Roberti in Bologna, and Squarcione had similar problems with his collection of drawings by famous artists in Padua. However, Lippi, Lorenzo Ghiberti and, later, Andrea del Verrocchio were evidently prepared, in certain circumstances, to make their drawings available to less creative masters.[41] Leading artists may well have expected their *concetti* to be viewed by others as, in some sense, their intellectual property. It has been demonstrated that motifs invented by Ghiberti circulated before his finished works were in place.[42] In 1425 he lamented the fact that drawings of birds that he had lent to one Goro, probably a fellow goldsmith, in Siena had been used by Goro's heir, Domenico dei Cori, a wood-worker, without his permission.[43] In this one instance, therefore, Ghiberti had licensed their imitation by a colleague, and was angered only because the designs had then moved beyond his control. It can thus be assumed that he was complicit in many of these borrowings.

The commercial arrangements of Marco del Buono, who ran several other businesses, and Apollonio make it likely not only that standard motifs could be combined by either one of them in a single composition, or copied by any of their assistants or apprentices in delegated work, but also that there was considerable movement of drawings, particularly those by the latter, *between* their various shops. Works were executed through a kind of cut-and-paste procedure. It is revealing that many of the figures and other elements these works have in common were not originally the invention of either master.

Patrons required artists, whose *ingegno* may not have been rated highly, to show their *arte* by the incorporation of trend-setting inventions by the city's leading artists (and it would probably have varied whether or not the precise origins of these quotations were always supposed to be pinpointed). Even though a client might have decided that a

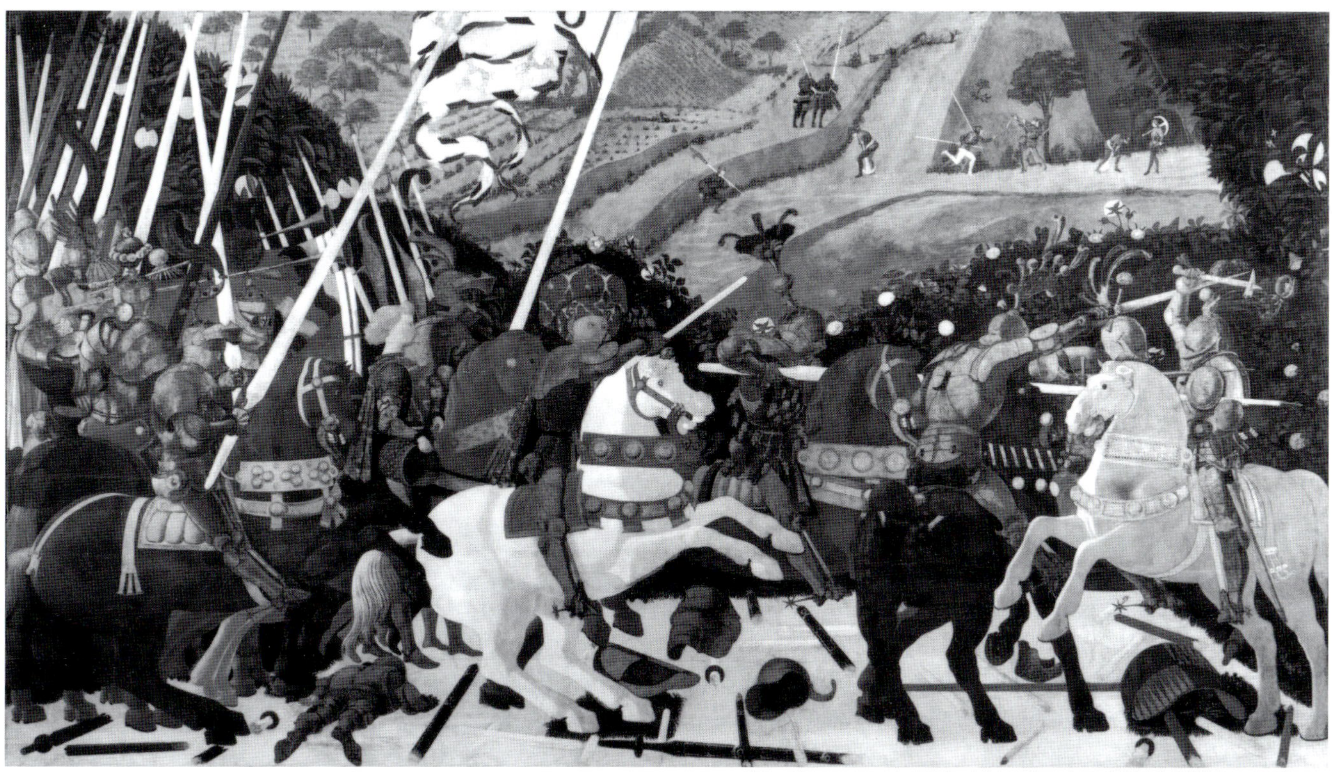

commission was too specialized or too unimportant to warrant the expertise or expense of an artist-designer of the highest calibre, craftsmen painting *cassoni* or ceramics were expected to adopt the style and vocabulary of autograph efforts by those artists. Apollonio, for example, combined in his works many motifs associated with paradigmatic artists like Uccello (fig. 192), Lippi and Ghiberti – as well as Domenico Veneziano, Benozzo Gozzoli and even Donatello.[44] His battle scenes almost always contain rearing and bucking horses in the manner of Uccello. Poses adopted by various of his figures can be traced to Ghiberti: his Polyphemus in the several Apollonio workshop depictions of the Odysseus legend (fig. 193) is loosely copied from the Adam in Ghiberti's relief of *The Creation* (fig. 194) on the Florence Baptistry 'Gates of Paradise'[45] (which itself derived from a seated Adonis on a well-known ancient sarcophagus fragment).[46] By doing so he was fulfilling exactly the expectations that we have come to associate with the word *arte*. Pliny's words on the sculptor Polycleitus make the point: 'He also made what artists called a "canon" [an exemplary model], as they drew their artistic outlines from it as a sort of standard; and he alone of mankind is deemed by means of one work of art to have created the art itself.'[47]

Such images and styles were best disseminated through works on paper. However, the occasional circulation of models by leading artists did not guarantee that most others operating in the field of art production had access to them. The proliferation of prints from the 1460s changed the situation. While we have seen in Chapter Four that not all prints were made with this purpose, some may have been originally conceived as models to be copied into other media. Certainly by the early Cinquecento *artefici* working in a wide range of media employed prints of designs by celebrated painters (and copied from famous antiquities) as recognized canons. *Istoriato* maiolica, in particular, depended on woodcuts and engravings for its sources, and specialists have spent a great deal of effort in identifying these and analysing the way in which they were used.[48]

It is clear that this method does not lessen the status of these pieces as works of *arte*. The question remains as to whether such objects could more completely fulfil the double demand of *arte* and *ingegno*. It is true that maiolica painters were sometimes handed designs to copy by better-known artists who specialized in fresco, canvas- or panel-painting.[49]

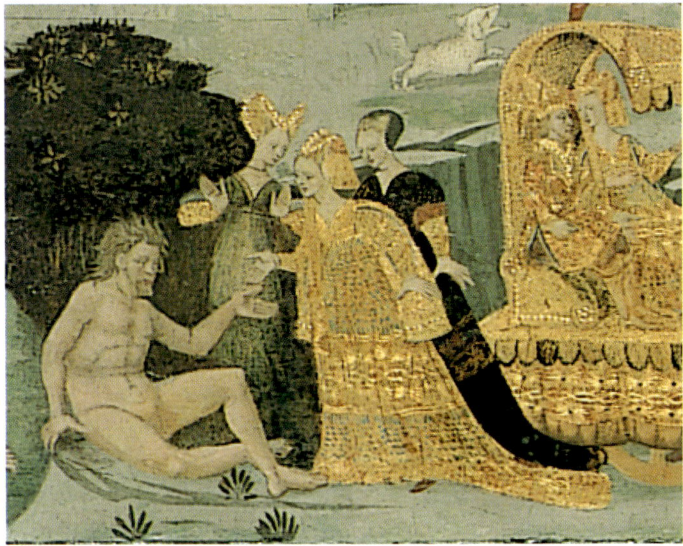

193 Apollonio di Giovanni and Marco del Buono (workshop), detail from fig. 191 with figure of Polyphemus

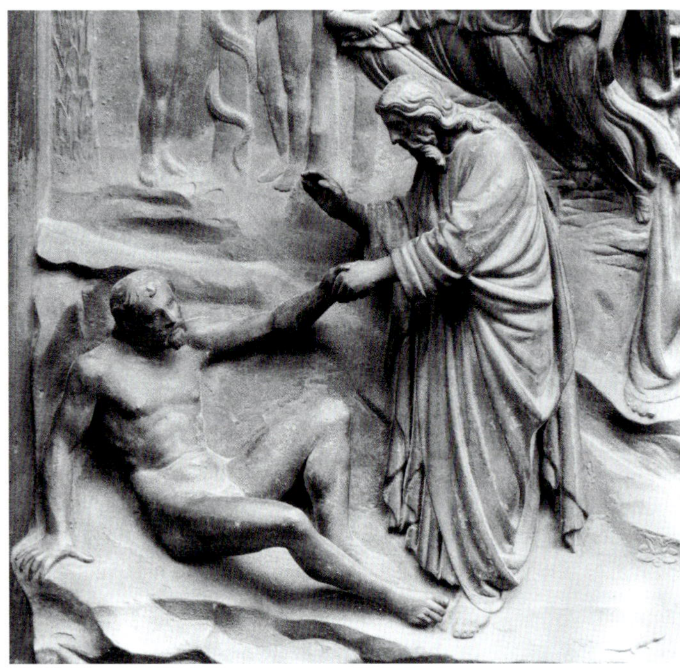

194 Lorenzo Ghiberti, *Creation* (detail with figure of Adam) from the 'Gates of Paradise'; gilded bronze; Florence, *c.*1426–52. Baptistry, Florence

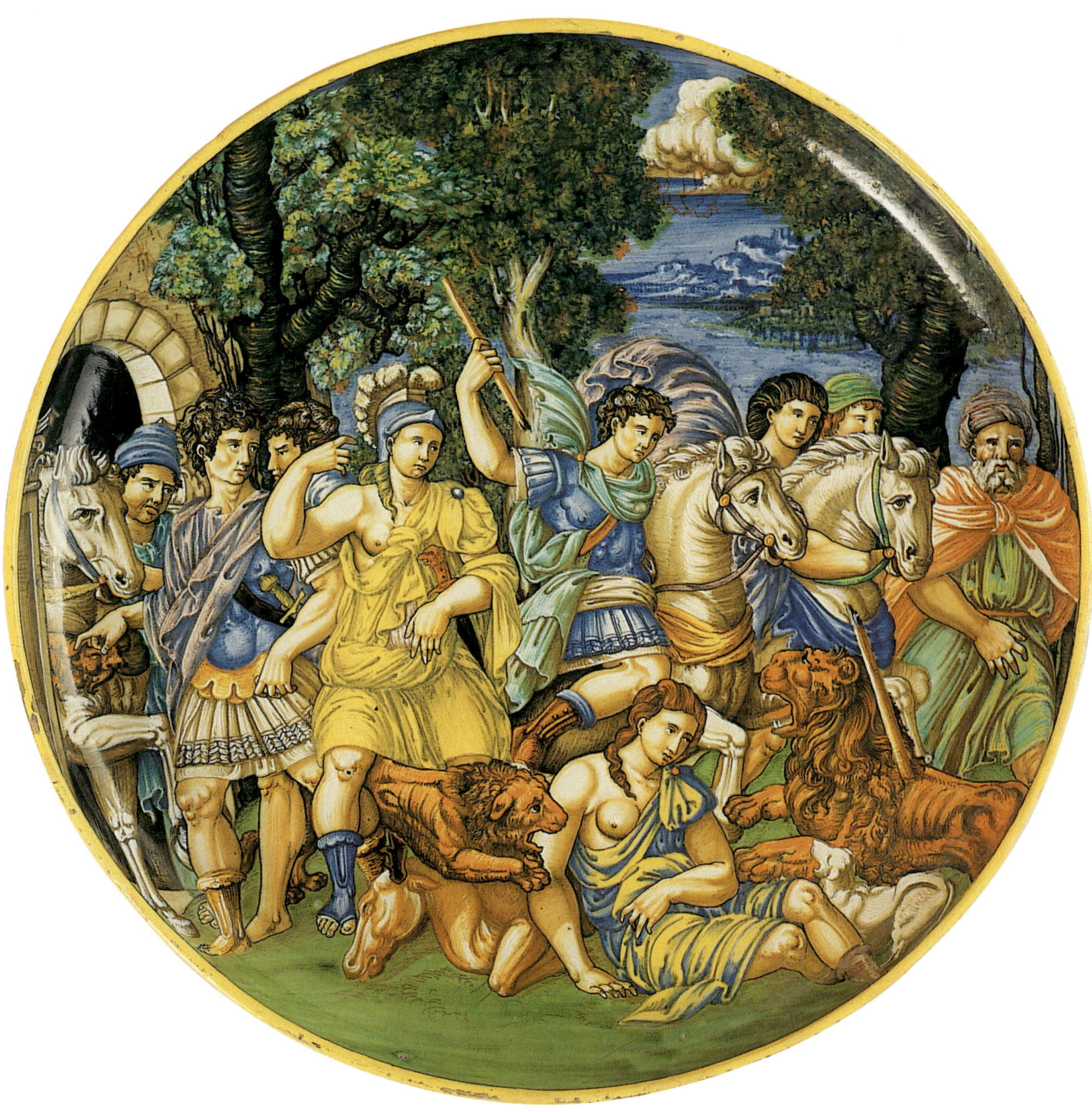

195 Francesco Xanto
Avelli da Rovigo
(attributed) after
Marcantonio Raimondi,
dish with scene of a
lion hunt copied
from a sarcophagus
relief; tin-glazed
ceramic (maiolica);
Urbino, *c*.1528–30.
The British Museum,
London

They seem also to have employed less-well-known sources for particular types of ornament: Muranese glass, linens from Perugia, and Lucchese silks.[50] Nevertheless, one must ask if their reliance on printed source material always limited their appreciation to one of perceived skill. Vasari judged maiolica painters as being especially in need of engraved sources – 'poor painters who do not have much *disegno*'.[51] But this, as we have seen, might equally apply to painters such as Apollonio. Vasari's assessment may therefore be anachronistic, written from the point of view of a court artist in the second half of the Cinquecento, and one with a declared artistic agenda.

The meaning of quotations might change according to the ways in which sources were used. The copying of a whole composition, for example, could be read in much the same

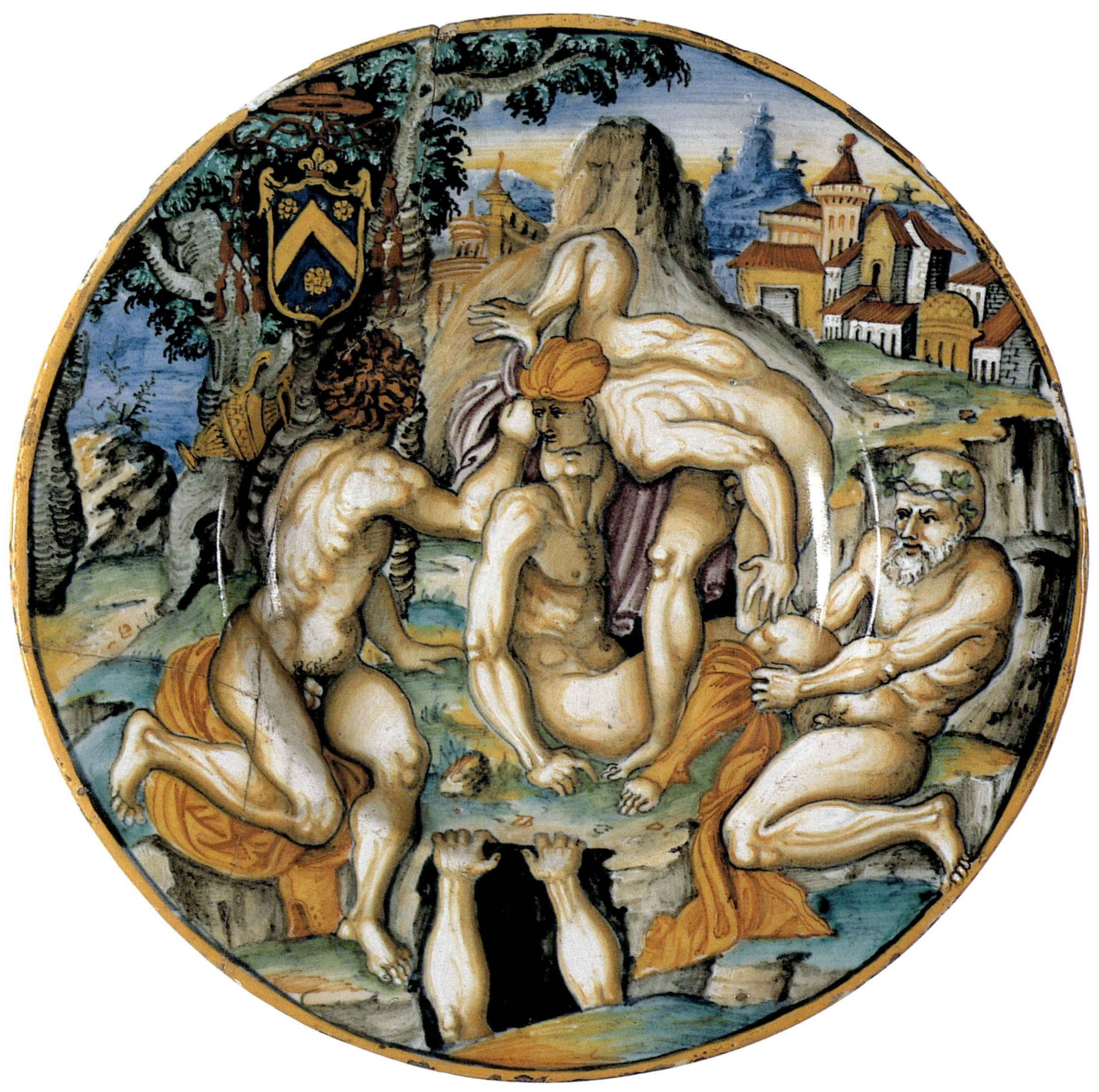

196 After Agostino Veneziano, plate with scene reproducing figures from Michelangelo's *Battle of Cascina* cartoon and arms of Cardinal Pietro Bembo; tin-glazed ceramic (maiolica); Urbino, 1539–47. The British Museum, London

way as Bernardi's use of Michelangelo's presentation drawings. Like rock-crystal, maiolica was a medium worthy of receiving distinguished designs. These might be ancient. Xanto Avelli signed a dish which took as its source a Raimondi print of a sarcophagus that stood outside St Peter's in Rome. Raimondi had claimed that by his print he had made the design better known: 'The tombs which stood almost out of sight of strangers are now seen and judged by anyone …'. Xanto copied these lines onto the reverse of his dish (fig. 195).[52]

The designs used by maiolica painters might equally be by modern masters. A striking instance is a plate made in Urbino between 1539 and 1547 for Pietro Bembo, who was made cardinal in 1539 (fig. 196). Since his arms appear beneath a cardinal's hat on the plate, we know it was made after 1539 and before his death in 1547.[53] The subject matter is

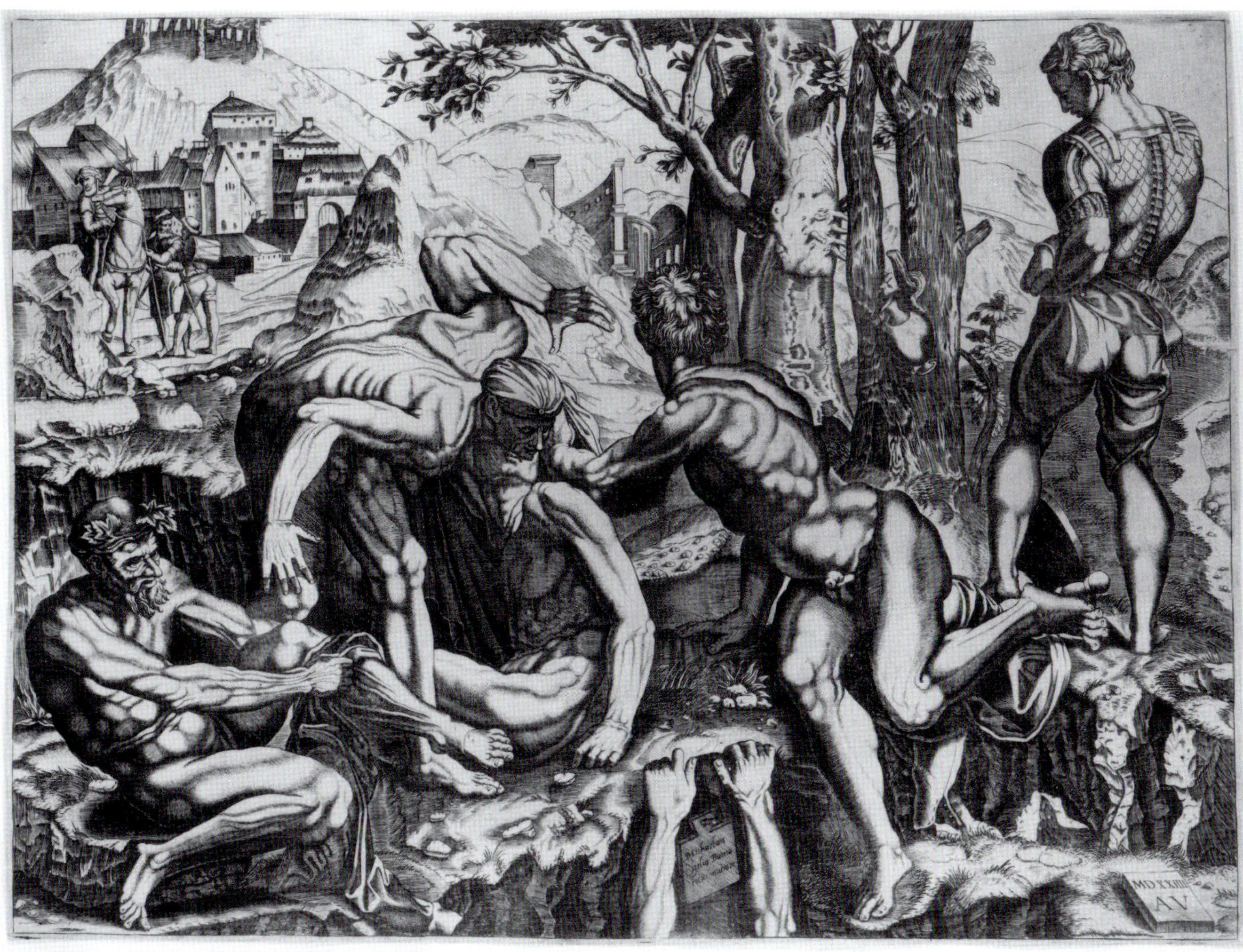

197 Agostino Veneziano
in part after Michelangelo,
Bathers; engraving;
Florence or Rome, 1524.
The British Museum,
London

unimportant compared with the dignity of the source of the composition, the cartoon for
the unexecuted *Battle of Cascina* fresco of 1504 by Michelangelo, parts of which were later
engraved by Marcantonio Raimondi and Agostino Veneziano (fig. 197).[54] Cellini's
description of the cartoon has given us a sense of how such a design would have been
appreciated and evaluated on maiolica in the elite papal circles to which Bembo belonged.

It is equally clear that individual technological skill could confer value on a ceramic
piece. Maestro Giorgio Andreoli of Gubbio started to sign the works lustred in his
workshop from 1518. In 1519 he was described, when his tax exemptions were being
renewed, as 'an excellent master without rival in the art of maiolica, whose work brings
honour to the lord, city and people of Gubbio in all the nations to which the pottery of
his workshop is exported, as well as the great income it brings in customs dues'.[55] Through
his particular skills, therefore, he brought recognition to his town in much the same way as
the collective efforts of the potters and painters of Faenza and Deruta did to theirs. Asking
for renewal of privileges in 1552, he mentioned the facilities he had been granted in
Gubbio to exercise 'the noble art of maiolica', but at the same time demanded continued

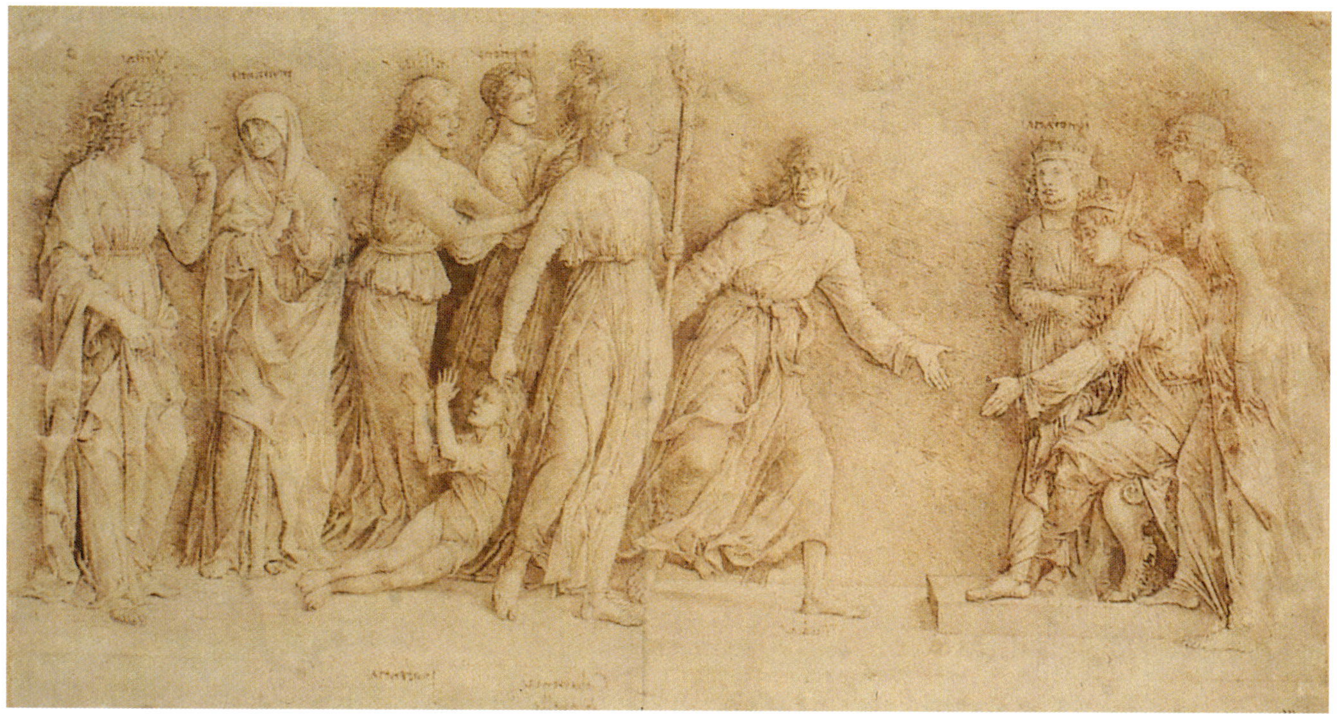

recognition for his *virtù*.[56] Here, then, is an example of *arte* being converted into something like *ingegno*.

It is clear, moreover, that some maiolica painters were keen to associate themselves with the particularly elevated status claimed for painters by Alberti and his successors. There survive two plates, in Oxford and Amsterdam, on which are depicted *The Calumny of Apelles*. The Oxford plate is by Nicola da Urbino; the other is not but probably also derives from Urbino (fig. 199).[57] Both Botticelli and Mantegna (fig. 198) had re-created this famous lost painting, the masterpiece by Apelles described in detail by the ancient Greek author Lucian.[58] In doing so they were affirming parity with their ancient predecessor. The work had long been recognized as a notional paradigm. Filarete, for example, had advocated that the artist should be well read so that he could devise 'beautiful inventions' as Apelles did in his *Calumny*.[59] It is true that neither of the painters of these plates signed themselves. However, to find the scene represented on a plate at all shows something about the fact that the famous image was deemed appropriate for the medium, and something about the status of the painters. The fact that both plates probably derive from a lost work executed by Luca Signorelli in the Palazzo Petrucci does not alter our reading of these objects or diminish the artistic claim that is the subject of the allegory.[60] Indeed, Nicola raises the stakes still higher; he has added the bull, the emblem of St Luke, patron of painters, to the Oxford plate. Thus the entire object becomes a manifesto for the status of the ceramic painter.

Some known *istoriato* painters had favourite sources that reveal that they were literate and had access to certain printed books; Francesco Durantino, for instance, refers to the 1493 Italian edition of Livy as a source of both subjects and decoration,[61] while Nicola da Urbino repeatedly used the 1497 Venetian paraphrase of Ovid's *Metamorphoses* on his pieces, exemplified by the *istorie* he painted for the service commissioned for Isabella

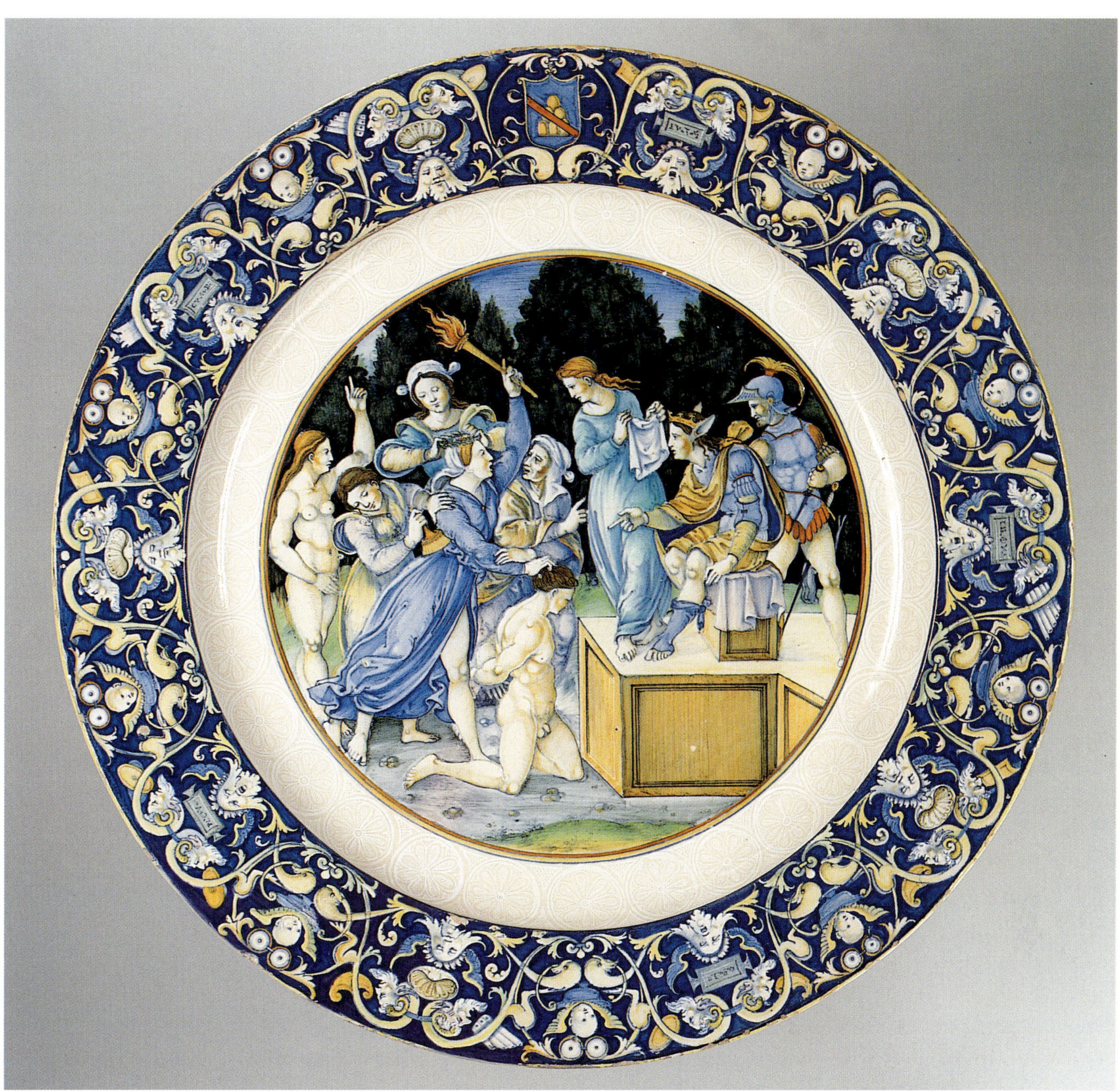

199 Dish with *The Calumny of Apelles*, grotesque and *bianco sopra bianco* borders; tin-glazed ceramic (maiolica); Urbino (?), *c.*1520–5. The Rijksmuseum, Amsterdam

d'Este. He copied a woodcut (fig. 200) to form the basis of his treatment of the Apollo and Daphne legend, for example (see fig. 181).[62] Both painters were using these books between twenty and forty years after they were printed. Nicola seems to have favoured these schematic woodcuts more than the complex prints by Marcantonio and others, which he knew by 1524 and to which he turned as sources in the later 1520s.[63] His dependence on the 1497 woodcuts must have been a deliberate choice, as his visual understanding was certainly sophisticated.

In these works, unlike the dishes which repeat whole compositions, the painters were not acting as literal copyists. Instead, they were taking elements from different sources and combining them in new compositions. By doing so, were they obeying Petrarch's influential dictum of *imitatio*: 'He who imitates must have a care that what he writes be

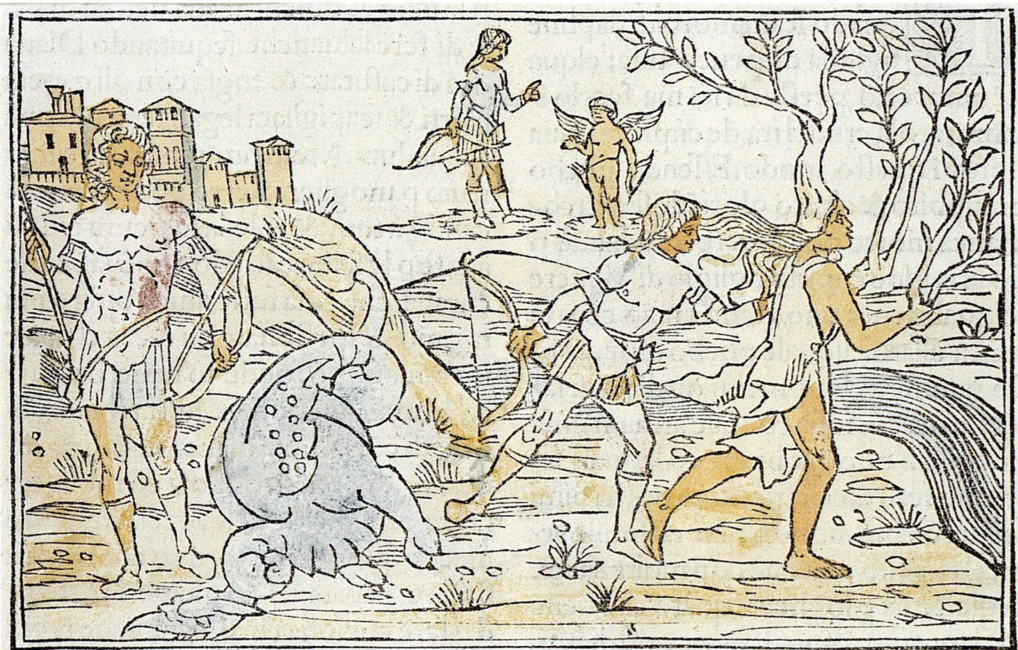

200 *Apollo and Daphne*; hand-coloured woodcut illustration from paraphrase of Ovid's *Metamorphoses*; Venice, 1497, fol. vii r. The British Library, London

similar, not identical [with his model] … We should therefore make use of another man's inner quality and tone, but avoid his words. For the one kind of similarity is hidden and the other protrudes; the one creates poets, the other apes.'[64] The question seems to hinge on whether and how their sources were intended to be recognized. It may be approached through an examination of the work of a particularly self-aggrandizing maiolica painter.

The art of Xanto Avelli

Francesco Xanto Avelli is one of the outstanding figures in the history of Renaissance maiolica, a painter who laid claim not just to *arte* but also to inventive *ingegno*.[65] His biography can be pieced together from three types of evidence: a small number of documents in the Urbino archives; the many detailed inscriptions on his pieces; and biographical details gleaned from his sonnet sequence, *The Portrait*, in praise of his patron, Francesco Maria della Rovere, Duke of Urbino.[66] The three sources work with each other to flesh out the details of his biography and career. He seems to have been born as Francesco Santo or Santini around 1500, and from the way he signed himself in the early 1530s as being 'da Rovigo' or 'Rovigese', it is assumed that he was born in Rovigo in the Veneto.[67] This has some bearing on the form of his name that he adopted some time before 1530, when he altered his family name, Santini, to Xanto. This is the local pronunciation of Santo, so by altering the spelling, Xanto was accentuating his Rovigese origin.[68] The new name also recalled the river-god, Xanthus, who fought for the Trojans against Achilles in Homer's *Iliad*. Xanto proclaimed this play on his name in his sonnet sequence, when he mentions 'the sacred river of my surname' *(il sacro fiume de' mei cognome)*.[69] The name makes another classical allusion, being Greek for 'curly-haired' or 'fair-haired', the equivalent therefore of Filarete's claim, through his name, to be a lover of virtue.[70]

Xanto himself claimed to value his 'two equal skills of poetry and painting' (*due di par canto e coloro*), and by doing so emphasized the intellectual element of the latter.[71] In the same sonnet he described painting as his 'wet-nurse', as the inspiration not only to paint but to write poetry. Thus he identifies painting as an art derived from nature.[72] Moreover, he used every strategy available to the Renaissance *artefice* to proclaim his individual status, ones that had been tried and tested by more established figures. First, the *all'antica* persona signalled by the classicized version of his name.[73] Second, he advertised his status as someone familiar with key ancient (and modern) texts in the number and nature of inscriptions on his work, revealing the extent of his reading.[74] Third, and here the difficulty lies, he raided the work of a wide range of leading draughtsmen – Raphael, Giulio Romano and Baccio Bandinelli – through the medium of prints, using up to fifty-seven engraved sources to create his own complex narrative style and celebrate his own inventiveness in

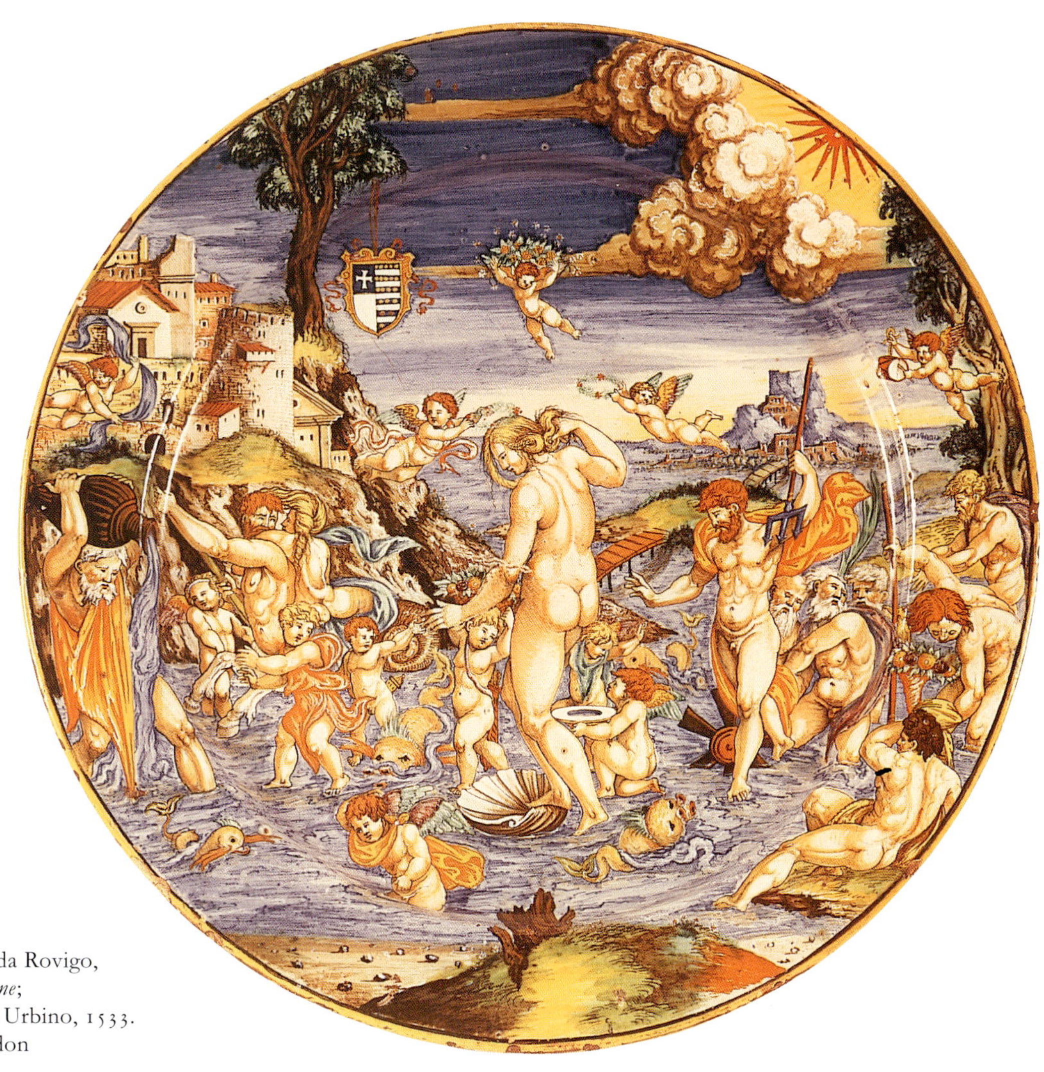

201 Francesco Xanto Avelli da Rovigo,
dish with *The Triumph of Alcyone*;
tin-glazed ceramic (maiolica); Urbino, 1533.
The Wallace Collection, London

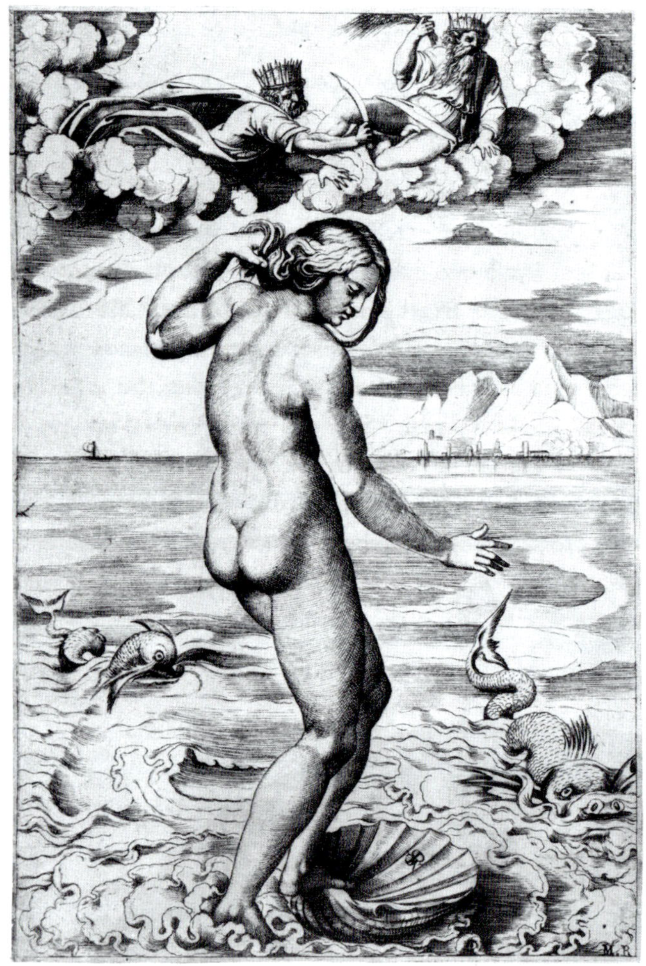

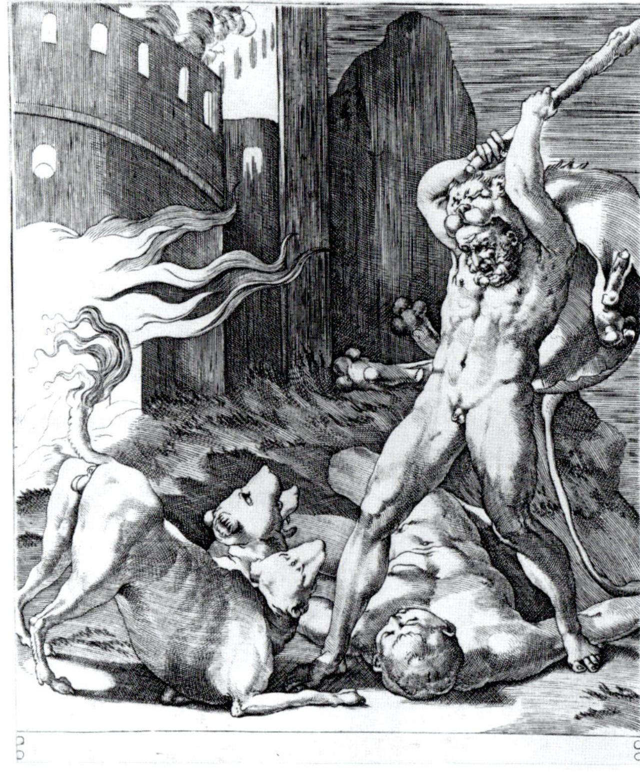

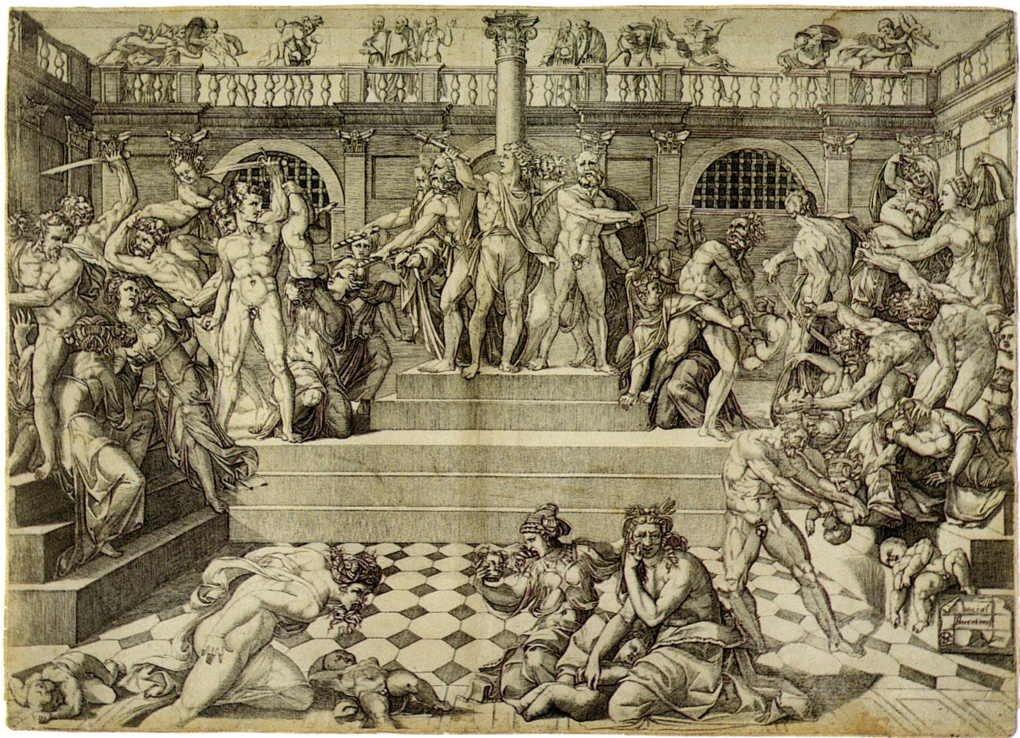

202 (*Above, left*)
Marcantonio Raimondi
after Raphael, *Venus*;
engraving; Rome, *c.*1515.
The British Museum,
London

203 (*Above, right*)
Gian Jacopo Caraglio after
Rosso Fiorentino, *Slaying
of Cerberus*; engraving;
Rome, *c.*1524–7.
The British Museum,
London

204 Marco Dente after
Baccio Bandinelli, *Massacre
of the Innocents*; engraving;
Rome, *c.*1520–1.
The British Museum,
London

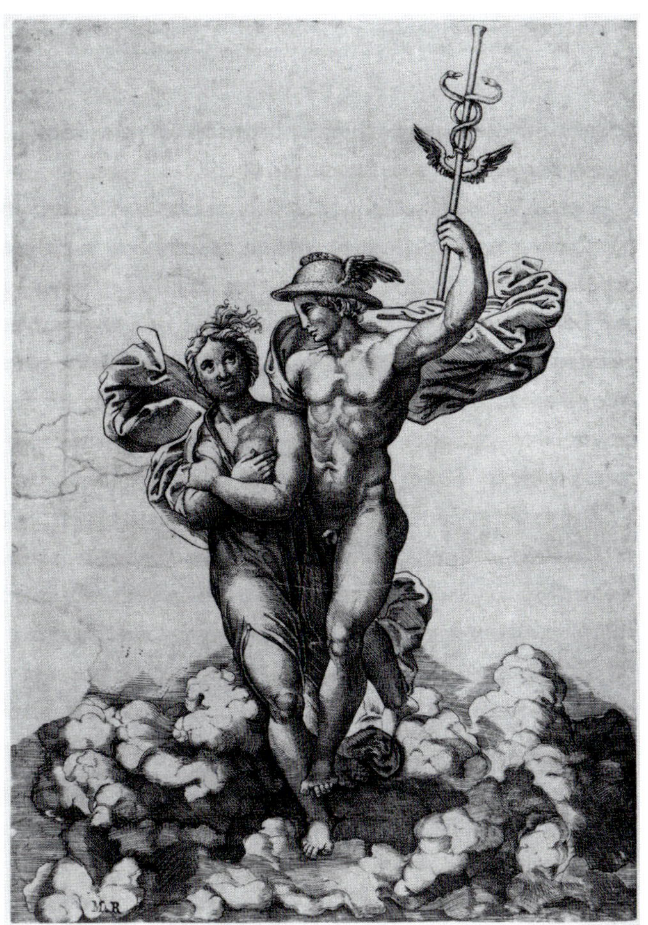

205 Gian Jacopo Caraglio after
Raphael, *Mercury conducting Psyche to
Olympus*; engraving; Rome, *c*.1526.
The British Museum, London

206 Marcantonio Raimondi
after Baccio Bandinelli,
Martyrdom of St Lawrence;
engraving; Rome, after 1525.
The British Museum, London

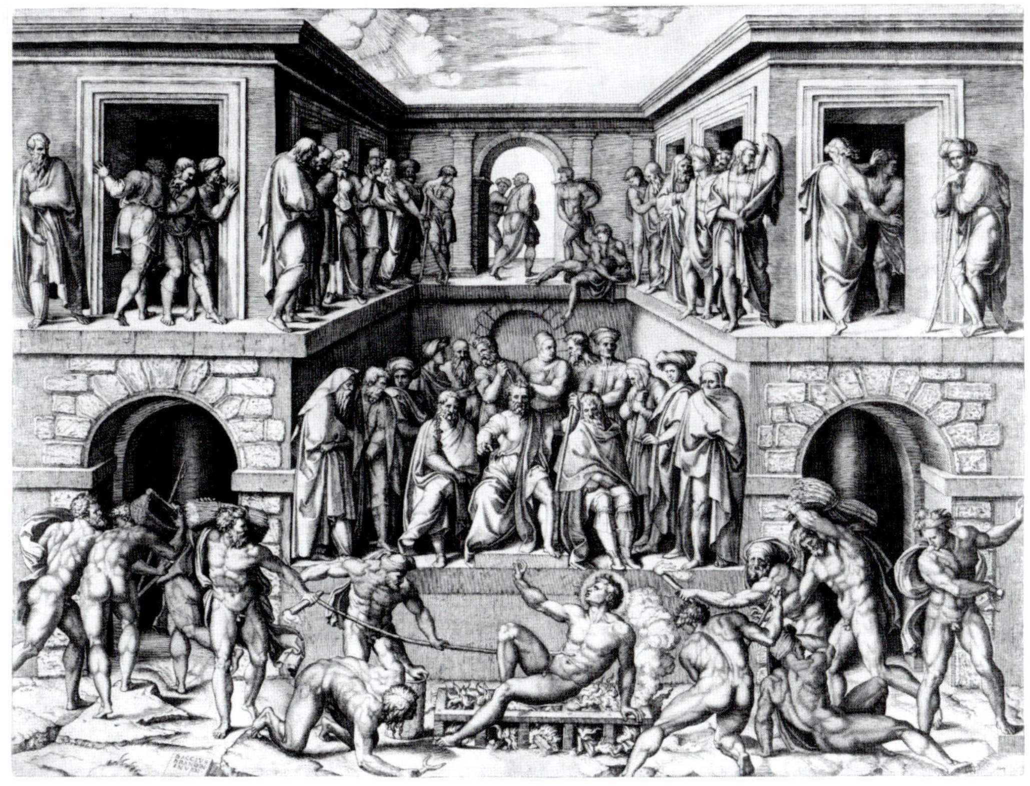

adapting these sources for his purposes.[75] By this means, he seems deliberately to shape his *ingegno* through proper imitation.

A plate in the Wallace Collection in London exemplifies Xanto's manner of working, in combining text and image and in assembling a narrative from figures excerpted from different prints. The subject is from Ovid, *The Triumph of Alcyone*, while the inscription on the back is from the Italian paraphrase of Ovid published in 1497 (fig. 201). The scene painted on the front incorporates figures from nine print sources, some of them reversed; five of them are shown here (figs 202–6).[76] Many of these figures were to be used several times over in other works, reconstituted in different groupings to illustrate different mythological or historical subjects, which are identified with quotations on the reverses.

The earliest hard evidence for Xanto's career dates from 1530, by which time he was established in Urbino, where he may – to judge by stylistic evidence – have been working on and off for over a decade.[77] It was in this year that he began to sign his works unequivocally, his name appearing on a plate signed on the reverse: F.X.A.R., for Francesco Xanto Avelli Rovigese.[78] The reason for his sudden interest in signing himself in this way has been linked to a trade dispute between maiolica painters and the workshop owners who employed them on contract, recorded in an Urbino document of 1530.[79] Five master potters agreed to boycott twelve named maiolica painters, including Xanto, who had joined together to force a rise in their wages. The painters' bid may have had more to do with money than with artistic status;[80] another pottery town, Faenza, had seen a similar dispute only a few months earlier, and there it was the potters rather than the painters who were trying to buttress their position and establish a minimum wage.[81]

However, this document has been seen as reflecting a positive move by Xanto and others to raise their status to more than mere client painters working for a succession of workshop owners on short-term contracts.[82] According to this interpretation, the document has a visual parallel in a famous plate in the Victoria and Albert Museum made in Cafaggiolo around 1510, showing a maiolica painter with his clients or patrons, in which his dress and demeanour proclaim him to be their social equal.[83] Xanto's claims, as made through his inscriptions on maiolica, did not go unchallenged. This is confirmed by the fact that on those pieces finished with lustre in the Gubbio workshop of Maestro Giorgio Andreoli between 1531 and 1533, Xanto's name and the inscription 'in Urbino' have been covered over and often obliterated in lustre, while the description of the subject is left uncovered (fig. 207). The intention is undeniable, but the effect is apparent only when handling the pieces, as the lustre gleams and obscures the underlying inscription in cobalt blue.[84] Might this represent an attempt to deny Xanto's role as the sole creator of the pieces by an *artefice* who was equally keen to establish the *virtuosi* credentials of his town and his technique?

That Xanto was the only painter (with the single exception of his closest follower, Giulio da Urbino) treated to this brand of censorship may reflect the manner in which he insisted on an elevated status.[85] Particularly noticeable is the way in which he advertises not only his literacy, but his literary ambition.[86] It is thought that he might have studied at vernacular school in his native Rovigo, where literary texts or Latin classics in translation were often read.[87] His sonnet cycle in praise of the duke of Urbino, which survives in a fair

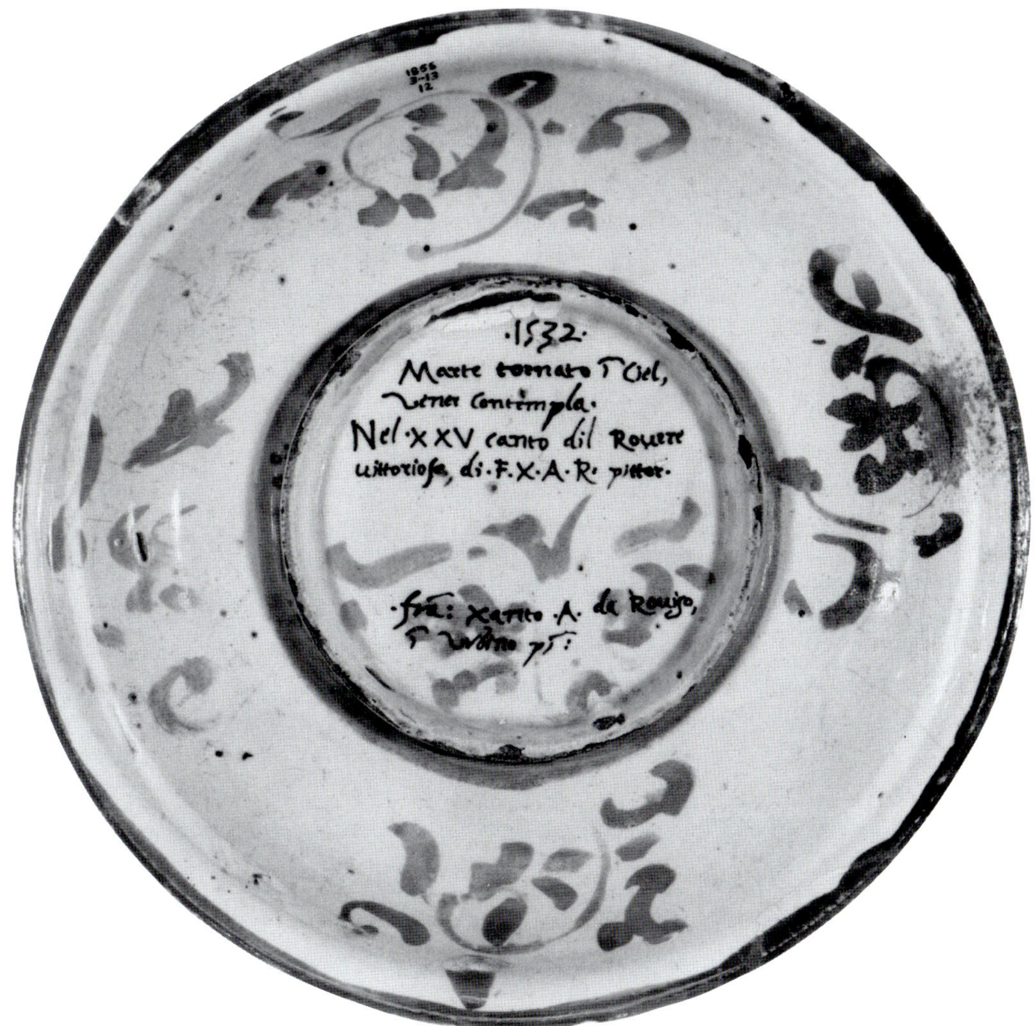

copy in an elegant italic script (not Xanto's own), is written in a competent Petrarchan manner.[88] A dish in The British Museum claims to illustrate one of the sonnets: Venus lies on a cloud, suckling Cupid, while Mars uncovers her (fig. 208). The inscription on the reverse (see fig. 207) reads '1532. Mars, returned to the sky, contemplates Venus. From canto 25 of Rovere the Victorious by F.X.A.R, painter.' Beneath this, overpainted with lustre, is the signature proper: 'Francesco Xanto Avelli da Rovigo in Urbino painted this.' Xanto was therefore calling himself a painter and a poet in one breath.[89]

His use of poetry is indicative of his priorities as a painter. His inscriptions on the reverses of his maiolica are often laid out, and read, as poetry.[90] The same inscriptions indicate that he was very familiar with Petrarch's *Trionfi* and with a contemporary commentary on it, to the extent that he seems to have viewed both ancient and contemporary history through the lens of Petrarch's poetry.[91] When, for instance, he constructed allegories of the 1527 sack of Rome, it was to Petrarch that he turned for lines that expressed his moral stance on the events portrayed.[92] He knew, but was less intimate with, the poetry of Dante and of his own contemporary, Ariosto.[93] There is no evidence that he could read Latin, but his inscriptions show that he had read at least parts of Ovid, Virgil and the works of ancient historians in Italian translation.[94] One of his most popular subjects, for example, *The Betrayal of Amphiaraus* (fig. 209) was attributed by him to Ovid in his inscription, but, in fact, it appears only in the Italian paraphrase of the *Metamorphoses*, which must have been his source.[95] He often misquoted or paraphrased his literary sources, and although he gives what look like precise citations, they can be incomplete or inaccurate.[96] He was more interested in allusion and suggestion than in illustration. His earliest works, attributed to him on the grounds of style and the type of inscription, include the words 'fable' and 'history' as pointers; others end with the command that the viewer should 'take note'.[97] That his scenes are rarely straightforward illustrations of the subject given on the reverse,[98] may show that he expected image and text to work in parallel – like the allegories and inscriptions on so many medal reverses – rather than that he was merely perfunctory in his use of images. His quotations are designed to amplify the images. When, for example, he represented Aeneas carrying his father, Anchises (fig. 210), he attributed

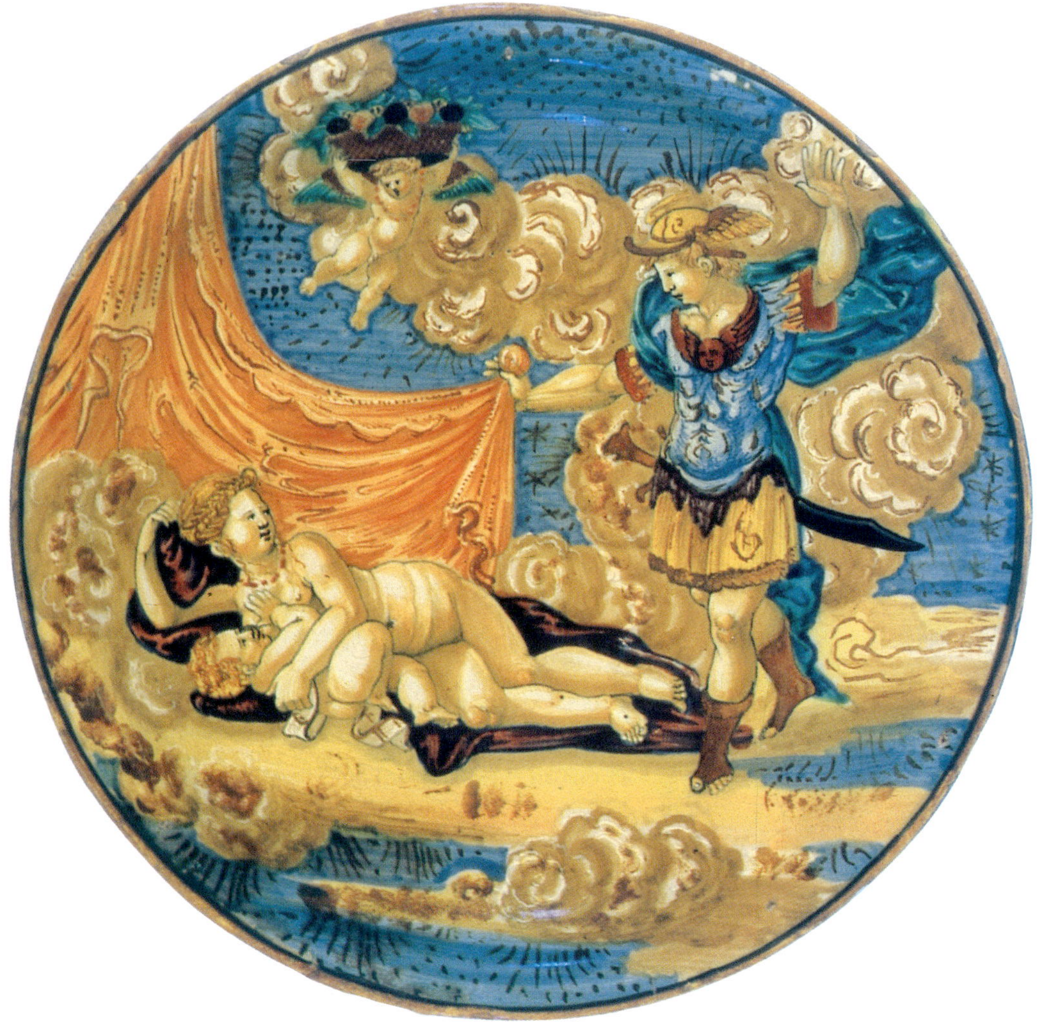

208 Francesco Xanto Avelli da Rovigo, dish with *Mars, Venus and Cupid*; tin-glazed ceramic (maiolica) with lustred decoration; painted in Urbino, perhaps lustred in Gubbio, 1532. The British Museum, London

209 Francesco Xanto
Avelli da Rovigo, dish
with *The Betrayal of
Amphiaraus*; tin-glazed
ceramic (maiolica) with
lustred decoration; painted
in Urbino and perhaps
lustred in Gubbio, 1533.
The British Museum,
London

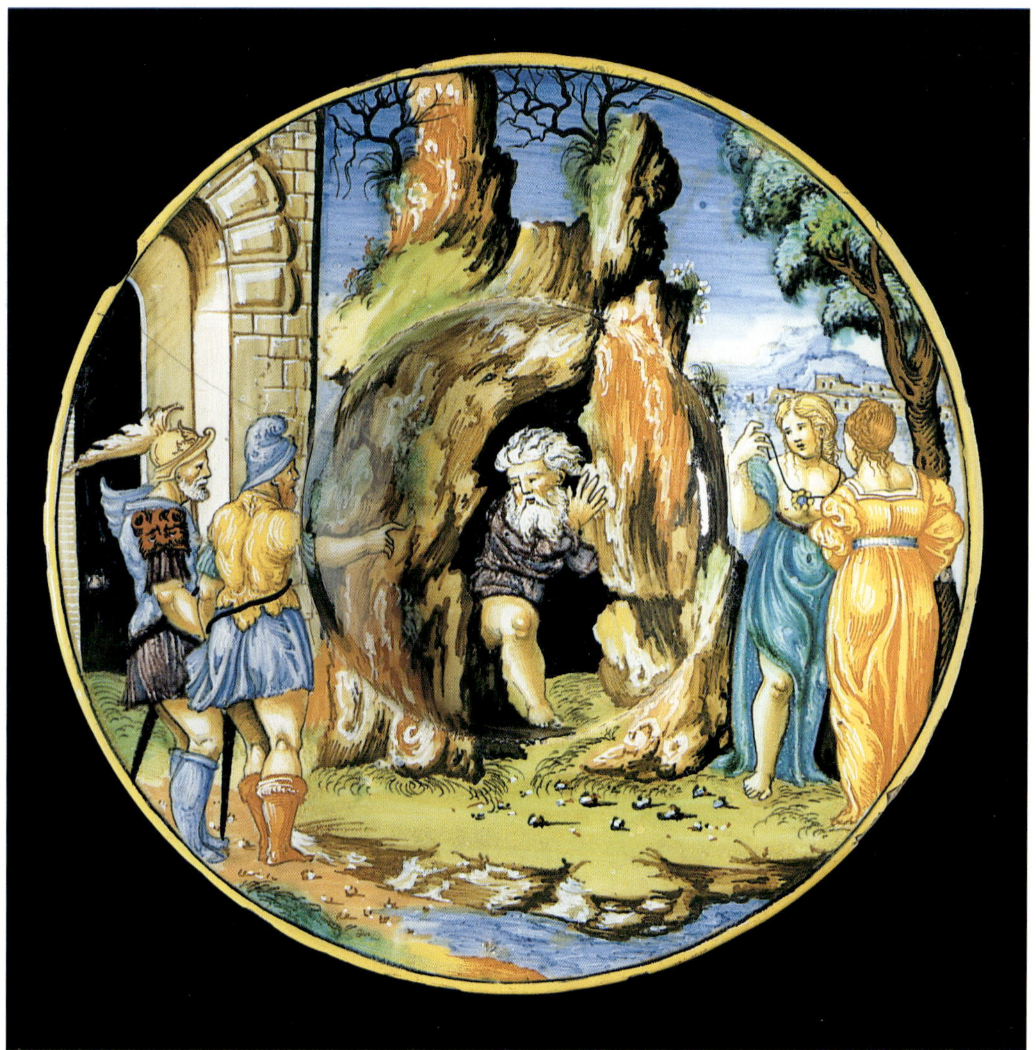

the subject to Petrarch rather than Ovid, adapting Petrarch's line to make the identification with Aeneas more obvious: 'This is he who wept under Antandro' (fig. 211).[99] As a result, his imagery can be sometimes obscure, resisting easy reading in (again) the same way as many medallic reverses. His *Allegory of the Battle of Pavia* in The British Museum is a good case in point; if the subject were not given, the iconography would be completely unintelligible (fig. 212).[100] As it is, only one figure, adapted from one of Marcantonio's celebrated (though banned) series of prints of sexual positions illustrating Aretino's pornographic poems – *I Modi* – can be identified as representing the fallen Francis I, King of France.[101] His visual source for the Aeneas plate was the same print by Caraglio after Raphael's *Fire in the Borgo* that had been employed by Valerio Belli in his medal of Aeneas (see figs 96, 97).

And there the real problem lies. Though his literary knowledge was perhaps more restricted than he would have liked, he has this in common with many of the better-known painters of his day (and, indeed, some of their patrons who also preferred to read their

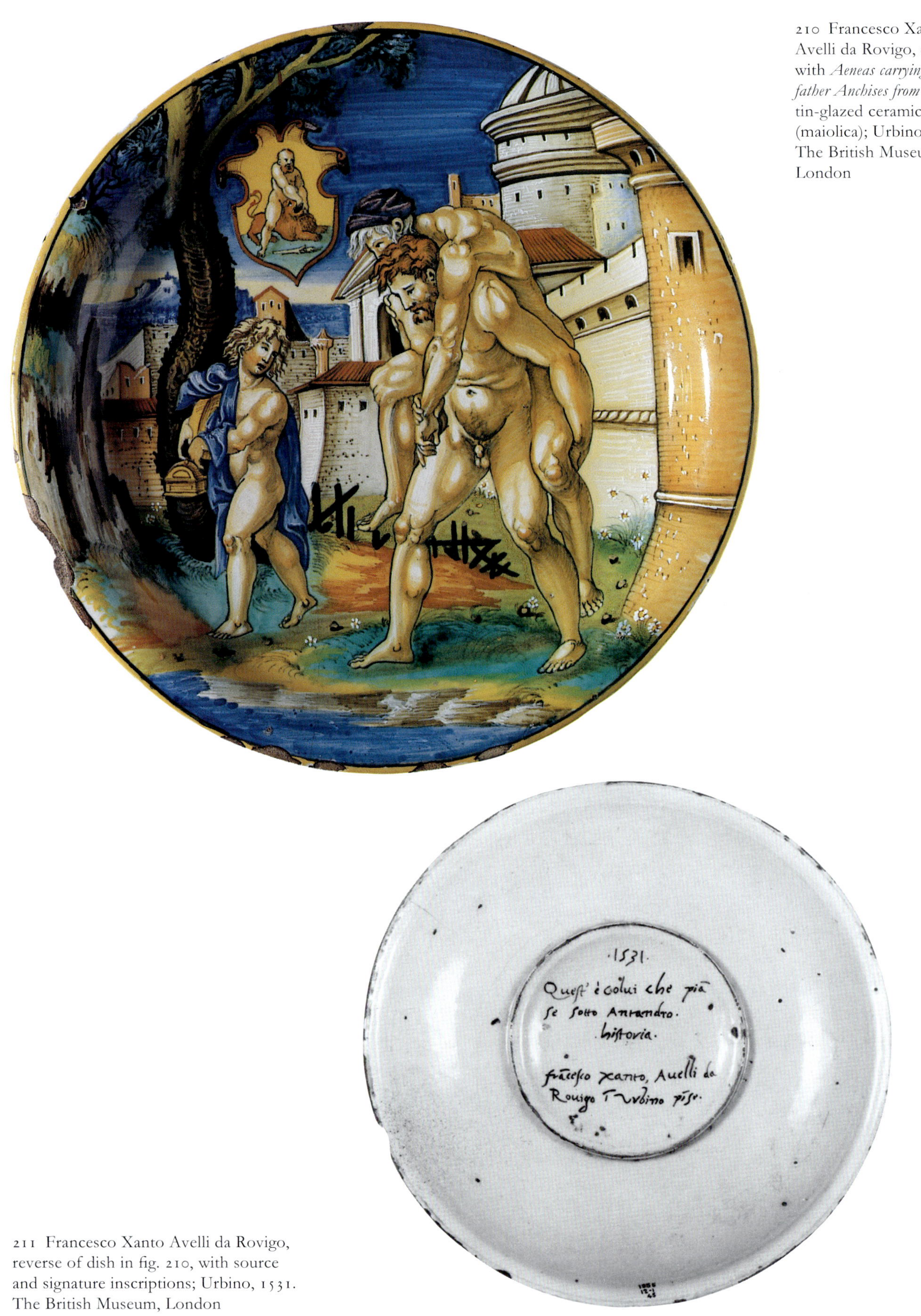

210 Francesco Xanto
Avelli da Rovigo, dish
with *Aeneas carrying his
father Anchises from Troy*;
tin-glazed ceramic
(maiolica); Urbino, 1531.
The British Museum,
London

211 Francesco Xanto Avelli da Rovigo,
reverse of dish in fig. 210, with source
and signature inscriptions; Urbino, 1531.
The British Museum, London

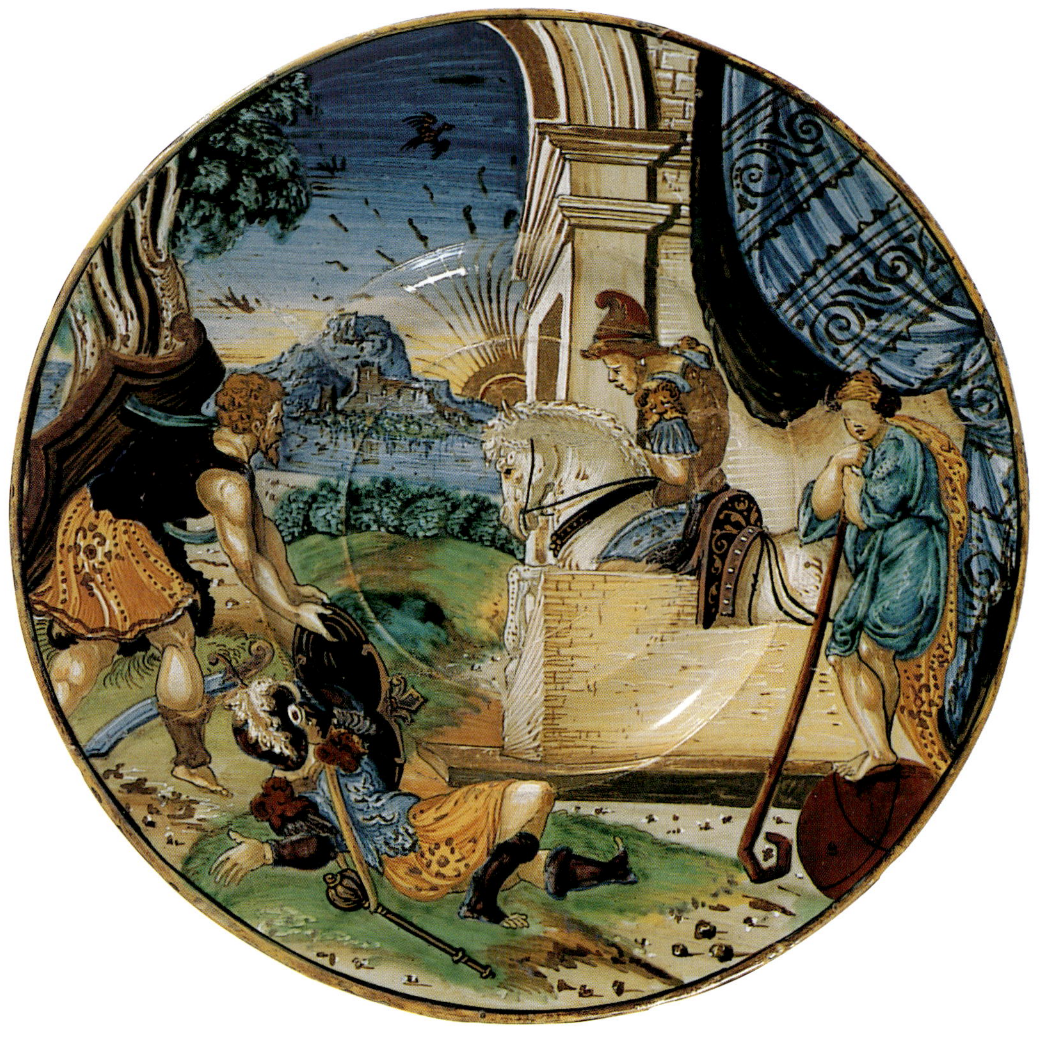

classics in the vernacular). Nevertheless, in writing his sonnet sequence he makes constant reference to Italian poems by celebrated contemporaries and forebears.[102] Are we then entitled to read his visual quotations in the same way – as Petrarchan *imitatio*? By the third decade of the sixteenth century we have seen that the works of particular heroicized painters and sculptors – Raphael, Michelangelo and Giulio, to take the most obvious instances – were considered canonical. Models need no longer be local and could justifiably be sought in their works, in exactly the same way as artists continued to cite ancient visual paradigms. By combining them in new compositions in landscapes and architectural settings of their own invention, Xanto, and the other ceramic painters who worked in this way, follow precisely Alberti's advice in the second book of his treatise *On Painting* on the composition of *istorie* – depending on the way the figures are posed in relation to one another, and in which the beholder should be delighted by the 'copiousness' and 'variety': 'Composition is that rule of painting by which the parts of the things seen fit together in the painting.'[103] And by doing so they were not differing substantially from painters like Rosso Fiorentino, whose inventiveness was not doubted, when he borrowed figures in action from Raphael.[104]

The history of the Marcantonio prints, suppressed as scandalous in Rome in 1524 so that no complete set has survived, however, raises an obvious question, given their appropriation in the two plates discussed here.[105] Was the notorious origin of Xanto's two excerpted figures meant to be recognizable? It has been suggested, for example, that Xanto's adaptation of a female figure to represent the fallen Francis I reduces him to impotence and offers a commentary on the King's defeat.[106] There may, indeed, have been a close match in the Renaissance mind between the Petrarchan and other moralizing comments about a corrupt papacy and papal city, which appear on the back of these plates, and the use of a lascivious or pornographic female figure to personify these qualities.[107]

However, in other contexts the quotation is iconographically meaningless. The deployment of a straining male figure from *I Modi*, known from a woodcut copy (fig. 213), as a shepherd carrying the infants Romulus and Remus out onto the mountainside (fig. 214) is extracted completely from its original sexual context and has apparently no relevance to the story represented.[108] That is not necessarily to imply that it was not recognizable or recognized. However, it may have been spotted as a quotation by the visually literate in exactly the same way as a reference to Dante or Petrarch in his poems. By turning a man in a complicated act of copulation into a shepherd, Xanto was using Giulio's 'quality and tone' (and he seems to have selected figures often on the basis of the *difficoltà* they display) but not his 'words'. Beyond the fame of a figure or group of figures that might or might not have been recognized, what counted was the ingenuity *and* the skill with which they were appropriated and adapted to a different use. And, of course, if they were not recognized by all of their restricted audience their ambition could be taken for Xanto's own. In this way a plate could move beyond *arte* and begin, even if a little clumsily, to display *ingegno*. A demanding medium had become, even if only for a brief period, an elite modern art form.

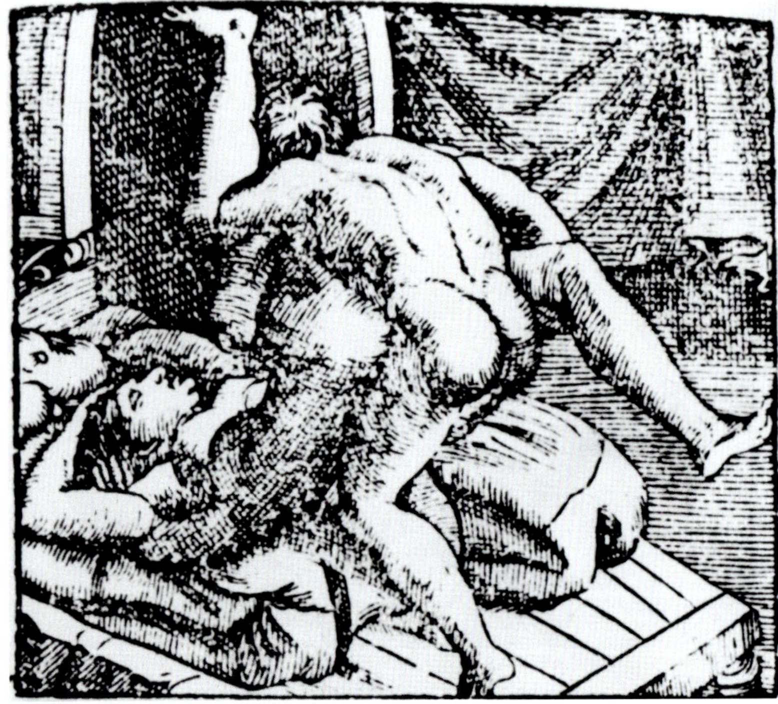

213 After Marcantonio Raimondi (after Giulio Romano), *Position Eight*; woodcut illustration to Pietro Aretino's *I Modi*. Former Toscanini volume, private collection, Switzerland

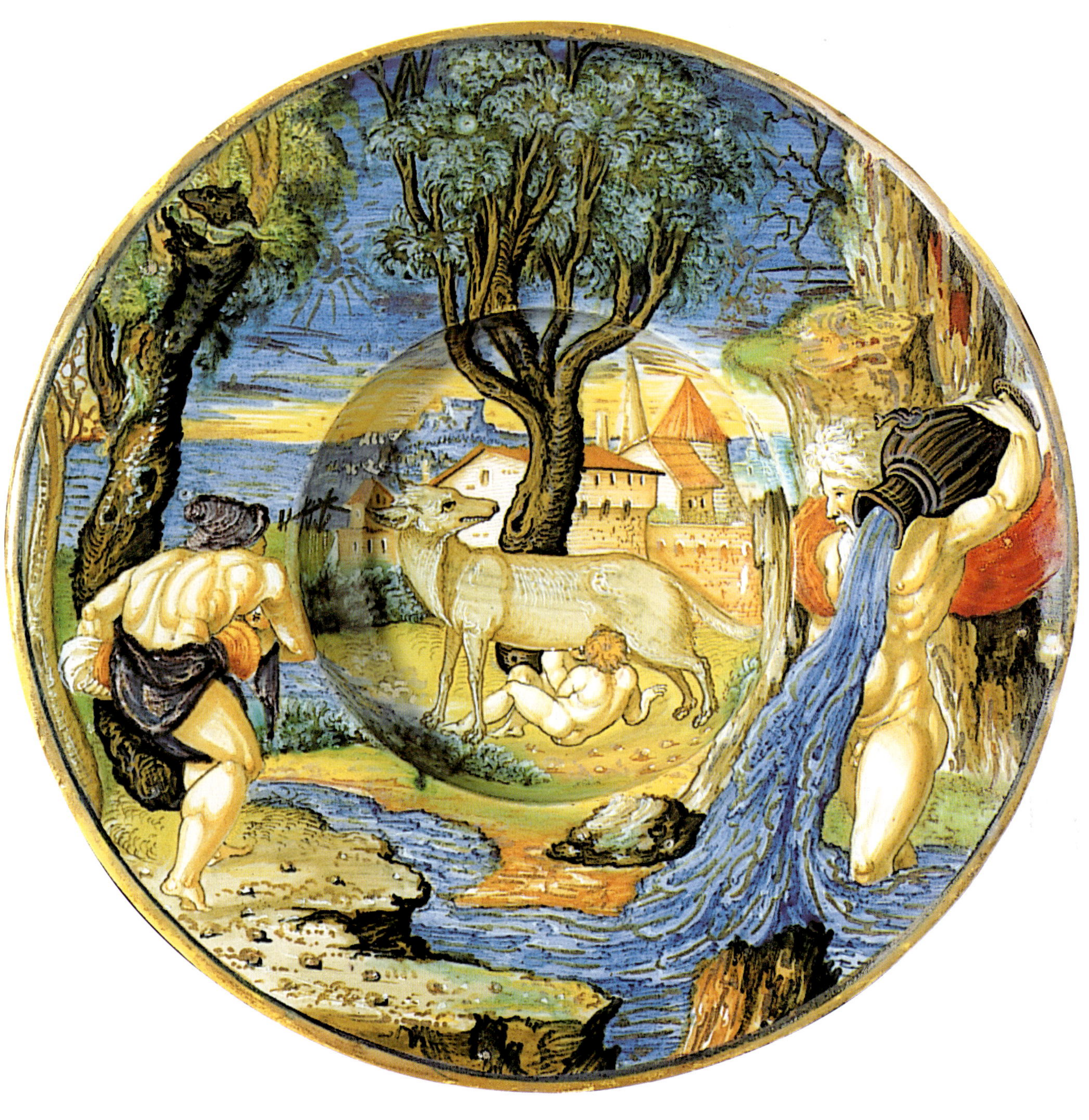

214 Francesco Xanto Avelli da Rovigo, dish with *Romulus and Remus;* tin-glazed ceramic (maiolica) with lustred decoration; Urbino, 1533, perhaps lustred in Gubbio. The British Museum, London

Notes

Chapter 1

1 R. Goldthwaite, *Wealth and the Demand for Art in Italy, 1300–1600*, Baltimore and London, 1993, pp. 193–22; P.L. Rubin, 'Patrons and Projects' in P.L. Rubin and A. Wright, *Renaissance Florence: The Art of the 1470s*, exh. cat., National Gallery, London, London, 1999, pp. 32–75.

2 For *liberalitas*, for example, see M. Warnke, *The Court Artist: On the Ancestry of the Modern Artist* (trans. D. McLintock), Cambridge, 1993, pp. 148–50.

3 Guarino Guarini, *Epistolario di Guarino Veronese*, 3 vols, ed. R. Sabbadini, Venice, 1915–19, I, 1915, p. 263; A. Grafton and L. Jardine, *From Humanism to the Humanities: Education and the Liberal Arts in Fifteenth- and Sixteenth-Century Europe*, London, 1986, p. 2.

4 E. Garin (ed.), *Prosatori latini del Quattrocento*, Milan and Naples, 1952, pp. 390–2; Grafton and Jardine, *From Humanism*, p. 34.

5 This high-brow genre became more popular in the sixteenth century. See R.M. Bell, *How to Do It: Guides to Good Living for Renaissance Italians*, Chicago, 1999, *passim*.

6 Leonardo Bruni, *De Militia*, written *c.* 1421; see G. Griffiths, J. Hankins and D. Thompson (eds), *The Humanism of Leonardo Bruni*, Binghamton, NY, 1987, pp. 107–11,127–45; A. Butterfield, 'Monument and Memory in Early Renaissance Florence' in G. Ciapelli and P.L. Rubin, *Art, Memory and Family in Renaissance Florence*, Cambridge, 2000, pp. 135–62, esp. p. 155.

7 An idea suggested by Johan Huizinga, *The Waning of the Middle Ages*, London 1924, p. 60; quoted by Butterfield, 'Monument and Memory', p. 157.

8 F. Barbaro, 'On Wifely Duties', trans. B.G. Kohl, in B.G. Kohl and R. Witt (eds), *The Earthly Republic: Italian Humanists on Government and Society*, Philadelphia, 1978, pp. 179–230; L. Haas, *The Renaissance Man and his Children: Childbirth and Early Childhood in Florence, 1300–1600*, New York, 1998, pp. 17–36, esp. pp. 19–20.

9 I. Kajanto, *Poggio Bracciolini and Classicism: a Study in Early Italian Humanism*, Helsinki, 1987, p. 16.

10 B. Platina, *De principe*, ed. G. Ferraù, Palermo, 1979; N. Rubinstein, 'The *De optimo cive* and the *De Principe* by Bartolomeo Platina in R. Cardini *et al.* (eds), *Letteratura umanistica e tradizione classica per Alessandro Perosa*, Rome, 1985, pp. 375–89.

11 M.E. Milhan, 'New Aspects of *De honeste voluptate ac valitudine*' in A. Campana and P. Medioli Masotti (eds), *Bartolomeo Sacchi, il Platina (Piadena 1421–Roma 1481). Atti del convegno internazionale di studi per il V centenaria (Cremona 14–15 novembre 1981)*, Padua, 1986, pp. 91–6.

12 Leon Battista Alberti, *Opere volgari*, I, *I libri della famiglia*, ed. C. Grayson, Bari, 1960, p. 67; R. Neu Watkins (ed. and trans.), *The Family in Renaisssance Florence: a translation of* I libri della famiglia *by Leon Battista Alberti*, Columbia, SC, 1969, pp. 79–80.

13 Matteo Palmieri, *Libro della vita civile*, Florence, 1529, p. 22; P. Tinagli, 'Womanly Virtues in

14 M. Lowry, *Nicolas Jensen and the Rise of Venetian Publishing in Renaissance Europe*, Oxford, 1991, pp. 122–3.

15 M. Ajmar, 'Exemplary Women in Renaissance Italy: Ambivalent Models of Behaviour' in Panizza, *Women in Italian Renaissance Culture*, pp. 244–64.

16 C. Jordan, *Renaissance Feminism: Literary Texts and Political Models*, Ithaca, NY and London, 1990, p. 47; M. Ajmar and D. Thornton, 'When is a Portrait not a Portrait? *Belle donne* on Maiolica and the Renaissance Praise of Local Beauties' in N. Mann and L. Syson (eds), *The Image of the Individual: Portraits of the Renaissance*, London, 1998, pp. 138–53, esp. p. 141.

17 G. Ianziti, *Humanistic Historiography under the Sforzas: Politics and Propaganda in Fifteenth-Century Milan*, Oxford, 1988, *passim*; J.M. McManamon, *Funeral Oratory and the Cultural Ideals of Italian Humanism*, Chapel Hill, NC and London, 1989, *passim*; P. Burke, 'L'art de la propagande à l'époque de Pisanello' in D. Cordellier and B. Py (eds), *Pisanello: Louvres conférences et colloques*, I, Paris, 1998, pp. 253–62.

18 J.J.G. Alexander (ed.), *The Painted Page: Italian Renaissance Book Illumination, 1450–1550*, exh. cat., Royal Academy of Arts, London, The Pierpont Morgan Library, New York, London and Munich, 1994.

19 F. Lollini, 'Le Vite di Plutarco all Malatestiana (S. XV.1, S. XV.2, S. XVII.2): proposte ed osservazioni per il periodo di transizione tra tardogotico e rinascimento nella miniatura settentrionale' in F. Lollini and P. Lucchi (eds), *Libraria Domini: I manoscritti della Biblioteca Malatestiana, testi e decorazioni*, Bologna, 1995, pp. 189–224.

20 V.H. Paltsits, 'A Renaissance Illuminated Ms. of Valerius Maximus', *New York Public Library Bulletin*, XXXIII, 1929, pp. 847–53; Alexander, *Painted Page*, pp. 106–8, cat. no. 41.

21 M.M. Donato, 'Gli eroi romai tra storia ed exemplum: I primi cicli umanistici di uomini famosi' in S. Settis (ed.), *Memoria dell'antico nel-l'arte italiana*, 3 vols, II, Turin, 1986, pp. 97–152, esp. p. 125.

22 K. Weil-Garris and J.F. D'Amico, 'The Renaissance Cardinal's Ideal Palace: a Chapter from Cortesi's *De Cardinalatu*' in H.A. Millon (ed.), *Studies in Italian Art and Architecture, 15th through 18th Centuries, Memoirs of the American Academy in Rome*, XXXV, 1980, p. 91.

23 R. Wilkins Sullivan, 'Three Ferrarese Panels on the Theme of "Death rather than Dishonour" and the Neapolitan Connection', *Zeitschrift für Kunstgeschichte*, LVII, 1994, pp. 610–25.

24 R. Bartalini in L. Bellosi (ed.), *Francesco di Giorgio e il Rinascimento a Siena, 1450–1500*, exh. cat., Chiesa di Sant'Agostino, Siena, Milan, 1993, pp. 462–9, cat. no. 103.

25 Weil-Garris and D'Amico, 'Renaissance Cardinal's Ideal Palace', p. 95.

26 G. F. Hill, *A Corpus of Italian Medals of the Renaissance before Cellini*, London, 1930, p. 8, cat. no. 23.

27 C. Brink, *Arte et Marte: Kriegskunst und Kunstliebe im Herrscherbild des 15. und 16. Jahrhunderts in Italien*, Munich and Berlin, 2000, *passim*.

28 Hill, *Corpus*, p. 12, cat. no. 41.

29 Ibid., p. 62, cat. no. 241.

30 A.D. Fraser Jenkins, 'Cosimo de' Medici's Patronage of Architecture and the Theory of Magnificence', *Journal of the Warburg and Courtauld Institutes*, XXXIII, 1970, pp. 162–70; P.L. Rubin, 'Magnificence and the Medici' in F. Ames-Lewis (ed.), *The Early Medici and their Artists*, London, 1995, pp. 37–51.

31 R. Neu Watkins, *Humanism and Liberty: Writings on Freedom from Fifteenth-Century Florence*, Columbias, SC, 1978, p. 132; Goldthwaite, *Wealth*, p. 177.

32 Platina, *De principe*, pp. 69–75; see also pp. 134–42 for his parallel views on liberality and magnificence.

33 Leon Battista Alberti, *On Painting and On Sculpture: The Latin Texts of De pictura and De statua*, ed. and trans. C. Grayson, London, 1972, pp. 106–7.

34 J. von Schlosser (ed.), *Lorenzo Ghiberti's Denkwürdigkeiten: I commentarii*, Berlin, 1912, p. 41.

35 S. Tumidei, 'Un tableau perdu de Pisanello pour l'empereur Sigismond' in Cordellier and Py, *Pisanello*, pp. 15–27, esp. p. 20.

36 W.L. Gundersheimer, *Art and Life at the Court of Ercole d'Este: the De Triumphis religionis of Giovanni Sabadino degli Arienti*, Geneva, 1972, p. 30.

37 Alberti, *Opere volgari*, I, p. 141; Neu Watkins, *Family in Renaissance Florence*, p. 142; cited by J. Woods-Marsden, *The Gonzaga of Mantua and Pisanello's Arthurian Frescoes*, Princeton, 1988, p. 141.

38 R. Goldthwaite, *The Building of Renaissance Florence: An Economic and Social History*, Baltimore and London, 1980, p. 83.

39 Goldthwaite, *Wealth*, p. 208.

40 D.S. Chambers, *A Renaissance Cardinal and His Wordly Goods: the Will and Inventory of Cardinal Francesco Gonzaga*, London, 1993, p. 81.

41 Woods-Marsden, *Gonzaga of Mantua*, p. 141.

42 Goldthwaite, *Wealth*, p. 206.

43 A. Dillon Bussi, 'Aspetti della miniatura ai tempi di Lorenzo il Magnifico' in *All'ombra del lauro: documenti della cultura in età Laurenziana*, exh. cat., Biblioteca Medicea-Laurenziana, Florence, 1992, pp. 149–60, esp. p. 152; Alexander, *Painted Page*, pp. 97–8, cat. no. 35.

44 Cited by J. Hankins, 'Cosimo de' Medici as Patron of Humanistic Literature' in F. Ames-Lewis (ed.), *Cosimo 'Il Vecchio' de' Medici*, Oxford, 1992, p. 84.

45 F.W. Kent, *Giovanni Rucellai ed il suo Zibaldone: A Florentine Patrician and his Palace*, London, 1981, II, pp. 9–98, esp. p. 40.

46 Rubin, 'Patrons and Projects', p. 46.

47 Goldthwaite, *Building*, p. 83.

48 G. Clarke, 'Magnificence and the City: Giovanni il Bentivoglio and Architecture in Fifteenth-Century Bologna', *Renaissance Studies*, XIII, 1999, pp. 397–411.

49 Gundersheimer, *Art and Life*, p. 51; Clarke, 'Magnificence and the City'.

50 Fraser Jenkins, 'Cosimo de' Medici's Patronage', pp. 162–70; Goldthwaite, *Wealth*, p. 221.

51 Weil-Garris and D'Amico, 'Renaissance Cardinal's Ideal Palace', p. 87.

52 Rubin, 'Magnificence', p. 41.

53 Weil-Garris and D'Amico, 'Renaissance Cardinal's Ideal Palace', p. 87.

54 Goldthwaite, *Building*, p. 84.

55 Luca Landucci, *Diario fiorentino dal 1450 al 1516*, ed. I De Badia, Florence, 1883, p. 62; F.W. Kent, ' "Più superba di quella di Lorenzo": Courtly and Family Interest in the Building of Filippo Strozzi's Palace', *Renaissance Quarterly*, XXX, 1977, pp. 311–23.

56 R. Goldthwaite, 'The Construction of the Strozzi Palace: the Construction Industry in Renaissance Florence', *Studies in Medieval and Renaissance History*, X, 1973, pp. 97–194; Kent, ' "Più superba" '; A. Lillie, 'The Palazzo Strozzi and Private Patronage in Fifteenth-Century Florence' in H. Millon and V. Lampugnani (eds), *The Renaissance from Brunelleschi to Michelangelo: The Representation of Architecture*, London, 1994, pp. 518–21.

57 Kent, ' "Più superba" ', pp. 317–18.

58 N. Rubinstein, review of Goldthwaite, *Building*, in *Renaissance Quarterly*, XXXV, 1982, pp. 274–8, esp. p. 274.

59 Rubin, 'Patrons and Projects', pp. 43–5.

60 Goldthwaite, *Wealth*, pp. 121–5.

61 A. Brown, 'Cosimo's Wit and Wisdom' in Ames-Lewis, *Cosimo*, pp. 95–114, esp. p. 108.

62 N. Machiavelli, quoted by P.L. Rubin, 'Art and the Imagery of Memory' in Ciapelli and Rubin, *Art*, pp. 67–85, esp. p. 70.

63 F.W. Kent, 'Individuals and Families as Patrons of Culture in Quattrocento Florence' in A. Brown (ed.), *Language and Images of Renaissance Italy*, Oxford, 1995, pp. 171–92, esp. p. 181.

64 S.K. Cohn, 'Burckhardt Revisited from Social History' in Brown, *Language and Images*, pp. 217–34.

65 Matteo Palmieri, *Della vita civile*, ed. Felice Battaglia, Bologna, 1944, p. 154.

66 Rubin, 'Magnificence', p. 39.

67 Giovanni Rucellai, *Il zibaldone quaresimale*, ed. A. Perosa, I, London, 1960, p. 118; P. Thornton, *The Italian Renaissance Interior 1400–1600*, London, 1991, p. 11.

68 On this aspect of Pontano's thought, see Goldthwaite, *Wealth*, pp. 208–9; E.S. Welch, *Art and Society in Italy, 1350–1500*, Oxford, 1997, p. 297.

69 Giovanni Pontano, *I trattati delle virtu sociali*, ed. Francesco Tateo, Rome, 1965, pp. 129, 131–2 for Latin text, pp. 270, 272 for Italian translation.

70 Palmieri, *Della vita civile*, p. 154.

71 Quoted in D. Thornton, *The Scholar in His Study: Ownership and Experience in Renaissance Italy*, New Haven and London, 1997, p. 177.

72 Goldthwaite, *Wealth*, p. 211; Rubin, 'Patrons and Projects', p. 41

73 R. Jones, 'Palla Strozzi e la sagrestia di Santa Trinita', *Rivista d'arte*, ser. iv, I, 1984, pp. 9–106, doc.140.

74 Thornton, *The Scholar*, p. 57.

75 C. Kovesi Killerby, 'Practical Problems in the Enforcement of Italian Sumptuary Law, 1200–1500' in T. Dean and K. Lowe (eds), *Crime, Society and the Law in Renaissance Italy*, Cambridge, 1994, pp. 99–120, esp. pp. 114–15; P. Allerston, 'Wedding Finery in Sixteenth-Century Venice' in T. Dean and K. Lowe, *Marriage in Italy 1300–1650*, Cambridge, 1998, pp. 25–40, esp. p. 28; J. Bridgeman, ' "Pagare le pompe": Why Quattrocento Sumptuary Laws did not work' in Panizza, *Women in Italian Renaissance Culture*, pp. 209–26.

76 Bridgeman, ' "Pagare le pompe" '.

77 R. Hale (ed.), *The Travel Journal of Antonio de Beatis*, London, 1979, p. 166; cited by Goldthwaite, *Wealth*, p. 203.

78 L. Gabel (ed.), *Memoirs of a Renaissance Pope: the Commentaries of Pius II*, New York, 1959, p. 114.

79 Poem by Il Pistoia (Antonio Camelli), quoted in A. Morselli, 'Il corredo nuziale di Caterina Pico (1474)', *Atti e memorie della Deputazione di Storia Patria per le Antiche Provincie Modenesi*, ser. viii, VIII, 1956, p. 10.

80 C. Cordiè (ed.), *Opere di Baldassare Castiglione, Giovanni della Casa, Benvenuto Cellini*, Milan and Naples, 1960, II, xxvii, p. 123.

81 Vespasiano da Bisticci, *Vite di uomoni illustri del sec. XV*, eds P. d'Ancona and E. Aeschlimann, Milan, 1951, pp. 72–3; Vespasiano da Bisticci, *Memoirs: Lives of Illustrious Men of the Fifteenth Century*, trans. W. George and E. Waters, Toronto, 1997, pp. 72–3.

82 Pontano, *I trattati*, p. 270; quoted (and translated differently) in Welch, *Art and Society*, p. 297.

83 R. Goldthwaite, 'The Economic and Social World of Italian Renaissance Maiolica', *Renaissance Quarterly*, XLII, 1989, pp. 1–32, esp. p. 25.

84 Vespasiano da Bisticci, *Vite di uomoni*, pp. 442–3; Vespasiano da Bisticci, *Memoirs,* 1997, p. 402; R. Goldthwaite, 'The Empire of Things' in P. Simons and F.W. Kent (eds), *Patronage, Art and Society in Renaissance Italy*, Oxford, 1987, pp. 153–76, esp. p. 172.

85 D. Thornton, 'Valerio Belli and After: Renaissance Gems in the British Museum', *Jewellery Studies*, 1998, pp. 11–20, esp. p. 11.

86 Rubin, 'Art and the imagery', p. 71.

87 Gundersheimer, *Art and Life*, p. 293.

88 Giovanni Boccaccio, *Opere minori in volgare: Filocolo*, Milan, 1969, II, p. 170.

89 Brown, 'Cosimo de' Medici's wit and wisdom', p. 108.

90 Thornton, *The Scholar*, p. 7.

91 D.S. Chambers (ed.), *Patrons and Artists in the Italian Renaissance*, London, 1970, pp. 47–8, doc. 24; M. Baxandall, *Giotto and the Orators: Humanist Observers of Painting in Italy and the Discovery of Pictorial Composition, 1350–1450*, Oxford, 1971, p. 19.

92 von Schlosser, *Lorenzo Ghiberti's Denkwürdigkeite*, pp. 41–2.

93 Thornton, *Italian Renaissance Interior*, p. 256, n. 9. On the status of ultramarine as a pigment, see M. Baxandall, *Painting and Experience in Fifteenth-Century Italy*, Oxford, 1972, p. 11.

94 E.S. Welch, *Art and Authority in Renaissance Milan*, New Haven and London, 1995, pp. 226–7.

95 Ibid.

96 Ibid.

97 Ibid.

98 Thornton, *Italian Renaissance Interior*, pp. 253–60, figs 281–9.

99 Ibid., p. 253.

100 S.S. Strocchia, *Death and Ritual in Renaissance Florence*, Baltimore and London, 1992, esp. pp. 149–77; Welch, *Art and Society*, pp. 189–210.

101 Welch, *Art and Society*, p. 191, 197; Cohn, 'Burckhardt Revisited', pp. 225–9; S.S. Strocchia, 'Remembering the Family: Women, Kin and Commemorative Masses in Renaissance Florence', *Renaissance Quarterly*, XLIII, 1990, pp. 635–55.

102 S.K. Cohn, *The Cult of Remembrance and the Black Death: Six Renaissance Cities in Central Italy*, Baltimore, 1992; for the tomb of Cosimo de' Medici, see D. Kent, *Cosimo de' Medici and the Florentine Renaissance: The Patron's Oeuvre*, New Haven and London, 2001, pp. 377–84; for the significance of a particular tomb type, see Butterfield, 'Monument and Memory', pp. 135–62.

103 Quoted by Kent, 'Individuals and Families', p. 183.

104 Pontano, *I trattati*, p. 249.

105 C.E. Gilbert (ed.), *Italian Art 1400–1500, Sources and Documents*, Evanstown, Ill., 1992 (rev. edn) p. 166.

106 Butterfield, 'Monument and Memory', p. 157.

107 The account of this funeral is taken from Strocchia, *Death and Ritual*, pp. 194–5.

108 A. Molho, *Marriage Alliance in Late Medieval Florence*, Cambridge, Mass., and London, 1994, pp. 341–4.

109 Pontano, *I trattati*, pp. 112–14, 256–8.

110 Ibid., pp. 113, 256.

111 Ibid., pp. 113, 257.

112 C. Kidwell, *Pontano: Poet and Prime Minister*, London, 1991, p. 271.

113 Ibid.

114 F.P. Luiso, *Studi su l'epistolario di Leonardo Bruni*, Rome, 1980, p. 77.

115 Kent, *Cosimo de' Medici*, p. 217.

116 P. Viti (ed.), *Opere letterarie e politiche di Leonardo Bruni*, Turin, 1996, pp. 44, 640.

117 We are grateful to Caroline Elam and Alison Brown for this translation and for their comments.

118 Allerston, 'Wedding Finery', p. 29.

119 Welch, *Art and Society*, p. 280.

Chapter 2

1 C. Grayson, 'Una intercenale inedita di L.B. Alberti: *Uxoria*', *Italia medioevale e umanistica*, III, 1960, pp. 291–307; Leon Battista Alberti, *Dinner Pieces: a Translation of the* Intercenales, ed. and trans. D. Marsh, Binghamton, NY, 1987, pp. 135, 140, 147; R. Cardini, 'Per *Uxoria* dell' Alberti', *Rivista di letteratura italiana*, XI, 1–2, 1993, pp. 215–81.

2 Neu Watkins, *The Family in Renaissance Florence*, pp. 110–15; see also pp. 115–19 on beauty and dowries.

3 R. Hyatte, 'Complementary Humanistic Models of Marriage and Male *Amicitia* in Fifteenth-Century Literature' in J. Haseldine (ed.), *Friendship in Medieval Europe*, Thrupp, Glos., 1999, pp. 251–61, esp. pp. 251–3, 257.

4 J.K. Lydecker, The Domestic Setting of the Arts in Renaissance Florence, PhD thesis, Johns Hopkins University, Baltimore, 1987, Ann Arbor Microfilms, pp. 145–65.

5 A. Molho, *Marriage Alliance in Late Medieval Florence*, Cambridge, Mass. and London, 1994, pp. 182–3.

6 A. Franceschini, *Artisti a Ferrara in età umanistica e rinascimentale: testimonianze archivistiche*, 2 vols, Ferrara and Rome, I, 1993, p. 394, doc. 705a.

7 Ibid., pp. 302–3, doc. 604d. Doc. 604e records the subject matter and expensive pigments of the two images of the Virgin (a Virgin and Child and a Coronation) purchased for Camilla and Beatrice.

8 J. Manca, *The Art of Ercole de' Roberti*, Cambridge, 1992, pp. 199–205, docs 22, 24, 26, 29, 31, 35.

9 See e.g. L. Beltrami, *La guardaroba di Lucrezia Borgia*, Milan, 1903, *passim*.

10 Marco Antonio Altieri, *Li Nuptiali* , ed. E. Narducci, Rome, 1995, pp. 12, 51.

11 For Florentine patrician practice, see B. Witthoft, 'Marriage Rituals and Marriage Chests in Quattrocento Florence', *artibus et historiae*, III, 1982, pp. 43–59; for customs of Venetian patricians and citizens, see P. Allerston, 'Wedding Finery in Sixteenth-Century Venice' in T. Dean and K. Lowe (eds), *Marriage in Italy, 1300–1650*, Cambridge, 1998, pp. 25–40; D.S. Chambers and B. Pullan (eds), *Venice: A Documentary History, 1450–1630*, Oxford, 1992, pp. 263–5; for Roman patricians, see Altieri, *Li Nuptiali*, *passim*.

12 Molho, *Marriage Alliance*, p. 143; Francesco Guicciardini, *Opere inedite, Ricordi*, Florence, 1867, p. 117.

13 Guicciardini, *Opere inedite*; Molho, *Marriage Alliance*, p. 143.

14 C. Murphy, 'Lavinia Fontana and Female Life Cycle Experience in Late Sixteenth-Century Bologna' in G.A. Johnson and S.F. Matthews Grieco (eds), *Picturing Women in Renaissance and Baroque Italy,* Cambridge 1997, pp. 111–38, esp. pp. 113–14.

15 E. Rosenthal, 'The Position of Women in Renaissance Florence: Neither Autonomy nor Subjection' in P. Denley and C. Elam (eds), *Florence and Italy: Essays in honour of Nicolai Rubinstein*, London,1988, pp. 368–81; S. Chojnacki, 'The power of Love: wives and husbands in Renaissance Venice' in M. Erler and M. Kowaleski (eds), *Women and Power in the Middle Ages*, Athens, Ga., 1988, pp. 126–48; C. Klapisch Zuber, 'The Griselda Complex: Dowry and Marriage Gifts in the Quattrocento', *Women, Family and Ritual in Renaissance Italy*, Chicago, 1985, pp. 213–47.

16 Cited by J. Musacchio, *The Art and Ritual of Childbirth in Renaissance Italy*, New Haven and London, 1999, p. 20.

17 Molho, *Marriage Alliance*, pp. 27–49; Musacchio, *Art and Ritual*, p. 19.

18 Thornton, *Italian Renaissance Interior*, p. 151, fig. 166.

19 On clothing, see E.S. Welch, 'New, old and secondhand culture: the case of the Renaissance sleeve' in G. Neher and R. Shepherd (eds), *Revaluing Renaissance Art*, Aldershot, 2000, pp. 101–20.

20 R. Levi Pisetzky, *Storia del costume in Italia*, Milan, 1966, III, pp. 111–21.

21 A. Ceruti, 'Il corredo nuziale di Bianca M. Sforza–Visconti, sposa dell'imperatore Massimiliano I', *Archivio storico lombardo*, II, 1875, pp. 51–75, esp. p. 61.

22 Beltrami, *La guardaroba di Lucrezia Borgia*, p. 26.

23 Molho, *Marriage Alliance*, pp. 128–9.

24 H. Gregory (ed.), *Selected Letters of Alessandra Strozzi*, bilingual edn, Berkeley, Los Angeles and London, 1997, pp. 29–31, translation altered here. Cited in Molho, *Marriage Alliance*, pp. 128–9.

25 A.W.B. Randolph, 'Performing the Bridal Body in Fifteenth-Century Florence', *Art History*, 21/2, January 1998, pp. 183–200, esp. p. 191.

26 Gregory, *Selected Letters*, pp. 150–1, translation altered; Randolph, 'Performing the Bridal Body', p. 192.

27 Randolph, 'Performing the Bridal Body', p. 187.

28 Klapisch Zuber, 'The Griselda Complex', p. 225, n. 9; Randolph, 'Performing the Bridal Body', pp. 190–1.

29 C. Mazzi, *Due provisioni suntuarie fiorentine*, Florence, 1908, p. 5; translated by Randolph, 'Performing the Bridal Body', p. 189.

30 Francesco di Matteo Castellani, *Ricordanze*, ed. G. Ciapelli, Florence, 1992, p. 86.

31 Ibid., p. 128.

32 Ibid., p. 129.

33 Randolph, 'Performing the Bridal Body', pp. 188–9.

34 L. Beltrami, *Gli sponsali di Galeazzo Maria Sforza*, Milan, 1893, *passim*; F. Malaguzzi Valeri, *Pittori lombardi del Quattrocento*, Milan, 1902, p. 128.

35 G.F. Hill, *A Corpus of Italian Medals of the Renaissance before Cellini*, London,1930, p. 21.

36 J. Manca, *Cosmè Tura: The Life and Art of a Painter in Estense Ferrara*, Oxford, 2000, p. 19.

37 A. Luzio, 'Isabella d'Este e Francesco Gonzaga, promessi sposi, *Archivo storico lombardo*, ser. iv, IX, 1908, pp. 34–68, esp. p. 56.

38 M.G. Ciardi Dupre Dal Poggetto (ed.), *L'oreficeria nella Firenze del Quattrocento*, exh. cat., Florence, 1977, p. 296; P.L. Rubin and A. Wright, *Renaissance Florence: The Art of the 1470s*, exh. cat. National Gallery, London, 1999, p. 79, fig. 51.

39 Randolph, 'Performing the Bridal Body', p. 187.

40 G.H. Tait (ed.), *Jewellery through 7000 Years*, London, 1976, p. 162, cat. no. 269 and references; J. Cherry, 'The Medieval Jewellery from the Fishpool, Nottinghamshire, Hoard', *Archaeologia*, 104, 1973, pp. 307–21, esp. pp. 315–16; *Catalog der Kunstsammlungen des Hugo Garthe*, sale cat., Cologne, 28 May 1877, lots 761–3; K. Reynolds Brown, 'Six Gothic brooches at the Cloisters' in E.C. Parker (ed.), *The Cloisters: Studies in Honor of the Fiftieth Anniversary*, New York, 1992, pp. 409–19, esp. p. 417, fig. 10a for related jewel; *The Middle Ages: Treasures from the Cloisters and the Metropolitan Museum of Art*, exh. cat., Los Angeles County Museum, Los Angeles, 1970, p. 249; M. Rosenberg, 'Studien uber Goldschmiede-kunst in der Sammlung Figdor, Wien', *Kunst und Kunsthandwerk,* XIV, 1911, p. 329 for a similar jewel.

41 R.W. Lightbown, *Medieval European Jewellery with a catalogue of the collection in the Victoria & Albert Museum*, London, 1992, p. 177.

42 S. Bandera in A. Mottola Molfino and M. Natale (eds), *Le muse e il principe: arte di corte nel Rinascimento padano*, exh. cat., Museo Poldi Pezzoli, Milan, Modena, 1991, I (*catalogo*), pp. 93–7, cat. no. 19.

43 P. Venturelli, 'Il *fermaglio cum l'angelo* di Bianca Maria Visconti Sforza nel dipinto alla Pinacoteca di Brera' in L. Golay, P. Luscher and P.A. Mariaux (eds), *Florilegium: scritti di storia dell'arte in onore di Carlo Bertelli*, Milan, 1995, pp. 116–18; P. Venturelli, *Gioelli e gioellieri milanesi: storia, arte, moda (1450–1630)*, Milan, 1996, pp. 78–9, pl. p. 79.

44 Venturelli, 'Il *fermaglio*', p. 116; P. Venturelli, *Glossario e documenti per la gioelleria milanese (1459–1631)*, Milan, 1999, pp. 145–6.

45 Tait, *Jewellery*, p. 162, cat. no. 269.

46 On the wearing life of silks, see L. Mola, *The Silk Industry in Renaissance Venice*, Baltimore and London, 2000, p. 95.

47 J. Pope-Hennessy and K. Christiansen, *Secular Painting in Fifteenth-Century Tuscany: Birth Trays,* Cassone *Panels and Portraits*, Metropolitan Museum of Art, New York, 1980, p. 63; Y. Hackenbroch, *Renaissance Jewellery*, Munich, 1979, p. 8; Venturelli, 'Il *fermaglio*', p. 118;

48 Venturelli, 'Il *fermaglio*', p. 118, n. 17; Randolph, 'Performing the Bridal Body', pp. 194–5, figs 11–12.

49 See A. Verde, 'Inventario e divisione dei beni di Pierfilippo Pandolfini', *Italian medioevale e umanistica*, XXXI, 1988, pp. 259–395, esp. p. 314 for items put aside for the dowry gifts for his daughter Cornelia; Randolph, 'Performing the Bridal Body', p. 192.

50 J. Herald, *Renaissance Dress in Italy*, London, 1981, pp. 178–9, 201, figs 111, 128; M. Koster, 'Reconsidering St Catherine of Bologna with three donors by the Baroncelli Master of Bruges', *Simiolus*, 26, 1–2, 1998, pp. 5–17; N. Roio, 'Francesco Francia e il Maestro dei ritratti Baroncelli', *Studi di storia dell'arte*, 10, 1999, pp. 261–5. Herald and Koster date the panel to the 1490s or even later; Lorne Campbell, however, considers the panel to date to about 1470. We are grateful to him and to Ernst Wegelin for their views on this painting.

51 M. Davies, *National Gallery Catalogues: the Early Italian Schools*, rev. edn, London, 1961, pp. 221–2; C. Baker and T. Henry, *The National Gallery: Complete Illustrated Catalogue*, London, 1995, p. 18.

52 Randolph, 'Performing the Bridal Body', p. 187.

53 Ibid.

54 Chambers and Pullan, *Venice*, p. 265 for marriage of Giustina Zaccaria to Lodovico Bianco.

55 A.M. Hind, *Nielli, chiefly Italian, of the XV Century: Plates, Sulphur Casts and Prints Preserved in the British Museum*, London 1936, p. 34, cat. nos 89–94.

56 Hackenbroch, *Renaissance Jewellery*, p. 10, n. 4.

57 Ibid., fig. 24; Venturelli, *Gioelli*, p. 111; Welch, *Art and Authority*, pp. 243–4, p. 253, fig. 135.

58 Welch, *Art and Authority*, p. 244, fig. 135.

59 H. Brigstocke, *A Poet in Paradise, Lord Lindsay and Christian Art*, exh. cat., National Gallery of Scotland, Edinburgh, 2000, p. 94, cat. no. 27.

60 E. Cropper, 'The Beauty of Woman: Problems in the Rhetoric of Renaissance Portraiture' in M.W. Ferguson, M. Quilligan and N.J. Vickers (eds) *Rewriting the Renaissance: the Discourses of Sexual Difference in Early Modern Europe*, Chicago and London, 1986, pp. 175–90; P. Simons, 'Women in Frames: the Eye, the Gaze, the Profile in Renaissance Portraiture', *History Workshop Journal*, 25, 1988, pp. 4–30; P. Simons, 'Portraiture, Portrayal and Idealization: Ambiguous Individualism in Representations of Renaissance Women' in Brown, *Language and Images*, Oxford, 1995, pp. 263–311; L. Syson, 'Consorts, Mistresses and Exemplary Women: the Female Medallic Portrait in Fifteenth-Century Italy' in S. Currie and P. Motture (eds), *The Sculpted Object, 1400–1700*, Aldershot, 1997, pp. 43–64.

61 Marsilio Ficino, *Commentarium in Convivium Platonis: De amore*, ed. R. Marcel, Paris, 1956, pp. 178–9.

62 J. Giacomotti, *Catalogue des majoliques des Musées Nationaux*, Paris, 1974, p. 245, cat. no. 801; M. Ajmar and D. Thornton, 'When is a Portrait not a Portrait? *Belle donne* on Maiolica and the Renaissance Praise of Local Beauties' in Mann and Syson, *The Image of the Individual*, pp. 138–49, esp. p. 145, n. 33.

63 Hill, *Corpus*, pp. 206–7, cat. no. 796; L. Syson in S.K. Scher (ed.), *The Currency of Fame: Portrait Medals of the Renaissance*, exh. cat., National Gallery of Art, Washington, The Frick Collection, New York, New York, 1994, p. 121, cat. no. 36.

64 K. Lydecker, 'Il patriziato fiorentino e la committenza artistica per la casa' in *I ceti dirigenti nella toscana del Quattrocento*, Impruneta, 1987, p. 216 for a mirror acquired for a marital bedchamber in 1472; Thornton, *Italian Renaissance Interior*, pp. 236, 385; Rubin and Wright, *Renaissance Florence*, p. 264, cat. no. 80.

65 See e.g. J.M. Fletcher, 'Bernardo Bembo and Leonardo's portrait of Ginevra de' Benci', *Burlington Magazine*, CXXXI, July–December 1989, pp. 811–16; A. Dülberg, *Privatporträts: Geschichte und Ikonologie einer Gattung im 15. und 16. Jahrhundert*, Berlin, 1990, pp. 228–9, 237–8, cat. nos 169, 185, pls 55, 56, 68; M. Warnke, 'Individuality as Argument: Piero della Francesca's Portrait of the Duke and Duchess of Urbino' in Mann and Syson, *Image of the Individual*, pp. 81–91, esp. p. 83.

66 J. Pope-Hennessy, *Catalogue of Italian Sculpture in the Victoria and Albert Museum*, London, 1964, Vol. 1, pp. 270–1, cat. no. 284.

67 B. Rackham, *The Victoria and Albert Museum, Catalogue of Italian Maiolica*, 2 vols, London, 1940, I, p. 121, cat. no. 351; T. Wilson, *Ceramic Art of the Italian Renaissance*, exh. cat., British Museum, London, 1987, p. 146, cat. no. 227; Ajmar and Thornton, 'When is a Portrait … ?', p. 144.

68 G.H. Tait, *The Golden Age of Venetian Glass*, London, 1979, p. 36, cat. no. 22; P. Hills, *Venetian Colour: Marble, Mosaic, Painting and Glass, 1250–1550*, New Haven and London 1999, p. 125.

69 T. Clarke, '*Lattimo*: a Group of Venetian Glass Enamelled on an Opaque White Ground', *Journal of Glass Studies*, XVI, 1974, pp. 22–56, esp. p. 35.

70 C. Dempsey, *The Portrayal of Love: Botticelli's Primavera and Humanist Culture in the Time of Lorenzo Il Magnifico*, Princeton 1992, pp. 111–12; Rubin and Wright, *Renaissance Florence*, p. 339, cat. no. 89.

71 Rubin and Wright, *Renaissance Florence*, p. 339, cat. no. 89.

72 J. Russell Sale, 'An Iconographic Program by Marco Parenti', *Renaissance Quarterly*, no. 27, 1974, pp. 293–9.

73 Ibid., p. 299 for the letter; Kent, *Cosimo de' Medici* pp. 108–10.

74 Venturelli, *Gioelli*, pp. 183–4; Welch, *Art and Authority*, p. 7, fig. 5.

75 G.H. Tait, *Seven Thousand Years of Jewellery*, London 1986, p. 144, cat. no. 330.

76 Hind, *Nielli*, p. 56, cat. no. 247.

77 Lightbown, *Medieval European Jewellery*, pp. 327–9, p. 328 for this plaque.

78 Hind, *Nielli*, p. 34, cat. no. 87–8.

79 See e.g. Baker and Henry, *National Gallery*; p. 633, cat. no. 923.

80 V. Cian (ed.), *Il Libro del Cortegiano del Conte Baldasar Castiglione*, Florence, n.d., p. 353 (III.26). The translation is from Baldassare Castiglione, *The Book of the Courtier* (trans. G. Bull), rev. edn, London, 1973, p. 241.

81 P. Tinagli, 'Womanly Virtues in Florentine Marriage Furnishings' in Panizza, *Women in Italian Renaissance Culture and Society*, pp. 265–84.

82 Johnson and Matthews Grieco, *Picturing Women*, p. 3.

83 J. Musacchio, 'The Rape of the Sabine Women on Marriage Panels' in Dean and Lowe, *Marriage in Italy*, pp. 66–89, fig. 8.

84 Hackenbroch, *Renaissance Jewellery*, p. 24, fig. 41.

85 D.A. Brown, P. Humfrey and M. Lucco, *Lorenzo Lotto, Il Genio inquieto del Rinascimento*, exh. cat., Accademia Carrara, Bergamo, 1998, p. 187, cat. no. 38.

86 Ibid., pp. 185–7, cat. no. 38.

87 Ibid., pp. 184–7, cat. no. 38; N. Penny and J. Dunkerton, 'Two paintings by Lorenzo Lotto in the National Gallery', *National Gallery Technical Bulletin*, 19, 1998, pp. 57–63; Johnson and Matthews Grieco, *Picturing Women*, pp. 2–3.

88 On Lucretia and how she was viewed in the Renaissance, see C. Baskins, *Cassone Painting, Humanism and Gender in Early Modern Italy*, Cambridge,1998, pp. 128–59.

89 Randolph, 'Performing the Bridal Body', p. 196; Fra Bernardino of Siena, *Le prediche volgari inedite*, ed. P. Dionisio Pacetti, Siena, 1935, p. 413.

90 I. Origo, *The World of San Bernardino*, London, 1963, pp. 55–9.

91 Randolph, 'Performing the Bridal Body', p. 196.

92 Witthoft, 'Marriage Rituals', pp. 43–59, esp. p. 45.

93 Thornton, *Italian Renaissance Interior*, pp. 204, 383.

94 Ibid., p. 383.

95 O.M. Dalton, *Ivory Carving of the Christian Era with Examples from Mohammedan Art and Carvings in Bone in the Department of British and Medieval Antiquities in the British Museum*, London, 1909, p. 139, cat. no. 403 for casket from the Meyrick gift; for its attribution, see E. Merlini, 'La Bottega degli Embriachi e i cofanetti eburnei fra

Trecento e Quattrocento: una proposta di classificazione', *Arte Cristiana*, 727, 1988, pp. 267–82; on Susanna, see C. Baskins, '*La festa di Susanna*: Virtue on Trial in Renaissance Sacred Drama and Painted Wedding Chests', *Art History*, 14, 1991, pp. 329–44.

96 J. Bliss, 'A Cuir Bouilli Case and other Decorative Arts from the Italian Renaissance', *Arts in Virginia*, 29/1, 1989, pp. 16–39, esp. p. 33, n. 56.

97 Dempsey, *Portrayal of Love*, p. 111.

98 Rubin and Wright, *Renaissance Florence*, pp. 340–2, cat. nos 90–2.

99 G. Swarzenski, 'A Marriage Casket and its Moral', *Bulletin of the Museum of Fine Arts, Boston*, XLV, no. 261, 1947, pp. 55–62; A.M. Hind, *Early Italian Engraving*, London, 1938, vol. 1, pp. 85–7.

100 For a letter of 1513 from Caterina Imhoff in Nuremberg to Enders Imhoff in Venice, asking him to procure her there a Virgin and Child with a candlestick in the lower part of the frame as seen in Venetian bedchambers, see T. Eser, 'Bring mir ein Marienbild mit', *Spiegel der Seligkeit, privates Bild und Frömmigkeit im Spätmittelalter*, Nuremberg, 2000, p. 49. Caterina went on to announce a birth in the family.

101 G. Johnson, 'Art or Artefact? Madonna and Child Reliefs in the Early Renaissance' in Currie and Motture *Sculpted Object*, pp. 1–17, esp pp. 5, 9; J. Musacchio, 'The Madonna and Child, a Host of Saints, and Domestic Devotion in Renaissance Florence' in G. Neher and R. Shepherd (eds), *Revaluing Renaissance Art*, Aldershot, 2000, pp. 147–64.

102 Johnson, 'Art or Artefact?', p. 15, n. 27.

103 Klapisch Zuber, *Women, Family and Ritual*, pp. 311–13.

104 Musacchio, *Art and Ritual*, p. 137, fig. 130.

105 J. Cherry, *The Middleham Jewel and Ring*, York, 1994, p. 30.

106 Ibid.

107 C. Santoro, 'Un registro di doti sforzesche', *Archivio storico lombardo*, LXXXX, 1953, pp. 177–84, esp. pp. 177–8; Venturelli, *Glossario e documenti*, p. 154 for Anna Sforza, p. 156 for Angela Sforza Visconti.

108 G. Aiazzi, *Ricordi storici di Filippo di Cino Rinuccini dal 1282 al 1460 colla continuazione di Alamanno e Neri suoi figli*, Florence, 1840, p. 260.

109 J. Cherry, 'Containers for Agnus Dei', forthcoming article for a festschrift for David Buckton, ed. C. Entwistle; Tait, *Jewellery through 7000 Years*, cat. no. 273 and references; Klapisch Zuber, *Women, Family and Ritual*, p. 149, fig. 7.1 for painting of the Madonna della Pergola by Bernardino di Antonio Detti, Museo Civico, Pistoia. This painting and the charms illustrated in it are to be discussed in detail by Jacqueline Musacchio in a forthcoming article; other accessories associated with fertility and childbirth are discussed by the same author in 'Weasels and Pregnancy in Renaissance Italy', *Renaissance Studies*, XV/2, 2001, forthcoming.

110 J.W. Pommeranz, *Pastigliakästchen*, Münster and New York, 1995, p. 127, no. 32.

111 Musacchio, *Art and Ritual*, pp. 129–31, figs 122–32.

112 Ibid., pp. 66, 129, fig. 120.

113 Ibid., p. 132.

114 J. Musacchio, 'Imaginative conceptions in Renaissance Italy' in Johnson and. Matthews Grieco, *Picturing Women*, pp. 42–60, esp. p. 54 for the origins of this saying.

115 Witthoft, 'Marriage Rituals', p. 45.

116 Altieri, *Li Nuptali*, p. 12 for explanation and p. 51 for text.

117 Witthoft, 'Marriage Rituals', p. 45.

118 Giacomotti, *Catalogue des majoliques*, p. 222, cat. no. 724.

119 G. Ruggieri, *The Boundaries of Eros: Sex Crime and Sexuality in Renaissance Venice*, Oxford, 1985, pp. 28, 30.

120 Thornton, *The Scholar*, p. 95.

121 J. Mallet, 'Un calamaio in maiolica di Boston', *Faenza*, LXII, 1976, pp. 79–81, fig. XXV.

122 M. Miglio and A. Modigliani, *Li Nuptiali di Marco Antonio Altieri pubblicati da Enrico Narducci*, Rome, 1995, p. 9; Klapish Zuber, *Women, Family and Ritual*, pp. 247–60.

123 Miglio and Modigliani, *Li Nuptiali*, p. 51.

124 Witthoft, 'Marriage Rituals', p. 46; Chambers and Pullan, *Venice*, pp. 263–5.

125 Klapisch Zuber, *Women, Family and Ritual*, pp. 213–47 esp. pp. 231–41.

126 Ibid., p. 231, n. 67.

127 A. Ward, J. Cherry, C. Gere and B. Cartledge, *The Ring from Antiquity to the Twentieth Century*, London, 1981, p. 84, cat. no. 197.

128 O.M. Dalton, *The Franks Bequest: Catalogue of the Finger Rings, Early Christian, Byzantine, Teutonic, medieval and later*, London, 1912, p. 157, cat. no. 984.

129 Beltrami, *La guardaroba di Lucrezia Borgia*, p. 33.

130 L. Frati, *La vita privata di Bologna*, Bologna, 1900, p. 55.

131 Witthoft, 'Marriage Rituals', p. 49.

132 Tait, *Venetian Glass*, p. 34, cat. no. 17.

133 C. James, 'The Palazzo Bentivoglio in 1487', *Mitteilungen des Kunsthistorischen Institutes in Florenz*, XLI, 1997, pp. 188–94; B. Preyer, 'Planning for Visitors at Florentine Palaces', *Renaissance Studies*, 12, 1998, pp. 357–72, esp. pp. 362, 369–70.

134 Thornton, *Italian Renaissance Interior*, fig. 101.

135 Castellani, *Ricordanze*, p. 50.

136 Cited in R.W. Lightbown, 'Giovanni Chellini, Donatello and Antonio Rosellino', *Burlington Magazine*, CIV, 1962, pp. 102–4, p. 103.

137 W. Boulting, *Woman in Italy*, London, 1910, p. 90.

138 The beginning of this tradition is impossible to trace. But see G. Ballardini, 'Una coppa d'amore al Museo Nazionale di Ravenna' in G. Ballardini, *Note di critica ceramica*, Faenza, 1929, pp. 123–45, esp. pp. 135, 137; J. Poole, *Italian Maiolica and Incised Slipware in the Fitzwilliam Museum, Cambridge*, Cambridge, 1995, p. 183, cat. no. 255.

139 Rackham, *Italian Maiolica*, I, pp. 49–50, cat. no. 162.

140 Ibid., cat. no. 408.

141 Cited by Baskins, *Cassone Painting*, p. 21.

142 E. Callmann, *Apollonio di Giovanni*, London, 1974, p. 71, cat. no. 45, fig. 189; Witthoft, 'Marriage Rituals', pp. 46–7.

143 Franceschini, *Artisti a Ferrara*, I, p. 295, doc. 600y, pp. 302–3, doc. 604d.

144 Rubin and Wright, *Renaissance Florence*, p. 315, cats 78–9.

145 For recent studies see B. Witthoft, 'Riti nuziali e loro iconografia' in M. De Giorgio and C. Klapisch Zuber (eds), *Storia del matrimonio*, Rome and Bari, 1996, p. 138; Baskins, *Cassone Painting, passim*; Musacchio, 'Rape of the Sabine Women'; Rubin and Wright, *Renaissance Florence*, p. 316, cat. nos 78–9; Tinagli, 'Womanly Virtues', pp. 265–84.

146 E.H. Gombrich, 'Apollonio di Giovanni: a Florentine Cassoni Workshop seen through the Eyes of a Humanist Poet', *Norm and Form: Studies in the Art of the Renaissance*, I, 4th edn, Oxford, 1985, pp. 11–28, esp. p. 16; Musacchio, *Art and Ritual*, p. 132, fig. 128.

147 Thornton, *Italian Renaissance Interior*, p. 204.

148 M. Phillips, *The Memoir of Marco Parenti*, London, 1987, pp. 40–1; Lydecker, Domestic Setting, pp. 112–23; Lydecker, 'Il patriziato fiorentino', pp. 209–21, esp. pp. 213–24.

149 Callmann, *Apollonio*, pp. 25–38.

150 Ibid., p. 25.

151 Baskins, *Cassone Painting*, pp. 2, 21.

152 Giovanni Bocaccio, *The Decameron*, trans. G.M. Rigby, 2 vols, London, 1930, I, 2.5, p. 81.

153 Ibid., II, p. 199 (8.8).

154 R.M. San Juan, 'Mythology, Women and Private Life: The Myth of Eurydice in Italian Furniture Painting', *Art History*, 15, 1992, pp. 127–45; Baskins, *Cassone Painting*, pp. 128–86.

155 Thornton, *Italian Renaissance Interior*, figs 107, 113–16.

156 J. Pope-Hennessy, *Italian Renaissance Sculpture*, London, 1958, p. 12.

157 Lydecker, Domestic Setting, p. 173, n. 40.

158 Rubin and Wright, *Renaissance Florence*, p. 317.

159 J. Bruce Ross, 'The Middle Class Child in Urban Italy, 14th to early 16th Centuries' in L. de Mause (ed.), *The History of Childhood*, New York, 1974, pp. 183–228.

160 See e.g. Isabella d'Este, for whom, L. Frati, 'Giuochi ed amori alla corte d' Isabella d'Este', *Archivio storico lombardo*, ser. ii, IX, 1898, pp. 350–65, esp. p. 352; Thornton, *Italian Renaissance Interior*, p. 288.

161 Leon Battista Alberti, *De re aedificatoria*, V.17.

162 I. MacLean, *The Renaissance Notion of Women: a Study in the Fortunes of Scholasticism and Medical Science in European Intellectual Life*, Cambridge, 1980, pp. 54, 61–2.

163 Welch, *Art and Society*, pp. 285–6

164 Callmann, *Apollonio*, pp. 36–7.

165 Thornton, *The Scholar*, p. 4.

166 Musacchio, *Art and Ritual*, pp. 73–7, figs 57–8; Thornton, *The Scholar*, p. 6.

167 C.M. Kauffmann, *Victoria and Albert Museum: Catalogue of Foreign Paintings*, I, *Before 1800*, London, 1973, p. 13, cat. no. 10; Musacchio, *Art and Ritual*, p. 72, fig. 56.

168 G. Vasari, *Le Vite de' più eccellenti pittori, scultori ed architettori*, 9 vols, ed. G. Milanesi, Florence, 1878–1906, II, 1878, pp. 147–8.

169 Baskins, *Cassone Painting*, 1998, pp. 9–10 and references.

170 Thornton, *The Scholar*, p. 86.

171 Lydecker, Domestic Setting, pp. 286–7.

172 R. Jones, 'Palla Strozzi e la sagrestia di Santa Trinita', *Rivista d'arte*, ser. iv, XXXVII, 1984,

pp. 95–101, esp. p. 101; trans. A. Lillie, 'Memory of Place: *Luogo* and Lineage in the Fifteenth-Century Florentine Countryside' in Ciapelli and Rubin, *Art*, pp. 195–214, esp. p. 209.

Chapter 3

1 T. Wilson, *Ceramic Art of the Italian Renaissance*, exh. cat., British Museum, London, 1987, pp. 87–8, cat. no. 134.

2 P.P. Bober, *Drawing after the Antique by Amico Aspertini: Sketchbooks in the British Museum*, Studies of the Warburg Institute, 21, London, 1957, p. 49, fig. 11; P.P. Bober and R. Rubinstein, *Renaissance Artists and Antique Sculpture: A Handbook of Sources*, Oxford, 1986, p. 109, no. 74; G. Agosti, 'Precisioni su un "Baccanale" perduto del Signorelli', *Prospettiva*, XXX, 1982, pp. 70–7; B.L. Holman, 'A "subtle artifice": Giulio Romano's *Salt Cellar with Satyrs* for Federico II Gonzaga', *Quaderni di Palazzo Te*, VIII, 2000, pp. 56–67, esp. p. 67, n. 91.

3 Diodorus Siculus, *Bibliotheke Historike*, 4.84.

4 E. Wind, *Pagan Mysteries in the Renaissance*, London, 1958, pp. 158–76.

5 U. Geese, 'Antike als Programm: Der Statuenhof des Belvedere im Vatikan' in *Natur und Antike*, exh. cat., Liebighaus, Museum alter Plastik, Frankfurt, 1985, pp. 24–50, esp. pp. 42–6; H.H. Brummer, *The Statue Court in the Vatican Belvedere*, Stockholm, 1970, pp. 146–52.

6 D.S. Chambers, *Patrons and Artists in the Italian Renaissance*, London, 1970, pp. 25–9, doc. 15.

7 'Il poeta el pittor Vanno di pare
Et tira il lor ardire tutto ad un segno
Si come espresso in queste carte appare
Fregiare dopre e dartificio degno
Di questo Roma ci puo essempio dare
Roma ricetto dogni chiaro ingegno
Da le cui grotte ove mai non saggiorna
Hor tanta luce a si bella arte torna.'
K. Oberhuber, 'Observations on Perino as a Draughtsman', *Master Drawings*, IV, 1966, pp. 170–82, esp. p. 172; E.H. Gombrich, *The Sense of Order: A Study in the Psychology of Decorative Art*, London, 1984, p. 280; M. Snodin and M. Howard, *A Social History of Ornament since 1450*, London and New Haven, 1996, pp. 38–9; T. Clifford and M. Connell in T. Clifford (ed.), *Designs of Desire: Architectural and Ornament Prints and Drawings, 1500–1850*, exh. cat., The Burrell Gallery, Glasgow, and the National Gallery of Scotland, Edinburgh, Edinburgh, 1999, pp. 58–9, cat. no. 11.

8 G. Pontano, *Trattati delle virtù sociali*, ed. F. Tateo, Rome, 1965, pp. 133, 274.

9 B. Corio, *Historia di Milano*, Venice, 1565, p. 1031, who called it a 'triumphant spectacle'; C.A. Vianello, 'Testimonianze venete su Milano e la Lombardia negli anni 1492–95', *Archivio storico lombardo*, n.s., IV, 1939, pp. 402–23, esp. p. 413. In addition to the coins the ambassadors saw 'around sixty very large silver vases of supreme beauty, all worked with enamels and most minutely'.

10 L. Fusco and G. Corti, 'New Documents for Lorenzo de' Medici as a Collector of Antiquities and Rare Objects, 1465–92', forthcoming. We are very grateful to Laurie Fusco for sharing this

document, which has been published only fragmentarily, with us.

11 R. Hatfield, 'Some Unknown Descriptions of the Medici Palace in 1459', *The Art Bulletin*, LII, 1970, pp. 232–49.

12 Thornton, *The Scholar*, p. 32.

13 C.M. Brown, ' "Lo insaciabile desiderio nostro de cose antique": new documents on Isabella d'Este's collection of antiquities' in C.H. Clough (ed.), *Cultural Aspects of the Italian Renaissance: Essays in Honour of Paul Oskar Kristeller*, Manchester and New York, 1976, pp. 330, 347, n. 37.

14 V. Mancini, *Antiquari, virtuosi e artisti: Saggi sul collezionismo tra Padova e Venezia alla metà del cinquecento*, Padua, 1995, pp. 41–3.

15 E.H. Gombrich, 'The Style *all'antica*: Imitation and Assimilation' in E.H. Gombrich, *Norm and Form: Studies in the Art of The Renaissance I*, 3rd edn, London and New York, 1978, pp. 122–8.

16 G. Campori, *Raccolta di cataloghi ed inventarii inediti*, Modena, 1870, p. 1. Also, for fabric, *uno drapo da cuna lavora de oro et de seta facto alanticha*, part of the dowry of Caterina Pico of Mirandola, see A. Morselli, 'Il corredo nuziale di Caterina Pico (1474)', *Atti e memorie della Deputazione di Storia Patria per le Antiche Provincie Modenesi*, ser. viii, VIII, 1956, p. 10 [offprint]; for jewellery, *uno anelo al'anticha* in 1496 inventory of the estate of Gianfrancesco Gonzaga, see A. Hersey Allison, 'The bronzes of Pier Jacopo Alari-Bonacolsi, called Antico', *Jahrbuch der kunsthisorischen Sammulungen in Wien*, 89/90, 1993–4, p. 272, doc. 10; for silver, Manca, *Cosmè Tura*, pp. 214–15, doc. 79 (1473); Campori, *Raccolta*, p. 11; for picture frames, Campori, *Raccolta*, p. 219, doc. 89 (1475: *una anchona de intaio cum foiami minuti minuti e lavori alantiqua*).

17 Brown, 'New Documents', p. 331.

18 D. Cordellier (ed.), 'Documenti e Fonti su Pisanello (1395–1581 circa)', *Verona Illustrata: Rivista del Museo di Castelvecchio*, VIII, 1995, pp. 160–2, doc. 74.

19 L. Barkan, *Unearthing the Past: Archaeology and Aesthetics in the Making of Renaissance Culture*, New Haven and London, 1999, pp. 89–117.

20 Pliny, *Natural History*, XXXVII, 20.

21 R. Bagemihl, 'The Trevisan Collection', *Burlington Magazine*, CXXXV, 1993, pp. 559–63.

22 M. Spallanzani and G. Bertelà (eds), *Libro d'inventario dei beni di Lorenzo il Magnifico*, Florence, 1992, p. 36.

23 M. Spallanzani (ed.), *Inventari Medicei, 1417–1465*, Florence, 1984, p. 94; A.G. Vianello, 'Un inventario di cose appartenute a Cicco Simonetta', *Archivio storico lombardo*, XLV, 1918, pp. 580–2.

24 E. Motta, 'Ambrogio Preda e Leonardo da Vinci (nuovi documenti)', *Archivio storico lombardo*, ser. ii, XI, 1893, pp. 972–89, esp. pp. 988–90; A. Giulini, 'Una corniola ducale', *Archivio storico lombardo*, ser. iv, XXXIX, 1912, p. 584.

25 G.G. Trivulzio, 'Gioie di Ludovico il Moro messe a pegno', *Archivio storico lombardo*, II, 1876, pp. 530–4; G. Agosti, 'Scrittori che parlano di artisti, tra Quattro e Cinquecento in Lombardia' in B. Agosti *et al.*, *Quattro pezzi lombardi (per Maria Teresa Binaghi)*, Brescia, 1998, pp. 41–93, esp. p. 74; P. Venturelli, *Glossario e documenti per la gioielleria milanese (1456–1631)*, Florence, 1999, pp. 157–8, doc. 26.

26 C.M. Brown, L. Fusco and G. Corti, 'Lorenzo de' Medici and the Dispersal of the Antiquarian Collections of Cardinal Francesco Gonzaga', *Arte Lombarda*, 90/91, 3–4, 1989, pp. 86–103; Chambers, *Renaissance Cardinal*, 1992; L. Jardine, *Worldly Goods: A New History of the Renaissance*, London, 1996, pp. 66–7, 102, 117–18, 421–4.

27 A. Luzio, 'Lettere inedite di Fra Sabba da Castiglione', *Archivio storico lombardo*, XIII, 1886, pp. 91–112, esp. pp. 92–3, n. 3.

28 A. Giuliano in N. Dacos, A. Giuliano and U. Pannuti, *Il tesoro di Lorenzo il Magnifico*, I, *Le gemme*, Florence, 1973, pp. 39–66. The addition, and its precise date, of the 'aquiletta' to a group of Roman coins remains controversial. See R. Riva and B. Simonetta, ' "Aquiletta" estense o "Aquiletta" Gonzaga?', *Quaderni Ticinesi di numismatica e antichità classiche*, VIII, 1979, pp. 359–73; L. Reggiani, 'De l'"aquiletta" estense', *Annotazioni numismatiche*, 8, December 1992, pp. 160–4.

29 F. Haskell, *History and Its Images: Art and the Interpretation of the Past*, New Haven and London, 1993, p.13.

30 R. Weiss, *The Renaissance Discovery of Classical Antiquity*, Oxford, 1969, pp. 37–8, 85.

31 C. Malagola, *Della vita e delle opere di Antonio Urceo detto Codro: studi e ricerche*, Bologna, 1878, pp. 439–40. Cited by S. De Maria, 'Fra corte e studio: la cultura antiquaria a Bologna nell'età dei Bentivoglio' in G.A. Mansuelli and G. Susini (eds), *Il contributo dell' Università di Bologna alla storia della città: l'Evo Antico: Atti del 10 convegno, Bologna, 11–12 March 1988*, Bologna, 1989, pp. 151–216, esp. p.155.

32 P. Bracciolini, *La vera nobilità*, ed. and Ital. trans. D. Canfora, Florence, 1998, pp. 28–35 (including Latin text); C.E. Gilbert (ed.), *Italian Art, 1400–1500: Sources and Documents*, Evanston, Ill., 1992 (rev. edn), p. 169; A. Rabil Jr (ed. and trans.), *Knowledge, Goodness and Power: the Debate over Nobility among Quattrocento Humanists*, Binghamton, NY, 1991, pp. 64–5.

33 Bracciolini, *La vera nobilità*, pp. 28–35; Gilbert, *Italian Art*, p. 169; Rabil Jr, *Knowledge, Goodness and Power*, pp. 64–5.

34 C. Acidini Luchinat, 'La "santa antichità", la scuola, il giardino' in F. Borsi (ed.), *'Per bellezza, per studio, per piacere': Lorenzo il Magnifico e gli spazi dell'arte*, Florence, 1991, pp. 143–60, esp. p. 146 and n. 21.

35 G.F. Hill, 'Classical Influence on the Renaissance Medal', *Burlington Magazine*, XVIII, 1910–11, pp. 259–68, esp. p. 260.

36 A. Chastel, *Art et Humanisme à Florence au temps de Laurent le Magnifique: Études sur la Renaisance et l'Humanisme platonicien*, Paris, 1959, p. 72, pl. XI; L. Beschi, 'Le antichità di Lorenzo il Magnifico: caratteri e vicende' in P. Barrochi and G. Ragionieri (eds), *Gli Uffizi: quattro secoli di una galleria*, Atti del convegno internazionale di studi (Firenze 20–24 settembre 1982), Florence, 1982, pp. 161–76, esp. p. 172.

37 G. Biadego, *Variazioni e divagazione a proposito di due sonetti di Giorgio Sommariva in onore di Gentile e Giovanni Bellini (per nozze Gerola-Cena)*, Verona, 1907, p. 20. Cited by J.M. Fletcher, 'Harpies, Venus and Giovanni Bellini's Classical Mirror: Some Fifteenth-Century Venetian Painters' Responses to the Antique' in I. Favaretto and G. Traversari (eds), *Venezia e l'archeologia: un importante capitolo nella storia del gusto dell'antico nella cultura artistica Veneziana*, Rome, 1990, pp. 170–6, esp. p. 170, n. 11.

38 C.M. Brown, ' "Una testa di Platone antica con la punta del Naso di Cera": Unpublished Negotiations between Isabella d'Este and Niccolò and Giovanni Bellini', *Art Bulletin*, LI, 1969, pp. 373–7.

39 J. Woods-Marsden, '*Ritratto al naturale*: Questions of Realism and Idealism in Early Renaissance Portraits', *Art Journal*, XLVI, 1987, pp. 209–16; L. Syson, 'Alberti e la ritrattistica' in J. Rykwert and A. Engel (eds), *Leon Battista Alberti*, exh. cat., Palazzo Te, Mantua, Milan, 1994, pp. 46–53.

40 Antonio Averlino detto il Filarete, *Trattato di architectura*, eds A.M. Finoli and L. Grassi, 2 vols, Milan, 1972, II, pp. 687–8; J.R. Spencer (ed. and trans.), *Filarete's Treatise on Architecture, Being the Treatise by Antonio Averlino, Known as Filarete*, 2 vols, New Haven and London, 1965, I, p. 320 (for a rather loose translation); cited by M. Kemp, *Behind the Picture: Art and Evidence in the Italian Renaissance*, New Haven and London, 1997, pp. 143–4, 149, 153.

41 B. Castiglione, *Il libro del cortegiano*, 2nd edn, ed. B. Maier, Turin, 1964, p. 179; A. Hobson, *Humanists and Bookbinders: the Origins and Diffusion of Humanistic Bookbinding, 1459–1559*, Cambridge, 1989, p. 91.

42 Sabba da Castiglione, *I ricordi*, Venice, 1560, pp 58–9; Thornton, *The Scholar*, p. 117.

43 A. Traversari, *Latinae Epistolae*, 1759, II (reprinted), lib. VIII, col. 417, ep. 48; cited by Hill, 'Classical Influence', p. 260.

44 Weiss, *Renaissance Discovery*, p. 186; P. Fortini Brown, *Venice and Antiquity*, New Haven and London, 1996, p. 85; D. Thornton, 'Valerio Belli and After: Renaissance Gems in the British Museum', *Jewellery Studies*, VIII, 1998, pp. 11–20, esp. p. 11.

45 Weiss, *Renaissance Discovery*, p. 74.

46 J. Kraye, 'Francesco Filelfo's lost letter *De ideis*', *Journal of the Warburg and Courtauld Institutes*, XLII, 1979, pp. 236–49, esp. pp. 240, 246.

47 F. Malaguzzi Valeri, 'Artisti lombardi a Roma nel Rinascimento: nuovi documenti su Cristoforo Solari, Bramante e Caradosso', *Repertorium für Kunstwissenschaft*, XXV, 1902, pp. 57–64, esp. p. 61.

48 Baxandall, *Giotto and the Orators*, p. 91.

49 F. Nicolini, *L'arte napoletano del Rinascimento*, Naples, 1925, p. 170.

50 M. Benedetti, 'Nuovi documenti sullo sculptore Vincenzo de' Grandi', *Studi Trentini*, IV, 1923, pp. 28–40, esp. p. 35. We are grateful to Peta Motture and Jeremy Warren for sharing this document with us.

51 Ibid.

52 J. von Schlosser (ed.), *Lorenzo Ghibertis Denkwürdigkeiten: I commentarii*, Berlin, 1912, pp. 24, 25.

53 Gilbert, *Italian Art*, p. 168.

54 R.W. Lightbown, *Mantegna*, Oxford, 1986, p. 95.

55 Ibid.

56 P. Kristeller, *Andrea Mantegna*, Berlin and Leipzig, 1902, p. 524, doc. 36.

57 Brummer, *The Statue Court*, p. 75; Bober and Rubinstein, *Renaissance Artists*, pp. 152–5, esp. 153, cat. no. 122.

58 Barkan, *Unearthing the Past*, pp. 111–12.

59 V. Golzio, *Raffaello nei documenti*, Vatican City, 1936, pp. 39–40.

60 R. Weiss, 'Andrea Fulvio Antiquario Romano (c.1470–1527)', *Annali della Scuola Normale Superiore di Pisa: Classe di lettere, storia e filosofia*, ser. ii, XXVIII, 1959, pp. 1–44, esp. pp. 11–12; P. Jacks, *The Antiquarian and the Myth of Antiquity: the Origins of Rome in Renaissance Thought*, Cambridge, 1993, pp. 189–90.

61 G. Mardersteig, *Felice Feliciano Veronese. Alphabetum Romanum*, Verona, 1960, p. 26.

62 Golzio, *Raffaello*, pp. 39–40; Barkan, *Unearthing the Past*, p. 39.

63 F. Ames-Lewis, *The Intellectual Life of the Early Renaissance Artist*, New Haven and London, 2000, pp. 76, 79–84.

64 E.W. Bodnar, *Cyriacus of Ancona and Athens*, Brussels, 1960, pp. 85, 105.

65 Spallanzani, *Inventari Medicei*, pp. 114, 117; C.M. Brown, 'Little Known and Unpublished Documents concerning Andrea Mantegna, Bernardino Parentino, Pietro Lombardo, Leonardo da Vinci and Filippo Benintendi, Part One', *L'Arte*, VI, 1969, pp. 152–64; L. Leoncini, 'The Mantegna Codex and the Gonzaga: Model Books and Drawings after the Antique at the Court of Mantua' in C. Mozzarelli, R. Oresko and L. Ventura (eds), *La Corte di Mantova nell'età di Andrea Mantegna: 1450–1550*, Rome, 1997, pp. 273–9.

66 G. Schweikhart, *Der Codex Wolfegg: Zeignungen nach der Antike von Amico Aspertini*, London, 1986, *passim*.

67 E. Parlato, 'Il gusto all'antica di Filarete scultore' in A. Cavallaro and E. Parlato (eds), *Da Pisanello alla nascita dei Musei Capitolini: l'antico a Roma all vigilia del Rinascimento*, exh. cat. Musei Capitolini, Rome, Rome and Milan, 1988, pp. 115–23, esp. p. 118.

68 A. Cavallaro, 'I sarcofagi mitologici' in Cavallaro and Parlato, *Da Pisanello*, pp. 147–60, n. 62; L. Scalabroni, 'Il sarcofago bacchico di S. Maria Maggiore' in Cavallaro and Parlato, *Da Pisanello*, pp. 161–73; B. Blass-Simmen, 'Pisanellos Tätigkeit in Rom' in B. Degenhart and A. Schmitt (eds), *Pisanello und Bono da Ferrara*, Munich, 1995, pp. 81–117.

69 R. Rubinstein, 'A Bacchic Sarcophagus in the Renaissance', *The British Museum Yearbook*, I, *The Classical Tradition*, London, 1975, pp. 103–50.

70 B. Scardeone, *De antiquitate urbis Patavi*, Basel, 1560, pp. 371; cited by D. Chambers, J. Martineau and R. Signorini, 'Mantegna and the Men of Letters' in J. Martineau (ed.), *Andrea Mantegna*, exh. cat., Royal Academy of Arts, London, and Metropolitan Museum of Art, New York, Milan, 1992, pp. 8–30.

71 K. Oberhuber, 'Ein unbekannte Zeichnung Raffaels in den Uffizen', *Mitteilungen des kunsthistorisches Instituts in Florenz*, XII, 1966, pp. 225–44, esp. p. 227; D. Ekserdjian in Martineau, *Andrea Mantegna*, pp. 445–7, cat. no. 145.

72 A. Martindale, *The Triumphs of Caesar by Andrea Mantegna in the Collection of H.M. the Queen at Hampton Court*, London, 1979; C. Hope in Martineau, *Andrea Mantegna*, pp. 350–72, cat. nos 108–15; E.A. Halliday, 'The Literary Sources of Mantegna's Triumphs of Caesar', *Annali della Scuola Normale Superiore di Pisa (Classe di lettere e filosofia)*, ser. iii, XXIV, 1, 1994, pp. 337–96.

73 N. Dacos, *La Découverte de la Domus Aurea et la formation des grotesques à Renaissance*, London and Leyden, 1969.

74 N. Dacos, 'Graffiti de la Domus Aurea', *Bulletin de l'Institut historique belge de Rome*, XXXVIII, 1967, pp. 145–75.

75 N. Dacos, 'Ghirlandaio et l'antique', *Bulletin de l'Institut historique belge de Rome*, XXXIV, 1962, pp. 419–55; M. Faietti and A. Nesselrath, ' "Bizar più che reverso di medaglia": un codex avec grotesque, monstres et ornements du jeune Amico Aspertini', *Revue de l'art*, CVII, 1995, pp. 44–88.

76 J. Schulz, 'Pinturicchio and the Revival of Antiquity', *Journal of the Warburg and Courtauld Institutes*, XXV, 1962, pp. 35–55.

77 C. Acidini Luchinat, 'La grottesca' in G. Previtali (ed.), *Storia dell'arte italiana*, II, *L'artista e il pubblico*, Turin, 1979, pp. 152–200, fig. 247; Wilson, *Ceramic Art*, pp. 87–90, cat. nos 134–6.

78 T. Wilson, 'Girolamo Genga: designer for maiolica?' in T. Wilson (ed.), *Italian Renaissance Pottery: Papers written in association with a colloquium at The British Museum*, London, 1991, pp. 157–65.

79 J.J.G. Alexander, 'Patrons, Libraries and Illuminators in the Italian Renaissance' in J.J.G. Alexander (ed.), *The Painted Page: Italian Renaissance Book Illumination, 1450–1550*, exh. cat., Royal Academy of Arts, London, and Pierpont Morgan Library, New York, London and Munich, 1994, p. 15.

80 C.M. Brown, 'Little Known and Unpublished Documents', pp. 140–64.

81 Luzio, 'Lettere inedite di Fra Sabba da Castiglione', pp. 92–3, n. 3.

82 T. Tonelli (ed.), *Poggi Epistulae*, Florence, 1832, IV, pp. 12, 15, 18, 21, VII, p. 14; E. Müntz, *Les Collections des Médicis au quinzième siècle*, Paris, 1888, pp. 8–10; E. Walser, *Poggius Florentinus*, Leipzig and Berlin, 1914, p. 147; Beschi, 'Le antichità di Lorenzo', pp. 161–76.

83 I. Favaretto, *Arte antica e cultura antiquaria nelle collezioni venete al tempo della Serenissima*, Rome, 1990, pp. 45–9; M. Landolfi, 'Ciriaco e il collezionismo di antichità greche nel Piceno' in G. Paci and S. Sconocchia (eds), *Ciriaco d'Ancona e la cultura antiquaria dell'Umanesimo: Atti del convegno internazionale di studio, Ancona, 6–9 febbraio 1992*, Reggio Emilia, 1998, pp. 443–9.

84 Matteo Maria Boiardo, *Opere volgari*, Bari, 1962, p. 275 (CXXXVII). They had been found by a peasant and would cost 2 ducats, 44 soldi each.

85 E. Müntz, *Les arts à la cour des papes*, Paris, II, 1879, p. 207.

86 Bagemihl, 'The Trevisan Collection', pp. 559–63. We are grateful to Alison Wright for drawing to our attention the fact that this inventory was witnessed by goldsmiths and for suggesting the identity of one of them.

87 C.M. Brown and S. Hickson, 'Caradosso Foppa (ca. 1452–1526/7)', *Arte Lombarda*, 119, 1997/1, pp. 9–39, esp. p. 18.

88 von Schlosser, *Lorenzo Ghibertis Denkwürdigkeiten*, p. 47; Lorenzo Ghiberti, *I commentarii*, ed. and intro. L Bartoli, Biblioteca Nazionale Centrale di Firenze, II, I, 33, Florence, 1998, p. 94.

89 Müntz, *Les arts*, II, pp. 117–18.

90 A. Bertolotti, *Le arte minori alla Corte di Mantova*, Milan, 1889, p. 280; A. Luzio and R. Renier, 'Il lusso di Isabella d'Este', *Nuova antologia*, ser. iv, LXIV, 1896, pp. 300–10, esp. p. 310; M. Perry, 'Wealth, Art and Display: the Grimani Cameos in Renaissance Venice', *Journal of the Warburg and Courtauld Institutes*, LVI, 1993, pp. 268–73, esp. p. 271.

91 Bertolotti, *Le arte*; Luzio and Renier, 'Il lusso di Isabella d'Este'; Perry, 'Wealth, Art and Display'.

92 L. Gargan, 'Oliviero Forzetta e le origini del collezionismo veneziano' in I. Favaretto and G. Traversari (eds), *Venezia e l'archeologia: un importante capitolo nella storia del gusto dell'antico nella cultura artistica Veneziana*, Rome, 1990, pp. 13–21.

93 U. Rossi, 'Cristoforo Geremia', *Archivo storico dell'arte*, I, 1888, pp. 404–11, esp. p. 409.

94 Ibid., esp. p. 408.

95 Ibid., esp. pp 408–9.

96 See Traversari, *Epistolae*, col. 411, lib. VIII, ep. 45; Weiss, *Renaissance Discovery*, p. 170.

97 Rossi, 'Cristoforo Geremia', p. 411.

98 Brown and Hickson, 'Caradosso Foppa', p. 16.

99 L. Tondo in *Magnificenza all corte dei Medici: arte a Firenze alle fine del Cinquecento*, exh. cat., Museo degli Argenti, Palazzo Pitti, Florence, Milan, 1997, p. 84, cat. no. 45; cf. Benvenuto Cellini, *La Vita*, ed. G. Davico Bonino, Turin, 1973, p. 56.

100 F. Caglioti and D. Gasparotto, 'Lorenzo Ghiberti, il "Sigillo di Nerone", e le origini della placchetta "antiquaria" ', *Prospettiva*, 85, January 1997, pp. 2–38, esp. p. 16.

101 Luzio, 'Lettere inedite de Fra Sabba da Castiglione', pp. 92–3, n. 3.

102 N. Dacos, 'Le rôle des plaquettes dans la diffusion des gemmes antiques: le cas de la collection Médicis', in A. Luchs (ed.) *Italian Plaquettes: Studies in the History of Art*, 22, National Gallery of Art, Washington DC, 1989, pp. 71–91, esp. p. 73, n. 102.

103 Caglioti and Gasparotto 'Lorenzo Ghiberti', pp. 2–38.

104 Now in Cabinet des Médailles, Bibliothèque nationale de France, Paris (inv. 2080).

105 G.F. Hill, *A Corpus of Italian Medals of the Renaissance before Cellini*, London 1930, p. 200, cat. no. 773.

106 P. Cannata, *Rilievi e placchette dal XV al XVIII secolo*, exh. cat., Palazzo Venezia, Rome, Rome, 1982, pp. 32–5, nn. 2–3.

107 P. Motture, 'The Decoration of Italian Renaissance Hand-Bells' in S. Currie and P. Motture (eds), *The Sculpted Object, 1400–1700*, Aldershot, Hants, 1997, pp. 99–116, esp. pp. 105–6.

108 Brown and Hickson, 'Caradosso Foppa', p. 26.

109 Ibid.

110 A. Butterfield, *The Sculptures of Andrea del Verrocchio*, New Haven and London, 1997, pp. 212–13; N. Penny in P.L. Rubin and

A. Wright, *Renaissance Florence: the Art of the 1470s*, exh. cat., National Gallery, London, London, 1999, pp. 152–3, cat. no. 12.

111 Rossi, 'Cristoforo Geremia', p. 408. The urn is now to be found as part of the eighteenth-century tomb of Pope Clement XII at the Lateran in Rome. See S. Butters, *The Triumph of Vulcan: Sculptor's Tools, Porphyry, and the Prince in Ducal Florence*, I, Florence, 1996, p. 116.

112 A. Radcliffe, 'Two Early Romano-Mantuan Plaquettes' in Luchs, *Italian Plaquettes*, pp. 93–103.

113 T. Frimmel, *Der Anonimo Morelliano (Marcanton Michiel's Notizia d'opere del disegno)*, Vienna, 1888, p. 96; G. Vasari, *Le vite de' più eccellenti pittori, scultori ed architettori*, 7 vols., ed. G. Milanesi, V, Florence, 1880, pp. 370–1.

114 Fusco and Corti, 'Giovanni Ciampolini', pp. 7–46.

115 Ibid.

116 L. Tondo, *Le gemme dei Medici e dei Lorena nel Museo Archeologico di Firenze*, Florence, 1990, pp. 173, 206, cat. no. 88.

117 B. Cellini, *I trattati dell'oreficeria e della scultura*, ed. G. Milanesi, Florence, 1857, p. 116. For a loose translation see C.R. Ashbee (trans.), *The Treatises of Benvenuto Cellini on Goldsmithing and Sculpture*, New York, 1967, p. 72.

118 Castiglione, *Ricordi*, p. 56.

119 H. Horne, *Alessandro Filipepi, commonly called Sandro Botticelli, Painter of Florence*, London, 1908, p. 28.

120 A. Burnett, 'Renaissance forgeries of ancient coins' in M. Jones (ed.), *Fake? The Art of Deception*, exh. cat., British Museum, London, 1990, pp. 136–8; A. Burnett, 'Coin Faking in the Renaissance' in M. Jones (ed.), *Why Fakes Matter: Essays on Problems of Authenticity*, London, 1992, pp. 15–22.

121 Burnett, 'Renaissance forgeries'; Burnett, 'Coin Faking'.

122 Burnett, 'Renaissance forgeries'; Burnett, 'Coin Faking'.

123 Vasari, *Vite*, p. 223; for mosaic and other *cose degli antichi Romani*, see p. 232.

124 Hill, *Corpus*, p. 4, cat. nos 10–11; Weiss, *Renaissance Discovery*, p. 54; A.M. Stahl and L. Waldman, 'The Earliest Known Medalists: the Sesto Brothers of Venice', *American Journal of Numismatics*, ser. ii, V–VI, 1993–4, pp. 167–88.

125 F. Panvini Rosati, 'Ispirazione classica nella medaglia italiana del Rinascimento' in *La medaglia d'arte: atti del primo convegno internazionale di studio, Udine 10–12 ottobre 1970*, Udine, 1973, pp. 95–105.

126 B. Nogara (ed.), *Scritti inediti e rari di Biondo Flavio*, Rome, 1927, pp. 159–60.

127 J. Raby, 'Pride and Prejudice: Mehmed the Conqueror and the Italian Portrait Medal' in J.G. Pollard (ed.), *Italian Medals: Studies in the History of Art*, 21, National Gallery of Art, Washington DC, 1987, pp. 171–94, esp. pp. 187–8.

128 See e.g. R. Rugolo in L. Puppi (ed.), *Pisanello: una poetica dell'inatteso*, Milan, 1996, pp. 138–93; L. Syson, '*Opus pisani pictoris*: les médailles de Pisanello et son atelier' in D. Cordellier and B. Py (eds), *Pisanello: Louvres conférences et colloques*, I, Paris, 1998, pp. 379–426.

129 M. Salmi, 'La "Divi Julii Caesaris Effigies" del Pisanello', *Commentari*, VIII, 1957, pp. 91–5.

130 D. Cordellier in *Pisanello: le peintre aux sept vertus*, exh. cat., Musée du Louvre, Paris, 1996, pp. 287–9, cat. no. 186.

131 Woods-Marsden, '*Ritratto al naturale*', pp. 209–16; L. Syson, 'Alberti e la ritrattistica' in J. Rykwert and A. Engel (eds), *Leon Battista Alberti*, exh. cat., Palazzo Te, Mantua, Milan, 1994, pp. 46–53.

132 Plutarch, *de Alexandri Fortitudine seu Virtute*, 2.2.3 (*Moralia* 335A–B).

133 For the medals see M. Jones, 'The First Cast Medals and the Limbourgs: the Iconography and Attribution of the Constantine and Heraclius Medals', *Art History*, II, 1979, pp. 35–44; S.K. Scher in S.K. Scher (ed.), *The Currency of Fame: Portrait Medals of the Renaissance*, exh. cat., National Gallery of Art, Washington, Frick Collection, New York, New York, 1994, pp. 32–7, cat. nos 1–2; for the location of the Heraclius, see G. Bertoni and E.P. Vicini, 'Il Castello di Ferrara ai tempi di Niccolò III', *Documenti e studi pubblicati per cura della Deputazione di Storia patria per le Provincie di Romagna*, 3, Bologna, 1909, p. 92, cat. nos 1650–1.

134 C. Seymour Jr in his article 'Some Reflections on Filarete's Use of Antique Visual Sources', *Arte Lombarda*, 38–39, XVIII, 1973, pp. 36–47, was the first to connect a group of medals attributed by Hill to a Lombard master working at the end of the Quattrocento with Filarete. J.R. Spencer, 'Filarete, the Medallist of the Roman Emperors', *Art Bulletin*, LXI, 1979, pp. 550–61, developed the idea, attributing the works to Filarete himself. This view was modified by Parlato, 'Il gusto all'antica', pp. 115–34, who considered the medals as the products of Filarete's workshop based on models provided for the doors by Filarete himself.

135 Hill, *Corpus*, pp. 186–7, cat. no. 732; Parlato, 'Il gusto all'antica', pp. 80–1, cat. no. 16.

136 Hill, *Corpus*, p. 187, cat. no. 734.

137 Ibid., p. 197, cat. no. 755; S. Danesi Squarina in Cavallaro and Parlato, *Da Pisanello*, p. 84, cat. no. 21.

138 Hill, *Corpus*, pp. 235–6, cat. no. 906.

139 Ibid., pp. 196–7, cat. no. 754; S. Danesi Squarina in Cavallaro and Parlato, *Da Pisanello*, p. 83, cat. no. 20.

140 Hill, *Corpus*, pp. 197–8, cat. no. 756.

141 Ibid., p. 200, cat. no. 733; R. Weiss, 'Un umanista veneziano – Papa Paolo II', *Civiltà Veneziana, Saggi*, 4, Venice, 1958, p. 59.

142 L.A. Waldman, ' "The Modern Lysippus": a Roman Quattrocento Medallist in Context', in S.K. Scher (ed.), *Perspectives on the Renaissance Medal*, New York, 2000, pp. 97–113.

143 Hill, *Corpus*, pp. 51–3, cat. nos 206–15; Allison, 'The bronzes', pp. 77–87, cat. nos 1–9.

144 Hill, *Corpus*, pp. 55–6, cat. no. 221; A. Norris, 'Gian Cristoforo Romano: the courtier as medallist' in Pollard, *Italian Medals*, pp. 131–41; K. Schulz, 'Die Medaille Gian Christophoro Romanos auf Isabella d'Este und die Medaillenkunst ihrer Zeit' in S. Ferino-Pagden (ed.), *'La prima donna del mondo': Isabella d'Este, Fürstin und Mäzenatin der Renaissance*, exh. cat. Kunsthistorisches Museum, Vienna, 1994,

pp. 373–8; L. Syson, 'Reading faces: Gian Cristoforo Romano's Medal of Isabella d'Este' in Mozzarelli, Oresko and Ventura, *La corte di Mantova*, pp. 281–94.

145 L. Syson in Scher, *Currency of Fame*, p. 114; C.M. Brown and A.M. Lorenzoni, 'Caradosso Foppa and the Roman Mint', *artibus et historiae*, XXII, 43, 2001, pp. 41–4.

146 Hill, *Corpus*, pp. 224–6, cat. nos 866–72; Butters, *The Triumph of Vulcan*, pp. 144, 159–68, 198–9, 282.

147 Hill, *Corpus*, pp. 115–21, esp. cat. nos 444–8, 458–62; P. Grotemeyer, 'Drei Medaillen von Camelio', *Münchner Jahrbuch der Bildenden Kunst*, XII, 1937/8, pp. x–xi; W. Schwabacher, 'Ein unkendt Renaissance medaille auf Camelio', *Konsthistorisk Tidskrift*, XIII, 1944, pp. 92–5; R. Weiss, 'Vittore Camelio e la medaglia veneziana del Rinascimento' in V. Branca (ed.), *Rinascimento Europeo e Rinascimento Veneziano, Civiltà Europea, Aspetti e problemi*, 3, Venice and Florence, 1967, pp. 327–37; G.F. Hill, *Medals of the Renaissance*, revd G. Pollard, London, 1978, pp. 58, 178, n. 40, pl. 31, fig. 4.

148 B. Jestaz, 'Les antiquités dans les inventaires vénitiens du XVIe siècle' in Favaretto and Traversari, *Venezia e l'archeologia*, pp. 35–40, esp. p. 37.

149 Hill, *Corpus*, p. 118, cat. no. 446; Fortini Brown, *Venice*, p. 234, fig. 260.

150 Francisco da Hollanda, *Dialogos en Roma*, ed. J. da Felicidade Alves, Lisbon, 1984, p. 71; Francisco da Hollanda, *Diálogos em Roma (1538): Conversations on Art with Michelangelo Buonarroti*, ed. G.D. Folliero-Metz, Heidelberg, 1998, pp. 120–1; S.E. Lawrence, 'Imitation and Emulation in the Numismatic Fantasies of Valerio Belli', *The Medal*, 29, Autumn 1996, pp. 18–29; M. Barausse, 'Documenti e testimonianze' in H. Burns, M. Collareta and D. Gasparotto (eds), *Valerio Belli Vicentino, 1468 –c.1546*, Vicenza, 2000, pp. 389–453, esp. 441.

151 D. Gasparotto, 'Una galleria metallica di personaggi illustre: le medaglie all'antica' in Burns, Collareta and Gasparotto, *Vicentino*, pp. 137–59, 369–86 (cat. nos 195–253), 454–62.

152 D. Gasparotto in Burns, Collareta and Gasparotto, *Vicentino*, pp. 366–7, cat. no. 189; Barausse, 'Documenti', pp. 389–453, esp. p. 413.

153 F. Cessi with B. Caon, *Giovanni da Cavino: medaglista padovano del Cinquecento*, Padua, 1969, p. 100, cat. no. 91; Burnett, 'Renaissance forgeries', pp. 136–8.

154 Cessi, *Giovanni da Cavino*, p. 105, cat. no. 100.

155 D. Myers in Scher, *Currency of Fame*, pp. 183–5, cat. no. 71.

156 Alberti, *On Painting*, pp. 100–1.

157 Vasari, *Vite*, III, p. 389.

158 Gombrich, 'The Style *all'antica*', p.123.

159 M. Collareta, 'Testimonianze letterarie su Donatello, 1450–1600' in P. Barocchi *et al.* (ed.), *Omaggio a Donatello: Donatello e la storia del Museo*, exh. cat., Muzeo Nazionale del Bargello, Florence, 1985, pp. 7–47, esp. p. 20.

160 Castiglione, *Ricordi*, p. 56.

161 See e.g. G. Corti and F. Hartt, 'New documents concerning Donatello, Luca and Andrea della Robbia, Desiderio, Mino, Uccello, Pollaiuolo, Filippo Lippi, Baldovinetti and others', *The Art*

Bulletin, XVIV, 1962, pp. 155–67, esp. p. 157, n. 12; D. Pincus, 'Tullio Lombardo as a restorer of antiquities', *Arte Veneta*, XXXIII, 1979, pp. 29–42.

162 A. Nesselrath, 'Simboli di Roma' in Cavallaro and Parlato, *Da Pisanello*, pp. 195–205, esp. pp. 202–4.

163 F. Caglioti, 'Due "restauratori" per le antichità dei primi Medici: Mino da Fiesole, Andrea del Verrocchio e il "Marsia rosso" degli Uffizi. I', *Prospettiva*, 72, 1993, pp. 17–42.

164 R.E. Stone, 'Antico and the Development of Bronze Casting in Italy at the End of the Quattrocento', *The Metropolitan Museum Journal*, XVI, 1981, pp. 87–116.

165 Müntz, *Les arts*, II, pp. 94–5.

166 A. Nesselrath, 'Antico and Monte Cavallo', *The Burlington Magazine*, CXXIV, 1982, pp. 353–7.

167 Allison, 'The bronzes', pp. 37–310, esp. p. 287, docs 54, 55.

168 A. Nesselrath in Cavallaro and Parlato, *Da Pisanello*, p. 235, cat. no. 82.

169 H.J. Hermann, 'Pier Jacopo Alari-Bonacolsi, gennant l'Antico', *Jahrbuch der kunsthistorischen Sammlungen in Wien*, XXVIII, 1910, pp. 201–88, esp. pp. 214–19.

170 Frimmel, *Der Anonimo Morelliano*, p. 28.

171 Brown and Hickson, 'Caradosso Foppa'

172 See e.g. Allison, 'The bronzes', pp. 138–51.

173 Ibid.

174 D. Lewis, 'On the Nature of Renaissance Bronzes' in M. Leithe-Jasper, *Renaissance Master Bronzes from the Collection of the Kunsthistorisches Museum, Vienna*, exh. cat., Smithsonian Institution Travelling Exhibition Service, London, 1986, pp. 19–24, esp. p. 23.

175 Beschi, 'Le antichità di Lorenzo', p. 166, n. 23.

176 C. Parisi Presicce, *La Lupa Capitolina*, exh. cat., Musei Capitolini, Rome, Rome, 2000, pp. 83–8.

177 Müntz, *Les collections*, p. 85; M. Cruttwell, *Antonio Pollaiulo*, London and New York, 1907, p. 81; L.D. Ettlinger, *Antonio and Piero Pollaiuolo*, London, 1978, p. 187, cat. no. 18; A. Wright, 'Dimensional Tension in the Work of Antonio Pollaiuolo' in Currie and Motture, *The Sculpted Object*, pp. 65–79, esp. pp. 66–9.

178 J.D. Draper, *Bertoldo di Giovanni: Sculptor of the Medici Household*, Columbia, Mo. and London, 1992, pp. 176–85, cat. no. 18; for mounted Hercules see pp. 153–9, cat. no. 14.

179 P. Barolsky, *The Faun in the Garden: Michelangelo and the Poetic Origins of Italian Renaissance Art*, University Park, Penn., 1994, pp. 66–7.

180 M. Hirst in M. Hirst and J. Dunkerton, *The Young Michelangelo: Making and Meaning*, exh. cat., National Gallery, London, 1994, pp. 20–8; K. Weil-Garris Brandt, 'Sogni di un *Cupido dormiente smarrito*' in K. Weil-Garris Brandt, C. Acidini Lucinat, J.D. Draper and N. Penny (eds), *Giovinezza di Michelangelo*, exh. cat. Palazzo Vecchio, Casa Buonarroti, Florence, 1999, pp. 315–23; N. Baldini, D. Lodico and A.M. Piras, 'Michelangelo a Roma: i rapporti con la famiglia Galli e con Baldassare del Milanese' in ibid., pp. 149–62.

181 A. Condivi, *Vita di Michelagnolo Buonarotti*, ed. G. Nencioni, Florence, 1998, p. 17.

182 Hirst in Hirst and Dunkerton, *Young Michelangelo*,

pp. 29–35; C.L. Frommel, 'Raffaele Riario, la Cancelleria, il teatro e il *Bacco* di Michelangelo' in Weil-Garris Brandt, Acidini Lucinat, Draper, and Penny, *Giovinezza di Michelangelo*, pp. 143–62.

183 Hirst in Hirst and Dunkerton, *Young Michelangelo*, pp. 29–35; Frommel, 'Raffaele Riario', pp. 143–62.

184 Vasari, *Vite*, VII, pp. 147–9.

185 Hirst in Hirst and Dunkerton, *Young Michelangelo*, pp. 29–35.

186 Condivi, *Vita*, p. 19.

Chapter 4

1 S.J. Campbell, *Cosmè Tura of Ferrara: Style Politics and the Renaissance City, 1450–1495*, New Haven and London, 1997, p. 12.

2 P. Kristeller, *Andrea Mantegna*, Berlin and Leipzig, 1902, p. 546, doc. 103; C. Elam, 'Mantegna at Mantua' in D. Chambers and J. Martineau (eds), *Splendours of the Gonzaga*, exh. cat., Victorian and Albert Museum, London, 1981, p. 15.

3 Kristeller, *Mantegna*, p. 535, doc. 79.

4 G. Milanesi and C. Pini, *La scrittura di artisti italiani (sec. XIV–XVII)*, Florence, 1876, I, n.p., doc. 60; J.D. Draper, *Bertoldo di Giovanni: Sculptor of the Medici Household*, Columbia, Mo. and London, 1992, pp. 277–8, doc. 12; F.W. Kent, 'Bertoldo "sculptore" e Lorenzo de'Medici' *Burlington Magazine*, CXXXIV, 1992, pp. 248–9, esp. 249, n. 9.

5 Useful summaries of this issue are to be found in Baxandall, *Giotto and the Orators*, pp. 15–17, 51; M. Warnke, *The Court Artist: On the Ancestry of the Modern Artist*, trans. D. McLintock, Cambridge, 1993, p. 9; M. Kemp, *Behind the Picture: Art and Evidence in the Italian Renaissance*, New Haven and London, 1997, pp. 229–35.

6 J. Manca, *The Art of Ercole de' Roberti*, Cambridge, 1992, p. 207, doc. 39.

7 For a useful discussion see B.L. Holman in B.L. Holman (ed.), *Disegno: Italian Renaissance Designs for the Decorative Arts*, exh. cat., Cooper-Hewitt National Design Museum, New York, 1997, pp. 3–14.

8 Francesco di Giorgio Martini, *Trattati di architettura ingegneria e arte militare*, 2 vols, Milan, 1967, I, pp. 36–7.

9 F. Malaguzzi Valeri, *La corte di Lodovico il Moro*, 4 vols, Milan, 1913–23, IV, 1923, p. 1.

10 J. von Schlosser (ed.), *Lorenzo Ghiberti's Denkwürdigkeiten: I commentarii*, Berlin, 1912, p. 23; Ghiberti, *I commentari*, p 3.

11 G. Vasari, *Le vite de' più eccellenti pittori, scultori ed architettori*, 9 vols, ed. G. Milanesi, Florence, 1880, I, p. 168.

12 G. Visconti, *I canzonieri per Beatrice d'Este e Bianca Maria Sforza*, ed. P. Bongrani, Milan, 1979, p. 27 (XXXII.17): a '*balasso che aveva una dama ad una orecchia fingendo sia una ferita d'Amore*'.

13 Goldthwaite, *Building*, pp. 399–400; T. Tuohy, *Herculean Ferrara: Ercole d'Este, 1471–1505, and the Invention of a Ducal Capital*, Cambridge, 1996, pp. 225 (wall-hangings), 311, 326, 337; for fresco cycle, A. Franceschini, *Artista a Ferrara in età umanistica e rinascimentale: testimonianze archivistiche*, 2 vols, Ferrara and Rome, 1993–5, II.1, p. 25, doc. 25.

14 K. Schulz, 'Die Medaille Gian Christophoro Romanos auf Isabella d'Este und die Medaillenkunst ihrer Zeit' in S. Ferino-Pagden (ed.), '*La Prima Donna del Mondo' Isabella d'Este: Fürstin und Mäzenatin der Renaissance*, exh. cat. Kunsthistorisches Museum, Vienna, 1994, pp. 373–8.

15 E. Müntz, *Les arts à la cour des papes pendant le XVe et le XVIe siècles*, Paris, 1882, III, pp. 297–8.

16 G. Meconcelli Notarianni, in A. Mottola Molfino and M. Natale (eds), *Le muse e il principe: arte di corte nel Rinascimento padano*, exh. cat., Museo Poldi Pezzoli, Milan, Modena, 1991, I, *Catalogo*, pp. 243–6, cat. nos 65, 66.

17 Tuohy, *Herculean Ferrrara*, p. 230.

18 In relation to the dismantlement of works by 'Gusmin' see Schlosser (ed.), *Ghiberti*, 1912, p. 44.

19 E. Plon, *Benvenuto Cellini: orfévre, médailleur, sculpteur*, Paris, 1883, p. 392, doc. VII; J. Pope-Hennessy, *Cellini*, London, 1985, pp. 107–16.

20 E. Ruhmer, *Tura: paintings and drawings*, London, 1958, pp. 82–3.

21 Manca, *Cosmè Tura*, pp. 214–16, doc. 79.

22 See e.g. Franceschini, *Artista a Ferrara*, I, pp. 211, 231, 262, 684, doc. 462p, 493z, 553a, 1097 a.

23 Manca, *Cosmè Tura*, pp. 220, doc. 91.

24 Bernardino Zambotti, *Diario Ferrarese dall' anno 1476 sino al 1504*, ed. G. Pardi, *Rerum italicarum scriptores*, XXIV.7, Bologna, 1934–7, pp. 22, 60–1, 76, 84; A. Luzio, 'Isabella d'Este e Gian Francesco Gonzaga, promesi sposi', *Archivo storico lombardo*, ser. iv, IX, 1908, pp. 34–68, esp. p. 47.

25 Benvenuto Cellini, *La Vita*, ed. G. Davico Bonino, Turin, 1973, pp. 40–1.

26 Ibid., p. 43.

27 J.F. Hayward, *Virtuoso Goldsmiths and the Triumph of Mannerism 1540–1620*, London, 1976, pp. 24–5.

28 J. Babelon, *Jacopo da Trezzo et la construction de l'Escurial*, Paris, 1922, pp 275–6, doc. 6.

29 Thornton, *The Scholar*, pp. 146–8.

30 G. Pozzi and L.A. Ciappini (eds), *Hypnerotomachia Poliphili*, Padua, 1964, p. 87.

31 Ibid., p. 83.

32 A. Luzio and R. Renier, 'Il lusso di Isabella d'Este', *Nuova antologia*, ser. iv, LXIV, July 1896, pp. 300–1.

33 Holman, *Disegno*, pp. 5, 13, n. 36.

34 U. Bazzotti, 'Disegni per argenteria' in E.H. Gombrich *et al.*, *Giulio Romano*, exh. cat., Palazzo Te, Palazzo Ducale, Mantua, Milan, 1989, pp. 454–7, esp. p. 454.

35 U. Rossi, 'Cristoforo Geremia', *Archivo storico dell'arte*, I, 1888, pp. 404–11, esp. pp. 406, 408–9.

36 Ibid.

37 Luzio and Renier, 'Il lusso di Isabella d'Este', p. 303.

38 F. Canuti, *Il Perugino*, 2 vols, Siena, 1931, II, p. 127, doc. 327–8; Lightbown, *Mantegna*, p. 190.

39 L. Artusi, *Le arti e i mestieri di Firenze*, Rome, 1990, pp. 87–98. For goldsmiths in Florence, see M.G. Ciardi Dupre (ed.), *L'oreficeria nella Firenze del Quattrocento*, exh. cat., Florence, 1977, pp. 139–200.

40 Vasari, *Vite*, VI, p. 135.

41 R. Krautheimer, *Lorenzo Ghiberti*, 2nd edn, Princeton, 1970, p. 17.

42 G. Bironi, 'Documenti inediti per Bramantino', *Arte Lombarda*, 3/4, 1988, p. 42; P. Venturelli,

Gioelli e gioiellieri milanesi: storia, arte, moda (1450–1630), Milan, 1996, p. 22.

43 R. Bartoli in A. Petrioli Tofani (ed.), *Il disegno fiorentino del tempo di Lorenzo il Magnifico*, exh. cat., Uffizi, Florence, 1992, p. 61, cat. no. 2.18; L. Melli, *Maso Finiguerra: I disegni*, Florence, 1992, p. 81, cat. no. 68.

44 A. Perosa (ed.), *Giovanni Rucellai ed il suo Zibaldone*, London, 1960, I, pp. 23–4; A. Wright, 'Antonio Pollaiuolo: *maestro di disegno*' in E. Cropper (ed.), *Florentine Drawing at the Time of Lorenzo the Magnificent*, Papers of the Villa Spelman Colloquium 1992, Bologna, 1994, VI, pp. 131–46.

45 C. Mitchell, 'Felice Feliciano *Antiquarius*', *Proceedings of the British Academy*, LXVII, 1961, pp. 197–221, esp. pp. 199–200.

46 For Maso's nielli and the art in general see A.M. Hind, *Nielli, Chiefly Italian of the XV Century: Plates, Sulphur Casts and Prints Preserved in the British Museum*, London, 1936. For the Bargello pax, see M. Collareta and A. Capitanio, *Oreficeria sacra italiana: Museo Nazionale del Bargello*, Florence, 1990, pp. 136–41, cat. no. 39.

47 M. Cruttwell, *Antonio Pollaiuolo*, London and New York, 1907, pp. 45–60, 260, 273–7, 279–80; L.D. Ettlinger, *Antonio and Piero Pollaiuolo*, London, 1978, pp. 166–8.

48 E. Steingräber, 'Eine unbekannte Arbeit des Antonio Pollaiuolo für das Kloster S. Gaggio bei Florenz', *Mitteilungen des Kunsthistorisches Institutes in Florenz*, VII, 1955, pp. 87–92; M. Collareta, *La croce del Pollaiolo*, Florence, 1982. The quality of these pieces is somewhat uneven, but there can be little doubt that the attribution of the plaques with St John the Evangelist, the Virgin, and God the Father is correct.

49 Alberti, *On Painting*, p. 143.

50 Krautheimer, *Ghiberti*, pp. 4, 6, 203.

51 For Maso, see M. Haines, *The 'Sacrestia delle Messe' of the Florentine Cathedral*, Florence, 1983, pp. 140, 162–5; for Pollaiuolo, see Cruttwell, *Pollaiuolo*, pp. 261–3; A. Venturi, 'Il paliotto di Sisto IV', *L'arte*, IX, 1906, pp. 218–22.

52 A.M. Hind, *Early Italian Engraving: a Critical Catalogue*, Part 1, *Florentine Engravings and Anonymous Prints of Other Schools*, New York and London, 1938, I, p. 82, no. AIII.6a, II, pl. 124.

53 Maso made such casts from 1447 at the latest. See Alesso Baldovinetti, *I Ricordi di Alesso Baldovinetti, pittore fiorentino nel secolo XV*, ed. G. Pierotti, Lucca, 1868, p. 9; R. Wedgwood Kennedy, *Alesso Baldovinetti: a Critical and Historical Study*, New Haven, 1938, p. 236; J.A. Levenson, K. Oberhuber and J.L. Sheehan, *Early Italian Engravings from the National Gallery of Art*, exh. cat., Washington, 1973. pp. 1–9, 13–21.

54 Hind, *Early Italian Engravings*, 1938, pp. 189–92, no. D.I.1; L. Richards, 'Antonio Pollaiuolo: Battle of the Naked Men', *Bulletin of the Cleveland Museum of Art*, LV, 1968, pp. 63–70.

55 Sabba da Castiglione, *I Ricordi*, Vencie, 1559, p. 57.

56 M. Faietti, 'Stampe a niello bolognesi ed emiliane' in M. Faietti and K. Oberhuber, *Bologna e l'umanesimo, 1490–1510*, exh. cat., Pinacoteca Nazionale, Bologna, 1988, pp. 323–40.

57 Krautheimer, *Ghiberti*, 1970, p. 6; F. and S. Borsi, *Paolo Uccello*, Milan, 1992, pp. 318–21.

58 Haines, '*Sacrestia delle Messe*', pp. 140–1. Baldovinetti was paid 3 florins.

59 See D. Cordellier, 'Documenti e fonti su Pisanello (1395–1581 circa)' in D. Cordellier (ed.), *Verona Illustrata: Rivista del Museo di Castelvecchio*, 1995, VIII, pp. 151–3, doc. 68. We are grateful to Caroline Elam for her translation.

60 M. Fossi Todorow, *I disegni del Pisanello e della sua cerchia*, Florence, 1966, pp. 88–91, 116–21, cat. nos 73–80, 152–65, D. Cordellier in *Pisanello: peintre aux sept vertus*, exh. cat., Musée du Louvre, Paris, 1996, pp. 415–53, cat. nos 290–7, 301–2, 308–18.

61 See Ruhmer, *Tura*, 1958, pp. 79–84 for a good chronological account of the range of Tura's activities at court revealed in the documents.

62 Franceschini, *Artista a Ferrara*, II.1, p. 96, doc. 117f; Manca, *Cosmè Tura*, p. 219, doc. 89.

63 C. Rosenberg, 'Francesco Cossa's Letter Reconsidered', *Musei Ferraresi*, V/VI, 1975–6, pp. 11–16.

64 F. Varignana, 'Le vetrate di San Giovanni in Monte' in F. Varignana (ed.), *Tre artisti nella Bologna dei Bentivoglio*, Bologna, 1985, pp. 7–113.

65 A. Bacchi, *Francesco del Cossa*, Soncino, 1991, p. 5.

66 C.G.E. Bunt, *The Goldsmiths of Italy: Some Account of Their Guilds, Statutes and Work*, London, 1926, pp. 56–7.

67 G. Agosti, 'Piccole asservazioni nell' area dello Squarcione' in A. De Nicolò Salmazo (ed.), *Francesco Squarcione: 'Pictorum gymnasiarcha singularis'*, Padua, 1999, pp. 53–78, esp. p. 75.

68 E. Motta, 'I medaglioni di Galeazzo Maria Sforza e di Bona da Savoia', *Rivista italiana di numismatica*, XXIX, 1916, pp. 239–46; L. Syson, 'The Circulation of Drawings for Medals in Fifteenth-Century Italy' in M. Jones (ed.), *Designs on Posterity: Drawings for Medals*, London, 1994, pp. 10–26, esp. pp. 11–12.

69 J. Meyer zur Capellen, *Gentile Bellini*, Stuttgart, 1985, p. 108, doc. 13 (1476).

70 T. Frimmel, 'Urkunden, Regesten und artistisches Quellenmaterial aus der Bibliothek der Kunsthistorischen Sammlungen des Allerhöchsten Kaiserhauses', *Jahrbuch der Kunsthistorischen Sammlungen des Allerhöchsten Kaiserhauses*, 1887, V, 2, pp. xv–xvi, doc. 4020; E. Motta, 'Ambrogio Preda e Leonardo da Vinci (nuovi documenti)', *Archivio storico lombardo*, ser. ii, XI, 1893, pp. 972–89, esp. pp. 979–85; Venturelli, *Gioielli*, p. 25.

71 Kristeller, *Mantegna*, p. 526, doc. 42.

72 K. Clark, 'Andrea Mantegna', *Master Drawings*, IV, 1929–30, pp. 60–2; D. Ekserdjian in J. Martineau (ed.), *Andrea Mantegna*, exh. cat., Royal Academy of Arts, London, and Metropolitan Museum of Art, New York, 1992, pp. 223–4, cat. no. 50.

73 L. Syson, 'Circulating a Likeness? Coin Portraits in Late Fifteenth-Century Italy' in N. Mann and L. Syson (eds), *The Image of the Individual: Portraits in the Renaissance*, London, 1998, pp. 113–25, esp. p. 120.

74 U. Rossi, 'I medaglisti del Rinascimento all corte di Mantova', *Rivista italiana di numismatica*, I, 1888, pp. 433–54; Kristeller, *Mantegna*, pp. 541, docs 84–5.

75 For his other tactics, see J. Woods-Marsden, *Renaissance Self-Portraiture: the Visual Construction of Identity and the Social Status of the Artist*, New Haven and London, 1998, pp. 85–97; F. Ames-Lewis, *The Intellectual Life of the Early Renaisssance Artist*, New Haven and London, 2000, pp. 20, 62–3, 101–6, 242, 268.

76 E. Lincoln, 'Mantegna's Culture of Line', *Art History*, XVI, 1, 1993, pp. 33–57, A. Wright, 'Mantegna and Pollaiuolo: artistic personality and the marketing of invention' in S. Currie (ed.), *Drawing, 1400–1600: Invention and Innovation*, Aldershot, 1998, pp. 72–90.

77 See D. Landau, 'Mantegna as Printmaker', in Martineau, *Andrea Mantegna*, pp. 44–54; S. Boorsch, 'Mantegna and the Printmakers', in ibid., pp. 56–66; K. Christiansen, 'The Case for Mantegna as a Printmaker', *Burlington Magazine*, CXXXV, 1993, pp. 604–11; J.A. Levenson, 'Mantegna and the Emergence of Engraving in Italy' in C. Mozzarelli *et al.* (eds), *La corte di Mantova nell'età di Andrea Mantegna: 1450–1550*, Rome, 1997, pp. 197–205.

78 A bronze statuette of a young boy, the best example of which is preserved in Houston, was depicted from different angles in paintings and prints by Mantegna and his circle, leading to the plausible suggestion that it was designed by Mantegna himself, and executed under his supervision. See W. Stedman Sheard, *Antiquity in the Renaissance*, exh. cat., Smith College Museum of Art, Northampton, Mass., 1978, no. 6; see also Lightbown, *Mantegna*, *passim*.

79 Landau, 'Mantegna as Printmaker', pp. 279–81, 285–7, cat. nos 74–5, 79.

80 Ibid., pp. 48–52.

81 L. Beltrami, 'Bramante e Leonardo praticarono l'arte del bulino? Un incisore sconosciuto, Bernardino Prevedari', *Rassegna d'arte*, XVII, 1917, pp. 187–94; E. Borea, 'Stampa figurativa e pubblico dalle origini all'affermazione nel Cinquecento' in G. Previtali (ed.), *Storia dell'arte italiana*, II, *L'artista e il pubblico*, Turin, 1979, pp. 319–413; esp. pp. 346–7; Venturelli, *Gioielli*, p. 25.

82 K. Oberhuber, 'Marcantonio Raimondi: gli inizi a Bologna ed il primo periodo romano' in Faietti and Oberhuber, *Bologna e l'umanesimo*, pp. 51–88; D. Landau and P. Parshall, *The Renaissance Print, 1470–1550*, New Haven and London, 1994, pp. 76, 99–100, 117–19.

83 See J. Warren, 'Francesco Francia and the Art of Sculpture in Renaissance Bologna', *Burlington Magazine*, CXLI, 1999, pp. 216–25; E. Negro and N. Roio, *Francesco Francia e la sua scuola*, Modena, 1999, pp. 69–124 (attributions should be treated with caution).

84 Brown and Hickson, 'Caradosso Foppa', pp. 9–39.

85 S. Fermor, *The Raphael Tapestry Cartoons: Narrative, Decoration, Design*, London, 1996, *passim*.

86 K. Oberhuber, 'Raffaello e l'incisione' in *Raffaello in Vaticano*, exh. cat., Vatican, Rome, 1984, pp. 333–42; Landau and Parshall, *Renaissance Print*, pp. 121–2.

87 V. Golzio, *Rafaello nei documenti*, Vatican City, 1936, pp. 22–3.

88 See A. Luzio and R. Renier, *Mantova e Urbino: Isabella d'Este ed Elisabetta Gonzaga*, Turin, 1893, pp. 230–4; Holman, *Disgeno*, p. 12, n. 5.

89 J.A. Gere and N. Turner, *Drawings by Raphael*, exh. cat., British Museum, London, 1983, pp. 149–50, cat. no. 123; Holman, *Disgeno*, pp. 1–2; M. Clayton, *Raphael and his Circle: Drawings from Windsor Castle*, London, 1999, pp. 83–5. A second drawing related to this sheet is in the Ashmolean (Parker 572).

90 Bunt, *Goldsmiths of Italy*, pp. 77–80.

91 E. Parma Armani, *Perin del Vaga: l'anello mancante*, Genoa, 1986, pp. 177–208; J. Hayward, *Virtuoso Goldsmiths and the Triumph of Mannerism*, London, 1976, pp. 134–6.

92 See Pope-Hennessy, *Cellini*, p. 29; Hayward, *Virtuoso Goldsmiths*, pp. 56–7, 146–7; for a combination of precious stones and figurative elements, see C.M. Brown, 'The Archival Scholarship of Antonino Bertolotti – a Cautionary Tale: the Galeazzo Mondella (Moderno) Model for a Diamond *Saint George Brooch*', *artibus et historiae*, XXXV, 1997, pp. 65–71.

93 Cellini, *Vita*, pp. 38, 43–4; Hayward, *Virtuoso Goldsmiths*, pp. 56–7.

94 F. Hartt, *Giulio Romano*, New Haven, 1958, p. 73, doc. 69.

95 B.L. Holman, 'A "subtle artifice": Giulio Romano's *Salt Cellar with Satyrs* for Federico II Gonzaga', *Quaderni di Palazzo Te*, VIII, 2000, pp. 56–67, esp. p. 62.

96 C.M. Brown and G. Delmarcel, *Tapestries for the Courts of Federio II, Ercole and Ferrante Gonzaga, 1552–63*, Seattle and London, 1996, *passim*.

97 Bazzotti, 'Disegni per argenterie', pp. 455.

98 G. Vasari, *Vite*, V, 1880, pp. 537–9.

99 Chambers and Martineau, *Gonzaga*, p. 195.

100 Ibid., p. 196.

101 Hartt, *Giulio Romano*, I, cat. nos 48–132.

102 Chambers and Martineau, *Gonzaga*, pp. 197–8, cat. no. 192.

103 Ibid., pp. 196–7, cat. no. 189.

104 D.J. Jansen, 'Jacopo Strada antiquario mantovano e la fortuna di Giulio Romano' in *Giulio Romano: atti del convegno internazionale di studi*, Mantua, 1989, pp. 361–74.

105 J.F. Hayward, 'Ottavio da Strada and the Goldsmiths' Designs of Giulio Romano', *Burlington Magazine*, CXII, 1970, pp. 10–14; Hayward, *Virtuoso Goldsmiths*, pp. 24–6.

106 Franceschini, *Artisti a Ferrara*, II.1, p. 336, doc. 487n.

107 L. Fairbairn, *Italian Renaissance Drawings from the Collection of Sir John Soane's Museum*, London 1998, p. 33, cat. no. 31.

108 Hayward, *Virtuoso Goldsmiths*, p. 85.

109 Ibid., p. 338, cat. no. 8; E. Miller, *16th-Century Italian Ornament Prints in the Victoria and Albert Museum*, London, 1999, p. 228, cat. no. 65.

110 C. Monbeig Goguel in C. Monbeig Goguel (ed.), *Francesco Salviati (1510–1563) o la Bella Maniera*, exh. cat., Villa Medici, Rome, Musée du Louvre, Paris, Milan, 1998, pp. 276–7, cat. no. 109; Miller, *Italian Ornament Prints*, pp. 223–5, cat. no. 63a.

111 Cf. T.L. Rebanks in Holman, *Disegno*, pp. 91–3, cat. no. 20.

112 Miller, *Italian Ornament Prints*, pp. 229–32, cat. no. 66.

113 Cordellier *Pisanello*, pp. 110–11, cat. no. 59.

114 F. Ames-Lewis, *Drawing in Early Renaissance Italy*, New Haven and London, 1981, pp. 4–5.

115 C. Monbeig Goguel in Monbeig Goguel, *Francesco Salviati*, pp. 272–3, cat. no. 107.

116 Hayward, *Virtuoso Goldsmiths*, p. 36.

117 Vasari, *Vite*, VII, 1881, p. 194.

118 Ibid., pp. 192, 198.

119 Hayward, *Virtuoso Goldsmiths*, p. 134.

120 Vasari, *Vite*, VII, p. 383; J. Wilde, *Italian Drawings in the Department of Prints and Drawings at the British Museum: Michelangelo and his Studio*, London, 1953, p. 105, cat. no. 66; document translated by Hayward, *Virtuoso Goldsmiths*, p. 343.

121 Cellini, *Vita*, p. 26.

122 For Cavalieri, see E. Steinmann and H. Pogatscher, *Die Sixtinische Kapelle*, 2 vols, Munich, 1901–5, II, 1905, pp. 500–2, 511; A. Perrig, 'Cavalieri, Tommaso de", *Dizionario biografico degli italiani*, XXII, Rome, 1979, pp. 678–80 for ref. For the drawings, see M. Hirst, *Michelangelo and his Drawings*, New Haven and London, 1988, pp. 105–16; P. Joannides, *Michelangelo and his Influence: Drawings from Windsor Castle*, exh. cat., National Gallery of Art, Washington, Queen's Gallery, London, 1998, p. 56, cat. no. 9a. For the sarcophagus source of the Phaeton composition, now in the Uffizi, Florence, see P. Bober and R. Rubinstein, *Renaissance Artists and Antique Sculpture: A Handbook of Sources*, Oxford, 1986, p. 27, cat. no. 27.

123 Joannides, *Michelangelo*, p. 57.

124 Vasari wrote: 'These cartoons secured M. Tommaso a good success, such as Michelangelo had already to Fra Bastiano of Venice; indeed, M. Tommaso has preserved these wonderful drawings as keepsakes, and courteously allows other artists to use them.' See Vasari, *Vite*, VII, 1881, p. 272; M. Hirst, *Sebastiano del Piombo*, Oxford, 1981, pp. 41–75.

125 See M. Roliti *et al.* (ed.), *Fortuna di Michelangelo nell'incisione*, exh. cat., Museo del Sannio, Benevento, 1964, pp. 64–71 (which should be treated with some caution).

126 M. McCrory, 'The Symbolism of Stones: Engraved Gems at the Medici Grand-Ducal Court' in C.M. Brown (ed.), *Engraved Gems: Survivals and Revivals, Studies in the History of Art*, LIV, Washington, 1997, pp. 158–79, esp. pp. 169–71.

127 See J.A. Gere, 'Two late Frescoes by Perin del Vaga: the Massimi Chapel and the Sala Paolina', *Burlington Magazine*, CII, 1960, pp. 9–19, esp. p. 13; V. Donati, *Pietre dure e medaglie del rinascimento: Giovanni da Castel Bolognese*, Ferrara, 1989, pp. 108–9, 114–21, 144–7, 168–71, 182–3; D. Jaffe, 'Drawings for Renaissance Medals' in M. Jones (ed.), *Designs on Posterity: Drawings for Medals*, London, 1994, pp. 48–50; Monbeig Goguel, *Francesco Salviati*, pp. 244–7, 260–1, 264–5, cat. nos 93–4, 101, 103.

128 By Adamo Ghizi, see S. Boorsch and J. Spike (eds), *The Illustrated Bartsch*, XXXI (15.4), p. 175 (23.424), where Giulio's drawing is mistakenly said to be after the gem rather than a design for it.

129 B. Marsolin, 'Valerio Vicentino nelle *Vite* di Giorgio Vasari', *Atti del reale Istituto Veneto di Scienze, Lettere ed Arte*, ser. vi, XLIV, 1885–6, pp. 1093–1121, esp. pp. 1117–21. For the British Museum gem, see Thornton, 'Valerio Belli', pp. 11–20, esp. pp. 12–13, cat. no. 1.

130 C.M. Brown, 'Isabella d'Este Gonzaga's *Augustus and Livia* Cameo and the *Alexander and Olympias* Gems in Vienna and Saint Petersburg', in Brown, *Engraved Gems*, pp. 84–107, esp. pp. 99–100.

131 Donati, *Pietre dure e medaglie*, pp. 80–6; C. Robertson, Il gran cardinale: *Alessandro Farnese, Patron of the Arts*, New Haven and London, 1992, pp. 38–41, esp. fig. 24, Thornton, 'Valerio Belli', p. 15.

132 Donati, *Pietre dure e medaglie*, pp. 80–5.

133 E. Kris, *Meister und Meisterwerke der Steinschneiderkunst*, Vienna, 1929, I, pp. 64–5.

Chapter 5

1 A. Bayer, 'Dosso's Public: the Este Court at Ferrara' in A. Bayer (ed.), *Dosso Dossi: Court Painter in Renaissance Ferrara*, exh. cat., Galleria d'Arte Moderna e Contemporanea, Ferrara, Metropolitan Museum of Art, New York, J. Paul Getty Museum, Los Angeles, 1998–9, pp. 27–54, esp. pp. 28–9.

2 Manca, *Ercole de' Roberti*, p. 221, doc. 72.

3 A. Venturi, 'L'arte ferrarese nel periodo d'Ercole I d'Este', *Atti e memorie della R. Deputazione di Soria Patria per le provincie di Romagna*, ser. iii, VI, 1888, pp. 91–119, 350–422, esp. pp. 352–3, VII, 1888–9, pp. 386–412; Bayer, 'Dosso's Public', p. 28.

4 Paolo Giovio, *La vita di Alfonso da Este, duca di Ferrara, scritta da il vescovo Iovio. Tr. in lingua toscana da Giovanbattista Gelli*, Venice, 1553, pp. 16; cited by Bayer, 'Dosso's Public', p. 28.

5 Pliny, *Natural History*, XXXIV, I.1, III.5.

6 D. Heikamp, *Mediceischen Glaskunst*, Florence, 1986, p. 44.

7 C.S. Smith and M. Teach Gnudi (eds and trans), *The* Pirotechnia *of Vannoccio Biringuccio*, New York, 1990, pp. ix–x on dating.

8 Ibid., p. 127; P.P. McCray, *Glassmaking in Renaissance Venice: The Fragile Craft*, Ashtead, Surrey, 1999, p. 66.

9 Letter from Lorenzo da Pavia to Isabella d'Este of 28 September 1503, quoted in C.M. Brown and A.M. Lorenzoni, *Isabella d'Este and Lorenzo da Pavia*, Geneva, 1982, p. 77, doc. 80.

10 See Brown and Lorenzoni, *Isabella d'Este*, pp. 213–19.

11 For sources on Renaissance glass, see McCray, *Glassmaking*, pp. 4–8.

12 L. Zecchin, *Vetro e vetrai di Murano*, 3 vols, Venice, 1987–90, I, pp. 6, 46.

13 D. Jacoby, 'Raw materials for the Glass Industries of Venice and the Terraferma, about 1370–1460', *Glass Studies*, XXXV, 1993, pp. 65–90, esp. pp. 67–73.

14 Ibid., pp. 85–6.

15 R. Schmidt, *Das Glas*, Berlin, 1912, p. 118. We are grateful to Reino Liefkes for this reference.

16 R. Brown (ed.), *Calendar of State Papers and Manuscripts relating to English Affairs, existing in the archives and collections of Venice*, V, *1534–1554*, London, 1873, p. 311, doc. 648, for petition of Muranese glassmakers in London of February

1550 [1549]; A. Hartshorne, *Old English Glasses*, London and New York, 1897, pp. 148–50. For Venetian glassworkers in Belgium, see L. Engen (ed.), *Le verre en Belgique des origines à nos jours*, Liège, 1989, p. 71. On emigration of glass-workers in general, see McCray, *Glassmaking*, pp. 157–63.

17 C. Hess and T. Husband, *European Glass in the J. Paul Getty Museum*, Los Angeles, 1997, p. 8.

18 On the Aldrevandin Group and the beaker itself, see J. Clark, 'Medieval Enamelled Glasses from London', *Medieval Archaeology*, XXVII, 1983, pp. 152–6; E. Baumgartner and I. Krueger, *Phoenix aus Sand und Asche: Glas des Mittelalters*, Bonn, 1988, pp. 125–54; I. Freestone, 'Looking at Glass' in S. Bowman (ed.), *Science and the Past*, London, 1991, pp. 37–56, esp. pp. 51–2; I. Krueger, 'An Enamelled Beaker from Stralsund: A Spectacular New Find' in R. Ward (ed.), *Gilded and Enamelled Glass from the Near East*, London, 1998, pp. 107–9; I. Freestone and C. Stapleton, 'Composition and Technology of Islamic Enamelled Glass of the Thirteenth and Fourteenth Centuries' in Ward, *Gilded and Enamelled Glass*, pp. 122–8.

19 G.H. Tait, *Five Thousand Years of Glass*, London, 1991, p. 152.

20 Smith and Teach Gnudi, *Pirotechnia*, pp. 130–1.

21 D. Whitehouse, 'Glass in the Epigrams of Martial', *Journal of Glass Studies*, XIV, 1999, pp. 73–82, esp. p. 80, n. 61. The same passage had been translated with directly opposite meaning by M. Vickers, 'Rock Crystal: the Key to Cut Glass and Diatreta in Persia and Rome', *Journal of Roman Archaeology*, IX, 1996, pp. 48–65, esp. p. 48.

22 McCray, *Glassmaking*, pp. 97–125 for detailed account of this development.

23 Jacoby, 'Raw materials', pp. 65–90; for the Florentine treatise, see G. Milanesi (ed.), *Dell'arte del vetro per musaico: tre tratatelli dei secoli XIV e XV*, Bologna, 1864, p. 111.

24 Zecchin, *Vetro e vetrai*, I, 1987, pp. 237–40, esp. p. 238; J.V.G. Mallet, 'Tiled Floors and Court Designers in Mantua and Northern Italy' in C. Mozzarelli, R. Oresko and L. Ventura (eds), *The Court of the Gonzaga in the Age of Mantegna: 1450–1550*, Rome, 1997, pp. 253–72, esp. p. 258.

25 Zecchin, *Vetro e vetrai*, I, p. 51 for documents of 1457; McCray, *Glassmaking*, pp. 99–100 for analysis.

26 Zecchin, *Vetro e vetrai*, I, p. 52 for accord of 1460; Jacoby, 'Raw materials', p. 89.

27 Both techniques illustrated in Tait, *Five Thousand Years*, pp. 219–21, figs 56–7 for Roman technique, pp. 228–9, fig. 209 for Renaissance version; A.-E. Theuerkauff-Liederwald, *Venezianisches Glas der Veste Coburg*, Lingen, 1994, pp. 58–60.

28 Zecchin, *Vetro e vetrai*, I, p. 49.

29 McCray, *Glassmaking*, p. 122.

30 P. Venturelli, *Glossario e documenti per la gioielleria milanese*, Milan, 1999, p. 10.

31 R.W. Lightbown, *Medieval European Jewellery with a catalogue of the collection in the Victoria & Albert Museum*, London, 1992, p. 19.

32 O.M. Dalton, *Franks Bequest: Catalogue of the Finger Rings, Early Christian, Byzantine, Teutonic,*

medieval and later*, London, 1912, cat. no. 859; Chambers, *A Renaissance Cardinal*, p. 163, item 586; J. Goodall, 'Papal Rings, a Quattrocento Reference', *The Antiquaries Journal*, 73, 1993, pp. 157–8.

33 Chambers, *Renaissance Cardinal*, 1992, p. 5.

34 Zecchin, *Vetro e vetrai*, I, p. 52.

35 M. Spallanzani, *Le ceramiche orientali*, Florence, 1978, p. 165, doc. 23; Zecchin, *Vetro e vetrai*, III, pp. 378–82.

36 G.H. Tait, *The Golden Age of Venetian Glass*, exh. cat., British Museum, London, 1979, p. 74.

37 C.A. Levi, *L'arte del vetro in Murano nel Rinascimento e i Berroviero*, Venice, 1895, p. 20.

38 Tait, *Five Thousand Years*, p. 119, fig. 147.

39 Ibid., p. 128, fig. 160; M.G. Diani, 'Contributo alla carta di distribuzione di alcune forme vitree de età Romana colate a stampo e soffiate a stampo' in *Il vetro dall' antichita all' età contemporanea: aspetti technologici, funzionale e commerciali*, Milan, 1998, pp. 31–8 (esp. p. 36), 296.

40 R. Liefkes (ed.), *Glass*, London, 1997, p. 44; McCray, *Glassmaking*, p. 123.

41 P. Hills, *Venetian Colour: Marble, Mosaic, Painting and Glass, 1250–1550*, New Haven and London 1999, p. 127, n. 36.

42 Liefkes, *Glass*, p. 45, fig. 49.

43 Tait, *Five Thousand Years*, p. 235 for an example.

44 A. Moore Valeri, 'Venetian Beakers with Enamel Decoration and Tuscan Mould-Blown Vessels in an Early Sixteenth-Century Wall Painting in Florence', *Journal of Glass Studies*, XXXIX, 1997, pp. 200–6, esp. p. 202.

45 Letter of 20 April 1496: Brown and Lorenzoni, *Isabella d'Este*, p. 214; McCray, *Glassmaking*, p. 93.

46 Zecchin, *Vetro e vetrai*, III, p. 109

47 McCray, *Glassmaking*, p. 143.

48 Zecchin, *Vetro e vetrai*, III, pp. 125–35; F.A. Dreier and J.V.G. Mallet, *The Hockemeyer Collection: Maiolica and Glass*, Bremen, 1998, pp. 54–103, p. 84.

49 Zecchin, *Vetro e vetrai*, I, pp. 217–20, III, pp. 116–20, esp. p. 118.

50 Levi, *L'arte del vetro*, p. 13; Tait, *Five Thousand Years*, p. 157; Zecchin, *Vetro e vetrai*, I, p. 48.

51 Zecchin, *Vetro e vetrai*, I, p. 62.

52 Levi, *L'arte del vetro*, p. 21; T. Clarke, 'Lattimo – a Group of Venetian Glass Enamelled on an Opaque-White Ground', *Journal of Glass Studies*, XVI, 1974, pp. 22–56, esp. p. 23.

53 Levi, *L'arte del vetro*, p. 23; Zecchin, *Vetro e vetrai*, I, p. 62.

54 Levi, *L'arte del vetro*, p. 21; Clarke, 'Lattimo', p. 25.

55 Clarke, 'Lattimo', pp. 36, 50, 51.

56 H. Read, *The Waddesdon Bequest*, London, 1899, p. 26; D.B. Harden, K.S. Painter, R.H. Pinder-Wilson and G.H Tait, *Masterpieces of Glass*, London, 1968, cat. no. 208; Tait, *Golden Age*, p. 36, cat. no. 21; Tait, *Five Thousand Years*, p. 160.

57 Tait, *Golden Age*, cat. no. 22; Hills, *Venetian Colour*, p. 126, fig. 154.

58 Zecchin, *Vetro e vetrai*, I, pp. 237–8, II, pp. 200–2; McCray, *Glassmaking*, pp. 98–100.

59 Antonio Averlino detto Il Filarete, *Trattato di architettura*, eds A.M. Finoli, L. Grassi, Milan

1972, pp. 258–9; J.R. Spencer (ed.), *Filarete's Treatise on Architecture, Being the Treatise by Antonio Averlino, Known as Filarete*, New Haven and London, 1965, I, pp. 115–16; Mallet, 'Tiled Floors', pp. 253–72, esp. p. 257.

60 Mallet, 'Tiled Floors', p. 258.

61 Ibid., citing a glass tile in The British Museum with a portrait of Doge Andrea Gritti (1523–38) made by slumping glass over a relief portrait copying from a contemporary bronze medal, figs 1A and B.

62 Ibid.

63 *Dizionario biografico degli italiani*, VI, Rome, 1964, p. 492. Lodovico Carbone's epitaph, dedicated to Barovier as *optimum artificem crystallinorum vasorum*, is published in Levi, *L'arte del vetro*, p. 13.

64 We are grateful to Tim Wilson for his comments.

65 F. Tateo, *I Trattati delle virtù sociali*, Rome, 1965, p. 273; McCray, *Glassmaking*, p. 80.

66 Tait, *Five Thousand Years*, p. 160; McCray, *Glassmaking*, pp. 84–5.

67 Hess and Husband, *European Glass*, pp. 87–9, figs 20c–d.

68 Tait, *Glassmaking*, p. 159.

69 Bagemihl, 'The Trevisan Collection', pp. 559–62.

70 On the glass in this collection, see later in this chapter. On rock-crystal, see Chambers, *Renaissance Cardinal*, p. 159, items 498–503.

71 Ibid., p. 163, item 590.

72 Tait, *Golden Age*, cat. nos 13, 14.

73 M. Spallanzani and G. Gaeta Bertelà (eds), *Libro d'inventario dei beni di Lorenzo Il Magnifico*, Florence, 1992, p. 6.

74 Thornton, *The Scholar*, pp. 83, 209; McCray, *Glassmaking*, p. 85.

75 R. Signorini, 'New Findings about Andrea Mantegna: his Son Ludovico's Post-Mortem Inventory', *Journal of the Courtauld and Warburg Institutes*, LIX, 1996, pp. 103–18, p. 112.

76 Ibid., p. 104.

77 Moore Valeri, 'Venetian Beakers', p. 205, n. 19.

78 Pomponius Gauricus, *Treatise on Sculpture*, 1504, ed.1969, p. 232. We are grateful to Jeremy Warren for this reference and for the information about the bronze bust in the Ca d'Oro in Venice.

79 A. Radcliffe and C. Avery, 'The Chellini Madonna by Donatello', *Burlington Magazine*, CXVIII, 1976, pp. 377–87.

80 M.T. Sillano (ed.), *Le ricordanze di Giovanni Chellini da San Miniato*, Milan, 1984, p. 218; R.W. Lightbown, 'Giovanni Chellini, Donatello and Antonio Rosellino', *Burlington Magazine*, CIV, March 1962, pp. 102–4, esp. p. 104.

81 Liefkes, *Glass*, p. 46.

82 Hess and Husband, *European Glass*, p. 8.

83 Brown and Lorenzoni, *Isabella d'Este*, p. 213.

84 Smith and Teach Gnudi, *Pirotechnia*, p. 132; McCray, *Glassmaking*, p. 124.

85 A. Dawson *et al.*, 'Recent Acquisitions of Post-Medieval Ceramics and Glass in the British Museum's Department of Medieval and Later Antiquities (1982–1988)', *Burlington Magazine*, CXXX,1988, pp. 399–404, esp. p. 399; Tait, *Five Thousand Years*, p. 168, fig. 215.

86 R. Charleston, 'New Light on Renaissance Glass in England', *Journal of Glass Studies*, XXV, 1988, pp. 129–34, p. 131; R. Brown, *Calendar of State Papers*, doc. 648, pp. 311–12.

87 Zecchin, *Vetro e vetrai*, I, p. 235.

88 Tait, *Glass*, p. 166, fig. 212.

89 Leandro Alberti, *Descrittione di tutta Italia*, Bologna, 1550, p. 468.

90 Liefkes, *Glass*, p. 44 on enamelling.

91 Hess and Husband, *European Glass*, pp. 12–13.

92 Zecchin, *Vetro e vetrai*, I, p. 235.

93 See discussion of Aretine pottery, pp. 214–15.

94 Alberti, *Descrittione*, p. 468.

95 For moulded glass, see Tait, *Golden Age*, pp. 97–102, cat. nos 148–57. For Aretine wares, see F. Paturzo, *Arretina vasa*, Cortona, 1996, pp. 31–3.

96 Zecchin, *Vetro e vetrai*, I, p. 235.

97 Hess and Husband, *European Glass*, p. 9, fig. 11.

98 T. Wilson, *Ceramic Art of the Italian Renaissance*, exh. cat., British Museum, London, 1987, pp. 10, 148–9, 164–70; R. Goldthwaite, 'The Economic and Social World of Italian Renaissance Maiolica', *Renaissance Quarterly*, XLII, 1989, pp. 1–32, esp. p.13.

99 D. Ferrari (ed.), *Giulio Romano: Repertorio di fonti documentarie*, Rome, 1992, I, pp. 106, 109, 125–6.

100 For the price of maiolica, see G. Vitaletti, *Francesco Xanto Avelli*, Urbino, 1912, pp. 7–8; J.V.G. Mallet, 'Mantua and Urbino: Gonzaga Patronage of Maiolica', *Apollo*, XIV, 1981, pp. 162–9, esp. p. 167; B.L. Holman, *Disegno: Italian Renaissance Designs for the Decorative Arts*, exh. cat. Cooper-Hewitt Museum, New York, 1997, p. 95 for the cost of silver designed by Giulio Romano. We are grateful to Tim Wilson for referring us to these figures.

101 Vitaletti, *Avelli*, p. 8; Mallet, 'Mantua and Urbino', p. 167.

102 Niccolò Perotti, 'Ad Thadeum', quoted in A. Campana, 'Poesie umanistiche relative a ceramiche', *Faenza*, XXXII, 1946, pp. 59–68, esp. pp. 60–1.

103 *Matthias Corvinus und die Renaissance in Ungarn 1458–1541*, exh. cat., Schloss Schallaburg, 1982, p. 296.

104 G. Busti, 'Riverberi del terzo fuoco: la tecnica del lustro', *CeramicAntica*, V, no. 5, 1995, pp. 48–53; T. Wilson, 'The Beginnings of Lustreware in Renaissance Italy', *Handbook of the International Ceramics Fair and Seminar*, London, 1996, pp. 35–43.

105 C. Ravanelli Guidotti, *Mediterraneum: ceramica spagnola in Italia tra medioevo e Rinascimento*, Viterbo, 1992; A. Ray, *Spanish Pottery, 1248–1898*, London, 2000.

106 J.G. Hurst, D.S. Neal and H.J.E. van Beuningen (eds), *Pottery Produced and Traded in North-west Europe*, Rotterdam, 1986; T. Wilson, 'Maioliche rinascimentali armoriate con stemmi fiorentini', *L'araldica: fonti e metodi*, Florence, 1989, pp. 128–38, esp. p. 128.

107 A. Ray, 'The Rothschild Alfabeguer and other Fifteenth-Century Spanish Lustred "Basil Pots" ', *Burlington Magazine*, CXLII, no. 1167, June 2000, pp. 371–5.

108 M. Spallanzani, 'Maioliche di Valenza e di Montelupo in una casa pisana del 1480', *Faenza*, LXXII, 1986, pp. 164–70.

109 Thornton, *The Scholar*, p. 78, fig. 50.

110 Spallanzani, 'Maioliche di Valenza', p. 166.

111 M. Spallanzani, *Le ceramiche orientali a Firenze*, Florence, 1978, p. 152, doc. 11.

112 Ibid., pp. 152–3.

113 Spallanzani, 'Maioliche di Valenza', p. 165.

114 Thornton, *The Scholar*, p. 49, fig. 32.

115 Wilson, *Ceramic Art*, pp. 31, cat. no. 16; Wilson, 'Maioliche rinascimentali armoiate', pp. 129–30; N. Penny in P.L. Rubin and A. Wright, *Renaissance Florence: The Art of the 1470s*, exh. cat., National Gallery, London, 1999, p. 323, cat. no. 81.

116 Wilson, *Ceramic Art*, p. 31, cat. no. 16; Wilson, 'Maioliche rinascimentali armoriate', pp. 129–30.

117 Spallanzani and Gaeta Bertelà, *Libro d'inventario*, p. 141.

118 M. Spallanzani, 'Il vaso Medici Orsini in un documento d'archivio', *Faenza*, LX, 1974, pp. 88–90.

119 Ibid.

120 Goldthwaite, 'Italian Renaissance Maiolica', pp. 3–6; Wilson, *Ceramic Art*, p. 32.

121 T. Wilson, 'Italian Maiolica around 1500: Some Considerations on the Background to Antwerp Maiolica', in D. Gaimster (ed.), *Maiolica in the North*, London, 1999, p. 10, n. 6.

122 Wilson, *Ceramic Art*, pp. 39, 65.

123 Goldthwaite, 'Italian Renaissance Maiolica', pp. 7–9.

124 Cipriano Piccolpasso, *The Three Books of the Potter's Art*, 2 vols, trans and eds R. Lightbown and A. Caiger-Smith, London, 1980.

125 Ibid., I, pp. xxi–xxiv.

126 Ibid., I, p. xxxi; II, pp. 6–7.

127 We are grateful to Timothy Wilson for sharing this idea with us.

128 Piccolpasso, *Potter's Art*, I, p. 19; II, p. 105.

129 A.V.B. Norman, *The Wallace Collection: Catalogue of Ceramics*, I, Pottery, Maiolica, Faience, Stoneware, London, 1976, p. 4; Piccolpasso, *Potter's Art*, I, p. xvi; II, section 197, pp. 14–16, esp. p. 16.

130 Piccolpasso, *Potter's Art*, II, p. 13; W.M. Watson, *Italian Renaissance Maiolica from the William A.Clark Collection*, Washington, 1986, p. 173, cat. no. 69; T. Wilson, 'Maiolica in Renaissance Venice', *Apollo*, CXXV, 1987, pp. 184–9.

131 Watson, *Italian Renaissance Maiolica*, p. 16.

132 Piccolpasso, *Potter's Art*, II, p. 54.

133 Wilson, *Ceramic Art*, p. 24.

134 Piccolpasso, *Potter's Art*, II, pp. 56–84.

135 Norman, *Wallace Collection*, p. 7; Piccolpasso, *Potter's Art*, II, pp. 552–3; Watson, *Italian Renaissance Maiolica*, p. 21.

136 M. Lama, *Il libro di conti di un maiolicaro del Quattrocento*, Faenza, 1939, p. 36.

137 Wilson, 'Beginnings of lustreware', p. 39; G. Busti, 'Tecnica e produzione della decorazione a lustro nella storia della Ceramica Umbria' in C. Fiocco and G. Gherardi, *Ceramiche Umbria dal Medioevo allo Storicismo*, Faenza, 1989, vol. 2, pp. 629–44, esp. p. 639.

138 B. Rackham, *Victoria and Albert Museum: Catalogue of Italian Maiolica*, London, 1940, p. 247, cat. no. 746; Piccolpasso, *Potter's Art*, II, p. 33.

139 Piccolpasso, *Potter's Art*, II, pp. xvii, 29, 39.

140 Dreier and Mallet, *Hockmeyer*, p. 19.

141 A. Ladis, *Italian Renaissance Maiolica from Southern Collections*, Georgia, 1989, p. 16.

142 B.L. Holman, 'A "subtle artifice": Giulio Romano's *Salt Cellar with Satyrs* for Federico II Gonzaga', *Quaderni di Palazzo Te*, VIII, 2000, pp. 56–67, esp. p. 62.

143 Watson, *Italian Renaissance Maiolica*, p. 98, cat. no. 38; Wilson, *Ceramic Art*, pp. 108, cat. nos 172–3.

144 Piccolpasso, *Potter's Art*, II, pp. 45–6.

145 Ibid., p. 44.

146 Ibid., p. 30; O. Mazzucato, 'La bottega di un vasaio della fine del XVI secolo' in M. Nota (ed.), *Archaeologia nel centro storico*, Rome, 1986, pp. 131–3.

147 Wilson, *Ceramic Art*, p. 12.

148 Piccolpasso, *Potter's Art*, II, pp. xiv, 69.

149 Wilson, *Ceramic Art*, p. 13.

150 Piccolpasso, *Potter's Art*, II, pp. 53–6, 61–88; Watson, *Italian Renaissance Maiolica*, p. 14.

151 Piccolpasso, *Potter's Art*, II, p. 104; Wilson, *Ceramic Art*, pp. 119–20, cat. no. 188.

152 Piccolpasso, *Potter's Art*, II, pp. xvii, 105–6.

153 Ibid., p. 40.

154 Ibid.; Mazzucato, 'La bottega', p. 137.

155 Piccolpasso, *Potter's Art*, II, p. 106.

156 G.Vannini (ed.), *La maiolica di Montelupo: scavo di un carico di fornace*, Montelupo, 1977, p. 21.

157 Wilson, *Ceramic Art*, pp. 13–14; A. Caiger-Smith, *Lustre Pottery: Technique, Tradition and Innovation in Islam and the Western World*, London, 1985, pp. 129–54; Wilson, 'Beginnings of Lustreware', pp. 35–43.

158 Wilson, 'Beginnings of Lustreware', p. 40.

159 Goldthwaite, 'Italian Renaissance Maiolica', p. 12; Vannini, *Maiolica di Montelupo*, 1977, p. 21; H. Blake, 'Archaeology and Maiolica' in Wilson, *Ceramic Art*, p. 15; Wilson, 'Beginnings of lustreware', p. 38.

160 Wilson, 'Beginnings of lustreware', p. 39, with comments on likely retail prices for lustre.

161 Ibid., pp. 38–41; C. Fiocco and G. Gherardi, *La ceramica di Deruta dal XIII al XVIII secolo*, Faenza, 1994, pp. 214–58.

162 Wilson, 'Beginnings of lustreware', p. 37.

163 Piccolpasso, *Potter's Art*, II, pp. 100–1.

164 G. Cesare Tonducci, *Descrittione della città di Faenza*, Faenza, 1675.

165 Piccolpasso, *Potter's Art*, II, p. 103.

166 Ibid., pp. 103–4.

167 Letter to Gianjacopo Calandra from 'El Poeta' in Urbino, dated 1 August 1530; Vitaletti, *Avelli*, p. 7; Mallet, 'Mantua and Urbino', p. 167.

168 J.R. Spencer, *Leon Battista Alberti on Painting*, New Haven and London, 1966, pp. 23–7; M. Baxandall, *Giotto and the Orators: Humanist Observers of Painting in Italy and the Discovery of Pictorial Composition, 1350–1450*, Oxford, 1971, pp. 129–35.

169 M. Collareta, ' "Encaustum vulgo smaltum": note sulla percezione umanistica delle tecniche figurative', *Annali della Scuola Normale di Pisa*, ser. iii, XIV, 1984, pp. 757–9 for discussion of use of language by humanists to describe contemporary techniques.

170 Wilson, *Ceramic Art*, p. 103, cat. no. 160; Wilson, 'Il pittore delle maioliche *Lu Ur*: compagno e seguace di Francesco Xanto Avelli', *Fimantiquari*, II, 1993, pp. 19–31, esp. p. 19.

171 Wilson, *Ceramic Art*, pp. 11–12.

172 Piccolpasso, *Potter's Art*, I, p. xxii, on the 'typical workshop'.

173 Goldthwaite, 'Italian Renaissance Maiolica', p. 8, n. 11.

174 Lama, *Maiolicaro del Quattrocento*, p. 38; Piccolpasso, *Potter's Art*, I, p. xxii; Goldthwaite, 'Italian Renaissance Maiolica', p. 9.

175 Wilson, *Ceramic Art*, pp. 61, 66, cat. nos 83, 94.

176 Goldthwaite, 'Italian Renaissance Maiolica', p. 9; Wilson, *Ceramic Art*, p. 14; for Masci and Andreoli, see Fiocco and Gherardi, *Ceramica di Deruta*, pp. 23, 24, 45–6, 50, 55, 68; Wilson, 'Beginnings of Lustreware', pp. 38–9; for the Fontana and Calamelli, see Wilson, *Ceramic Art*, pp. 59, 65, 149–50, 152–3.

177 T. Clifford and J.V.G. Mallet, 'Battista Franco as a designer for maiolica', *Burlington Magazine*, CXVIII, 1976, pp. 387–410.

178 G. Vasari, *Le Opere di Giorgio Vasari*, 9 vols, ed. G. Milanesi, Florence, 1906, VI, p. 581.

179 E. Müntz, *Les collections des Médicis au quinzième siècle*, Paris, 1888, p. 57; R. Weiss, *The Renaissance Discovery of Classical Antiquity*, Oxford, 1969, p. 189.

180 P.L. Rubin, *Giorgio Vasari, Art and History*, New Haven and London, 1995, p. 61.

181 P. Roberts, 'Mass-Production of Roman Finewares' in I. Freestone and D. Gaimster (eds), *Pottery in the Making*, exh. cat., British Museum, London, 1997, pp. 188–93, esp. p. 190.

182 P. Bocci Picini, 'La riscoperta dell'antico' in K. Weil-Garris Brandt *et al.* (eds), *Giovinezza di Michelangelo*, exh. cat. Palazzo Vecchio, Florence, 1999, pp. 31–48, esp. p. 39.

183 Paturzo, *Arretina vasa*, pp. 31–3.

184 Ladis, *Maiolica from Southern Collections*, p. 24; Rubin, *Vasari*, p. 61.

185 Ladis, *Maiolica from Southern Collections*, p. 24.

186 P. Berardi, *L'antica maiolica di Pesaro*, Pesaro, 1984, pp. 43–4; T. Wilson, *Italian Maiolica of the Renaissance*, Milan, 1996, p. xiv.

187 A. Rossi, 'Documenti inediti per la storia delle maioliche', *Archivio storico dell'arte*, II, 1889, pp. 308–9; Wilson, 'Italian Maiolica around 1500', p. 6.

188 Wilson, 'Italian Maiolica around 1500', p. 11, n. 21.

189 Wilson, *Italian Maiolica*, pp. xiv–xv.

190 Wilson, 'Italian Maiolica around 1500', p. 6.

191 Piccolpasso, *Potter's Art*, I, pp. 10v–11r; II, pp. 30–1; J. Musacchio, *The Art and Ritual of Childbirth in Renaissance Italy*, New Haven and London, 1999, pp. 100–1, fig. 87.

192 Wilson, *Ceramic Art*, pp. 58–9, cat. no. 78.

193 M. Spallanzani, *Ceramiche alla corte dei Medici nel Cinquecento*, Modena, 1994, p. 129; Dreier and Mallet, *Hockemeyer*, p. 36.

194 Spallanzani, *Ceramiche alla corte dei Medici*, p. 129; Dreier and Mallet, *Hockemeyer*, p. 36.

195 Dreier and Mallet, *Hockemeyer*, p. 35; J. Giacomotti, *Catalogue des majoliques des musées nationaux*, Paris, 1974, p. 259, cat. no. 841; T. Crépin Leblond and P. Ennès, *Le Dressoir du Prince*, exh. cat., Musée National de la Renaissance, Ecouen, 1995, pp. 66, cat. no. 31.

196 Will of Lucia Bischizi, widow of Maestro Paolo, *finestraio*, Ferrara 1483. A. Franceschini, *Artisti a Ferrara in età umanistica e rinscimentale: testimonianze archivistiche*, Rome and Ferrara, II, 1995, p. 301, doc. 436.

197 Oil painting by unknown painter in the Convent of the Augustinian Canonesses at Modigliana, dating to around 1580: G. Viroli, *Arte Rinfrescata: interventi di restauro in territorio forlivese finanziati dalla Cassa dei Risparmi di Forlì*, Cesena, 1999, pp. 163–6. We are grateful to Jeremy Warren for drawing this to our attention.

198 See e.g. J. Rasmussen, *The Robert Lehman Collection*, X, *Italian Maiolica*, Metropolitan Museum of Art, New York, New York and Princeton, 1989, pp. 66–7, cat. no. 38.

199 The quotation is from Benedetto di Falco, *Descrizione dei luoghi antichi di Napoli e del suo amenissimo distretto*, Naples 1535; M. Galeotti Minola, 'Maiolica napoletana dell'età viceregnale', *Faenza*, LVIII, 1975, pp. 87–94, esp. p. 87; Goldthwaite, 'Italian Renaissance Maiolica', p. 19.

200 Galeotti Minola, 'Maiolica', p. 88.

201 F. Cioci, 'L'epigrafe sul boccale', *Faenza*, LXXVIII, 1992, pp. 257–69.

202 Thornton, *The Scholar*, p. 30.

203 Giovanni Pontano, *Carmina, Ecloghe, Elegie, Liriche*, ed. J. Oeschger, Bari, 1948; *Eridanus*, XL, p. 413, line 11.

204 M. Palvarini Gobio Casali, *La ceramica di Mantova*, Ferrara, 1987, pp. 180–92; C. Ravanelli Guidotti, 'Un singolare ritrovamento: un piatto del servizio di Isabella d'Este-Gonzaga', in T. Wilson (ed.), *Italian Renaissance Pottery: Papers written in association with a colloquium at the British Museum*, London, 1991, pp. 13–23.

205 Palvarini Gobio Casali, *Ceramica*, pp. 180–92.

206 F. Negroni, 'Nicola Pelliario, ceramista fantasma', *Notizie di Palazzo Albani,* XIV, 1986, pp. 13–19.

207 J. Poole, *Italian Maiolica and Incised Slipware in the Fitzwilliam Museum, Cambridge*, Cambridge, 1995, pp. 305–7, cat. no. 376.

208 Ibid.; Wilson, *Ceramic Art*, p. 47, cat. no. 53.

209 Wilson, *Ceramic Art*, p. 46, cat. no. 52.

210 B. Rackham, 'Niccolo Pellipario and Bramante', *Burlington Magazine*, LXXXVI, 1945, pp. 144–9. Wilson, *Ceramic Art*, p. 46, cat. no. 52.

211 T. Haussmann, *Majolica: spanische und italienische Keramik vom 14. bis zum 18.*, Berlin, 1972, pp. 232–5, cat. no. 171.

212 Ibid.

213 B.E. Wallen, A Maiolica Service for Isabella d'Este, MA thesis, Institute of Fine Arts, New York, 1966.

214 P.P. Bober and R. Rubinstein, *Renaissance Artists and Antique Sculpture: A Handbook of Sources*, Oxford, 1986, pp. 99–101, cat. no. 64,

215 For Gonzaga devices, see M. Praz, 'The Gonzaga devices' in D.S. Chambers and J. Martineau (eds), *Splendours of the Gonzaga*, exh. cat., Victoria and Albert Museum, London, 1981, pp. 65–80; Wilson, *Ceramic Art*, p. 46, cat. no. 52.

216 Chambers and Martineau, *Gonzaga*, p. 178, cat. no. 137; Wilson, *Ceramic Art*, p. 46, cat. no. 52.

217 T. Wilson, 'History on a Plate', *Art Quarterly*, no. 14, Summer 1993, pp. 20–3

218 M. Brodie, 'Un piatto di Nicola da Urbino proveniente dalla credenza di Isabella d'Este-Gonzaga nel Philadelphia Museum of Art', *Ceramic Antica*, VII, 73, 1997, pp. 36–62.

219 Wilson, *Ceramic Art*, p. 45, cat. no. 51.

220 P. Fortini Brown, *Art and Life in Renaissance Venice*, New York, 1997, pp. 138–9.

221 Campana, 'Poesie umanistiche', p. 59–68.

222 Ibid., esp. pp. 62–4.

223 Ibid., p. 63.

224 Signorini, 'New findings', pp. 103–18, esp. p. 109.

225 C. Piancastelli, 'Notizia di due piatti faentini del 1540', *Faenza*, VIII, 1920, pp. 49–60.

226 Ibid., pp. 51, 57, 59.

Chapter 6

1 Alberti, *On Painting*, pp. 61–2.

2 Baxandall, *Giotto and the Orators*, pp. 15–17; M. Kemp, *Behind the Picture: Art and Evidence in the Italian Renaissance*, New Haven and London, 1997, pp. 80–5.

3 See A. Luzio, *La galleria dei Gonzaga venduta all'Inghilterra nel 1627–28*, Milan, 1913, p. 200, for Isabella's desire to substitute a painting of *Christ among the Doctors* by Leonardo for her own proposed portrait, suggesting that the subject mattered less than the artist responsible. For Isabella's relationship with Bellini, see J. Fletcher, 'Isabella d'Este and Giovanni Bellini's *Presepio*', *Burlington Magazine*, CXIII, 1971, pp. 703–12; R. Goffen, *Giovanni Bellini*, New Haven and London, 1989, pp. 265–8. For her attempt to acquire a painting by Giorgione, see J. Anderson, *Giorgione: The Painter of 'Poetic Brevity'*, Paris and New York, 1997, p. 17.

4 J. Pope-Hennessy, *Paolo Uccello*, London, 1950, p. 154; G. Robertson, *Giovanni Bellini*, Oxford, 1968, p. 104; C. Gould, *National Gallery Catalogues: the Sixteenth-Century Italian Schools*, London, 1975, pp. 199–201; L. Armstrong, *The Paintings and Drawings of Marco Zoppo*, New York and London, 1976, pp. 331–2, doc. 10; R. Lightbown, *Sandro Botticelli*, London, 1978, 2 vols, II, pp. 47–51, 101–6; Goffen, *Bellini*, pp. 224, 226–68; A. Angelini in *Domenico Beccafumi e il suo tempo*, exh. cat., Chiesa di Sant'Agostino, Pinacoteca Nazionale di Siena, Siena, Milan, 1990, pp.138–9; Manca, *The Art of Ercole*, pp. 199–203, 205–6, doc. 19–20, 23–4, 26, 29–30, 33–5; R. Bartoli in A. Cecchi and A. Natali (eds), *L'officina della maniera: varietà e fierrezza nell'arte fiorentina del Cinquecento fra le due repubbliche (1494–1530)*, exh. cat., Uffizi, Florence, Venice and Florence, 1996, pp. 248–59, cat. nos 82–7; M. Folchi in P. Torriti (ed.), *Beccafumi*, Milan, 1998, pp. 92–7, cat. nos P28–P30.

5 H. Wohl, 'Domenico Veneziano Studies: the Sant' Egidio and Parenti Documents', *Burlington Magazine*, CXIII, 1971, pp. 635–41.

6 Although between 1446 and 1463 the price for a pair of chests went as high as 75 florins, a sizeable majority was sold for around 28–35 florins. See E. Callmann, *Apollonio di Giovanni*, Oxford, 1974, pp. 76–81.

7 Horace, *Ars poetica*, 408–12.

8 A. Markham Schulz, *Giammaria Mosca called Padovano, a Renaissance Sculptor in Italy and Poland*, University Park, Penn., 1998, p. 190, doc. 1A.

9 Benvenuto Cellini, *I trattati dell'oreficeria e della sculura*, ed. C. Milanesi, Florence, 1857, pp. 7–8.

10 C. Casati, *Notices sur les faïences de Deruta d'apres des documents nouveaux*, Paris, 1874, p. 7; T. Biganti, 'La produzione di ceramica a lustro a Gubbio e Deruta tra la fine del secolo XV e l'inizio del secolo XVI. Primi resultati di una ricerca documentaria', *Faenza*, LXXIII, 1987, pp. 209–25, esp. p. 215.

11 M. Ricci, 'Maiolica di età rinascimentale e moderna' in D. Manacorda (ed.), *Archaeologica urbana a Roma: il progetto della Crypta Balbi*, III, *Il giardino del conservatorio di S. Caterina della Rosa*, Florence, 1985, pp. 303–424.

12 G. Ballardini, 'Antologia ceramica', *Faenza*, V, 1919, pp. 60–3, esp. p. 61.

13 Ibid.

14 T. Wilson, *Ceramic Art of the Italian Renaissance*, exh. cat. British Museum, 1987, p. 91.

15 Piccolpasso, *Potter's Art*, II, p. 113.

16 A. Giulini, 'Drusiana Sforza, moglie di Jacopo Piccinino' in *Miscellanea di studi storici in onore di Antonio Manno*, II, Turin, 1912, pp. 163–214, esp. pp. 193–4.

17 See e.g. in 1465 'a table-cut ruby set *alla Vinitiana*' owned by Piero de' Medici, and his pointed diamond mounted in the same way: E. Müntz, *Les collections des Médicis au quinzième siècle*, Paris, 1888, p. 36.

18 L.A. Gandini, *Tavola, cantina e cucina della corte di Ferrara nel Quattrocento*, Modena, 1889, p. 20.

19 G. Campori, *Raccolta di cataloghi ed inventarii inediti*, Modena, 1870, p. 11.

20 A. Morselli, 'Il corredo nuziale di Caterina Pico (1474)', *Atti e memorie della Deputazione di Storia Patria per le Antiche Provincie Modenesi*, ser. viii, VIII, 1956, pp. 19–20, 25 [offprint], items 78–9, 214.

21 L. Beltrami, *La guardaroba di Lucrezia Borgia*, Milan, 1903, p. 33.

22 J. Woods-Marsden, *The Gonzaga of Mantua and Pisanello's Arthurian Frescoes*, Princeton, NJ, 1988, p. 73.

23 U. Rossi, 'Cristoforo Geremia', *Archivio storico dell'arte*, I, 1888, pp. 404–11, esp. p. 411, and n. 2.

24 E. Kris, *Meister und Meisterwerke der Steinschneiderkunst*, I, Vienna, 1929, p. 35; E.H. Gombrich, *Norm and Form: Studies in the Art of the Renaissance*, 3rd edn, London and New York, 1978, p. 56.

25 G. Gaye, *Carteggio inedito d'artisti*, I, Florence, 1839, pp. 354–7, esp. pp. 354–5; translated by Gombrich, *Norm and Form*, pp. 54–5.

26 F.W. Kent, 'Patron-Client Networks in Renaissance Florence and the Emergence of Lorenzo as "Maestro della Bottega"' in B. Toscani (ed.), *Lorenzo de' Medici: New Perspectives*, New York, 1993, pp. 1279–313, esp. pp. 1280, 1303, n. 4.

27 Benedetto Dei, *La Cronica dall'anno 1400 all'anno 1500*, ed. R. Barducci, Florence, 1984, p. 82; C.E. Gilbert (ed.), *Italian Art, 1400–1500: Sources and Documents*, Evanston, Ill., 1992 (rev. edn), pp. 181–4.

28 C. Elam, 'Lorenzo de' Medici's sculpture garden', *Mitteilungen des Kunsthistorischen Institutes in Florenz*, XXXVI, 1992, pp. 41–84. In this article she corrected some errors of documentation that led to the identification of the wrong Medici garden in the otherwise useful article by L. Borgo and A.H. Sievers, 'The Medici Gardens at San Marco', *Mitteilungen des Kunsthistorischen Institutes in Florenz*, XXXIII, 1989, pp. 237–56. See also P. Barocchi (ed.), *Il Giardino di San Marco: maestri e compagni del giovane Michelangelo*, exh. cat., Casa Buonarroti, Florence, 1992, *passim*.

29 D. Benati, 'Per il problema di 'Vicino da Ferrara' (alias Baldassare d'Este)', *Paragone*, 393, XXXIII, 1982, pp. 3–26, esp. p. 21; M. Molteni, *Ercole de' Roberti*, Milan, 1995, p. 30.

30 G. Campori, *Notizie storiche e artistiche della maiolica e porcellana di Ferrara nei secoli XV e XVI*, Modena, 1871, p. 13.

31 A.M. Visser Travagli in A. Mottola Molfino and M. Natale (eds) *Le muse e il principe: arte di corte nel Rinascimento padano*, exh. cat., Museo Poldi Pezzoli, Milan, Modena, 1991, I, *Catalogo*, pp. 254–6, cat. no. 69.

32 J. Shell, *Pittori in bottega: Milano del Rinascimento*, Turin, 1995, pp. 77–99. See e.g. J. ffoulkes and R. Maiocchi, *Vincenzo Foppa of Brescia, Founder of the Lombard School: His Life and Work*, London and New York, 1909, pp. 298–302, 304, 306–8, docs 20–1, 24, 27–8.

33 G.C. Sciolla (ed.), *Ambrogio da Fossano detto il Bergognone: un pittore per la Certosa*, exh. cat. Castello Visconteo, Pavia, Certosa di Pavia, Milan, 1998 (esp. M.T. Fiorio, 'Bergognone e la pittura a Milano e a Pavia', pp. 77–86, 'Ambrogio Bergognone e la decorazione ad affresco della Certosa', pp. 255–68).

34 E. Steingräber, 'Lombardisches Malerei um 1500' in F. Piel and J. Traeger, *Festschrift Wolfgang Braunfels*, Tübingen, 1977, pp. 371–87.

35 E.H. Gombrich, 'Apollonio di Giovanni: a Florentine Cassone Workshop seen through the Eyes of a Humanist Poet' in Gombrich, *Norm and Form*, pp. 11–28, esp. pp. 12, 26–7; C. Lloyd, *Italian Paintings before 1600 in the Art Institute of Chicago: a Catalogue of the Collection*, Chicago, 1993, pp. 6–9.

36 R.W. Scheller, *Exemplum: Model-Book Drawings and the Practice of Artistic Transmission in the Middle Ages (ca.900–ca.1470)*, Amsterdam, 1995, *passim*.

37 H. Glasser, Artists' Contracts of the Early Renaissance, unpublished PhD, Columbia University, NY, 1965, pp. 73–78. See also e.g. an altarpiece commissioned from Giovan Francesco Maineri in Ferrara: S. Zamboni, *Pittori di Ercole I d'Este*, Ferrara, 1975, p. 40.

38 S. Orlandi, 'Su una tavola dipinta da Fra Filippo Lippi per Antonio del Branca nel febbraio 1451', *Rivista d'arte*, ser. iii, XXIX, 1954, pp. 199–201; J. Ruda, *Fra Filippo Lippi*, London, 1993, pp. 525–6, doc. 2.

39 See F. Heinemann, *Giovanni Bellini e i belliniani*, 3 vols, Venice, 1963, I, p. 291, no. MB19 for a Virgin and Child with Donor, a shop work that bears Bellini's signature. For a signed and dated (1512) panel by Francia's shop, see G. Lipparini, *Francesco Francia*, Bergamo, 1913, pp. 85–6.

40 D. Carl, 'Documenti inediti su Maso Finiguerra e la sua famiglia', *Annali della Scuola Normale Superiore di Pisa*, XIII, 2, 1983, pp. 507–54; A. Franceschini, *Artisti a Ferrara in età umanistica e rinascimentale: testimonianze archivistiche*, 2 vols, Ferrara and Rome, 1992–5, I, p. 797, doc. 1235; Manca, *Cosmè Tura*, pp. 204–6, doc. 6.

41 G. Gronau, 'Über des sogenannte Skizzenbuch des Verrocchio', *Jahrbuch der preussichen Kunstsammlungen*, XVII, 1896, p. 71; A. Butterfield, *The Sculptures of Andrea del Verrocchio*, New Haven and London, 1997, p. 26.

42 R. Krautheimer, *Lorenzo Ghiberti*, 2nd edn, Princeton, 1970, pp. 208–11.

43 A. Thomas, *The Painter's Practice in Renaissance Florence*, Cambridge, 1995, p. 157.

44 Callmann, *Apollonio di Giovanni*, pp. 15, 18, 33, 68.

45 Ibid.

46 Bober and Rubinstein, *Renaissance Artists and Antique Sculpture*, p. 65, no. 22.

47 Pliny, *Natural History*, XXXIV, xix, 55.

48 T. Wilson, 'Xanto and Ariosto', *Burlington Magazine*, CXXXII, 1046 (May 1990), pp. 321–7, esp. p. 324, n. 18; P. Collins, 'Prints and the development of *istoriato* painting on Italian Renaissance maiolica', *Print Quarterly* 4, 1987, pp. 223–35; F. Ames-Lewis, 'Nicola da Urbino and Raphael', *Burlington Magazine*, CXXX, 1988, pp. 690–2; A. Gentilini, C. Ravanelli Guidotti and G. Morello, *L'istoriato: libri a stampa e maioliche italiane del Cinquecento*, Città del Vaticano, 1993, *passim*; J.V.G. Mallet, 'Michelangelo on maiolica: an *istoriato* dish at Waddesdon', *Apollo*, April 1994, pp. 50–5.

49 Wilson, *Ceramic Art*, pp. 133–4, 117–20, cat. nos 40–1, 186, 203; Wilson, *Italian Renaissance Pottery*, pp. 157–65; Ames-Lewis, 'Nicola da Urbino and Raphael'; T. Clifford, 'Some Unpublished Drawings for Maiolica and Federico Zuccaro's role in the Spanish Service' in Wilson, *Italian Renaissance Pottery*, pp. 166–76; T. Clifford and J.V.G. Mallet, 'Battista Franco as a Designer for Maiolica', *Burlington Magazine*, CXVIII, 1976, pp. 387–410.

50 A. Moore Valeri, 'La mezzaluna dentata, le sue origini ed il suo sviluppo', *Faenza*, LXX, 1984, pp. 5–6, 375–80; Moore Valeri, 'Florentine *zaffera a rilievo* maiolica', *Archaeologia Medievale*, XI, 1984, pp. 477–500.

51 Wilson, 'Xanto and Ariosto', p. 324, cat. no. 18.

52 Wilson, *Ceramic Art*, p. 103; for doc. text see Pietro Mattei Tonina Cecchetti, *Mastro Giorgio l'uomo, l'artista, l'imprenditore*, Perugia, 1995, pp. 66–7.

53 Wilson, *Ceramic Art*, pp. 133–4, opp. p. 56, cat. no. 203.

54 Bartsch XIV, p. 318, no. 423; Mallet, 'Michelangelo on Maiolica', p. 51.

55 G. Vanzolini, *Istorie delle fabbriche di majoliche metaurensi*, Pesaro, 1879, II, p. 245.

56 Wilson, *Ceramic Art*, pp. 45–6, cat. nos 49–50; F. Liversani, 'Notiziario', *Quaderni dell' Emil Ceramica*, Faenza, 1987, n.p.

57 Wilson, *Ceramic Art*, pp. 54, 61, cat. nos 70, 83.

58 J.M. Massing, *Du texte à l'image: la Calomnie d'Apelle et son iconographie*, Strasbourg, 1990, pp. 256–68, esp. pp. 264–6, cat. nos 4A, 6A.

59 J.R. Spencer (ed. and trans.), *Filarete's Treatise on Architecture, Being the Treatise by Antonio Averlino, Known as Filarete*, 2 vols, New Haven and London, 1965, I, p. 315; Antonio Averlino detto il Filarete, *Trattato di architettura*, eds A.M. Finoli and L. Grassi, 2 vols, Milan, 1972, II, p. 677.

60 Wilson, *Ceramic Art*, p. 54, cat. no. 70.

61 Ibid., p. 61, cat. no. 83.

62 Watson, *Italian Renaissance Maiolica*, pp. 112–13, cat. no. 45; J. Poole, *Italian Maiolica and Incised Slipware in the Fitzwilliam Museum, Cambridge,* Cambridge 1995, pp. 305–7, cat. no. 376; Wilson, *Ceramic Art*, p. 45, 49, cat. nos 51, 60.

63 T. Wilson, 'History on a Plate', *The Art Quarterly*, 14, Summer 1993, pp. 20–3, esp. p. 22.

64 E.H. Gombrich, 'The Style *all'antica*: Imitation and Assimilation' in Gombich, *Norm and Form,* pp. 122–8, esp. p. 122.

65 For the status of Xanto, see Wilson 'Xanto and Ariosto'. The principal literature on Xanto is most recently summarized in Poole, *Italian Maiolica*, p. 326.

66 J. Triolo, The Armorial Maiolica of Francesco Avelli, unpublished PhD thesis, University of Pennsylvania, 1996, pp. 97–101.

67 J.V.G. Mallet, 'La biografia di Francesco Xanto Avelli alla luce dei suoi sonnetti', *Faenza*, LXX, 1984, pp. 398–402; Triolo, Armorial Maiolica, pp. 97–8.

68 F. Cioci, *Xanto e il duca d'Urbino*, Milan, 1987, pp. 190–1; F. Negroni, 'Niccolo Pellipario: ceramista fantasma', *Notizie da Palazzo Albani,* Urbino 1986, pp. 13–19, esp. p. 18; B. Talvacchia, 'Professional Advancement and the Use of the Erotic in the Art of Francesco Xanto', *Sixteenth-Century Journal*, XXVI, 1994, pp. 121–53, esp. p. 122.

69 Talvacchia, 'Professional Advancement', p. 122; Triolo, Armorial Maiolica, p. 99; Poole, *Italian Maiolica*, pp. 324–5.

70 We are grateful to Tim Wilson, who signalled to us the Greek meaning of the word.

71 Cioci, *Xanto*, pp. 96–7; Mallet, 'La biografia', p. 400; Talvacchia, 'Professional Advancement', p. 131.

72 Cioci, *Xanto*, pp. 96–7, 100–1.

73 T. Wilson, 'Renaissance Ceramics', *The Collections of the National Gallery of Art, Systematic Catalogue: Western Decorative Arts, Part I,* Washington DC, Cambridge 1993, p. 201, n. 11; Triolo, Armorial Maiolica, p. 99; Talvacchia, 'Professional Advancement', p. 122.

74 Wilson, *Ceramic Art*, p. 52; J.V.G. Mallet, 'Xanto: i suoi compagni e seguaci', *Francesco Xanto Avelli da Rovigo: atti del Convegno Internazionale di Studi, 1980,* Rovigo, 1987, pp. 67–108; A. Holcroft, 'Francesco Xanto Avelli and Petrarch', *Journal of the Warburg and Courtauld Institutes*, LI, 1988, pp. 225–34; Wilson, 'Xanto and Ariosto', pp. 321–7.

75 Wilson, 'Xanto and Ariosto', p. 321; Poole, *Italian Maiolica*, p. 323.

76 A.V.B. Norman, *Wallace Collection, Catalogue of Ceramics*, London, 1976, p. 179, C89.

77 Poole, *Italian Maiolica*, p. 323; Triolo, Armorial Maiolica, pp. 100–11; Mallet, 'Xanto: i suoi compagni', pp. 67–8.

78 J. Petruzzellis-Scherer, 'Le opere di Francesco Xanto Avelli al Castello Sforzesco', *Rassegna di Studi e di Notizie del Castello Sforzesco, Milan*, 8, 1980, pp. 322–6.

79 Discussed and partly published in Vanzolini, *Istorie delle fabriche*, p. 337; Negroni, 'Niccolo Pellipario', p. 18; full text in Triolo, Armorial Maiolica, pp. 388–9.

80 Wilson, 'Xanto and Ariosto', p. 322.

81 P. Marsili, 'Ars Orcelariorum: la corporazione dei maiolicari di Faenza', *Faenza*, 1982, 68, pp. 20–1; Triolo, Armorial Maiolica, p. 100.

82 Talvacchia, 'Professional Advancement', pp. 139–40.

83 B. Rackham, *Victoria and Albert Museum, Catalogue of Italian Maiolica*, London 1940, cat. no. 307 for the plate; Wilson, *Ceramic Art*, p. 10.

84 Mallet, 'Xanto: i suoi compagni', pp. 67–8; Talvacchia, 'Professional Advancement', p. 130; Triolo, Armorial Maiolica, p. 101.

85 Wilson, 'Xanto and Ariosto', p. 322.

86 Ibid.; Holcroft, 'Francesco Xanto Avelli', p. 225; Poole, *Italian Maiolica*, pp. 323–51.

87 P.F. Grendler, 'What Zuanne read in school: Vernacular Texts in Sixteenth Century Venetian Schools', *Sixteenth Century Journal*, XIII, 2, 1982, pp. 41–53, esp. p. 42.

88 Reproduced with commentary in Cioci, *Xanto*, pp. 88–197; Triolo, Armorial Maiolica, p. 104.

89 Wilson, *Ceramic Art*, p. 57, cat. no. 75; Cioci, *Xanto*, pp. 60–1; Wilson, 'Xanto and Ariosto', p. 322.

90 Cioci, *Xanto*, p. 41.

91 Holcroft, 'Francesco Xanto Avelli', pp. 225–34.

92 Talvacchia, 'Professional Advancement', pp. 121–54; Triolo, Armorial Maiolica, p. 299, cat. no. 7.2; D. Thornton, 'An Allegory of the Sack of Rome by Giulio da Urbino', *Apollo*, CLI, June 1999, pp. 11–18, esp. p. 15.

93 Wilson, 'Xanto and Ariosto', p. 322.

94 Holcroft, 'Francesco Xanto Avelli', pp. 232–5.

95 Ibid., p. 231; Wilson, *Ceramic Art*, p. 58, cat. no. 77.

96 Wilson, *Ceramic Art*, p. 58, cat. no. 77; Holcroft, 'Francesco Xanto Avelli', pp. 231–2.

97 J.V.G. Mallet, 'Maiolica at Polesden Lacey III: A New Look at the Xanto Problem', *Apollo*, March 1971, pp. 170–83; Poole, *Italian Maiolica*, p. 323 and cat. nos 385, 387.

98 A point made by both Holcroft, 'Francesco Xanto Avelli', p. 234, and Wilson, 'Xanto and Ariosto', p. 327.

99 Holcroft, 'Francesco Xanto Avelli', p. 230; Wilson, *Ceramic Art*, p. 58, cat. no. 77.

100 Wilson, *Ceramic Art*, p. 143, cat. no. 220.

101 Ibid.; Talvacchia, 'Professional Advancement', p. 138.

102 B. Talvacchia, *Taking Positions: on the erotic in Renaissance culture*, Princeton, 1999, pp. 142–7; Thornton, 'An Allegory of the Sack of Rome', p. 14.

103 Alberti, *On Painting*, pp. 70–1; Baxandall, *Giotto and the Orators*, pp. 121–39; C. Hope, 'Composition from Cennini and Alberti to Vasari' in P. Taylor and F. Quiviger (eds), *Pictorial Composition from Medieval to Modern Art,* Warburg Institute Colloquia, 6, London and Turin, 2000, pp. 27–44; T. Puttfarken, *The Discovery of Pictorial Composition: Theories of Visual Order in Painting, 1400–1800,* New Haven and London, 2000, pp. 53–68, esp. p. 55.

104 D. Ekserdjian, 'Rosso Fiorentino and Raphael: a Question of Influence', *Apollo*, CLIII, February 2001, pp. 34–8.

105 Talvacchia, *Taking Positions*, pp. 3–47 on the prints and their history.

106 Talvacchia, 'Professional Advancement', pp. 138, 153.

107 Thornton, 'An Allegory of the Sack of Rome', p. 15; Triolo, Armorial Maiolica, p. 299, cat. no. 7.2.

108 Wilson, *Ceramic Art*, pp. 57–8, cat. no. 76.

Illustration Acknowledgements

Illustrations not listed below originate from
The British Museum.

Frontispiece The J. Paul Getty Museum, Los Angeles,
86.SB.688

3 Biblioteca Apostolica Vaticana, Vatican

5 Kunsthistorisches Museum, Vienna

6 Biblioteca Malatestiana, Cesena (photo: Ivano
Giovannini)

7 Spencer Collection, New York Public Library,
Astor, Lennox and Tilden Foundations, New
York

8 Kimbell Art Museum, Fort Worth, Texas
(photo: Michael Bodycomb)

9 Andrew W. Mellon Collection, photograph
© 2001 Board of Trustees, National Gallery of
Art, Washington

10 Barber Institute of Fine Arts, University of
Birmingham/The Bridgeman Art Library

13 © 2001 BPK/Staatliche Museen zu Berlin –
Preußischer Kulturbesitz, Münzkabinett

16 Biblioteca Laurenziana, Florence (photo: Scala,
Florence)

17 Palazzo Medici-Riccardi, Florence (photo: Scala,
Florence)

18 Samuel H. Kress Collection, photograph
© 2001 Board of Trustees, National Gallery of
Art, Washington

19 Fratelli Alinari 2001

21 Pinacoteca di Brera, Milan (photo: Scala,
Florence)

22 Galleria Buonarroti/Fratelli Alinari 2001

24 The Metropolitan Museum of Art, Bequest of
Edward S. Harkness, 1950. (50.135.3)
Photograph © 2001 Metropolitan Museum of
Art

25 © 2001 BPK/Staatliche Museen zu Berlin –
Preußischer Kulturbesitz, Gemäldegalerie
(photo: Jörg P. Anders)

26 The Courtauld Institute Gallery, London

27 © The National Gallery, London

29 Widener Collection, photograph © 2001 Board
of Trustees, National Gallery of Art, Washington

30 In a private Scottish collection (photo: Antonia
Reeve)

32 V&A Picture Library

34 Bibliothèque nationale de France

37 Gabinetto dei Disegni, Uffizi, Florence. Su
concessione del Ministero dei Beni e le Attività
Culturali, Firenze

38 © The National Gallery, London

39 Biblioteca Riccardiana

43 Ashmolean Museum, Oxford

44 Courtesy, Museum of Fine Arts, Boston.
Reproduced with permission. © 2000 Museum
of Fine Arts, Boston. All rights reserved.

48 Palazzo Altemps (photo: by permission of the
Soprintendenza Archeologica di Roma)

49 The Fitzwilliam Museum, University of
Cambridge

50 V&A Picture Library

51 The Metropolitan Museum of Art, John Stewart
Kennedy Fund, 1913. (14.39) Photograph
© 1986 Metropolitan Museum of Art

53 The Metropolitan Museum of Art, Purchase in
memory of Sir John Pope-Hennessey: Rogers
Fund, the Annenberg Foundation, Drue
Heinze Foundation, Annette de la Renta,
Mr and Mrs Frank E. Richardson, and The
Vincent Astor Foundation Gifts, Wrightsman
and Gwynne Andrews Funds, special funds,
and Gift of the children of Mrs Harry Payne
Whitney, Gift of Mr and Mrs Joshua Logan,
and other gifts and bequests by exchange, 1995.
(1995.7) Photograph © 1995 Metropolitan
Museum of Art

54 Lee Collection, The Courtauld Institute
Gallery, London

56 V&A Picture Library

57 Palazzo Medici-Riccardi, Florence
(photo: Scala, Florence)

59 Museo Nazionale di Napoli/Fratelli Alinari 2001

61 Palazzo Medici-Riccardi/Fratelli Alinari 2001

62 © 2001 BPK/Staatliche Museen zu Berlin –
Preußischer Kulturbesitz, Antikensammlung
(photo: Johannes Laurentius)

63 Santa Costanza, Rome (photo: Scala, Florence)

64 Fratelli Alinari 2001

65 Fratelli Alinari 2001

66 Vatican Museum/Fratelli Alinari 2001

70 © Photo RMN

71 Schloss Wolfegg, Germany

72 Albertina, Wien

73 The Royal Collection © 2001, Her Majesty
Queen Elizabeth II (photo: A.C. Cooper Ltd)

74 Museo Archeologico Nazionale, Naples

75 Bibliothèque nationale de France

76 Samuel H. Kress Collection, photograph
© Board of Trustees, National Gallery of Art,
Washington

78 © Rijksmuseum-Stichting Amsterdam

79 V&A Picture Library

82 Museo Archeologico, Florence

83 The American Numismatic Society

84 © Photo RMN (Michèle Bellot)

86 Samuel H. Kress Collection, photograph
© 2001 Board of Trustees, National Gallery of
Art, Washington

87 Bibliothèque nationale de France

91 Kunsthistorisches Museum, Vienna

102 Musei Capitolini/Fratelli Alinari 2001

103 V&A Picture Library

104 Museo Nazionale, Firenze/Fratelli Alinari 2001

105 Kunsthistorisches Museum, Vienna

106 Casa Buonarroti, Florence (photo: Scala,
Florence)

107 Museo Nazionale, Firenze/Fratelli Alinari 2001

108 Galleria e Museo Estense, Modena, Italy/The
Bridgeman Art Library

109 Kunsthistorisches Museum, Vienna

111 Gabinetto dei Disegni, Uffizi, Florence. Su
concessione del Ministero dei Beni e le Attività
Culturali, Firenze

112 Bargello, Florence/Fratelli Alinari 2001

113 Bargello, Florence (photo: Scala, Florence)

114 Duomo, Florence/Fratelli Alinari 2001

119 Pinacoteca Nazionale, Bologna

120 © National Gallery, London

121 © Photo RMN (Michèle Bellot)

126 The Royal Collection © 2001, Her Majesty
Queen Elizabeth II

127 Palazzo Te, Mantua (photo: Scala, Florence)

128 Massimo Listri/Gilbert Collection, Somerset
House

131 Devonshire Collection. By permission of the
Duke of Devonshire and the Chatsworth
Settlement Trustees

132 By courtesy of the Trustees of Sir John Soane's
Museum

134 V&A Picture Library

136 Museo del Bargello (photo: Nicolò Orsi
Battaglini)

138 Gabinetto dei Disegni, Uffizi, Florence. Su
concessione del Ministero dei Beni e le Attività
Culturali, Firenze

139 Ashmolean Museum, Oxford

141 The Royal Collection © 2001, Her Majesty
Queen Elizabeth II

143 Gallerie dell'Accademia, Venice/Fratelli
Alinari, 2001

144 The Royal Collection © 2001, Her Majesty
Queen Elizabeth II

146 The Walters Art Museum, Baltimore

149 By permission of The British Library

156 Kunsthistorisches Museum, Vienna

157 Galleria 'Giorgio Franchetti' alla Ca d'Oro,
Venice

158 V&A Picture Library

162 The Metropolitan Museum of Art, Robert
Lehman Collection, 1975. (1975.1.1015)
Photograph © 1988 The Metropolitan
Museum of Art

163 © 2001 BPK/Staatliche Museen zu Berlin –
Preußischer Kulturbesitz, Gemäldegalerie
(photo: Jörg P. Anders)

166 Gift of the Women's Committee with
additional funds from Robert H. Tannahill.
Photograph © 1987 The Detroit Institute of
Arts

167 National Art Library, V&A

168 National Art Library, V&A

169 National Art Library, V&A

173 By permission of The British Library

174 V&A Picture Library

176 © Photo RMN

177 © Photo RMN

180 © 2001 BPK/Staatliche Museen zu Berlin –
Preußischer Kulturbesitz, Kunstgewerbe
Museum (photo: Saturia Linke)

182 © The National Gallery, London

185 National Art Library, V&A

186 Palazzo Schifanoia, Ferrara (photo: Scala,
Florence)

188 Castello Sforzesco, Milan. By kind permission
of Foto Saporetti

189 The Metropolitan Museum of Art, Bequest of
Benjamin Altman, 1913. (14.40.705). All rights
reserved, The Metropolitan Museum of Art

190 Niedersächsisches Landesmuseum,
Landesgalerie, Hannover

191 Mr and Mrs Martin A. Ryerson Collection,
1933.1006. The Art Institute of Chicago.
All rights reserved

192 © The National Gallery, London

193 Mr and Mrs Martin A. Ryerson Collection,
1933.1006. The Art Institute of Chicago.
All rights reserved

194 Baptistry, Florence/Fratelli Alinari 2001

199 Rijksmuseum, Amsterdam

200 By permission of The British Library

201 By kind permission of the Trustees of the
Wallace Collection

213 Private collection, Switzerland

Select Bibliography

Primary Texts

Alberti, Leon Battista, *Opere volgari*, I, *I libri della famiglia*, ed. C. Grayson, Bari, 1960.

Alberti, Leon Battista, *The Family in Renaissance Florence: a Translation by Renée Neu Watkins of* I libri della famiglia, Columbia, SC, 1969.

Alberti, Leon Battista, *On Painting and On Sculpture: The Latin Texts of De pictura and De statua*, ed. and trans. C. Grayson, London, 1972.

Alberti, Leon Battista, *Dinner Pieces: a Translation of the* Intercenales, ed. and trans. D. Marsh, Binghamton, NY, 1987.

Averlino detto il Filarete, Antonio, *Trattato di architectura*, 2 vols, eds A.M. Finoli and L. Grassi, Milan, 1972.

Baldovinetti, Alesso, *I Ricordi di Alesso Baldovinetti, pittore fiorentino nel secolo XV*, ed. G. Pierotti, Lucca, 1868.

Barbaro, F., 'On Wifely Duties', trans. B.G. Kohl, in B.G. Kohl and R. Witt (eds), *The Earthly Republic: Italian Humanists on Government and Society*, Philadelphia, 1978, pp. 179–230.

Bisticci, Vespasiano da, *Vite di uomini illustri del sec. XV*, eds P. d'Ancona and E. Aeschlimann, Milan, 1951.

Bisticci, Vespasiano da, *Memoirs: Lives of Illustrious Men of the Fifteenth Century*, trans. W. George and E. Waters, Toronto, 1997.

Boiardo, Matteo Maria, *Opere volgari*, Bari, 1962.

Bracciolini, Poggio, *La vera nobilità*, ed. and Ital. trans. D. Canforda, Florence, 1998.

Castellani, Francesco di Matteo, *Ricordanze*, ed. G. Ciapelli, Florence, 1992.

Castiglione, B., *Il libro del cortegiano*, ed. B. Maier, Turin, 1964.

Castiglione, Sabba da, *I ricordi*, Venice, 1560.

Cellini, Benvenuto, *I trattati dell'oreficeria e della scultura*, ed. G. Milanesi, Florence, 1857.

Cellini, Benvenuto, *La Vita*, ed. G. Davico Bonino, Turin, 1973.

Condivi, Ascanio, *Vita di Michelagnolo Buonarotti*, ed. G. Nencioni, Florence, 1998.

Dei, Benedetto, *La Cronica dall'anno 1400 all'anno 1500*, ed. R. Barducci, Florence, 1984.

Ficino, Marsilio, *Commentarium in Convivium Platonis: De amore*, ed. R. Marcel, Paris, 1956.

Fra Bernardino of Siena, *Le prediche volgari inedite*, ed. P. Dionisio Pacetti, Siena, 1935.

Frimmel, T., *Der Anonimo Morelliano (Marcanton Michiel's Notizia d'opere del disegno)*, Vienna, 1888.

Gabel, L. (ed.), *Memoirs of a Renaissance Pope: the Commentaries of Pius II*, New York, 1959.

Giorgio Martini, Francesco di, *Trattati di architettura, ingegneria e arte militare*, 2 vols, Milan, 1967.

Gregory, H. (ed.), *Selected Letters of Alessandra Strozzi*, bilingual edn, Berkeley, Los Angeles and London, 1997.

Guicciardini, Francesco, *Opere inedite, Ricordi*, Florence, 1867.

Gundersheimer, W.L., *Art and Life at the Court of Ercole d'Este: the* De Triumphis religionis *of Giovanni Sabadino degli Arienti*, Geneva, 1972.

Hale, R. (ed.), *The Travel Journal of Antonio de Beatis*, London, 1979.

Hollanda, Francisco da, *Dialogos en Roma*, ed. J. da Felicidade Alves, Lisbon, 1984.

Kent, F.W., *Giovanni Rucellai ed il suo Zibaldone: A Florentine Patrician and his Palace*, II, London, 1981.

Lama, M., *Il libro dei conti di un maiolicaro del Quattrocento*, Faenza, 1939.

Landucci, Luca, *Diario fiorentino dal 1450 al 1516* (ed. I. De Badia), Florence, 1883.

Miglio, M. and Modigliani, A., *Li Nuptiali di Marco Antonio Altieri pubblicati da Enrico Narducci*, Rome, 1995.

Milanesi, G. (ed.), *Dell'arte del vetro per mosaico: tre tratatelli dei secoli XIV e XV*, Bologna, 1864.

Nogara, B. (ed.), *Scritti inediti e rari di Biondo Flavio*, Rome, 1927.

Palmieri, Matteo, *Della vita civile*, ed. Felice Battaglia, Bologna, 1944.

Phillips, M., *The Memoir of Marco Parenti*, London, 1987.

Piccolpasso, Cipriano, *The Three Books of the Potter's Art*, 2 vols, trans and eds R. Lightbown and A. Caiger-Smith, London, 1980.

Pontano, Giovanni, *Carmina, Ecloghe, Elegie, Liriche*, ed. J. Oeschger, Bari, 1948.

Pontano, Giovanni, *I trattati delle virtu sociali*, ed. Francesco Tateo, Rome, 1965.

Pozzi, G. and Ciappini, L.A. (eds), *Hypnerotomachia Poliphili*, Padua, 1964.

Rucellai, Giovanni, *Il zibaldone quaresimale*, ed. A. Perosa, London, 1960.

Sillano, M.T. (ed.), *Le ricordanze di Giovanni Chellini da San Miniato*, Milan, 1984.

Smith, C.S. and Teach Gnudi, M. (eds and trans), *The* Pirotechnia *of Vannoccio Biringuccio*, New York, 1990.

Spencer, J.R. (ed. and trans.), *Filarete's Treatise on Architecture, Being the Treatise by Antonio Averlino, Known as Filarete*, 2 vols, New Haven and London, 1965.

Tonelli, T. (ed.), *Poggi Epistulae*, Florence, 1832.

Vasari, Giorgio, *Le Vite de' più eccellenti pittori, scultori ed architettori*, 9 vols, ed. G. Milanesi, Florence, 1878–1906.

Visconti, Gaspare, *I canzonieri per Beatrice d'Este e Bianca Maria Sforza*, ed. p. Bongrani, Milan, 1979.

Viti, P. (ed.), *Opere letterarie e politiche di Leonardo Bruni*, Turin, 1996.

von Schlosser, J. (ed.), *Lorenzo Ghiberti's Denkwürdigkeiten: I commentarii*, Berlin, 1912.

Weil-Garris, K. and D'Amico, J.F., 'The Renaissance Cardinal's Ideal Palace: a Chapter from Cortesi's *De Cardinalatu*' in H.A. Millon (ed.), *Studies in Italian Art and Architecture, 15th through 18th Centuries, Memoirs of the American Academy in Rome*, XXXV, 1980.

Zambotti, Bernardino, *Diario Ferrarese dall' anno 1476 sino al 1504, Rerum italicarum scriptores*, ed. G. Pardi, Bologna, XXIV.7, 1934–7.

Secondary Texts

Acidini Luchinat, C., 'La grottesca', in *Storia dell'arte italiana*, II, *L'artista e il pubblico*, Turin, 1979.

Acidini Luchinat, C., 'La "santa antichità", la scuola, il giardino' in F. Borsi (ed.), *'Per bellezza, per studio, per piacere': Lorenzo il Magnifico e gli spazi dell'arte*, Florence, 1991, pp. 143–60.

Agosti, G., 'Precisioni su un "Baccanale" perduto del Signorelli', *Prospettiva*, XXX, 1982, pp. 70–7.

Agosti, G., 'Scrittori che parlano di artisti, tra Quattro e Cinquecento in Lombardia' in B. Agosti *et al.*, *Quattro pezzi lombardi (per Maria Teresa Binaghi)*, Brescia, 1998, pp. 41–93.

Alexander, J.J.G. (ed.), *The Painted Page: Italian Renaissance Book Illumination, 1450–1550*, exh. cat., Royal Academy of Arts, London, The Pierpont Morgan Library, New York, London and Munich, 1994.

Allison, A. Hersey, 'The bronzes of Pier Jacopo Alari-Bonacolsi, called Antico', *Jahrbuch der kunsthisorischen Sammulungen in Wien*, 89/90, 1993–4.

Ames-Lewis, F., *Drawing in Early Renaissance Italy*, New Haven and London, 1981.

Ames-Lewis, F. (ed.), *Cosimo 'Il Vecchio' de' Medici*, Oxford, 1992.

Ames-Lewis, F. (ed.), *The Early Medici and their Artists*, London, 1995.

Ames-Lewis, F., *The Intellectual Life of the Early Renaissance Artist*, New Haven and London, 2000.

Angelini, A. in *Domenico Beccafumi e il suo tempo*, exh. cat., Chiesa di Sant'Agostino, Pinacoteca Nazionale di Siena, Siena, Milan, 1990, pp. 138–9.

Armstrong, L. *The Paintings and Drawings of Marco Zoppo*, New York and London, 1976.

Artusi, L., *Le arti e i mestieri di Firenze*, Rome, 1990.

Bacchi, A., *Francesco del Cossa*, Soncino, 1991.

Bagemihl, R., 'The Trevisan Collection', *Burlington Magazine*, CXXXV, 1993, pp. 559–63.

Ballardini, G., 'Antologia ceramica', *Faenza*, V, 1919, pp. 60–3.

Ballardini, G., *Note di critica ceramica*, Faenza, 1929, pp. 123–45.

Barkan, L., *Unearthing the Past: Archaeology and Aesthetics in the Making of Renaissance Culture*, New Haven and London, 1999.

Barocchi, P. (ed.), *Il Giardino di San Marco: maestri e compagni del giovane Michelangelo*, exh. cat., Casa Buonarroti, Florence, 1992.

Barolsky, P., *The Faun in the Garden: Michelangelo and the Poetic Origins of Italian Renaissance Art*, University Park, Penn., 1994.

Baxandall, M., *Giotto and the Orators: Humanist Observers of Painting in Italy and the Discovery of Pictorial Composition, 1350–1450*, Oxford, 1971.

Baxandall, M., *Painting and Experience in Fifteenth-Century Italy*, Oxford, 1972.

Bayer, A., 'Dosso's Public: the Este Court at Ferrara' in A. Bayer (ed.), *Dosso Dossi: Court Painter in Renaissance Ferrara*, exh. cat., Galleria d'Arte Moderna e Contemporanea, Ferrara, Metropolitan Museum of Art, New York, J. Paul Getty Museum, Los Angeles, 1989.

Bazzotti, U., 'Disegni per argenterie' in Gombrich *et al.*, *Giulio Romano*, pp. 454–7.

Bellosi, L. (ed.), *Francesco di Giorgio e il Rinascimento a Siena, 1450–1500*, exh. cat. Chiesa di Sant'Agostino, Siena, Milan, 1993.

Beltrami, L., *Gli sponsali di Galeazzo Maria Sforza*, Milan, 1893.

Beltrami, L., *La guardaroba di Lucrezia Borgia*, Milan, 1903.

Beltrami, L., 'Bramante e Leonardo praticarono l'arte del bulino? Un incisore sconosciuto, Bernardino Prevedari', *Rassegna d'arte*, XVII, 1917, pp. 187–94.

Benedetti, M., 'Nuovi documenti sullo sculptore Vincenzo de' Grandi', *Studi Trentini*, IV, 1923, pp. 28–40.

Bertolotti, A., *Le arte minori alla Corte di Mantova*, Milan, 1889.

Bertoni, G. and Vicini, E.P., 'Il Castello di Ferrara ai tempi di Niccolò III', *Documenti e studi pubblicati per cura della Deputazione di Storia patria per le Provincie di Romagna*, 3, Bologna, 1909.

Beschi, L., 'Le antichità di Lorenzo il Magnifico: caratteri e vicende' in P. Barrochi and G. Ragionieri (eds), *Gli Uffizi: quattro secoli di una galleria*, Atti del convegno internazionale di studi (Firenze 20–24 settembre 1982), Florence, 1982, pp. 161–76.

Biadego, G., *Variazioni e divagazione a proposito di due sonetti di Giorgio Sommariva in onore di Gentile e Giovanni Bellini (per nozze Gerola-Cena)*, Verona, 1907.

Bironi, G., 'Documenti inediti per Bramantino', *Arte Lombarda*, 3/4, 1988, p. 42.

Bober, P.P., *Drawing after the Antique by Amico Aspertini: Sketchbooks in the British Museum* (Studies of the Warburg Institute, 21), London, 1957.

Bober P.P. and Rubinstein, R., *Renaissance Artists and Antique Sculpture: A Handbook of Sources*, Oxford, 1986.

Borea, E., 'Stampa figurativa e pubblico dalle origini all'affermazione nel Cinquecento, in G. Previtali (ed.), *Storia dell'arte italiana*, II, *L'artista e il pubblico*, Turin, 1979, pp. 319–413.

Brink, C., *Arte et Marte: Kriegskunst und Kunstliebe im Herrscherbild des 15. und 16. Jahrhunderts in Italien*, Munich and Berlin, 2000.

Brown, A. (ed.), *Language and Images of Renaissance Italy*, Oxford, 1995.

Brown, C.M., 'Little Known and Unpublished Documents concerning Andrea Mantegna, Bernardino Parentino, Pietro Lombardo, Leonardo da Vinci and Filippo Benintendi, Part One', *L'Arte*, VI, 1969, pp. 152–64.

Brown, C.M., ' "Una testa di Platone antica con la punta del naso di cera": unpublished negotiations between Isabella d'Este and Niccolò and Giovanni Bellini', *Art Bulletin*, LI, 1969, pp. 373–7.

Brown, C.M., ' "Lo insaciabile desiderio nostro de cose antique": new documents on Isabella d'Este's collection of antiquities' in C.H. Clough (ed.), *Cultural Aspects of the Italian Renaissance: Essays in Honour of Paul Oskar Kristeller*, Manchester and New York, 1976, pp. 330–47.

Brown, C.M. (ed.), *Engraved Gems: Survivals and Revivals, Studies in the History of Art*, LIV, Washington, 1997.

Brown, C.M. and Delmarcel, G., *Tapestries for the Courts of Federico II, Ercole and Ferrante Gonzaga, 1552–63*, Seattle and London, 1996.

Brown, C.M., Fusco, L. and Corti, G., 'Lorenzo de' Medici and the Dispersal of the Antiquarian Collections of Cardinal Francesco Gonzaga', *Arte Lombarda*, 90/91, 34, 1989, pp. 86–103.

Brown, C.M. and Hickson, S., 'Caradosso Foppa (ca. 1452–1526/7)', *Arte Lombarda*, 119, 1997/1, pp. 9–35.

Brown, C.M. and Lorenzoni, A.M., *Isabella d'Este and Lorenzo da Pavia*, Geneva, 1982.

Brummer, H.H., *The Statue Court in the Vatican Belvedere*, Stockholm, 1970.

Bunt, C.G.E., *The Goldsmiths of Italy: Some Account of their Guilds, Statutes and Work*, London, 1926.

Burnett, A., 'Coin Faking in the Renaissance' in M. Jones (ed.), *Why Fakes Matter: Essays on Problems of Authenticity*, London, 1992, pp. 15–22.

Burns, H., Collareta, M. and Gasparotto, D. (eds), *Valerio Belli Vicentino, 1468– c.1546*, Vicenza, 2000.

Butterfield, A., *The Sculptures of Andrea del Verrocchio*, New Haven and London, 1997.

Butters, S., *The Triumph of Vulcan: Sculptor's Tools, Porphyry, and the Prince in Ducal Florence*, Florence, 1996.

Caglioti, F., 'Due "restauratori" per le antichità dei primi Medici: Mino da Fiesole, Andrea del Verrocchio e il "Marsia rosso" degli Uffizi. I', *Prospettiva*, 72, 1993, pp. 17–42.

Caglioti, F. and Gasparotto, D., 'Lorenzi Ghiberti, il "Sigillo di Nerone", e le origini della placchetta "antiquaria" ', *Prospettiva*, 85, January 1997, pp. 2–38.

Callmann, E., *Apollonio di Giovanni*, London, 1974.

Campana, A., 'Poesie umanistiche relative a ceramiche', *Faenza*, XXXII, 1946, pp. 59–68.

Campana, A. and Medioli Masotti, P. (eds), *Bartolomeo Sacchi, il Platina (Piadena 1421–Roma 1481). Atti del convegno internazionale di studi per il V centenaria (Cremona 14–15 novembre 1981)*, Padua, 1986.

Campbell, S.J., *Cosmè Tura of Ferrara: Style, Politics and the Renaissance City, 1450–1495*, New Haven and London, 1997.

Campori, G., *Raccolta di cataloghi ed inventarii inediti*, Modena, 1870.

Campori, G., *Notizie storiche e artistiche della maiolica e porcellana di Ferrara nei secoli XV e XVI*, Modena, 1871.

Cannatta, P., *Rilievi e placchette dal XV al XVIII secolo*, exh. cat., Palazzo Venezia, Rome, Rome, 1982.

Cantelli, G., *Storia dell'oreficeria e dell'arte tessile in Toscana dal Medioevo all'età moderna*, Florence, 1996.

Capellen, J. Meyer zur, *Gentile Bellini*, Stuttgart, 1985.

Carl, D., 'Documenti inediti su Maso Finiguerra e la sua famiglia', *Annali della Scuola Normale Superiore di Pisa*, XIII, 2, 1983, pp. 507–54.

Casati, C., *Notices sur les faiences de Deruta d'apres des documents nouveaux*, Paris, 1874.

Cavallaro, A. and Parlato E. (eds), *Da Pisanello alla nascita dei Muisei Capitolini: l'antico a Roma all'vigilia del Rinascimento*, exh. cat., Musei Capitolini, Rome, Rome and Milan, 1988.

Cecchetti, Pietro Mattei Tonina, *Mastro Giorgio l'uomo, l'artista, l'imprenditore'*, Perugia, 1995.

Cecchi, A. and Natali, A. (eds), *L'officina della maniera: varietà e fierrezza nell'arte fiorentina del Cinquecento fra due repubbliche (1494–1530)*, exh. cat., Uffizi, Florence, Venice and Florence, 1996.

Ceruti, A., 'Il corredo nuziale di Bianca M. Sforza Visconti, sposa dell'imperatore Massimiliano I', *Archivio storico lombardo*, II, 1875, pp. 51–75.

Cessi, F. with Caon, B., *Giovanni da Cavino: medaglista padovano del Cinquecento*, Padua, 1969.

Chambers, D.S. (ed.), *Patrons and Artists in the Italian Renaissance*, London, 1970.

Chambers, D.S., *A Renaissance Cardinal and his Worldly Goods: the Will and Inventory of Cardinal Francesco Gonzaga*, London, 1992.

Chambers, D.S. and Martineau, J. (eds), *Splendours of the Gonzaga*, exh. cat., Victoria and Albert Museum, London, 1981.

Chambers, D.S. and Pullan, B. (eds), *Venice: A Documentary History, 1450–1630*, Oxford, 1992.

Chastel, A., *Art et Humanisme à Florence au temps de Laurent le Magnifique: Études sur la Renaissance et l'Humanisme platonicien*, Paris, 1959.

Christiansen, K., 'The Case for Mantegna as a Printmaker', *Burlington Magazine*, CXXXV, 1993, pp. 604–11.

Ciapelli, G. and Rubin, P.L., *Art, Memory and Family in Renaissance Florence*, Cambridge, 2000.

Ciardi Dupre Dal Poggetto, M.G. (ed.), *L'oreficeria nella Firenze del Quattrocento*, exh. cat., Florence, 1977.

Clarke, G., 'Magnificence and the City: Giovanni il Bentivoglio and Architecture in Fifteenth-Century Bologna', *Renaissance Studies*, XIII, 1999, pp. 397–411.

Clayton, M., *Raphael and his Circle: Drawings from Windsor Castle*, London, 1999.

Clifford, T. (ed.), *Designs of Desire: Architectural and Ornament Prints and Drawings, 1500–1850*, exh. cat., The Burrell Gallery, Glasgow, and the National Gallery of Scotland, Edinburgh, Edinburgh, 1999.

Cohn, S.K., *The Cult of Remembrance and the Black Death: Six Renaissance Cities in Central Italy*, Baltimore, 1992.

Collareta, M., *La croce del Pollaiuolo*, Florence, 1982.

Collareta, M. and Capitanio, A., *Oreficeria sacra italiana: Museo Nazionale del Bargello*, Florence, 1990.

Cordellier, D. (ed.), 'Documenti e Fonti su Pisanello (1395–1581 circa)', *Verona Illustrata: Rivista del Museo di Castelvecchio*, 8, 1995.

Cordellier, D. (ed.), *Pisanello: peintre aux sept vertus*, exh. cat., Musée du Louvre, Paris, 1996, pp. 287–9, 415–53.

Cordellier, D. and Py, B. (eds), *Pisanello: Louvres conférences et colloques*, I, Paris, 1998.

Corti, G. and Hartt, F., 'New documents concerning Donatello, Luca and Andrea della Robbia, Desiderio, Mino, Uccello, Pollaiuolo, Filippo Lippi, Baldovinetti and others', *The Art Bulletin*, XVIV, 1962, pp. 155–67.

Cruttwell, M., *Antonio Pollaiuolo*, London and New York, 1907.

Currie, S. and Motture, P. (eds), *The Sculpted Object, 1400–1700*, Aldershot, 1997.

Dacos, N., 'Ghirlandaio e l'antique', *Bulletin de l'Institut historique belge de Rome*, XXXIV, 1962, pp. 419–55.

Dacos, N., 'Graffiti de la Domus Aurea', *Bulletin de l'Institut historique belge de Rome*, XXXVIII, 1967, pp. 145–75.

Dacos, N., *La Découverte de la Domus Aurea et la formation des grotesques à Renaissance*, London and Leyden, 1969.

Dacos, N., Giuliano, A. and Pannuti, U., *Il tesoro di Lorenzo il Magnifico*, I, *Le gemme*, Florence, 1973.

Davies, M., *National Gallery Catalogues: the Early Italian Schools*, rev. edn, London, 1961.

Dean, T. and Lowe, K. (eds), *Crime, Society and the Law in Renaissance Italy*, Cambridge, 1994.

Dean, T. and Lowe, K. (eds), *Marriage in Italy 1300–1650*, Cambridge, 1998.

Degenhart, B. and Schmitt, A. (eds), *Pisanello und Bono da Ferrara*, Munich, 1995.

De Maria, S., 'Fra corte e studio: la cultura antiquaria a Bologna nell'età dei Bentivoglio' in G.A. Mansuelli and G. Susini (eds), *Il contributo dell' Università di Bologna alla storia della città: l'Evo Antico: Atti del 10 convegno, Bologna, 11–12 March 1988*, Bologna, 1989, pp. 151–216.

De Nicolò Salmazo, A. (ed.), *Francesco Squarcione: 'Pictorum gymnasiarca singularis'*, Padua, 1999.

Distelberger, R. et al., *The Collections of the National Gallery of Art, Systematic Catalogue: Western Decorative Arts, Part I*, Washington DC, Cambridge, 1993.

Donato, M.M., 'Gli eroi romani tra storia ed exemplum: I primi cicli umanistici di uomini famosi' in S. Settis (ed.), *Memoria dell'antico nell'arte italiana*, 3 vols, Turin, 1986, II, pp. 97–152.

Draper, J.D., *Bertoldo di Giovanni: Sculptor of the Medici Household*, Columbia, Mo. and London, 1992.

Dreier, F.A. and Mallet, J.V.G., *The Hockemeyer Collection: maiolica and glass,* Bremen, 1998.

Elam, C., 'Lorenzo de' Medici's Sculpture Garden', *Mitteilungen des Kunsthistorischen Institutes in Florenz*, XXXVI, 1992, pp. 41–84.

Ettlinger, L.D., *Antonio and Piero Pollaiuolo*, London, 1978.

Faietti, M. and Oberhuber, K., *Bologna e l'umanesimo, 1490–1510*, exh. cat., Pinacoteca Nazionale, Bologna, 1988.

Fairbairn, L., *Italian Renaissance Drawings from the Collection of Sir John Soane's Museum*, London, 1998.

Favaretto, I., *Andrea Mantova Benavides: Inventario delle antichità di casa Mantova Benavides*, Padua, 1978.

Favaretto, I., *Arte antica e cultura antiquaria nelle collezioni venete al tempo della Serenissima*, Rome, 1990.

Favaretto, I. and Traversari, G. (eds), *Venezia e l'archeologia: un importante capitolo nella storia del gusto dell'antico nella cultura artistica Veneziana*, Rome, 1990.

Fermor, S. *The Raphael Tapestry Cartoons: Narrative, Decoration, Design*, London, 1996.

Ferrari, D. (ed.), *Giulio Romano: Repertorio di fonti documentarie*, Rome, 1992.

ffoulkes, J. and Maiocchi, R., *Vincenzo Foppa of Brescia, Founder of the Lombard School: His Life and Work*, London and New York, 1909.

Fiocco, C. and Gherardi, G., *La ceramica di Deruta dal XIII al XVIII secolo*, Faenza, 1994.

Fletcher, J.M., 'Isabella d'Este and Giovanni Bellini's *Presepio*', *Burlington Magazine*, CXIII, 1971, pp. 703–12.

Fletcher, J.M., 'Bernardo Bembo and Leonardo's portrait of Ginevra de' Benci', *Burlington Magazine*, CXXXI, 1989, pp. 811–16.

Fortini Brown, P., *Venice and Antiquity*, New Haven and London, 1996.

Fortini Brown, P., *Art and Life in Renaissance Venice*, New York, 1997.

Fossi Todorow, M., *I disegni del Pisanello e della sua cerchia*, Florence, 1966.

Franceschini, A., *Artisti a Ferrara in età umanistica e rinascimentale: testimonianze archivistiche*, 2 vols, Ferrara and Rome, 1993–5.

Fraser Jenkins, A.D., 'Cosimo de' Medici's Patronage of Architecture and the Theory of Magnificence', *Journal of the Warburg and Courtauld Institutes*, XXXIII, 1970, pp. 162–70.

Frati, L., 'Giuochi ed amori alla corte d'Isabella d'Este', *Archivio storico lombardo*, ser. ii, IX, 1898, pp. 350–65.

Frati, L., *La vita privata di Bologna*, Bologna, 1900.

Fusco, L. and Corti, G., 'Giovanni Ciampolini (d. 1505), a Renaissance Dealer in Rome and his Collection of Antiquities', *Xenia*, 21, 1991.

Fusco, L. and Corti, G., New Documents for Lorenzo de' Medici as a Collector of Antiquities and Rare Objects, 1465–92, forthcoming book.

Gandini, L.A., *Tavola, cantina e cucina della corte di Ferrara nel Quattrocento*, Modena, 1889.

Gaye, G., *Carteggio inedito d'artisti*, Florence, 1839.

Geese, U., 'Antike als Programm: Der Statuenhof des Belvedere im Vatikan' in *Natur und Antike*, exh. cat., Liebighaus Museum alter Plastik, Frankfurt, 1985, pp. 24–50.

Gere, J.A. and Turner, N., *Drawings by Raphael*, exh. cat., British Museum, London, 1983.

Giacomotti, J., *Catalogue des majoliques des Musées Nationaux*, Paris, 1974.

Gilbert, C.E. (ed.), *Italian Art, 1400–1500: Sources and Documents*, Evanston, Ill., 1992.

Giulini, A., 'Drusiana Sforza, moglie di Jacopo Piccinino' in *Miscellanea di studi storici in onore di Antonio Manno*, II, Turin, 1912, pp. 163–214.

Glasser, H., Artists' Contracts of the Early Renaissance, unpublished PhD thesis, Columbia University, NY, 1965.

Goffen, R., *Giovanni Bellini*, New Haven and London, 1989.

Goldthwaite, R., *The Building of Renaissance Florence: An Economic and Social History*, Baltimore and London, 1980.

Goldthwaite, R., 'The Economic and Social World of Italian Renaissance Maiolica', *Renaissance Quarterly*, XLII, 1989, pp. 1–32.

Goldthwaite, R., *Wealth and the Demand for Art in Italy, 1300–1600*, Baltimore and London, 1993.

Golzio, V., *Raffaello nei documenti*, Vatican City, 1936.

Gombrich, E.H., *Norm and Form: Studies in the Art of the Renaissance*, 3rd edn, London and New York, 1978.

Gombrich, E.H., *The Sense of Order: A Study in the Psychology of Decorative Art*, London, 1984.

Grafton, A. and Jardine, L., *From Humanism to the Humanities: Education and the Liberal Arts in Fifteenth- and Sixteenth-Century Europe*, London, 1986.

Grayson, C., 'Una intercenale inedita di L.B. Alberti: *Uxoria*', *Italia medioevale e umanistica*, III, 1960.

Hackenbroch, Y., *Renaissance Jewellery*, Munich, 1979.

Haines, M., *The 'Sacrestia delle Messe' of the Florentine Cathedral*, Florence, 1983.

Hartt, F., *Giulio Romano*, New Haven, 1958.

Haussmann, T., *Majolica: spanische und italienische Keramik vom 14. bis zum 18.*, Berlin, 1972.

Hayward, J.F., *Virtuoso Goldsmiths and the Triumph of Mannerism 1540–1620*, London, 1976.

Herald, J., *Renaissance Dress in Italy*, London, 1981.

Hermann, H.J., 'Pier Jacopo Alari-Bonacolsi, gennant l'Antico', *Jahrbuch der kunsthistorischen Sammlungen in Wien*, XXVIII, 1910, pp. 201–88.

Hill, G.F., 'Classical Influence on the Renaissance Medal', *Burlington Magazine*, XVIII, 1910–11, pp. 259–68.

Hill, G.F., *A Corpus of Italian Medals of the Renaissance before Cellini*, London, 1930.

Hill, G.F., *Medals of the Renaissance*, revd G. Pollard, London, 1978.

Hills, P., *Venetian Colour: Marble, Mosaic, Painting and Glass, 1250–1550*, New Haven and London, 1999.

Hind, A.M., *Nielli, chiefly Italian, of the XV Century: Plates, Sulphur Casts and Prints Preserved in the British Museum*, London, 1936.

Hind, A.M., *Early Italian Engraving, Part 1: Florentine Engravings and Anonymous Prints of Other Schools*, London, 1938.

Hirst, M., *Sebastiano del Piombo*, Oxford, 1981.

Hirst, M., *Michelangelo and his Drawings*, New Haven and London, 1988.

Hirst, M. and Dunkerton, J., *The Young Michelangelo: Making and Meaning*, exh. cat., National Gallery, London, 1994.

Hobson, A., *Humanists and Bookbinders: the Origins and Diffusion of Humanistic Bookbinding, 1459–1559*, Cambridge, 1989.

Holcroft, A., 'Francesco Xanto Avelli and Petrarch', *Journal of the Warburg and Courtauld Institutes*, LI, 1988, pp. 225–34.

Holman, B.L. (ed.), *Disegno: Italian Renaissance Designs for the Decorative Arts*, exh. cat., Cooper-Hewitt National Design Museum, New York, 1997.

Holman, B.L., 'A "subtle artifice": Giulio Romano's *Salt Cellar with Satyrs* for Federico II Gonzaga', *Quaderni di Palazzo Te*, VIII, 2000, pp. 56–67.

Hope, C., 'Composition from Cennini and Alberti to Vasari' in P. Taylor and F. Quiviger (eds), *Pictorial Composition from Medieval to Modern Art*, Warburg Institute Colloquia, 6, London and Turin, 2000, pp. 27–44.

Hyatte, R., 'Complementary Humanistic Models of Marriage and Male *Amicitia* in Fifteenth-Century Literature' in J. Haseldine (ed.), *Friendship in Medieval Europe*, Thrupp, Glos, 1999, pp. 251–61.

Ianziti, G., *Humanist Historiography under the Sforzas: Politics and Propaganda in Fifteenth-Century Milan*, Oxford, 1988.

Jacks, P., *The Antiquarian and the Myth of Antiquity: the Origins of Rome in Renaissance Thought*, Cambridge, 1993.

Jansen, D.J., 'Jacopo Strada antiquario mantovano e la fortuna di Giulio Romano' in *Giulio Romano: atti del convegno internazionale di studi*, Mantua, 1989, pp. 361–74.

Jardine, L., *Worldly Goods: A New History of the Renaissance*, London, 1996.

Joannides, P., *Michelangelo and his Influence: Drawings from Windsor Castle*, exh. cat., National Gallery of Art, Washington, Queen's Gallery, London, 1998.

Johnson, G.A. and Matthews Grieco, S.F. (eds), *Picturing Women in Renaissance and Baroque Italy*, Cambridge, 1997.

Jones, M. (ed.), *Fake? The Art of Deception*, exh. cat., British Museum, London, 1990.

Jones, M. (ed.), *Designs on Posterity: Drawings for Medals*, London, 1994.

Kemp, M., *Behind the Picture: Art and Evidence in the Italian Renaissance*, New Haven and London, 1997.

Kennedy, R. Wedgwood, *Alesso Baldovinetti: a Critical and Historical Study*, New Haven, 1938.

Kent, D., *Cosimo de' Medici and the Florentine Renaissance: The Patron's Oeuvre*, New Haven and London, 2001.

Kent, F.W., ' "Più superba di quella di Lorenzo": Courtly and Family Interest in the Building of Filippo Strozzi's Palace', *Renaissance Quarterly*, XXX, 1977, pp. 311–23.

Kent, F.W., 'Patron-Client Networks in Renaissance Florence and the Emergence of Lorenzo as "Maestro della Bottega" ' in B. Toscani (ed.), *Lorenzo de' Medici: New Perspectives*, New York, 1993, pp. 279–313.

Kidwell, C., *Pontano: Poet and Prime Minister*, London, 1991.

Klapisch Zuber, C., *Women, Family and Ritual in Renaissance Italy*, Chicago, 1985.

Krautheimer, R., *Lorenzo Ghiberti*, 2nd edn, Princeton, 1970.

Kris, E., *Meister und Meisterwerke der Steinschneiderkunst*, Vienna, 1929.

Kristeller, P., *Andrea Mantegna*, Berlin and Leipzig, 1902.

Ladis, A., *Italian Renaissance Maiolica from Southern Collections*, Georgia, 1989.

Landau, D. and Parshall, P., *The Renaissance Print, 1470–1550*, New Haven and London, 1994.

Lawrence, S.E., 'Imitation and Emulation in the Numismatic Fantasies of Valerio Belli', *The Medal*, 29, Autumn 1996, pp. 18–29.

Levenson, J.A., Oberhuber, K. and Sheehan, J.L., *Early Italian Engravings from the National Gallery of Art*, exh. cat., National Gallery of Art, Washington, 1973.

Levi, C.A., *L'arte del Vetro in Murano nel Rinascimento e i Berroviero*, Venice, 1895.

Levi Pisetzky, R., *Storia del costume in Italia*, Milan, 1966.

Lewis, D., 'On the Nature of Renaissance Bronzes' in M. Leithe-Jasper, *Renaissance Master Bronzes from the Collection of the Kunsthistorisches Museum, Vienna*, exh. cat., Smithsonian Institution Travelling Exhibition Service, London, 1986, pp. 19–24.

Lightbown, R.W., 'Giovanni Chellini, Donatello and Antonio Rosellino', *Burlington Magazine*, CIV, 1962, pp. 102–4.

Lightbown, R.W., *Mantegna*, Oxford, 1986.

Lightbown, R., *Medieval European Jewellery, with a catalogue of the collection in the Victoria & Albert Museum*, London, 1992.

Lillie, A., 'The Palazzo Strozzi and Private Patronage in Fifteenth-Century Florence' in H. Millon and V. Lampugnani (eds), *The Renaissance from Brunelleschi to Michelangelo: The Representation of Architecture*, London, 1994, pp. 518–21.

Lincoln, E., 'Mantegna's Culture of Line', *Art History*, XVI, 1, 1993, pp. 33–57.

Lollini, F. and Lucchi, P. (eds), *Libraria Domini: I manoscritti della Biblioteca Malatestiana, testi e decorazioni*, Bologna, 1995.

Luchs, A. (ed.), *Italian Plaquettes: Studies in the History of Art*, 22, National Gallery of Art, Washington DC, 1989.

Luiso, F.P., *Studi su l'epistolario di Leonardo Bruni*, Rome, 1980.

Luzio, A., 'Lettere inedite di Fra Sabba da Castiglione', *Archivio storico lombardo*, XIII, 1886, pp. 99–112.

Luzio, A., 'Isabella d'Este e Francesco Gonzaga, promessi sposi', *Archivio storico lombardo*, ser. iv, IX, 1908, pp. 34–68.

Luzio, A., *La galleria dei Gonzaga venduta all'Inghilterra nel 1627–28*, Milan, 1913.

Luzio, A. and Renier, R., 'Il lusso di Isabella d'Este', *Nuova antologia*, ser. iv, LXIV, 1896, pp. 300–10.

Lydecker, J.K., The Domestic Setting of the Arts in Renaissance Florence, PhD thesis, Johns Hopkins University, Baltimore, 1987.

Lydecker, J.K., 'Il patriziato fiorentino e la committenza artistica per la casa' in *I ceti dirigenti nella Toscana del Quattrocento*, Impruneta, 1987.

McCray, P.P., *Glassmaking in Renaissance Venice: The Fragile Craft*, Ashtead, Surrey, 1999.

MacLean, I., *The Renaissance Notion of Women: a Study in the Fortunes of Scholasticism and Medical Science in European Intellectual Life*, Cambridge, 1980.

McManamon, J.M., *Funeral Oratory and the Cultural Ideals of Italian Humanism,* Chapel Hill, NC and London, 1989.

Malaguzzi Valeri, F., *Pittori lombardi del Quattrocento*, Milan, 1902.

Malaguzzi Valeri, F., *La corte di Lodovico il Moro*, 4 vols, Milan, 1913–23.

Mallet, J.V.G., 'Maiolica at Polesden Lacey III: a new

look at the Xanto problem', *Apollo*, March 1971, pp. 170–83.

Mallet, J.V.G., 'Mantua and Urbino: Gonzaga Patronage of Maiolica', *Apollo*, XIV, 1981, pp. 162–9.

Mallet, J.V.G., 'La biografia di Francesco Xanto Avelli alla luce dei suoi sonnetti', *Faenza*, LXX, 1984, pp. 398–402.

Mallet, J.V.G., 'Xanto: i suoi compagni e seguaci', *Francesco Xanto Avelli da Rovigo: atti del Convegno Internazionale di Studi, 1980*, Rovigo, 1987, pp. 67–108.

Manca, J., *The Art of Ercole de' Roberti*, Cambridge, 1992.

Manca, J., *Cosmè Tura: The Life and Art of a Painter in Estense Ferrara*, Oxford, 2000.

Mancini, V., *Antiquari, virtuosi e artisti: Saggi sul collezionismo tra Padova e Venezia alla metà del cinquecento*, Padua, 1995.

Mann, N. and Syson, L. (eds), *The Image of the Individual: Portraits in the Renaissance*, London, 1998.

Mardersteig, G., *Felice Feliciano Veronese. Alphabetum Romanum*, Verona, 1960.

Marsili, P., 'Ars Orcelariorum: la corporazione dei maiolicari di Faenza', *Faenza*, 1982, pp. 20–1.

Marsolin, B., 'Valerio Vicentino nelle *Vite* di Giorgio Vasari', *Atti del reale Istituto Veneto di Scienze, Lettere ed Arte*, ser. vi, XLIV, 1885–6, pp. 1093–1121.

Martineau, J. (ed.), *Andrea Mantegna*, exh. cat., Royal Academy of Arts, London, and Metropolitan Museum of Art, New York, Milan, 1992.

Massing, J.M., *Du texte à l'image: la Calomnie d'Apelle et son iconographie*, Strasbourg, 1990.

Mazzi, C., *Due provisioni suntuarie fiorentine*, Florence, 1908.

Melli, L., *Maso Finiguerra: I disegni*, Florence, 1992.

Milanesi, G. and Pini, C., *La scrittura di artisti italiani (sec. XIV–XVII)*, Florence, 1876.

Miller, E., *16th-Century Italian Ornament Prints in the Victoria and Albert Museum*, London, 1999.

Molho, A., *Marriage Alliance in Late Medieval Florence*, Cambridge, Mass., and London, 1994.

Monbeig Goguel, C. (ed.), *Francesco Salviati (1510–1563) o la Bella Maniera*, exh. cat., Villa Medici, Rome, Musée du Louvre, Paris, Milan, 1998.

Morselli, A., 'Il corredo nuziale di Caterina Pico (1474)', *Atti e memorie della Deputazione di Storia Patria per le Antiche Provincie Modenesi*, ser. viii, VIII, 1956.

Motta, E., 'Ambrogio Preda e Leonardo da Vinci', *Archivio storico lombardo*, XX, 1893, pp. 988–90.

Mottola Molfino, A. and Natale, M. (eds), *Le muse e il principe: arte di corte nel Rinascimento padano*, exh. cat., 2 vols, Museo Poldi Pezzoli, Milan, Modena, 1991.

Mozzarelli, C., Oresko, R. and Ventura, L. (eds), *La Corte di Mantova nell'età di Andrea Mantegna: 1450–1550*, Rome, 1997.

Müntz, E., *Les arts à la cour des papes pendant le XVe et le XVIe siècles*, Paris, 1882.

Müntz, E., *Les collections des Médicis au quinzième siècle*, Paris, 1888.

Musacchio, J., *The Art and Ritual of Childbirth in Renaissance Italy*, New Haven and London, 1999.

Negroni, F., 'Nicola Pellipario, ceramista fantasma', *Notizie di Palazzo Albani,* XIV, 1986, pp. 13–20.

Neher, G. and Shepherd, R. (eds), *Revaluing Renaissance Art*, Aldershot, 2000.

Nesselrath, A., 'Antico and Monte Cavallo', *Burlington Magazine*, CXXIV, 1982, pp. 353–7.

Neu Watkins, R., *Humanism and Liberty: Writings on Freedom from Fifteenth-Century Florence*, Columbia, SC, 1978.

Norman, A.V.B., *The Wallace Collection: Catalogue of Ceramics*, I, Pottery, Maiolica, Faience, Stoneware, London, 1976.

Oberhuber, K., 'Raffaello e l'incisione' in *Raffaello in Vaticano*, exh. cat., Vatican, Rome, 1984, pp. 333–42.

Origo, I., *The World of San Bernardino*, London, 1963.

Orlandi, S., 'Su una tavola dipinta da Fra Filippo Lippi per Antonio del Branca nel febbraio 1451', *Rivista d'arte*, ser. iii, XXIX, 1954, pp. 199–201.

Palvarini Gobio Casali, M., *La ceramica di Mantova*, Ferrara, 1987.

Panizza, L. (ed.), *Women in Italian Renaissance Culture and Society*, Oxford, 2000.

Parisi Presicce, C., *La Lupa Capitolina*, exh. cat., Musei Capitolini, Rome, Rome, 2000, pp. 83–8.

Paturzo, F., *Arretina vasa*, Cortona, 1996.

Perry, M., 'Wealth, Art and Display: the Grimani Cameos in Renaissance Venice', *Journal of the Warburg and Courtauld Institutes*, LVI, 1993, pp. 268–73.

Petrioli Tofani, A. (ed.), *Il disegno fiorentino del tempo di Lorenzo il Magnifico*, exh. cat. Uffizi, Florence, 1992.

Pincus, D., 'Tullio Lombardo as a restorer of antiquities', *Arte Veneta*, XXXIII, 1979, pp. 29–42.

Plon, E., *Benvenuto Cellini: orfévre, médailleur, sculpteur*, Paris, 1883.

Pollard, J.G. (ed.), *Italian Medals: Studies in the History of Art*, 21, National Gallery of Art, Washington DC, 1987.

Pommeranz, J.W., *Pastigliakästchen*, Münster and New York, 1995.

Poole, J., *Italian Maiolica and Incised Slipware in the Fitzwilliam Museum, Cambridge*, Cambridge, 1995.

Pope-Hennessy, J., *Cellini*, London, 1985.

Pope-Hennessy, J. and Christiansen, K., *Secular Painting in Fifteenth-Century Tuscany: Birth Trays, Cassone Panels and Portraits*, Metropolitan Museum of Art, New York, 1980.

Puttfarken, T., *The Discovery of Pictorial Composition: Theories of Visual Order in Painting, 1400–1800*, New Haven and London, 2000.

Rackham, B., *The Victoria and Albert Museum, Catalogue of Italian Maiolica*, 2 vols, London, 1940.

Radcliffe, A. and Avery, C., 'The Chellini Madonna by Donatello', *Burlington Magazine*, CXVIII, 1976, pp. 377–87.

Randolph, A.W.B., 'Performing the Bridal Body in Fifteenth-Century Florence', *Art History*, 21/2, January 1998, pp. 183–200.

Rasmussen, J., *The Robert Lehman Collection*, X, *Italian Maiolica*, Metropolitan Museum of Art, New York, New York and Princeton, 1989.

Richards, L., 'Antonio Pollaiuolo: Battle of the Naked Men', *Bulletin of the Cleveland Museum of Art*, LV, 1968, pp. 63–70.

Robertson, C., Il gran cardinale: *Alessandro Farnese, Patron of the Arts*, New Haven and London, 1992.

Rosenberg, C., 'Francesco Cossa's Letter Reconsidered', *Musei Ferrarese*, V/VI, 1975–6, pp. 11–16.

Rossi, A., 'Documenti inediti per la storia delle maioliche', *Archivio storico dell'arte*, II, 1889, pp. 308–9.

Rossi, U., 'Cristoforo Geremia', *Archivo storico dell'arte*, I, 1888, pp. 404–11.

Rubin, P.L. and Wright, A., *Renaissance Florence: The Art of the 1470s*, exh. cat., National Gallery, London, 1999.

Rubinstein, N., 'The *De optimo cive* and the *De Principe* by Bartolomeo Platina' in R. Cardini *et al.* (eds), *Letteratura umanistica e tradizione classica per Alessandro Perosa*, Rome, 1985, pp. 375–89.

Rubinstein, R., 'A Bacchic Sarcophagus in the Renaissance', *The British Museum Yearbook*, I, *The Classical Tradition*, London, 1975, pp. 103–50.

Russell Sale, J., 'An Iconographic Program by Marco Parenti', *Renaissance Quarterly*, no. 27, 1974, pp. 293–9.

Rykwert, J. and Engel, A. (eds), *Leon Battista Alberti*, exh. cat., Palazzo Te, Mantua, Milan, 1994.

San Juan, R.M., 'Mythology, Women and Private Life: the Myth of Eurydice in Italian Furniture Painting', *Art History*, 15, 1992, pp. 127–45.

Santoro, C., 'Un registro di doti sforzesche', *Archivio storico lombardo*, LXXXX, 1953, pp. 177–84.

Scheller, R.W., *Exemplum: Model-Book Drawings and the Practice of Artistic Transmission in the Middle Ages (ca. 900–ca. 1470)*, Amsterdam, 1995.

Scher, S.K. (ed.), *The Currency of Fame: Portrait Medals of the Renaissance*, exh. cat., National Gallery of Art, Washington, Frick Collection, New York, New York, 1994.

Scher, S.K. (ed.), *Perspectives on the Renaissance Medal*, New York, 2000.

Schulz, J., 'Pinturicchio and the Revival of Antiquity', *Journal of the Warburg and Courtauld Institutes*, XXV, 1962, pp. 35–55.

Schweikhart, G., *Der Codex Wolfegg: Zeignungen nach der Antike von Amico Aspertini*, London, 1986.

Sciolla, G.C. (ed.), *Ambrogio da Fossano detto il Bergognone: un pittore per la Certosa*, exh. cat. Castello Visconteo, Pavia, Certosa di Pavia, Milan, 1998.

Seymour Jr, C., 'Some Reflections on Filarete's Use of Antique Visual Sources', *Arte Lombarda*, 38–39, XVIII, 1973, pp. 36–47.

Shell, J., *Pittori in bottega: Milano del Rinascimento*, Turin, 1995.

Signorini, R., 'New Findings about Andrea Mantegna: his Son Ludovico's Post-Mortem Inventory', *Journal of the Courtauld and Warburg Institutes*, LIX, 1996, pp. 103–18.

Snodin, M. and Howard, M., *A Social History of Ornament since 1450*, London and New Haven, 1996.

Spallanzani, M., 'Il vaso Medici Orsini in un documento d'archivio', *Faenza*, LX, 1974, pp. 88–90.

Spallanzani, M., *Le ceramiche orientali a Firenze*, Florence, 1978.

Spallanzani, M. (ed.), *Inventari Medicei, 1417–1465*, Florence, 1984.

Spallanzani, M. and Bertelà, G. (eds), *Libro d'inventario dei beni di Lorenzo il Magnifico*, Florence, 1992.

Spencer, J.R., 'Filarete, the Medallist of the Roman Emperors', *Art Bulletin*, LXI, 1979, pp. 550–61.

Stahl, A.M. and Waldman, L., 'The Earliest Known Medalists: the Sesto Brothers of Venice', *American Journal of Numismatics*, ser. ii, 5–6, 1993–4.

Stedman Sheard, W., *Antiquity in the Renaissance*, exh. cat., Smith College Museum of Art, Northampton, Mass., 1978.

Steingräber, E., 'Eine unbekannte Arbeit des Antonio Pollaiuolo für das Kloster S. Gaggio bei Florenz', *Mitteilungen des Kunsthistorisches Institutes in Florenz*, VII, 1955, pp. 87–92.

Steingräber, E., 'Lombardisches Malerei um 1500' in F. Piel and J. Traeger, *Festschrift Wolfgang Braunfels*, Tübingen, 1977, pp. 371–87.

Stone, R.E., 'Antico and the Development of Bronze Casting in Italy at the End of the Quattrocento', *The Metropolitan Museum Journal*, XVI, 1981, pp. 87–116.

Strocchia, S.S., *Death and Ritual in Renaissance Florence*, Baltimore and London, 1992.

Syson, L. and Gordon, D., *Pisanello: Painter to the Renaissance Court*, London, 2001.

Tait, G.H. (ed.), *Jewellery through 7000 Years*, London, 1976.

Tait, G.H., *The Golden Age of Venetian Glass*, exh. cat., British Museum, London, 1979.

Tait, G.H., *Seven Thousand Years of Jewellery*, London, 1986.

Tait, G.H., *Five Thousand Years of Glass*, London, 1991.

Talvacchia, B., 'Professional Advancement and the Use of the Erotic in the Art of Francesco Xanto', *Sixteenth Century Journal*, XXVI, 1994, pp. 121–53.

Talvacchia, B., *Taking Positions: on the erotic in Renaissance culture*, Princeton, 1999.

Thomas, A., *The Painter's Practice in Renaissance Florence*, Cambridge, 1995.

Thornton, D., *The Scholar in His Study: Ownership and Experience in Renaissance Italy*, New Haven and London, 1997.

Thornton, D., 'An Allegory of the Sack of Rome by Giulio da Urbino', *Apollo*, CLI, June 1999, pp. 11–18.

Thornton, P., *The Italian Renaissance Interior 1400–1600*, London, 1991.

Tondo, L., *Le gemme dei Medici e dei Lorena nel Museo Archeologico di Firenze*, Florence, 1990.

Triolo, J., The Armorial Maiolica of Francesco Avelli, unpublished PhD thesis, University of Pennsylvania, 1996.

Tuohy, T., *Herculean Ferrara: Ercole d'Este, 1471–1505, and the Invention of a Ducal Capital*, Cambridge, 1996.

Varignana, F. (ed.), *Tre artisti nella Bologna dei Bentivoglio*, Bologna, 1985.

Venturelli, P., 'Il *fermaglio cum l'angelo* di Bianca Maria Visconti Sforza nel dipinto alla Pinacoteca di Brera' in L. Golay, P. Luscher and P.A. Mariaux (eds), *Florilegium: scritti di storia dell'arte in onore di Carlo Bertelli*, Milan, 1995, pp. 116–18.

Venturelli, P., *Gioielli e gioiellieri milanesi: storia, arte, moda (1450–1630)*, Milan, 1996.

Venturelli, P., *Glossario e documenti per la gioellieria milanese (1459–1631)*, Milan, 1999.

Venturi, A., 'L'arte ferrarese nel periodo d'Ercole I d'Este', *Atti e memorie della R. Deputazione di Soria Patria per le provincie di Romagna*, ser. iii, VI, 1888, pp. 91–119, 350–422.

Vianello, A.G., 'Un inventario di cose appartenute a Cicco Simonetta', *Archivio storico lombardo*, XLV, 1918, pp. 580–2.

Vianello, C.A., 'Testimonianze venete su Milano e la Lombardia negli anni 1492–95', *Archivio storico lombardo*, n.s., IV, 1939, pp. 402–23.

Vitaletti, G., *Francesco Xanto Avelli*, Urbino, 1912.

Wallen, B.E., A Maiolica Service for Isabella d'Este, MA thesis, Institute of Fine Arts, New York, 1966.

Warnke, M., *The Court Artist: On the Ancestry of the Modern Artist*, trans. D. McLintock, Cambridge, 1993.

Watson, W.M., *Italian Renaissance Maiolica from the William A. Clark Collection*, Washington, 1986, pp. 216–25.

Weil-Garris Brandt, K., Acidini Lucinat, C., Draper, J.D. and Penny, N. (eds) *Giovinezza di Michelangelo*, exh. cat., Palazzo Vecchio, Casa Buonarroti, Florence, 1999.

Weiss, R., 'Andrea Fulvio Antiquario Romano (c.1470–1527)', *Annali della Scuola Normale Superiore di Pisa: Classe di lettere, storia e filosofia*, ser. ii, XXVIII, 1959, pp. 1–44.

Weiss, R., *The Renaissance Discovery of Classical Antiquity*, Oxford, 1969.

Welch, E.S., *Art and Authority in Renaissance Milan*, New Haven and London, 1995.

Welch, E.S., *Art and Society in Italy, 1350–1500*, Oxford, 1997.

Whitehouse, D., 'Glass in the Epigrams of Martial', *Journal of Glass Studies*, XIV, 1999, pp. 73–82.

Wilde, J., *Italian Drawings in the Department of Prints and Drawings at the British Museum: Michelangelo and his Studio*, London, 1953.

Wilkins Sullivan, R., 'Three Ferrarese Panels on the Theme of "Death rather than Dishonour" and the Neapolitan Connection', *Zeitschrift für Kunstgeschichte*, LVII, 1994, pp. 610–25.

Wilson, T., *Ceramic Art of the Italian Renaissance*, exh. cat., British Museum, London, 1987.

Wilson, T., 'Maiolica in Renaissance Venice', *Apollo*, CXXV, 1987, pp. 184–9.

Wilson, T., 'Maioliche rinascimentali armoriate con stemmi fiorentini', *L'araldica: fonti e metodi*, Florence, 1989, pp. 128–38.

Wilson, T., 'Xanto and Ariosto', *Burlington Magazine*, CXXXII, 1046, May 1990, pp. 321–7.

Wilson, T. (ed.), *Italian Renaissance Pottery: Papers written in association with a colloquium at the British Museum*, London, 1991.

Wilson, T., *Italian Maiolica of the Renaissance*, Milan, 1996.

Wind, E., *Pagan Mysteries in the Renaissance*, London, 1958.

Witthoft, B., 'Marriage Rituals and Marriage Chests in Quattrocento Florence', *artibus et historiae*, III, 1982, pp. 43–59.

Woods-Marsden, J., *The Gonzaga of Mantua and Pisanello's Arthurian Frescoes*, Princeton, 1988.

Wright, A., 'Antonio Pollaiuolo: *maestro di disegno*' in E. Cropper (ed.), *Florentine Drawing at the Time of Lorenzo the Magnificent, Papers of the Villa Spelman Colloquium, 1992*, Bologna, 1994, VI, pp. 131–46.

Wright, A., 'Mantegna and Pollaiuolo: artistic personality and the marketing of invention' in S. Currie (ed.), *Drawing, 1400–1600: Invention and Innovation*, Aldershot, 1998, pp. 72–90.

Zecchin, L., *Vetro e Vetrai di Murano*, 3 vols, Venice, 1987–90.

Index

Page numbers in italics refer to
illustrations.